The Batman Filmography
Second Edition

The Batman Filmography

Second Edition

MARK S. REINHART

McFarland & Company, Inc., Publishers
Jefferson, North Carolina, and London

ALSO BY MARK S. REINHART

Abraham Lincoln on Screen: Fictional and Documentary Portrayals on Film and Television, 2d ed. (McFarland 2009; paperback 2012)

Frontispiece: The first-ever screen Batman—
Lewis Wilson as Batman in *Batman* (1943).

LIBRARY OF CONGRESS CATALOGUING-IN-PUBLICATION DATA

Reinhart, Mark S., 1964–
The Batman filmography / Mark S. Reinhart. — Second edition.
    p.   cm.
Includes bibliographical references and index.

ISBN 978-0-7864-6891-1
softcover : acid free paper ∞

1. Batman films—Catalogs.
I. Title.
PN1995.9.B34R45 2013   791.43'651—dc23   2013024310

BRITISH LIBRARY CATALOGUING DATA ARE AVAILABLE

© 2013 Mark S. Reinhart. All rights reserved

No part of this book may be reproduced or transmitted in any form or by any means, electronic or mechanical, including photocopying or recording, or by any information storage and retrieval system, without permission in writing from the publisher.

Front cover images © 2013 Shutterstock

Manufactured in the United States of America

*McFarland & Company, Inc., Publishers
Box 611, Jefferson, North Carolina 28640
www.mcfarlandpub.com*

For Jill, Taylor, Keaton and Jenna —
all of the heroes in my Batcave

Table of Contents

Acknowledgments ix
Introduction 1

1 — The Creation of Batman and His World, 1939–1942   5
2 — *Batman* (1943)   15
3 — Between the Serials, 1943–1948   32
4 — *Batman and Robin* (1949)   35
5 — Changing with the Times, 1950–1965   52
6 — *Batman* (1966)   59
7 — Exile from the Big Screen, 1967–1989   80
8 — *Batman* (1989)   99
9 — Between Burton's Batman Films, 1989–1991   121
10 — *Batman Returns* (1992)   123
11 — *Batman: Mask of the Phantasm* (1993)   139
12 — Between Burton and Schumacher, 1993–1995   149
13 — *Batman Forever* (1995)   152
14 — Between Schumacher's Batman Films, 1996–1997   172
15 — *Batman and Robin* (1997)   177
16 — Iconic Character, Dormant Film Franchise, 1998–2004   193
17 — *Batman Begins* (2005)   208
18 — *The Dark Knight* (2008)   230
19 — "Non-Nolan" Batman Works During the Nolan Cinematic Batman Era   257
20 — *The Dark Knight Rises* (2012)   272
21 — The Adventure Goes On and On   297

Chapter Notes 301
Bibliography 305
Index 307

Acknowledgments

As a lifelong Batman fan, writing the first edition and now the second edition of this book has fulfilled my dream of making a small contribution to the history of this wonderful character. Though this book is primarily about Batman's big screen adventures, it is important to recognize the fact that Batman was born on the comics page. So first and foremost, I would like to thank the talented artists, writers and editors at DC Comics who have created Batman comic stories since 1939—so many of you have entertained, amazed and inspired me, both as a little boy and as a grown man.

I would particularly like to thank the late Bob Kane, Batman's creator. Like so many other Batman fans, I have often been flippant about Kane. History shows that Bill Finger was so instrumental in helping Kane to develop Batman that he probably should have been given an equal byline in the character's creation. History also shows that Kane came across as ungenerous by keeping that byline all for himself for so many years.

That said, however, as I really studied the history of Batman's creation, it struck me that Kane was the one who initially undertook the task to create a new costumed comic hero in the wake of Superman's success. Finger helped Kane flesh out all of the costume and character details that made Batman so memorable, and of course a huge number of subsequent artists and writers created works that made Batman the icon he is today—but it all started with Bob Kane. Batman is indisputably a product of his ambition. Thank you for bringing Batman into our world, Mr. Kane.

I also need to specifically thank another legend in the history of the Batman character as well. Michael Uslan decided to take on the task of producing a serious live-action Batman big screen work in the late 1970s, a time when most everyone in the world could only see the character as a washed-up camp craze. It took Uslan a decade of hard work to realize his goal through the release of the 1989 film *Batman*.

When *Batman* took the world by storm, the way the general public viewed Batman was totally changed. The movie introduced millions upon millions of people to "our" Batman, the dark hero we serious Batman fans loved. This incredible shift in the general public's perception of Batman would not have happened had the film never been made—and the film never would have been made without Uslan's vision and tenacity. Thank you for giving us the 1989 *Batman*, Mr. Uslan.

I would also like to thank a few Batman scholars who are personal friends of mine. Bill Ramey, creator of the wonderful Batman website Batman-on-Film, has been a great help to my research over the years. And Ross Bagby was very kind to provide me with information and insight regarding Batman's 1940s radio adventures.

I would like to thank my parents, Larry and Sally Reinhart, who have said on more than one occasion that I was practically born with a cape tied around my neck. They bought me so many great Batman books and toys when I was a child, and when I grew up they patiently waited for me to "grow out" of my Batman obsession like most all other kids did. Well, I never did, but they didn't seem to mind and they still loved me anyway — thanks, Mom and Dad.

My biggest thank you goes out to my wife Jill, our sons Taylor and Keaton, and our daughter Jenna for always sharing in my enthusiasm for Batman and his world. Many times over the years as Halloween rolled around they were good sports, donning capes and masks with me and running out into the autumn night by my side. And I have especially treasured the opportunity to witness Taylor, Keaton and Jenna become knowledgeable Batman fans in their own right. We have shared countless Batman adventures together, and getting the chance to see the character through their eyes as well as my own has been one of the greatest joys of my life. Thanks Jill, Taylor, Keaton and Jenna — you truly are my "Batman Family."

Introduction

When I started writing the first edition of this book in 2003 (published by McFarland in 2005), the history of Batman feature films was not a particularly rich one. Even though the Batman character had been so successful for so many years, there simply had been very few Batman big screen works ever made — eight, to be exact. And the first two of these films, the 1943 serial *Batman* and the 1949 serial *Batman and Robin,* were not even officially available to the home video market on any high-quality format. And most depressing of all, Warner Bros. Studios had yet to release a new Batman film to erase the bad memory of director Joel Schumacher's almost universally-despised 1997 movie *Batman and Robin.*

Here we are a decade later, and the history of Batman feature films is so much richer than it was back in 2003. Warner re-imagined their Batman film franchise with three hugely successful films by director Christopher Nolan: *Batman Begins* (2005), *The Dark Knight* (2008), and *The Dark Knight Rises* (2012). Also, the 1943 *Batman* and the 1949 *Batman and Robin* were released on DVD in 2005, ensuring that *every* Batman feature film could be obtained on high-quality home video format.

There was even more good news relating to Batman feature films during this time — many of them were released in vastly upgraded home video versions. *Batman* (1966), *Batman* (1989), *Batman Returns* (1992), *Batman Forever* (1995), *Batman and Robin* (1997), and *Batman Begins* (2005) were all released on Blu-ray between mid–2008 and early 2009. Each of these Blu-rays boasted fabulous picture quality, and were loaded with special features that detailed their particular film's creation. (Of course, *The Dark Knight* and *The Dark Knight Rises* never had to be upgraded in this fashion because they were rolled out in lavish Blu-ray packages upon their initial home video release.)

The history of Batman feature films may have changed for the better, but the reason I first wanted to write a book about these films has stayed much the same. Many film critics tend to be very dismissive of the Batman character's overall history when they review Batman feature films. This observation is not meant to be an insult to film critics — I am simply noting the fact that they generally write reviews of Batman feature films that are intended for general moviegoers, not serious Batman fans. Most critics and moviegoers view Batman solely as a big screen property, and have little connection to the character other than these major motion picture events that bring them to the theater every few years. Only serious Batman fans tend to give much thought as to how Batman feature films might have been inspired by the character's comic adventures, or how these films might fit into the character's history as a whole.

So this book is intended for serious Batman fans, and I think I can sum up why I wanted to write it for them in a single sentence. The purpose of this book is to provide analysis and criticism of Batman feature films that is always mindful of the character's 70-plus year history.

Remaining mindful of that history when examining Batman feature films can be a bit of a complicated task. The films produced to date have been fairly independent of Batman's comic book origins. In the motion pictures, time-honored characters have been drastically changed, new characters have been created, and Gotham City has been portrayed as a place quite removed from the comic book Gotham. While serious Batman fans have often seen these alterations as sacrilege, it is not hard to understand why motion picture studios have chosen to make such changes. After all, serious Batman fans make up a very small percentage of general moviegoers, so motion picture studios have been less concerned about pleasing those fans than they have been about pleasing mainstream audiences. Unfortunately, a number of these film rewrites were vastly inferior to the comic material that inspired them, so they ended up pleasing almost *nobody*—but that is a subject we'll address later.

One might argue that if Batman motion pictures have been critically neglected in terms of serious Batman fans, isn't the same also true of Batman television productions? Why not include those productions in this book? Well, to be honest, I wish I could have. But this project would not be just one single book if I had tried to do that — it probably would have been about four books! And even though I could not cover the history of Batman television productions in great detail in these pages, the book still does contain summaries of all of those productions.

And I'm happy to report that several major Batman television series such as *Batman* (ABC, 1966–68) and *Batman: The Animated Series* (Fox, 1992–95) have already been chronicled in full-length books. Readers who are interested in those series should find *The Official Batman Batbook* (the definitive work on ABC's *Batman* by Joel Eisner) and *Batman: Animated* (the definitive work on *Batman: The Animated Series* by Paul Dini and Chip Kidd). Somebody probably should do a book about the Batman television series that have been released in the past decade such as *The Batman* (Kid's WB, 2004–08) and *Batman: The Brave and the Bold* (Cartoon Network, 2008–11). Not me, though — after the past few years of obsessing over the character's big screen works, I need a break!

There is another big reason I wanted to write about Batman movies, one that is far more personal and far less tangible than the reason just outlined. There is just something magical about sitting in a darkened movie theater, seeing the Batman character come to life on the big screen. Batman so often looms in the darkness on the comic page, and watching his adventures unfold in a cavernous black room not unlike his Batcave is one of the ultimate Batman fan experiences. This book is a way for me to share that experience with other serious Batman fans.

I hope I've convinced you, the reader, that my book examining the history of Batman motion pictures is a worthwhile endeavor. Now I should take a moment to convince you why I'm qualified to write *The Batman Filmography*. Honestly, I don't have much to offer you in that regard, but here goes—I have an encyclopedic knowledge of Batman history, a sharp eye for film criticism, and a ton of determination. I can offer you some insight about these films that might lead you to see them in ways that you had not seen before.

Please allow me a moment to tell you a bit more about my own personal Batman obsession. It closely mirrors that of Chip Kidd, the graphic designer who authored the wonderful book about Batman merchandise entitled *Batman Collected* as well as the previously mentioned *Batman: Animated*. Like Kidd, I was a toddler when the ABC television show *Batman* premiered in 1966, and I was immediately hooked. Also like Kidd, while most everyone else seemed to "grow out" of being a Batman fan after the series ended its three-year run, I never did.

Sure, I got married, had three kids, worked in a public library, became a professional musician and wrote my first book (*Abraham Lincoln on Screen,* McFarland, 2009), but my Batmania always stayed with me. I followed the character through the Adams–O'Neil comic stories of the early 1970s and the Mego Toys action figure craze of the mid–1970s. I remained a fan through the debut of the first Batman graphic novel *Batman: The Dark Knight Returns* in 1986 and the astounding success of the 1989 film *Batman.* I was glued to my TV set for the 1992 premiere of the wonderful television program *Batman: The Animated Series.* I marveled at the realism of the stunning Paul Dini–Alex Ross oversized book *Batman: War on Crime* when it was released in 1999. I sat in awe experiencing Christopher Nolan's cinematic vision of the character for the first time in 2005's *Batman Begins.* Though not a gamer myself, I lived every moment of the hugely successful video games *Batman: Arkham Asylum* (2009) and *Batman: Arkham City* (2011), watching my sons play and beat them both. And I am anxiously awaiting all of the new Batman projects that are scheduled to debut even as you read this.

And if I may be so bold, let me say that I've also *been* a pretty good Batman over the years as well. At 5'11", and in possession of a decently chiseled chin and somewhat Adam West–like physique, I can pull off the character quite well, thank you. Okay, so maybe I wouldn't be in the running for a "major motion picture" Batman, but I make a solid "local" Batman. In fact, every Halloween for many years running, the public library where I worked asked me to appear at its Youth Services Halloween party and give a short speech about trick-or-treater safety to all of the costumed kids in attendance. And I'm proud to say that as Batman, I never won our staff association's "Best Employee Costume" award. It seemed to everyone at the library that it wasn't a costume but actually my uniform — I *was* Batman, and I was simply doing my job.

In fact, I maybe ended up being a little too convincing as Batman — some of the mommies accompanying their children to the Halloween party tried to hire me for birthday parties. For a moment, I would think about taking the gig — it would be the ultimate fanboy rush, to actually *be* Batman for a group of excited kids! Then my logical side would speak up — "What are you going to do when these kids start asking you to perform martial arts moves and backflips, or to jump off of a second story roof?" In the heat of the moment, I probably would have actually *tried* one of these maneuvers, and probably would have injured myself and given some poor kid a birthday memory he'd never forget. Thankfully my logical side always won out over my fanboy side in these situations, so Batman was not able to fit these parties into his busy crime fighting schedule.

But one mom finally convinced me to meet her halfway on her son's birthday celebration. I told her I was not prepared to "perform" as Batman at his party, but we struck a deal that I would come to their front door in costume just after dark and deliver a special Batman toy to him, and quickly run off into the night. The whole operation went off like clockwork — I parked my car far enough away that the birthday boy couldn't tell my Batmobile was actually a dark blue Toyota, and I hit the door fast. I handed him his present as he stared at me wide-eyed, grimly wished him a happy birthday and melted into the darkness. I jumped back into my car, still in full costume, and sped down the shadowed street.

It was at that moment that I best understood why Batman has appealed to both kids and adults for generations. Batman represents not only a powerful symbol of fantasy and adventure for kids, but also an equally powerful symbol of how much the human spirit is capable of for adults. I was just an ordinary man, but for a couple of seconds the costume had transformed me into a hero in that boy's eyes. Bruce Wayne was also an ordinary man, but to make sense of his life, he transformed himself into something much more. He pushed himself to be stronger, faster and smarter than seemed to be humanly possible — and then he put on just about the coolest costume anyone could dream up. When I put on that costume, I might not have been able to do all the great things that a "real" Batman might be capable of, but to a little boy I could convey that spirit of fantasy and adventure, and at the same time remind myself of how much potential that all of us "ordinary people" have.

Simply put, I believe in the spirit of the Batman character as much as many people believe in the spirit of Santa Claus as a representation of human generosity and goodness. Batman's relentless quest for justice serves to remind us that even though bad things happen in this world, we all have the courage and strength deep inside of us to help us rise above these bad things. I became a Batman fan as a child because of his cool costume and his great adventures but remained a fan as an adult because he never lets me forget that no matter how good or bad I think I'm doing in my own life, I can always try harder, do better.

I hope I've convinced you that my intentions are true, and that I am writing this book out of the deepest respect and affection for the Batman character. So this is where we'll go from here: We'll examine the history of Batman feature films in the context of the character's overall history. Of course, there will be chapters on each individual film, but there will also be chapters interspersed throughout the book that chronicle the general evolution of the Batman character. In the feature film chapters, I'll provide full cast and crew information, production and release details, plot synopsis and detailed analysis of that film's artistic and technical merits. I will have a lot to say about these films in terms of writing, directing, acting, construction, editing, continuity, sets, and so on that to my knowledge has not been explored in any previously published Batman books or reviews.

Many readers may disagree with the opinions I have about the Batman character and the movies in which he has appeared. In my previous book, *Abraham Lincoln on Screen*, I examined the history of Lincoln-related films and television shows. Since Lincoln was a real person, there was not as much room for personal opinion as there is in this book. It was easy for me to say, "This film is historically inaccurate because it depicts Lincoln traveling to the New Mexico territory to meet with an Indian chief, and this is something the real Lincoln never did." Obviously, there is no "real" Batman, he is a fictional character — so all of us have interpretations of him that are no more or less valid than anyone else's. This study of Batman films will be filtered through my own sensibilities regarding the character, and if I say something in these pages that you completely disagree with, feel free to write me, write my publisher or, better yet, write your own book that proves me wrong!

1

The Creation of Batman and His World, 1939–1942

His appearance has changed little in his 70-plus years—he wears a dark cowl outfitted with pointed ears. The cowl attaches to a voluminous dark cape with scallops cut into the bottom. When he spreads his arms wide, the cape opens and he creates a frightening image that looks like a giant version of his namesake. He wears a gray, form-fitting acrobat-style bodysuit with a bat emblem on his chest, dark gloves and boots. Around his waist is a combat-style utility belt, outfitted with climbing gear (known as the Batrope), boomerang (known as the Batarang) and various other items such as infrared flashlight, smoke pellets and knock-out gas. Only in his earliest adventures did he ever carry lethal weapons such as guns.

The colors and style of this basic costume have been subject to many revisions over the decades. Sometimes his cape, cowl, gloves and boots are blue, sometimes they are black. Sometimes his pointed ears are long, sometimes they are short. His bodysuit might be similar to regular clothing material, or it might be outfitted with heavy-duty body armor. Sometimes his eyes can be seen through his cowl, but often they appear as nothing more than eerie white slits. The bat emblem on his chest might just be a black bat silhouette, or it might be a black bat silhouette inside of a yellow oval. But in all of these incarnations, he is immediately recognizable as the master crimefighter Batman.

The history of Batman began with the publishing company that has always owned the rights to the character, DC Comics. "DC" was an acronym for *Detective Comics*, one of the company's initial comic book titles first published in March 1937. The company would adopt several different official names as it grew during its first few decades of existence, but it was almost always popularly known as "DC"—in fact, its comic titles began carrying the "DC" logo on their covers as early as 1940. Consequently, we'll refer to the company as DC Comics throughout this book.

Batman was created for DC in 1939 by Bob Kane, a 23-year-old artist from New York City. The success of Superman, who made his debut in DC's *Action Comics* the previous year, was so great that the company was anxious to introduce new characters that might capitalize on their readers' interest in costumed heroes. DC editor Vin Sullivan suggested to Kane that he ought to design such a character, which led Kane to come up with the idea of a costumed hero called "Batman." Kane took his idea to Bill Finger, a writer with whom Kane had collaborated on several comic series published in 1938 and early 1939, and the two began to piece together Batman's appearance and personality. Though Kane would receive a solo byline for creating Batman from DC, in reality the finished character was the result of his collaboration with Finger.[1]

In developing their hero, Kane and Finger were influenced by a number of diverse sources. The idea of Batman's scalloped cape came from Leonardo da Vinci's drawing of a glider he had designed called the "ornithopter," which was outfitted with bat-like wings. The idea of a heroic figure conversely clad in a dark, sinister-looking costume like a villain's came from pulp magazine characters such as Johnston McCulley's Zorro and Walter Gibson's The Shadow. The concept of that hero being a seemingly idle socialite by day and a masked vigilante by night was drawn from the Zorro character as well. Zorro's influence on Batman did not end there — Kane singled out the first Zorro film adaptation, the 1920 motion picture *The Mark of Zorro* starring Douglas Fairbanks in the title role, as being one of his biggest inspirations to create Batman.

The Mark of Zorro was not the only motion picture to shape Batman's creation. The 1930 film *The Bat Whispers* was instrumental in helping Kane to formulate the idea of a bat motif for his character. *The Bat Whispers* was directed by Roland West, and based on the 1920 hit Broadway play *The Bat* by Mary Roberts Rinehart and Avery Hopwood. The film's plot revolved around a murderer known as "The Bat" who stalked his victims while wearing a black mask and cloak. The bat-like shadows that "The Bat" cast in a number of the film's scenes would have an immediate and profound influence on the manner in which Kane would render Batman.[2]

Since Kane was an artist, he was primarily seeing Batman as a visual character. This meant that it was up to Finger the writer to flesh out just what going on inside Batman's mind. Inspired by Sir Arthur Conan Doyle's classic detective character Sherlock Holmes, Finger decided to make Batman a master detective. Batman's incredible investigative and deductive abilities would become as important to his persona as his cape and cowl.[3]

"The Bat-Man" in his comic book debut "The Case of the Chemical Syndicate," *Detective Comics* #27, May 1939. Art by Bob Kane.

All of these different literary and visual elements were synthesized into Kane and Finger's Batman. "The Bat-man," as he was initially billed, first appeared in a story entitled "The Case of the Chemical Syndicate" in *Detective Comics* #27, May 1939. Remarkably, from this very first appearance much of the Batman mythos that would endure for generations was already firmly in place. The opening panel of the story featured the Bat-man standing on a city rooftop, seen only in silhouette, with his arms outstretched so that his cape looked like giant bat wings. In "The Case of the Chemical Syndicate," the Bat-man was portrayed as an ordinary man with no superhuman powers like Superman — he was simply a dark-costumed vigilante who was both a skilled fighter and detective. Commissioner Gordon appeared in the story as well, though he and the Bat-man were not yet confidants.

In the story, the Bat-man encounters Alfred Stryker, a crooked businessman who is murdering his fellow business partners in order to gain control of their jointly owned chemical corporation. The Bat-man thwarts Stryker's scheme, and at the end of the story Stryker suffers a fatal fall into one of his own chemical tanks after being punched out by the cowled crimefighter. Upon Stryker's death, the Bat-man says "a fitting end for his kind." The last panels of "The Case of the Chemical Syndicate" revealed that the man behind the cowl was secretly Bruce Wayne, a young socialite. The biggest difference between this early Bat-man and the character he would evolve into was that he was not opposed to seeing criminals killed.

As previously mentioned, the pulp magazine hero the Shadow was one of a number of characters that Kane and Finger drew on to create Batman. But Batman's debut story owed its existence exclusively to the Shadow. As Finger went about writing "The Case of the Chemical Syndicate," he borrowed liberally from writer Theodore Tinsley's 1936 Shadow pulp story "Partners of Peril." In "Partners of Peril," the Shadow battles a crooked businessman who is trying to murder all of his fellow business partners in order to gain control of their jointly owned chemical corporation. In other words, most every key plot point found in "Partners of Peril" is in "The Case of the Chemical Syndicate" with the Bat-man standing in for the Shadow![4]

This fact might lead one to question just how original a character Batman ever really was. After all, we have seen that Batman was derivative of a number of literary and visual works, most of them classics in their own right. And now we see that his first story was an exact trace-over of one of these works. Perhaps the answer to this question is that Batman *wasn't* all that original — but original or not, he was such a fascinating blend of diverse influences that comic audiences were instantly drawn to him. Batman's quick success left no reason to debate his originality. The timeless appeal of the character seemed to be a forgone conclusion even as the ink was drying on his first few comic appearances. He was just, well, *Batman*, and that's all there was to it.

Batman's initial success let Kane, Finger and DC Comics know they were really on to something, and it was obvious that such a strong character needed an equally strong origin. Kane and Finger delivered the goods, providing Batman with a very memorable background story. The two-page "Legend — The Batman and How He Came to Be" served as a preface to the *Detective Comics* #33, November 1939 story "Batman Wars Against the Dirigible of Doom." It revealed that Batman was born from a horrific event — Bruce Wayne's parents were murdered by a thief right in front of Bruce's eyes when he was just a boy.

Bruce, Thomas and Martha Wayne had just come out of a movie theater when a robber came up to them and demanded their valuables. He tried to take Martha's necklace, and when Thomas Wayne tried to stop him, the robber shot both of them. Bruce was left an orphan, and the tragedy so traumatized him that he vowed to spend the rest of his life waging war on all criminals to avenge his parents' deaths. Over the years, Bruce trained himself to physical and mental perfection, until he was a great athlete, scientist and detective. He decided to wear a costume when he was fighting crime because he felt that criminals were a "superstitious, cowardly lot" and a disguise would "strike terror into their hearts." As he was sitting in his study thinking about what his costume should be, a bat flew in the open window. He said, "It's an omen ... I shall become a *bat*!"

Batman's success led Kane to bring in additional creative talent to help develop new Batman comic stories. The most notable of Kane's assistants during Batman's early years was artist Jerry Robinson. At first Robinson simply worked on adding lettering and backgrounds to Kane's finished work. But Robinson's work was so good that Kane soon entrusted him with the task of inking and embellishing most *all* of Kane's rough pencil sketches. Since Robinson's style of drawing was generally more realistic than Kane's cartoonish renderings based on the look of newspaper strips such as Chester Gould's *Dick Tracy*, Batman comic stories began to evolve into more visually complex works.[5]

Kane's willingness to allow Robinson to incorporate his own style of drawing into Batman comics was a decision that would have far-reaching implications for the visual appearance of the character. The task of plotting Batman's adventures was a collaborative effort right from the start—Kane relied on DC Comics writers like Bill Finger and Gardner Fox to supply his visuals with a strong narrative. But the art in those first Batman comics was Kane's. Once Kane let Robinson change his original image of Batman, it paved the way for numerous artists to develop their own distinctive interpretations of the character. Though well into the 1960s Batman stories would carry the sole byline of "Bob Kane," in reality the character would grow into a visual icon not through the efforts of Kane, but the many uncredited artists who subsequently drew him. (We'll be examining a number of these uncredited artists throughout this book.)

In *Detective Comics* #38, April 1940, Kane and company gave Batman a young sidekick. Robin made his debut in a story entitled "Robin—The Boy Wonder." In the story, Robin wore a costume consisting of a red tunic emblazoned with a yellow "R," a yellow cape, and a black mask. The costume also featured green short sleeves, short pants, gloves, and boots. The Robin costume would not be subjected to the same number of changes that the Batman costume would be over the years—amazingly, Robin would be depicted wearing this exact same costume in virtually all of his comic book appearances from 1940 up until the early 1990s!

In "Robin—The Boy Wonder," a young circus performer named Dick Grayson suffers a tragedy much like the one that led Bruce Wayne to become Batman. Dick and his parents have a trapeze act called "The Flying Graysons," and Dick's parents are killed when their trapeze ropes fail during a performance. But their deaths are not an accident—the ropes were sabotaged by a group of gangsters demanding protection money from the owner of the circus. Bruce happens to be attending the circus the night of the Grayson murders; because Dick's heartbreak so closely mirrors his own, he decides to take the boy on as a junior partner. Bruce reveals his secret life as Batman to Dick, and trains him in the ways of fighting crime. Dick adopts the guise of Robin, a "young Robin Hood of today." Together Batman and Robin bring the gangsters responsible for the Grayson murders to justice.

It seems strange that Kane and his Batman collaborators would have chosen to pair their dark, lone crimefighter with a brightly costumed, smiling child. But Kane felt that since the majority of comics readers were children, a heroic character close to their own age would have great appeal to them. And Kane proved to be right — after Robin's debut, sales of *Detective Comics* soared.[6]

But even though Robin would become an iconic character almost as recognizable as Batman himself, his presence in Batman's world led to a debate among Batman fans that continues to this day. Many Batman fans feel that the character works best when he is a lone vigilante, while others have argued that Robin's bright costume and sunny disposition serve as an effective contrast to Batman's dark persona. But no matter how one feels about Robin, there is no denying the fact that from his 1940 debut up until the present he has remained an integral part of the Batman mythos.

At any rate, by early 1940 Batman and Robin were so popular that, like their fellow DC character Superman, they received their own comic book title. *Batman* #1, Spring 1940, was one of the most momentous single comics ever published. It was not only the first-ever comic strictly devoted to the adventures of Batman, but it also featured the first-ever appearances of the villains the Joker and the Catwoman (known simply as "the Cat" at the time). It also reprinted Batman's two-page origin first featured in *Detective Comics* #33.

The two Joker stories in *Batman* #1 were by far the most compelling ones in the comic book. The first, simply titled "The Joker," served as an introduction to the villain, whose chalk white face, blood red lips and green hair looked like the grinning court jester face found on the Joker cards in many playing card decks. Clad in a bright purple suit, the Joker was an insane, murderous and diabolically clever criminal.

In the story, the Joker interrupts a radio broadcast to announce that he will kill millionaire Henry Claridge and steal a rare diamond from him. The villain makes good on his

Batman and Robin in "the Joker," *Batman* #1, Spring 1940. Art by Bob Kane and Jerry Robinson.

promise when Claridge falls over dead, and his face locks in a ghastly smile. We learn that the Joker actually stole the diamond the night before, and at the same time injected the sleeping Claridge with his own mix of deadly "Joker venom" chemicals concocted to have a delayed reaction of 24 hours.

The sensational murder attracts the attention of Batman and Robin. Batman learns that a rival criminal with a grudge against the Joker plans to ambush and kill him. Batman is lying in wait unseen when the ambush goes down, but the criminals spot him and open fire on him instead of the Joker. Batman fights off the criminals while the Joker escapes in the confusion. Batman gives chase, and their first-ever confrontation ends in favor of the Joker, when the killer delivers a kick to Batman's head and knocks him off of a bridge into a river.

Later, Batman and Robin encounter the Joker while he is in the process of murdering a prominent judge who once sent him to prison. Robin follows the Joker as he leaves the scene of the crime, but the Joker delivers a surprise blow to the boy's head and knocks him out. The Joker is about to administer his Joker venom to Robin just as Batman bursts on the scene. He fights off the Joker and saves his partner, but the Joker again eludes capture. That same night, Batman and Robin are able to track down the Joker while he attempts another robbery. This time the crimefighters defeat him and send him to prison.

Unbelievably, "The Joker" contained another milestone in Batman history that would eventually become every bit as important as the Joker himself. In the story, Batman was referred to by the nickname "The Dark Knight" for the first time. After the previously-mentioned confrontation when the Joker knocks Batman into a river, a title tells us that "The shock of cold water quickly revives the Dark Knight." Those three words would not immediately be cemented to the Batman character after *Batman* #1 was published, but over the years they would be used to such great effect by important Batman writers that "The Dark Knight" would become DC's official second name for Batman.

The second Joker story in *Batman* #1, entitled "The Joker Returns," was set a scant two days after the first story. In "The Joker Returns," the ghastly criminal escapes prison and goes on a crime spree similar to the murders and robberies he committed in "The Joker." Batman and Robin again track him down and do battle with him, and this time during a fight the Joker is stabbed by his own knife, which he was wielding against the crimefighters. Batman and Robin leave the scene thinking the Joker is gone for good, but the last panel shows that the Joker's wound is not mortal, and he will live to plague the heroes yet again.

The Joker in "The Joker," *Batman* #1, Spring 1940. Art by Bob Kane and Jerry Robinson.

Interestingly, "The Joker Returns" was originally supposed to end with the villain actually dying. But DC Comics editor Whitney Ellsworth immediately recognized what a strong character the Joker was, and requested that the story be revised so that the Joker could be used in subsequent Batman stories.[7]

Ellsworth could not have been more right—in creating the Joker, the team of Kane, Finger and Robinson had struck gold yet again. From the first panels of "The Joker," the character was as memorable and fully formed as Batman and Robin had been in *their* debut stories. And it was immediately obvious that he was the *perfect* arch-enemy for the crimefighters, because everything about him was the complete opposite of Batman and Robin. Batman and Robin both had very intricately crafted origins so that readers knew who they were and how they had become such great heroes. The Joker had *no* origin—no one knew where he came from or who he was, his villainy just seemed to materialize from out of nowhere. Batman was a hero conversely clad in a dark costume much like a villain would wear, and the Joker was a villain conversely clad in a bright costume much like a harmless, funny clown would wear. Batman and Robin stood as powerful symbols of all that was noble and honorable, and the Joker stood as an equally powerful symbol of all that was chaotic and evil.

Like Batman, the Joker also was a character that was inspired by the motion picture medium. Kane's and Robinson's original drawings of the Joker were a direct copy of actor Conrad Veidt's makeup in *The Man Who Laughs* (1928), a silent historical drama based on the novel by Victor Hugo.[8] Veidt's character in *The Man Who Laughs* has been disfigured in a horrible way—his face and mouth have been cut into a permanent, grotesque smile. In the film, Veidt looks *exactly* like the drawings of the Joker in *Batman* #1—in fact, he looks far more like the traditional "comic book" version of the Joker than Cesar Romero, Jack Nicholson or Heath Ledger would look when they actually played the character on the big screen!

The Catwoman's debut in an untitled *Batman* #1 story was less auspicious than the Joker's. As previously mentioned, she was known only as "The Cat," and she was simply a jewel thief who wore ordinary street clothes. Still, one major aspect of her character that would both plague and thrill Batman was already in place—she was a very beautiful woman, and Batman was immediately attracted to her even though she was on the wrong side of the law. In fact, at the end of the story Batman and Robin capture the Cat, but Batman is so taken with her that he allows her to escape.

The character next appeared in another untitled story in *Batman* #2 that also featured the Joker. She still wore street clothes instead of a special costume in *Batman* #2, but she was now being billed as "The Cat-woman." By *Batman* #3, she was given her first costume: In "The Batman vs. the Cat-Woman," she wore a cloak and a mask that looked like a real cat. By the mid–1940s, she would lose the cat mask for a purple dress and cat-styled cowl. But that costume also would not last; in fact, over the years her appearance would vary more than any other major Batman adversary. She would eventually be depicted in no less than ten completely different costumes. However, her real name would never change—when not dressed as the Catwoman, she was known as Selina Kyle.

DC editor Whitney Ellsworth had made another Bat-decision that was every bit as important as his decision to preserve the character of the Joker for further use. Ellsworth informed Kane and company that he wanted the character to stop using lethal force against criminals in future Batman comics. Batman's use of such force had been a rarity over the course of his first adventures, but Ellsworth decreed that it cease entirely. This decision was reinforced by the fact that Batman now had a child as his junior partner, and it seemed inappropriate to depict Batman killing criminals with a youngster standing by his side.[9] Plus, Batman and Robin's aversion to lethal force made good narrative sense — the crimefighters had both suffered greatly over the murders of their loved ones, so it seemed only fitting that they would be completely opposed to taking another person's life. Once Batman gave up killing for good, he became an even more heroic character because he now held the moral high ground over his adversaries.

Not long after Batman stopped using lethal force on criminals, he also became a confidant of Gotham City's official law enforcement agencies. Police Commissioner Gordon had appeared in Batman's very first adventure, but at the time Gordon considered him an outlaw. Gordon changed his mind about Batman in *Batman #7*, October-November 1941: In the story "The People vs. The Batman," the Commissioner finally realized how valuable Batman was to Gotham as a crimefighter, so he appointed the masked man an honorary member of the Gotham City Police Department. The bond between Batman and Gordon, forged out of the two men's desire to see all criminals brought to justice, would become one of the most enduring elements of Batman comic stories over the years. However, this bond never led to Batman revealing his secret identity to the Commissioner.

Batman's character began to soften somewhat after he became a "legitimate" presence in Gotham City. He started to come across not so much as a grim avenger of evil, but as a benevolent, albeit strangely dressed, police officer. Some Batman fans regretted this change; they felt that the introduction of Robin had already diluted the character's power, and making him an officially sanctioned crimefighter further watered him down. In fact, throughout the years DC Comics writers would often concoct scenarios that pitted Batman against legitimate law enforcement agencies, even if only temporarily, in order to give the character back some of the edge he had in his 1939-40 adventures.

One might wonder why this is the first time in this discussion of Batman's history that Batman's hometown, the fictional Gotham City, has been mentioned by name. The reason for this is quite simple — Batman's city was not given the name "Gotham City" until *Batman #4*, Winter 1941, almost two years after the character's debut. From the very beginning, Kane and company depicted Batman operating in a large metropolitan area modeled after New York City — it just took them a while to settle on a final name for that metropolitan area.

Gotham City was not the only element of Batman's mythos that Kane and company introduced into Batman comic stories as a "work in progress." Batman's most recognizable piece of equipment in his crimefighting arsenal, his sleek, state-of-the-art car the Batmobile, also debuted in a not quite fully realized form. The first time Batman and Robin were shown driving a car that was referred to as "the Batmobile" was in "The Secret Cavern," a story that appeared in *Detective Comics #48*, February 1941 — but the car was a normal-looking red automobile without any bat-themed body stylings. A much more distinctive Batmobile debuted in *Batman #5*, Spring 1941, in a story entitled "The Riddle of the Missing Card." This Batmobile, dark blue in color, sported a stylized bat head on its grill and a large batwing-like tailfin on its roof. The Batmobile as it was drawn in "The Riddle of the Missing Card" would define the car's basic appearance well into the 1960s.

Batman's popularity continued to grow at such a rate that he and Robin began appearing regularly in a third DC comic title. *World's Best Comics #1*, published in Spring 1941, contained stories featuring DC's three most popular characters, Superman, Batman and Robin. The title of the comic was changed to *World's Finest Comics* the very next issue.

Though the covers of *World's Finest Comics* depicted the heroes appearing all together, Batman and Robin actually appeared in stories of their own, and Superman appeared in stories of his own. The three heroes would not begin teaming up in *World's Finest Comics* until 1954.

As previously mentioned, Bob Kane hired other artists to help him keep up with his Batman comic workload, and a number of these uncredited artists had a visual impact on the character that was as great as Kane's own. One of these artists was Dick Sprang, who began drawing Batman stories and comic covers in 1941. Sprang's imaginative, detailed renderings of Batman and his world were among the most memorable Batman images of the 1940s and '50s.[10]

In the opening of the Joker story "Case of the Costume-Clad Killers" (*Detective Comics* #60, February, 1942), the Batsignal was used to summon Batman and Robin for the first time. The Batsignal, a giant spotlight outfitted with a bat silhouette, was located on the roof of the Gotham City Police headquarters. Whenever Commissioner Gordon needed to consult with Batman and Robin, he would shine the spotlight into the night sky, projecting the bat silhouette so that it was visible throughout Gotham City. When Bruce and Dick saw the signal, they would change into their costumes and race to police headquarters.

The Joker and Catwoman had proven to be such immediate successes that Kane and company worked to create more costumed foes for Batman and Robin to square off against. Not all of their early villains were as memorable as the Joker or Catwoman, but a surprising number of them turned out to become icons in their own right. The Penguin, a short, portly criminal who wore a top hat and tuxedo in order to resemble his namesake, was introduced in late 1941. He always carried an umbrella, and these umbrellas usually served a more sinister purpose than just protecting him from getting wet — they were actually designed to conceal weapons such as guns and knockout gas dispensers. The Penguin was a dangerous villain, but his real name was quite comical — that name was Oswald Chesterfield Cobblepot!

In 1942, the villain Two-Face was introduced. Two-Face was originally a handsome, prominent Gotham City attorney named Harvey Kent whose face was horribly scarred by acid thrown at him by a crime boss. (Kent's name was changed to "Dent" not long after his debut appearance, perhaps because there was already a rather famous DC character with the last name of Kent!) More accurately, *half* of Kent's face was scarred — the acid hit only one side of him, leaving his face half-handsome and half-repulsive.

The tragedy unhinged Kent's mind, and he turned to crime. Because he had "two faces," he became obsessed with the concept of duality, and his crimes always related to the number two in some way. He carried a two-headed silver dollar with him at all times that had one clean, shiny side and one scarred side. He often flipped the coin to help him to decide whether or not to undertake his criminal schemes— only if the coin landed scarred side up would Two-Face would set his evil plans in motion.

So by the early 1940s, many of the elements were in place that would make Batman such a popular character for the next seven decades. He was a costumed crimefighter living in Gotham City who was opposed to the use of lethal force, and who was officially recognized by the Gotham Police Department. His adventures were published at least three different comic books, *Detective Comics*, *Batman* and *World's Finest Comics*. He was aided in his fight against crime by his young partner Robin. The pair maintained an arsenal of crimefighting equipment, including their custom car the Batmobile. And Batman and Robin had a number of costumed villains to fight who were as instantly recognizable as they were.

The motion picture serial was a popular form of film entertainment during these years that Batman's mythos was taking shape. Serials were multi-chapter films that were presented in theaters one chapter at a time in weekly installments. Most were action-adventure pieces, full of fight scenes, breathless chases and unapologetic melodrama. Obviously, serials were a perfect format for costumed comic characters like Batman. So Batman made his screen debut just five years after he was created, in the 1943 Columbia serial *Batman*. We'll examine *Batman* in detail in the next chapter.

2

Batman (1943)

Cast: Lewis Wilson (Batman/Bruce Wayne), Douglas Croft (Robin/Dick Grayson), J. Carrol Nash (Dr. Daka), Shirley Patterson [Shawn Smith] (Linda Page), William Austin (Alfred), Charles Wilson (Capt. Arnold), Gus Glassmire (Martin Warren), Charles Middleton (Ken Colton), Robert Fiske (Foster), Michael Vallon (Preston), John Maxwell (Fletcher), Karl Hackett (Wallace), Ted Oliver (Marshall), George Chesebro (Bernard), Stanley Price (Captured Henchman), Sam Flint (Dr. Borden), Frank Shannon (Dr. Hayden), Earle Hodgins (Box Office Attendant), I. Stanford Jolley (Brett), Anthony Warde (Stone), George J. Lewis (Burke), Jack Ingram (Kline), Kenne Duncan (Aircraft Worker #1), Lynton Brent (Aircraft Worker #2), Terry Frost (Hospital Attendant), Tom London (Andrews), Dick Curtis (Croft), Lester Dorr (Lawson), Eddie Kane (Bail Officer), Bud Osborne (Zombie Brown), Pat O'Malley (Police Officer), Knox Manning (Narrator). *Producer:* Rudolph C. Flothow. *Director:* Lambert Hillyer. *Screenplay:* Victor McLeod, Leslie Swabacker, Harry Fraser (based on Batman comic magazine features appearing in *Detective Comics* and *Batman* magazines). *Batman Creator:* Bob Kane. *Director of Photography:* James S. Brown, Jr. *Film Editors:* Dwight Caldwell, Earl Turner. *Music:* Lee Zahler. *Sound Engineer:* Jack Goodrich. *Studio:* Columbia. *Length:* Approximately 260 minutes in 15 separate chapters. *United States Release Dates:* July 16–October 22, 1943.

Chapter Titles

1. "The Electrical Brain" (Released July 16, 1943)
2. "The Bat's Cave" (Released July 23, 1943)
3. "The Mark of the Zombies" (Released July 30, 1943)
4. "Slaves of the Rising Sun" (Released August 6, 1943)
5. "The Living Corpse" (Released August 13, 1943)
6. "Poison Peril" (Released August 20, 1943)
7. "The Phoney Doctor" (Released August 27, 1943)
8. "Lured by Radium" (Released September 3, 1943)
9. "The Sign of the Sphinx" (Released September 10, 1943)
10. "Flying Spies" (Released September 17, 1943)
11. "A Nipponese Trap" (Released September 24, 1943)
12. "Embers of Evil" (Released October 1, 1943)
13. "Eight Steps Down" (Released October 8, 1943)
14. "The Executioner Strikes" (Released October 15, 1943)
15. "The Doom of the Rising Sun" (Released October 22, 1943)

The Batman character first appeared on the screen in the 1943 Columbia serial *Batman*, an odd but fascinating mixture of Batman comic mythos, World War II propaganda and cheaply crafted cliffhanger clichés. The production starred Lewis Wilson as Batman/Bruce Wayne and Douglas Croft as Robin/Dick Grayson. *Batman* was a black-and-white, 15-chapter film originally presented in theaters one chapter at a time in weekly installments. Each of *Batman*'s chapters ended with a scene showing its heroes facing seemingly inescapable mortal danger.

Unfortunately, Batman's screen debut was most definitely *not* a well-realized, big-budget production — in fact, Columbia Pictures considered *Batman* such a low priority that they actually subcontracted the filming of the serial out to a smaller independent production company, Larry Darmour Productions. Darmour made *Batman* as cheaply and quickly as possible — all 260 minutes of it were filmed in the Los Angeles area between early June and mid–July 1943![1] Not surprisingly, Columbia's offhand treatment of Batman as a screen property resulted in *Batman* leaving much to be desired in terms of quality.

In fact, even *before Batman* started shooting, it was apparent that Columbia did not think enough of Bob Kane and company's wonderful Batman comic book work to put any serious effort into faithfully adapting it for the screen. Instead of taking the time and care to base *Batman* on some of Kane's best Batman comic stories, they employed their own writers, Victor McLeod, Leslie Swabacker and Harry Fraser, to throw together a plot for Batman's motion picture debut. Their script was a flimsy wartime adventure tale full of unimaginative cliffhanger clichés, a work so generic that it could have featured most *any* action hero as the main character, costumed or not. *Batman*'s script did not render the character completely unrecognizable from his comic book self, but he certainly did not come across as being as complex or unique as he had proven to be on the comics page.

It is likely that this decision to deviate from the "comic book" Batman in *Batman* had less to do with any negative opinions the writers might have had regarding Kane's work, and more to do with Columbia's wish to have Batman's adventures reflect the United States' preoccupation with World War II. After all, many films of the early 1940s were not looked upon as just entertainment, they were also looked upon as a means to help keep American wartime morale high. *Batman* definitely was such a motion picture — it was as much about exhorting Americans to fight the Axis Powers, especially the Japanese, as it was about Batman.

Consequently, *Batman* adopted a World War II–themed plot that ignored all of the classic villains found in Batman's comic book world. The Japanese criminal mastermind Dr. Daka was *Batman*'s only villain — all 15 chapters of the serial revolved around Batman and Robin's efforts to bring him to justice. The character was portrayed by an American actor, J. Carrol Naish, made up with slicked-back dark hair and eyeliner in order to look Japanese.

Daka was a ruthless and insidiously clever agent of the Japanese government, determined to see the American way of life wiped off the face of the earth. From his secret base of operations in a deserted area of Gotham City known as "Little Tokyo," he aided Japan in their efforts to conquer the United States and turn all Americans into slaves of a vast Japanese empire. Naish evidently considered America's anti–Japanese sentiments as his own personal license to ham it up in *Batman* — he played Daka's villainy up for all its worth, making the character seem all the more evil. (In fact, Naish was so gloriously dastardly as Daka that one wishes the serial had given him the opportunity to play an established Batman villain like the Joker — he probably would have been tremendous.)

While America's concerns regarding Japanese aggression during the World War II years were all too real, *Batman*'s depiction of Daka and his Japanese spy operation were completely

Lewis Wilson as Batman and Douglas Croft as Robin in *Batman* (1943).

fictional. In fact, "fanciful" might be an even better word—for example, Daka had an outlandish, "mad scientist"–looking machine in his lair that altered human beings' brain waves and turned them into "zombies." Daka used his "zombie machine" to turn decent, patriotic Americans into his own personal slaves—he would then force these slaves to help him carry out his plans to destroy the United States. The slaves were fitted with a metal headpiece that was connected directly to their brain (just *how* these headpieces were connected was a question the serial never bothered to answer) so that Daka could communicate with them from his hideout through a remote microphone. Daka was also able to transmit images the slaves saw through their own eyes onto a screen in his lair, allowing him to spy through his slaves.

Daka's hand-held "radium gun" emitted a lightning bolt–like blast so powerful it could destroy virtually anything it was directed at. Much of *Batman*'s plot dealt with Daka trying to obtain enough radium to build a larger gun that could be used as a weapon of mass destruction. Daka never realized his plans of building a large radium gun in *Batman*, but his hand-held model wreaked plenty of havoc in the opening chapters.

Batman's anti–Japanese sentiments come across now as bigoted and hysterical, and they appear all the more Neanderthal when coupled with such outrageously silly science fiction. In fact, most every time *Batman* has been publicly screened since its initial 1940s run, it has been screened for laughs—it has become widely regarded as a camp howler, a film so bad it is good. (I'll discuss this interpretation of *Batman* and how it affected the 1960s *Batman* television show and motion picture in detail a bit later.)

One might be tempted to write *Batman* off as a total loss for its low production values, for basically ignoring Batman comic stories, for its offensive racial stereotypes, and for its ridiculous science fiction elements. And we haven't even gotten around to actually discussing *Batman*'s depiction of Batman and Robin yet!

One of *Batman*'s biggest problems in terms of attempting to bring Batman and Robin to life was the characters' costumes— their uniforms were designed as offhandedly as everything else in the serial was. Obviously, Kane and company were able to make Batman and Robin's costumes appear more dramatic and well-tailored on the one-dimensional comics page than they ever could have been in real life, but *Batman*'s uncredited costume designers did not make much of an effort to close this gap between comic book fantasy and reality.

Batman's costume was by far the worse of the two. Its cowl was lumpy and misshapen, and the bat ears pointed in crazy, asymmetric angles off the top of it! Plus, the cowl's eye holes were cut at a severe angle, making it almost impossible to see out of it. Its cape was far too short, and it did not wrap around the front of the costume to give the appearance of bat wings like it did in the comics. And even though *Batman* was filmed in black and white, it was obvious that the cape, cowl, gloves and boots were all slightly different colors from one another. Its utility belt was an oversized, shiny, Santa Claus–style belt that did not even have proper compartments to store crimefighting equipment in. Finally, its bodysuit was made of a heavy fabric that bunched up so much it resembled pajamas more than it did acrobatic gear. Incidentally, the costume *did* have at least one positive feature worth mentioning — the bat emblem on its chest was well-crafted.

Granted, *Batman* was made in the 1940s, well before the age of fabrics like spandex — but even when giving the serial's costume designers this allowance, the fact remains that they certainly could have done a better job of capturing Batman's comic book look. One need only to look at the excellent costuming found in other comic book serials of the time like *Adventures of Captain Marvel* (1941) or *Superman* (1948) to realize how poor Batman's costume here really was.

Batman's Robin costume was decidedly better, closely resembling the look of the 1940s-era comic book Robin. Also, the costume had medieval-looking long laces running up the front of its "R" emblazoned tunic that recalled the character's original Robin Hood inspiration. However, it still had one glaring problem — its mask was nothing more that a cheap oval-shaped dime store mask that covered far more of the face than it should have. One would think that *Batman*'s costume designers would have thought to take a minute or two to trim the mask with a pair of scissors so that it looked like more like the comic book Robin's mask.

Not only did *Batman* not give Batman and Robin proper costumes, it also did not give them a Batmobile. The heroes were forced to drive Bruce Wayne's rather plain-looking convertible around Gotham City while they were fighting crime. This obviously made no narrative sense — if Batman and Robin were so determined to keep their real identities a secret, why would they venture out in public in Bruce Wayne's car? Furthermore, even by the early 1940s the Batmobile had become one of the most recognizable elements of the Batman mythos— depicting Batman without his Batmobile was like depicting the Lone Ranger without his horse Silver. Columbia's decision not to bother with creating a Batmobile was further proof of how little the studio cared about the serial's quality.

Batman and Robin's fight scenes in *Batman* were just about the most unimaginatively staged film fight scenes of all time. At least once in every episode, the heroes would encounter Daka's henchmen and a fight would break out. More often than not, everyone would basically stand in one place and flail their arms at one another until the criminals were able to momentarily overpower Batman or Robin. Then the henchmen would run off, and Batman and Robin would pull themselves together so that they could try to track the criminals down yet again. Simply put, Batman and Robin almost *never* won a fight in *Batman*, whether they were fighting two men or ten. Obviously, this is the way the action in most all serials was structured—Batman and Robin could not win their battle against Daka and his men too quickly, or the serial would not have lasted 15 chapters.

Still, director Lambert Hillyer certainly could have done a better job of varying the serial's action scenes so they would not become so mind-numbingly repetitive. Furthermore, would it really have thrown off *Batman*'s narrative thread that much if Batman and Robin were allowed to win at least a *few* of their battles? After all, the characters of Batman and Robin were supposed to be skilled hand-to-hand combatants—but *Batman* depicts them as being so maddeningly inept in this regard that they couldn't have won a fight against a group of grade schoolers.

So we can add *Batman*'s shoddy treatment of the Batman and Robin characters to the list of deficits. But *Batman* did have a number of good moments, many of them attributable to Lewis Wilson's Batman and Douglas Croft's Robin. Wilson and Croft had almost everything going against them in *Batman*, still they managed to bring their characters to life quite well in a number of scenes.

Twenty-three-year-old Lewis Wilson's good looks and sturdy physique made him perfectly suited for the role of Batman/Bruce Wayne. He played Batman in a straightforward, square-jawed action hero manner that at times transcended his ill-fitting costume. And he did an excellent job of capturing the dual nature of Bruce Wayne's character. Wilson did Wayne's "bored playboy" routine as well or better than any other actor who would ever play the role, and he also was effective in conveying Wayne's grim determination when his playboy guise was dropped.

Douglas Croft was equally good as Robin/Dick Grayson. Croft had one major advantage over every other actor that would ever play the role—namely, he was closer in age to the character than they were. To date, Croft has been the screen's only true "*Boy* Wonder"— he was about 16 years old when *Batman* was filmed, and he looked even younger than that. His youthful appearance was complemented by a naturally exuberant demeanor, making him perfectly suited for the part. Croft had only one feature that was markedly different from the comic book Robin: His head was covered with a wiry, slightly unruly hair. But even this feature was in keeping with *Batman*'s depiction of Robin as a free-spirited, adventurous boy.

It is interesting to note that *Batman* is the only live-action Batman screen work to feature a juvenile Robin operating within Batman's world of murder, death and destruction. The serial played up the harder-edged crime drama aspects found in many Batman comic plots of the 1940s. Consequently, the youngster was faced with some pretty horrific scenes in *Batman*, such as people being crushed in mine collapses or devoured by ravenous alligators.

The interaction between Wilson and Croft in the serial made their performances all the more effective. Because Croft was so young when *Batman* was filmed, the relationship between Bruce/Batman and Robin/Dick seemed quite believable. The characters came across like their comic book selves in the serial as well as any other live-action screen portrayal of Batman and Robin. Batman and Robin's rapport mirrored the way they operated in their comic book world—they were like a "father-son" team, a team forged out of a love of adventure and a wish to see justice prevail over evil. Perhaps "mentor-pupil" might be even better words to use to phrase their relationship — because even though Dick was unquestionably a minor under Bruce's care, he still had enough say in their partnership to question Bruce's actions at times during the serial.

Lee Zahler's musical score contained several brooding, memorable melodies that were quite effective in setting the mood for Batman and Robin's adventures. The untitled theme that accompanied *Batman*'s opening credits was perhaps the best of his compositions — in fact, its opening notes are suspiciously similar to the distinctive first few notes of Danny Elfman's "Batman Theme" composed for the 1989 *Batman*. If Elfman did indeed steal this motif from Zahler, he should not feel too guilty about it — Zahler himself stole several key musical phrases for his *Batman* music from Richard Wagner's 1840 opera *Rienzi*. (I'll discuss the similarity between Zahler's and Elfman's Batman themes in more detail in Chapter 8.)

The visual design of *Batman*'s opening credits should also be singled out for praise. Each chapter opened with a richly rendered painting of the familiar Batman logo featuring a bat silhouette with Batman's face on the head. The title of the serial, main credits and individual chapter title rolled over this painting, resulting in an image that was perhaps as powerful as anything else found in *Batman*.

Perhaps *Batman*'s greatest strength was that it introduced a number of elements into the Batman mythos that would end up becoming as vital to the character as his cape and cowl. First, the Batcave was entirely an invention of *Batman*'s screenwriters. It was actually referred to as the "Bat's Cave" in *Batman*, but its name was just about the only element of it that would be changed from the screen to the comic page. In *Batman*'s first scenes, the "Bat's Cave" was established as Batman's secret base of operations, located under Bruce Wayne's residence in Gotham City. It was made up of a dimly lit main chamber that featured a bat insignia on one of its rocky walls and a state-of-the-art crime laboratory in a separate room. *Batman*'s "Bat's Cave" certainly was not as elaborate as the comic book Batcave would become over the years, but it holds the distinction of being Batman's first official "home."

Batman also was responsible for creating one of Batman's most memorable supporting characters — Alfred, Bruce Wayne's faithful English butler. Alfred, played by William Austin, was an essential but slightly bumbling member of Batman's crimefighting team and the only person who knew that Bruce and Dick were actually Batman and Robin. Many times during the course of the serial he was called into service to assist them. *Batman*'s writers likely created Alfred to be a "comic relief sidekick," much like the characters "Gabby" Hayes and Smiley Burnette played in Western films. Alfred was unquestionably a "good guy" in the serial, but one who often found himself on the receiving end of Bruce and Dick's wisecracks and practical jokes.

Batman's writers evidently informed DC Comics that they had created the Alfred character for the serial, because Alfred was written into Batman's comic book world several months before the premiere of *Batman*'s first chapter.[2] The character made his first comic appearance in "Here Comes Alfred," a story featured in *Batman* #16, April-May 1943.

In "Here Comes Alfred," Alfred unexpectedly arrives from England to assume the duties of Bruce's butler. Alfred explains that he has come to attend to Bruce at the request of his father, who for many years worked as a butler for *Bruce's* father. Bruce and Dick are concerned about letting Alfred, an amateur detective, stay with them because he might stumble onto the fact that they are actually Batman and Robin. But Bruce does not have the heart to immediately send him away, so he allows him to stay for one night. Of course, in that one night Alfred does accidentally find out about Bruce and Dick's alter egos, so the heroes have no choice but to make him a member of their team.

Apparently, no one at DC was given the opportunity to find out what William Austin was going to look like in the role of Alfred before the creation of "Here Comes Alfred"—in the story, Alfred was portly and clean-shaven, while Austin's Alfred was tall, thin and sported a moustache. Not long after *Batman* began running in theaters, DC figured out a way to reconcile these conflicting versions of the character—in the story "Accidentally on Purpose" which appeared in *Detective Comics* #83, January 1944, Alfred went on a diet and grew a moustache! Alfred's comic book look has continued to be modeled on Austin right up to the present day.

Alfred would eventually evolve into a far more respected member of Batman's inner circle that he was shown to be in *Batman*, "Here Comes Alfred," and "Accidentally on Purpose." Over the years, he would become something of a wise father figure for Bruce and Dick, and certainly their closest confidant. He would also be given a last name, or more accurately, *two* last names—in the comics, his name was first revealed to be Alfred Beagle, but that name was changed to Alfred Pennyworth. "Pennyworth" was the name that caught on with Batman comic writers, so the character has been known as Alfred Pennyworth for most of his existence. At any rate, Alfred would become such an important part of Batman's mythos that he would become the only character other than Batman himself to appear in *every* Batman-related film and television project. Even though *Batman*'s Alfred was not the fully realized character he would eventually turn out to be, he was quite fun to watch thanks to Austin's light, comedic performance.

It should be noted that Alfred's origin as depicted in "Here Comes Alfred" was in no way a part of *Batman*'s storyline. This is hardly surprising, because the serial also made no effort to incorporate the origins of Batman and Robin into its narrative. Like most Batman comic stories, *Batman* simply began its story with the premise that Batman and Robin were already well-established crimefighters.

However, there was one major difference in terms of how well-established they were in the comics and how well-established they were in the serial—namely, the Gotham City Police still considered Batman and Robin to be vigilantes who operated outside the law. In the comics, Commissioner Gordon had appointed Batman an honorary member of Gotham's Police Department. For some unknown reason, *Batman*'s writers chose not only to ignore this element of Batman comic stories, but also to ignore Commissioner Gordon altogether—he was not included in the serial's storyline in any way.

The Gotham Police Department was instead represented by a character created specifically for the serial, Captain Arnold. The befuddled captain (Charles Wilson) spent most of his scenes wondering who Batman and Robin were and why they were so much better crimefighters than any of the officers on his force. *Batman*'s decision to ignore Gordon and the crimefighters' "official" relationship with the Gotham Police did not really hamper the serial in any way, because it simply harkened back to those very first Batman stories when Batman *was* a true vigilante.

Batman also featured a love interest for Bruce Wayne. The character of Bruce's girlfriend Linda Page was pulled from early 1940s Batman comic stories in order to give Batman a "damsel in distress" to rescue in most every chapter. Like the comic version of Linda, the movie version of Linda would often be annoyed with Bruce because he was seemingly wasting his life away as a self-centered, lazy playboy. Of course, neither version of Linda ever caught on to the fact that Bruce behaved the way he did in order to keep people from figuring out that he was actually Batman. The part of Linda was played by Shirley Patterson in *Batman*, and her performance was amiable enough — though it certainly did not rise above the decidedly clichéd nature of her character.

Chapter 1 of *Batman*, "The Electrical Brain," starts out promisingly enough. Batman is seen sitting behind a desk in his "Bat's Cave," wearing a grim expression on his face. A narrator explains that the crimefighter is planning his latest assault on the forces of evil. Batman's thoughts are interrupted when Robin runs up to him. Batman smiles, puts his arm around his junior partner and the two of them dash out of the cave.

The heroes call the Gotham City Police Station to tell them to pick up a "package" they have left for Capt. Arnold — two criminals neatly tied up with bat insignias stamped on their heads. Before Batman and Robin leave the scene, one of the criminals brazenly tells them that they will suffer Dr. Daka's wrath for their interference. The heroes do not stick around to find out more about Daka, because Bruce Wayne and Dick Grayson are due to meet Bruce's girlfriend Linda Page at her place of employment, the Gotham City Foundation. (The Foundation seems to be some sort of medical facility, though its purpose is never really explained during the serial's 15 chapters.)

At the Foundation, Bruce puts on his "bored playboy" ruse while talking to Linda, and she is put off by his seeming laziness. When she leaves the room, Dick advises Bruce to drop the act and let her know that he is really Batman. Bruce rejects this suggestion, saying he doesn't want Linda to worry about him; also, the U.S. government is planning on giving Batman and Robin ultra-secret wartime intelligence assignments, so they must not let *anyone* know about their crimefighting identities.

The next day, Bruce, Dick and Alfred accompany Linda on a trip to pick up Linda's Uncle Martin, who is just being released from prison. Martin was unjustly convicted of a crime five years ago, and he is eager to make a fresh start. Just before Linda and company arrive, his old cellmate Foster, who had been released from prison some months before, intercepts him at the prison gates. Foster tricks Martin into leaving the prison with him by saying that Linda had sent him. When Martin gets suspicious, Foster pulls a gun on him and forces him into a waiting car. Linda, Bruce, Dick and Alfred see Martin being driven off, but they are unable to catch up with the car.

Foster takes Martin to an area of Gotham called "Little Tokyo," which used to be populated by Japanese immigrants. However, now that the Japanese have bombed Pearl Harbor and the U.S. has entered World War II, the area is almost deserted because the country's "wise government has rounded up the shifty-eyed Japs," as the narrator phrases it.

This is undoubtedly *Batman*'s most repugnantly racist moment — obviously, America's decision to imprison over 100,000 Japanese-Americans who lived in the western part of the U.S. during the World War II years simply because they were of Japanese descent was a monstrously unjust one. It was an action that Americans should have been ashamed of, even during the uncertainty of the war years, not one to be celebrated in a fantasy movie serial geared mainly for young audiences. Simply put, this moment in *Batman* spews the kind of propaganda one might have expected to hear from our fascist enemies, not from the United States. Luckily, *Batman* would not touch on real-life World War II issues again — most all of its anti–Japanese sentiment from this point on would be directed at the fictional Dr. Daka.

Foster forces Martin into an amusement park–style attraction called the "Japanese Cave of Horrors." This attraction, the only business still operating in Little Tokyo, features wax figures depicting the history of Japan's villainy throughout the years. But the "Japanese

Cave of Horrors" is not what it seems — its real purpose is not to expose Japan's villainy, but to *conceal* it. Deep inside the attraction is the secret headquarters of Foster's boss Daka.

When Martin is brought before Daka, Daka explains that as a servant of the Japanese Emperor Hirohito, he has been charged with the duty of helping to "destroy the democratic forces of evil in the United States to make way for the new order, an order that will bring about the liberation of the enslaved people of America." To achieve this goal, Daka has assembled a group of American businessmen who are experts in fields of industry and commerce — these men are helping Daka in his efforts. Daka "asks" Martin to join their cause, at the same time warning him that if he should refuse this request, he will be *forced* to join. Martin refuses, saying that no amount of torture can compel him to turn against his country.

Daka explains that he will force Martin to serve him by using his "zombie machine" to turn Martin into a mindless drone who responds only to his (Daka's) commands. Daka demonstrates his zombie technology by commanding one of these zombies to come into the room. The drone, one of Martin's old business partners, does not even recognize Martin. Martin is frightened by this demonstration, but he still refuses to cooperate with Daka.

Daka chooses not to turn Martin into a zombie at this point; instead, he injects Martin with truth serum in order to find out what he knows about the Gotham City Foundation's radium supply. Martin tells Daka that a small amount of radium is kept in the Foundation's safe. Daka has in his possession a radium gun which is so powerful it can destroy virtually anything it is aimed at. Daka tells his men that if he can obtain enough radium, he can build a much larger gun that could be used as a weapon of mass destruction. Daka sends Foster and some of his other henchmen to the Foundation to steal the radium.

Bruce and Dick are at the Foundation when the criminals arrive. Recognizing the men as the ones Martin drove off with, they decide to investigate as Batman and Robin.

Daka's henchmen force their way into the Foundation, overpower Linda and use the radium gun to blow up the safe holding the radium. Before they can flee, Batman and Robin crash through a window and begin fighting them. The heroes chase the criminals onto the roof of the building, where they narrowly escape being struck by several blasts from the radium gun. The criminals eventually overpower Batman and Robin and throw Batman off of the roof. The chapter closes with Batman plummeting to his doom.

Chapter 2 of *Batman*, "The Bat's Cave," opens with a brief recap of Chapter 1's climactic moments. We then see that Batman survives his fall from the roof because he lands on a painter's scaffolding several floors down. Climbing back up to the roof, he and Robin apprehend one of Daka's men and take him and the radium gun to the Bat's Cave.

At the cave, they interrogate the henchman, who is spooked by all of the bats flying around in the darkness. He tells the heroes that he was hired to help steal the Gotham City Foundation's radium supply and then take it to a low-rent hotel called the House of the Open Door. The heroes deliver the hood to Captain Arnold at the Gotham Police Station.

Daka, furious over the loss of the radium gun, assumes that the weapon must still be somewhere in the Foundation and he instructs his men to interrogate Linda regarding its whereabouts. One of Daka's thugs calls Linda, pretending to be Martin, and sets up a meeting with her at a nightclub. Bruce finds out about this meeting and fears it might be a trap. He and Dick follow her, but their efforts are in vain — Daka's men kidnap her and spirit her away to the House of the Open Door.

Based on the information they received from Daka's hood in the Bat's Cave, Batman and Robin decide to check out the House of the Open Door. The heroes burst into the hotel just as the thugs are getting rough with Linda. A fight ensues and a fire breaks out in the chaos. Batman and Robin climb out a window to safety, walking on a utility line like high-wire artists. Robin makes it to the ground, but Batman, who is carrying the unconscious Linda, falls when one of the hoods shorts out the line, causing it to break. The chapter ends with Batman and Linda apparently falling to their death.

Chapter 3, "The Mark of the Zombies," recaps Batman and Linda's fall, and then reveals that Robin saves the pair by throwing them a rope at the last second. (Or rather, this *seems* to be what Robin does—the action is so unclear in this scene it is almost impossible to make out!)

Daka makes plans to hijack a government train carrying a supply of radium, and also makes good on his threat to turn the uncooperative Martin into a zombie. Meanwhile, Batman places an anonymous notice in the paper advertising the discovery of the radium gun in the hopes of luring Daka or his men out of hiding. Daka takes the bait, sending his men to meet with the finder of the weapon. Batman and Robin do not keep this appointment themselves; they send Alfred to meet with Daka's men, staying close in case of trouble.

Of course, there *is* trouble—the hoods pull a gun on Alfred, and the heroes jump in to save him. The thugs give Batman and Robin more trouble than they bargained on, so Alfred ends up saving *them* by grabbing the gun and firing it wildly into the air, scaring the hoods off. Because of the fight, Foster inadvertently left behind a map detailing Daka's train hijack plans. The train is just about to reach the bridge that Daka intends to destroy in order to stop it, so Batman and Robin leap into action and confront Daka's men on the bridge. The heroes are able to prevent the destruction of the bridge, but Batman is knocked out in the struggle. He lies unconscious on the railroad bridge with the train bearing down on him as the chapter ends.

In Chapter 4, "Slaves of the Rising Sun," we see that Robin saves Batman by pushing him off the bridge to safety right before the train reaches him. They both fall into a shallow creek as the train thunders by. Daka is furious with his men when he learns that both the radium gun and the government radium shipment have slipped through their fingers. In fact, he becomes so furious that Foster tells him he is quitting their gang right then and there. But Daka will have none of this insubordination. He drops Foster through a hidden trapdoor right in the middle of his lair. The trapdoor leads down into a pit filled with Daka's "pets," a bunch of ravenous alligators. As Foster meets his horrible fate, Daka tells his remaining men that they would be wise to avoid harboring the kind of mutinous thoughts that their late colleague did.

Daka hatches another scheme to capture Linda, who is carrying papers containing information about a shipment of radium due to arrive at the Foundation. Daka's hoods do not succeed in nabbing Linda, but they are able to steal the papers. Learning the details of the shipment, they hijack the armored car carrying the radium. As they flee in the armored car, Batman and Robin pursue them. Robin drives as Batman leaps out of their car and onto the armored car. Using the radium gun, he blasts his way into the car and overpowers the hoods. The chapter closes with Batman struggling with the armored car's driver as it careens off the edge of a cliff.

Chapter 5, "The Living Corpse," reveals that Batman falls out of the armored car right before it goes over the cliff. Some time later, the corpse of a Japanese soldier is delivered to Daka, who (using a special electrical apparatus) is able to briefly bring him back to life. During those moments, the soldier tells Daka that a new airplane motor has been designed by the Americans at the Lockwood Aircraft Factory, and that the Japanese government wants

Daka to steal it. The soldier then lapses back into death, happy that he has served his country.

Bruce and Dick also learn about the new airplane motor, though not through anything as diabolical as a "living corpse." They get a letter from the U.S. government containing a seemingly blank sheet of paper. But when Bruce submerges the paper in a special chemical, writing appears on the paper telling the heroes to be on the lookout for saboteurs at Lockwood. (This scene contains one of *Batman*'s funniest gaffes—the address on the letter reads "Mr. Bruce Wayne/1918 Hill Road/Los Angeles, Calif." Even though the serial was being filmed in California, one would think that *Batman*'s prop department would have remembered that Batman was supposed to be operating in Gotham City!)

Daka is able to turn two Lockwood employees into zombies and sends them back to the factory to steal the plane containing the new motor. The zombies knock out the plane's pilots and fly the craft into the sky themselves, unaware that Batman has stowed away on board. Batman attacks the zombies, and during their struggle the plane goes out of control and crashes.

Chapter 6, "Poison Peril," reveals that Batman and the zombies *were* inside the plane when it crashed—the solution to this cliffhanger is simply that Batman walks away from the crash miraculously unharmed! In fact, his costume isn't even dirtied or torn. (*Batman*'s writers were seemingly running out of escape ideas for Batman only five chapters into the serial.) As Batman makes his way back to town, he looks at a road sign that says "Garden City—58 miles"—it seems that *Batman*'s prop department was still having problems understanding that Batman's adventures were supposed to be taking place in *Gotham* City!

Bruce and Dick are eventually able to get back home, where they find Linda waiting for them. She has come to tell them that Martin's friend Ken Colton has come to town. Colton had entered into a joint mining venture with Martin, and it just so happens that their mine has yielded a rich supply of (you guessed it) radium. Bruce, Dick and Colton meet over at Linda's apartment that night so that Colton can tell them all about his good fortune.

Someone else listens in on this conversation: Daka has bugged Linda's apartment in order to find out her connection to Batman. (He has figured out that there must be *some* connection between the two, because every time she is in trouble, Batman comes to her rescue.) However, right before Colton tells them where the mine is, Dick finds the bug and disconnects it. Daka then sends his men to break into Colton's hotel room to try to find out the location of the mine. But Colton comes back to his room while they are there, and a fight ensues. Luckily for Colton, Batman and Robin burst in and chase the thugs off.

Daka still will not give up on finding the location of Colton's mine, so he commands Martin to call Colton. Under Daka's influence, Martin asks Colton to meet him at a chemical warehouse. Bruce learns of Martin's call and assumes that it is meant to lead Colton into a trap. He has Alfred dress up as Colton and go to the warehouse. Of course, it *is* a trap—Daka's men arrive and start to rough up "Colton." Batman and Robin come to Alfred's rescue, but the thugs overpower them. To make matters worse, some chemicals are ignited during the fight, trapping Batman, Robin and Alfred. The chapter ends with the trio facing what looks to be certain doom as the fire bursts into a fierce explosion.

In Chapter 7, "The Phoney Doctor," Robin and Alfred take refuge from the explosion in a large safe, and Batman is saved by collapsing steel beams that form a protective arch above him. Later, Bruce calls Colton to warn him that someone is still trying to find the location of his mine. But this warning is not enough to keep Colton out of danger—one of Daka's men, posing as a doctor, abducts the miner. Bruce and Dick check in on Colton and realize he has been forcibly taken. The handkerchief soaked in chloroform used to drug Colton has been left at the scene, and Bruce sees a Japanese laundry mark on it. Investigating the Japanese laundromat, Bruce and Dick see some of Daka's men. They change to Batman and Robin and jump the criminals. They are overpowered, and Batman is thrown down an elevator shaft. (Or rather, a laughably bad dummy in a Batman costume is thrown down an elevator shaft!) The elevator car is just about to come down on him as the chapter ends.

In Chapter 8, "Lured by Radium," Robin stops the elevator car right before it can crush Batman. (However, it does not explain how Batman was able to survive the 20-foot-plus fall right on his face that preceded his close call with the elevator.) Later, Linda convinces Bruce and Dick to accompany her on a visit to Colton's mine. Since Martin and now Colton have gone missing, Linda thinks that maybe they can find a clue as to their whereabouts inside of Colton's cabin located near the mine's entrance. Linda, Bruce, Dick and Alfred set off for the mine, carrying a trailer full of supplies with them.

Daka is holding Colton prisoner, and he is able to persuade the miner to reveal the location of the mine. Daka sends his men and Colton out to the mine to retrieve some radium for him. Daka's men go the entrance of the mine, and Colton manages to escape from them. Bruce and Dick decide to walk to the entrance of the mine and check it out as well, and there they see the car belonging to Daka's men. They decide to investigate as Batman and Robin.

Colton exits the mine through a secret passage that leads to a trapdoor located in the floor of the cabin. As he comes up through the trapdoor, he is surprised to find Linda and Alfred there. Colton tells them he is going to blow the mine up with dynamite and finish off Daka's men. Alfred fears that Bruce and Dick are still in the mine, so he rushes off to warn them. But he doesn't get far—two of Daka's men capture him. When Linda realizes that Alfred has not been able to warn Bruce and Dick, she follows Colton through the trapdoor to try to find them. Linda is confronted by several more of Daka's men. Batman and Robin come to her rescue, and a chaotic fight ensues. During the struggle, one of the thugs lands on the dynamite detonator, which sets off a tremendous explosion. The chapter closes as the explosion brings the walls of the mine crashing down.

In Chapter 9, "The Sign of the Sphinx," we learn that Batman, Robin and Linda get clear of the explosion and falling rubble. Batman and Robin capture one of Daka's men, a hood named Marshall. Colton has been killed in the explosion.

Batman and Robin sneak away, change out of their costumes and return to the cabin. Bruce and Dick explain their absence to Linda by telling her they never went into the mine—they laid down under a tree and took a nap! She is furious with them, and tells them that Colton is dead. In another one of *Batman*'s funniest gaffes, Bruce asks her what happened to Colton—but Linda simply says, "I don't want to talk about it, let's get out of this place"—and then everyone just leaves the cabin for home! Their friend has been brutally killed, and they all brush it off as if it were of no more concern than a bad day at work—they don't even bother to try to find a way to recover his body!

The heroes take Marshall back to the Bat's Cave, and through him they learn that Daka's men are hiding out at a waterfront dive called the Sphinx Club. Bruce assumes the guise of a cheap gangster and, calling himself Chuck White, he goes to the club. One of Daka's men, Fletcher, becomes suspicious of Bruce, pulls a gun on him and prepares to search him. Just then, Robin shines a bat signal flashlight through the window on the wall next to Bruce, and Fletcher and Daka's other hoods are momentarily distracted. Bruce breaks free of them and changes to Batman. As the criminals attack Robin outside the club, Batman appears on a nearby rooftop, spreading his arms wide to make a giant bat silhouette with his cape just before he pounces on them. Unfortunately, this dramatic entrance doesn't help the heroes' chances in the fight—they are overpowered and Batman is knocked out under a loading ramp. The chapter ends with one of the gangsters cutting a rope that seemingly sends the ramp crashing down on Batman.

Chapter 10, "Flying Spies," reveals that Batman is able to roll out of the way of the ramp right before it lands on him. Later, the heroes decide to turn Marshall over to the police. However, they do not tell the police about the Sphinx Club and the fact that Daka's men are hiding there. The heroes hope that Fletcher or one of the other men will lead them to the brains of their organization. (Batman and Robin still have no idea they are up against Daka—they haven't heard his name mentioned since the very opening of Chapter 1.)

Daka receives word that a shipment of radium will soon be dropped from a plane for him. As he prepares to receive this shipment, Batman and Robin also receive word about the radium drop from the U.S. government. Bruce again dons his Chuck White disguise and returns to the Sphinx Club. He allows himself to be recruited as a member of Daka's gang, and his first assignment is to help Daka's men retrieve the radium. As they wait for the plane to fly overhead and drop the shipment, several of Daka's men again become suspicious of Bruce. When they confront him, he runs out of sight and changes into Batman. The radium is dropped via parachute, and Batman drives off in one of the criminals' cars in order to get to it. But one of Daka's men shoots out a tire on the car. The car careens off a road and bursts into flames.

In Chapter 11, "A Nipponese Trap," Batman jumps free of the car before it crashes and burns. (There is no explanation as to why the car caught on fire in the first place—after all, it only suffered a punctured tire!) Batman, smarting over his failure to keep the radium shipment out of the criminals' hands, forms another plan to catch up with the criminals. Again disguising himself as Chuck White, he gets himself thrown into the prison cell next to Marshall. Bruce strikes up a conversation with Marshall, telling him that he knows where Batman's Bat's Cave is located. Marshall gives Bruce the address of yet another hideout that Daka's men are using, and tells him to go there and relay the information about the Bat's Cave.

Batman and Robin go to the address Marshall has provided and attack Daka's men who are stationed there. But they are yet again overpowered and knocked out. The criminals unmask Batman, but Bruce is still disguised as Chuck White—so they assume that Chuck White is Batman. Robin regains consciousness, and from the other room he radios the police for help. Realizing their cover is blown, the criminals decide to dynamite the hideout so that the police will not find any clues there. The chapter ends with Batman and Robin apparently still inside the hideout as it is destroyed by a huge explosion.

Chapter 12, "Embers of Evil," reveals that the heroes are able to escape the explosion through a trapdoor in the hideout floor. Later, Daka hatches yet another scheme to capture Batman. Using Martin as bait, Daka draws Linda into a trap, and this time she does not escape his clutches. Now using *Linda* as bait, Daka lures Batman and Robin to a factory where Daka's men are holding her hostage. A fight breaks out between the heroes and the henchmen, and the factory catches fire in the melee. Everyone escapes except for Batman, who as the chapter ends is trapped in the inferno.

In Chapter 13, "Eight Steps Down," Batman gets out of the factory right before it collapses. He and Robin return to the Sphinx Club (shut down by Capt. Arnold since Daka's men were discovered to be hiding there) to look for clues regarding Linda's disappearance. They capture one of Daka's thugs, Bernie, still hiding out in the building, and take him back to the Bat's Cave to interrogate him. Bernie tips them off to still *another* one of Daka's hideouts, one located on Bell Street. There the heroes find a hidden tunnel leading from it to Daka's lair.

Meanwhile, Linda is taken to Daka and comes face-to-face with him for the first time. Daka tries to force Linda to lead Bruce Wayne to him; Daka has finally come to the conclusion that the connection between Linda and Batman might be that Wayne and Batman are the same person. Linda refuses, so Daka prepares to turn her into a zombie. Just as he is strapping her to the zombie machine, Batman sets off an alarm in the tunnel outside of Daka's lair. Daka opens a trapdoor under Batman's feet and he falls into a pit with spikes lining the walls. (This is another one of *Batman*'s most unintentionally funny scenes. The spikes in the pit do not look sharp at all, they are shaped like — well, to be perfectly blunt, they are extremely phallic-looking! If Fredric Wertham, author of the 1954 anti-comic diatribe *Seduction of the Innocent*, had ever gotten the chance to see this scene, he would have had a field day with it.) The walls suddenly start to close in as the chapter ends.

In Chapter 14, "The Executioner Strikes," Batman wedges a crowbar between the walls to keep from being impaled by the spikes. Daka destroys the Bell Street tunnel leading to his hideout, so Batman and Robin resolve to find another way in. Daka also makes good on his threat to turn Linda into a zombie; he then instructs her to write Bruce a letter asking him to meet her. Bruce receives the letter and, even though he is convinced it is meant to lead him into a trap, he goes to the location of the meeting as Batman. Two of Daka's men jump him, knock him out and place him in a large coffin-like crate. (One would think that the mighty Batman would be on his guard a bit more when walking into a situation that he knew was a trap.) In a quick succession of scenes, we see the crate being taken to Daka's lair and Daka dumping it into his alligator pit.

In Chapter 15, "The Doom of the Rising Sun," we learn that Chapter 14's final scenes were basically an out-and-out cheat accomplished through editing: Well before the crate is taken to Daka, Robin rescues Batman from his predicament. The heroes then place one of Daka's men in the crate, and *he* meets his end in the alligator pit. Meanwhile, Batman and Robin have followed the men who took the crate to Daka's lair, so they have finally found a way to get to their as-yet-unknown foe.

The heroes make their way through the "Japanese Cave of Horrors," trying to locate the entrance into Daka's lair. Via one of his remote viewing devices Daka sees Batman and Robin in the cave, and he sends his men out to capture them. The heroes overcome all of the thugs (yes, they finally get to decisively win a fight — after all, we are in the last chapter of the serial!) and Batman makes his way into the main chamber of Daka's lair.

Before Batman can get to Daka, two zombies grab him. Daka prepares to turn Batman into a zombie, but before he does he cannot resist the chance to gloat a bit, bringing out his zombies Martin and Linda to show Batman how complete his triumph is. Robin bursts in and throws a lasso around Daka, capturing him. Batman then makes the bound Daka walk him through the process of "de-zombifying" Linda and Martin.

In going through Daka's papers, Batman learns that Martin was convicted and sent to prison on the basis of false testimony from one of Daka's men, so Martin can now begin a fresh start in life as an exonerated man. While Batman has been looking over these papers, Daka has loosened his bonds. He jumps up and takes Linda hostage as he tries to make his escape. Batman yells to Robin to hit the switch that closes the automatic door leading out of the lair, but Robin mistakenly hits the switch that opens the trapdoor leading to the alligator pit. As luck would have it, Daka is standing on the trapdoor — he falls into the pit and is devoured by his alligator "pets."

Capt. Arnold arrives on the scene but the officer still is not able to find out who Batman and Robin really are because the heroes escape through one of the lair's hidden doors. Arnold offers to take Linda home just as Bruce and Dick come in looking for her. (Capt. Arnold probably should have been able to guess Batman and Robin's real identities by this *extremely* coincidental appearance of Bruce and Dick, but he makes no such deduction.) The serial ends with Bruce, Dick and Linda all headed for home, happy in the knowledge that good has vanquished over evil.

After "The Doom of the Rising Sun" finished its run in the autumn of 1943, Batman's big screen debut was a matter of history. And not particularly momentous history at that. *Batman* performed well enough for Columbia, but its quality was such that there was really nothing to distinguish the production from the dozens of other similar low-budget serials that premiered in the mid–1940s. So, generally speaking, *Batman* went from the theaters to obscurity almost overnight — the serial was given a very low profile re-release by Columbia in 1954, and after that, it gathered dust in the studio's archives. *Batman* remained there for over a decade, apparently destined to be forgotten by all but the most avid film buffs and comic book fans.

Then in 1965, a very strange thing happened to *Batman*. As the concept of "camp" entertainment became popular in the 1960s, and younger audiences looked to find works so outrageously bad they were good, Columbia re-released the serial in its 15-chapter entirety under the title *An Evening with Batman and Robin*. The marathon film played in selected cities across the country, mainly in college towns, and it drew huge crowds who howled with laughter at Batman and Robin's efforts to vanquish Daka's forces of evil. In fact, this release of *Batman* as a camp piece actually brought the film far more attention than it had ever received as a straight action-adventure piece. *Time* magazine even ran a national story on the serial in November 1965 which stated "Wilson and Croft prompt more laughter than any other pair since Laurel and Hardy."[3]

Batman's 1965 resurrection as a camp hero was certainly troubling to the character's loyal comic book fans — after all, DC Comics had just performed a major Bat-revamp the previous year to make him a more plausible, "serious" character than he had been in his 1950s incarnation. But in all fairness, *Batman* arguably worked far better as camp entertainment than it ever had as an action-adventure work. Simply put, from a modern perspective much of *Batman was* ridiculous — so why not enjoy it as comedic, escapist entertainment?

Holy foreshadowing, Batman! In an amazing coincidence, guess what television show was going into production just as *Batman* was enjoying its run as an unintentional comedy? The ABC prime-time series *Batman* premiered in January 1966, right on the heels of *An Evening with Batman and Robin*'s improbable success. So the 1943 *Batman* turned out to be the work that started to shape the general public's perception of Batman as a camp hero. Of course, ABC's *Batman* was the work that would cement this perception for decades, but the 1943 *Batman* should be credited (perhaps serious Batman fans would prefer the word "faulted") for getting the "Batman as camp" ball rolling.

In his autobiography *Batman and Me*, Bob Kane expressed his disappointment over seeing his creation come to the screen for the first time in such a low-budget, poorly-realized production. He visited the set while *Batman* was being filmed, and was distressed to learn that Columbia wasn't even giving Batman and Robin a Batmobile to drive around in. Kane was also decidedly unimpressed with the serial's uninspired World War II–themed plot. In short, Batman's creator didn't think any more of *Batman* than the 1960s audiences who viewed it as a camp work did.[4]

Interestingly, *Batman was* treated as somewhat of a more "serious" work when it was released on home video formats in the years following its 1960s camp revival. Due to the success of *An Evening with Batman and Robin* and ABC's *Batman*, Columbia edited the serial into a roughly hour-long, six-chapter version entitled *The Adventures of Batman* and offered it for sale on 8mm and Super 8mm film at stores throughout the country in the late 1960s. *The Adventures of Batman* was packaged in brightly colored boxes that featured a dramatic painting of Batman clad in a parachute harness, bearing down on a criminal. The art was accompanied by the tag line "Mightiest Hero of All Action Serials!"

Obviously, this art was not particularly representative of the action found in *The Adventures of Batman*. In fact, its image of Batman was actually taken from posters used to advertise the 1949 serial *Batman and Robin*. But still, it presented *The Adventures of Batman* in the spirit that the 1943 *Batman* was originally intended to be taken — namely, as an action-adventure piece rather than a camp piece. Unfortunately, Columbia short-changed this home movie version of *Batman* by choosing to release it as a silent film with subtitles rather than as a sound film. When stripped of sound, *The Adventures of Batman* simply did not have the same kind of impact that the serial had in its original 1943 form.

In the 1970s, Columbia released a second home movie version of *Batman* which was far superior to *The Adventures of Batman*. The serial was presented under its original title on Super 8mm sound film as part of a series called *Columbia Pictures: The Condensed Features Collection*. This version of *Batman* not only restored sound to the serial, but also presented it in its full 15-chapter format. The Super 8mm sound version of *Batman* was packaged in boxes that featured colorful pop art–style renderings of Batman, Robin, Linda Page and Dr. Daka.

Batman was released to the general public on VHS videotape in 1990 by GoodTimes Home Video. Unfortunately, the two-tape set was unquestionably a "cheapie" designed to cash in on the character's newfound popularity following the blockbuster success of the 1989 film *Batman*. It was recorded at a substandard playback speed, which resulted in picture and sound being considerably less sharp than most pre-recorded videotapes. It also contained some decidedly amateurish dialogue edits in its audio track; these edits were meant to tone down the serial's anti–Japanese content, replacing the word "Japs" with the word "thugs," for example. Since this VHS version of *Batman* was likely going to be viewed by very young Batman fans, the edits were definitely reasonable ones — however, they should have been handled with considerably more finesse.

Like the box art for the *Batman* home movies, the box art for the GoodTimes VHS version of *Batman* advertised the serial as an action-adventure piece. It featured a dramatic, though highly retouched photograph of Lewis Wilson in his Batman costume, leaping through a cloud of smoke. The most amusing thing about the photo was that the bat ears on Wilson's cowl were severely cropped so that they did not point off in crazy, asymmetric angles the way they really did in the serial!

Batman was finally treated to a high-quality home video release in late 2005, when Sony Pictures Home Entertainment presented the serial on a 2-disc DVD set. The overall picture and sound quality of the set was reasonably good, although it varied from chapter to chapter — some chapters seemed almost pristine, while others appeared to be derived from inferior quality prints. Perhaps the set's biggest drawback was that it offered no bonus features or printed material dealing with the making of the serial. That said, however, the Sony DVD release of *Batman* was a vast improvement over the previous home video versions of *Batman*.

Interestingly, Sony chose not to remove any of *Batman*'s anti–Japanese sentiments in their DVD release of the serial. As previously mentioned, the GoodTimes VHS version of *Batman* altered some of the serial's most bigoted dialogue, presumably because GoodTimes was anticipating that their product would be watched by very young Batman fans. Sony certainly had to assume that their version of the serial would also attract the attention of youngsters, but they decided to let the serial's unpleasant racial stereotypes stand as a matter of historical record.

Like previous home video versions of *Batman*, the *Batman* DVD set was packaged in a manner that was both visually striking and decidedly misleading. The cover of the set was adorned with dramatic, sepia-toned artwork depicting Batman and Robin swooping down from out of the sky, an image far more stylish and striking than anything found in the serial itself! Obviously, the artwork was a not-so-subtle attempt to market the set as a kind of counterpart to the 2005 blockbuster film *Batman Begins*, which had first been advertised through a series of sepia-toned posters. Just in case anyone missed Sony's attempt to connect the two works, there was a tag line displayed prominently on *Batman*'s back cover that read "SEE HOW BATMAN REALLY BEGAN!" And just in case *that* didn't get the point across, the *Batman* DVD set was released on the very same week that *Batman Begins* was first released on DVD!

It has now been seven decades since *Batman* was first released, and Sony's *Batman* DVD set has guaranteed that the serial will be accessible to anyone who wishes to see it for a long, long time. *Batman* is basically such a poor motion picture work that one might argue it is not deserving of the longevity it has ended up enjoying. But this author feels that *Batman* is worthy of remembrance. After all, the serial *does* represent the first time Batman ever appeared on screen — and despite all its flaws, *Batman*'s best moments are just about as memorable and enjoyable as any screen depiction of the character to date. Granted, these moments *are* few and far between. But scenes such as the ones showing Batman and Robin interrogating thugs in the Bat's Cave, or Batman spreading his arms wide to make a giant bat silhouette with his cape just before he pounces on a group of criminals, are "classic Batman," as true to the character as any Batman image put on film in the 70-plus years since. *Batman* might not be very good, but it is still good enough to always stand as a very important milestone in the character's history.

3

Between the Serials, 1943–1948

As we have seen in the previous two chapters, the Batman character's first five years were extremely eventful ones. During those years, Batman skyrocketed from being nothing more than a young artist's rough preliminary sketch to being a nationally-known character appearing in multiple comic titles and a motion picture serial. Batman's next five years were not quite as momentous, but they still contained several notable events in the character's history.

In late 1943, Batman was given his own newspaper comic strip, entitled *Batman and Robin*. The McClure Syndicate offered *Batman and Robin* to newspapers around the country from October 1943 until November 1946. Though McClure discontinued the strip because it was not being carried by enough newspapers to make it profitable, it still managed to bring Batman to the attention of millions of non–comic book readers throughout the United States during its run.

Bob Kane worked on the pencil sketches for *Batman and Robin*, leading him to focus his attention away from the character's comic book titles. *Batman and Robin* was inked by Charles Paris. Paris' association with the Batman character began with the strip, but it did not end there — after *Batman and Robin* folded, Paris continued to ink Batman comic stories all the way up until 1964![1]

The strip holds the distinction of being the first print work to feature a fully realized version of the Batcave. As discussed last chapter, the "Bat's Cave," Batman's secret headquarters located in a cave under Bruce Wayne's Gotham City home, was created for the 1943 serial *Batman*. In the months since the serial's first chapters had premiered, Kane decided to expand on the idea of the Batcave for use in *Batman and Robin*. So for the first time, the Batcave was depicted in its familiar form of an incredibly elaborate underground center of operations.

Another form of media helped to broaden Batman and Robin's audience during this time period. The characters reached millions of radio listeners when they appeared on the Mutual Broadcasting System's popular radio serial *The Adventures of Superman*. Batman and Robin first teamed up with Superman on the serial in "The Mystery of the Waxmen," a storyline which aired in March 1945. In "The Mystery of the Waxmen," the part of Batman was voiced by Stacy Harris and the part of Robin was voiced by Ronald Liss. The characters would continue to work with Superman on *The Adventures of Superman* up through the end of the 1940s. The serial's storylines that featured Batman and Robin had several different actors other than Harris playing the part of Batman — the character was usually voiced by either Matt Crowley or Gary Merrill. The part of Robin was always voiced by Liss.[2]

It is interesting to note that *The Adventures of Superman* was the first work of any kind

3—Between the Serials, 1943–1948

to feature stories that depicted Superman and Batman regularly teaming up to fight crime. As mentioned in Chapter 1, *World's Finest Comics* contained stories featuring the characters, but Superman actually appeared in stories of his own, and Batman appeared in stories of his own. The heroes would not begin working together in *World's Finest Comics* until 1954, almost a decade after their first team-up on *The Adventures of Superman*.

Though Batman's adventures with Superman on *The Adventures of Superman* certainly helped the character to win new fans, it should be mentioned that the serial never seemed all that interested in depicting him with any real depth. Many of the elements that were so essential to the Batman character were never worked into the serial at all. For example, *The Adventures of Superman* never established that Batman's home was Gotham City — it simply appeared that like Superman, Batman was based in Metropolis. Also, the serial never got around to mentioning that Batman's crimefighting operations were headquartered in his Batcave. Perhaps if Batman had ever gotten his own radio serial, his world would have been fleshed out in greater detail — but his presence on the radio would never rise above him being simply a supporting character for Superman on *The Adventures of Superman*.

DC Comics continued to do their fair share of the work in terms of keeping Batman and Robin's popularity growing. Starting in February 1947, Robin was featured in solo stories appearing in the DC title *Star Spangled Comics*. Robin's adventures in *Star Spangled Comics* would continue up until July 1952.

A number of classic Batman comic stories were published in the mid– to late 1940s. Perhaps the most notable of these was "The Origin of Batman," which was featured in *Batman* #47, June-July 1948. The story re-examined and expanded upon Batman's origin story that was first published back in late 1939. In "The Origin of Batman," Batman encounters a small-time hood named Joe Chill whom the crimefighter recognizes as the thief who gunned down his father many years ago. (The story made one major change regarding Bruce's parent's deaths. In Batman's 1939 origin, the thief who attacked the Waynes shot both Bruce's father and mother. In "The Origin of Batman," Chill did not shoot Bruce's mother — instead, she died of a heart attack upon the shock of seeing her husband killed.)

Batman tells Robin that at long last he has located the man responsible for the death of his parents, and he plans on hunting this criminal down — without Robin's aid. Batman feels that he alone must confront the criminal who brought about his existence. Batman goes to Chill and tells him he knows that he killed Thomas Wayne, and that even after all these years, Bruce Wayne would still be able to identify him. When Chill reacts to this information with disbelief, Batman removes his mask and tells Chill that it is true, Wayne can identify him — because Batman and Bruce Wayne are one and the same person, and Wayne became Batman as a result of Chill's long-ago murderous deed.

In panic, Chill runs away from Batman. He meets up with a group of thugs who work for him, and tells them that he is in real trouble — he killed Batman's father, and now Batman is after him for the crime. When the thugs learn that the only reason that their hated enemy Batman came into existence was because of Chill, they fly into a rage and shoot Chill, mortally wounding him. The thugs then try to get Chill to tell them who Batman really is before he dies, but Batman attacks them and prevents them from learning his true identity. "The Origin of Batman" ends with Chill dying in Batman's arms, and the crimefighter declaring the case of his father's death "closed."

"The Origin of Batman" has remained an important part of Batman's mythos for over 60 years. Even though DC Comics has often tinkered with the details of Batman's origin since the story was first published, the Joe Chill character has almost continually been known in the comics as the villain who was responsible for the deaths of Thomas and Martha Wayne.

Batman might have finally brought the criminal responsible for his creation to justice, but there were still an infinite number of adventures in store for the character. He returned to the big screen for the second time Columbia's 1949 serial *Batman and Robin*. We'll examine *Batman and Robin* in detail in the next chapter.

4

Batman and Robin (1949)

Cast: Robert Lowery (Batman/Bruce Wayne), Johnny Duncan (Robin/Dick Grayson), Jane Adams (Vicki Vale), Lyle Talbot (Commissioner Gordon), Eric Wilton (Alfred), Ralph Graves (Harrison), Don Harvey (Nolan), William Fawcett (Prof. Hamill), Leonard Penn (Carter), Rick Vallin (Barry Brown), Michael Whalen (Dunne), Greg McClure (Evans), House Peters, Jr. (Earl), Jim Diehl (Jason), Rusty Wescoatt (Ives), John Doucette (Dan), Marshall Bradford (Morton), Hal Landon (Jimmy Vale), Allan Ray (Mac Lacey). *Producer:* Sam Katzman. *Director:* Spencer Bennet. *Screenplay:* George H. Plympton, Joseph F. Poland, Royal K. Cole (based on Batman comic magazine features appearing in *Detective Comics* and *Batman* magazines). *Batman Creator:* Bob Kane. *Director of Photography:* Ira H. Morgan. *Art Director:* Paul Palmentola. *Film Editors:* Dwight Caldwell, Earl Turner. *Set Decorator:* Sidney Clifford. *Music:* Mischa Bakaleinikoff. *Production Manager:* Herbert Leonard. *Studio:* Columbia. *Length:* Approximately 257 minutes in 15 separate chapters. *United States Release Dates:* May 26–September 1, 1949.

Chapter Titles

1. "Batman Takes Over" (Released May 26, 1949)
2. "Tunnel of Terror" (Released June 2, 1949)
3. "Robin's Wild Ride" (Released June 9, 1949)
4. "Batman Trapped" (Released June 16, 1949)
5. "Robin Rescues Batman" (Released June 23, 1949)
6. "Target: Robin" (Released June 30, 1949)
7. "The Fatal Blast" (Released July 7, 1949)
8. "Robin Meets the Wizard" (Released July 14, 1949)
9. "The Wizard Strikes Back" (Released July 21, 1949)
10. "Batman's Last Chance" (Released July 28, 1949)
11. "Robin's Ruse" (Released August 4, 1949)
12. "Robin Rides the Wind" (Released August 11, 1949)
13. "The Wizard's Challenge" (Released August 18, 1949)
14. "Batman vs. Wizard" (Released August 25, 1949)
15. "Batman Victorious" (Released September 1, 1949)

Columbia's 1943 serial *Batman* was by no means a commercial failure, but it certainly did not achieve any great level of success that made the studio want to immediately follow it up with another Batman serial. In fact, Columbia waited until 1949 before deciding to produce its second and last Batman serial, *Batman and Robin*. *Batman and Robin* starred Robert Lowery as Batman/Bruce Wayne and Johnny Duncan as Robin/Dick Grayson. Like *Batman*, the serial was a black-and-white, 15-chapter film.

As *Batman and Robin* was going into production, it looked as if Columbia was going to show more respect for the Batman character in the serial than they had in *Batman*. The studio was fresh off their recent triumph in bringing a live-action version of Superman to the screen for the very first time — their 1948 serial *Superman* starring Kirk Alyn in the title role had proven to be resoundingly popular with moviegoers. *Superman*'s success led Columbia to assign most of the serial's principal creators to *Batman and Robin*. *Batman and Robin* would be produced by Sam Katzman, directed by Spencer Bennet, and written by George H. Plympton, Joseph F. Poland and Royal K. Cole, all *Superman* alums. It certainly seemed likely that this pool of talent who had contributed so much to *Superman* would be up to the task of creating a Batman serial that was superior to *Batman*.

Unfortunately, this did not turn out to be the case — *Batman and Robin* ended up being every bit as poorly realized as its predecessor. Almost every element of *Batman and Robin* was sorely lacking in quality — bad writing, stale acting, unconvincing special effects, shoddy costuming and props, and wildly inappropriate shooting locations. Simply put, *Batman and Robin* demonstrated the same lack of interest in the Batman character as a screen property on Columbia's part that *Batman* did.

Batman and Robin was filmed on the same kind of ridiculously tight shooting schedule that *Batman* was, ample evidence that Columbia still did not think much of Batman. All 257 minutes of *Batman and Robin* was filmed in the Los Angeles area in just one month, in February 1949![1] Obviously, *nothing* about the serial was going to end up being very good if it had to be done in that short of a time period

It would probably be unfair to say that *Batman and Robin* was all that much worse than *Batman* was. But it certainly was not any better. There seems to be no consensus among Batman aficionados as to which serial was superior. For example, out of all the books and articles offering appraisals of the two serials that this author has examined, roughly half of them thought that *Batman* was the stronger work, and the other half preferred *Batman and Robin*. To put it bluntly, both serials are on the whole so bad that neither one has a noticeable advantage over the other. In other words, Batman fans, choose your poison.

This particular Batman fan is of the opinion that *Batman and Robin* is the worse poison. As evidenced by this book's examination of *Batman* in Chapter 2, I cannot by any means give *Batman* a wholehearted thumbs up — but I feel it still has considerably more style and spirit than *Batman and Robin* does. Plus, one must remember that *Batman* was made a scant four years after the character's comic book debut, during which time many key elements of his mythos were still in their infancy. Since these elements could not possibly be viewed as "time-honored traditions" in 1943, it is hard to find fault with the serial for not sticking to the comic book version of Batman all that closely.

But *Batman and Robin* does not deserve this same allowance. The serial was made a full decade after the character's comic book debut, by which point most every key element of his mythos was firmly established. In other words, by 1949 these elements *were* starting to be looked upon as "time-honored traditions." Still, *Batman and Robin* changed or ignored many elements of the comic book version of Batman, even after the character had proven his popularity. Columbia should have treated Batman with more respect when making *Batman and Robin* than they did when making *Batman*, because by 1949 he had become a character that possessed a certain degree of "longevity." But instead, the studio treated him every bit as offhandedly as they had six years earlier, and basically doomed *Batman and Robin* to failure even before the cameras started rolling.

For example, Columbia *still* did not provide Batman with a Batmobile in *Batman and*

4—Batman and Robin *(1949)* 37

Robert Lowery as Batman and Johnny Duncan as Robin in *Batman and Robin* (1949).

Robin! By 1949, Batman simply was not Batman without a Batmobile — the car had become *that* important a part of the character's mythos. But Columbia cared so little about *Batman and Robin*'s quality that they sent their title characters off to fight crime in a standard convertible that was every bit as plain as the one in *Batman*!

And just like in *Batman*, *Batman and Robin* depicted Batman's and Bruce Wayne's car as being one and the same. As discussed last chapter, this obviously made no narrative sense—if Batman and Robin were so determined to keep their real identities a secret, why would they have ventured out in public in Bruce Wayne's car? The new serial called for the heroes to be involved in at least a dozen car chases; in scene after scene, they were shown pursuing criminals in their modest convertible. These car chases would have come across as infinitely less tedious if Batman and Robin were shown driving a sleek Batmobile similar like the one in their comic book adventures.

Batman and Robin also lacked a decent villain. By 1949, the Joker, Catwoman, Penguin, Riddler and Two-Face were all regularly bedeviling Batman. But *Batman and Robin*'s writers ignored all of these memorable characters in favor of creating a villain specifically for the serial. The villain they came up with was an appallingly bland character called "The Wizard."

The Wizard was *Batman and Robin*'s only villain—all 15 chapters of the serial revolved around Batman and Robin's efforts to find him and bring him to justice. The villain concealed his identity from everyone in *Batman and Robin*, including all of the members of his own gang. Part of the "fun" of *Batman and Robin* for audiences was to try to figure out which character featured in the serial was actually the Wizard. But as we will see, the end of *Batman and Robin* completely cheated these audiences by revealing the villain to be a character that never really even appeared on screen until the final moments of the last chapter!

The Wizard wore a dark mask that covered his entire face, with nothing cut into it except for two small eyeholes, and a long dark cape. (He and Batman might have been on opposite sides of the law, but they obviously shared the same fashion sense.) He did not come across as particularly frightening or menacing; during the course of the serial's 15 chapters, he was never actually shown killing anyone. But he *was* undoubtedly very grouchy—he constantly snapped at his men about their incompetence and made threats that he would finish off Batman and Robin for good.

The Wizard maintained an elaborate base of operations in a hidden underground cavern located near Gotham City. (Along with fashion sense, Batman and the Wizard also shared the same taste in hideouts.) From this base, the Wizard operated a "remote control machine" that projected a beam of energy capable of locking in on and operating any piece of motorized machinery within a 50-mile range. With this device, the Wizard planned on extorting money from transportation companies by threatening to seize control of their cars, trains, planes, etc. The Wizard peered through some sort of some sort of viewer attached to the remote control machine that allowed him visual access to whatever he chose to aim the machine's beams at. The remote control machine used diamonds for fuel, so he was often trying to steal diamonds to keep it in operation. The Wizard also had in his possession a "neutralizer" which had the ability to make objects invisible when its beam was coupled with the beam from the remote control machine.

Now, all of us Batman fans must admit that the character has appeared in plenty of comic stories that contained, for lack of a better term, "junk science fiction"—that is, science fiction that is all fiction and no science. In fact, the 1943 *Batman*'s zombie machine would certainly classify as a "junk science fiction" plot device. But *Batman and Robin*'s remote control machine and neutralizer made *Batman*'s zombie machine seem downright realistic.

In *Batman and Robin*, we are told that the remote control machine and the neutralizer emit beams that allow them to perform their respective functions. In other words, if the remote control machine is going to be able to seize control of an automobile, it needs to aim its beam directly at this automobile. As previously mentioned, the Wizard operates these devices from his underground hideout—and he has not constructed an antenna of any kind on the ground above his lair. So how in the world is he able to transmit beams from his devices through the air, and then to any point in and around Gotham City that he pleases? And furthermore, how is he able to aim these devices so narrowly that he can affect just one vehicle, or so broadly that he can affect the entire city?

Also, how is the Wizard able to see virtually anywhere he wants within the Gotham City area from his hideout? He is continually looking through his viewer that allows him visual access to anything or anyone he pleases, but just how this viewer could possibly be connected to his remote control machine is never explained. And how could the remote control machine, or *any* machine for that matter, be powered by grinding up diamonds? Simply put, *Batman and Robin*'s "junk science fiction" was so far removed from reality that it came across as nothing more than annoying gibberish.

So basically, the Wizard was a complete dud of a character—he had no real identity, he was not particularly dangerous, and his gadgets did not make the least bit of sense. Again, one can more easily forgive *Batman* for choosing to concoct a new villain for its storyline. The serial's writers had a very concrete reason for creating the Dr. Daka character—he was designed to reflect America's involvement in World War II. *Batman and Robin*'s writers had no such excuse.

Another of *Batman and Robin*'s particularly noticeable flaws was Columbia's choice of shooting locations for the serial. Even though *Batman and Robin* was set in the large metropolis of Gotham City, it seemed that the majority of the serial's action scenes were scripted to take place outside of Gotham's city limits. The real-life terrain that was supposed to represent the area outside of Gotham in *Batman and Robin* was the hills around Los Angeles. Consequently, many of its scenes featured Batman and Robin scaling jagged rock slopes or running down dusty trails lined with scrubby trees and brush. In other words, Batman and Robin often looked as if they had been accidentally turned loose in the middle of a Western movie!

Also, several of the structures that *Batman and Robin* used for the Wizard's men to hide out in were ramshackle little wooden cabins that also looked like they belonged in a Western. Obviously, the cabins must have originally been constructed for some of Columbia's Westerns, and the studio simply decided to use them in the serial instead of spending money on new, more appropriate sets. These outdoor locations and sets greatly compromised *Batman and Robin*'s sense of atmosphere. Gotham City had always been patterned after New York City in the comics, so *Batman and Robin*'s Gotham should have had an "Eastern United States" feel to it, not a "Western United States" feel.

To make matters worse, some of the music featured in the serial consisted of themes that were originally composed for earlier Columbia releases, including the 1948 western *Relentless*. Not surprisingly, since some of these themes were first meant for a Western film, they sounded as if they *belonged* in a Western film, not in a Batman film. These recycled melodies helped to reinforce the impression that *Batman and Robin*'s creators seemed to think they were making a cowboy picture, not a costume adventure set in a large urban area.

But the very worst thing about *Batman and Robin* was simply the manner in which the serial portrayed its title characters. Batman and Robin came across as so unbelievably flat and uninspired that they hardly resembled their comic book selves. After *Batman and Robin*'s creators saddled the characters with a pathetic automobile and an equally pathetic adversary, they further burdened them with terrible costumes, unbearably stiff dialogue and howlingly bad action sequences.

First off, Batman's and Robin's costumes in the serial were every bit as poor as their costumes were in the 1943 *Batman*. Batman's cowl sported ears that pointed sideways off his mask, one out to the left and one out to the right; they looked more like devil's horns than they did bat ears. And the cowl's nose was so long, and came to such a sharp point, that from certain angles it resembled the beak of a bird. Finally, the cowl's eye holes were cut too low, making it almost impossible to see out of.

His utility belt looked more like a sash than a belt. It did have a buckle in the front, but other than that it was nothing more than a wide strip of shiny fabric, with no pouches on it for carrying crimefighting equipment. One large loop of fabric sewn on it off to the side could be used for carrying objects. (This loop was used only once in *Batman and Robin*, in the opening scenes of Chapter 7—the scene is so ridiculous that it deserves an in-depth explanation, so I will provide one in my rundown of the entire serial a bit later.)

Batman's badly designed gloves consisted of regular-length heavy work gloves with fabric sewn onto the ends of them so that they would resemble long gauntlets. Even though the serial was filmed in black and white, it was obvious that the gloves were far lighter in color than the fabric sewn onto them!

In fairness to *Batman and Robin*'s costume designers, they did a better job with Batman's bodysuit than *Batman*'s costume designers did—it was much more form-fitting, and it had a very well-crafted bat emblem sewn onto its chest. Also, Batman's cape in *Batman and Robin* was longer and much better tailored than was his cape in *Batman*. But obviously, these positives were far outweighed by all of the negatives mentioned above.

Once again, Robin's costume was better designed than Batman's. It had the same style of medieval-looking long laces running up the front of its "R"-emblazoned tunic that *Batman*'s Robin costume did, which recalled the character's original Robin Hood inspiration. However, the costume was generally darker in color than *Batman*'s Robin costume. In fact, it did not have a light colored cape to approximate the comic book Robin's yellow cape; instead, it sported a black cape. But this change actually looked quite good on screen. Since the serial was filmed in black and white, the black cape gave the costume as a whole more definition. Unfortunately, *Batman and Robin*'s Robin costume had one glaring problem, a problem that *Batman*'s Robin costume had as well—namely, its mask was nothing more that a cheap oval-shaped dime store mask that covered far too much of the face.

Batman's and Robin's dialogue in *Batman and Robin* was every bit as ill-conceived as their costumes; all of their lines were so mundane and stilted that the characters came across as having no personality at all. Perhaps their blandness was due to the fact that, unlike *Batman*, they were depicted as working very closely with the Gotham City Police Department. Consequently, *Batman and Robin* depicted the presence of the heroes in Gotham as an unremarkable, everyday event, as if seeing them on the street would be as regular of an occurrence as seeing a traffic cop on his beat. (As discussed in the introduction of this book, this same problem also adversely affected the comic book Batman—the character lost some of its bite once he gave up his vigilante status and became a "legitimate" law enforcement officer.) At any rate, *Batman and Robin*'s decision to portray Batman and Robin as rather unexceptional citizens of Gotham just seemed to take all of the mystery and fun out of the characters.

And not only did *Batman and Robin* not give its heroes much of anything to say, it also did not give them much of anything to do. They were thrown into dozens of scenes that were ripe with cheaply crafted cliffhanger clichés, scenes that obligated them to escape the usual burning buildings, gas-filled rooms and out-of-control cars with mind-numbing regularity.

In fairness to *Batman and Robin* director Spencer Bennet, the serial did feature a number of well-staged fight sequences. In fact, generally speaking the serial had far better fight scenes than did *Batman*—*Batman*'s fight scenes usually consisted of everyone basically standing in one place and flailing their arms at one another. And unlike *Batman*, *Batman and Robin* even allowed its heroes to decisively win some of their battles.

Robert Lowery's portrayal of Batman/Bruce Wayne and Johnny Duncan's portrayal of Robin/Dick Grayson did very little to offset all of the negatives the actors had been given to work with. Lowery and Duncan's performances were uninspired, to say the least. While Lewis Wilson and Douglas Croft gave energetic performances in *Batman* that at times managed to rise above the serial's many faults, Lowery and Duncan blandly delivered most of their lines as if they were reading them for the first time.

When *Batman and Robin* was filmed, Lowery was 35 years old, a little over six feet tall, and athletically built—so he certainly looked the part of Batman/Bruce Wayne. But Lowery's glum acting seemed to suggest that he considered the role to be far beneath him. And honestly, who could blame him? Watching *Batman and Robin*, one cannot help but feel sorry for him as he struggles to see out of his ridiculous cowl with devil's horns and a bird's beak nose, and has to spout line after line of atrocious dialogue. Fortunately for Lowery, *Batman and Robin* would end up being little more than an undistinguished entry on his acting resume—he would go on to appear in many successful film and television productions all the way up through the late 1960s.

Duncan's performance as Robin/Dick Grayson was even more problematic, because he was simply far too old for his role—he was 26 years of age when the serial was filmed! Duncan was youthful-looking and considerably shorter than Lowery, so the pair bore a decent enough physical resemblance to their comic book counterparts. But whenever Duncan talked, it was glaringly obvious that he was about a decade removed from being a "boy wonder." To make matters worse, in Duncan's scenes as Dick Grayson he was outfitted with a sports coat that had very prominent shoulder pads, making him appear more broad-shouldered than Lowery! The last thing *Batman and Robin*'s costume designers should have done was to put Duncan in clothes that made him look even *more* manly!

Batman and Robin incorporated several elements drawn from Batman's comic book world that did not make it to the screen in the 1943 *Batman*. Gotham City Police Commissioner Gordon appeared on screen for the first time in the serial. The part of Gordon was played by Lyle Talbot, who turned in a likable, low-key performance. Also, the Batsignal made its screen debut; it was kept in Gordon's office, and when he wanted to summon Batman and Robin he would shine it out of his window and into the sky. Unfortunately, *Batman and Robin*'s Batsignal looked like nothing more than a standard-sized television set with a bat silhouette pasted on the screen, and the image it supposedly projected was an unconvincing process shot of that bat silhouette superimposed on some low clouds. In fact, the same shot was used every time the signal was lighted during the 15 chapters, so it was always shown shining on the exact same cloud formation!

The Batcave was one of the few bright spots of the serial. It was a much larger set than the one used in the 1943 *Batman*, complete with laboratory gear and large banks of electrical equipment. (What purpose this electrical equipment served was never revealed.) However, *Batman and Robin*'s Batcave had one absurdly obvious weakness—it evidently had no passageway to allow the crimefighters to discreetly enter and exit the Wayne home! Whenever Batman and Robin were shown leaving from or returning to the Wayne home, they simply walked between the side door of the house and their car, which was parked right out in the driveway! What would be the point of having a secret base of operations if the only way in and out of it could be easily spotted by all of your neighbors?

And Wayne's neighbors *would* have seen Batman and Robin passing in and out of the house. *Batman and Robin*'s creators must have forgotten that, in the comics, Wayne was a very wealthy man who owned a large estate situated on lots of acreage—because in the serial, they set him up in a rather modest-looking suburban home with a very small yard! The inside of the Wayne house was decidedly "un–millionaire-like" as well—it was appointed with the kind of generic furnishings and decor that one would find in a home that belonged to a family with 2.5 children, a dog and a barbecue grill on the back porch. Both *Batman and Robin*'s Batcave and Wayne home served to reinforce the impression that the serial's creators simply had very little familiarity with the Batman character.

Batman and Robin's writers were able to concoct one character for the serial that would become a mainstay of Batman's comic book world throughout the 1950s and early 1960s. Just as Alfred had been created for the 1943 *Batman*, Bruce Wayne's girlfriend Vicki Vale was created for *Batman and Robin*. Bob Kane stated in his autobiography *Batman and Me* that he first learned about the character when he visited the Columbia lot in 1948, as *Batman and Robin* was going into production, so he decided to introduce her into Batman comic stories.[2]

Kane also stated in *Batman and Me* that the comic book Vicki's appearance was based on Marilyn Monroe. Kane claimed to have met the actress and spent some time with her both in 1943, when he visited Hollywood during the production of *Batman*, and in 1948, during his *Batman and Robin* Hollywood visit.[3] (It is worth pointing out that Kane's autobiography is filled with many colorful anecdotes that seem quite far removed from actual truth—so his claim to have rubbed elbows with Marilyn Monroe should probably not be taken too seriously.)

At any rate, *Batman and Robin*'s Vicki Vale looked nothing at all like Marilyn Monroe—the part was played in the serial by a dark-haired actress named Jane Adams. In *Batman and Robin*, Vicki Vale was basically a retread of Superman's girlfriend Lois Lane. Lois worked as a news reporter and Vicki worked as a news photographer—and, just like Lois, Vicki was always getting herself into perilous situations that required a caped hero to come and rescue her. (The character would be used in the same manner 40 years later, in the 1989 *Batman* film.) Adams was pleasant enough as Vicki in *Batman and Robin*, but her performance was no more inspired than the derivative character she played.

Each chapter opens with a dramatic title shot showing the heroes against a dark background, looking intently around them as if searching for something or someone. (Given the quality of the serial, perhaps they are trying to find their way *off* of the screen.) Chapter 1, "Batman Takes Over," opens with a number of banner newspaper headlines proclaiming the heroes' success in putting an end to a Gotham City crime wave. We then see Batman and Robin entering the Batcave, where they receive a call from Alfred, who informs them that Vicki Vale, Bruce Wayne's girlfriend and a photographer for *Picture* magazine, has arrived at the Wayne home for a visit. Bruce has not revealed the fact that he is actually Batman to Vicki, so he changes out of his costume and goes upstairs to the living room where she is waiting for him. As they chat, he puts on his "bored playboy" act for her, much to her annoyance.

Meanwhile, Police Commissioner Gordon is placing a call to a Gotham City electrical research facility that has just completed work on an experimental remote control machine. The device projects a beam of energy that is capable of locking in on and operating any piece of motorized machinery within 50 miles. Gordon tells the facility that the federal government has requested that the Gotham Police provide extra security. But soon after Gordon's call, thieves break into the facility and steal the device.

Gordon, Batman and Robin go to the facility, where they are given a demonstration of how the remote control machine works. They learn that the device is powered by diamonds, so Batman urges Gordon to post extra officers everywhere in Gotham where diamonds might be kept. Their conference is interrupted by the entrance of Prof. Hamill, developer of the remote control machine. Hamill, who is confined to a wheelchair, has been in such poor health that he had to bow out of the final construction phases of the device. He is furious with the facility, Gordon and even Batman and Robin over the loss of his life's work.

Later, at his home, Hamill is being attended by his servant Carter. When Carter leaves the room, Hamill locks the door and wheels himself over to a chair equipped with odd-looking electronic devices. He sits in the chair and flips a switch attached to it. After the chair buzzes and flashes for several moments, Hamill is suddenly able to stand on his own. He walks through a secret door located in his fireplace and out of sight.

We are then transported to the hidden underground cavern that serves as a hideout for the Wizard. His real identity shrouded by a dark mask and cloak, the Wizard is revealed to be the mastermind behind the theft of the remote control machine. He sends some of his henchmen to steal diamonds necessary for the machine's operation. The henchmen attempt to rob a jewelry warehouse, but they are thwarted by Batman and Robin.

The Wizard, angry that the crimefighters have interfered with his operation, plans another diamond heist; he has learned that a shipment of diamonds is being transported by plane from the Gotham Airport, and he hatches a scheme to obtain them. (Incidentally, before many of the Wizard's major scenes in the serial, we see Hamill sitting down in this strange chair, reviving his legs and walking through his secret fireplace door. Obviously, we are being led to believe that Hamill is the Wizard.)

Batman and Robin also learned of the diamond shipment and replace the plane's regular pilots in case someone makes a grab for the diamonds. The Wizard fires up the remote control machine and takes over the plane, forcing it to land. Once the crimefighters are on the ground, the Wizard's henchmen meet the plane and take the package of diamonds from them at gunpoint. With Batman and Robin still in the plane, the Wizard again targets the craft with the remote control machine. This time, the Wizard causes it to burst into flames and explode, seemingly with the heroes still aboard.

Chapter 2, "Tunnel of Terror," opens with Batman and Robin running out of the plane before it is destroyed. Stowing away on a plane carrying the Wizard's men, Batman and Robin listen to their conversation and hear the name of the Wizard for the first time. Batman is able to steal back the diamonds by replacing the package with another of the same size and weight that is full of pebbles. (Exactly why Batman just happens to be carrying a package full of pebbles that exactly matches the diamond package is a question the serial does not answer.)

The plane lands and the henchmen make their way to the Wizard's hideout. Batman and Robin attempt to follow, but the heroes lose sight of them just before they pass through the hideout's hidden entrance. As Batman and Robin head back to the Batcave, they notice that Prof. Hamill's house is located close to the area where they lost the Wizard's men.

Some time later, Bruce and Dick are listening to a radio news broadcast by reporter Barry Brown, who seems to consistently have inside information regarding Gotham criminal activity. Brown predicts that thieves will attempt to steal a shipment of unspecified material that is being moved through Gotham by train that very day. Bruce and Dick learn that the material targeted for theft is a powerful new explosive known as X–90 and that the train carrying the explosive has just left a Gotham train station. They change to Batman and Robin and race to intercept the train.

The heroes catch up with the train just as the Wizard's men board it. As Robin drives, Batman leaps from their car onto the moving train. He climbs up the side of the train and begins fighting the Wizard's men atop one of the freight cars. As they fight, the train approaches a tunnel. The chapter closes with Batman seemingly about to be smashed against the top of the tunnel.

Chapter 3, "Robin's Wild Ride," shows the crimefighter duck down and avoid the top of the tunnel. The tunnel provides the momentary distraction the Wizard's men need to radio their boss and tell him to use the remote control machine to halt the train. Once the train is stopped, they grab the explosive, but Batman leaps down from the top of the train at them. Batman is momentarily overpowered during the fight and the criminals are able to escape with the explosive. Batman and Robin try to pursue the fleeing thugs in their car, but the Wizard disables it using the remote control machine.

The criminals present the Wizard with the box containing the X–90. But the Wizard's triumph is short-lived, because his men forgot to steal the box containing the special detonators required to set off the explosive. The Wizard sends his men to kidnap Wesley Morton, the inventor of X–90. The criminals take the inventor to one of their secret hideouts, where the Wizard appears and hypnotizes him. Morton reveals that the detonators are being stored at the electrical research facility where the remote control machine was developed.

Later, Hamill and Carter are shown visiting the facility. Then someone's hand is shown pressing a button to unlock the facility vault where the detonators are stored, but just whose hand it *is* remains a mystery.

The Wizard's men enter the vault and steal the detonators, but as they make their escape in a truck they are intercepted by Batman and Robin. The heroes chase the Wizard's men in their car. For some inexplicable reason, the criminals stop their truck and get out of it for a cigarette break while Batman and Robin are still closely pursuing them. This pause gives Batman the opportunity to scale a rocky hillside and pounce on the hoods. During the struggle, the Wizard uses the remote control machine to electrify a metal crowbar with which one of the hoods is trying to strike Batman. Batman grabs onto the crowbar and electrical bolts fly from it—the crimefighter is lifted off the ground, his legs jerking back and forth as if he is performing some kind of crazy Charleston-style dance. The chapter closes with Batman, still holding onto the crowbar, plummeting down a steep hillside.

(Obviously, *Batman and Robin*'s narrative has already collapsed into an incomprehensible heap by only the third chapter. Why did the criminals stop their truck and get out of it for a cigarette break while they were still being chased by Batman and Robin? How did the Wizard manage to electrify a crowbar with the remote control machine when the device is only supposed to affect motorized machinery? Why is Batman dancing around like a 1920s flapper? Why is this episode entitled "Robin's Wild Ride" when Robin never takes a wild ride?)

Chapter 4, "Batman Trapped," shows Batman grab a tree limb before he falls too far. Robin, overpowered by the criminals, is thrown in the back of the truck and brought to a cabin used as an outpost by the Wizard. Robin opens a valve on an oil drum in the back of the truck, and the oil that spills out leaves a trail for Batman to follow.

At the cabin, the Wizard tries to force Morton to give him details about all of X–90's destructive capabilities. After rescuing Robin from the Wizard's men, Batman bursts into the cabin. There the heroes get their first look at the Wizard—but in reality, it is not the villain himself. Rather, it is a projection of his image on a large television screen cleverly disguised to look like a doorway. Since the Wizard is not really there and his henchmen have all fled, there is nothing left for Batman and Robin to do but to take Morton, who has been slightly injured during his interrogation, to the hospital.

At the hospital, Morton reveals that all of his data regarding the X–90 explosive are at his office. Through a radio transmitter placed in Morton's room, the Wizard has now learned this as well. The Wizard's men break into the office to steal the formula, where they are met by Batman and Robin. During a fight, Batman is knocked into a large electrical device. The device emits a fierce shower of sparks and Batman falls to the floor.

Chapter 5, "Robin Rescues Batman," reveals that the electrical device Batman short-circuited lost power before the crimefighter was harmed. However, the Wizard's men are able to escape with Morton's X–90 formula. As they flee Morton's office, Vicki arrives on the scene with her camera and snaps a picture of them. When she develops the picture, she is shocked to see her brother Jimmy in the photo—he is a member of the Wizard's gang! The Wizard's men realize that Vicki's photo could not only compromise Jimmy, but all of them, so they have Jimmy call her and arrange a meeting at a local park in order to confiscate the picture. Vicki mentions the planned meeting to Bruce, who fears that it is some sort of trap and decides to keep an eye on her as Batman.

Vicki goes to the park, but Jimmy does not; instead, another member of the Wizard's gang meets her. He tries to forcibly take the picture from her as Batman and Robin arrive on the scene. The heroes fight him off, but the negative falls into a campfire. Batman scoops up the charred photo and takes it with him back to the Batcave. There he is able to reconstruct it and identifies another hood in the photo, Mac Lacey. Mac is known to hang out at a waterfront dive called the Harbor Club.

The heroes find Mac and capture him. As they are placing the bound criminal in their car, they hear a woman's scream from a nearby pier. It is Vicki—she has also learned that the Harbor Club is a place that the Wizard's men frequent and has come to look for her brother. She has not found him, but she *has* found trouble: The Wizard's men have caught her snooping around and grabbed her. Batman comes to her rescue, but a stray bullet fired at him pierces a large gasoline tank on the pier, causing gas to pour into the water. Vicki falls in the water during the struggle and Batman jumps in to save her. One of the thugs throws a lit kerosene lantern into the water close to them, and the gasoline in the water bursts into flame. The chapter ends with Batman and Vicki seemingly surrounded by the fire.

Chapter 6, "Target: Robin," reveals that Batman and Vicki simply swim through the burning water without being harmed. (Obviously this is not a particularly compelling or believable solution to the previous chapter's cliffhanger, but given *Batman and Robin*'s overall quality, one takes what one can get!) Bruce disguises himself as Mac and returns to the Harbor Club, hoping to infiltrate the Wizard's gang. The Wizard's men are suspicious of "Mac," but they allow him to accompany them to one of their hideouts. Robin trails them to keep an eye on Bruce.

At the hideout, the Wizard's men listen to Barry Brown's radio broadcast as Brown reveals that Mac Lacey is still in police custody. Obviously forced to drop the pretense that he *is* Mac, Bruce tells the Wizard's men that he is a friend of Mac's, and he disguised himself in order to get the gang to take him as a member. The hoods are still suspicious of Bruce, so they give him an important task in order to test his loyalty. The criminals have found Robin hiding outside, grabbed him and tied him up. Bruce is handed a gun and told to shoot Robin.

Incredibly, Bruce does just that, and Robin falls to the floor. But Bruce then shoots out the light in the room and helps Robin to his feet, and the two of them dash out of the hideout. It turns out that Bruce aimed for Robin's belt buckle, so the youngster was not hurt at all. Some time later, Batman and Robin make their way back to a warehouse in the waterfront area, where Mac Lacey has told police the Wizard will strike next. But Mac's information is simply a trap set by the Wizard to lure the crimefighters to the warehouse. The Wizard's men are able to lock Batman and Robin in a room, which the hoods begin filling with carbon dioxide. The chapter ends with the heroes gasping for air, seemingly without hope of escape.

In Chapter 7, "The Fatal Blast," Batman pulls a blowtorch from a loop on his utility belt and cuts through the door in order to escape the poison gas. (This is the only scene in which Batman uses his utility belt, and it is howlingly unrealistic. The blowtorch is at least a foot tall, and he was not carrying it in the scenes leading up to its use!)

Later, the Wizard plans to blackmail the Associated Rail Company by threatening to disrupt their train traffic with the remote control machine. On his radio program, Barry Brown reports that company president Winslow Harrison is traveling to Gotham to discuss the situation with Commissioner Gordon. Upon hearing the broadcast, the Wizard plans to kidnap Harrison before he can meet with Gordon. Batman and Robin have also heard the broadcast, so they race to intercept the Wizard's men before they can grab Harrison. Vicki Vale hurries after Batman and Robin in her car in search of a story.

The heroes realize they are being tailed, so they pull over and force Vicki to stop. In one of the serial's most bizarre moments, Vicki asks Batman, "Does Bruce Wayne know that you're driving his car?" Batman simply answers, "Of course!" (As previously mentioned, having Batman and Bruce Wayne drive the same car makes no sense, since Batman is supposedly trying to keep his identity a secret. So evidently *Batman and Robin*'s writers decided to address this issue by simply having Batman infer that his borrowing of Wayne's car was no big deal, that it shouldn't give anyone any reason to suspect that Batman and Wayne were one and the same person!) Batman does not want Vicki in harm's way, so he takes her car keys and tells her to wait with her car, and he will send Bruce to pick her up. But after the heroes drive off, Vicki pulls out a spare set of keys and continues after them.

Batman and Robin find the Wizard's men just as they are confronting Harrison. Batman is able to rescue Harrison, and the two men take refuge in a small nearby cabin that the Wizard has been using as an outpost. (This is a different cabin than the one seen in Chapter 4 — the Wizard's taste in real estate obviously leans toward cabins!) But one of the Wizard's men has left an explosive device in the cabin. The chapter ends with the cabin being destroyed by a fierce explosion.

Chapter 8, "Robin Meets the Wizard," reveals that Batman and Harrison escape the explosion by exiting the cabin through a trapdoor hidden in the cabin's floor. Batman then takes Harrison to his meeting with Commissioner Gordon. Batman convinces the men to tell the Wizard that the railroad company has decided to give in to his demands. But the ransom money that will be delivered to the criminal will be obsolete bills treated with a radioactive substance that will burst into flames when exposed to air.

Batman and Robin monitor the money drop, hoping if they follow the hoods who pick up the money box they will be led to the Wizard. They trail the criminals to a warehouse in the waterfront district, where Batman ends up in a confrontation with the hoods. Robin is knocked out by the Wizard, who has come to the warehouse to get the ransom money. As Batman struggles with the hoods, the radioactive money ignites and sets the warehouse ablaze. The thugs overpower Batman, knocking him to the ground. The chapter ends with Batman lying unconscious, about to be engulfed by flames.

In Chapter 9, "The Wizard Strikes Back," Batman regains consciousness and makes his way out of the burning warehouse. He finds Robin, who has recovered from the blow the Wizard inflicted on him. The heroes see Barry Brown and Dunne, a private detective, lurking around the warehouse, and they discuss the possibility that one of these men may be the Wizard. Batman suggests that perhaps Hamill is the Wizard, but Robin dismisses this theory since Hamill is in such poor health and confined to a wheelchair.

The Wizard, furious that the railroads would not bow to his blackmail scheme, attempts to turn the remote control machine loose on all of Gotham City in order to give everyone a taste of his power. The diamonds in the machine burn out during this attempt, and the Wizard is now without his main weapon. He hatches a new scheme to obtain diamonds, one involving Vicki's brother Jimmy.

Jimmy pretends to break ties with the Wizard and goes to Commissioner Gordon, supposedly to rat the criminal out. But in reality, Jimmy is simply looking for information regarding a batch of synthetic diamonds manufactured at the research facility. He finds out where the diamonds are being held and relays this information to the Wizard. The Wizard's men steal the diamonds, but they are pursued by Batman and Robin. The Wizard fires up his remote control machine and forces the heroes' car off of a cliff. (Why the villain was able to use the machine on Batman and Robin when earlier in the chapter he said it was out of order is a question the serial does not answer.) The chapter ends with Batman and Robin seemingly killed as the car crashes.

In Chapter 10, "Batman's Last Chance," the heroes bail out of the car right before it goes over the cliff. Meanwhile, Jimmy heads to a downtown Gotham office building that the Wizard's men are using for a hideout, unaware that Vicki is trailing him. The Wizard's men grab Vicki and hold her hostage. From the office building, Vicki is able to call Bruce's home and let Alfred know that she is being held prisoner.

Alfred relays this message to Bruce, who races to the building with Robin. Once Batman gets inside the building, he is knocked out when he touches an office doorknob electrified by the Wizard as a security precaution. Jimmy finds the unconscious Batman in the hallway, unmasks him and realizes that Batman is actually his sister's boyfriend Bruce Wayne. He drags Batman around a corner. Then, almost immediately, Batman is shown back on his feet, rushing in to free Vicki. The Wizard's men see Batman, rushing him and pushing him out of a window. The chapter closes with Batman plummeting to earth. (Actually, this shot is pulled directly from the cliffhanger ending of "The Electrical Brain," the first chapter of the 1943 *Batman* serial — it is glaringly obvious that the Batman costume in the shot does not match *Batman and Robin*'s Batman costume!)

In Chapter 11, "Robin's Ruse," we learn that the man in the Batman costume was killed — but that man was not Bruce Wayne. Dressed in Jimmy Vale's clothes, Wayne runs out of the building, finding Robin waiting for him. Robin is so shocked to see him, he pulls off his own mask when he asks Bruce what happened. Bruce explains that Jimmy dragged him into a room while he was unconscious and removed his costume. Jimmy then changed

Bruce into *his* clothes and put on the Batman costume himself. So it was Jimmy who rescued Vicki, and then was pushed out of the window by the Wizard's men. Bruce assumes that Jimmy did all of this to make things right by his sister. Bruce and Robin drive back home, leaving Jimmy's body on the street; in fact, no one mentions Jimmy for the rest of the serial, including his sister Vicki.

(This is another one of those moments when *Batman and Robin*'s plot completely falls apart. How in the world did Jimmy switch clothes with the unconscious Bruce in a matter of only a few seconds? Why does Robin rip off his mask while he is standing on a street in broad daylight? Why is Jimmy never mentioned again? Doesn't his sister care enough about him to mourn his loss just a little bit, or at least plan his funeral?)

The Wizard's men spot Bruce Wayne leaving with Robin and begin to suspect that Bruce is actually Batman. The Wizard learns that Wayne is having dinner with Vicki that night, so two of the Wizard's men abduct him at gunpoint and take him to yet another one of their hideouts. (In a previous scene, Bruce had casually mentioned his date with Vicki to Prof. Hamill, so we are again led to believe that Hamill must be the Wizard.) Bruce is able to let Robin know that he has been kidnapped, as well as where he is being taken, so Robin comes to his rescue. He shines a flashlight that projects a bat insignia into the room where Bruce is being held, and the criminals run outside assuming Batman is after them. They see Batman running by, so they assume that they are wrong about Wayne being the crimefighter. After Bruce rescues Robin, we learn that it was Alfred who dressed up as Batman to throw the hoods off the track.

The Wizard himself has come to the hideout to question Bruce, but since Robin has broken up the interrogation, the criminal is forced to flee. Bruce changes into his costume and the heroes chase the Wizard's car. The Wizard releases a smokescreen from his car, causing Batman and Robin to lose sight of the criminal. The chapter ends with the heroes unable to see the road, heading right for a stone embankment.

Chapter 12, "Robin Rides the Wind," shows Batman stopping the car without hitting the stone. Later, through the private detective Dunne, Batman acquires blueprints for a "neutralizer" machine that will counter the effects of the remote control machine. The device is being developed by Prof. Hamill, but it has not yet been perfected.

Batman develops a plan to use the neutralizer to draw the Wizard out. It is publicly announced that work on the device has been completed and that it is being shipped by armored car. But the neutralizer is not in the armored car — it is merely bait meant to trap the Wizard. The Wizard's men take the bait. From an airplane, they drop bombs close to the armored car to try to force it off the road. The chapter closes with the vehicle going over a cliff, seemingly with driver Robin still aboard. (Actually, this shot is pulled directly from the cliffhanger ending of "Slaves of the Rising Sun," the fourth chapter of the 1943 *Batman*.)

In Chapter 13, "The Wizard's Challenge," Robin leaps out of the armored car before it goes off the cliff. Later, Hamill is shown to have finished work on the neutralizer; he gives the device, which is secured in a crate, to his servant Carter. Hamill tells Carter to deliver the crate to the research facility. The Wizard's men attack Carter and try to steal the crate, but they are chased off by Batman and Robin. When the crate is opened, it is revealed to be empty — the Wizard's men have obtained the neutralizer after all.

When the neutralizer is delivered to the Wizard, he demonstrates how he plans to use the device in his criminal schemes. By merging the beams from the remote control machine and the neutralizer, he is able to make any object in the path of the beams invisible. The

Wizard then goes to the research facility to steal plans for a new super jet plane the facility is developing. When he gets there, he has one of his men point the remote control machine and the neutralizer directly at him. Invisible, the Wizard walks into the facility undetected. (As previously mentioned, this invisibility beam story angle makes no sense whatsoever — how are beams aimed from machines located underground possibly reaching the Wizard, who is above ground miles away? And where did this super jet plane story angle come from all of a sudden? Furthermore, just why is the facility developing a super jet plane in the first place? It is supposed to be an *electrical* research facility!)

Batman is also at the facility, because reporter Barry Brown had announced that the Wizard was planning on stealing the jet plane plans. The invisible Wizard makes his way into the facility and puts an explosive device in a safe where Batman is hiding. The chapter ends with the explosive device detonating.

Chapter 14, "Batman Vs. Wizard," reveals that Batman retreated into the far corner of the safe right before the explosive went off, and consequently was protected from the blast. The remote control device and the neutralizer have started to overheat, so the Wizard again becomes visible. In his rush to get back to his hideout, he drops one of his gloves.

Batman takes the glove and performs a fingerprint check on it. The fingerprints belong to Carter, Hamill's servant, so it seems that Carter is the Wizard. But when Batman, Robin and Gordon go to Hamill's house to arrest Carter, they find that he has been shot to death by an unknown assailant.

In what has to be the crowning moment of *Batman and Robin*'s stupidity, Hamill *walks* in the room to find Batman, Robin and Gordon standing over Carter's body. Don't forget, the serial has reminded us over and over that no one thinks Hamill could be the Wizard since he is confined to a wheelchair — plus, we have been subjected to many scenes showing Hamill climbing into his ultra-secret experimental chair and reviving his legs without anyone else's knowledge. Now in Chapter 14, he simply strides into a room, and no one even questions the fact that all of a sudden he can walk again!

At any rate, it would seem that the case is closed: Carter was the Wizard, and now he is dead. But Barry Brown is suddenly attacked by an invisible assailant right in the middle of a broadcast in which he warned that the Wizard is alive and planning on attacking Commissioner Gordon. Upon hearing this news, Batman and Robin guard Gordon in his office (Vicki is there as well). Batman has surmised that the Wizard has found a way to make himself invisible using the remote control machine and the neutralizer, so he has Vicki place a special infrared bulb in her camera lens that enables her camera to detect anything that might be shielded from the naked eye by the Wizard's devices.

The invisible Wizard hangs on a rope right outside of Gordon's office window holding a gun. He fires, and instinctively Vicki snaps a picture. The chapter ends without revealing whether the Wizard shot anyone in the room.

In Chapter 15, "Batman Victorious," we learn that the Wizard was not able to get off a shot before Vicki snapped a picture. When the film is developed, everyone is shocked to see that it is a photo of Carter. This does not seem possible, since Carter was killed in the previous chapter. Whoever the Wizard really is, Batman surmises that he will try to get back to his hideout. Since he and Robin once lost the trail of the Wizard's men before in an area near Prof. Hamill's home, Batman sends Robin to the area to keep an eye out for the Wizard.

The Wizard makes his way back through the area where Robin is lying in wait, entering his lair through a door hidden among the trees and rocks. Robin radios Batman with this information. Batman meets up with his partner and the two enter the Wizard's hideout. As they burst into the Wizard's secret laboratory, the Wizard flees to Prof. Hamill's home. Batman and Robin follow, finding Hamill and Carter sitting in Hamill's study. The crimefighters seem not the least bit surprised to see Carter, supposedly a dead man, very much alive. Hamill tells Batman that he is ready to confess—*he* is the Wizard. Carter says that he and his twin brother were forced to take orders from Hamill, and that it was his twin brother who was actually shot to death. No one was even aware that Carter had a twin brother. Batman does not buy this story, so he jumps Carter. It turns out that Carter is holding a gun on Hamill, forcing a fake confession from the Professor. Carter, the one and only Wizard, will not escape justice this time.

After Carter is taken into custody, he reveals that it was his twin brother who worked as Hamill's servant—not him. He forced his brother to give him information about the Professor's work, which he then put to use in his criminal schemes. Every scene in the serial that featured Carter did *not* actually feature Carter, but his twin brother, who was never even given the courtesy of a name. So the *real* Carter, the actual villain of the serial, did not even appear on screen *sans* his Wizard costume until the final minutes of the serial's last chapter. In other words, *Batman and Robin*'s final insult to its viewers was to cheat them out of being able to solve the mystery they had been puzzling over for the past 15 chapters.

Later, Batman, Robin, Vicki and Commissioner Gordon talk over the Wizard case in Gordon's office. Vicki invites Batman to join her and Bruce Wayne for dinner that evening, and Batman accepts the invitation. Just then, a phone call comes for Vicki—it is Bruce. Actually, it is Alfred, playing a phonograph record of Bruce's voice canceling his date with Vicki. Disgusted, Vicki puts the phone down and tells Batman that she thought she had figured out his secret identity—she thought he was Bruce Wayne—but she now knows she was wrong. Everyone shares a hearty laugh over the notion of Wayne being Batman as the serial comes to a close. (Actually, Batman has a bit *too* hearty of a laugh—Lowery, who has been so stiff for 15 chapters, all of a sudden lets out a spooky cackle that keeps rising in volume until he starts to sound like the Joker! Perhaps he was just relieved that this nightmare of a serial was finally over.)

I hope this summary indicates to the reader how bad *Batman and Robin* is. It just seems to go on and on forever, and it contains far more awful scenes than just the ones described above. Simply put, just about every foot of *Batman and Robin* is sadly lacking in one capacity or another, and it makes for very depressing viewing—especially if you are a Batman fan.

After *Batman and Robin* completed its initial theatrical run in the late summer of 1949, it disappeared into obscurity much like Columbia's first Batman serial *Batman*. But as discussed last chapter, *Batman* enjoyed an improbable return to the spotlight when Columbia re-released it under the title *An Evening With Batman and Robin* in 1965, at which time audiences delighted in its outrageous campiness. For some reason, *Batman and Robin* enjoyed no such large-scale revival as an unintentional comedy—perhaps this was because, even though it was certainly bad enough to be considered camp, it simply did not have the hammy energy of its predecessor.

Columbia did release the serial almost in its entirety on Super 8mm film in the mid–1970s. However, it was slightly edited—to make all 15 chapters of uniform length, Columbia omitted several Chapter 1 scenes involving Bruce talking with Vicki. (Like most all serials, the *Batman and Robin*'s first chapter was slightly longer than the rest of the chapters in order to establish main characters and plot.)

Batman and Robin was also released on VHS videotape in 1990 by GoodTimes Home Video. The two-tape set was unquestionably a "cheapie" designed to cash in on the character's newfound popularity following the blockbuster success of the 1989 film *Batman*. It was recorded in a substandard playback mode, which resulted in less-than-ideal picture and sound quality. (GoodTimes also released the 1943 *Batman* in this same economy format.) The GoodTimes version of *Batman and Robin* retained the edits of Chapter 1 found in the home movie version of the serial.

Batman and Robin was treated to a high-quality home video release in early 2005, when Sony Pictures Home Entertainment presented the serial on a 2-disc DVD set. The set's picture and sound quality was very good, uniformly better than Sony's 1943 *Batman* DVD set. (As mentioned in Chapter 2, that set varied in quality from chapter to chapter.) The *Batman and Robin* DVD set also restored the footage from Chapter 1 that had been edited out of the previous home video versions of the serial. Unfortunately, like the 1943 *Batman* DVD set, the *Batman and Robin* DVD set did not offer any bonus features or printed material dealing with the making of the serial. That said, however, Sony's DVD release of *Batman and Robin* was a vast improvement over the previous home video versions of *Batman and Robin*.

Also like the 1943 *Batman* DVD set, the *Batman and Robin* DVD set featured some interesting artwork on its cover — perhaps *too* interesting. The cover featured a dramatic full-color image of Batman and Robin standing on a rooftop, the night sky above them lit up by a huge Batsignal. Batman and Robin were outfitted in costumes that looked like a modern comic book cover — the bat ears on Batman's cowl were long and imposing, and Robin was wearing a full bodysuit that was red and green in color. In other words, the image looked nothing like anything contained in the serial itself! It could be argued that Sony was doing more than a little bit of false advertising by marketing their product in this manner.

In the final analysis, serious Batman fans should have a look at *Batman and Robin* despite all of its flaws. There are at least a few scenes in the serial that are worth watching. A number of the fight scenes are well staged, and there are fleeting moments when Lowery and Duncan are able to bring some life their characters. But if you took all of *Batman and Robin*'s "good" moments and spliced them together, they would probably not add up to be much longer than the running time of just one of the serial's individual chapters.

With the advent of television, the motion picture serial format became less and less popular with audiences throughout the late 1940s and early 1950s — in fact, the genre was extinct by the mid-1950s. Since *Batman and Robin* was made during the twilight of the chapter play era, Columbia chose not to produce a third *Batman* serial. It would be almost two decades before the characters would return to the big screen — but as we will discuss later in this book, when he came back, he came back in a *big* way.

5

Changing with the Times, 1950–1965

By the early 1950s, Batman was again a character who generally appeared only in the pages of comic books published by DC Comics— and DC continued to turn out a number of memorable Batman stories during this time period. One of these was "The Man Behind the Red Hood!" published in *Detective Comics* #168, February 1951. As Batman's origin was examined in "The Origin of Batman," the Joker's origin was examined in "The Man Behind the Red Hood!" However, the story stopped well short of actually providing a detailed backstory for the villain.

In "The Man Behind the Red Hood!," the Joker was revealed to have originally been an unnamed criminal who called himself the Red Hood. In his first clash with Batman, the Red Hood jumped into a vat of chemicals to escape pursuit— this permanently dyed his skin white and his hair green, giving him the appearance of a hideous clown. Elements of the story would eventually be incorporated into the Joker depictions found in the 1988 graphic novel *Batman: The Killing Joke* and the 1989 motion picture *Batman*.

The comic book industry in general, and Batman in particular, suffered a substantial setback with the 1953 publication of the book *Seduction of the Innocent* by Fredric Wertham. Wertham was a psychiatrist who believed that comic books, with their stories featuring elements of crime, violence and sexuality, were extremely damaging to the mental health of young readers. Dr. Wertham laid out all of his arguments against the comics industry in *Seduction of the Innocent*, including his infamous assertion that the relationship between Batman and Robin was rife with homosexual overtones. According to Wertham, Batman and Robin represented "a wish dream of two homosexuals living together."[1]

Seduction of the Innocent created a sensation upon its release, and led to public hearings regarding the comic book industry held by the Subcommittee to Investigate Juvenile Delinquency in the United States. Wertham himself testified at these hearings, claiming that comic books were a major factor in leading young people to become juvenile delinquents and deviants. As a result of these hearings, the Senate determined that a standards code needed to be developed for the comics industry in order to eliminate the objectionable material found in some comics. In order to appease the Senate, the comic book industry formed a self-regulating committee called the Comics Code Authority, which examined the content of all new comic books before they were published. If these new comics met with the standards of the committee, they were printed with a Comics Code Authority logo displayed on their covers, which signified that they were "safe" reading material for children.

5—Changing with the Times, 1950–1965

The public backlash against comics following the publication of *Seduction of the Innocent* led to a number of comic book publishers going out of business, but DC Comics was able to soldier on. And even though DC's Batman was one of Wertham's primary targets in the book, the character weathered the storm as well. Like all comic titles published after the uproar surrounding *Seduction of the Innocent*, sales of Batman comic titles fell dramatically—but Wertham's accusations did not put an end to the Caped Crusader's career. In the long run, Batman's strength as a character turned out to be far more potent than any attack that a homophobic and paranoid psychiatrist could level at him.

Wertham's analysis of the relationship between Batman and Robin was obviously misguided in many ways, but perhaps its biggest flaw was that it failed to recognize the fact that Batman comic stories of the time were crafted not for a homosexual or heterosexual audience, but for a basically *asexual* audience. The vast majority of comic book readers during the 1940s and 1950s were grade school–age boys—they were interested in action, adventure and fantasy, not matters of romance of *any* kind. To most young male Batman fans, Robin represented the kind of life they wished *they* could lead, one full of heroism, intrigue and hi-tech gadgetry. (Not to mention one basically devoid of dull responsibilities such as school, homework and chores.) And Batman represented the ultimate father–big brother figure, someone that continually took you on fantastic adventures and treated you as a complete equal.

This view of Batman and Robin was not a realistic one, to be sure. On the comic page, Robin was empowered by Batman in a manner that could never be translated into actual life—after all, any responsible adult who would put a real child into perilous situations would be prosecuted for child endangerment! But no one involved with the creation of Batman comics during the 1940s and 1950s would have argued that they were anything more than harmless fantasy, pure and simple. Most comic readers took this fantasy in the spirit it was intended—only Wertham chose to look for a subliminal meaning in Batman and Robin's adventures. However ridiculous Wertham's accusations might seem to us today, it still must be noted that they certainly cast a long shadow. In fact, they still have the power to incite discussion among present-day comic book fans and students of popular culture, six decades after *Seduction of the Innocent* was first published.

The uproar over *Seduction of the Innocent* and the resulting creation of the Comics Code Authority continued the general trend of Batman's "softening" as a character, a trend that began when Robin was first introduced back in 1940. In order to comply with the Code and avoid any further public criticism of Batman, in the mid–1950s DC Comics set about making the character more benign than he had been in his 1940s–early 1950s incarnation. Batman comic stories placed less and less emphasis on scenarios relating to real-life crime and detective work, and more and more emphasis on science fiction. The ruthless gangsters and homicidal madmen who had plagued Batman and Robin in the past gave way to an assortment of outlandish-looking space aliens and mad scientists who continually passed through Gotham City in their quest for world domination. Of course, none of these aliens and scientists ever had any luck conquering the world, because Gotham's friendly caped crimefighters were always on hand to save the day. And when Batman's classic villains such as the Joker or the Penguin *were* used, they were usually placed in such silly scenarios that they were far removed from their 1940s incarnations.

In fairness, it should be pointed out that many Batman comic stories had contained elements of science fiction and fantasy since the character was introduced in the late 1930s. But the increased sci-fi/fantasy content found in Batman comic stories during this period had the effect of basically stripping the character of his identity — he was not so much Batman, but "Superman in a Batman costume." Most everything Batman did in his mid–1950s–early 1960s adventures was far more suited to Superman than it was to Batman — the character traveled into outer space, went back and forth in time and was mutated into countless weird forms, including a giant, a baby and a merman.

Batman's ties to Superman were made even stronger during this time period, because in 1954 the characters started regularly appearing in adventures together in *World's Finest Comics*. The title had been running stories that featured Superman, Batman and Robin since the early 1940s, but Superman appeared in stories of his own, and Batman and Robin appeared in stories of their own. In *World's Finest Comics* #71, July-August 1954, the characters teamed up in the title for the first time in a story called "Batman — Double for Superman!" The pairing of Superman and Batman in *World's Finest Comics* would prove to be a very long-lasting alliance — most every issue of the title published after #71 would feature the heroes working together, all the way up until its final issue #323 published in January 1986!

Since Wertham's attacks on Batman and Robin in *Seduction of the Innocent* included the assertion that the characters were homosexual, DC decided to create some female costumed heroes for Gotham City in order to "prove" that Batman and Robin were indeed interested in members of the opposite sex. The first of these characters made her debut in *Detective Comics* #233, July 1956, in a story simply titled "The Batwoman." The story revealed Batwoman to be Kathy Kane, a former circus performer who admired Batman so much that she designed her own yellow, red and black bat–themed costume and began to fight crime. Batwoman was joined by Bat-Girl, who made her debut in the story "Bat-Girl" (*Batman* #139, April 1961). Bat-Girl was actually Kathy Kane's teenage niece Betty, who designed her own red and green bat–costume after discovering that Kathy was Batwoman so that she too could join in on all the fun.

Since Batwoman was about Batman's age and Bat-Girl was about Robin's age, romance was in the air for all four of Gotham's costumed crimefighters. But even though Batwoman and Bat-Girl were introduced into Batman's world so that Batman and Robin could be shown to have romantic feelings for them, most all of the stories featuring the characters depicted the women pursuing the men, not the other way around. In fact, Batman and Robin were most always shown trying to stoically fend off Batwoman's and Bat-Girl's advances. It is anyone's guess as to why DC thought that Batman's and Robin's heterosexuality could best be established by depicting them rejecting romantic overtures from beautiful masked women.

As if all of this science fiction and awkward romance weren't enough to render Batman's comic book world a completely bizarre place, an interdimensional imp named Bat-Mite made his debut in the story "Batman Meets Bat-Mite" (*Detective Comics* #267, May 1958). Looking like an elf in an ill-fitting Batman costume, Bat-Mite considered himself Batman's biggest fan. He showed up from time to time in order to try to "help" the Caped Crusaders in their fight against crime, but of course, his efforts always backfired and chaos ensued. The introduction of Bat-Mite into Batman's world was the most obvious sign that DC was trying to mold Batman into Superman's image — the character was a direct copy of the Superman villain Mr. Mxyzptlk, an elflike interdimensional imp who regularly appeared on Earth in order to harass the Man of Steel.

Well, there *was* at least one other equally obvious sign that DC was trying to mold Batman into Superman's image. In March 1955, Superman was given a pet dog named

"The Batman Family" in the 1950s — Batman, Bat-Mite, Robin, Alfred, Bat-Girl, Commissioner Gordon, and Batwoman. (And that is Ace the Bat-Hound in front!) Art by Sheldon Moldoff.

Krypto the Superdog, which led DC to decide to give Batman a pet dog as well — so Ace the Bat-Hound was introduced into Batman's comic world in July 1955. Ace even wore a dark cowl like his master — but of course, that cowl did not need to be fitted with pointed ears, since Ace already had them! At any rate, Ace still manages to periodically show up in the DC Universe to this day. For example, the pooch was featured in the 2005–06 Cartoon Network kids' animated series *Krypto the Superdog*.

A few characters created for Batman comic stories during the late 1950s and early 1960s did become regular fixtures of the Batman universe. One of these was Mr. Zero, who first appeared in a story in *Batman* #121, February 1959, called "The Ice Crimes of Mr. Zero." In the story, Mr. Zero is a criminal scientist who works to create an ice gun. He succeeds in creating his weapon, but in the process he accidentally spills some sort of freezing chemical solution all over himself which makes him unable to stand warm temperatures. He dons an air-conditioned costume and goes on a crime spree in Gotham City, leading Batman and Robin to bring him to justice. Mr. Zero would eventually be renamed Mr. Freeze (we'll discuss that change in the next chapter), and become one of Batman's regularly-featured villains.

In 1960, DC introduced a new superhero team that featured Batman as one of its charter members. The Justice League of America debuted in *The Brave and the Bold* #28, February-March 1960, and its original lineup included Superman, Batman, Wonder Woman, Flash, Green Lantern, Aquaman, and Martian Manhunter. The team proved to be so popular that it was given its own comic title in October 1960. The League has undergone numerous changes in members and name over the decades, but Batman has continued to be involved in their adventures right up until the present day.

As discussed in Chapter 1, Bob Kane's actual hands-on involvement in the creation of Batman comic art began to lessen almost from the character's first few comic appearances — he had brought in additional creative talent to bolster his work even before *Batman* #1 was published. By the 1950s, Kane was contributing almost nothing to the Batman comic art that was being produced, even though that art still carried his name on the byline. Kane's most prominent ghost artist during this time was Sheldon Moldoff, who worked for Kane from 1953 all the way up until 1967. Moldoff's bold, cartoonish style perfectly fit the sunnier, sci-fi/fantasy-oriented Batman stories of the 1950s.[2]

In spite of Moldoff's excellent work, Batman's future was in serious doubt by the early 1960s. All of the stories burdened with second-rate sci-fi and characters that had been running in DC Comics' Batman titles for the past decade had made the character less and less popular with readers. Plus, as previously mentioned, Wertham's mid–1950s attack on the comics industry in general had brought about a sharp decline in sales of most all comic book titles, including Batman's. Batman's fortunes had fallen so low that there was even some discussion at DC about canceling the character's titles altogether.[3]

But instead of canceling Batman, DC turned the character over to editor Julius Schwartz. Schwartz had a proven track record of taking over DC characters that had grown stale and successfully revamping them. Schwartz wasted no time in bringing about changes to Batman and his world. Gone were Batwoman, Bat-Girl and Bat-Mite, as well as all of the aliens and mad scientists that Batman and Robin had been fighting since the mid–1950s. With all of these distractions out of the way, Batman comic stories again began to focus on more realistic crime and detective work scenarios.

And the art found in Batman comic stories was radically changed as well. Schwartz gave DC artist Carmine Infantino the assignment of designing a new visual style for Batman.

The "New Look" Batman and Robin, 1966. Art by Carmine Infantino and Murphy Anderson.

The one-dimensional, cartoonish look of 1950s–early 1960s Batman comic book stories gave way to Infantino's more realistic style of drawing — his detailed renderings of Batman and Robin looked far more like actual, flesh-and-blood people than any previous print versions of the characters.

All of these changes also brought about some modifications to Batman's costume and crimefighting arsenal. The bat emblem on the character's chest, which since 1939 had consisted of a simple black bat silhouette, was redesigned as a black bat silhouette inside of a yellow oval. Also, the Batmobile, which since 1941 had been drawn as a large sedan with a stylized bat head on its grill and a huge batwing-like tailfin on its roof, was redesigned into a sleek sports car with batwing-like rear fender tailfins.

DC dubbed the Schwartz Batman revamp the "New Look," and this New Look Batman premiered in *Detective Comics* #327, May 1964, in the story "The Mystery of the Menacing Mask." "Menacing Mask" did not include any of Batman's classic costumed villains, but Schwartz wasted little time in returning some of the character's most memorable foes to more regular action than they had seen during the 1950s and early 1960s. Early New Look stories featured the Joker, Penguin and the Riddler battling the Dynamic Duo.

The Riddler's return was particularly welcome. He had initially appeared in two stories in the late 1940s, and even though he seemed like a character with great potential, he was never used again until Schwartz revived him in 1965. Clad in a skintight green bodysuit emblazoned with black question marks, the Riddler delighted in leaving Batman clues relating to the criminal schemes he was planning in the form of riddles. In fact, it seemed that he was perhaps actually more interested in posing riddles to Batman than he was in committing crimes. Even the Riddler's real name suggested that his riddles were more important to him than anything else — he was really Edward Nigma, which when shortened to "E. Nigma" became another word for "riddle." Though the meaning of his real name would never change, its spelling would — in the 1990s, the "Nigma" would be dropped in favor of "Nygma." At any rate, the Riddler's New Look comic stories began the process of making the villain every bit as important a character as the Joker, Penguin and Catwoman.

Ironically, not long after DC Comics instigated Batman's New Look and returned the character to his more realistic, "serious" roots, the ABC Television Network decided to bring the character for the first time in a manner that was about as far removed from "serious" as possible. In early 1966, the half-hour action comedy *Batman* made its debut on ABC. The show starred Adam West as Batman/Bruce Wayne and Burt Ward as Robin/Dick Grayson. *Batman* turned out to be a hit of monumental proportions, and it spawned the 1966 feature film of the same name. In the next chapter we'll examine the film in detail, and set it within the context of the television show's run.

6

Batman (1966)

Cast: Adam West (Batman/Bruce Wayne), Burt Ward (Robin/Dick Grayson), Lee Meriwether (Catwoman/Kitka), Cesar Romero (The Joker), Burgess Meredith (The Penguin), Frank Gorshin (The Riddler), Alan Napier (Alfred), Neil Hamilton (Commissioner Gordon), Stafford Repp (Chief O'Hara), Madge Blake (Aunt Harriet Cooper), Reginald Denny (Commodore Schmidlapp), Milton Frome (Vice Admiral Fangschliester), Gil Perkins (Bluebeard), Dick Crockett (Morgan), George Sawaya (Quetch). *Producer:* William Dozier. *Director:* Leslie H. Martinson. *Screenplay:* Lorenzo Semple, Jr. (Based on characters created by Bob Kane). *Cinematography:* Howard Schwartz. *Editor:* Harry Gerstad. *Music:* Nelson Riddle. *Studio:* 20th Century–Fox. *Length:* 105 minutes. *United States Release Date:* July 30, 1966.

Nearly two decades after his last big screen appearance in the lackluster 1949 serial *Batman and Robin*, Batman made a triumphant return to movie theaters in the 1966 action comedy *Batman*. *Batman* was a very successful film in its own right, but its history is completely intertwined with that of the wildly popular television program of the same name that aired on ABC from 1966 until 1968. Both the film and the TV show starred Adam West as Batman/Bruce Wayne and Burt Ward as Robin/Dick Grayson.

Batman the movie also starred Lee Meriwether as the Catwoman, Cesar Romero as the Joker, Burgess Meredith as the Penguin and Frank Gorshin as the Riddler. Romero, Meredith and Gorshin all had made numerous appearances on the *Batman* television show as well, but Meriwether had not. She was cast as the film Catwoman because Julie Newmar, the actress who played the part in the television show during its first two seasons, was unavailable during the weeks that *Batman* was filming.

Any examination of the film must begin by providing background on the television show. In early 1965, ABC acquired the rights to the Batman character from DC Comics. The network's decision to develop a Batman television show was likely influenced by several major art and entertainment trends that were taking place in the mid–1960s.

First, the Pop Art movement was in full swing at the time. Pop artists took everyday images such as advertisements for commercial products and comic strip panels, and incorporated them into their works. Consequently, the public had a heightened interest in comic imagery since prominent artists like Andy Warhol and Roy Lichtenstein were painting pieces inspired by comic art. Also, the success of the James Bond film series, beginning with the release of *Dr. No* in 1962, suggested that the public might be receptive to other larger-than-life action hero characters.

Adam West as Batman and Burt Ward as Robin in *Batman* (1966).

Interestingly, ABC considered developing shows based on several other comic characters before settling on Batman. Both Superman and Dick Tracy were actually the network's first choices for a comic-themed show, but the rights to these characters were not available at the time. Since Batman's rights were available, Batman became "their" hero.[1]

ABC entrusted the development of their *Batman* television show to veteran producer William Dozier and his production company Greenway Productions. Dozier took the job knowing almost nothing about Batman at all — he had never read a Batman comic story until he became involved with the project. Dozier enlisted writer Lorenzo Semple, Jr. to craft a pilot script that would set the tone for the series, and what Semple came up with was startlingly original. His script "Hi Diddle Riddle" featuring the Riddler could be enjoyed on two completely separate levels—its campy dialogue, outrageous characters and absurd situations would play as hip, Pop Art–inspired comedy for adults, and its comic book action would play as straight-ahead adventure for young children. And *everyone* could enjoy the show's imagery of a comic page brought to life, complete with wild costumes, brightly colored sets and hi-tech gadgetry.

ABC matched Dozier and Semple's ambitious concept for *Batman* with equally ambitious production values. The network entered into an agreement with 20th Century–Fox to co-produce the show, which meant that the *Batman*'s creators would have at their disposal Fox's very large, high-quality production facilities. Dozier began developing costumes, sets and props for *Batman* that were both lavish and marvelously inventive. After being treated so offhandedly by Columbia Pictures in the 1940s, the Batman character was finally getting a "big-budget" screen treatment.

The downside of this treatment, at least for longtime fans of Batman comics, was that the character was going to be presented in a manner that was intentionally comedic. After all, DC Comics had just performed the New Look revamp on Batman in 1964 in order to make him a more plausible, serious character than he had been in his mid–1950s, early 1960s incarnation. But in all fairness, even many New Look Batman comic stories of the mid–1960s were still fanciful enough that most non–comic book readers would have found them ridiculous. (In fact, a number of *Batman*'s episodes would actually end up being based on New Look stories.) Simply put, a 1965 Batman comic story was unapologetically escapist, often silly, entertainment—so ABC's decision to realize the Batman character on the screen in a lighthearted manner made perfect sense. Batman would have his day as a serious screen action hero, but that day would not come during the years that he was a property of ABC.

But at least the day had finally arrived that a screen version of Batman would be given a Batmobile to drive! And along with that Batmobile, he would be given a huge Batcave, a Batcycle, a Batcopter, a Batboat and dozens of crimefighting bat gadgets. Plus, he would finally get the chance to square off against memorable comic book adversaries such as the Joker, Penguin, Riddler and Catwoman. ABC and Fox would bring Batman's world to life in a stylish and imaginative manner that made Columbia's 1940s serials look positively anemic in comparison.

However, this new *Batman* was not above borrowing a trick or two from the Columbia serials. ABC planned on airing *Batman twice* a week, Wednesdays and Thursdays at 7:30 P.M. Scheduling the show in this manner meant that the Wednesday episode could end with a "cliffhanger" situation like the old movie serial chapters did, and then the "cliffhanger" could be resolved in the Thursday episode. And also like the serials, the dialogue and action in *Batman* would be overplayed to the point of being absurdly melodramatic—only this time around, the melodrama was intentionally meant to create laughter. (Incidentally, the 1943 Columbia serial *Batman* would end up having an even more direct effect on this new *Batman* before it premiered. I'll discuss the odd turn of events that led to this a bit later.)

Because of *Batman*'s groundbreaking style and content, it was going to be a far more complex and expensive program to produce than an "average" half-hour television show. Consequently, Dozier envisioned producing a *Batman* film prior to the release of the *Batman* television show. The film would facilitate the production of the television show in several ways. First, it could serve to introduce the show and its many different characters to the public. Also, many of the scenes featuring expensive props such as the Batcopter, the Batboat and the Batcycle could be filmed for the movie, and then those scenes could be lifted directly from the film for use in episodes of the television show. This recycling of footage would help to trim the television show's special effects budget.[2]

Now that *Batman* had both a well-realized concept and a shrewd production strategy, it needed actors. Dozier's casting choices for the show's major parts were inspired, to say the least. Adam West was hired for the role of Batman/Bruce Wayne. West was a handsome 37-year-old who had been working steadily in film and television productions since the late 1950s. In 1964, he appeared in several commercials for the powdered chocolate milk mix Nestle Quik as "Captain Quik," a spoof of the James Bond character. These commercials brought him to the attention of ABC and Fox, who thought he might have the right combination of seriousness and silliness for the role of Batman. Upon meeting with Dozier, West immediately grasped the nature of the part. He understood the producer's reasoning that Batman needed to be played as earnestly as possible in order to both enthrall youngsters and amuse adults.[3] And at 6'2" and of reasonably good build, West was also physically just right for the role.

Bert Gervis, Jr., was cast as Robin/Dick Grayson. Gervis was 19 when he won the role, and it was his first professional acting job. Amusingly, ABC somehow failed to communicate to Gervis the fact that he had actually been given the part. For a number of weeks, the studio kept contacting him regarding measurements for his Robin costume — since he was so new to the business, he assumed all of these fittings were still just a part of the audition process![4] At any rate, Gervis' inexperience as an actor probably worked to his advantage while playing Robin. The character was designed to be outrageously corny, with all of his "Holy —" (this or that) exclamations and wide-eyed naïveté, and Gervis' lack of subtlety perfectly captured that corniness. Also, at 5'8" and appearing even younger than his age, he was physically very well suited for the part. The only thing Gervis really had to change about himself for *Batman* was his name — he adopted the much more punchy stage name of Burt Ward before the show's premiere.

Not only were West and Ward individually perfect for their roles, they were perfect together as well. The chemistry between the two actors was definitely one of the elements that would make the show so successful. Plus, since Ward came across as being younger than his age, Batman and Robin's rapport in *Batman* could mirror the way they operated in their comic book world — they would be very much like a "father-son" team.

Batman's creators now set about providing these actors with ideal costumes. *Batman*'s costume designer Jan Kemp created Batman and Robin uniforms that were marvelously faithful to the characters' mid–1960s comic book appearance in terms of style and color. In fact, to this day the *Batman* television show and its companion movie are the *only* live-action screen depictions of Batman and Robin to feature the characters in their standard "comic book" garb.

Kemp's Batman costume featured a cape, cowl, trunks, gloves and boots that were all fashioned out of dark blue satin. Because of all of the different kinds of lighting used during the filming of *Batman*, the camera would sometimes register this dark blue material as a brighter shade of blue, purple or even black. The cowl was crafted out of a plastic skullcap under its satin finish, giving it a smooth, seamless look. The costume also featured a gray leotard and gray tights that when worn together, looked like a one-piece, form-fitting bodysuit. On the chest area of the leotard was the familiar bat emblem, a black bat silhouette inside of a yellow oval. One of the costume's most prominent elements was its yellow utility belt with a large, bat-engraved gold buckle.

Perhaps the costume's only major weakness was that its cowl's bat ears were so short that they often completely blended into the cowl when filmed from certain angles. The mid–1960s comic book Batman did have short ears on his cowl, but they were still not quite as short as Kemp designed them. But even with this flaw, the costume was so memorably designed and well-tailored that it became one of *Batman*'s most potent visuals.

Kemp's Robin costume was equally well-crafted. It featured a bright yellow satin cape. Its form-fitting red tunic sported a yellow "R" encircled in black, and yellow laces running up the front. The costume also featured green short sleeves, gloves, trunks and boots. (The comic book Robin was usually depicted as being bare legged, but presumably in the interest of modesty Kemp outfitted his version of the costume with skin-colored tights.) And finally, it featured a well-sewn black fabric, "bandit-style" mask.

Adam West's Batman and Burt Ward's Robin turned out to be so iconic that it might seem hard to imagine *Batman* being done with anyone else but them. But Dozier did seriously consider two other actors as Batman and Robin — amazingly, those other actors were so good in the roles that they might well have made them their own just as West and Ward ended up doing. Lyle Waggoner was considered for the part of Batman, and Peter Deyell was considered for the part of Robin. Screen test footage has survived that shows Waggoner and Deyell doing two scenes from "Hi Diddle Riddle." The first scene features them as Bruce and Dick in Wayne Manor, trying to figure out a clue the Riddler has purposely left for them. The second scene features them in their Batman and Robin costumes in the Batcave, getting ready to head out and confront the Riddler. West and Ward's screen test featuring them doing the exact same scenes has also survived.

It is fascinating to compare Waggoner and Deyell to West and Ward in these screen tests. Waggoner was perhaps a more conventional action hero-style of actor than West, with a squarer jaw and a more reserved pattern of speech. And Deyell came off as being even more boyish than Ward, mainly because of his noticeably high-pitched speaking voice. In short, Waggoner and Deyell were very good in the roles, and gave West and Ward more than just a bit of competition. Of course, as wonderful as West and Ward turned out to be in *Batman*, Dozier certainly made the right choice in picking them over Waggoner and Deyell. But Waggoner and Deyell's screen test suggests that if *they* had been picked, they could have very possibly ended up being the "right" choice as well!

Another aspect of these screen tests that is so interesting is that they provide a glimpse of *Batman*'s early attempts at costuming and set design. The Batman costume used in the screen tests had much taller ears on its cowl than the TV show's cowl, and its bat emblem did not include a yellow oval like the TV show's bat emblem did. In other words, the Batman costume in the screen test looked very much like the pre–New Look Batman costume found in comic stories of the 1950s and early 1960s. And the Batcave set used in the screen tests was markedly different from the Batcave set that would be created for the TV show. The TV show's Batcave would end up being an expansive space jammed with hi-tech crimefighting equipment, while the screen test's Batcave established a much more intimate, mysterious tone by featuring less equipment and multiple layers of dimly-lit rock formations. (We'll discuss the TV show's Batcave set in more detail a bit later)

Batman's main villains would be every bit as well realized as West and Ward were in their roles, both in terms of casting and costuming. Like *Batman*'s Batman and Robin uniforms, the villains' costumes were designed by Jan Kemp. The villains were always billed as "guest villains" on the show, because none of them appeared as episode-to-episode regulars. During *Batman*'s first two seasons, a specific villain was usually featured in both the show's Wednesday night "cliffhanger" episode and Thursday night "resolution" episode, and then a different villain would be given the spotlight in the Wednesday and Thursday episodes the following week.

The villains featured most regularly on the series were also the villains slated to be in the *Batman* motion picture. Burgess Meredith (the Penguin) had enjoyed a long and distinguished career on both the stage and screen as a dramatic actor, but his appearances in *Batman* catapulted him to far greater fame than did all of his "serious" roles. As the Penguin, Meredith wore a long false nose, black tuxedo with tails, and purple top hat — and, of course, he almost always had one of his trick umbrellas in hand. Meredith was so good as the Penguin that he waddled and squawked his way through more episodes of *Batman* than any other guest villain.

Another veteran, Cesar Romero, was hired for the role of the Joker. Romero seemed to be a very unlikely choice for the part — he had appeared in scores of films since the 1930s, often playing suave, romantic leading roles. Plus, he sported a moustache that he considered to be his show business trademark, so he refused to shave it off for his Joker role. *Batman*'s makeup crew solved this problem by simply applying layer upon layer of white makeup on Romero's face until his moustache was for the most part obscured — however, one does not have to look too hard at Romero in *Batman* to spot it! Still, Romero ended up making a wonderful Joker. Clad in a wild purple suit, and sporting a green wig and blood red lipstick, he cackled his way through nearly as many episodes of *Batman* as Meredith did.

Another of *Batman*'s regular guest villains was a much younger, up-and-coming performer. Frank Gorshin, an impressionist-actor who had appeared in numerous movies and television shows throughout the late 1950s and early 1960s, was given the part of the Riddler. Wearing a skintight green bodysuit emblazoned with black question marks, Gorshin's manic energy elevated the Riddler character from a relatively minor Batman comic book villain to one of the Caped Crusader's most recognizable foes.

Of course, *Batman* would feature far more villains than just the Penguin, the Joker and the Riddler. Some of them, such as the Catwoman, first appeared in the pages of Batman comic stories. (We'll discuss the Catwoman's *Batman* debut a bit later.) Another Batman comic villain selected for use on the show was given a name change — Mr. Zero was renamed "Mr. Freeze" by *Batman*'s creators and used in six episodes of the series. Mr. Freeze never became identified with one specific actor during *Batman*'s run — he was played by three different actors, George Sanders, Otto Preminger, and Eli Wallach. Many other villains, such as the Bookworm, King Tut and Egghead, were created specifically for the show.

The strength of *Batman*'s "non-costume" supporting cast was equal to its cast of heroes and villains. Veteran British actor Alan Napier played the role of Alfred, and though he did not physically resemble the Alfred of the comics, his low-key performance perfectly captured the trustworthy nature of Bruce and Dick's closest confidant. Neil Hamilton, who began his acting career playing leading roles in several of director D.W. Griffith's silent features, was cast as Gotham City Police Commissioner Gordon. Hamilton also did not particularly resemble his comic book counterpart, but his earnest portrayal of Gotham's top cop was very effective. Stafford Repp played a character specifically created for the show, Police Chief O'Hara. Repp laid on a heavy Irish brogue while playing O'Hara, making the part come across as a rather clichéd stereotype, but his energetic performance was still quite enjoyable.

Some of the casting choices Dozier made regarding *Batman*, such as the hiring of veteran "serious" actors like Burgess Meredith, Cesar Romero and Neil Hamilton, were surprising. But his choice for the actor to provide the show's voiceover narration was the most surprising of all — namely, himself! He kept auditioning narrators to try to find someone who could ham the dialogue up in just the right melodramatic, movie serial-like fashion. But he never found anyone who could do the job as well as he could, so he added the job of *Batman*'s narrator to his producer duties.

The most striking thing about *all* of the actors in *Batman*, heroes, villains and supporting players alike, was that they played their parts with the utmost seriousness. Dozier had communicated the fact to Adam West that *Batman*'s camp comedy would be stronger if West played Batman/Bruce Wayne completely straight, as if there was nothing funny about the part. Obviously, the rest of the cast was given this directive as well — and just as obviously, they took it completely to heart. For the most part, *Batman* was acted as straight drama. Granted, many of the villain's parts were of such a broad nature that they could not help but ham up their material to some degree, but on the whole, even they played their parts as if they were appearing in a serious dramatic work. *Batman* was shaping up to be a very unusual show with this combination of comedic material, dramatic acting and breathless comic book action.

In an odd coincidence, *Batman* got an unexpected boost in terms of pre-publicity from the 1943 Columbia serial *Batman*. The 15-chapter action-adventure was re-released as a camp piece under the title *An Evening with Batman and Robin* in 1965. The marathon film played in selected cities across the country, mainly in college towns, and it drew huge crowds who howled with laughter at Batman and Robin's efforts to vanquish Daka's forces of evil. *Time* Magazine ran a national story on the serial in November 1965.[5]

ABC originally planned on premiering their *Batman* during the start of their fall 1966 season, but they likely realized they had a golden opportunity to release the show while *An Evening with Batman and Robin* was still fresh in the minds of the general public. Also, many of the network's prime time shows that premiered during the fall 1965 season were failing, so they were looking for something to shore up their schedule. Consequently, ABC decided to rush *Batman* into full production mode and premiere it as a midseason replacement in January 1966.[6]

This premiere date change had a huge impact on the production of the show. Plans to film and release a *Batman* motion picture before the television show hit the airwaves were altered — the film would still be made, but not until filming of the television show's first season was completed. Consequently, the *Batman* motion picture would no longer be used to introduce American audiences to all of the television show's main characters. However, the film could still be used to sell the television show to overseas markets. And the film could still be used to help trim the television show's special effects budget — expensive props such as the Batcopter, the Batboat, and the Batcycle could be filmed for the movie, and then those scenes could be lifted directly from the film for use in second season episodes.

After working to bring Batman's world to life with just the right actors and costumes, *Batman*'s creators started work on perfecting the vast arsenal of crimefighting gadgetry and vehicles they had created for Batman and Robin to use on the show. With the show's premiere date moved up approximately eight months, they now had far less time to get this arsenal together than previously planned.

Batman's early debut forced a major change in plans regarding the construction of the show's Batmobile. The car was originally going to be built by custom car designer Dean Jeffries, but Jeffries was not able to fit the project's new deadline into his work schedule.

So Dozier contracted custom automotive designer George Barris to design and build the car — in a matter of just several weeks!

Barris was able to complete this formidable task because he chose not to design and build a Batmobile from scratch. Instead, he reworked an experimental 1955 Lincoln automobile known as the Futura into the Batmobile. The Futura he used had actually already appeared on the screen — in bright red paint, the car was seen in the 1959 motion picture *It Started with a Kiss* starring Glenn Ford and Debbie Reynolds. The Futura was already equipped with hooded headlights, bubble dome windshields and large tailfins, so Barris' main tasks were to accessorize the car with Batman-themed items, reshape the body so that it featured some batwing-like scallops and repaint it. He also added one of the Batmobile's most distinctive features — a jet engine–like afterburner that shot flames from the rear of the car. Incidentally, much of the Futura's bodywork was not actually done by Barris himself; he subcontracted the work out to another car customizer, Bill Cushenbery.[7]

While many of the gadgets and vehicles featured in *Batman* were spectacular, the most spectacular of them all was Barris' Batmobile. Painted a sleek jet black with red-orange pinstriping and bat insignias, the Batmobile was simply a fabulous looking car. For the first time, a screen version of Batman would have a Batmobile that was every inch the icon the car had become on the comics page. Incidentally, the Batmobile turned out to be so popular with the public that Barris built a number of replicas of the car strictly for "public appearance" purposes, and these replicas were exhibited at automobile shows throughout the country. But the only Batmobile that was ever used on the show or in the *Batman* film was Barris' original Futura remodel.

Batman's giant Batcave set was also a wonder to behold. Surrounded by walls of jagged rock, the Batcave was jammed with high tech crimefighting devices such as computers, radar equipment and chemical analyzers. The Batmobile could be driven directly into the cave via a secret entrance hidden off of a small dirt road just outside of the cave walls. (Bronson Cave in Bronson Canyon near Los Angeles was used for all of the Batcave secret entrance exterior shots in the series.) A turntable inside the cave turned the Batmobile 180 degrees so that it could be driven directly out the entrance. Just behind the Batmobile's turntable was a towering nuclear generator used to power the car. Two fire station–like poles known as the "Batpoles" led down into the cave from Wayne Manor above, and these were equipped with an "instant costume change" lever that allowed Bruce and Dick to magically change into their costumes during their descent. (Obviously, the Batcave's absurdly efficient equipment was played up as one of *Batman*'s major comedic aspects.)

The "guest villain hideout" sets were also one of the show's visual highlights. Often filmed at odd angles and lighted with garish colors, these sets appeared as if they had jumped directly off of a comic book page and onto the television screen. Another highlight of the show was its scenes showing Batman and Robin scaling the outside walls of buildings using their Bat ropes. These wall-scaling scenes were accomplished through very low-tech camera trickery. The "walls" were flat on the ground, and the camera was turned on its side so that it appeared the walls were vertical instead of horizontal. Then West and Ward would slowly walk along the walls holding onto their ropes, acting as if they were having to expend a great deal of effort in their "climb."

Probably the most memorable visual highlight of *Batman* was the crazily lettered onomatopoeia words that flashed on the screen during the show's fight scenes. Whenever anyone took a big hit, "POW!," "BAM!" or some other wildly expressive word was cut into the action, just like words would be drawn into a comic book panel.

Batman's creators also understood the importance of creating a recognizable Gotham City for the show; along with the visuals specifically relating to Batman and his adversaries, the city itself needed to be visually well-defined as well in order to bring Batman and his world to life. The Gotham City sets wonderfully captured Batman's hometown as the bustling, East Coast city it had been in the comics for 25 years.

Batman's strong visuals were matched up with one of the best theme songs ever written for a television show. Neal Hefti's classic, instantly recognizable "Batman Theme" kicked off every episode, and was also used as background music most every time that Batman and Robin were shown jumping into the Batmobile and speeding out of the Batcave. The song was driven by a buzzing guitar riff (the "nah-nah-nah-nah-nah-nah" part that most everyone sings when they quote the song) and punctuated by blaring brass. This instrumentation was accompanied by layered, somewhat dissonant vocals (the word "Batman" over and over again). On paper, the song might not seem all that compelling—but most everyone needs to hear it just once to have it burned into their memory.

Hefti did not write the many other pieces of background orchestral music that were used in the show; they were written by the legendary composer and musical arranger Nelson Riddle. Riddle's dramatic musical contributions to *Batman* were essential in helping the show to realize its goal of being a breathless, thrill-a-minute affair.

Amidst a blitz of publicity, ABC premiered *Batman* on Wednesday, January 12, 1966, at 7:30 P.M. The first episode to air was the pilot "Hi Diddle Riddle" written by Semple. In "Hi Diddle Riddle," Batman mentioned that he had become a masked crimefighter because his parents were murdered—this marked the first time the character's comic book origin was translated to the screen in any form. On the following night, January 13, 1966, the follow-up to this episode entitled "Smack in the Middle" aired at the same Bat time, same Bat channel. (This was the show's catch phrase used to close many of the "cliffhanger" episodes of the series.)

Batman was a smash from the first moment it hit the airwaves. ABC of course was thrilled at the show's meteoric success, but they also had ample reason to feel relieved—because when the network showed the first episodes to test audiences before the premiere, they scored as poorly as any program they had ever produced. Consequently, ABC wasn't worried so much about whether or not *Batman* would be a hit—they were more worried about the show being a bomb of epic proportions. Obviously, these test audiences simply did not know how to take *Batman*—they could not decide whether they were watching a comedy or an action show. But the general public "got" Dozier's concept of creating tongue-in-cheek humor by mixing Batman's comic book world with the real world, and they got it in a *big* way.

Batman quickly became much more than just a hot new television show, it became a national craze. Throughout 1966, "Batmania" swept the country—Batman seemed to be everywhere. His television theme song was a huge radio hit, he was on the cover of *Life* Magazine, and countless kids were running around with capes tied around their necks. Plus, thousands of products bearing his likeness (toys, dolls, model kits, books, bubble gum cards, clothes, etc.) were available for purchase.

All of this Batman merchandise spawned by the Batmania of 1966 had a tremendous impact on the history of the character. Generally speaking, in Batman's first quarter century of existence, almost no non-print merchandise relating to the character was manufactured. But starting in 1966, Batman fans had the option of not only enjoying the character through his comic book adventures, but also through the collecting of non-comic Batman material. Consequently, from 1966 on, the buying of "Batman stuff" would become a major part of the Batman fan experience. The amount of Bat-related merchandise available to fans over the years would directly depend on how interested in the character the general public was at a specific point in time—but Batman's retail presence which began with the Batmania of 1966 has continued without pause right up until the present day.

Not surprisingly, sales of Batman comic titles skyrocketed after the television show's debut. DC Comics took advantage of this phenomenon by creating Batman comic stories that had the look and feel of the *Batman* TV show — in other words, they became more self-consciously campy than the original New Look Batman stories had been. Also, DC introduced Batman into a comic title that had not previously been devoted to the character's adventures. *The Brave and the Bold* originally carried stories featuring a variety of DC heroes— as we discussed last chapter, the title featured the first Justice League of America story ever published. With the onslaught of Batmania, DC made Batman a permanent fixture of *The Brave and the Bold*. Batman was featured in "team-up" stories in most every issue of the comic from late 1966 until the title was canceled in 1983, giving him the chance to interact with heroes he would not normally have worked with in his other comic titles. In fact, Batman ended up sharing adventures with most every hero in the DC universe in the pages of *The Brave and the Bold*.

In spite of all of this incredible success, the Batman character still had a bit of unfinished business he had to take care of, one more frontier he had yet to conquer — the movies. 20th Century–Fox's *Batman* motion picture which was originally supposed to introduce the public to the character and his world would now instead become one of the high watermarks of Batmania.

Principal photography for *Batman* commenced in late April 1966, almost immediately after the filming of the first season TV episodes ended. The film finished shooting by late May 1966; obviously, the movie was on the same kind of breakneck production schedule the television show had been on during its first season. The majority of the creative talent behind the television show's first season was also behind the movie. The film was produced by Dozier, written by Semple, and directed by Leslie Martinson, who had directed two first season episodes of the show, "The Penguin Goes Straight" and "Not Yet He Ain't." The film featured most all of the first season's essential cast members, with one notable exception — a new actress was hired to play the Catwoman.

Julie Newmar was cast in the role for the television show shortly after *Batman* actually premiered and appeared in two first season episodes. But she only needed those two episodes to make an indelible mark as the character. Newmar's Catwoman was a devastatingly beautiful femme fatale clad in a skintight black bodysuit and cat ears, and her combination of sexuality and wicked comedic wit was perfect for the role. The Catwoman was to play a major part in the storyline of the *Batman* film, but unfortunately Newmar was unavailable during the weeks that *Batman* was filming.

Because *Batman* was being done so quickly in between seasons of the TV show, the casting of Lee Meriwether as the film's Catwoman was handled with similar speed. The film had already commenced principal photography before Meriwether was even hired to replace Newmar! Meriwether played the part quite well in *Batman* considering how abruptly she was thrown into the production. That said, however, her Catwoman was not quite as memorable as Newmar's slinky take on the character. (Incidentally, Dozier would continue to have a problem with revolving Catwomen. Newmar returned to play the part for *Batman*'s second season, but due to another scheduling conflict she had to bow out of the role before the show's third season. In season three, the Catwoman was played by Eartha Kitt.)

Burgess Meredith (the Penguin), Frank Gorshin (the Riddler), Lee Meriwether (Catwoman/Kitka), and Cesar Romero (the Joker) in *Batman* (1966).

Another element of the *Batman* motion picture that was markedly different from the TV show was its use of new Bat vehicles. The scenes showing these new bat vehicles in action were filmed at outdoor locations; consequently, the *Batman* movie had a more expansive, "big budget" feel to it than did the TV show.

Batman's Batcopter was actually a 1964 Bell 47 helicopter owned by the California company National Helicopter Service, and was numbered N3079G. For the movie, it was outfitted with canvas "Batwings" to make it appear more bat-like. These Batwings actually made the helicopter very difficult to fly because they created so much wind resistance. *Batman*'s Batcopter scenes were filmed over a period of five days in April 1966, mainly at the National Helicopter hangar in Van Nuys and at Marineland in Palos Verdes. After filming, N3079G had its Batwings removed and was returned to regular service.

However, N3079G has since been restored to its former Batcopter glory. In 1996, pilot Eugene Nock bought the N3079G; he had studied the copter's log books, and he realized that it was a unique piece of Batman film and television history. He set about restoring the machine to look like it did when it was the Batcopter, complete with bright red-orange paint and bat insignias. (He did not try to reinstall the problematic canvas batwings.)

For any Bat-fan, just seeing the Batcopter would make for a memorable experience. But Mr. Nock ended up offering something much more memorable—a *ride* in it. Nock took the restored N3079G to numerous festivals and fairs around the country, giving countless Batman fans the opportunity to soar into the sky in the Batcopter. One of those fairs was the Ohio State Fair in Columbus—I am a resident of Columbus, so I probably don't have to tell you that I have taken quite a few Batcopter rides! In my personal opinion, Mr. Nock owns one of the coolest Batman toys that anyone could ever have.

The movie's Batboat was a modified 1966 Glastron V-174 Fiberglas sporting boat. The Glastron Company itself actually performed all of the Bat-modifications, which included designing and building a scalloped tail fin adorned with bat insignias. Like the Batmobile and the Batcopter, the Batboat became an instantly recognizable part of 1960s Batman mythos.

Batman's Batcycle was a modified 1966 Yamaha Catalina outfitted with a detachable sidecar. It was designed by Dan Dempski, a mechanic who worked with George Barris. While the Batcycle looked good on film, it was quite difficult to maneuver. Hubie Kerns (West's stuntman) and Victor Paul (Ward's) were the ones who actually had to ride the cycle. Kerns and Paul never crashed on it, but neither found their time with the Batcycle to be particularly enjoyable.[8]

Some of *Batman*'s best scenes were the ones showing all of these vehicles in action. Because they were real-life, powerful machines that actually drove, flew or sped across the water, the scenes were quite believable and exciting. Their realism would provide a refreshing counterpoint to all of the film's intentional silliness.

Batman was edited and assembled just about as quickly as it had been filmed, and was ready for its world premiere by late July 1966. The premiere was held at the Paramount Theatre in Austin, Texas, on July 30, with West, Meredith, Romero and Meriwether in attendance. In fact, these *Batman* stars did more than just *attend* the premiere—they appeared in costume, and were driven in open cars to the theatre so that thousands of Bat-fans lining the streets of Austin could get a real-life peek at them! Interestingly, a short video clip from that day has survived which features Austin television host Jean Boone interviewing Meriwether, Romero and West, all of them in costume. Boone's low-key interviews provide a fascinating behind-the-scenes look at the Batmania of 1966. Incidentally, Austin was chosen to debut the film because the Glastron Boat Company was located in that city. Glastron displayed their Batboat out front of the Paramount so those who attended the premiere could get a close-up look.[9]

Batman opens with a terrific title sequence, as stylish and fun as any Batman-related image ever committed to film. As the credits flash on the screen, a series of night scenes illuminated only by a bright spotlight depict Batman, Robin, Catwoman, Joker, Penguin and Riddler stepping momentarily into the light, and then disappearing back into the darkness. The spotlight keeps changing color as it illuminates each character, flashing bright shades of blue, red, green, purple and yellow, suggesting the vivid colors of a comic book page. These character shots are intertwined with shots of an unidentified criminal dressed in a long, film noir–style trenchcoat and a hat that hides his face, running down dark city streets, illuminated only by the same spotlight.

This sequence is accompanied by an equally striking main title theme composed by Nelson Riddle, who wrote all of the film's musical score except for Neal Hefti's "Batman Theme." Riddle's opening music for the film incorporates the feel, if not the actual notes, of the "Batman Theme." It then builds on this feel, adding bursts of big band brass and swirling orchestral passages that briefly quote all of the individual melodies that Riddle wrote for each of the film's main characters. In other words, the main title theme plays like an ingenious, compact overture for the entire film. Riddle's score remains every bit as strong throughout the entire movie as it is in this opening sequence. (As previously mentioned, Riddle also composed equally memorable music for the *Batman* television program.)

6—Batman (1966)

While this opening sequence suggests Batman's "creature of the night" origins, the rest of *Batman* is infinitely sunnier and sillier—most all of the film's scenes take place in broad daylight, and are played for laughs. *Batman* wastes no time in setting up its plot and getting into the action. An anonymous source has informed the Gotham City authorities that a yacht carrying the wealthy English whisky maker Commodore Schmidlapp is in danger of being hijacked. Schmidlapp is traveling to the United States to demonstrate his revolutionary invention, known as a "dehydrator," which can instantly remove all of the water content from any object.

Batman and Robin race from the Batcave in their Batmobile to the Gotham airport, where their Batcopter is hangared. After transferring from the Batmobile to the Batcopter, they fly out over the ocean, hoping to intercept the Commodore's yacht. They see the yacht, and Batman climbs down a rope ladder attached to the underside of the Batcopter in order to board it. But just as he is about to set foot on the yacht, it disappears right out from under him. Batman sinks into the ocean, and as Robin starts to take the helicopter back into the sky, a shark bites into Batman's leg. As Batman struggles with the shark, Robin climbs down the ladder and hands Batman a can of shark repellent batspray. Batman gives the shark a healthy dose of the spray, causing the shark to let go of his leg and plummet down toward the ocean. As the shark hits the water, it explodes.

Back at the office of Gotham City Police Commissioner Gordon, Batman, Robin, Gordon and Chief O'Hara organize a press conference regarding the mysterious disappearance of Schmidlapp. A beautiful reporter from the *Moscow Bugle* by the name of Kitka is in attendance, and Batman is obviously smitten with her. Afterwards, the lawmen talk candidly about the fact that whoever is behind Schmidlapp's disappearance must also be the anonymous source who tried to lure Batman out into the ocean so that he could meet his doom in the jaws of the shark stuffed full of explosives. Realizing that the Penguin, Joker, Riddler and Catwoman are all currently at large, they fear these crimes might signal the fact that these supercriminals have joined forces.

Their fears are well founded—Kitka is actually the Catwoman in disguise, and she reports back to a hideout above a seedy waterfront tavern where the Penguin, Joker and Riddler are waiting. The criminals are bitterly disappointed to learn that Batman was not killed by the Penguin's trained exploding shark, but they gloat over the fact that they were able to hijack Schmidlapp's yacht and steal his dehydrator. They realize that their criminal plans involving the dehydrator can never be pulled off with Batman and Robin around to stop them. Assuming that the Caped Crusaders will make their way back out into the ocean where Schmidlapp's yacht disappeared in order to look for clues, the Penguin, Joker and Riddler board the Penguin's customized Penguin submarine and head out to sea to intercept them.

Via the Batboat, Batman and Robin travel back to the spot in the ocean where they thought they saw Schmidlapp's yacht. There they find a projection unit cleverly disguised as a bell buoy—the yacht was never there in the first place, it was just an illusion meant to lead Batman into the shark trap. And now another trap is waiting for them—a powerful magnet inside the buoy pins Batman and Robin to its sides via all of the metallic objects in their utility belts. As they struggle, the villains fire torpedoes at them from their sub. Batman is able to pry loose a transmitter from his utility belt and use it to send waves of super energy toward the torpedoes, causing them to explode before they reach the buoy. The last torpedo almost gets to them because the transmitter's batteries go dead. However, a porpoise hurls itself in front of the missile right before it reaches the buoy, nobly giving its life for the Dynamic Duo.

Back at their hideout, the Penguin, Joker, Riddler and Catwoman discuss their main criminal objective — to kidnap all of the multinational members of the United World Security Council and hold them for ransom. They still feel that their scheme cannot succeed while Batman and Robin are alive, so they devise yet another attempt to kill the crimefighters. They will kidnap a prominent citizen and hold him hostage at their hideout. When the Dynamic Duo burst into the hideout to rescue this citizen, they will step on a gigantic jack-in-the-box that will propel them out into the ocean and into the arms of a gigantic exploding octopus. (*Batman*'s screenwriter Semple must have been harboring some sort of grudge against large sea animals.) The Riddler suggests the perfect do-gooding citizen to kidnap — Bruce Wayne.

Disguised as Kitka, the Catwoman goes to see Wayne claiming that she has received two riddles from the Riddler. Batman and Robin figure out the answers to the riddles, and interpret their meanings to be a threat against Kitka's life. Bruce asks Kitka out to dinner in order to keep watch over her. Back at Kitka's penthouse after dinner, the date turns decidedly romantic. Just then, the Penguin, Joker and Riddler burst in riding on jet pack umbrellas and abduct Bruce. The villains take Bruce back to their hideout and wait for Batman and Robin to come to Bruce's rescue. Bruce cleverly tricks them into untying him for a moment, at which point he attacks them and escapes.

The Penguin uses the dehydrator to remove all the water from five of his henchmen, reducing them all to powder. He then stores the powder in five separate vials for easy rehydrating when he comes face-to-face with Batman and Robin again.

Batman and Robin race back to the hideout to try to apprehend the criminals and rescue Kitka, but they find it deserted. They *do* find that something has been left behind for them — a large lit bomb. Batman grabs the bomb and dashes outside to try to find a place to throw it where it will not hurt anyone when it explodes. As he runs around the waterfront area, he dodges crowds of people, mothers pushing babies in strollers, and even a Salvation Army band! He is finally able to throw the bomb into a deserted area and take cover just before it explodes.

All of a sudden, the Penguin waddles up to them disguised as Commodore Schmidlapp. They see through his disguise immediately, but when they attempt to run a fingerprint check on him to prove he *is* the Penguin, they find that he has had his fingerprints surgically removed. "Schmidlapp" agrees to a retinal eye scan using equipment at the Batcave to prove his identity, so the crimefighters give him a whiff of knockout Bat gas and take him to their headquarters.

Once they are at the Batcave, the Penguin rehydrates his henchmen and orders them to fight Batman and Robin. But it does not amount to much of a fight, because the Penguin has accidentally rehydrated the thugs with hard water, leaving their molecular structure highly unstable. In fact, the slightest impact causes them to disappear into thin air. After the henchmen have vanished, Batman pretends to believe that the Penguin is Schmidlapp, and offers to give him another whiff of bat gas and take him back to the city.

On their way back, the Penguin sprays the crimefighters with a knockout gas of his own, kicks them out of the Batmobile and drives off. But Batman and Robin have only feigned unconsciousness to allow the Penguin to escape — they assume that he will then lead them back to the rest of his criminal gang. The Dynamic Duo commandeer their Batcycle (hidden near the stretch of road where the Penguin stole their car), transfer from the Batcycle to the Batcopter and give chase to the Penguin by air.

From the Penguin submarine, the Riddler fires off a missile which skywrites two riddles regarding the criminals' plot to kidnap all of the members of the United World Security Council. Coincidentally, the missile almost strikes the Batcopter, forcing Batman and Robin to crash land. When they see the riddles, the Caped Crusaders realize the grave danger the Council members are in and race on foot to United World Headquarters. But they are too late — the criminals have forced their way into the building and dehydrated all of the Council members and poured them into vials.

Assuming that the criminals will use their sub to escape, Batman and Robin pursue them in the Batboat. They catch up with the sub and pummel it with blasts of energy fired from their batcharge launcher. The batcharges force the sub to surface and the Caped Crusaders climb aboard. They are met by the Penguin, Joker, Riddler and a host of henchmen. A wild fight ensues, complete with the same style of onscreen "POWs" and "BAMs" first featured in the TV *Batman* brawls. The Dynamic Duo triumphs over all of the villains and then give chase to the Catwoman, whose mask falls off. They are shocked to see that the Catwoman is the object of Bruce's affection, Kitka. Robin tries to offer his sympathy to Batman, but Batman quickly cuts him off, saying anything he might say could turn out to be compromising. Batman stoically says that this disappointment means nothing, and tells Robin to cuff her.

Just then, the real Commodore Schmidlapp walks in. (During the entire film, he has never become aware of his predicament — the villains fooled him into thinking that his yacht has simply been held up in heavy fog on the way to America!) He trips and knocks over the vials containing the dehydrated members of the United World Security Council. The vials are smashed and Schmidlapp sneezes right into the powder, scattering it all over the place.

Later, Batman and Robin are in the Batcave, laboring to sort what powder belongs to what Council member. The entire world, including U.S. president Lyndon B. Johnson, waits breathlessly to find out if the Dynamic Duo can restore the Council members to their rehydrated selves. Back at the United World Headquarters building, the heroes prepare to commence the rehydrating process. The process is successful, except for one hitch — all of the council members are speaking the wrong languages! Batman expresses his hope that maybe this bizarre mixing of minds and bodies will help to further understanding among all nations of the world. The film ends with the Caped Crusaders quietly exiting the building through the window, descending toward the ground on their batropes.

Since the *Batman* motion picture was basically an expanded version of the *Batman* television series, there is no need for a long discussion regarding the film's actors, costumes, props, sets and dialogue — I have already covered all of these elements in my discussion of the TV show. However, there are a number of differences between the film and the TV show that are worth mentioning. First and foremost, the film was able to play up some of the more "adult" aspects of *Batman* without having to worry about running afoul of the network television censors. The most notable of these aspects is the fact that Bruce makes no secret of his desire to sleep with Kitka — the script even allows for Bruce to utter a few rather daring yet subtle double entendres to this effect. And the scenes featuring the two of them back at her penthouse, with Kitka "slipping into something more comfortable" before she joins Bruce on the couch, are far racier than anything the TV show could have ever depicted.

Adam West's acting was always deadly serious on the television show, but in the film, he is allowed to play Batman/Bruce in a more grim, determined manner than he could ever get away with on TV. For example, in the scene where he is being held hostage by the villains, he confronts them about the whereabouts and safety of Kitka. He tells them that if they have harmed her, he will kill them all. There is not a hint of lightheartedness in this scene — given the absurd nature of the majority of the film, his intensity at this particular moment is rather startling. It makes one think that if West had been asked to play Batman in a screen work that placed more emphasis on drama and action than it did comedy, he probably would have been every bit as good of a serious Batman as he was a comedic Batman.

Even with these slight differences, *Batman* basically played like a "supersized" TV episode. Keeping in mind the old adage "if it ain't broke, don't fix it," director Leslie Martinson generally stuck closely to the formula of the TV show. But Martinson still was able to add a few of his own personal touches to the project. For example, Batman's wild waterfront scramble to dispose of the bomb the villains have left for him, in which he dodges crowds of people, mothers pushing babies in strollers, and even a Salvation Army band, was Martinson's idea. He improvised the sequence while *Batman* was actually being shot, and it turned out to be one of the film's funniest and most memorable moments.

The speed with which the film was made does not affect its quality in the least — it is every bit as well-written, acted and produced as the best episodes of the *Batman* TV show. This is likely due to the fact that the *Batman* team had simply found their groove while producing the first season episodes and they just kept smoothly rolling through the production of the film.

Critics were not particularly kind to the film. This probably had less to do with their opinions of the film itself than it did with the fact that most everyone in America was beginning to show signs of "Batman overload," for lack of a better term. The relentless avalanche of Batmania that 1966 had brought was starting to grow a little tiresome. After all, the TV show's wildly hyped first season ran from mid–January to early May, the film was released in late July, and the show's second season was scheduled to premiere just a few weeks after that, in early September. To put it bluntly, the Batman character was starting to suffer from a massive case of overexposure. Also, many critics perceived the *Batman* motion picture as nothing more than a crass attempt to milk the Batman cash cow before it went dry.

In spite of lackluster reviews, *Batman* did well at the box office — the character's star may have stopped rising so meteorically, but it was certainly nowhere near falling yet. Children all over the country were thrilled by Batman's big screen adventure — and, just like the TV show, there was more than enough humor in the film to keep Mom and Dad entertained as well. So *Batman* finished out its initial theatrical run as an indisputable success, just as the *Batman* television program began its second season.

During this second season (September 1966 to March 1967), the bloom started to come off of the rose. First off, *Batman*'s cast and crew were simply exhausted from all of the work they had done since late 1965. They had jumped from rushing the show into production so that it would be ready for an early premiere date, to rushing a movie out between the show's first and second seasons, to rushing out new second season episodes of the show. By late 1966 they were all so burned out by that they could not possibly sustain the level of enthusiasm they felt for the show when it first commenced production.

But *Batman* faced a much bigger problem than on-set weariness: The show was slipping in the ratings. Much of *Batman*'s initial popularity was attributable to its novelty, and now that novelty had worn off and, consequently, many viewers were tuning out. The show seemed so fresh and original when it first premiered, but once audiences knew what to expect from it, its format and humor had become downright predictable. *Batman* tried to combat this problem by adding more celebrity guest stars and playing the show's comedy more broadly, but this only made the series come across as all the more forced and stale. Simply put, everyone had seen so much of Batman over the past year or so that they had grown bored with him. Now, as the show's second season came to a close, the character's star *was* truly starting to fall.

ABC decided to renew *Batman* for a third season, but demanded that some substantial changes be made in an attempt to cut production costs and increase ratings. First off, the show was cut back to airing only once a week instead of twice. Most of the third season episodes would be self-contained, and not end with a cliffhanger—the cliffhangers were suspended because the network felt that trying to carry a cliffhanger scenario all the way to next week's episode would make the show confusing to follow for its youngest viewers. Also, *Batman* would have to make do with less elaborate ("expensive" might perhaps be a better word) props and sets. Unfortunately, this decision would result in many third season episodes looking almost amateurish in comparison to the lavishly produced first and second season episodes.

William Dozier thought that *Batman*'s ratings might improve if the show were to introduce a new regularly-featured female character. He presented this idea to Batman editor Julius Schwartz at DC Comics, which led DC to hit upon the concept of a "Batgirl."[10] DC artist Carmine Infantino designed this new character—her costume consisted of a blue cape and bat-eared cowl, yellow utility belt, gloves, boots, and a black bodysuit emblazoned with a yellow bat emblem. Batgirl made her first-ever appearance in "The Million Dollar Debut of Batgirl" in *Detective Comics* #359, January 1967. In the story, Batgirl was revealed to secretly be mild-mannered librarian Barbara Gordon, the daughter of Commissioner Gordon.

In "The Million Dollar Debut of Batgirl," Barbara makes her costume only to be worn at a Gotham Police Masquerade Ball. But on her way to the event she encounters a bizarre moth-costumed criminal known as Killer Moth, who is trying to kidnap Bruce Wayne. Batgirl saves Wayne from Killer Moth, which of course allows Wayne to begin his pursuit of the criminal as Batman. Batman learns that Killer Moth was trying to kidnap his alter ego in order to frighten him into paying the criminal protection money. Batgirl also joins in the pursuit of Killer Moth—Barbara has decided that being a costumed crimefighter is just what she needs to spice up her humdrum life. With Batgirl's help, Batman and Robin are able to track Killer Moth down, foil his extortion racket and put him behind bars. The story ends with Batman saying that he would welcome Batgirl's aid in future cases, even though he still does not know her true identity.

As we discussed last chapter, there was a previous comic book Bat-Girl, who (along with Batwoman) appeared in Batman comic stories of the 1950s and early 1960s. The Barbara Gordon Batgirl was a completely new character, with no continuity ties to her predecessor. This new Batgirl proved to be a far more enduring character than either Batwoman or Bat-Girl. She seemed far less "gimmicky" than these earlier heroines—perhaps this was because Batman's comic writers wisely stayed away from placing her in the kind of "romantic longing for Batman and Robin" scenarios that had made Batwoman and Bat-Girl seem so silly. She was depicted first and foremost as a crimefighter, just like Batman, Robin and her father. While Batgirl would never become as popular as her male counterparts, she nevertheless would become a regular fixture of Batman's comic book world.

Batman's creators stayed generally faithful to the comic book Batgirl when creating their television Batgirl—she too was Barbara Gordon, the Commissioner's daughter and a librarian-turned-crimefighter. (In fact, to introduce the character to the executives at ABC,

Batman's producers actually filmed an adaptation of "The Million Dollar Debut of Batgirl." This short film was never officially released to the public in any form.) However, her costume was quite removed from the character's comic book costume — she was clad in a garish purple bodysuit with a purple cowl, and purple cape that sported bright yellow lining. She was given an equally garish purple Batgirl motorcycle to ride.

The part of Batgirl/Barbara Gordon was played by Yvonne Craig. Craig was an attractive, dark-haired actress who had appeared in a number of films during the late 1950s and early 1960s. An accomplished ballet dancer, she possessed the kind of physical dexterity that the role of Batgirl required. Craig's performance in *Batman* was very enjoyable, but it did nothing to help stop the show's slide in the ratings. *Batman*'s third season aired from September 1967 to March 1968, and then the series was cancelled.

The 1960s screen *Batman* ended up producing 120 half-hour television episodes and one feature film during its three years of existence, and its impact on the history of the character cannot be overstated. Simply put, audiences have *never* stopped watching this screen version of Batman. The TV series was sold into syndication even before it finished its third season run — consequently, it was rerunning on television stations all over the world almost immediately after its cancellation. As of 2013, this pattern of *Batman* television reruns has not ended. It is likely that a television station somewhere on this planet is broadcasting an episode of the series for their viewers to enjoy even as you read these words.

And the film proved to be just as ubiquitous as the TV series — countless movie theatres around the globe continued to feature it at revival screenings. Also, the film was sold into syndication just like the TV series had been — so it found an even *bigger* audience on television stations all over the world. And of course, our planet has continued to turn and new children have continued to be born — these children who weren't alive to be a part of Batmania the first time around discovered the TV series and the movie, and they loved this screen version of Batman as much as the kids of 1966 did.

One of the main reasons that *Batman* continued to appeal to generation after generation of youngsters was that the show truly had a timeless quality to it. Since *Batman* was so well-made and visually unique, it just never seemed to go out of date. *Batman*'s Gotham City was a place that was not connected to any particular time period at all — it was a comic book page come magically to life, and it was every bit as compelling to youngsters of the 1970s, '80s, '90s and beyond as it had been to youngsters who watched the show in its heyday.

So much of this chapter has been about the connection between the *Batman* television series and the *Batman* motion picture. Ironically, there has not been any connection between the two in terms of their home video release history. As of 2013, a legal agreement has never been reached between all of the corporations with a financial interest in the *Batman* TV series that would allow the series to be released on home video. Hopefully someday such an agreement will be reached, but that seems like a remote possibility at this time.

The home video release history of the *Batman* movie has been exactly the opposite of the *Batman* TV show's home video release history. The movie has been available on home video basically since magnetic tape became the standard home video format in the mid-1980s. Countless *Batman* videotapes were popped into Beta and VHS players around the world until DVD became the standard home video format in the late 1990s. In 2001, *Batman* was released on DVD for the first time by 20th Century–Fox Home Video. The DVD included a wealth of bonus material along with the film, such as an audio commentary track recorded by Adam West and Burt Ward, a featurette about the making of the film, and an up-close video tour of the Batmobile.

DVD remained the highest-quality home video format until the introduction of the Blu-ray disc in 2006. Of course, the continuing popularity of the *Batman* film on home video all but guaranteed that not too much time would pass before the movie would be upgraded to Blu-ray. In July 2008, 20th Century–Fox Home Video released *Batman* on Blu-ray for the first time to coincide with the theatrical release of Christopher Nolan's film *The Dark Knight*. The picture and sound quality of *Batman* on Blu-ray was nothing short of remarkable — on the disc, the film looked and sounded every bit as vibrant as it did the day it was theatrically released. The *Batman* Blu-ray also contained new short documentaries about the film created especially for the Blu-ray release, as well as all of the bonus material found on the 2001 DVD.

Another home video release relating to the 1960s screen *Batman* warrants mention here. In 2004, Image Entertainment released a 2-disc DVD set that examined the 1960s screen Batman phenomenon entitled *Batman: Holy Batmania!* The bulk of the DVD set's running time consisted of four documentaries produced for the cable television network The Biography Channel in the early 2000s. The titles of the documentaries were "Batman: Holy Batmania!," "Adam West: Behind the Cowl," "Cesar Romero: In a Class By Himself," and "Julie Newmar: The Cat's Meow." The DVD set also included a number of interesting bonus features, such as the original *Batman* TV series screen tests featuring Adam West, Burt Ward, Lyle Waggoner and Peter Deyell.

Not surprisingly, Adam West and Burt Ward have not been able to step out of the long shadow that the *Batman* TV series and film ended up casting. When the series was cancelled, they found that *Batman*'s incredible success had left them more than simply typecast — in the public's eyes, they *were* Batman and Robin, and nothing in the world would ever change that fact. *Batman*'s timeless appeal trapped West and Ward in the same state of suspended animation. They both managed to land some post–*Batman* parts but, generally speaking, their names were never publicly mentioned without the "B-word" following closely behind.

Consequently, West and Ward acted in "non–Batman" productions as much as they could, but they still suited up to reprise their famous roles from time to time. They made a number of personal appearances in costume, together and separately, throughout the 1970s and 1980s — West in particular made many solo costumed appearances with the Batmobile at automobile shows all over the country. Also, they played the characters in a 1979 NBC two-part television comedy special entitled *Legends of the Super-Heroes*. The special marked the only time that the Batman and Robin characters appeared in a live-action screen production between *Batman*'s 1968 cancellation and the 1989 Warner Bros. motion picture *Batman*. (We'll discuss the special in more detail next chapter.)

West and Ward did some voice-only work for Batman animated television productions during this time period as well. The actors provided the voices for Batman and Robin in *The New Adventures of Batman* (1977), and West provided Batman's voice in *Super Friends: The Legendary Super Powers Show* (1984) and *Super Powers Team: The Galactic Guardians* (1985). In *Super Friends* and *Super Powers Team*, Robin was voiced not by Ward, but by Casey Kasem. (We'll discuss these animated shows in more detail in the next chapter.)

Ironically, after working to move beyond their Batman and Robin roles for over 20 years, West and Ward had to be somewhat forced to let go of the characters once Warner Bros. began developing their "serious" Batman film in the late 1980s. The film's title would be the same as West and Ward's 1966 Batman film, but that was about where the similarities ended. Warner was moving as far away from the "camp Batman" of the 1960s as possible, so they did not want West and Ward's names anywhere near their film.

Not surprisingly, it was difficult for West and Ward to see a brand new wave of Batmania start to heat up that had nothing to do with them. West even went so far as to publicly complain about not being given the chance to appear as Batman in Warner's film.[11] Of course, because West was so closely identified with his comedic portrayal of the character, he was completely wrong for the kind of Batman that this new *Batman* was hoping to depict. Still, he was understandably hurt that Warner would not even consider him for a part that he was already world-famous for playing. Ward also voiced his opposition to the film, but since it was not even going to feature the character of Robin, he did not have as much reason to feel slighted by it as West did. At any rate, their complaints did not make much of an impression on anyone, least of all on Warner Bros., so the film moved ahead without them.

Even though Warner Bros. shut West and Ward out of participating in the 1989 *Batman*, the actors were able to reap some benefits from the new wave of Batmania that the film spawned. Because of the renewed interest in the 1960s TV show and film, West and Ward were asked to appear on a number of TV talk shows and entertainment news programs and reminisce about their years in capes and tights. Batman's newfound popularity also led both men to write books about their Bat experiences.

West's 1994 book *Back to the Batcave* was an entertaining look at 1960s Batmania from the perspective of the man at the center of it all. The book also revealed West to be surprisingly introspective regarding his perceptions of the Batman character in general. West made it plain that even though his Batman performance might have hindered his subsequent acting career, he never regretted taking the role; on the contrary, he still had great affection for the character, and was pleased that his Batman portrayal had been enjoyed by so many people all over the world for so many years.

Ward's 1995 book, *Boy Wonder: My Life in Tights*, was quite another story. Featuring a cover photo of a man's midsection clad in Robin-style green trunks adorned with a "bat-zipper," and a woman's hand pulling down that zipper, the book was a trashy tell-all that devoted most of its pages to recounting Ward's many sexual escapades during the years he played Robin. In *Boy Wonder: My Life in Tights*, Ward seemed to not have the slightest bit of interest in the Robin character, or in the fact that *Batman* was loved by so many people around the world. Instead, the book appeared to be nothing more than an excuse for Ward to degrade the entire *Batman* experience while at the same brag about his own "accomplishments."

Some of the anecdotes featured in *Back to the Batcave* and *Boy Wonder: My Life in Tights* were the inspiration for the 2003 CBS television movie *Return to the Batcave: The Misadventures of Adam and Burt*. The production was an unusual mix of comedy, fantasy and historical dramatization—it featured West and Ward playing themselves, hot on the trail of some unknown thieves who have stolen the original 1966 Batmobile. As they pursue the thieves, they recall some of the most memorable events that took place during the years they were making *Batman*. These reminiscences are re-created in flashbacks that feature young actors playing the *Batman*-era West and Ward. The end of the production reveals the Batmobile thieves to be none other than Frank Gorshin and Julie Newmar, who are out to finish off West and Ward once and for all so that they can claim *Batman*'s legacy for the show's *real* stars—namely, the villains! *Return to the Batcave* was a slight piece, but its irreverently affectionate look back at the 1960s *Batman* phenomenon was quite entertaining—especially for longtime Batman fans. The production was released on DVD to the home video market in 2005.

There are a substantial number of Batman fans that feel the 1960s *Batman* TV series and film are insults to the character because they chose to play Batman for laughs. This author is not one of them. Generally speaking, both the TV show and the movie were very well produced, written and acted — but most importantly, they were *fun*. They were fun for the kids who enjoyed them as straight action, and they were fun for adults who enjoyed them as comedy.

And since *Batman*'s action sequences were played so straight and filmed with such high production values, it is no wonder that they have captivated young children for almost 50 years now. I personally will never forget the first time I saw the *Batman* movie when I was a child. Watching Batman and Robin roar out of the Batcave in the Batmobile, and then soar into the sky in the Batcopter in the film's opening scenes was thrilling — there was nothing funny about those scenes at all to me. Of course, now that I am an adult I see that the exploding shark hanging onto Batman's leg as he dangles beneath the Batcopter was meant to be funny — and it *is* funny.

But when all is said and done, the point of *Batman* really does not have to do with whether one finds it funny or not — because either way, the good guys win, the bad guys lose, and a marvelous time is had by all along the way. With all of the troubles in this world, this author sees nothing wrong at all with a screen Batman that has brought happiness to people of all ages for generations.

7

Exile from the Big Screen, 1967–1989

After the cancellation of the *Batman* TV series in 1968, the character basically disappeared from view as far as the general public was concerned. The camp craze that surrounded *Batman* came to an abrupt end, and all of the "POWs," "BAMs" and "ZAPs" that went along with it faded from the national spotlight. However, the years immediately following the show's demise were incredibly eventful ones for the Batman of the comic books. DC Comics was left with a commodity that to the majority of the general public appeared to be washed up — but to many comic book fans, Batman remained a treasured icon. So in an ironic twist, the end of the TV series and Batman's widespread popularity would end up leading to a major revitalization of the character.

But before we start examining that revitalization in detail, we need to back up just a bit and look at what was happening in the world of Batman comics during the last half of the *Batman* TV series' three-year run. In 1967, Batman's premier New Look artist Carmine Infantino was promoted to editorial director of DC Comics. Since Infantino's modernized visual interpretation of Batman did not jibe with Bob Kane's "old school" approach, Kane found himself increasingly at odds with DC over the character he had created. But as we have noted earlier in this book, even though Kane had received sole credit for the creation of the Batman character, Kane's Batman comic art had almost always been a collaborative effort. Indeed, Kane had begun hiring uncredited ghost artists to help him illustrate Batman stories within the first few months of the character's existence. Since the efforts of so many individual artists were responsible for making Batman into the icon he had become, it was probably inevitable that Kane's influence regarding the character's development would eventually wane to nothing.

This fact obviously did not sit well with Kane. There is no doubt that he loved all of the limelight and financial gain he received for being Batman's sole creator — and he was content to enjoy those spoils while basically doing none of the day-to-day work required to create the Batman comic art that bore his name. But by the mid–1960s, Kane certainly had to see the handwriting on the wall. His character had evolved to a point where he would never have any significant control over it again, and DC was starting to make sure that the writers and artists who were creating new Batman comic stories *would* be publicly credited for their work — the era of Kane's ghost artists doing all the work and Kane getting all the credit was over.

It is sad to note that after doing so little and receiving so much, Kane's final years at DC were marked by him brazenly asserting that he deserved even *more* creative credit for

7—Exile from the Big Screen, 1967–1989

Batman than he had been given. The most glaring example of Kane's selfishness relating to the Batman character occurred in September 1965, when he wrote an open letter to a Batman fanzine called *Batmania*. Kane wrote the letter in order to respond to public comments made by Bill Finger earlier that year—in these comments, Finger had stated that he was far more involved in the creation of the Batman character than he had ever been given credit for. Kane was furious over Finger's claim that he was as responsible for the existence of Batman as Kane was.

Kane's long letter to *Batmania* is fascinating to read, because in vociferously defending himself against Finger's claim, he basically resorts to telling out-and-out lies about how involved he was in the creation of Batman comics during the 1940s, 1950s and 1960s. In the letter, Kane states that in the "Golden Age" of the character, he penciled, inked and lettered the strip himself. He goes on to claim that ninety percent of the mid–1960s New Look Batman stories were drawn by him as well. Obviously, these were outrageously false assertions—earlier in this book, we have examined a number of artists who ghosted for Kane during this time period such as Jerry Robinson, Dick Sprang, and Sheldon Moldoff. In the letter, Kane even accidentally reveals how totally disconnected he had become from the Batman character by the mid–1960s—for example, at one point he refers to the 1950s Batwoman character as one of his "villains."[1]

In fairness to Kane, he still made a point of recognizing Finger's valuable contributions to the development of the Batman character in his letter. But this small gesture of goodwill does not make up for the fact that he was willing to be so deceitful in order to portray himself as the sole architect of Batman's continuing success. In short, Kane certainly deserved credit for creating Batman, perhaps even sole credit because he was the one who initially undertook the task to create a new costumed comic hero in the wake of Superman's success. That said, however, the untruths Kane was willing to put forth regarding his ongoing involvement in Batman comics, untruths like the ones found in this letter, will always stand as a mark against his personal character. Incidentally, *Batmania* might very well have been uncomfortable with the amount of shameless self-interest found Kane's letter—they chose not to publish it in the fanzine until 1967. By that time, it was obvious that Kane's efforts to retain control of the Batman character would not succeed. Kane retired from DC and regular Batman comic work that same year, not long after Infantino's promotion to editorial director.[2]

Even though Kane would no longer be a part of Batman's ongoing development at DC, he would continue to enjoy the spoils of being recognized as the character's sole creator. The income he had earned through Batman comics and the 1960s Batman screen projects made him a wealthy man. And the staggering success of the 1960s screen Batman also brought him a certain degree of celebrity. Kane's Batman fortune and fame would continue to grow over the years, reaching its zenith in 1989—that year, he would get the opportunity to be a focal point of the Batmania surrounding the character's fiftieth anniversary and the release of the 1989 film *Batman*. (We'll discuss Kane's involvement with the Warner Bros. Studios Batman film series later in the book.)

There is another point I feel I need to make before we completely leave the era of the 1960s camp Batman behind. As I mentioned at the end of the last chapter, there are a substantial number of Batman fans that feel the 1960s *Batman* TV series and film are insults to the character because they chose to play Batman for laughs. These fans feel much the same way about the Batman comic stories of the late 1960s, because during this time DC basically hopped on the camp bandwagon and created stories featuring the character that had the look and feel of the *Batman* TV show. But I find it fascinating to note that even during the camp Batman's peak period, Batman was still *Batman*— in other words, he never lost his uniqueness or his timeless appeal.

To illustrate this point, please allow me a moment to recap one of my favorite Batman comic stories of all time. "Hunt for a Robin-Killer" was first published in *Detective Comics* #374, April 1968. The story was written by Gardner Fox, penciled by Gil Kane and inked by Sid Greene. The story is not one that is considered "great" by most Batman comic fans — in fact, it never has been reprinted in any sort of "Best of Batman" anthology released by DC Comics. But it has remained a personal favorite of mine because it presented such a compelling depiction of Batman as a crimefighter and detective.

"Hunt for a Robin-Killer" tells the tale of Batman tracking down a vicious criminal named Jim Condors after Condors brutally beats Robin almost to death. At the opening of the story, Batman and Robin are raiding the hideout of a gang of criminals. During the raid, Condors makes a sneak attack on the Boy Wonder while Batman is occupied taking down the gang. (Condors holds a grudge against Robin because the young hero apprehended Condors's brother during a solo case.) Batman finds Robin, bloodied, bruised, and perilously close to death, and rushes the boy to a nearby hospital. Overcome with grief, Batman then goes on a manhunt to find the criminal who had come so close to killing his junior partner. Batman has a hard time keeping his feelings of rage and vengeance under control during this intensely personal case, but in the end he uses his superior detection skills to find Condors and bring him to justice. The story ends with Robin being released from the hospital, still weak, but ready to take his place alongside his mentor.

"Hunt for a Robin-Killer" is a well-written, realistic crime drama that features Batman and Robin fighting non-costumed thugs similar to characters one might find in a 1940s film noir production. And Kane and Greene's art is every bit as strong as Fox's story — their work features unusual panel layouts, deep perspective, and wonderfully realistic, expressive characters. Fox, Kane and Greene perfectly capture the essence of Batman and his world in "Hunt for a Robin-Killer." In the tale, Batman descends on criminals with a vengeance that fills them with terror. At one point, he even appears in menacing silhouette in a doorway, a dark vigilante bent on apprehending Robin's attacker. "Hunt for a Robin-Killer" depicted Batman in a manner not that far removed from the character's late 1930s–early 1940s adventures — and it hit the newsstands just as the *Batman* TV series was airing the last of its third season episodes! To me, the story stands as proof that all of the camp silliness that the 1960s Batman craze delivered did nothing to lessen the power of the Batman character.

And that power was about to grow even stronger with the cancellation of the *Batman* TV series. Free from the masses who enjoyed regarding Batman as a silly, throwaway piece of pop culture, DC Comics decided to let a new breed of comic book writers and artists return the character to his dark late 1930s roots. This new era in Batman comic history began with a story that appeared in *Batman* #217, December 1969, entitled "One Bullet Too Many." The story was written by Frank Robbins, penciled by Irv Novick and inked by Dick Giordano. In "One Bullet Too Many," Dick Grayson moves out of Wayne Manor in order to attend college at Hudson University outside of Gotham City — obviously, this means the end of Batman and Robin working regularly together as a team. Bruce Wayne decides that this major change in his life should bring about major changes in Batman's career as well — Batman will once again become a mysterious figure who prowls the night as a lone vigilante.

Writer Denny O'Neil and artist Neal Adams were the most notable storytellers in this

7—*Exile from the Big Screen, 1967–1989*

Batman in 1974, returned to his dark roots. Art by Neal Adams.

new era of Batman comics; their first Batman collaboration was the story "The Secret of the Waiting Graves" published in *Detective Comics* #395, January 1970. In the tale, they depicted Batman as a grim detective whose costume featured the long ears, angular cowl and dramatically flowing cape of Bob Kane's and Bill Finger's original vision. In "The Secret of the Waiting Graves," Batman travels to Mexico and encounters a wealthy couple by the name of Muerto that have discovered a rare kind of flower which has the power of conferring immortality on anyone who regularly smells its fragrance. But the fragrance also drives anyone who smells it long enough completely mad, so Batman decides to destroy all of the flowers. After he does so, the Muertos age over a century in just the matter of a few seconds and fall over dead. "The Secret of the Waiting Graves" ends with Batman standing over the Muertos' fresh graves, a grim expression on his face. O'Neil's dark, emotionally complex script and Adams' intricate figural renderings made the story's Batman seem far more realistic than any previous version of the character had been. But at the same time, the supernatural forces he faced in the tale also gave him a mysterious, horror movie–type of quality.

Comic book fans immediately embraced the O'Neil-Adams version of Batman. Throughout the first half of the 1970s, they created a host of tales featured in *Batman* and *Detective Comics* that were hailed as Batman classics from the moment they were released. Their story "The Joker's Five-Way Revenge!," published in *Batman* #251, September 1973, was especially important, because in it they returned the Joker from the silly prankster he had become in 1950s and 1960s comics to the leering, homicidal madman found in Kane and Finger's original work.

In "The Joker's Five-Way Revenge!" the villain is ruthlessly hunting down members of his old gang because one of them betrayed him to Batman and the Gotham Police, leading to his arrest. The Joker kills his former henchmen one by one, with Batman hot on his trail. Batman finally catches up to the Joker at a seaside aquarium that has been closed due to a recent oil spill. The Caped Crusader manages to save the Joker's last surviving henchman just as the villain throws the henchman into a tank containing a ravenous shark. Batman then chases the Joker down on the oil-slicked beach, bringing him to justice with several savage punches. "The Joker's Five-Way Revenge!" delivered the first modern age view of a dark hero in cape and cowl battling a murderous, mirthless clown in a moody, film noir–like setting. In other words, it virtually provided a blueprint for all of the classic Batman/Joker confrontations that would follow in the coming decades.

O'Neil and Adams were also responsible for creating one of Batman's all-time greatest comic book foes, Ra's Al Ghul. Ra's appeared to be a middle-aged man of far eastern descent who was in possession of great wisdom and strength—but basic appearances could not begin to scratch the surface of his *real* history. Thousands of years old, Ra's Al Ghul was able to rejuvenate himself in a bubbling cauldron of chemicals known at the Lazarus Pit. Ra's felt that the planet was on the verge of being destroyed by the reckless actions of twentieth century humankind, so he wanted to wipe out most everyone on Earth in order to restore the planet to what he considered to be its "natural balance." Obviously, Batman opposed Ra's' plan to purge the planet of most of its humans, but his relationship with the villain was far more complex than a standard "good guy vs. bad guy" scenario.

Batman first met Ra's Al Ghul in "Daughter of the Demon," a story published in *Batman* #232, June 1971. Right from the first panels, it was obvious that Ra's was going to be unlike any other villain Batman had ever faced. In the story, Batman learns that Robin has been kidnapped and is being held prisoner by an unknown criminal. (Even though Dick Grayson had been sent off to college, Robin still made occasional appearances with Batman in Batman comic titles.) Just as Batman begins to investigate his partner's abduction, Ra's steps out of the shadows of the Batcave and tells the crimefighter that he has deduced his secret identity. Ra's also reveals that his beautiful daughter Talia, whom Batman had met on an earlier case, has been kidnapped in a similar manner. Ra's proposes that they work together to rescue Robin and Talia.

Clues left by the kidnappers lead Ra's and Batman to the hideout of an organization known as the Brotherhood of the Demon, located high in the Himalayan Mountains. But by the time he reaches the hideout, Batman has deduced that the person behind Robin and Talia's abduction is none other than Ra's himself. When Batman confronts Ra's with this information, Ra's admits it is true that he staged the entire scenario. Ra's then reveals why he went to all this trouble. Talia is in love with Batman, and Ra's wants to retire from running his criminal organization — so he set up a test to see if Batman was worthy of becoming his son-in-law and heir! Ra's informs Batman that he has passed this test, and the story ends with Talia kissing the stunned crimefighter on the cheek.

Needless to say, Batman did not take Ra's and Talia up on their offers. In fact, over the years he worked to thwart a number of Ra's' schemes to wipe out most of the people on Earth. But opposing Ra's did not keep Batman from having feelings for Talia — he was captivated by her beauty and spirit, even though she was in his eyes every bit as much of a criminal as Ra's himself. And opposing Batman did not keep Ra's from having feelings for his enemy — Ra's kept Batman's secret identity a secret in the hopes that the crimefighter would one day change his mind about joining his organization and marrying his daughter. In other words, though Batman and Ra's were mortal enemies, there were deep psychological connections between them that almost bordered on a familial relationship. These connections helped to make some of Batman's battles against Ra's Al Ghul among the best Batman comic stories ever published.

While Neal Adams' Batman art is often given the majority of the credit for visually returning the character to his "creature of the night" roots, there were a number of other talented artists who produced equally memorable Batman images during the 1970s. Dick Giordano not only inked a substantial amount of Adams' Batman art, but he also was the main illustrator of many excellent Batman stories featured in *Batman* and *Detective Comics*. (Just a few pages back, we noted Giordano's inking efforts on the story which began this new era in Batman comic history, "One Bullet Too Many.") Also, Jim Aparo's excellent Batman renderings, which featured the realism of Adams' style coupled with the strong lines of more traditional comic artwork, were a welcome fixture of countless stories featured in *The Brave and the Bold* and *Detective Comics*. Aparo's close association with the character continued well into the late 1990s, making him one of the most prolific Batman artists of all time.

As Batman's comic book world began to grow darker and more sophisticated, the first-ever reference books designed for serious Batman fans were published. The 1971 anthology book *Batman from the 30s to the 70s* contained classic Batman comic stories ranging from his 1939 debut all the way up to O'Neil-Adams works such as "The Secret of the Waiting Graves." And the 1976 book *The Encyclopedia of Comic Book Heroes Volume 1: Batman* by Michael J. Fleisher provided a wealth of information on the thousands of characters appearing in Batman comic stories between 1939 and 1965. Unfortunately, while that book was very comprehensive, its focus was too narrow — it made no attempt to cover all of the changes the character had gone through during the camp Batman craze of the 1960s and the O'Neil-Adams led revamp of the 1970s.

Batman's comic book world might have been growing more serious during the 1970s, but the character's lighthearted 1960s screen works kept right on winning new fans. Since youngsters were still being drawn to this incarnation of Batman, the character was featured in a variety of kiddie television cartoon series from the late 1960s all the way up to the 1980s.

The first of these series was Filmation's *The Batman-Superman Hour*, which first aired on CBS in late 1968 and early 1969. Contrary to the program's name, Batman and Superman never appeared together—they each starred in their own cartoon adventures. Batman's cartoons in the series were very similar in tone to the third season of the live-action *Batman* TV series—they featured Robin and Batgirl working with the Caped Crusader, battling familiar villains such as the Joker, Penguin, Riddler and Catwoman. In 1969, CBS repackaged *The Batman-Superman Hour*'s Batman cartoons into a Batman-only series entitled *Batman with Robin the Boy Wonder*. Like so many Saturday morning kiddie cartoons, Filmation's 1968–69 Batman cartoons were of decidedly poor quality—their animation was very cheaply produced, and their scripts were unbearably silly. In the cartoons, the part of Batman was voiced by Olan Soule and the part of Robin was voiced by Casey Kasem.

Filmation's next series of Batman cartoons, *The New Adventures of Batman*, was no better. *The New Adventures of Batman* first aired in 1977 on CBS, and it too was burdened with terrible production values. To make matters worse, Filmation decided to add a new character to the series—Bat-Mite! (As discussed in Chapter 5, Bat-Mite was an interdimensional imp in an ill-fitting Batman costume who appeared in Batman comic stories of the late 1950s and early 1960s.) *The New Adventures of Batman* was already bad enough due to its poor animation and stories, but adding one of the silliest regular characters ever to appear in the pages of Batman comics made them doubly awful. Incidentally, Adam West and Burt Ward provided the voices for Batman and Robin in *The New Adventures of Batman*, but not even the presence of the legendary screen Caped Crusaders of the 1960s could help to salvage the series.

The longest-running television cartoon program to feature Batman was the Hanna-Barbera series *Super Friends*, which premiered on ABC in 1973. The Super Friends were a team of DC heroes similar to the one found in the DC comic title *Justice League of America*. The team included Superman, Batman, Robin, Wonder Woman and Aquaman, as well as a variety of other heroes that appeared as occasional guest stars. The *Super Friends* series ran on ABC under slightly varying titles (*The All-New Super Friends Hour*, *Challenge of the Super Friends* and *The World's Greatest Super Friends*) until 1979. In all of these versions of *Super Friends*, the part of Batman was voiced by Olan Soule and the part of Robin was voiced by Casey Kasem, reprising their roles from the 1968–69 Filmation Batman cartoons.

The series was revived by Hanna-Barbera and ABC in 1984 under the title *Super Friends: The Legendary Super Powers Show*, and in 1985 under the title *Super Powers Team: The Galactic Guardians*. As he had for 1977's *The New Adventures of Batman*, Adam West provided Batman's voice in *Super Friends: The Legendary Super Powers Show* and *Super Powers Team: The Galactic Guardians*. In these *Super Friends* incarnations, the part of Robin was again played by Casey Kasem.

Like Filmation's Batman cartoons, the 1970s incarnations of *Super Friends* were by no means "high-class" productions—they featured lackluster animation and stories designed for very young audiences. The 1980s *SuperFriends* were far more ambitious than their predecessors, especially in terms of their scripts, presenting stories that thoughtfully adapted some of DC's most cherished comic book traditions.

For example, an October 1985 episode of *Super Powers Team: The Galactic Guardians* entitled "The Fear" depicted Batman's origin on screen for the very first time. The episode was written by Alan Burnett, who would go on to co-produce the landmark animated television series *Batman: The Animated Series* in the early 1990s. In "The Fear," Batman faces one of his longtime comic book foes, the Scarecrow, who dresses up like his namesake and is obsessed with inflicting fear on his victims. While chasing the Scarecrow, Batman inadvertently runs into the Gotham City alley where his parents were killed. The crimefighter is paralyzed with fright after memories of his parents' murders come flooding back to him. Batman realizes that in order to defeat the Scarecrow, he must overcome his fears surrounding his parents' deaths; he does just that, and the Scarecrow is captured at the end of the episode.

When surveying the history of the Batman character's screen appearances, "The Fear" stands out as sort of a "missing link." The episode bridged the gap between the campy, kiddie-oriented screen Batman found in the 1960s *Batman* TV series and film, and the darker, more emotionally complex screen Batman found in the Warner Bros. live-action Batman films. For the first time, Batman was brought to the screen as a character that was unequivocally scarred by deep personal tragedy. It is interesting to note that this first glimpse of a serious screen Batman featured none other than Adam West voicing the character! Ironically, the actor who was the icon of the 1960s camp Batman craze helped to usher in the era of a darker screen Batman.

Still, with the exception of "The Fear," most of Batman's cartoon appearances from the 1960s up through the 1980s were decidedly "kiddie" in nature. And since Batman was a character that appealed mainly to children during this time period, there was no shortage of Batman toys being produced. The most notable of these toys were the line of Batman action figures and accessories made by the Mego Company in the 1970s. Mego manufactured a line of 8" figures billed as "The World's Greatest Superheroes" which included Batman, Robin and Batgirl, as well as the villains the Joker, Penguin, Riddler and Catwoman.

The plastic figures themselves were outfitted in wonderfully detailed cloth costumes. Along with these figures, Mego offered accessories such as the Batmobile, the Batcycle and the Batcopter, as well as a large Batcave playset. All of Mego's Batman toys tended to reflect the look of the 1960s New Look comic stories, as well as the 1960s *Batman* TV show and film. For the first time, a large part of the Batman mythos had been realized in miniature form by one specific toymaker. By collecting Mego Batman toys, children could bring Batman's world to dazzling three-dimensional life right in their own homes.

Now, back to the world of Batman comics. While not as prolific as comic creators like O'Neil, Adams, Giordano or Aparo, writer Steve Englehart and artists Marshall Rogers and Terry Austin made a tremendous impact on the Batman character with a series of stories that appeared in *Detective Comics* from August 1977 through April 1978. These stories featured familiar allies such as Robin, Alfred and Commissioner Gordon, and familiar villains like the Joker and the Penguin, but several new Englehart characters thrown into the mix added a narrative depth not often found in comic books of the time.

One of these characters was Silver St. Cloud, a successful businesswoman with whom Bruce Wayne fell in love, and during the course of their romance she deduced that he was actually Batman. Another was Rupert Thorne, the corrupt President of Gotham City Council, who tried to stop Batman from interfering with his criminal activities by falsely accusing the Caped Crusader of being an outlaw. Englehart also resurrected a Batman villain that had not appeared in Batman comic stories since the early 1940s— Hugo Strange was an evil scientific genius whose criminal schemes accidentally led him to discover that Bruce Wayne was actually Batman. (In Englehart's stories, Batman had a much harder time than usual keeping his identity a secret!) Englehart's storytelling in these comics, a mixture of adventure, intrigue and romance featuring characters old and new, was so sophisticated that many readers considered his Batman to be the "definitive" depiction of the character.

Englehart's stories were made all the more compelling when coupled with the art of Rogers and Austin. While similar to the art of Neal Adams, Rogers and Austin's work rendered Batman and his world in a more strongly linear, almost architectural fashion. This style perfectly suited Englehart's complex plots, and made Batman seem closer to the "real" world than ever before.

The climax of the Englehart-Rogers-Austin Batman saga was a two-part Joker story that ended with Batman battling his arch nemesis high atop an unfinished skyscraper in a fierce thunderstorm. A bolt of lightning sends the Joker tumbling off of a girder to his apparent doom. (But as all Batman fans know, he'll find a way to survive and torment our hero yet again as he has many times before.) Just at this moment of triumph, Batman is handed a tremendous personal sorrow—Silver leaves him because she is unable to cope with his double life.

Englehart's *Detective Comics* scripting run featured a welcome addition to the Batman mythos that is worthy of note. In his stories, Englehart referred to Batman by the nickname "The Dark Knight." As we discussed in Chapter 1, this nickname was first used in the story "The Joker" which appeared in *Batman* #1, Spring 1940—but the nickname had been used very sparingly in Batman comic stories after that. Englehart's decision to resurrect the practice of referring to Batman as "The Dark Knight" would have far-reaching implications—eventually, the phrase would become DC's official second name for Batman.

Incidentally, the Englehart-Rogers-Austin Batman saga has remained very popular with serious Batman fans over the years, so it has been reprinted in a number of different book formats. For example, in 1999 the stories were published in a stand-alone book entitled *Strange Apparitions*.

Batman and Robin in "The Malay Penguin," *Detective Comics* #473, November 1977. Art by Marshall Rogers and Terry Austin.

The revitalization of the Batman character in 1970s comic stories, combined with the blockbuster success of the 1978 Warner Bros. motion picture *Superman* starring Christopher Reeve in the title role, led to the first attempts to produce a new live-action Batman screen work. In 1979, Michael Uslan and Benjamin Melniker set up a production company called BatFilm Productions to finance a Batman film that would be far more serious in tone than the 1960s TV show.[3]

The project was not realized at this time, but it laid the groundwork for Batman's return to the big screen a decade later. (We'll discuss Uslan's and Melniker's efforts in detail next chapter.)

The 1960s screen Batman works had been so staggeringly successful that Uslan and Melniker certainly had their work cut out for them in terms of trying to convince the entertainment industry that a Batman screen work could be so much deeper than a silly camp romp. Ironically, this point probably could not have been made any more clearly than it was by a television production featuring Batman and Robin released the very same year that Uslan and Melniker formed BatFilm Productions. Adam West and Burt Ward reprised their roles as Batman and Robin in the 1979 NBC two-part television comedy special entitled *Legends of the Super Heroes*. The special was produced by Hanna-Barbera as sort of a live-action companion to their *Super Friends* cartoon series. *Legends of the Super Heroes* marked the only time that the Batman character appeared in a live-action screen production between the *Batman* TV show's 1968 cancellation and the 1989 Warner Bros. motion picture *Batman*.

The first part of *Legends of the Super Heroes* was called "The Challenge," and it featured Batman, Robin, and a host of DC heroes battling a host of DC villains who had created a bomb that was powerful enough to kill everyone in the entire world. The only one of these villains from Batman's mythos was the Riddler—the part was played by Frank Gorshin, reprising his role from the 1960s *Batman* TV show and film. The second part of *Legends of the Super Heroes* was called "The Roast," and it featured Ed McMahon as himself, hosting a celebrity roast–style event for the DC heroes who had appeared in "The Challenge," including Batman and Robin.

Simply put, *Legends of the Super Heroes* was a torturously bad production. The production's attempts to create tongue-in-cheek humor by mixing the comic book world with the real world never really had a chance to succeed—that strategy had worked so well for the 1960s screen *Batman*, but it came across as dreadfully stale by the late 1970s. Being painfully unfunny was not the only problem that *Legends of the Super Heroes* had—it also suffered from ridiculously cheap-looking sets and woefully bad special effects.

Adam West and Burt Ward must have been mortified once they realized just what a mess they had gotten themselves into by agreeing to appear in the show. Poor Adam West looked as if he had to suffer even more than Burt Ward did. West was fitted with a new cowl for *Legends of the Super Heroes* that wasn't long enough in the neck area to allow it to smoothly taper down to his shoulders. Consequently, the loose cowl flopped around his neck the entire program, making it look like he was sporting a double (or triple) chin!

Whether one is a fan of the 1960s Batman screen works or not, one must admit that those works were very well-crafted—their writing, acting, costumes and production values were almost always top-notch. *Legends of the Super Heroes* was every bit as bad as the 1960s screen *Batman* was good. Fortunately, *Legends of the Super Heroes* basically dropped out of sight immediately after it first aired—if too many viewers had gotten the chance to see the special, the general public's opinion of Batman might well have fallen so low that the entertainment industry would *never* have risked producing a new Batman screen work!

Eventually, the special did make its way to the home video market—it was released on DVD by Warner Bros. in 2010. One might wonder why Warner Bros. even bothered to release such an awful program on home video. The most likely answer to that question is that *Legends of the Super Heroes* is one of those productions that is so bad it has become sort of, well, *legendary*. Trust me, it *is* so bad that you really have to see it to believe it—so if you are brave enough, it is out there waiting for you!

Fortunately for Batman fans, a much better Batman work with the word "legends" in the title appeared the year after *Legends of the Super Heroes* first aired. In 1980, DC published the landmark three-part series entitled *The Untold Legends of the Batman*. *The Untold Legends of the Batman* marked the first time the character appeared in a stand-alone miniseries, and it retold the origins of all of the major characters in Batman's world, heroes and villains alike. In the series, Batman is afraid that one of his enemies has discovered his secret identity because someone has been leaving him threatening messages in the Batcave. As he tries to deduce who the culprit might be, he recalls the events that led him to become a crimefighter, as well as some of his most memorable cases. At the end of the series, he discovers that he himself actually left the messages — his bizarre actions are the result of a brain trauma he suffered during a recent case, which has caused him to suffer from temporary schizophrenia. Written by Len Wein and illustrated by Jim Aparo and John Byrne, *The Untold Legends of the Batman* served as an excellent "summing up" of over 40 years of Batman history, as well as an homage to all of the talented artists and writers who had contributed to that history.

In the early 1980s, Batman was in somewhat of a creative slump. Over a decade had passed since DC's new generation of writers and artists had revitalized the character, and as wonderful as that revitalization had been, it seemed as if it was time for something new to happen in Batman's world. In 1983, DC Comics tried to force the issue by introducing a second Robin character. Jason Todd was introduced in issues of *Batman* and *Detective Comics* as a young circus aerialist who performed in a trapeze act with his mother and father, Trina and Joseph. Trina and Joseph were helping Batman to find Killer Croc, a criminal with freakish, reptilian-like skin. Croc was becoming a very powerful figure in Gotham's underworld, and he had vowed to become even more powerful by murdering the Caped Crusader.

Detective Comics #526, May 1983, marked Batman's five hundredth appearance in the magazine and, to commemorate this auspicious anniversary, the Jason Todd storyline was brought to a dramatic climax. The issue featured a 50-plus page story written by Gerry Conway entitled "All My Enemies Against Me," which depicted dozens of Batman's foes, including the Joker, Penguin, Riddler and Two-Face, teaming up to kill Batman before Killer Croc could get to him. In the story, Batman is able to round up and defeat all of his enemies, including Killer Croc, but not before Croc murders Trina and Joseph Todd. At the end of the story, Bruce Wayne decides to make the orphaned Jason his ward, just as he had done with Dick Grayson many years earlier.

"All My Enemies Against Me" set the stage for Jason to adopt the identity of Robin. Of course, Dick Grayson was still fighting crime as Robin, so for the next year or so, the plots of both *Batman* and *Detective Comics* moved Jason toward becoming Robin, and Dick toward adopting a new crimefighting identity. Finally, in *Batman* #368, February 1984, Dick passed on his costume to Jason, formally ending his partnership with Bruce. This decision was reached without any rancor between Bruce and Dick — Bruce wanted Jason to become Batman's full-time partner, and Dick was ready to establish a life outside of Batman's shadow. Dick then designed a sleek, capeless costume that was primarily blue in color, and dubbed himself "Nightwing."

The Robin character's return to Batman's world on a basically full-time basis was met with generally negative reviews from Batman fans. Many felt that tradition dictated that Dick Grayson should be the only character to ever don the Robin costume. Plus, the Dick Grayson Robin's occasional presence in Batman stories kept both "pro–Robin" and "anti–Robin" Batman fans happy — a part-time Robin allowed for appearances of the Batman and

Batman and the Joker in *Batman: The Dark Knight Returns* #3, "Hunt the Dark Knight" (1986). Art by Frank Miller, Klaus Janson and Lynn Varley.

Robin team, as well as solo Batman appearances. Fans were also put off by Jason's origin being such an obvious retread of Dick's origin. Nevertheless, the Jason Todd Robin remained a fixture of Batman's comic book world for the next few years.

A form of the comic book commonly referred to as a "graphic novel" was beginning to grow in popularity in the mid–1980s. Graphic novels were basically very high-quality comic books— they featured more pages, heavier paper and better printing than their dime-store counterparts. In 1986, the first-ever Batman graphic novel was published, and it presented a complex, startlingly new version of Batman that completely changed the course of the character's history. Writer-artist Frank Miller's four-part *Batman: The Dark Knight Returns* was set in an indefinite future, and it told the story of what the end of Bruce Wayne's Batman career might be like.

In *Batman: The Dark Knight Returns*, Wayne is a 55-year-old alcoholic who has given up fighting crime because his second Robin Jason Todd was brutally murdered by the Joker a decade earlier. Gotham City has been overrun by criminals, and Wayne feels powerless to do anything about it. But finally he comes to the realization that he cannot just remain idle while his city crumbles, so he dons his costume for a last series of adventures. One of the first criminals he brings to justice is Harvey Dent, who had supposedly been rehabilitated from his Two-Face persona through plastic surgery and psychiatric counseling.

Batman faces off against a very dangerous and powerful Gotham street gang known as the Mutants, who have vowed to murder his longtime ally Commissioner Gordon. He brings down the leader of the Mutants with the help of an adventurous young girl named Carrie Kelley. Like her predecessors Dick Grayson and Jason Todd, she too adopts the guise of Robin. This new Batman and Robin team is soon faced with an even deadlier enemy, the

Joker. The madman snaps out of the catatonic state he has been in for a number of years upon learning that Batman has returned to action. The Joker's reign of terror finally ends once and for all — Batman gravely wounds the villain when the two fight at a county fair. There the Joker chooses to end his own life, twisting his neck until his spine snaps.

The United States government wants the new Batman and Robin team stopped because they feel they are lawless vigilantes, so they send one of their special agents to put them out of commission. That special agent is none other than Superman, who has just returned from defending the United States from a nuclear attack launched by the Soviet Union. In nuclear winter conditions, Batman and Superman engage in an apocalyptic battle on the very street where Bruce Wayne's parents were murdered decades earlier.

Superman "wins" the battle because Batman fakes his own death. Carrie is in on the plan, so after Bruce Wayne's elaborate funeral, she exhumes his body and he goes right back to fighting crime. But not as Batman — he has given up that identity forever, and he will now continue his war on crime as a far more covert operative.

Batman: The Dark Knight Returns was beautifully written and stunningly illustrated, but it was Miller's richly detailed vision of Batman that really made the series so special; his Batman inhabited a world even more closely tied to reality than the O'Neil-Adams Batman or the Englehart-Rogers-Austin Batman. And the reality Miller created for Batman in *Batman: The Dark Knight Returns* was an immensely tragic one. The murder of Bruce Wayne's parents had filled Bruce with a grief that was so crushing, so all-encompassing, that his Batman persona had become more than just a disguise — it had become a kind of psychological escape for Bruce, a wraithlike alter ego that was almost completely separate from his thoughts and actions..

Page after page in *Batman: The Dark Knight Returns*, Miller brought readers a Batman that was both haunted and hauntingly real. The physical peril he faced, the calculations he made while striving to prevent crime, the self-doubts he dealt with, all made him seem like an actual, flesh-and-blood person. And the reactions his quest for justice inspired were much the same reactions our world would likely have if there really was a Batman. In *Batman: The Dark Knight Returns*, politicians and pundits debated the legitimacy of his actions on television news programs, while the general public responded to him with varying degrees of hero worship. Miller's insights into how our culture perceives heroism, evil and social responsibility were by turns chilling, satirical, inspiring and depressing, but at all times riveting.

Batman: The Dark Knight Returns was a tremendous critical and commercial success, and this success ended up not being confined to the relatively small population of comic book fans. Warner Communications, the parent company of DC Comics, released the series as a one-volume paperback through their publishing company Warner Books. This version of *Batman: The Dark Knight Returns* sold very well at major bookstores throughout the country, and paved the way for the general public to start taking Batman more seriously than they did when he was viewed as a campy TV show character.

Batman's re-entry into the general public's consciousness via *Batman: The Dark Knight Returns* had a very positive effect on the plans for producing a new Batman motion picture that were commenced by Michael Uslan and Benjamin Melniker back in the late 1970s. Due to a number of corporate takeovers and partnership changes (we'll discuss those events in more detail next chapter), this Batman film project was now in the hands of Warner Bros.— and *Batman: The Dark Knight Returns* made Warner realize that a serious screen Batman could be a highly marketable property.

But before Batman would return to the movies, his comic book world underwent a number of radical changes brought on by the phenomenal success of *Batman: The Dark Knight Returns*. First off, DC Comics completely revamped his relationship with his old ally Superman. Since the mid–1950s, the two heroes had been sharing adventures in *World's Finest Comics* and were depicted to be the closest of friends. But Miller's portrayal of these titans as enemies resulted in DC making relations between Batman and Superman much chillier. DC canceled *World's Finest Comics* in January 1986, and from that point on, DC's two greatest heroes would maintain a relationship that ranged from strained to outright adversarial whenever they appeared together.

This change made for some interesting dramatic tension in stories that featured both Batman and Superman. Even though the heroes basically still worked to achieve the same goal of stopping crime wherever they might find it, their methods were so different that conflict would sometimes arise between them. Batman's frightening "creature of the night" approach to fighting crime was often at odds with Superman's straightforward "friendly public servant" approach. This rapport between the crimefighters seemed to be much more true to *both* of their characters than the three-decades-old tradition depicting them as close confidants.

Another 1980s Batman graphic novel that ended up having a long-range effect on the history of the character was *Batman: Son of the Demon*, which was written by Mike W. Barr and illustrated by Jerry Bingham. *Batman: Son of the Demon* was first published in 1987, and told the tale of Batman and his longtime foe Ra's al Ghul joining forces in order to hunt down a dangerous terrorist known as Qayin. Of course, in Batman's eyes, Ra's normally fell under the definition of "dangerous terrorist" as well, but Qayin was such a threat to the world that Batman was willing to work with Ra's to bring Qayin down.

In *Batman: Son of the Demon*, Batman and Ra's's daughter Talia finally give into their love for one another and become a couple. Talia becomes pregnant with Batman's child, and at first they are both thrilled at the prospect of starting a family together. But Talia eventually becomes so worried that Batman will unnecessarily risk his own life protecting the child that she lies to him about the pregnancy, saying she has suffered a miscarriage. The story ends with Talia giving birth to the child, a boy, and giving him up for adoption to an unnamed couple. It would take nearly two decades for the implications of *Batman: Son of the Demon* to greatly affect Batman's comic history — in 2006, writer Grant Morrison introduced Batman and Talia's son into the regular continuity of Batman comic stories. We'll discuss Morrison's version of the character, a young man named Damian Wayne, later in the book.

The success of *Batman: The Dark Knight Returns* led DC to contract Frank Miller to create another four-part Batman series. In the series, Miller would retell Batman's origin in a manner in keeping with the tone he established in *Batman: The Dark Knight Returns*. However, this series would not first be published as a graphic novel, but as stories appearing in regular issues of *Batman* comics. *Batman: Year One*, written by Miller and illustrated by David Mazzucchelli, ran in *Batman* #404, February 1987, through *Batman* #407, May 1987.

Batman: Year One focuses on Bruce Wayne's decision to become a costumed crimefighter, and his very first exploits as Batman. As Wayne is returning home to Gotham City after training himself as a fighter, detective and scientist, police officer James Gotham is moving to Gotham to start working for the Gotham City Police Department. Wayne's very first attempt at fighting crime goes very poorly — he is attacked by several prostitutes, including one named Selina Kyle, and shot by Gotham Police officers. Despite his wounds, he is able to make it home to Wayne Manor — as he sits in his home gravely injured, a huge bat

Batman in *Batman: Year One* #2, "War Is Declared" (1987). Art by David Mazzucchelli and Richmond Lewis.

crashes through the window, giving him the inspiration to don the disguise of a bat. Gordon's first days with the Gotham Police go just as badly—he immediately works to rid the force of corruption, which leads to him being brutally attacked by several corrupt cops.

Wayne dons his Batman disguise for the first time, and his exploits instantly become the stuff of legend. He even crashes a dinner party being attended by many of Gotham's crime bosses and crooked politicians to let them know that he plans on bringing them all to justice. This leads corrupt Gotham City Police Commissioner Gillian Loeb to order the Gotham Police to apprehend Batman by any means necessary. A Gotham Police SWAT team eventually corners Batman in an abandoned building, but Batman is able to elude capture by using a sonar device to attract all of the bats in a cave beneath Wayne Manor to him. In the chaos caused by the swarming bats, Batman makes it back to Wayne Manor. Batman's noble intentions begin to sway Gordon—Gordon begins to see Batman not as a criminal, but as a potential crimefighting ally.

Batman also has a deep effect on Selina Kyle, inspiring her to don a costume and fight crime—disguised as a cat, she attacks a major crime boss named Carmine Falcone. Falcone, hoping to gain back control of his city which has suddenly seemed to go so crazy, unleashes a plan to kidnap Gordon's son in order to force Gordon to end his fight against Gotham's corrupt system. Bruce Wayne, sans his Batman costume, is able to foil the kidnapping plot. Gordon is not able to get a look at the man who heroically saved his son, so Batman's identity still remains unknown to him—but Batman has proven that he is indeed Gordon's staunch ally. The final panels of *Batman: Year One* show Gordon on the roof of the Gotham City Police Department, waiting to meet with Batman about a criminal who has threatened to poison Gotham's water supply. That criminal refers to himself as "The Joker."

Batman: Year One's brilliant re-imagining of Batman's beginnings was hailed as an instant classic. Miller's compelling storytelling and Mazzucchelli's spare, no-nonsense artwork had captured Batman in a far more realistic manner than *any* previous Batman work ever had—indeed, most every panel in *Batman: Year One* could have been easily acted out in our real world. And Miller and Mazzucchelli's interpretations of Batman's supporting characters such as James Gordon and Selina Kyle were every bit as compelling as their interpretation of Batman himself.

Batman: Year One had rendered Batman and his world as an intricate, logical crime drama, and the results were so powerful that the series would prove to be one of the most influential Batman works of all time. (This fact will be made very obvious by the number of times we'll be discussing it later in this book.) After its initial run in *Batman*, *Batman: Year One* was released as a one-volume graphic novel, and enjoyed a commercial success equal to that of *Batman: The Dark Knight Returns*.

In addition to spawning *Batman: Year One*, *Batman: The Dark Knight Returns* also had a significant impact on the future of the Jason Todd Robin character. The graphic novel caused DC to rethink their inclusion of Jason in Batman's world because it had given voice to most Batman fans' dislike of Jason. Frank Miller's decision to have Jason meet his grisly end at the hands of the Joker seemed to be little more than a very thinly veiled expression of Miller's contempt for the character. This contempt mirrored how poorly Jason was being received by longtime Batman fans. Simply put, DC knew they had a problem in terms of where to go with the Jason Todd Robin, and Miller's "Jason editorializing" in *Batman: The Dark Knight Returns* only made the problem that much more obvious.

Premier Batman writer Denny O'Neil had been promoted to editor of DC's Batman comic titles in 1986. Right after *Batman: Year One* debuted, O'Neil immediately instigated changes to the Jason Todd Robin character in an effort to make him more popular. In the story "Did Robin Die Tonight?" (*Batman* #408, June 1987), Jason's origin, so meticulously set up over the course of dozens of issues of *Batman* and *Detective Comics*, was completely nullified.

In the opening of "Did Robin Die Tonight?" Dick Grayson was again Robin, and he and Batman were trying to capture the Joker. In the process, Robin was wounded and almost killed, which led Batman to decide to end Robin's career. Dick was unhappy about this, but he accepted it—but he also told his mentor that he would continue to fight crime in another guise. (Of course, this allowed Dick to continue appearing in other DC stories as Nightwing, which the character had been doing for the past two years or so.) Just as Batman returned to being a strictly solo crimefighter, he encountered a tough street kid named Jason Todd who was in the process of stealing the tires off of the Batmobile!

In subsequent issues of *Batman*, Batman eventually took Jason in just as he had Dick (and the first version of Jason!) and make him his partner. This second version of Jason proved to be just as unpopular as the first version. Consequently, O'Neil and company decided to do something very drastic to determine whether or not Jason would continue to be a part of Batman's world. DC held a phone-in poll for Batman fans to determine whether Jason would die at the hands of the Joker, in effect making Jason's fate as depicted in *Batman: The Dark Knight Returns* the character's "official" fate, or whether he would survive the Joker's attack. The poll was held in mid–September 1988 and, not surprisingly, the fans voted to kill off Jason. So in a series entitled "A Death in the Family" (*Batman* #426, December 1988 through *Batman* #429, January 1989), Jason was severely beaten by the Joker, and then killed in an explosion that the madman had set.

DC's decision to allow the Jason character to be killed off sparked quite a bit of media coverage. All of the major news media outlets knew a potentially compelling headline when they saw one, and "ROBIN THE BOY WONDER DEAD" certainly was a headline that would grab the public's attention. Of course, many people did not pay enough attention to the details of the story to realize that it was not the "classic" Dick Grayson Robin that DC had eliminated, but his very unpopular successor.

Most comic book fans had followed the genre long enough to know that even though Jason was gone, a new Robin was bound to be introduced before too long. After all, Robin remained one of the most recognizable comic book characters of all time — he was far too valuable a property to simply abandon. These comic book fans were right, of course: Plans were underway to introduce yet another Robin into Batman's comic book world even before the ink was dry on issues of "A Death in the Family." (We'll discuss this third Robin later in the book.) So DC's decision to portray "the death of Robin" as a major, irrevocable milestone in the history of the Batman character really amounted to nothing more than a crass publicity stunt.

The demise of another Batman icon was handled with considerably more thought and finesse in a graphic novel entitled *Batman: The Killing Joke*, released in late 1988. Written by Alan Moore and illustrated by Brian Bolland, it told the chilling tale of the Joker gunning down Barbara Gordon as part of an elaborate plan to drive Commissioner Gordon insane.

In *Batman: The Killing Joke*, the Joker thinks back on his life and contends that the only reason he became an insane, murderous criminal was because of monstrously bad luck. The Joker remembers himself as an unsuccessful comedian who agreed to help some

Batman and the Joker in *Batman: The Killing Joke* (1988). Art by Brian Bolland.

criminals pull off a robbery at a chemical plant where he had previously worked. Unknown to the comedian, the criminals had come up with a clever master plan to make their role in the robbery look insignificant — they made the comedian wear a red hood and cape, so it seemed that *he* was the costumed mastermind of the robbery.

The comedian's sole reason for taking part in the robbery was to obtain money for himself and his pregnant wife. But right before the robbery was to take place, his wife and unborn baby were killed in a freak accident. In spite of this tragedy, the criminals still forced him to don the guise of "the Red Hood" and help them. Batman broke up the robbery attempt and the comedian fell into a vat of acid, turning his skin white and his hair green.

As far as the Joker is concerned, the loss of his wife and his fall into the acid drove him insane — in fact, the Joker feels that *anyone* would be driven insane if they had to face the kind of horrific events he faced. In order to prove this theory, he shoots Barbara Gordon and photographs her terribly wounded body. The Joker then kidnaps Commissioner Gordon, holds him prisoner at a run-down amusement park, and forces him to look at these awful pictures of his beloved daughter over and over again — the criminal will drive the Commissioner mad just to prove that his actions are not his fault, it is the random cruelty of life that is responsible for his insanity.

Batman eventually tracks the Joker down and saves the Commissioner — in spite of all the Joker's efforts, Gordon has retained his sanity. And Barbara has survived the Joker's attack — but she will be confined to a wheelchair for the rest of her life. While in the process of apprehending the Joker, Batman tells the criminal that Gordon is still sane. Batman goes on to tell the Joker that Gordon has proved the criminal wrong, people *can* strive to overcome tragedy and lead meaningful lives. *Batman: The Killing Joke* ends with Batman trying to convince the Joker to try to rehabilitate himself — maybe Batman can even help him find his way out of the maze of insanity and violence that his life has become. The Joker tells Batman that it is far too late for that; consequently, the war between them will simply go on and on.

Batman: The Killing Joke's combination of Moore's emotionally deep storytelling and Bolland's realistic, beautifully detailed art made the graphic novel among the greatest Batman comic works of all time. And the book included an ingenious nod to the history of the Joker character — its exploration of the villain's origin as "the Red Hood" was inspired by the classic comic book story "The Man Behind the Red Hood!" which was first published in *Detective Comics* #168, 1952. (We discussed that story in detail in Chapter 5.)

But the most ingenious aspect of the book was that even though it gave the Joker a far more detailed backstory than he had ever received before, it was made clear that this backstory was only a *possible* origin of the criminal, not the "definitive" one. The Joker says during the course of the book that he *thinks* he remembers what happened to him in terms of his wife dying and his fall into the acid, but because he is so mentally unstable, his memories of these events tend to vary wildly. Consequently, *Batman: The Killing Joke* did not tie the character down to any specific pre–Joker identity, allowing the roots of his psychotic behavior to remain largely a mystery.

Batman: The Killing Joke's most long-ranging contribution to Batman mythos was that the Joker's horrific actions ended the crimefighting career of Batgirl. Batgirl's demise had far more impact on Batman fans than the death of Jason Todd in "A Death in the Family." As previously mentioned, killing off the unpopular Jason on the basis of a phone-in poll seemed like nothing more than a cheap publicity stunt, so it carried little emotional resonance for Batman fans. But the Barbara Gordon Batgirl had been a character that had remained popular with many Batman fans over the years, so seeing her taken out of action so completely was somewhat of a shock to them.

Barbara's injury turned out to be a plotline that lasted for decades. In the world of comic books, characters are often gravely injured or killed, but writers will often concoct some way to bring that character back to full strength after just a short time. This was not the case with Barbara — she remained paralyzed and confined to a wheelchair. She became a computer expert and, after dubbing herself "Oracle," began assisting Batman and other heroes in the gathering of information pertaining to cases they were working on. Barbara's transformation from Batgirl to Oracle seemed to emphasize *Batman: The Killing Joke*'s hopeful concept that people have the power to overcome adversity and find purpose in their lives, if they are only willing to look deep inside of themselves to find that power.

Incidentally, DC did eventually decide to rewrite Barbara's history so that she could return to action as Batgirl after the events of *Batman: The Killing Joke*—but that rewrite did not debut until late 2011, 23 years after *Batman: The Killing Joke* was first published. We'll discuss Barbara's second round of Batgirl adventures much later in the book.

Interestingly, Frank Miller's Batman works and the Moore-Bolland *Batman: The Killing Joke* ended up being widely regarded as the best Batman graphic novels of the 1980s, even though Miller's and Moore's interpretations of the character were so radically different from one another. Miller saw Batman as a soul so tortured that he was almost as unbalanced as the criminals he fought. Moore's Batman was undoubtedly very grim and driven, but he was most definitely not mentally unstable. In fact, the whole point of *Batman: The Killing Joke* was that heroes like Batman and the Gordons were able to find a way to hold themselves together in the wake of enormous personal tragedy. This characteristic was one of the main things that separated them from villains like the Joker.

Obviously, Moore's version of Batman was far closer in spirit to the way Batman had usually been portrayed since his 1939 debut. But while Miller's version of the character did not have the strength of tradition behind it, many Batman fans found it to be a compelling new way of interpreting their hero. At any rate, by the late 1980s there were many Batman fans who felt that the character should be portrayed as being mentally stable, and just about as many who felt that he should be portrayed as mentally *un*stable. Batman's adventures were about to begin proliferating at such an incredible rate that before long, there would be enough different kinds of Batman stories being published to keep *both* of these camps relatively happy.

Nineteen eighty-nine was the year that was going to mark the fiftieth anniversary of the Batman character's debut in *Detective Comics* #27, and DC Comics was preparing to celebrate the occasion very proudly and publicly just as they had when Superman turned 50 the year before. Of course, Batman's anniversary ended up being commemorated in a manner far larger than any celebration DC could have ever assembled. In June 1989, the long-awaited Warner Bros. motion picture *Batman* starring Michael Keaton as Batman and Jack Nicholson as the Joker was released, and it became one of the most commercially successful films of its time. We'll discuss that film in detail next chapter.

Batman (1989)

Cast: Michael Keaton (Batman/Bruce Wayne), Jack Nicholson (Joker/Jack Napier), Kim Basinger (Vicki Vale), Robert Wuhl (Alexander Knox), Pat Hingle (Commissioner Gordon), Billy Dee Williams (Harvey Dent), Michael Gough (Alfred Pennyworth), Jack Palance (Boss Carl Grissom), Jerry Hall (Alicia Hunt), Tracey Walter (Bob the Goon), Lee Wallace (William Borg), William Hootkins (Lt. Max Eckhardt), Richard Strange, Carl Chase, Mac McDonald (Goons), George Lane Cooper (Lawrence the Goon), Terence Plummer, Philip Tan (Goons), John Sterland (Grissom's Accountant), Edwin Craig (Antoine Rotelli), Vincent Wong (Crimelord 1), Joel Cutara (Crimelord 2), John Dair (Ricorso), Christopher Fairbank (Nic, Second Mugger), George Roth (Eddie, First Mugger), Kate Harper (Anchorwoman), Bruce McGuire (Peter McElroy, Anchorman), Richard Durden (TV Director), Kit Hollerbach (Becky, Action News Reporter), Lachelle Carl (Renee, TV Technician), Del Baker, Jazzer Jeyes, Wayne Michaels, Valentino Musetti, Rocky Taylor (Napier Hoods), Keith Edwards (Reporter), Leon Herbert (Reporter at City Hall), Steve Plytas (Plastic Surgeon), Anthony Wellington (Robert, Patrolman at Party), Amir Korangy (Wine Steward), Hugo E. Blick (Young Jack Napier), Charles Roskilly (Young Bruce Wayne), Philip O'Brien (Maitre d' at Museum), Michael Balfour (Scientist at Axis Chemicals), Liza Ross (Tourist Mom), Garrick Hagon (Harold, Tourist Dad), Adrian Meyers (Jimmy, Tourist Son), David Baxt (Dr. Thomas Wayne), Sharon Holm (Mrs. Martha Wayne), Clyde Gatell (Other Mugger), Jon Soresi (Medic), Sam Douglas (Gangster Lawyer), Elliott Stein (Man in Crowd), Denis Lill (Bob the Globe Cartoonist), Paul Birchard (Another Reporter), Paul Michael (Young Cop at Axis Chemicals), Carl Newman (Movement Double). *Producers:* Peter Guber, Jon Peters. *Co-Producer:* Chris Kenny. *Associate Producer:* Barbara Kalish. *Executive Producers:* Benjamin Melniker, Michael E. Uslan. *Director:* Tim Burton. *Screenplay:* Sam Hamm, Warren Skaaren (Story by Sam Hamm, based on characters created by Bob Kane). *Cinematography:* Roger Pratt. *Editor:* Ray Lovejoy. *Music:* Danny Elfman (Additional songs composed and performed by Prince). *Casting:* Marion Dougherty, Owens Hill. *Production Designer:* Anton Furst. *Art Directors:* Terry Ackland-Snow, Nigel Phelps. *Set Decorator:* Peter Young. *Costume Designer:* Bob Ringwood (Kim Basinger's costumes by Linda Henrikson). *Makeup:* Lynda Armstrong. *Joker Makeup Designer:* Nick Dudman. *Key Makeup:* Paul Engelen. *Prosthetic Makeup:* Suzanne Reynolds. *Chief Hair Stylist:* Colin Jamison (Kim Basinger's hair by Rick Provenzano) *Unit Manager:* Pat Harrison. *First Assistant Director:* Derek Cracknell. *Second Unit Director:* Peter MacDonald. *Supervising Art Director:* Les Tomkins. *Supervising Sound Editor:* Don Sharpe. *Special Effects Supervisor:* John Evans. *Visual Effects Production Manager:* Susan Ford. *Stunt Coordinator:* Eddie Stacey. *Batsuit Designers:* Paul Barrett-Brown, Vin Burnham. *Studio:* Warner Bros. *Length:* 126 minutes. *United States Release Date:* June 23, 1989.

It is hard to explain to anyone who was born after 1989 just what it was like to be a serious Batman fan in the years between the cancellation of the *Batman* TV show and the

Michael Keaton as Batman in *Batman* (1989).

release of the 1989 film *Batman*. Still, I feel I must try to do this before we really start to examine the 1989 *Batman*, because it will illustrate just how important the motion picture turned out to be in the history of the character. So listen up, all of you Batman fans in your twenties—this is what Batman fandom was like during the 1970s and 1980s.

During those years, it was almost impossible even to *tell* someone you were a serious Batman fan — unless that person was a hardcore comic book fan, that is. To everyone other than hardcore comic book fans, the words "serious" and "Batman" could not really even be placed next to each other in the same sentence. Batman was nothing more than Adam West in the campy TV show and movie, a silly character for kids, a craze that had died out a long time ago. Most people simply had no idea that Batman had originated in the comics as a dark avenger, as a man with a haunted past relentlessly fighting for justice.

Consequently, if you said to someone that you were a serious Batman fan and you thought the character could be appropriate entertainment for adults, you would almost always get very strange looks indeed. It was like saying to someone that you thought the "Neighborhood of Make-Believe" puppets from the PBS children's show *Mister Rogers' Neighborhood* would be the ideal cast to perform the definitive version of Shakespeare's *King Lear*. Most people could just not grasp the concept of Batman being rendered in a manner that was almost the complete opposite of the Adam West/kids' character Batman.

The phenomenal success of *Batman* in the summer of 1989 changed all that. Within a period of just a few months, the film introduced millions upon millions of people around the world to "our" Batman, the dark hero we serious Batman fans loved. There have been a lot of great moments in the history of the Batman character since *Batman*, and there are doubtless many more to come in the future. That said, however, the film's release holds an importance in Batman history that can never be equaled — it will forever stand as the first time a worldwide audience appreciated Batman in the way Bob Kane and Bill Finger had intended him to be appreciated when they created the first Batman comic story back in 1939.

One man in particular was responsible for bringing about this incredible shift in the way the general public perceived Batman, and his life story seemed to indicate that he had literally been born to do this job. Michael Uslan had become an avid comic book fan in the late 1950s when he was a young boy growing up in New Jersey, and he ended up being particularly drawn to Batman. He was a teenager when the *Batman* TV show premiered in 1966, and while he was thrilled to see his hero featured in a big-budget television show, he was bitterly disappointed that the show played Batman for laughs.

By the time Uslan was a law student at Indiana University in the early 1970s, he was actively working to get people to appreciate comic books as a serious art form. He developed a fully accredited college class for the university's Experimental Curriculum program on the history of comic books. Shortly after Uslan began teaching his class, it received an avalanche of attention from major news media outlets — at the time, the idea of a major university recognizing comic books as a legitimate academic subject was so novel that it warranted nationwide headlines.

This media attention led to both Marvel Comics and DC Comics contacting Uslan — both companies wanted to establish a relationship with this young man who was championing their work. DC ended up offering Uslan a job, which he happily accepted. Uslan's tenure at DC was a dream come true for him — he even got the chance to co-write several Batman stories for *Detective Comics* in 1976.

Jack Nicholson as the Joker in *Batman* (1989).

But Uslan's Batman dreams were far from over. In 1979, after working for the United Artists Studios' legal department for several years, he decided to take on the task of producing a new live-action Batman big screen work. The revitalization of the Batman character in 1970s comic stories and the blockbuster success of the 1978 Warner Bros. motion picture *Superman* led Uslan to feel that the time was just right to embark on such a project. Of course, Uslan envisioned this Batman film being far more serious in tone than the 1960s TV show — it would be inspired by the work of great Batman creators such as Bob Kane, Bill Finger, Denny O'Neil, Neal Adams, Steve Englehart and Marshall Rogers.

Uslan felt that he would need a preliminary script to help motion picture studios to understand his vision of Batman. The script he planned on using for this purpose was one entitled "The Return of The Batman" that he had co-written with one of his Indiana University friends in 1975. It is interesting to note that the script told the tale of Batman coming out of retirement in his mid–50s for a last series of adventures — in other words, it captured the Batman character in much the same manner that Frank Miller's groundbreaking four-part graphic novel *Batman: The Dark Knight Returns* would capture him ten years later![1]

Uslan knew that he would need the help of an experienced entertainment industry insider to sell his vision of a serious Batman film to motion picture studios. He was lucky enough to find the perfect ally in Benjamin Melniker, a former MGM Studios executive vice-president. Melniker agreed to enter into a partnership with Uslan on this venture, and in late 1979 the two men secured the film rights to the Batman character from DC Comics. Uslan and Melniker set up a production company called BatFilm Productions, and they set about pitching their film to major Hollywood studios.

Due to a number of corporate buyouts over the years, the interests of both DC Comics and Warner Bros. Pictures were controlled by a large parent company known as Warner Communications — so Warner was the studio that had the right of first negotiation for Uslan and Melniker's project. Warner was not interested, so the men went about contacting other studios. They were disappointed to find that no studio would even come close to accepting their proposal — it seemed that the entire film industry simply could not see the Batman character in any incarnation other than the campy Adam West version.[2]

Well, not quite the *entire* film industry. Uslan and Melniker finally found one studio that was willing to take on their Batman project. They pitched their film to producer Peter Guber at Casablanca Filmworks, and Guber immediately grasped where they were going with the Batman character. Uslan and Melniker entered into a joint venture with Casablanca to begin development on the film as 1979 came to an end, and it seemed that a new screen version of Batman was well on its way to becoming a reality. Uslan and Casablanca even staged an official announcement regarding the commencement of the film at the 1980 New York ComiCon.[3]

Uslan's dream of producing a new Batman motion picture was wholeheartedly supported by Bob Kane. Kane was thrilled that his creation was finally going to be interpreted in a "mysterioso" manner on the big screen. (Kane almost always used that word when explaining his vision of Batman.)[4] He had certainly been waiting for a long time to see his original incarnation of the Batman character make it to the screen — obviously, the cheaply-made 1940s serials and the campy 1960s screen Batman had not come anywhere close to being "mysterioso." (Of course, it turned out that Kane's wait was still about a decade from being over!)

Peter Guber's career continued on an upward trajectory while he worked to bring this new vision of Batman to the screen. He formed a partnership with Jon Peters, and the two men became head of PolyGram Pictures, the corporation that had purchased Casablanca Filmworks in full in 1980. Guber and Peters left PolyGram in 1982 and moved to Warner Bros., where they set up their own production company called Guber-Peters Entertainment. This move meant that the Batman film project was now in the hands of Warner, the very first studio to pass on the project several years earlier.

In the early 1980s, the Uslan-Melniker-Guber-Peters Batman team hired Tom Mankiewicz, creative consultant for the films *Superman* (1978) and *Superman II* (1980), to write a Batman screenplay. Titled *The Batman*, Mankiewicz's script was loosely based on the Batman comic stories by Steve Englehart, Marshall Rogers and Terry Austin that were originally published in *Detective Comics* in 1977–78. (We discussed these stories in detail last chapter.) The script featured the Englehart characters Silver St. Cloud and Rupert Thorne, as well as familiar characters such as Robin, the Joker and the Penguin. The screenplay resembled the 1978 *Superman* in that it was epic in tone, and chronologically followed Bruce Wayne's life from the time of his parents' murder through his metamorphosis into a master costumed crimefighter.[5]

Even at this early stage of planning the film, Jack Nicholson's name was mentioned as the major candidate for the role of the Joker. Michael Uslan in particular thought that Nicholson's volatile style of acting made him perfect for the part.[6] But it would be a long time before this Batman movie project would be developed to the point where it actually needed actors. Warner Bros. was not impressed enough with Mankiewicz's script to begin work on committing it to film, so the project languished in pre-production limbo for several years.

Then in 1986, a new comic version of Batman completely changed not only the course of the Batman movie project, but also the course of the character's history. Frank Miller's groundbreaking four-part graphic novel series *Batman: The Dark Knight Returns* was a tremendous critical and commercial success, and this success was not confined to the relatively small population of comic book fans. Warner Communications released the series as a one-volume paperback through their publishing company Warner Books. This version of *Batman: The Dark Knight Returns* sold very well throughout the country, paving the way for the general public to start taking Batman more seriously than they did when he was viewed as a campy TV show character. (We discussed *Batman: The Dark Knight Returns* in detail last chapter as well.)

Batman: The Dark Knight Returns made Warner Bros. realize that a serious screen Batman could be a highly marketable property, so they intensified their efforts to get their Batman film made. Since Warner had never warmed up to Mankiewicz's script *The Batman*, the studio elected to have some different writers try their hand at scripting the film. Because *The Batman* had been loosely based on the Englehart-Rogers-Austin Batman stories, the studio elected to bring in Steve Englehart as a script consultant in 1986; he even wrote several Batman treatments of his own using his Silver St. Cloud and Rupert Thorne characters.[7]

But the success of *Batman: The Dark Knight Returns* led Warner Bros. to move away from the Englehart-Rogers-Austin interpretation of Batman, and more toward Frank Miller's vision of the character. This line of thinking led the studio to consider hiring Tim Burton to direct their Batman film. Warner viewed Burton as a very promising young talent — his first major directorial effort was the offbeat comedy *Pee Wee's Big Adventure* (1985), which turned out to be a surprise hit for the studio. Burton began his film career as an animator, and his work possessed a cartoonish yet dark sensibility that seemed well-suited for bringing the kind of complex, tragic Batman found in *Batman: The Dark Knight Returns* to the big screen. However, Burton did have one major weakness as a prospective Batman director — he had no experience whatsoever in terms of directing an action film. Still, Warner liked what they saw in Burton, so he moved to the top of the studio's list of Batman directorial candidates.[8]

Warner Bros. hired writer Sam Hamm to fashion an all-new Batman screenplay, one that would reflect the darkness and edginess of *Batman: The Dark Knight Returns*. Hamm's screenplay, simply titled *Batman*, took shape through a number of drafts completed between late 1986 and early 1988. While Hamm was writing, he and Burton regularly met to flesh out their shared interpretation of Batman and his world. The two men shared a common disdain for the fanciful, melodramatic nature of comic books in general, and they wanted to steer their Batman away from being a one-dimensional "comic hero." Consequently, the early drafts of the screenplay featured far less of Batman in costume performing his usual heroics than many Batman comic fans would have liked. Each successive draft of the script moved closer toward a more traditional comic-style version of Batman, but even Hamm's final revision was darker and less costume-oriented than one might have expected.

The only classic Batman villain featured in *Batman* was the Joker. Unlike the Joker of the comics, the script's Joker was given a very detailed origin story. Before his transformation into the Clown Prince of Crime, he would be depicted in the film as Gotham City mobster Jack Napier. The character of Robin/Dick Grayson also was featured in the script.[9]

Warner's faith in Tim Burton grew even stronger with the success of his second feature, the dark fantasy comedy *Beetlejuice* (1988). After the film enjoyed a strong opening weekend, the studio officially hired Burton to direct *Batman*. *Beetlejuice* starred Michael Keaton as the grotesque, obnoxious ghost Betelgeuse, and the manic energy of his performance led Warner Bros. and Burton to think that he might be able to bring the same kind of intensity to the role of Batman.[10] (Obviously, we'll discuss that unusual casting idea in *much* more detail in just a bit!)

So by mid–1988, plans for *Batman* were truly beginning to fall into place. It would be a Warner Bros. film produced by Peter Guber and Jon Peters, directed by Tim Burton, and written by Sam Hamm. Unfortunately for Michael Uslan and Benjamin Melniker, the two men who originally initiated the creation of *Batman*, they had been forced out of their role as the film's producers. Guber and Peters's move to Warner in 1982 meant that Guber was no longer legally bound to the original partnership he had forged with Uslan and Melniker at Casablanca Filmworks back in 1979. Consequently, Guber, Peters and Warner Bros. relegated Uslan and Melniker to the far less influential and profitable role of executive producers.[11]

Uslan and Melniker vigorously protested this change, eventually filing lawsuits against Guber, Peters and Warner Bros.[12] Uslan and Melniker were unsuccessful in their litigation, but their relationship with Warner would eventually be smoothed over. In fact, they have been credited as executive producers of most every Batman film and television work that Warner Bros. has ever produced.

Even though Hamm had already revised his *Batman* script a number of times, Warner felt that the script needed still more work before the film went into production. But Hamm would not be available to make any further changes to *Batman*—the Writer's Guild of America went on strike from March 1988 to August 1988, and Hamm supported the strike by refusing to do any further work on his screenplay.[13] The studio turned to writer Warren Skaaren to revise *Batman*. Skaaren was the perfect choice for this job — he had done the final *Beetlejuice* script revisions for Burton the year before, so the two men were very comfortable working together.

Skaaren ended up making substantial changes to Hamm's *Batman* script. First off, he completely removed the Robin/Dick Grayson character from the screenplay. Robin had always seemed to be somewhat shoehorned into the script since he did not appear until the very end of the story, so dropping the entire Robin subplot in order to simplify the film and tighten its focus was a logical move. It was also a move that Warner Bros. had been resisting ever since they had begun to develop their Batman film. The studio had directed every Batman screenwriter before Skaaren to include Robin, because they felt that the character needed to be in the movie at least to some degree. But Warner finally began to see that this new screen version of Batman would actually work better without Robin, so the studio allowed Skaaren to cut him.

Another major change that Skaaren made to the script was that he reworked the pre–Joker Jack Napier character — Skaaren made Napier the murderer of Bruce Wayne's parents. In the comics, the Joker character never had anything whatsoever to do with the Wayne murders. By making the Joker responsible for the crime that created Batman, Skaaren intertwined the origins and motivations of these two adversaries, making their battle even more personal. This change created a neat symmetry in *Batman*'s narrative, but it would not sit well with many Batman comic fans when the film was released — since the late 1940s, the comics had always depicted the Joe Chill character as the villain who was responsible for the deaths of Thomas and Martha Wayne. (We discussed the comic story that introduced Chill, "The Origin of Batman," in detail in Chapter 3.)

Skaaren's changes to *Batman* were broader than just the removal or reworking of certain characters. He steered the screenplay as a whole away from Hamm's darker, "anti–comic book" vision of Batman. Skaaren toned down Hamm's interpretation of Bruce Wayne as a tortured soul, and played up the more traditional concept of Batman as an action hero. This change in focus allowed for more scenes of Batman in costume performing the kind of heroics that the general public associated him with, and gave the script a somewhat lighter overall tone.[14]

Now that *Batman* had a near-finished script, the task of casting the film began in earnest. After much negotiation, Guber and Peters were able to land Jack Nicholson for the role of the Joker/Jack Napier. As previously mentioned, many had considered the explosive Nicholson to be the perfect actor for the part when plans were first being formulated for a new Batman film in the early 1980s. But Nicholson's importance to *Batman* went far beyond simply being the perfect actor to play the Joker — just by agreeing to star in *Batman*, the legendary Oscar winner legitimized the production in a way that no amount of Warner-generated publicity ever could have. Jack Nicholson, one of the most respected film actors of the late 20th century, the star of classic movies like *Chinatown* (1974), *One Flew over the Cuckoo's Nest* (1975) and *The Shining* (1980), was going to star in *Batman*. This sent a powerful message to the general public that Batman could no longer be dismissed as just a silly character or washed-up camp craze — Batman was now serious business.

But just who was going to play that serious Batman in *Batman*? The answer to that question turned out to be quite a headache for Warner Bros. In July 1988, the studio announced that *Batman* would star Nicholson as the Joker/Jack Napier, and Michael Keaton as Batman/Bruce Wayne. Serious Batman fans were generally very pleased with the prospect of Nicholson playing the Joker, but they were mortified when they found out that Keaton had been cast as Batman. How could Warner cast a short, weak-chinned actor with a receding hairline, an actor best known for starring in light comedies like *Mr. Mom* (1983), as Batman? At 5'10" and of medium to slight build, Keaton was simply not physically right for the role — over the years, the Batman of the comics had always been portrayed as 6'2" and athletically built. This was supposed to be the serious Batman film that fans had long been waiting for, nothing at all like the 1960s TV show and movie — how could such a film feature "Mr. Mom" as Batman?

Burton responded to these criticisms by stating that Keaton would have the psychological complexity to capture the character's personality that was so dramatically split between Batman and Bruce Wayne. Having worked closely with Keaton on *Beetlejuice*, Burton felt that the actor had the kind of intensity and drive that his interpretation of Batman was going to require.[15]

This argument did not calm the fears of serious Batman fans in the least. They were convinced that Keaton would ruin *Batman*, and they worked very hard to communicate their dismay to Warner Bros. The studio was inundated with fifty thousand letters, most of them written by Batman fans, which protested Keaton's casting.[16] Warner was definitely unnerved by the backlash they faced over Keaton playing Batman, but that did not stop them from publicly and forcefully defending their decision to hire the actor for the part. The studio held firm in their belief that Keaton was indeed the right choice to play the serious Batman that fans had long been clamoring for.

Amusingly, the hiring of Keaton was not the only Batman casting controversy that Warner faced at this time. As mentioned in Chapter 6, Adam West publicly complained that he was not considered for the role of Batman in the new film — consequently, some fans of the 1960s *Batman* communicated their dismay to the studio because they felt West was being slighted. Of course, West was completely wrong for the kind of Batman that this new film was hoping to depict, so Warner dismissed the complaints of both the actor and his supporters with barely a second thought.[17]

The casting of Vicki Vale also proved problematic. Sean Young, hired to play Vicki Vale, broke her arm while horseback riding right before the film was due to start shooting, so she was replaced by Kim Basinger. (To add insult to injury, the only reason Young was riding a horse in the first place was to rehearse for a *Batman* scene that required her to be on horseback — and the scene was eventually cut from the script. She broke her arm and lost her part in the film all for nothing!) Luckily, the other major parts in *Batman* were filled without incident — they included Robert Wuhl as reporter Alexander Knox, Pat Hingle as Commissioner Gordon, Billy Dee Williams as Harvey Dent, Michael Gough as Alfred Pennyworth and Jack Palance as Carl Grissom.

Another name was officially connected to the movie, one very familiar to Batman fans: Bob Kane was hired as a "consultant" for *Batman*. His title was basically a ceremonial one, and he would have little to do with the actual making of the film — but Warner Bros. guaranteed some good publicity for themselves by including Kane in the project. (And after the Michael Keaton uproar, Warner needed all of the good publicity they could get!)

Batman was primarily filmed at Pinewood Studios near London, England. Huge outdoor sets depicting parts of Gotham City were constructed based on the designs of the movie's production designer, Anton Furst. To create Gotham's bleak, foreboding environment, Furst fused a number of different architectural styles together, some of which openly clashed with one another. The result was a city made up of a patchwork nightmare of dirty steel, brick and cement. *Batman* did rely on a considerable amount of location shooting in and around London to capture its vision of Batman's world as well. For example, the film's

Wayne Manor scenes were filmed at Knebworth House outside of London, and its scenes at a Gotham company called Axis Chemicals were filmed at Acton Lane Power Station in West London and Little Barford Power Station in Bedfordshire.[18]

Furst also designed another memorable element of the Batman mythos for *Batman*—the Batmobile. Furst's Batmobile was a flat black, jet engine–powered behemoth with scalloped batwing-like tailfins. Its body had the streamlined look of a Chevrolet Corvette, but it was much larger and more imposing than any kind of real-life commercial sports car. Interestingly, it sported the same style of afterburner that shot flames from the rear of the car as the 1960s Batmobile. The bold simplicity of Furst's Batmobile design was a perfect counterpoint to the chaos and squalor of the Gotham City streets.

At long last, the filming of *Batman* began in earnest in October 1988. Warner Bros., still concerned over the Keaton casting controversy, kept a very close watch over the production via producer Jon Peters. Another element that added to Warner's nervousness was the fact that Jack Nicholson's involvement led to the production having a far bigger budget than was originally projected—the final price tag for the film ended up being around $35 million.[19] In the studio's eyes, Tim Burton simply did not have all that long of a track record to be handling such a tricky and expensive project. As a result, Peters attempted to do no small amount of "hand holding" of Burton while he was making *Batman*.[20]

Peters' main concern was the script, particularly its climactic scenes. While Warren Skaaren's rewrites had strengthened the production as a whole and made Batman decidedly more heroic, Peters felt that Skaaren's revision of the final battle between Batman and the Joker in the Gotham Cathedral bell tower still was not a strong enough climax. Sam Hamm's original version called for Batman to be so injured that he was not even able to stand and fight the Joker. In Skaaren's rewrite, Batman's injuries were lessened so that he was given somewhat more mobility, but he still could not decisively beat the Joker in hand-to-hand combat.

This was still not the climax that Peters was looking for, so he forced Burton to completely rework *Batman*'s final act. Peters devised the scenario of a slightly injured but still very mobile Batman fighting and defeating the Joker and his henchmen in the Gotham Cathedral bell tower. And the bell tower would not just be several stories off of the ground—it would be a massively tall bell tower, like a skyscraper. Peters then left Burton with the task of committing this new ending to film.

Not surprisingly, Burton was unhappy about having to make such major last-minute changes. In fact, the ending of the film had become such a patchwork affair that *no one* seemed to have a clear idea of just how it was supposed to play out. As Nicholson was filming the scenes showing the Joker heading up the bell tower stairs with his captive Vicki Vale, he was trying to find out from Burton just where it was that his character was going—and at that moment poor Burton really had no idea how to answer these questions![21] But all of this confusion aside, the fact remains that Peters's instincts were right on target. The script changes he called for questionably shaped *Batman* into more of an action-oriented, "summer blockbuster" type of film.

Warner Bros. had every right to be concerned about making *Batman* as strong a motion picture as possible. As *Batman* was being committed to celluloid, it was becoming increasingly obvious that it was going to be more than just a film, it was truly going to be an "event." Of course, major movie studios have a tendency to try very hard to bill *all* of their high-profile releases as "events," but *Batman* was shaping up to be the real thing. Much of this was due to a simple fact of timing—1989 marked the fiftieth anniversary of the Batman character's debut in *Detective Comics* #27, and DC Comics was prepared to commemorate the occasion very proudly and publicly just as they had when Superman turned 50 the year before. So the Batman character would have likely received a good deal of mass media coverage even without the release of a new motion picture. But the twin events of Batman's fiftieth anniversary and the production of a major Batman motion picture featuring the likes of Jack Nicholson led to skyrocketing public interest. *Batman* was poised to ride a wave of popularity that might well surpass the Batman craze surrounding the 1960s TV show — that is, if the film itself turned out to be any good.

The first indication that *Batman* might well live up to all the buzz surrounding it was the film's first preview clip that was released to theaters in January 1989. Warner's nervousness over the Keaton casting controversy led them to release a rough trailer of the film six months before its premiere so that the public could see that this was indeed finally going to be a serious Batman film. Moviegoers got their first view of this new Batman, and he was a Batman totally unlike anything from the 1960s TV show and film.

In fact, he was even fairly far removed from the Batman of recent comics, thanks to the work of *Batman* costume designer Bob Ringwood. First off, Batman was outfitted in black from his cowl to his boots — the only color on his costume was his yellow utility belt and the yellow oval around the bat emblem on his chest. And the costume's bat emblem was markedly different from any previous bat emblems that had appeared either in the comics or on the screen — it could almost be considered a low relief sculpture, because it was slightly raised over the yellow oval, giving it a three-dimensional appearance. The bat emblem was further defined by its very sharply pointed scallops, giving it an overall look that recalled the style of Victorian architecture.

The costume itself was fitted with pieces of latex and plastic that were sculpted to look like futuristic body armor. The armor on its chest area was especially conspicuous, because it was sculpted to look like well-defined muscles. The costume's scalloped cape was huge and billowing, and was made of material that gave it the appearance of leathery bat wings. The costume's latex cowl was molded into an expression of a menacing scowl, and its bat ears were long and sharply pointed. Keaton wore black makeup around his eyes when he was wearing the costume, making it appear as if there was no separation at all between the cowl and his real face. (This eye makeup technique would end up being used by all of the actors who played Batman in Warner's live-action films.)

All in all, *Batman*'s Batman looked far more imposing and grim than any previous screen version of the character — he truly captured the spirit of the character's longtime nickname "The Dark Knight." It seemed that Warner Bros. was right all along — Keaton was going to play the part of a serious Batman very well, and serious Batman fans would finally get the film they had been waiting for.

The preview's scenes showing Jack Nicholson as the Joker were every bit as compelling as its scenes showing Michael Keaton as Batman. As the Joker, Nicholson's face was fitted with prosthetics to elongate his chin and force his face into a grotesque smile, and he was made up with bright green hair, chalk white skin and blood red lips. Nicholson's acting infused the character with a boundless amount of menacing energy — his Joker was surreal, funny and scary all at the same time. The general public was immediately intrigued by this new cinematic vision of these familiar characters; after the preview was released, *Batman* was being talked about across the country as a "must see" film. The fan complaints about Michael Keaton playing Batman dramatically subsided, Warner Bros. drew a sigh of relief, and a new round of Batmania really began to heat up.

There were further signs that this Batmania was beginning to take hold — in the months leading up to the premiere, retail stores all over the country were having a very difficult time keeping Batman-related merchandise in stock. There were literally hundreds of Batman items to choose from — even the most rabid Batman collectors had a hard time keeping up with all of the action figures, toys, dolls, books, comics, trading cards, mugs, T-shirts, hats, etc., being released. Some complained that this flood of Batman merchandise was nothing more than a cynical ploy on the part of Warner Bros. to promote their upcoming film, and make as much money off of it in any way they possibly could. While there is no doubt that Warner seized on the opportunity to reap the benefits of a Batman licensing bonanza, in fairness it must be pointed out that Batman's fiftieth anniversary was also instrumental in spawning the Batman merchandising frenzy of 1989.

By the late spring–early summer of 1989, Batman seemed to be everywhere. The movie was advertised with a simple but very striking poster that featured Batman's bat symbol against a black background, so thousands upon thousands of bat symbols dotted the urban landscape. Reports about the film's upcoming release dominated entertainment news TV shows, and countless people across the country were sporting new Batman T-shirts.

Several new *Batman* previews were released to theatres and to the media during this time, and they featured an element of the film that had not been featured in the first preview — that element was the film's dramatic musical soundtrack. Danny Elfman, composer of the musical score for Burton's film *Pee Wee's Big Adventure*, composed the orchestral music that comprised the majority of *Batman*'s score. Elfman's *Batman* music was dark and powerful, and wonderfully heightened the film's sense of mystery and adventure. (Incidentally, *Batman* would also end up featuring several minutes of music written by Prince. We'll discuss both Elfman's and Prince's music for the film in more detail later in the chapter.)

Amidst all of this new Batmania, *Batman*'s world premiere was held in Westwood, near Los Angeles, on June 19. Most of the film's principal onscreen and offscreen talent attended the event, including Keaton, Nicholson, Basinger and Burton. Many celebrities not connected to the film but every bit as anxious as the general public to finally see it also attended. Fittingly, the two men most responsible for *Batman*'s existence were at the premiere as well — Bob Kane was there to see his creation reach unparalleled new heights, and Michael Uslan was there to see his dream of creating a serious Batman film come true in spectacular fashion.[22]

As *Batman*'s United States premiere date of June 23, 1989, finally arrived, serious Batman fans all over the country held their breath. Would the film live up to all the hype? Would it truly depict the character in a serious, substantive manner? How would it fare with the critics? How would it fare at the box office?

Batman opens with the familiar Warner Bros. "WB shield" logo against its usual background of a bright blue sky. The sky turns a menacing dark blue against the ominous first orchestral notes of Elfman's "Batman Theme." The film's first scene takes us right into Gotham City, where a tourist couple with their young son mistakenly wander down a seedy alley. Two street punks attack and rob them, knocking the father out with the butt of a gun. The attack attracts the attention of a shadowed figure high atop Gotham Cathedral: Batman.

The punks retreat to a rooftop to divide up their loot. One of them is nervous, because he has heard rumors of a giant bat attacking criminals on Gotham rooftops. The other punk scoffs at these rumors, as a huge bat silhouette descends onto the roof some yards behind him. They jump up in terror, and fire a gun at Batman's chest. The bullet hits him, but he is unhurt because he is protected by body armor. Batman beats the punks up, leaps off the edge of the roof and disappears from sight.

The next day, Gotham Mayor Borg, Commissioner Gordon and District Attorney Harvey Dent are discussing the city's upcoming 200th anniversary festival. They fear it may have to be cancelled because Gotham is so riddled with crime. Meanwhile, *Gotham Globe* newspaper reporter Alexander Knox meets with photojournalist Vicki Vale. They want to find out the truth about the Batman rumors and be the first to report this sensational story.

Later that day, Grissom is holding a meeting with his advisors. Harvey Dent has become suspicious of one of Grissom's front companies in Gotham, Axis Chemicals, so Grissom sends his right-hand man Jack Napier to trash Axis' office and make off with the records connecting Axis to Grissom. Napier doesn't know that he is actually being set up: Through a crooked Gotham police lieutenant named Eckhardt, Grissom has learned that Napier is having an affair with Grissom's mistress. Axis' records have already been removed, and Grissom is only sending Napier to Axis so that Eckhardt can meet him there and kill him.

That night, Bruce Wayne is holding a "save the festival" benefit at his manor, with Vicki and Knox in attendance. Bruce and Vicki meet and are obviously interested in one another, but Wayne's butler Alfred interrupts to tell Bruce that Gordon just left the party because of what appeared to be very pressing police business. Bruce abruptly excuses himself from talking to Vicki and hastens to the Batcave, where he examines a surveillance tape from one of Wayne Manor's many hidden cameras. He plays back some conversation between Gordon and a police officer that took place right before Gordon left. In it, Gordon is told that Napier is robbing Axis Chemicals.

At Axis, a group of police led by Eckhardt burst in and start firing on Napier and his goons. Gordon arrives on the scene and tells the police that he wants Napier taken alive, contrary to Eckhardt's orders. As Napier tries to flee, Batman appears and begins putting all of the criminals out of action. When Batman comes face to face with Napier on a high catwalk, Napier tries to shoot Batman, but the bullet ricochets off Batman's costume and hits the mobster in the face. Napier flips off the catwalk, but his hand catches a railing. He dangles above a large vat of acid. Batman tries to help him up, but he loses his grip and falls into the acid. In the sewage pipes outside of Axis, a white hand emerges out of the water — Napier has survived his fall.

The next day, Bruce and Vicki have a quiet dinner at Wayne Manor. They are so taken with each other that they end up sleeping together. At the same time, Jack Napier makes his way to a seedy surgeon to repair his injured face. The surgeon can only do so much — when Napier sees his disfigurement, his mind becomes completely unhinged. He goes to Grissom's penthouse to settle the score with his double-crossing boss. The acid has turned his skin white and hair green, and the bullet wound has turned his mouth up in a ghastly grin — he looks like an evil clown. Before he kills Grissom, he says, "You can call me Joker."

The Joker holds a meeting with Gotham's major crime bosses. He tells them that he wants to unleash a crime wave on the city. One of the bosses does not agree, so the Joker electrocutes him with a lethal joy buzzer. Joker then sends one of his goons out to follow Knox and find out what he knows about Batman.

Vicki decides to find out more about Bruce. He leaves the Manor and visits a rundown alley in Gotham. As she trails him, she sees him put two roses on the dirty pavement.

The Joker sets up shop inside of Axis Chemicals and begins shipping out canisters filled with a chemical agent — a deadly form of nerve gas that causes its victims' facial muscles to lock into a hideous grin, one not unlike the Joker's own. Joker learns that Vicki is working with Knox on the Batman story. Smitten, the Joker forms a plan to meet her.

On a TV news set, two anchors are starting a broadcast. One of the anchors begins to laugh and falls over dead — then the broadcast is interrupted by the Joker, who tells viewers about his new product "Smylex"— the nerve gas with which he has poisoned thousands of everyday cosmetics products throughout the city. Bruce sees the broadcast, and immediately starts trying to figure out just what products the Joker has poisoned.

Several days later, Bruce receives a call from Vicki saying she will be late meeting Bruce at the art museum. Bruce is suspicious, because he had not made plans to meet with her. It turns out that the Joker had called Vicki pretending to be Bruce in order to lure her into meeting him. The Joker barges into the museum, where Vicki is waiting for Bruce. In his own crazed way, he tries to woo her, and when she resists his advances, he tries to spray her with acid.

Batman comes crashing through the museum skylight to save Vicki, whisking her on a spear gun–fired zip line out of the building. Batman and Vicki speed off in the Batmobile with the Joker's goons at their heels. They come upon a closed street, and Batman and Vicki are forced to leave the car. Batman tries to use his grappling hook gun to escape. But their combined weight is too heavy for the line, so Batman jumps back down where the Joker's goons are waiting for him. A fight ensues, and Batman is briefly knocked out. They try to shoot him, but the bullet does not penetrate his body armor. Vicki distracts the criminals by taking a flash picture. The distraction is all Batman needs to regain his senses and pound the goons.

Batman races with Vicki to the Batcave. There he tells her he has figured out which products the Joker has tainted, and that he wants her to take this information to the press. He also retrieves the film she shot during his fight with the Joker's men, so she is denied her hope of getting the first picture of Batman.

Some days later, Bruce goes to see Vicki to tell her that he is really Batman. Before he can do so, the Joker also calls on Vicki. Bruce tells the Joker that he knows he is really Jack Napier. The Joker pulls out a gun and asks, "Have you ever danced with the devil in the pale moonlight?" and shoots him in the chest.

The Joker leaves, and Vicki rushes over to tend to Bruce. But he is gone, and only a tray with a bullet imprint in it is on the floor where he fell. She realizes that he slipped the tray inside his shirt before the Joker shot him. Bruce has raced back to the Batcave, because the words that the Joker said to him before pulling the trigger made him realize something very important. Jack Napier is the criminal who killed his parents many years ago.

Bruce reaches the Batcave just as the Joker makes another one of his pirate broadcasts. Because of the terror the Joker has unleashed on Gotham, Mayor Borg has decided to cancel the city's anniversary festival. In his broadcast, the Joker says *he* will hold the festival, and he will give away $20 million in cash.

Bruce stares at the Joker's face on one of the Batcave's television screens. Through a flashback scene, we see young Bruce coming out of a theater with his parents. They enter an alley where a young Napier and another hood confront them — it is the same alley where Bruce had placed the two roses. The hood grabs at Bruce's mother's pearl necklace and Bruce's father tries to stop him. Napier savagely guns down both of them. He then trains his gun on Bruce, asking, "Have you ever danced with the devil in the pale moonlight?" But instead of shooting Bruce, he leaves him over his parents' dead bodies.

Bruce's memories are interrupted by Alfred. Alfred has told Bruce's secret to Vicki, and he has brought her down into the Batcave to talk with Bruce. Vicki has put all of the pieces together, and knows that the murder of Bruce's parents led him to devote his life to fighting crime as Batman. Bruce and Vicki profess their love for one another. Bruce says their romance will have to wait, because the Joker is out there and he needs to stop him from hurting anyone else.

At Axis Chemicals, Batman pilots the Batmobile by remote control to lead an assault on the Joker's lair. Using explosives, Batman demolishes the entire structure, but the Joker is unharmed. In his helicopter above the inferno, the Joker tauntingly waves at Batman.

The scene shifts to the Joker's perverse version of the city's anniversary festival. Huge balloons and floats make their way down a crowded Gotham street, with the Joker riding on one of the floats and throwing money. Vicki and Knox, covering the chaotic scene, realize the balloons are filled with Smylex gas—the Joker is planning on killing everyone. Batman swoops down in a futuristic bat-shaped aircraft and snares the balloons. He releases them in the sky where they will not hurt anybody. He then turns his attention to the Joker, firing bullets and small missiles at him. The Joker brings down Batman's aircraft with a single shot from a gun with an absurdly long barrel. The aircraft crashes in front of Gotham Cathedral. Vicki runs up and searches the wreckage for Batman, but does not find him. Instead, the Joker finds *her*, and leads her at gunpoint up the stairs of the Cathedral.

Batman, bloodied and bruised, emerges from the wreckage of the Batwing and follows the Joker and Vicki up the stairs. Batman reaches the belfry, but before he can confront the Joker, several of the Joker's goons attack him. Batman fights off the goons as the Joker whirls Vicki around in a grotesque ballroom dance.

Batman defeats the goons and sneaks up on the Joker. He beats the Joker savagely, telling him that he is going to kill him. Batman tells the Joker "you killed my parents," and then punches him so hard that he seemingly falls off the Cathedral's roof. The Joker lands on a lower level of the roof, and *he* pulls Batman and Vicki off. Batman and Vicki are able to grab hold of the edge of the roof, and the Joker laughs in triumph as he stands over them. He tries to knock them off, but before he succeeds, a helicopter piloted by his goons arrives to pick him up. The Joker grabs the helicopter's ladder, but as he starts to rise, Batman fires a bolo gun at him. The bolo wraps around both the Joker's ankle and a large stone gargoyle on the cathedral roof. The gargoyle breaks off of the roof, and its weight causes the Joker to lose his grip on the ladder. He plummets to his death. Batman and Vicki almost fall to their death as well when the edge of the roof they are hanging onto collapses, but Batman is able to save them by firing a line from his grappling hook gun.

Several days later, Gotham City officials hold a press conference to announce that the Joker's reign of terror is at an end. They also announce plans to contact Batman if trouble arises in the future. Gordon then flashes the Batsignal into the night sky for the first time. *Batman* closes with a shot of Batman atop a Gotham building, looking up at the Batsignal.

Batman lived up to its promise of being far more adult and sophisticated than any previous Batman screen work. And as a serious motion picture, it garnered respectable reviews from a number of nationally known film critics. But *Batman*'s real success was not measured by reviews, but by its incredible box office numbers. The film was a true blockbuster in every sense of the word—it earned over $40 million in its U.S. opening weekend alone, and ended up grossing over $250 million during its U.S. theatrical run. With a worldwide total gross of over $400 million, *Batman* was one of the most commercially successful motion pictures of its time.[23] In fact, the film turned out to be such a monumental hit that the Batmania that took hold of the general public in 1989 turned out to be an even bigger phenomenon than the Batmania of 1966.

Looking back at *Batman* almost 25 years after its release, it is easier now to separate the film from the Batmania surrounding it in order to accurately assess its strengths and weaknesses. And it is a film with very potent strengths, but equally potent weaknesses.

Chief among *Batman*'s strengths is Jack Nicholson as the Joker. The explosive, Oscar-winning actor turns in the over-the-top performance that most everyone expected of him — his Joker is evil, grotesque, menacing and completely insane. And he is funny, in a very black comedy kind of way. Nicholson's performance is greatly helped by the film's characterization of the Joker. In some ways it is not faithful to the Joker's comic book origins (in the comics he has never been given a definite backstory or pre–Joker name, and he has always been much closer in age to Batman than the film depicts) but it does contain many elements that are "classic Joker."

For example, the fall into a vat of acid that turns his skin white and his hair green are culled from the classic comic book story "The Man Behind the Red Hood!" which was first published in *Detective Comics* #168, 1952. (We discussed that story in detail in Chapter 5.) And the Joker's use of deadly chemicals to cause his victims' faces to lock in a ghastly smile is drawn from the character's first-ever comic book story, "The Joker" (*Batman* #1, 1940). Another memorable element of that particular story that was incorporated into *Batman* was the Joker's pirate use of the media to boast about his criminal plans. In the original story, the Joker announces the names of the people he plans to murder by interrupting legitimate radio broadcasts. (We discussed "The Joker" in detail in Chapter 2.) Finally, Nicholson's makeup and his wildly colorful Joker costumes are in keeping with the look of *all* of the character's comic book appearances, from "The Joker" to the present.

But perhaps the best thing about Nicholson's performance as the Joker in *Batman* is simply that he *is* Jack Nicholson. As previously mentioned, the involvement of such a revered Hollywood icon in the film was key to the production being taken seriously by critics and the general public, and was certainly one of the major reasons the film became such a spectacular success.

But many serious Batman fans found Nicholson's aura to be a sword that cut both ways — because in some respects, Nicholson turned out to be one of the film's main weaknesses. First and foremost, the actor simply could not really transform himself into the appearance of the comic book Joker. Nicholson would have been physically perfect for the part in the late 1970s–early 1980s when plans for a new Batman movie were first getting underway, but by the time production began, he was too old, doughy-faced and balding.

Batman screenwriter Warren Skaaren did find a way to incorporate the age difference between Nicholson and Keaton into the film's plot by making the Joker the murderer of Batman's parents. (As we discussed earlier in this chapter, this change did not sit well with many Batman comic fans when the film was released — since the late 1940s, the comics had always depicted the Joe Chill character as the villain who was responsible for the Wayne murders.) Still, the fact remains that the taut-skinned, long-faced Joker of the comics is a far more visually arresting character than Nicholson's pudgy, soft-edged Joker. In fact, Hugo E. Blick, who played the young Jack Napier, would have made a much better traditional Joker than Nicholson ever does in the movie.

The filmmakers worked very hard to overcome Nicholson's physical shortcomings. As previously mentioned, the actor was fitted with facial prosthetics for the role in order to elongate his chin and force his face into a grotesque smile. While these efforts worked to some degree, they never completely erased Nicholson's real-life appearance as a stocky, fleshy, middle-aged man. But even though Nicholson might not be a physically perfect

Joker in *Batman*, his performance has enough truly inspired moments to make his presence in *Batman* far more of a benefit than a deficit.

Unfortunately, the balance sheet runs quite a bit closer in terms of Michael Keaton's Bruce Wayne/Batman performance. To put it bluntly, many of the criticisms that Batman fans leveled at Keaton when he was first given the part were right on target. At 5'10" and of medium to slight build, he is simply too short and scrawny to be completely convincing in the role. Because of Keaton's limited physical stature, many of his scenes are underwhelming.

In fact, Kim Basinger (5'7") has to take off her shoes in the film no less than three times so that she does not appear taller than him! Since it would have looked ridiculous to have Vicki, the damsel in distress, towering over the mighty Batman, she simply throws off her footwear. The first time the shoes go are when Bruce is going to kiss her during their date at Wayne Manor. Next, she throws them out of the Batmobile when she and Batman are preparing to run through the streets of Gotham to avoid the Joker's goons. Finally, they fall off her feet when she is ascending the Gotham Cathedral staircase with the Joker. These "Vicki loses her shoes" scenes in *Batman* add nothing in terms of plot, character development, etc.—they are there simply because Keaton is too short for his role.

Keaton's Batman costume was designed to make him look more physically imposing than he is in real life — but this attempt at visual trickery backfires in several scenes, and actually ends up making him look even *less* physically imposing! For example, he wears a number of different cowls in *Batman*, one of which is constructed of extra-thick latex in order to make his head and shoulders appear larger. This particular cowl is used in several shots during the sequence when Batman takes Vicki to the Batcave. Keaton's headgear in these shots is so large and unwieldy that it looks like his head is shrinking inside of it!

Keaton's performance in the film does have some real strengths. He approaches the role with a combination of brooding intensity and nervous energy that makes both Bruce Wayne and Batman seem very believable, and not all that far removed from our own world. Keaton's understated acting as Bruce Wayne is often very effective in communicating Bruce's resolve to save others from going through the kind of torment he endured as a child, even if it means becoming a different person altogether. Many of his Batman scenes work equally well because he is able to do what Batman would likely do if he was a real person — Keaton takes an emotional step back when he is in costume, keeps quiet, and lets the cape and cowl do the acting for him.

That cowl had one particularly large effect on Keaton's performance that Batman fans still talk about. The manner in which the cowl was attached to the costume did not allow Keaton to turn his head while was wearing it. Consequently, whenever he had to turn his head to look and someone or something, he swung his whole body around to get his head where it needed to be! This maneuver became affectionately known as the "Bat-turn" among Batman fans— the cowl might have been very unwieldy, but it did give Keaton a memorable move for his character to perform in the film. (Incidentally, the phrase "Bat-turn" originated from the 1966 *Batman* TV show and movie — whenever Batman needed to perform a particularly tight turn in the Batmobile, he used the car's emergency bat turn lever!)

As Nicholson's performance is greatly helped by the film's characterization of the Joker, so is Keaton's performance helped by the film's characterization of Batman. For the first time on screen, Batman is presented as a complex, believable masked man, not just as a one-dimensional kiddie hero. He is tragic, dark, tough and determined, and he inhabits a Gotham City teeming with film noir–style gangsters.

He does use lethal force on these criminals, such as in the scenes where he destroys Axis Chemicals and he fires at the Joker from the Batwing, and this is a departure from the traditional comic book Batman who is completely opposed to killing. But even this is in keeping with Kane and Finger's first Batman stories of the late 1930s, when the character carried a gun and wasn't above using it from time to time. In fact, since *Batman* takes place at the very beginning of the character's career, it could be argued that Batman's use of lethal force in the film is actually very true to Kane and Finger's original vision. At any rate, *Batman* certainly depicts Batman in a manner that is very much in the spirit of Kane and Finger, O'Neil and Adams, Englehart and Rogers, and Miller — and Keaton works hard to live up to this spirit.

So is Michael Keaton good or bad in *Batman*? That is a very difficult question to answer. On the one hand, his acting is strong, his costume is for the most part impressive, and he is helped along by the film's intelligent, adult-oriented characterization of Batman. On the other hand, he is so physically wrong for the role that his undersized screen presence is a continual distraction.

But the biggest problem with Keaton's performance, at least from a serious Batman fan's perspective, was one that was not the actor's fault at all — namely, there is simply not *enough* of it. *Batman* focused more on the Joker than it did Batman in terms of character development and actual screen time. Obviously, the primary reason that the Jack Napier/Joker scenes were given more weight than the Bruce Wayne/Batman scenes was because Jack Nicholson was the top-billed star of the film. Since Nicholson represented the film's major draw for the general public, Batman fans had to live with the fact that Keaton would play second fiddle to his characterization of the Joker, at least to some degree.

And play second fiddle he does — there are only four sections of the film that actually show Keaton in his Batman costume. The first is the scene where he collars the two street punks, the second is the fight sequence at Axis Chemicals, the third is the Vicki museum rescue/trip to the Batcave sequence, and the fourth is the climactic Batwing/Gotham Cathedral battle with the Joker. Between the film's second and third "Batman" sections, the Batman costume does not appear on screen for about 45 minutes!

To make matters worse, even the scenes that actually show Keaton as Batman are often presented in such quick cuts that the viewer does not get a chance to study his costume, his actions or his expressions. *Batman* does not give the viewer, for lack of a better term, enough "postcard views" of its main character — in other words, medium shots of Batman lasting for more than a couple of seconds, designed to let the viewer to visually take him in and appreciate him.

Let's examine the 1978 *Superman* for a moment. The film features dozens of shots that show Superman in all his glory. After all of the creativity, time and money that went into designing his costume, it only made sense that the makers of *Superman* would want to let their title character linger on the screen a bit so that audiences could really enjoy him. Even with the increasingly hyperactive editing found in so much of modern filmmaking, this "postcard view" concept still has a place in more recent comic book films — for example, *Spider-Man* (2002) featured plenty of generous medium shots that allowed its title character to make maximum visual impact. *Batman* would have been a stronger, more memorable film if it had included more "postcard view" shots like the ones found in *Superman* and *Spider-Man*.

Batman's major supporting actors are generally strong. Though Michael Gough's Alfred does not physically resemble the Alfred of the comics, he is perhaps the best of the bunch —

he brings a warmth and sympathy to the role that is a welcome counterpoint to the overall darkness of the film. Pat Hingle as Commissioner Gordon is not quite as strong as Gough — like Gough, Hingle does not physically resemble his comic book counterpart, and he does not appear in enough scenes to make much of an impression.

The film's unluckiest actor has to be Billy Dee Williams as Harvey Dent. He is given even fewer scenes than Hingle, so he makes almost no impression at all. Of course, in the Batman comics Harvey Dent is eventually scarred by acid and becomes the villain Two-Face, so Williams probably took the part in *Batman* in the hopes that there would be a meatier part for him if a Batman sequel was ever produced. As we'll discuss later in the book, things wouldn't quite work out that way for him.

Kim Basinger as Vicki Vale is passable, though her performance never really rises above the cinematic cliché of a "damsel in distress." This is not really her fault — so many scenes in *Batman* call for her to scream, run away or faint that it would have been hard for her to bring much else to the role. That said, however, there is a general remoteness to her acting that keeps her from being very convincing in the film.

Some of *Batman*'s best supporting characters are ones that were created specifically for the film. Jack Palance only appears in several scenes as the powerful and menacing Gotham crime boss Carl Grissom, but his memorable performance is still one of the movie's high points. And Robert Wuhl is equally good as reporter Alexander Knox — Wuhl's acting nicely captures Knox's ambition to bring Batman's story to the world.

One of *Batman*'s major strengths is the film's production design. Anton Furst's Gotham City sets provide a wonderful sense of atmosphere that is realistic while at the same time fantastic. His Batcave set is also wonderfully moody, filled with just the right balance of jagged rock and high tech gadgetry. Furst's sets draw the viewer into a world only slightly, if nightmarishly, removed from our own. And the dark sets are often bathed in wonderful deep blue light, giving Batman's costume those bluish-black tones that comic book colorists have labored to put on paper for decades. Also, Furst's designs for the Batmobile resulted in a car that was as stylized and as immediately recognizable as the 1960s Batmobile. Furst's accomplishments on *Batman* were rewarded with a 1990 Academy Award for Best Art Direction, which he shared with the film's set decorator Peter Young.

Furst's efforts to design an aircraft for Batman to use in *Batman* were perhaps not quite as successful as his Batmobile design. Furst came up with the idea for a bat-shaped plane which was dubbed "the Batwing." The Batwing's design was very sci-fi in nature, resembling an X-wing starfighter from the *Star Wars* films — consequently, it could not be realized as a real-life, functioning mode of transport. This meant that all of *Batman*'s Batwing scenes had to be filmed using either miniature or partially constructed Batwings. *Batman*'s Batwing scenes are by no means completely awful, but the aircraft's sci-fi feel certainly detracts from the film's overall real world sensibility. In fact, the Batwing is at the center of one of the movie's silliest, most "comic booky" moments — the seemingly heavily-armed aircraft is somehow shot down with a single bullet from the Joker's impossibly long-barreled gun!

Batman's wonderful prop gadgetry is a perfect complement to Furst's production design. John Evans designed the weaponry and utility equipment that Batman used in the film, such as the grappling hook gun and the spear gun. These devices made Batman seem like a more plausible character than he had ever been in most of his comic adventures. In the comics, Batman was always shown throwing a rope attached to his Batarang into the air, and the rope would impossibly attach to some building or flagpole — then Batman would somehow pull himself up several stories high on the rope! Obviously, this cannot be done in real life, so *Batman*'s motor-fired grappling hook gun allowed Batman to ascend into the air in a much more believable manner. Incidentally, Evans also led the team of technicians who developed Furst's Batmobile designs into a real automobile. Amazingly, that formidable job took them only about three months to complete![24]

Another of *Batman*'s strengths is the film's "non-comic book" wardrobe. The actors' 1940s-style street clothes, especially those of the gangsters, give the movie a film noir feel. *Batman*'s combination of futuristic comic book costumes and antique clothing styles creates a visually arresting style of new and old. This keeps *Batman* from being tied to any specific time period, and as a result the film does not seem all that dated almost 25 years after its release.

Danny Elfman's marvelous musical score was also essential in establishing *Batman*'s overall atmosphere. His dark, sweeping orchestral compositions are a perfect complement to the film's images of Batman's mysterious figure and Gotham City's foreboding architecture. One only needs to hear the distinctive first few notes of Elfman's "Batman Theme" at the opening of the film to know how far removed this film is from the lighthearted world of the 1960s Batman.

As a musician I can't resist pointing out that those first notes that make up the main motif of the "Batman Theme" are suspiciously similar to Lee Zahler's opening orchestral music of the 1943 serial *Batman*. The music at the opening titles of the 1943 *Batman* starts with the notes "D-E-F-B." Elfman's "Batman Theme" is in a different key than is the 1943 music, but it opens with notes that are almost the exact same intervals—the notes are "C-D-D#-G#." In fact, if you moved the G# note in Elfman's piece up a half step to an A, they would be exactly the same! This is either a remarkable coincidence, or Mr. Elfman is guilty of a tiny bit of very clever musical thievery. Incidentally, Elfman's Batman compositions were conducted by Shirley Walker, who would go on to compose memorable Batman screen music of her own for works such as *Batman: The Animated Series* and *Batman: Mask of the Phantasm*. (We'll discuss those works later in the book.)

Surprisingly, *Batman*'s "official" musical soundtrack was not Elfman's score, but the pop album *Batman* by Prince. Prince's album, released to coincide with the premiere of the film, was met with widespread radio airplay and strong sales. However, *Batman* the film featured only several minutes of *Batman* the album! The movie's true musical soundtrack was Elfman's score, which was released as an album under the title *Batman: Original Motion Picture Score* some months after the movie bowed. Prince's songs fit nicely with the scenes in which they were featured, but they certainly were not important enough to the film as a whole to warrant Prince's album being called *Batman*'s "official" soundtrack. Still, Prince's *Batman* ended up being a wonderful promotional tool for the film—the album's first single, "Batdance," was a #1 hit in the United States during the film's theatrical run. "Batdance" was not featured in the film in any way, but the song contained snippets of the film's dialogue, and the song's music video prominently featured dancers in Batman and Joker costumes.

When *Batman* was released, many critics were quick to credit director Tim Burton for the artistry they perceived in the film. This assumption that *Batman*'s artistic virtues all stemmed from Burton is a problematic one, because some of the film's worst flaws come from glaring directorial lapses. For example, Burton's narrative skills seriously break down at the end of the film when Batman confronts the Joker atop Gotham Cathedral. In the scene, Batman says to the Joker "you killed my parents," and the Joker responds by saying

"I was a kid when I killed your parents." But in the film, Batman has never revealed he is actually Bruce Wayne to the Joker — so the Joker has no way of knowing who Batman's parents were, or when he would have killed them. (After all, the film has led us to believe that Jack/Joker has killed scores of people over the years.) Consequently, this line at the climactic moment of the film literally makes no sense whatsoever.

This narrative mistake happened because in the early versions of *Batman*'s script, the Joker was supposed to discover that Batman was Bruce Wayne during the final scenes of the film. However, this element of the story was dropped by the time filming began. Somehow, the Joker's line about being a kid when he killed Batman's parents made it all the way into the final cut of the film, even when it no longer matched up with the film's story. It is simply unacceptable for any director to overlook a narrative error that sizable, and at that critical of a moment in a film: Burton should have seen this mistake right away and somehow corrected it.

Also, Burton allowed a number of ridiculously shoddy special effects to be included in *Batman*. For example, the very first image of Batman featured in the film is a laughably unrealistic computer graphic shadow that defies any lighting or perspective found in the real world. And the scene where Batman and Vicki ascend to the catwalk high above the street using Batman's grappling hook gun is filmed with two unconvincing dolls that look as if they have been stapled together. And worst of all, *Batman*'s scenes showing the iconic Batsignal are made up of unconvincing process shots that are laid into the film with an awkward ripple effect.

In fact, *Batman*'s final scene of Batman looking up at the Batsignal is perhaps one of the most unsatisfying moments in the film. Not only is the Batsignal a poor image, but it is also obvious that it is not even Michael Keaton wearing the actual Batman costume looking up at it! It looks like an extra in a plain black bodysuit with a ski mask over his head, and a non-scalloped cape tied around his neck! Were both Michael Keaton and the batsuit unavailable for the last shot of the film? But seriously, it is puzzling that such a big budget, high profile film would elect to end with such a substandard scene.

It should also be pointed out that some of the visually inspired moments in the film that critics gave Burton credit for were not necessarily his to begin with. For example, *Batman*'s nightmarish Wayne family murder scene was directly based on panels from Frank Miller's 1986 graphic novel *Batman: The Dark Knight Returns*. The pearls that so chillingly fall from Martha Wayne's neck in the scene can be attributed to Miller's artistic vision much more so than to Burton's.

These criticisms of Tim Burton are not meant to imply that I feel Warner Bros. made a poor choice when they picked him to direct *Batman*. On the contrary, Burton's dark, quirky sensibilities proved to be very well-suited to bringing a serious Batman to the screen for the first time. And obviously, Burton has directed many hit films in the years since *Batman* was released — his resume speaks for itself, and I greatly respect his talent.

I simply want to make the point that I believe *Batman*'s incredible success was less about Burton's directorial skills than it was about the fact that the Batman character's moment of greatness truly had come. As we discussed earlier in this chapter, the release of *Batman: The Dark Knight Returns* and the commemoration of Batman's fiftieth anniversary paved the way for the general public to start taking Batman more seriously than they did when he was viewed as a campy TV show character. This huge shift in the way the general public perceived Batman perfectly set *Batman* up to ride an unprecedented wave of popularity. Burton's direction of *Batman* was good enough to allow the film to realize its enormous artistic and commercial potential, but not good enough to keep the film from ending up with some major flaws.

Needless to say, *Batman* was such a huge box office hit that it was also tremendously successful when it was first made available to the home video market by Warner Home Video. The film was released on VHS tape, Beta tape and laserdisc in November 1989, before it had even finished its theatrical run. Millions of home video copies of *Batman* were sold, most of them VHS tapes, before Warner first released the movie on DVD in 1997. This initial DVD version of *Batman* offered the film in its original widescreen format as well as in a format cropped to fit a standard television screen, but it offered no bonus features or printed material dealing with the making of the film.

The success of Warner's 2005 film *Batman Begins* led the studio to release their four previous Batman live-action features on 2-disc DVD sets late that same year. Each of these sets were loaded with special features that detailed their particular film's creation. Because *Batman* was the most groundbreaking and commercially successful of all of Warner's Batman movies, its set featured more bonus material than most of the other sets.

The program *Legends of the Dark Knight: The History of Batman* recounted the 60 plus-year history of the Batman character, and featured commentary from notable Batman creators such as Bob Kane, Denny O'Neil and Frank Miller. *Shadows of the Bat: The Cinematic Saga of the Dark Knight Parts 1–3* chronicled the making of *Batman* from Michael Uslan's initial efforts to produce a serious live-action Batman big screen work all the way up until the film's triumphant premiere. The program featured interesting insights from many of the individuals who played a major role in *Batman*'s creation, including Tim Burton, Peter Guber, Michael Uslan, Benjamin Melniker, Sam Hamm, Bob Kane, Michael Keaton, Jack Nicholson, and Kim Basinger. These insights were accompanied by a good deal of behind-the-scenes footage shot on the *Batman* set showing the film's cast and crew at work.

Shadows of the Bat: The Cinematic Saga of the Dark Knight Parts 1–3 even featured one scene that was deleted from *Batman*. The very brief scene showed Batman moving a little girl out of harm's way while fighting the Joker's goons, and the little girl asking him, "Is it Halloween?" (Incidentally, this scene must have been cut from the film at the last possible moment — photos of it were even included in the first *Batman* trading card set that was released at the time of the film's premiere.)

Beyond Batman was a program that consisted of featurettes about some of the specific elements that made *Batman* such a success. The titles of the featurettes were "Visualizing Gotham: The Production Design of *Batman*," "Building the Batmobile," "Those Wonderful Toys: The Props and Gadgets of *Batman*," "Designing the Batsuit, "From Jack to the Joker," and "Nocturnal Overtures: The Music of *Batman*." The DVD set also included featurettes on the main heroes and villains of the film, as well as footage showing Bob Kane visiting the *Batman* set while the film was in production. (Incidentally, Kane did make it into the actual *Batman* film in some form. Early in the film, a *Gotham Globe* cartoonist mocks Alexander Knox's interest in Batman by handing him a drawing of a bat-like man wearing a suit and tie. This drawing was actually done by Kane — his distinctive signature is clearly visible on the page!)

As we discussed earlier, the Robin character was cut from *Batman* before filming began — but Robin was able to make his way onto the *Batman* DVD set. The set included a short program entitled *Batman: The Complete Robin Storyboard Sequence* that used storyboard images to visualize Robin's part in one of Sam Hamm's early versions of the *Batman* script. In addition to all of the bonus material included in the set, the movie itself was enhanced with an audio commentary track recorded by Tim Burton.

This 2005 DVD set remained the definitive home video version of *Batman* until Warner released on the movie Blu-ray disc in early 2009. The *Batman* Blu-ray included all of the special features found on the DVD set, but it did not contain any new bonus material. Of course, the Blu-ray's main selling point was not its special features, but its presentation of the film itself. On Blu-ray, *Batman* looked and sounded far better than it ever had on any other home video format — in fact, it is really no exaggeration to say that the quality of the *Batman* Blu-ray came very close to matching the quality of the most pristine *Batman* film prints that first played in theatres during the summer of 1989.

I'll close my discussion of *Batman* with these thoughts. The film is far from perfect, but its flaws do not keep it from being one of the most stunning achievements in the history of the Batman character. As I said at the beginning of this chapter, *Batman*'s release will forever stand as the first time a worldwide audience appreciated Batman in the way Bob Kane and Bill Finger had intended him to be appreciated when they created the first Batman comic story back in 1939. For the first time, millions upon millions of people around the world saw Batman as the dark hero we serious Batman fans loved — and speaking as a serious Batman fan, let me just say *wow*, did that ever feel good! Now, *Batman Returns* — well, I personally didn't think *that* one felt anywhere near as good. We'll get to that story a bit later in the book.

9

Between Burton's Batman Films, 1989–1991

Before we move on to Tim Burton's second Batman film *Batman Returns* (1992), we have a bit of Batman comic history we need to attend to. Not surprisingly, the phenomenal success of Burton's *Batman* led DC Comics to undertake a tremendous number of new Batman-related projects. A new comic title devoted to Batman's early, pre–Robin exploits entitled *Batman: Legends of the Dark Knight* debuted in November 1989. The title was so well-received that it ran for almost two decades before being discontinued in early 2007. Also, more and more stand-alone Batman graphic novels were being released in the wake of *Batman*.

A number of these graphic novels (known as *Elseworlds* titles) placed Batman in times and places far removed from late twentieth century Gotham City. This allowed artists and writers to imagine the character in contexts that were very different from his usual self. Sometimes these contexts were rooted in reality—for example, he hunted down Jack the Ripper in the nineteenth century in *Batman: Gotham by Gaslight* (1989) and worked as an agent of the U.S. government during the Civil War years in *Batman: The Blue, the Grey and the Bat* (1992). However, these contexts might also be completely rooted in fantasy, such as his battle with Dracula in the 1991 *Elseworlds* tale *Batman: Red Rain*.

However, the most successful and influential Batman graphic novel that was published during this time was not an *Elseworlds* title. *Arkham Asylum: A Serious House on Serious Earth* made its debut in October 1989, and was written by Grant Morrison and illustrated by Dave McKean. The graphic novel explored the origin of Arkham Asylum, the Gotham City psychiatric hospital where many of Batman's deadliest and most insane adversaries had been held over the years. Arkham had first appeared in Batman comics back in the mid–1970s, but the graphic novel brought the hospital to a prominence in Batman mythos that it had never held before.

In *Arkham Asylum: A Serious House on Serious Earth*, Arkham's inmates have taken over the hospital, and Batman comes to the hospital to bring it under control and restore order. As he makes his way through the asylum, he battles many of his foes who have been incarcerated there. The most prominent of these foes is the Joker, who has been leading the inmates' revolt.

Batman eventually discovers that it is actually Arkham's administrator, Dr. Charles Cavendish, who has orchestrated the inmate uprising. Cavendish has gone insane himself, having become obsessed with the actions of Arkham's long-dead founder, Amadeus Arkham. Cavendish reveals to Batman that Arkham had descended into madness, believing that a bat-like evil spirit was haunting his family. Cavendish believes that Batman is the evil spirit that Arkham encountered, so Cavendish has set all of Arkham's inmates free to kill the crimefighter. Cavendish's insane plan fails—he is killed by one of the asylum's doctors, and Batman quells the inmate uprising. But Batman's victory comes at an enormous cost—his journey through the madness of the asylum and its inhabitants exacts an almost unbearable physical and mental toll on him.

Arkham Asylum: A Serious House on Serious Earth remains one of the most complex and challenging Batman works ever created. In the graphic novel, Morrison presented Batman and his world through a prism of deep psychological themes and shocking violence that was hard to comprehend and even harder to forget. And McKean's artwork was every bit and revolutionary as Morrison's writing—it was created with a wild juxtaposition of mediums, and was often so abstract that it was hard to figure out just what was happening in certain scenes. The graphic novel's depiction of the Joker was particularly compelling—his surreal appearance and horrifying actions made the character arguably more frightening than he had ever been in any previous Batman work.

Another major event in Batman comic history took place shortly after *Batman*'s premiere, when DC Comics gave Batman yet another Robin to work with in his comic adventures. This new Robin was introduced in a five-part series entitled *A Lonely Place of Dying*, which appeared in *Batman* #440–42, and *The New Titans* #60–61 in late 1989.

In *A Lonely Place of Dying*, a young man named Tim Drake deduced that Bruce Wayne and Dick Grayson were actually Batman and Robin because he had attended the circus the night that Dick's parents were killed while performing their trapeze act. When Tim saw Robin in action on a television news broadcast years later, he noticed Robin's trapeze-style maneuvers were the exact same moves he had seen Dick Grayson perform that fateful evening. Since Dick was now Bruce's ward, Tim assumed that if Dick was Robin, then Bruce had to be Batman. Tim was then able to deduce that Jason Todd took Dick's place as Robin, and was killed while acting as Batman's partner.

Fearing that Batman is losing his mind because he is unable to cope with Jason's loss, Tim decides to seek out Dick and tell him that Batman needs help. Tim eventually comes face-to-face with these heroes that he has admired from afar. Of course, Bruce and Dick are at first stunned that this boy has penetrated the secret of their crimefighting identities, but after they get to know Tim and see what an exceptional young man he is, Bruce decides to take him on as his third junior partner.

In a story entitled "Master of Fear" which appeared in *Batman* #457, December 1990, Bruce Wayne formally bestowed the mantle of Robin on Tim Drake. Bruce also gave Tim a newly created Robin costume to wear. Robin would now be outfitted in a full bodysuit that was red and green in color. The costume also featured a stylized yellow "R" on its chest, green mask, green gloves, black boots and a black cape with yellow lining. This Robin costume was designed by the legendary Batman comic artist Neal Adams, and was so well-received that it would be the basis of the character's standard appearance throughout the 1990s and right up to the present day. Over the years the costume's color patterns would vary, but one thing about it remained a constant—the current version of Robin always got to wear long pants instead of the short pants the character had been wearing for the past half-century!

The Tim Drake Robin turned out to be considerably more popular with Batman fans than the Jason Todd Robin. In the first half of 1991 he was featured in his own five-issue series, simply titled *Robin*, which was so successful that it was followed by two more Robin series in the early 1990s. The re-introduction of Robin into Batman's comic book world would intertwine with the development of *Batman Returns* in an unusual way—we'll look into that story when we examine the film in the next chapter.

10

Batman Returns (1992)

Cast: Michael Keaton (Batman/Bruce Wayne), Danny DeVito (The Penguin/Oswald Cobblepot), Michelle Pfeiffer (Catwoman/Selina Kyle), Christopher Walken (Max Shreck), Michael Gough (Alfred), Pat Hingle (Commissioner Gordon), Michael Murphy (Mayor of Gotham City), Cristi Conaway (Ice Princess), Andrew Bryniarski (Chip Shreck), Vincent Schiavelli (Organ Grinder), Jan Hooks (Jen), Steve Witting (Josh), John Strong (Swordswallower), Rick Zumwalt (Tattooed Strongman), Anna Katarina (Poodle Lady), Gregory Scott Cummins (Acrobat Thug One), Erika Andersch (Knifethrower Dame), Travis McKenna (Fat Clown), Doug Jones (Thin Clown), Branscombe Richmond (Terrifying Clown One), Flame (Snakewoman), Paul Reubens (Penguin's Father), Diane Salinger (Penguin's Mother), Stuart Lancaster (Penguin's Doctor), Cal Hoffman (Happy Man), Joan Jurige (Happy Woman), Rosie O'Connor (Adorable Little Girl), Sean Whalen (Paperboy), Erik Onate (Aggressive Reporter), Joey DePinto (Shreck Security Guard), Steven Brill (Gothamite 1), Neal Lerner (Gothamite 2), Ashley Tillman (Gothamite 3), Elizabeth Sanders (Gothamite 4), Henry Kingi (Mugger), Joan Giammarco (Female Victim), Lisa Guerrero (Volunteer Bimbo), Frank DiElsi (Security 1), Biff Yeager (Security 2), Robert Gossett (TV Anchorman), Adam Drescher (Crowd Member), Robert N. Bell, Susan Rossitto, Margarita Fernandez, Denise Killpack, Felix Silla, Debbie Lee Carrington (Emperor Penguins), Niki Botelho (Emperor Penguin/Baby Penguin). *Producers:* Denise Di Novi, Tim Burton. *Co-Producer:* Larry Franco. *Associate Producer/Production Manager:* Ian Bryce. *Executive Producers:* Jon Peters, Peter Guber, Benjamin Melniker, Michael E. Uslan. *Director:* Tim Burton. *Screenplay:* Daniel Waters (Story by Daniel Waters and Sam Hamm, based on characters created by Bob Kane). *Cinematography:* Stefan Czapsky. *Production Designer:* Bo Welch. *Art Directors:* Tom Duffield, Rick Heinrichs. *Set Decorator:* Cheryl Carasik. *Costume Designers:* Bob Ringwood, Mary Vogt. *Editor:* Chris Lebenzon. *Music:* Danny Elfman. *Casting:* Marion Dougherty. *Key Makeup:* Ve Neill. *Key Hair Stylist:* Yolanda Toussieng. *First Assistant Director:* David McGiffert. *Second Unit Director:* Billy Weber. *Second Unit Director/Stunt Coordinator:* Max Kleven. *Visual Effects Supervisor:* Michael Fink. *Mechanical Effects Supervisor:* Chuck Gaspar. *Studio:* Warner Bros. *Length:* 126 minutes. *United States Release Date:* June 19, 1992.

The 1989 motion picture *Batman* was such a tremendous box office success that even before it finished its first run in theaters, it was already a foregone conclusion that it would be followed by a sequel. Throughout 1990 and early 1991, rumors were flying in terms of whether or not *Batman*'s principal actors would return for another Batman film. There was also much speculation about what new villains might be featured in the movie, and which actors could play those villains.

Getting the *Batman* sequel off the ground took some serious negotiating on the part of Warner Bros., and the project was not spearheaded by the same production team that had made *Batman* a reality. In late 1989, Peter Guber and Jon Peters left Warner to head up Columbia Pictures after the Sony Corporation purchased both the Guber-Peters Entertainment Company and Columbia. *Batman* director Tim Burton had initially been reluctant to direct a *Batman* sequel for Warner, but the departure of Guber and Peters might well have made him more receptive to the idea of doing the film.[1] As we discussed last chapter, Burton was not happy about how much creative control the producers had over his work while he was directing *Batman*. Warner Bros. was able to heighten Burton's interest in directing the *Batman* sequel by giving him far more creative control over the film than he was allowed to have over *Batman*—for the *Batman* sequel, he would be both producer and director. Burton officially signed on to the project in the summer of 1990.

Turning the *Batman* sequel over to Burton so completely was a curious decision on the part of Warner Bros. The studio's input was instrumental in helping to shape *Batman* into a more action-oriented, "summer blockbuster" type of movie that would be more accessible to mainstream audiences—and now they would not be able to have that kind of input on its sequel. But whatever misgivings Warner might have had in terms of trusting Burton with the original *Batman* had evaporated in the wake of the finished product's phenomenal box office returns. The studio seemed very confident that a *Batman* sequel directed by Burton had a good chance of being a huge blockbuster as well. So in their zeal to secure Burton for a *Batman* sequel, Warner ignored the fact that one of the major reasons that *Batman* was such a success was that they had left themselves the option to have some degree of control over both the film and Burton. Now they had given away that option, gambling that this time around Burton, on his own, would give them the film they were hoping for.

Warner hired *Batman*'s primary screenwriter Sam Hamm to write a preliminary script for the sequel, at the time known only by its working title of *Batman 2*. Hamm's script basically picked up where *Batman* left off—Bruce's romance with Vicki Vale continued to progress, and as Batman he had to contend with two new costumed villains in Gotham City, the Penguin and the Catwoman. Also, much like the early drafts of Hamm's original *Batman* screenplay, his *Batman 2* screenplay introduced the Robin/Dick Grayson character in its final act. Though the *Batman 2* script retained the generally dark tone of *Batman*, it also had a decidedly happy ending—the Penguin and the Catwoman were defeated, Bruce proposed to Vicki, and Dick came to live at Wayne Manor, setting the stage for his transformation to Robin.[2]

Warner Bros. and Burton were not impressed with Hamm's *Batman 2* script, so they brought in screenwriter Daniel Waters to create a brand-new script for the sequel. While Waters was writing, he and Burton regularly met to share ideas for the screenplay with one another, much like Hamm and Burton had done while Hamm was writing *Batman*.[3] In May 1991, Waters finished his initial draft of the script for *Batman Returns*, the sequel's newly-decided upon official name. Most of the primary characters featured in Hamm's *Batman 2* screenplay remained in Waters' *Batman Returns* screenplay, with one notable exception—Waters completely cut Vicki Vale and her "happy ending" subplot from the film. The Robin character remained in the *Batman Returns* script, and he was depicted in a manner that recalled the comic book origin of the second Jason Todd Robin—Waters imagined Robin as a tough street kid who eventually becomes Batman's crimefighting partner. (We discussed this second version of the Jason Todd Robin character in detail in Chapter 7.)

Waters' *Batman Returns* script was very long, and needed to be considerably cut down to make it filmable. This task was performed by screenwriter Wesley Strick, who turned in his revised version of the script to Warner Bros. in August 1991—this version would make

Top: Michael Keaton as Batman in *Batman Returns* (1992). *Bottom:* Michelle Pfeiffer as the Catwoman and Danny DeVito as the Penguin in *Batman Returns* (1992).

it to the screen with only minor changes.⁴ One of the cuts Strick made to Waters' screenplay was to eliminate the Robin character, just as writer Warren Skaaren had cut the character from Hamm's *Batman* screenplay. This time around, the character was cut so late in the game that an actor had already been cast for the part—Marlon Wayans was to play Robin. One can imagine how disappointing it must have been for Wayans to have been pulled from such a high-profile film just a short time before its production was to begin.

Interestingly, the Robin character's connection to *Batman Returns* did not end with the dismissal of Wayans. Kenner Toys had obtained the licensing rights to produce action figures of the *Batman Returns* characters, and when they began designing their figures, Robin was still going to be featured in the film. Evidently Kenner was informed that Robin was cut from the film too late to stop production of their *Batman Returns* Robin action figure, so the figure ended up being displayed on toy store shelves all over the United States just as the film was premiering! This caused a bit of confusion among Batman fans of all ages — if there was a *Batman Returns* Robin action figure, why wasn't the character actually *in* the *Batman Returns* film? (Incidentally, Kenner based the design of their *Batman Returns* Robin figure on the Tim Drake version of the character, so it was the first modern-era Robin action figure ever to be produced.)

This miscommunication between Kenner Toys and Warner Bros. regarding Robin being in *Batman Returns* was a troubling sign of things to come. Warner was aggressively developing merchandising tie-ins to *Batman Returns* aimed at younger audiences, and Burton was just as aggressively working to craft *Batman Returns* into a film that was absolutely *not* intended for younger audiences. As we just discussed, Burton was very involved in the creation of the movie's script — a script which contained horrific images of cruelty to children and animals, gleeful sadism, senseless murder and kinky sexuality. Warner knew what was in this screenplay, so how could the studio ever have thought it would be appropriate to approve the release of countless *Batman Returns* children's products?

The most likely answer to this question is that the studio must have been holding out hope that Burton would eventually see the logic of softening the film in order to make it marketable to a broader audience. But this would not happen — simply put, there was a huge disconnect between Warner Bros. and Burton in terms of just who the target audience for *Batman Returns* was going to be. Warner envisioned the film's audience as one that would be made up of all age groups, including children who loved Batman, and parents who loved buying Batman products for those children — essentially the same audience that had made *Batman* such a runaway hit. That audience was unequivocally *not* the one Burton envisioned reaching with *Batman Returns*. The film's script alone was more than enough evidence that Burton had no interest in making *Batman Returns* into the kind of all-ages film that *Batman* was.

Burton had made it very clear that he was not trying to recapture the magical success of *Batman* with *Batman Returns*— in fact, on several occasions he had been quick to point out that he personally was not all that satisfied with *Batman*.⁵ His ambivalence toward *Batman* was hardly surprising, considering the fact that Warner Bros. had never allowed the movie to truly be *his* movie. But the deal that Burton had struck with Warner this time around did allow *Batman Returns* to be *his* movie — and he wasn't going to soften it just so the studio could sell a bunch of extra movie tickets and Batman toys.

In August 1992, *Empire* Magazine published a story about *Batman Returns* entitled "Three Go Mad in Gotham" that succinctly summed up the collision course that Burton and Warner Bros. had been on over the film. In the story, Burton stated that he was not happy about Warner's desire to market *Batman Returns* so aggressively — he said "I often felt they [Warner] forgot we were making a movie. It seems like they wished the process of making the film didn't have to happen and they could cut immediately to the merchandising."[6]

Here's one more thought regarding the *Batman Returns* screenplay. While Warren Skaaren received onscreen credit for his work on revising the *Batman* script, Wesley Strick's similar work on the *Batman Returns* script went uncredited. It seems odd that Strick did not receive some sort of credit for his contribution to the film — after all, Sam Hamm was credited for *his* work on *Batman Returns*, and his *Batman 2* script had been tossed aside in favor of Daniel Waters' script! (Hamm was credited as being the film's "story" co-creator with Waters.)

The casting of *Batman Returns* went relatively smoothly. In early 1991, Michael Keaton agreed to reprise his role as Batman/Bruce Wayne — and after the huge success of *Batman*, this time around he would not have to contend with huge numbers of serious Batman fans protesting him playing the part! Along with Keaton, several other *Batman* cast members would be reprising their roles in *Batman Returns*. Michael Gough was returning as Alfred, and Pat Hingle was returning as Commissioner Gordon.

Choosing an actor to play the role of Oswald Cobblepot/The Penguin turned out to be as easy a decision as choosing to bring back Keaton, Gough and Hingle. From the first talk of a Batman sequel, the Penguin was considered to be the most likely villain to appear in the film. And because the diminutive, sardonic actor Danny DeVito was such a perfect physical and cerebral match for the role, his name almost always came up when the subject of casting the Penguin was discussed. DeVito jumped at the chance to take the part — after all, *Batman Returns* was going to be one of the most hotly anticipated sequels of all time, and it seemed almost as if he was *born* to play the Penguin. Unfortunately, Burton and DeVito's interpretation of the Penguin would eventually prove to be one of the film's most problematic elements.

The only real problem that Burton and Warner Bros. faced while casting *Batman Returns* was finding the right actress to play the role of Selina Kyle/The Catwoman. Annette Bening was originally chosen for the role, but she had to bow out of the film after becoming pregnant. Michelle Pfeiffer was hired to replace her. The versatile, beautiful Pfeiffer had starred in a wide range of successful films since the mid–1980s, so her presence in *Batman Returns* was welcome news to film fans and Batman fans alike.

Amusingly, Sean Young, the actress originally slated to play Vicki Vale in *Batman*, campaigned very hard for the Catwoman part. She even went so far as to dress in a Catwoman-like costume and go to the Warner lot in an attempt to meet with Burton so that she could convince him to give her the role. She brought her own video crew with her to film this "storming the gates" audition — however, the whole plan backfired when Burton was unavailable (or perhaps simply unwilling) to give her an audience. She ended up prowling the lot in her costume, making everyone she encountered there, including Michael Keaton, rather uncomfortable. Obviously, she didn't end up with the part, but she did appear on the television talk show *The Joan Rivers Show* to share the story of her Catwoman adventure![7]

The script for *Batman Returns* also featured another villain that rated as much screen time as the Penguin and the Catwoman. Christopher Walken was cast as Max Shreck, a ruthless Gotham City businessman whose corrupt path intertwines with both of the film's costumed villains. Incorporating two classic Batman adversaries into *Batman Returns* was already a sign that Batman himself might not have enough screen time to make much of an impact. Adding a third villain created specifically for the film practically guaranteed that Batman would not really be the focal point of his own movie.

The script for *Batman Returns* had been the first major indication of how different the film was going to be from *Batman*. Another indication was where that script was going to be filmed. Warner Bros. decided not to return to Pinewood Studios in England, where the huge outdoor sets for *Batman* had been standing, waiting to be used for a Batman sequel. Burton wanted to make *Batman Returns* at the Warner Studios in Burbank, California, so the studio agreed to construct all-new sets designed by Bo Welch for the film.[8]

Moving the primary filming of *Batman Returns* proved to be a costly financial decision for Warner Bros. They had to spend millions of dollars on new sets when they had elaborate Batman sets sitting idle at Pinewood. To make matters worse, in many respects these new sets turned out to be far inferior to Pinewood's *Batman* sets, especially the ones depicting Gotham City. Anton Furst's Gotham City sets were brilliant and, equally important, they were outdoors and very large. They *looked* like a real city — in particular, they looked like some of the grimmer areas of New York City, the real-life inspiration for Gotham. All of Welch's Gotham City sets in *Batman Returns*, constructed indoors on sound stages, were just too cramped and artificial-looking to convey the kind of urban realism that Furst captured in his Gotham sets.

As a result, Gotham ended up looking like the setting of some sort of demented storybook land in *Batman Returns*, fanciful, claustrophobic and unreal. Batman's strength as a character had always come from the fact that he was much more closely tied to reality than most other comic book heroes, and Burton greatly undermined this strength by choosing to abandon Furst's concept of Gotham City. One final, and tragic, note regarding *Batman* set design — Anton Furst committed suicide in November 1991, during the making of *Batman Returns*.

Batman Returns was not going to end up looking much like *Batman*, but it would end up *sounding* much like *Batman*. Danny Elfman was brought on board to compose the orchestral score for *Batman Returns*, and he would end up using a number of the musical themes he first used in *Batman*, especially his memorable "Batman Theme."

Primary filming of *Batman Returns* took place between late 1991 and early 1992. The making of *Batman Returns* did not have the same level of off-screen dramatics that complicated the making of *Batman*. There were no major creative differences like the ones that arose between Burton and producer Jon Peters in 1988 and 1989.

While at the time Warner Bros. might have been pleased about the relative peace found on their *Batman Returns* sets, their pleasure would give way to no small measure of distress once they actually saw the finished movie in the spring of 1992. Burton had not softened the overall tone of *Batman Returns* from its original conceptualization at all — it was a dark, disjointed film full of horrific imagery and adult content. One can only imagine the panic Warner must have felt upon realizing that this problematic movie was the end result of all their efforts. *Batman Returns* was just too edgy to be a huge hit with audiences of all ages like *Batman* was.

And to make matters worse, *Batman Returns* actually cost the studio much more money to make than the 1989 *Batman* had. Given the success of their first Batman film, Burton and Keaton were able to command far larger salaries for their participation in *Batman Returns*—and as we just noted, Warner Bros. had to shell out millions for all new sets in order for the film to be made in California. Consequently, the final price tag for *Batman Returns* was around $80 million, more than twice *Batman*'s budget.⁹ This meant that *Batman Returns* was going to have to do extremely well at the box office in order to make any money at *all*.

Just as troubling, the great pains that Warner had taken to develop numerous merchandising tie-ins for *Batman Returns* could not possibly pay off now. All of their efforts to market the film would be construed as a cynical effort to entice young children to see a movie that they really had no business seeing. McDonald's Restaurants was going to be including *Batman Returns* toys with their "Happy Meal" children's meal packages—promotional tactics such as this were bound to unleash a firestorm of criticism. But there was no turning back for the studio now: *Batman Returns* was due to premiere nationwide in just a few weeks, on June 19, so there was little else they could do but release the movie and hope for the best.

Batman Returns opens with a series of scenes showing Oswald Cobblepot being born horribly deformed, and then being imprisoned in a cage by his parents at Christmastime. From his cage, baby Oswald is able to grab hold of the family cat by its tail. He pulls the cat into his cage, and a horrible racket ensues as the cat is presumably killed. This is the last straw for the Cobblepots—they wheel Oswald in his stroller out into the snowy night, and dump him off of a bridge into a fast-moving river. The water carries Oswald to an abandoned zoo, where a group of penguins adopt him as their own.

The scene then shifts to Christmastime in Gotham City, 33 years later. As Gotham's reigning beauty queen the Ice Princess is preparing to light the Christmas tree at Gotham Plaza, Oswald watches the scene from the sewers. Gotham's Mayor is on hand to attend the tree lighting ceremony, as is Max Shreck, Gotham's most successful businessman and owner of Shreck's Department Store. Before they attend the ceremony, Shreck tries to convince the Mayor to approve groundbreaking of Shreck's new power plant for Gotham. The Mayor refuses, saying Gotham already has enough power. Shreck's timid secretary Selina Kyle attempts to make a suggestion regarding the power plant, but Shreck rudely cuts her off, humiliating her in the process.

Shreck and the Mayor make their way to Gotham Plaza for the ceremony, but the festivities are interrupted by an attack on the Plaza by the Red Triangle Circus Gang, a group of criminals in cahoots with Oswald. Via the Batsignal, Commissioner Gordon summons Batman. The Batsignal triggers a number of smaller Batsignal lights mounted on the outside walls of Wayne Manor, which shine a Batsignal directly into Bruce Wayne's study. Bruce sees the signal and races to Gotham Plaza as Batman. Using hi-tech weapons concealed in the Batmobile, Batman subdues the Circus Gang. One of the gang members is a fire-eater, so Batman fights fire with fire by using the Batmobile's jet-fueled afterburner to set him ablaze.

In the chaos, Shreck runs into Gotham's extensive sewer system to escape the Circus Gang. There he comes face to face with Oswald. Shreck is amazed to learn that the urban legends that have been circulating throughout Gotham about a Penguin-like man with a long nose and flippers instead of fingers living in the city's sewers are actually true. Oswald wants Shreck to help him orchestrate a return to the civilized Gotham above the sewers, so that he can find out who his parents were and why they abandoned him. Shreck at first refuses—but when Oswald informs Shreck that he holds incriminating evidence regarding Shreck's illegal business dealings, including the severed hand of Shreck's long-missing former business partner, Shreck agrees to help him.

Returning to his office, Shreck discovers Selina working late. Selina tells him that she accessed his secret files regarding his proposed power plant, and she has learned that the plant will actually *rob* Gotham of power, not produce it. Enraged by her insubordination and worried that she might try to use this discovery against him, Shreck pushes her out of his office window. She plunges to the ground hundreds of feet below but, amazingly, is not killed. As she lies injured on the pavement, dozens of cats swarm over her body, licking her wounds. She returns to her apartment and goes completely berserk, smashing everything in sight. She sews a patchwork Catwoman costume out of a vinyl raincoat, using sewing needles for claws.

The next day, the Mayor holds a press conference to decry the violence that took place in Gotham Plaza the night before. While he is speaking, an acrobat from the Circus gang leaps in and snatches the Mayor's baby from the arms of the Mayor's wife. The acrobat leaps into the sewers, but the baby is seemingly rescued by Oswald, the "Penguin Man," and returned to the Mayor. Of course, the acrobat is actually part of Oswald's Circus Gang, so the entire rescue is a fake — part of Shreck's plan to bring Oswald back to the world above the sewers. The citizens of Gotham, unaware of this, are enthralled with this unlikely new hero.

At the Gotham Hall of Records, Oswald learns his given name, and he then goes to visit his parents' graves. Meanwhile, Bruce pores over old newspaper articles and learns that there is a connection between the Red Triangle Circus and Oswald. Also at this time, Selina makes her first "public appearance" as the black vinyl-clad, whip-wielding Catwoman — she stops a mugger from assaulting a woman, slashing the mugger's face with her claws.

The next day, Bruce meets with Shreck, who wants him to invest in his proposed power plant. Bruce refuses, saying Gotham has enough power already, and that he will fight Shreck's plans to build a new plant. While the two argue, Selina walks in, much to Shreck's surprise. Selina has no memory of Shreck's attempt to murder her, but she does have a keen interest in Bruce. The feeling is mutual — Bruce tells her he will call her for a date sometime soon.

Later, Shreck meets with Oswald and asks him to run for Mayor. Since Shreck can't get the current Mayor to go along with his power plant scheme, he wants to recall the Mayor and get Gotham's new hero Oswald Cobblepot elected to the office — then Oswald can give Shreck the permits he needs to build his plant. Oswald at first refuses, even going so far as to bite one of his potential "political consultants" on the nose, which sends the consultant's blood spurting all over the place. Shreck finally convinces the sexually frustrated Oswald to be a candidate by telling him the job will get him lots of women.

Oswald and Shreck devise a plan to turn Gotham against their current Mayor: They send out the Circus Gang to turn Gotham's streets into a battle zone so that it will appear that the Mayor has completely lost control of the city. As the Circus Gang runs wild, Batman appears on the scene and begins to fight them. He puts sticks of dynamite into one of the gang member's pants and pushes him down a sewer; the dynamite explodes, obviously killing the gang member. At the same time, the Catwoman breaks into Shreck Department Store, putting flammable chemicals in one of the store's microwave ovens, and tearing open a natural gas line. Batman then comes face to face with Oswald for the first time on the streets of Gotham in front of Shreck's Department Store, but their combative conversation is interrupted by the Catwoman. She vaults in, meows — and then the entire first floor of the store explodes into flame.

The Catwoman climbs up the facade of a nearby building and Batman gives chase.

They fight on a rooftop, but their fighting gives way to physical attraction for one another. However, the Catwoman interrupts the mood by suddenly and savagely piercing his torso with one of her sewing needle claws. He pushes her off the building, and she lands in a sand-filled dump truck.

The next day, Oswald officially kicks off his mayoral campaign, blaming the Mayor for the chaos on Gotham's streets. He gives a young female voter a campaign button, lewdly groping her in the process. He retreats to his office, where he finds the Catwoman waiting for him. She tells him she wants him to help her destroy Batman. However, the Penguin is so overcome with lust for her he has a difficult time concentrating on her request, instead concentrating on sniffing the heels of her boots and offering her body oils. Finally they begin to formulate a plan to frame Batman and make it appear that he is a criminal.

The scene shifts to the Ice Princess preparing for her appearance at the re-lighting of the Christmas tree in Gotham Plaza. The Penguin bursts in and knocks her out with a Batarang that Batman accidentally left behind in a previous battle. Meanwhile, Bruce and Selina are having a romantic evening together at Wayne Manor. But their evening is cut short by a news bulletin stating that Batman has kidnapped the Ice Princess. Both Bruce and Selina make awkward excuses to get away from one another, and they separately race to Gotham Plaza in costume.

Batman jumps out of the Batmobile to look for the Ice Princess—but as he leaves the car, members of the Circus Gang sneak up and start to sabotage its controls. Batman locates the Ice Princess bound in a building near Gotham Plaza, but as he tries to untie her, the Catwoman bursts in and starts fighting him. The Catwoman grabs the Ice Princess and drags her to the roof of the building. Batman gives chase and finds the Ice Princess standing on the edge of the building. She says that the Catwoman let her go, but before he can get to her, Oswald throws an umbrella filled with live bats at her, which causes her to fall to her death. The Gotham Police arrive on the scene and assume that Batman pushed the Ice Princess off the roof. They open fire on him, knocking him to a lower rooftop. The Catwoman finds him there and they are again attracted to one another, but Batman resists her advances and jumps off the roof, using bat glider wings built into his costume to sail down to the Batmobile.

The Penguin appears by the Catwoman's side on the roof, and tries to seduce her. When she rejects *his* advances, he attaches one of his flying umbrellas to her neck and sends her skyward. She frees herself from the umbrella, and her fall is broken by plants in a rooftop greenhouse. Batman climbs into the Batmobile, but he quickly finds that Oswald is remotely controlling the car. Oswald sends Batman on a destructive joyride through the streets of Gotham. Batman is able to find Oswald's controller on the bottom of the car—he punches through the floor of the car, discards the controller and regains control before Oswald can do any further damage.

The next day, Oswald prepares to give a speech in his bid to become mayor. From the Batcave, Bruce and Alfred sabotage *him*. Using a CD that Batman recorded of Oswald saying disparaging things about Gotham and its citizens, they jam the live speech and broadcast his rude remarks. The crowd immediately turns on Oswald, throwing vegetables at him. Enraged, he opens fire on the crowd with one of his umbrella guns and races back to his abandoned zoo hideout. There he hatches a plot with his Circus Gang to kidnap all of Gotham's first-born sons and murder them. He tells his gang not to call him Oswald—he is not human, he is the Penguin.

At a holiday ball at Shreck's Department Store, Bruce and Selina dance, and Selina reveals that she came to the ball to kill Shreck. While Bruce tries to calm her, they exchange words with one another that they had previously exchanged while they were in costume. They are both shocked to realize each other's secret identities. Before they can recover, the Penguin breaks through the floor riding in a bizarre vehicle that is shaped like a toy rubber duck. The villain is there to kidnap Shreck's first-born son Chip, who is also at the ball. Shreck convinces the Penguin to take him to his lair instead of Chip, so the two descend back into the sewers. The Penguin's gang rides through the Gotham streets in a parade-style circus train vehicle kidnapping all of the city's first-born sons. Batman intercepts them, and sends a note back to the Penguin telling him that his plan has been thwarted. The Penguin responds by sending an army of real penguins with missiles on their backs to destroy Gotham.

From the Batboat in the Gotham sewers, Batman jams the Penguin's signal sending instructions to the penguins and sends the birds back to the Penguin's lair. Batman intercepts the Penguin there as he tries to escape in his duck vehicle. Batman thwarts his escape, and the Penguin pushes the button to tell the penguins to fire their missiles—right at that moment, a bunch of bats fly out of the Batboat and swarm the villain. The Penguin falls into the pool where he and the penguins had been hiding for so many years. At the same time, the Catwoman shows up and attacks Shreck. Batman intervenes and tells Selina to let Shreck live—he will go to prison, and they can go back to Wayne Manor together. As he tells her this, he rips off his mask, exposing his true face to both Selina and Shreck. But Selina rejects Bruce, and starts after Shreck. He shoots her repeatedly, but she keeps after him—she grabs a downed power line and electrocutes him. The Penguin then rises out of the pool, bloodied, with inky black mucus running out of his nose and mouth. He falls over dead before he can confront Batman, and a group of Emperor Penguins slide his body back into the pool.

On Christmas Eve, Bruce and Alfred are driving through Gotham City. Bruce thinks he sees the Catwoman in a shadowy alley, and he jumps out of the car—but he only finds a black stray cat. He brings the cat back into the car with him, and he and Alfred wish each other a Merry Christmas. The Batsignal flashes in the sky, and in the film's final shot we see the Catwoman viewing it from the rooftops.

One does not have to study this synopsis too closely to see just why *Batman Returns* was not the film ripe with "summer blockbuster" potential that Warner Bros. was hoping for. But its initial reviews and opening box office numbers were actually very good. Many critics were greatly impressed by the film's surreal images and bizarre characters. It must be noted that most of these critics had no prior interest in Batman comic book characters, so they approached the film from an "art" perspective, not a "Batman fan" perspective. Also, given these critics' generally cynical nature, their favorable reviews seemed to be based on the notion that *Batman Returns* was going to defy mainstream audiences' expectations so completely as much as anything else. In other words, critics seemed to be amused by the idea that people were going to go see *Batman Returns* hoping for an action-packed good time, and would instead be walloped over the head by Burton's morose, edgy "art film."

Likely because of the strength of these early reviews, and because of the Batman brand name, audiences lined up in droves to see *Batman Returns*. At first it seemed that Burton's "art film" might well turn out to be as successful as the 1989 *Batman* (*Batman Returns* grossed over $45 million in the U.S. on its opening weekend). But once the initial wave of moviegoers actually *saw* the film, word began to get out about how dark, mean-spirited and inappropriate for younger audiences it actually was—and box office business dropped off very rapidly. In the end, *Batman Returns* grossed only about $160 million in the U.S., and about $270 million worldwide.[10]

Obviously, these are not unsubstantial figures — many filmmakers would feel blessed if their motion pictures made the amount of money that *Batman Returns* made. But as we noted earlier in the chapter, *Batman Returns* cost Warner Bros. well over twice as much money to make as *Batman* had — so the studio was certainly justified in viewing the film as a financial underachiever when it ended up making almost $150 million *less* than *Batman* did.

But Warner's woes over *Batman Returns* were by no means strictly financial ones. The studio engendered no small amount of ill will from the moviegoing public over the release of the film, especially from parents of young children. These parents were angry because they felt Warner Bros. had misled them by marketing *Batman Returns* as appropriate for children, when in reality it was not. In fairness, *Batman Returns* was rated PG-13, which should have alerted parents that the film contained unsuitable material. But the 1989 *Batman*, also rated PG-13, was not nearly as dark and disturbing. In other words, yes, *Batman* was a film that parents had to think carefully about before taking their children to see, but its "scary" scenes were generally as much fun as they were frightening. The same could not be said for *Batman Returns* — its "scary" scenes were frightening in an adult, horror movie manner. Also, *Batman Returns* contained far more sexual innuendo than its predecessor, making it doubly inappropriate.

This parental backlash against Warner Bros. over *Batman Returns* became a very public problem for the studio during the summer of 1992. *The New York Times* and *Entertainment Weekly* ran pieces detailing moviegoers' negative reaction to both the content of the film, and the manner in which had been marketed.[11]

So the problems that Warner Bros. feared they might encounter upon the release of *Batman Returns* ended up coming to pass. The studio did not make near as much money off of the film as they thought they would, and they had to endure a public relations nightmare created by their attempts to market the film. Leaving their Batman franchise solely in the hands of Tim Burton had proved to be their undoing. Only several weeks into *Batman Returns*'s theatrical run, Warner Bros. understood this fact all too well — privately they were already discussing finding a new director for their third Batman film.[12]

As a longtime Batman fan, I was shocked and profoundly disappointed by this film when it premiered. In my opinion, *Batman Returns* showed such disregard and outright contempt for the time-honored Batman characters that it was hard for me even to view the film as a "legitimate" Batman motion picture. But Batman is a fictional character, so all of us can have interpretations of him that are no more or less valid than anyone else's. I will try to keep this fact in mind while commenting on the film over the next few pages. Still, I feel that it is only right to inform you that my analysis of *Batman Returns* will reflect my overall negative opinion of the film.

First off, I believe that the manner in which Batman is portrayed in *Batman Returns* is an insult to the character's storied history. The Batman of the film is simply a cold-blooded killer. In the opening fight scene, he has no qualms with setting a thug ablaze using the Batmobile afterburners. And in a scene later in the film, he stuffs dynamite down another thug's pants and pushes him into a sewer. Batman offhandedly murders these criminals, which is behavior that runs completely counter to the comic book Batman's long-standing vow to never purposefully take a human life.

In fairness, it must be stated that the 1989 *Batman* also depicted Batman using lethal force on criminals, such as in the scenes where he destroys Axis Chemicals and when he fires at the Joker from the Batwing. But these actions do not seem quite so out of character for Batman considering that the film takes place at the very beginning of the crimefighter's career — after all, in Kane's first Batman stories of the late 1930s, the character carried a gun and wasn't above using it. Also, Batman's willingness to try to put an to end the Joker's life in *Batman* makes sense because his hatred of the Joker is so personal, the Joker being the man who murdered his parents many years earlier.

Whether one agrees with Batman's use of lethal force in *Batman* or not, the fact remains that the comic book Batman's resolve to see justice prevail over blind vengeance eventually led him to become completely opposed to killing. *Batman Returns* makes no attempt to honor this noble character trait. In the film, Batman is far enough down the road in his crimefighting career that he should be more of a hero than he was in *Batman*, not less. Instead, in *Batman Returns* we find him callously slaughtering human beings in ways that make him practically indistinguishable from the criminals he fights.

Also, Batman/Bruce Wayne is portrayed in *Batman Returns* as being unconfident and indecisive. He seems less interested in fighting crime than in trying to get Selina to go out on a date with him — and he is not even all that successful in that regard, because every time he tries to talk to Selina, he comes across as a bumbling idiot. He gets tongue-tied, he forgets what he is doing, and he seems unable to respond to even the simplest questions she poses to him. Obviously, the comic book Batman/Bruce Wayne has almost always been a dark character — but he has also almost always been impressive, efficient and in control. He has *not* been a wishy-washy sad sack, which is the way he is portrayed in *Batman Returns*.

If Michael Keaton's effectiveness in the role of Batman was limited by his physical stature in *Batman*, he is doubly limited in *Batman Returns*. At least Keaton's character was generally well-realized in *Batman*, whereas in *Batman Returns* he is given almost nothing positive to work with in terms of character development. He is frequently forced to stand sullenly off to the side, watching the villains gobble up the majority of the screen time — and then when he *is* allowed to step into the spotlight, the script calls for him to act in a decidedly unheroic manner.

One of the film's only bright spots regarding the Batman character is Bob Ringwood's new Batman costume design, which is a vast improvement over *Batman*'s Batman costume. It appears not to be as cumbersome, so Keaton seems to have a wider range of movement. And the simulated muscles on the chest of his previous costume have been replaced by more streamlined plated body armor. Also, several of Keaton's Batman fight scenes in *Batman Returns* are quite exciting, and far more coherent than many of the action sequences in *Batman* — in fact, the rooftop battle between Batman and the Catwoman is one of the most memorable Batman big-screen moments of all time. The scene does not suffer from the kind of hyperactive editing found in the previous film.

But these few positives cannot begin to outweigh the overwhelmingly negative manner in which Batman is portrayed in *Batman Returns*. Plus, as mentioned earlier, with three major villains running around in *Batman Returns*, Batman doesn't get enough screen time. The final shot of *Batman Returns* perfectly sums up how much more interested Burton was in the villains than in his title character. *Batman* closed with Batman standing tall on a Gotham rooftop, looking up at the Batsignal; the final shot of *Batman Returns* shows the Catwoman standing tall on a Gotham rooftop, looking up at the Batsignal.

The mean-spiritedness and hopelessness that Batman exudes in *Batman Returns* are by no means qualities that are unique to his character in the film — in fact, the film as a whole seems to revel in all of the anger, hatred, cruelty and senseless violence it depicts. The Oswald Cobblepot/Penguin character is a perfect summation of *Batman Returns'* sadistic nature — because Oswald is born deformed, the Cobblepots lock him up in a cage as a baby, and then dump him into a river and leave him for dead. These disturbing scenes are the first images we see in *Batman Returns*, and they set the tone for the rest of the film.

As horrific as these first scenes are, they seem almost tame in comparison to the scenes that follow featuring Danny DeVito as the grown-up Oswald/Penguin. Though his first scenes portray him in a slightly sympathetic manner, these quickly give way to monstrous images of a Penguin character like nothing that had ever been seen on the pages of any Batman comic book. DeVito's Penguin oozes inky black mucus from his nose and mouth, eats raw fish entrails with his shark-like teeth, makes sexual innuendoes about every woman he sees, and wants to murder as many children as he can get his hands on.

Burton and DeVito chose to discard almost everything that made the comic book and 1960s screen Penguin such a memorable character, and gleefully push him as far beyond the boundaries of good taste as they could. As the Penguin, DeVito seems to be saying to the viewer, "You think Jack Nicholson's Joker was something? Well, just watch me 'out-Nicholson' Nicholson!" As a result, his performance comes across as self-consciously over the top, never nearly as fun as it is labored. (Not to mention completely terrifying to most small children — the character was particularly reviled by the parents who were angry with Warner Bros. over the release and marketing of the film.) Given both his physical stature and sardonic nature, Danny DeVito should have made the perfect Penguin in *Batman Returns*. Instead, thanks to a lot of grotesque makeup and equally grotesque overacting, DeVito's Penguin turned out to be one of the film's most glaring missteps.

Michelle Pfeiffer fares considerably better in her role as Selina Kyle/The Catwoman. She turns in a slinky, explosive performance that is perhaps the highlight of the film. Like the Penguin, the Catwoman is changed substantially from her comic book form in *Batman Returns* — her "timid secretary transformed into a tigress by a near-death experience and a bunch of alley cats" origin is unique to the film. But this rewrite is not nearly as jarring as the revisions *Batman Returns* makes to the characters of Batman and the Penguin. Plus, it allows Pfeiffer to play Selina and the Catwoman as almost completely separate characters, showcasing her range as an actress.

In fact, Pfeiffer's sensuous dominatrix of a Catwoman proved to be just about the only element of *Batman Returns* that moviegoers really liked. The Catwoman's popularity with the general public led to rumors of Pfeiffer reprising the role in a future Batman film, or perhaps even in a spin-off film of her own. These rumors persisted for several years after the release of *Batman Returns*, but Pfeiffer's Catwoman never returned to the big screen. Still, plans for a Catwoman spin-off film refused to die — in July 2004, Warner Bros. and Village Roadshow Pictures released the movie *Catwoman* starring Halle Berry in the title role. The film's Catwoman had nothing to do with any previous comic, film or television version of the character — in fact, Batman was not connected to her in any way! Of course, this ended up being a good thing for the Batman character, because *Catwoman* turned out to be a spectacularly bad film that bombed with both the critics and the public.

As previously mentioned, *Batman Returns* tried to incorporate so many characters into its storyline that it was almost inevitable that the film would be saddled with a hopelessly tangled plot. Christopher Walken's Max Shreck is the character that truly throws *Batman Returns* into a narrative tailspin. His bogus power plant subplot takes up far too much screen time, and often slows the tempo of the film to a virtual standstill. Walken's trademark deadpan delivery is amusing at times, but generally his scenes just get in the way of the actions of the film's "Batman" characters.

In fact, two of the film's major "Batman" characters are almost completely forced off the screen in order to make room for all of *Batman Returns*' villains. Michael Gough's Alfred and Pat Hingle's Commissioner Gordon are relegated to little more than cameo roles in the film, reinforcing the impression that Burton has little use for *Batman Returns*' "good guys."

Gough and Hingle probably should have considered themselves lucky that they made it into *Batman Returns* at *all*, considering the fact that Burton chose to cut most of *Batman*'s most prominent supporting characters from the film. As previously mentioned, Vicki Vale was removed, and so were Harvey Dent, Alexander Knox, and Mayor Borg. Bo Welch's Gotham City sets had already made the Gotham of *Batman Returns* look nothing like the Gotham of *Batman*—the absence of familiar Gothamites was further proof that Burton wanted *Batman Returns* to be as far removed from *Batman* as possible.

It could be argued that when all is said and done in *Batman Returns*, Burton not only has a distaste for characters that would be categorized as "good guys," but also for just about anything that society at large would perceive as "good." In the film, Burton seizes on every opportunity he can to destroy anything that appears benign, cute or cuddly. A dollhouse is smashed to bits, a beauty queen is brutally murdered, stuffed animals are torn to shreds, pets are abused, and Christmas decorations are riddled with machine-gun fire. These scenes might give us a glimpse of what is going on in Tim Burton's head, but they do not seem all that connected to what the film is supposed to be about—namely, Batman.

Batman Returns' lack of interest in its title character and overall mean-spiritedness were not the film's only major problems—perhaps its biggest failing was that so much of it simply made no sense. Burton seemed to construct the film by placing style over substance, and effect over logic, at every turn. In fact, the film is so far removed from reality that at times it becomes almost impossible to follow. For example, consider all of the following questions that *Batman Returns* raises upon viewing it.

How could a human baby possibly survive being raised by penguins?

The "old zoo" that Penguin has made into his hideout for decades—it is in very close proximity to Gotham City's downtown, so how is it that it has never been detected by the millions of people living or working near it?

Bruce wants to keep his identity as Batman a secret—why would he mount large lighted Batsignals on the outside walls of Wayne Manor where they could be easily spotted by visitors?

How could Batman punch a hole through the floor of the Batmobile to get to the Penguin's remote control device? It is not even possible to punch a hole through the floor of a *regular* car, let alone the armored Batmobile.

How could Bruce move a compact disc back and forth like a 33⅓ r.p.m. record to make deejay-style beat sounds when he is jamming Oswald's speech? The digital disc format is a completely different technology from the grooved 33⅓ records, so creating such a sound from a CD is not possible.

How could the Penguin ever list and round up *all* of the first-born sons of Gotham? Gotham City would have hundreds of thousands of first-born sons—they would be no way for a small group of people to fan out across such a large city and round up so many children, especially when trying to collect them in a slow-moving, parade-style circus train vehicle. Several police cars could easily shut down the entire operation.

How could Shreck host his holiday masquerade ball on the ground floor of his department store? Just several days before the ball, the Catwoman ignited an explosion that turned the entire floor into a giant fireball.

If Batman's costume is so heavily armored, how can the Catwoman pierce his torso with a standard sewing needle, and why does his headgear tear off like an old plastic bag?

How can the Penguin's penguins understand the long speech he makes to them at the end of the film? And for that matter, how are they able fire his missiles, or to move his heavy, lifeless body along the ground using only their flippers?

How in the world is Batman able to keep a large number of bats in his Batboat? And how could he have commanded them to attack the Penguin?

How will Batman ever be exonerated for the crime of killing the Ice Princess? The only two people aware of his innocence are the Penguin, who is dead, and the Catwoman, who has gone into hiding.

From this Batman fan's perspective, Tim Burton must be held accountable for most all of *Batman Returns*' failings. In the film, he chose to depict Batman, Penguin, and Catwoman in ways that made them almost unrecognizable so that they would reflect his own morose sensibilities— they are not so much "Batman" characters in the film as they are "Burton" characters. Simply put, *Batman Returns* isn't about Batman, it is about Burton's perception of modern urban life as a lonely, often hopeless existence. If Burton wanted to make a film with this particular message, he should have made it using characters of his own invention, and left Batman and his world completely out of it.

Instead, Burton made *Batman Returns*, a "Burton" film disguised as a "Batman" film. Sure, that looks like Batman up there on the screen in *Batman Returns*— you can see him driving his Batmobile, and you can hear the strains of Danny Elfman's wonderful orchestral score playing in the background. And the character is surrounded by sets, props and special effects that are often dazzling to behold. But that Batman on the screen in *Batman Returns* has very little to do with the character as he has been portrayed in the comics for so many years.

Stung by the *Batman Returns* experience, Warner Bros. realized that Burton could no longer be trusted to helm their Batman franchise. They began their search for a new Batman director, one whose artistic sensibilities would mesh better with the interests of the franchise than Burton's had.

We have a bit more business relating to *Batman Returns* that we need to attend to before we move on. Because the film was not as theatrically successful as *Batman*, it also enjoyed less popularity on home video than its predecessor. Still, there was a large demand for *Batman Returns* VHS tapes and laserdiscs when Warner first released the movie to the home video market in late 1992. The first DVD version of *Batman Returns* was released by Warner in 1997. The DVD offered the film in its original widescreen format as well as in a format cropped to fit a standard television screen, but it offered no bonus features or printed material dealing with the making of the film.

The success of Warner's 2005 film *Batman Begins* led the studio to release their four previous Batman live-action features on 2-disc DVD sets late that same year. Each of these sets were loaded with special features that detailed their particular film's creation. The *Batman Returns* DVD set included a 1992 television documentary hosted by Robert Urich entitled *The Bat, the Cat, and the Penguin*. The short program was designed to introduce the public to *Batman Returns*, and featured commentary from members of the film's cast and crew, including Burton, Keaton, Pfeiffer and DeVito. Perhaps the most interesting thing about *The Bat, the Cat, and the Penguin* was the program's overall lighthearted tone, which ended up giving the impression of *Batman Returns* being a much more "fun" movie than it really was!

The DVD set also included newly-produced documentaries. The program *Shadows of the Bat: The Cinematic Saga of the Dark Knight Part 4* chronicled the making of *Batman Returns*. The program featured insights from many of the individuals who played a major role in the film's creation, including Tim Burton, Daniel Waters, Sam Hamm, Michael Keaton, Michelle Pfeiffer, and Danny DeVito. These insights were accompanied by a good deal of behind-the-scenes footage shot on the *Batman Returns* set showing the film's cast and crew at work.

The DVD set's program *Beyond Batman* consisted of featurettes about some of the specific elements of *Batman Returns*. The titles of the featurettes were "Gotham City Revisited: The Production Design of *Batman Returns*," "Sleek, Sexy and Sinister: The Costumes of *Batman Returns*," "Making-up the Penguin," "Assembling the Arctic Army," "Bats, Mattes and Dark Nights: The Visual Effects of *Batman Returns*," and "Inside the Elfman Studios: The Music of *Batman Returns*." The set also included featurettes on the main heroes and villains of the film.

This 2005 DVD set remained the definitive home video version of *Batman Returns* until Warner released the movie on Blu-ray disc in early 2009. The *Batman Returns* Blu-ray included all of the special features found on the DVD set, but it did not contain any new bonus material. Of course, the Blu-ray's main selling point was not its special features, but its presentation of the film itself. On Blu-ray, *Batman Returns* looked and sounded far better than it ever had on any other home video format.

I'll close my discussion of *Batman Returns* with these thoughts. The film certainly has its supporters, both Batman fans and non–Batman fans alike — and that is by no means a bad thing. As I mentioned earlier in this chapter, Batman is a fictional character, so all of us can have interpretations of him that are no more or less valid than anyone else's. But in my opinion, Batman as he is portrayed in *Batman Returns* is simply not the character as I understand and appreciate him.

Fortunately for all of us Batman fans disappointed by *Batman Returns*, a marvelous new animated Batman television program called *Batman: The Animated Series* debuted just several months after the premiere of the film. This series would end up being so successful that it would spawn a Batman motion picture of its own entitled *Batman: Mask of the Phantasm*— we'll discuss that film in detail in the next chapter.

11

Batman: Mask of the Phantasm (1993)

Cast (All Voice-only): Kevin Conroy (Batman/Bruce Wayne), Mark Hamill (The Joker), Dana Delany (Andrea Beaumont), Hart Bochner (Arthur Reeves), Abe Vigoda (Salvatore Valestra), Stacy Keach, Jr. (Phantasm, Carl Beaumont), Dick Miller (Chuckie Sol), John P. Ryan (Buzz Bronski), Efrem Zimbalist, Jr. (Alfred), Bob Hastings (Commissioner Gordon), Robert Costanzo (Detective Bullock). *Directors:* Eric Radomski, Bruce W. Timm. *Sequence Directors:* Kevin Altieri, Boyd Kirkland, Frank Paur, Dan Riba. *Producers:* Benjamin Melniker, Michael Uslan. *Co-Producers:* Alan Burnett, Eric Radomski, Bruce W. Timm. *Executive Producer:* Tom Ruegger. *Story:* Alan Burnett. *Screenplay:* Alan Burnett, Paul Dini, Martin Pasko, Michael Reaves (based on the DC Comics characters, Batman created by Bob Kane). *Editor:* Al Breitenbach. *Casting and Voice Supervision:* Andrea Romano. *Music:* Shirley Walker. *Studio:* Warner Bros. *Length:* 77 minutes. *United States Release Date:* December 25, 1993.

Even many ardent Batman fans probably do not think of *Batman: Mask of the Phantasm* as a Batman feature film, because its theatrical run was an absurdly brief one — it premiered in U.S. theatres on Christmas Day 1993, and was gone from those theatres by mid–January 1994! Still, its short time on the big screen does qualify it as a feature, so we will treat it as such in this book. The film's history is completely intertwined with that of the tremendous animated Batman television program *Batman: The Animated Series*.

Produced by Warner Bros. Animation, *Batman: The Animated Series* premiered on the Fox Kids Network in early September 1992. Executive producer Jean MacCurdy placed artists Bruce Timm and Eric Radomski in charge of creating and producing the series, and writers Alan Burnett and Paul Dini were brought on as the series' co-producers. An incredibly talented team of designers, artists, writers, directors and actors worked with these individuals to make *Batman: The Animated Series* not only one of the best Batman screen works, but also one of the best animated television programs of all time.

The initial Fox run of *Batman: The Animated Series* consisted of 70 half-hour episodes that aired between September 1992 and May 1994. Fox changed the title of the series to *The Adventures of Batman and Robin* in September 1994 and premiered an additional 15 episodes between September 1994 and September 1995.

These 85 episodes brought a depth and a level of detail to Batman's world that no previous Batman screen work had come close to matching. The reason for this was quite simple: Unlike most all of the creative forces behind the Batman film and television productions

Batman, the Joker and the Phantasm in *Batman: Mask of the Phantasm* (1993).

that had been released to date, Timm, Radomski and company were actually Batman *fans*. They treated the character and his comic book history with a respect that no creator of a previous Batman film or TV work had ever exhibited.

Because its creators had a great fondness and encyclopedic knowledge of all things Batman, *Batman: The Animated Series* drew on the character's rich history in both a visual and a literary sense. The series' visual depiction of Batman incorporated elements of the classic Batman comic renderings of Bob Kane, Neal Adams, Marshall Rogers and Frank Miller — Batman wore a dark blue and gray costume with a flowing cape and long ears on its cowl that was a perfect summation of the character's basic appearance from the late

1930s to the early 1990s. And the series perfectly captured the essence of Batman's personality as well. He was grim and determined, but he was still very much in control of his actions and emotions. There was darkness in his soul because he was born from great tragedy, but he still could still take some satisfaction in the fact that his mission was truly helping Gotham City and its citizens.

Interestingly, even though Timm, Radomski and company chose to feature the most well-known version of Robin in the series (the teenage Dick Grayson Robin), they depicted the character wearing a costume similar to the one worn by the Tim Drake Robin of the 1990s. This decision was a perfect example of the manner in which *Batman: The Animated Series* synthesized old and new elements of Batman history into a powerful, singular vision of the characters' world. Incidentally, Robin's origin was meticulously chronicled in one of the series' best episodes. The two-part "Robin's Reckoning" written by Randy Rogel was a thoughtful adaptation of the character's comic origin story "Robin — the Boy Wonder" (*Detective Comics* #38, April 1940).

Other episodes of *Batman: The Animated Series* were based on classic Batman comic book tales by writers such as Denny O'Neil and Steve Englehart. In fact, O'Neil actually adapted several of his landmark 1970s Ra's Al Ghul stories into scripts for the series. But even the tales featured in *Batman: The Animated Series* that were written specifically for the program often turned out to be every bit as powerful as Batman's best comic book adventures. The series' writers regularly captured the perfect blend of realistic crime drama and fanciful adventure that had made Batman such a popular character for over five decades.

The episodic nature of *Batman: The Animated Series* allowed its creators to take time to really develop their characters — and not just main characters like Batman, Robin, Joker, Penguin, Riddler and Catwoman. The series also explored "background" characters such as Batman's allies Commissioner Gordon and Alfred. It also presented depictions of a wide range of comic villains that had never been portrayed on screen before, such as Two-Face, Killer Croc, Rupert Thorne and the previously mentioned Ra's Al Ghul.

In fact, *Batman: The Animated Series*' depiction of several Batman comic villains turned out to be so powerful that many Batman fans ended up considering them to be the "definitive" versions of the characters. For example, the series imagined Mr. Freeze as much more than just a mad scientist with an ice gun. In an episode called "Heart of Ice" written by Dini and directed by Timm, Mr. Freeze was revealed to be Dr. Victor Fries, a cryogenic researcher who was desperately trying to save his beloved wife Nora from an incurable disease.

And the series' depiction of Two-Face was especially riveting. In a two-part episode simply called "Two-Face," Gotham City District Attorney Harvey Dent was revealed to have been suffering from dual personality disorder long before the accident that disfigured half of his face and turned him to a life of crime. So the dark side of Dent was very much there even before his disfigurement — his transformation into Two-Face basically just revealed the troubled person that he had *always* been. "Two-Face" was written by Burnett and Rogel, and directed by Kevin Altieri. Giving characters such as Mr. Freeze and Two-Face backstories that explained their motivations made them more emotionally deep and tragic than they had ever been before.

Batman: The Animated Series' depiction of the Penguin was very interesting, because it was directly inspired by the *Batman Returns* version of the character. In the series, the Penguin looked almost exactly like Danny Devito's Penguin, complete with flipper-like hands. The Penguin was essentially the only character in *Batman: The Animated Series* that was a direct carryover from Warner's live-action Batman films. Of course, since *Batman: The Animated Series* was very much a program designed for younger audiences, the Penguin's crimes in the series were nowhere near as grotesque or violent as the crimes of the *Batman Returns* Penguin!

Batman: The Animated Series even created a few new characters that ended up becoming regulars in Batman's comic book world. The most memorable of these was the Joker's female assistant Harley Quinn. Clad in a red and black harlequin costume complete with a three-pointed jester hat, Harley first appeared as a very minor background character. But the series' creators realized they had a character with great potential on their hands and expanded her role, making her a regular (and very vocal) presence in most every Joker episode. For some inexplicable reason, Harley was in love with her demented boss, so their relationship was a nightmarish mix of horribly skewed domesticity, insanity and violence. The scenes between the Joker and Harley were often quite funny, but at times the emotional and physical abuse that Joker regularly inflicted on Harley also made them very disturbing.

Batman: The Animated Series featured backgrounds that were every bit as memorable as its depictions of Batman and his supporting cast. The series rendered Gotham City in dark tones that recalled the ominous feel of the 1989 *Batman* film. *Batman: The Animated Series* followed *Batman*'s lead in another way as well — like the film, the series featured non-costumed gangsters who looked as if they had been pulled from a 1940s film noir movie. This mix of fantastic costumes and antique clothing styles worked every bit as well in *Batman: The Animated Series* as it had worked in *Batman*, creating a visually arresting clash of new and old that kept the series from being tied to any specific time period.

Batman: The Animated Series also featured memorable designs of Batman's crimefighting equipment. Its Batmobile was a sleek auto that blended the streamlined look of the 1940s with the imposing power of a modern race car. And the series' Batcave boasted an incredible array of computers, communication equipment and weaponry.

Perhaps *Batman: The Animated Series*' only real weakness was the varying quality of its animation. Because a number of different animation companies actually created the images used to animate individual episodes, the overall consistency of the series suffered — some episodes looked incredibly detailed and realistic, while others looked like not particularly well-made kiddie cartoons. However, this weakness seemed like a very minor one given the high quality of the series as a whole.

Batman: The Animated Series featured great voice acting as well as great visuals and storytelling. Voice director Andrea Romano chose the perfect actors to voice all of the characters in Batman's world. Batman was played by Kevin Conroy, whose deep, determined voice perfectly meshed with the Caped Crusader's appearance and personality. Conroy was equally good at playing Bruce Wayne, adopting a light, carefree tone that served to illustrate that in many ways Bruce Wayne was a mask for Batman, not the other way around.

Conroy's performance was matched in quality by series regulars Loren Lester as Robin/Dick Grayson, Efrem Zimbalist, Jr. as Alfred, and Bob Hastings as Commissioner Gordon. The dialogue of Batman's villains was memorably realized by actors such as Mark Hamill (The Joker), Paul Williams (The Penguin), Adrienne Barbeau (The Catwoman), John Glover (The Riddler), Richard Moll (Two-Face), and Arleen Sorkin (Harley Quinn). Mark Hamill's portrayal of the Joker was particularly inspired — he brought a menacing lunacy to the part that served as the perfect counterpoint to Conroy's controlled, no-nonsense portrayal of Batman.

Batman: The Animated Series also featured a number of notable guest stars who provided voices for individual episodes, including Ed Begley, Jr., Heather Locklear and Malcolm McDowell. But the most notable of these stars was probably the 1960s TV Batman Adam West: In an episode entitled "Beware the Gray Ghost," he played an actor named Simon Trent who had found fleeting TV fame playing a costumed character called the Gray Ghost.

The musical score for *Batman: The Animated Series* was essential in helping the series to set its darkly adventurous tone. Danny Elfman's most memorable Batman film composition served as the program's musical starting point. He reworked his "Batman Theme" from the 1989 *Batman* into a theme for the series that opened and closed most of its episodes. A number of different composers wrote music specifically for the program, including Shirley Walker, Lolita Ritmanis, and Michael McCuistion. (As we discussed earlier in the book, Walker was the conductor of Elfman's *Batman* music.) Their *Batman: The Animated Series* music consisted almost entirely of memorable, dramatic orchestral pieces that stayed true to the spirit of Elfman's theme music.

Because of its extremely high quality, *Batman: The Animated Series* reaped far greater commercial and critical success than one would expect from a half-hour animated TV show primarily geared for younger viewers. The series had been so well-received that Fox chose to insert the program into its prime-time schedule in late 1992–early 1993 in an effort to give the show a chance to attract more adult viewers. While it did not generate the kind of prime-time viewership necessary to convince Fox to keep it in an prime-time slot long-term, the very fact that the network was willing to give the show such a slot in the first place demonstrated how highly regarded the program had become.

The success of *Batman: The Animated Series* led Warner Bros. to request that the series' creative team make a direct-to-video film based on the program. The film would be directed by Timm and Radomski, and written by Burnett and Dini. Two other *Batman: The Animated Series* writers, Martin Pasko and Michael Reaves, would work on scripting the film as well. In early 1993, Warner Bros. decided that *Batman: The Animated Series* deserved a shot at an even larger audience — they upgraded the film to a theatrical work. So Timm, Radomski and company were given a very tight schedule to prepare their film for a late 1993 theatrical release.[1] They made this deadline, and their film *Batman: Mask of the Phantasm* premiered in U.S. theatres on Christmas Day 1993.

Batman: Mask of the Phantasm was set within the continuity of *Batman: The Animated Series*, but the film introduced a number of new characters into that continuity. The most notable of these characters were Andrea Beaumont, a woman who Bruce Wayne fell in love with before adopting the guise of Batman, and the Phantasm, a costumed criminal who was murdering a number of Gotham City mobsters. We'll discuss the surprise connection between the two characters as we go over the film.

Batman: Mask of the Phantasm opens with Batman raiding the operation of a Gotham City gangster named Chuckie Sol. As Sol tries to escape from Batman, he is attacked by a mysterious cloaked figure with a skull-like mask that looks much like the popular personification of death known as the Grim Reaper. The figure even wears a scythe-bladed handpiece that recalls the Grim Reaper's fabled scythe. Sol tries to kill the figure by running over it with his car, but instead ends up dead himself when the car crashes.

The next day, Gotham City Councilman Arthur Reeves holds a press conference blaming Batman for Sol's death. Soon after, Reeves has a phone conversation with his old friend Andrea Beaumont — Reeves worked for Andrea's father Carl in the years before he began his political career. Andrea has been away from Gotham for quite some time, and she is returning to take care of some financial matters. Reeves then attends a party at Wayne Manor, and he brings up the subject of Andrea to Bruce. Bruce pretends to be unfazed by the mention of Andrea's name, but inwardly he is heartbroken.

Bruce's relationship to Andrea is then revealed in a flashback sequence. Bruce had first met Andrea when he was a young man, while he was standing in front of his parents' graves. He was immediately attracted to her, but he could not give in to that attraction because of his "plan." Of course, this plan was to become a masked crimefighter in order to avenge the murder of his parents.

Not long after meeting Andrea, Bruce put his plan into action for the first time. He donned a ski mask to hide his identity and attacked a group of burglars, but he was almost killed when he jumped on the top of a speeding truck that one of the burglars was fleeing in. Back at Wayne Manor, Bruce told Alfred that his plan was working, but he needed to find a way to make criminals fear him. Their discussion was interrupted by a visit from Andrea—this time around, Bruce gave in to his attraction and kissed her.

Back to the present day—Gotham gangster Buzz Bronski goes to visit Sol's fresh grave, but his visit is interrupted by the same cloaked figure that had attacked Sol. The figure attacks Bronski as well, killing him by crushing him under a massive grave marker. Reeves blames Batman for Bronski's murder as well as Sol's, and presses Commissioner Gordon to bring the crimefighter into custody. Batman goes to the cemetery where Buzz was killed in order to investigate the crime, which happens to be the same cemetery where his parents are buried. He visits their graves, and Andrea sees him there—this leads her to deduce that Batman's true identity is Bruce Wayne.

In another flashback sequence, we learn that the relationship between Bruce and Andrea had grown quite serious. While visiting the Gotham World's Fair, Andrea convinced Bruce to go to her home to meet her father Carl for the first time. Bruce's chat with Carl was cut short when a Gotham gangster named Salvatore Valestra showed up at the Beaumont home to meet with Carl. Bruce was immediately suspicious of Valestra's intentions, and even *more* suspicious of one of his underlings, a menacing young man with a noticeably long face.

However, Bruce's suspicions had to take a backseat to a more pressing problem—he and Andrea encountered a shopkeeper being robbed by a biker gang. Bruce fought the gang, but they got the best of him because he was distracted by worrying about Andrea's safety. This led Bruce to think that Andrea was compromising his plan, and he didn't know what to do. He went to his parents' graves and told them that he would not be able to keep his vow to fight crime because Andrea had made him happy. Not long afterward, Bruce proposed to Andrea outside of Wayne Manor—she accepted, but their happiness was interrupted by a huge swarm of bats that flew out from a cave underneath the manor.

Bruce took Andrea home so that they could tell their wonderful news to Carl, but he was again meeting with Valestra. They decided to wait until the next day to tell him, but that day would not come. Carl had been embezzling money from Valestra, as well as Valestra's partners Chuckie Sol and Buzz Bronski—the mobsters had discovered this, and they threatened to kill Carl if he did not pay them back their money immediately. Unable to raise the money to pay the gangsters, Carl chose to flee the country and take Andrea with him. Obviously, this put an end to the engagement of Andrea and Bruce. Bruce was then left alone with his plan, and he donned his Batman costume for the first time.

Back to the present day again—Valestra goes to the abandoned, broken down Gotham World's Fair site, because the site is being used as a hideout by the Joker. Valestra meets with the Joker and tries to persuade him to kill Batman, because Valestra is convinced that it is Batman who killed Sol and Bronski. Valestra tells the Joker that Batman might even come after *them* as well. The Joker says he will help Valestra because he wants to see him smile.

While investigating the mobster murders, Batman connects Sol and Bronski to Valestra. The crimefighter goes to Valestra's house to question him. Batman does not find Valestra, but he does find a photo of the gangsters with Carl Beaumont. Batman finally meets up with Andrea again at her hotel room to question her about her father's connection to the mobsters. She won't answer any of his questions, so he angrily leaves.

Later, the cloaked figure goes to Valestra's home to kill him, but the figure only finds Valestra's corpse — the Joker has killed the gangster by injecting him with his Joker venom. The Joker has also rigged Valestra's home with explosives in the hopes of killing Batman should the crimefighter try to attack Valestra. The figure escapes the Joker's trap, but is then intercepted by Batman, who gives chase in his Batwing aircraft. Batman ejects the Batwing while pursuing the figure, but he ends up in far more trouble than he bargained for — the Gotham Police swarm him, trapping him at a construction site. A Gotham Police SWAT team almost brings Batman down, but the crimefighter is able to momentarily escape when he diverts the SWAT's attention by placing his cape and cowl on a sawhorse. Wounded and unmasked, he runs through the streets of Gotham with seemingly no way out of his predicament, but just then Andrea pulls up in her car and takes him back to Wayne Manor.

At the manor, Bruce and Andrea reconcile, and hope that the time has truly come for their love for one another. Andrea tells Bruce that she believes the mobster-killing figure is really her father. This leads Bruce to fear that his pursuit of Carl will stand between him and Andrea. But it turns out that they face far more unfinished business than just Andrea's father. Bruce looks at a photo of Carl, Valestra, Sol and Bronski, and notices that the gangsters' underling that had bothered him years ago is in the photo as well. It dawns on Bruce that the underling is none other than the Joker — the madman was working for the gangsters before he took the fall into the vat of chemicals that turned his skin white and his hair green.

Meanwhile, the Joker goes to see Reeves because he has figured out the connection between the councilman, Carl Beaumont and the mobsters. The Joker injects Reeves with his Joker venom, sending Reeves to the hospital. Batman comes into the hospital to question Reeves, and Reeves tells the crimefighter that *he* was the one who divulged Beaumont's whereabouts to the mobsters years ago. Batman goes to Andrea's hotel to share this information with her, but she is not there — what *is* there is a bomb flown in by the Joker, which he escapes. However, the bomb was never meant for Batman, it was meant for Andrea — the Joker has figured out that the real identity of the cloaked figure is Andrea.

In a final flashback sequence, we learn that the "pre–Joker" Joker was sent by the mobsters to find Carl Beaumont and kill him. Andrea walked in right after the murder and saw the madman leaving the scene. So it is not Carl, but his daughter, who has been seeking revenge against the gangsters all of this time.

Back to the present day again — Andrea, dressed in her cloak and scythe, goes to the Joker's World's Fair hideout to finally settle her score with the madman. They fight, but the Joker escapes. Batman arrives on the scene to help Andrea, but also to tell her that she needs to end her insane thirst for revenge. She refuses his appeal, and disappears in a cloud of smoke. Batman then engages in an epic battle with the Joker, who has rigged the World's

Fair grounds with tons of explosives. Just as Batman defeats the Joker, Andrea reappears and grabs the Joker, whisking him away in another cloud of smoke.

Later, Batman has returned to the Batcave, where he sits physically and emotionally drained. Alfred praises him for never having fallen into an abyss of vengeance the way that Andrea did. Andrea is then shown on a cruise ship, basically headed for nowhere, tormented and alone. The film closes with Batman leaping from a building, responding to the Batsignal.

Unfortunately, Warner Bros. did not back up *Batman: Mask of the Phantasm*'s release with any significant promotional efforts, so the film did very little box office business. As mentioned at the beginning of the chapter, the movie was in and out of theatres within a matter of just a few weeks. But the diehard Batman fans who sought out the film were given the opportunity to see their hero return to the big screen in a motion picture that was much more true to the character than *Batman Returns*.

That said, however, *Batman: Mask of the Phantasm* was not necessarily perfect. The film's plot was so ambitious that it ended up coming across as rather muddled. The movie tried to tackle Batman's origin, the Joker's "pre-Joker" past, the Phantasm's origin, the love of Bruce Wayne's life, and the maneuvers of several powerful Gotham mobsters. To make matters worse, the film was trying to cram all of these story elements into an extremely short run time — *Batman: Mask of the Phantasm* clocked in at only 77 minutes!

The Phantasm turned out to be a particularly confusing character for a number of reasons. First off, the character was never referred to by name throughout the entire movie! You might have noticed that in my synopsis of the film, I always referred to the character as the "cloaked figure"—now you know I did that because the name "Phantasm" was never uttered even one time in the film.

This confusion was compounded by the fact that the Phantasm looked and acted almost exactly like a differently-named villain that had been prominently featured in a popular 1987 Batman comic series. The characters were so similar that it is worth taking a moment to examine the series in some detail. *Batman: Year Two* initially ran in *Detective Comics* #575, June 1987, through *Detective Comics* #578, September 1987, and was basically a sequel to Frank Miller's 1986 series *Batman: Year One*. *Batman: Year Two* was written by Mike W. Barr and primarily illustrated by Todd McFarlane, an artist who would eventually go on to become one of the comic industry's most influential creators.

In the series, Batman confronts a seemingly unbeatable villain known as the Reaper who is a vigilante crimefighter like Batman, but with one major difference—he is willing to kill the criminals he fights. The Reaper is mysterious cloaked figure with a skull-like mask that looks much like the popular personification of death known as the Grim Reaper. The Reaper even wears scythe-bladed handpieces that recall the Grim Reaper's fabled scythe. When Batman is unable to best the Reaper in hand-to-hand combat, he decides to start carrying a gun for the first time. But it is not just *any* gun — it is the gun that Joe Chill used to murder Bruce Wayne's parents.

Batman's turmoil is eased by the happiness that his alter ego has found — Bruce Wayne has fallen in love with a woman named Rachel Caspian, and Bruce and Rachel become engaged. Batman ends up forming an alliance with some Gotham gangsters in order to hunt down the Reaper, and one of these gangsters is none other than Joe Chill. While Batman and Chill are hunting the Reaper together, Batman eventually confronts Chill about the Wayne murders. Batman is prepared to use Chill's own gun on the criminal to avenge his parents' deaths, but before he can make this fateful decision the Reaper intervenes and murders Chill. The Reaper then commits suicide during his final struggle with Batman.

The true identity of the Reaper turns out Rachel's father, Judson. To atone for her father's sins, Rachel breaks off her engagement with Bruce and decides to become a nun. At the end of the series, Bruce decides that he will go back to fighting crime as Batman without the use of the gun that killed his parents—he will not let the evil that created him lead him down a path of murderous vengeance.

Obviously, this synopsis of *Batman: Year Two* clearly illustrates the fact that the Reaper and the Phantasm were *very* similar characters—they both wore the same style of costume, murdered criminals, and had a father/daughter dynamic that intertwined with Bruce Wayne's life. Timm, Radomski and company undoubtedly based the Phantasm on the Reaper, and their decision to do this was certainly warranted—after all, fictional characters are constantly being revised and tweaked by their creators. That said, however, when *Batman: Mask of the Phantasm* was released, there had to have been quite a few Batman fans who were confused as to whether the Phantasm was a brand-new character, or one that was somehow tied to the events of *Batman: Year Two*.

I hate to make things even *more* confusing, but I feel I should point out that there was yet another skull-masked, cloak-wearing, scythe-wielding villain called the Reaper that Batman faced in the comics. This version of the Reaper appeared in only one story, but it was a memorable one—in fact, it became widely regarded as one of the best Batman comic stories of all time. "Night of the Reaper" was written by Denny O'Neil and illustrated by Neal Adams, and was originally published in *Batman #237*, December 1971. In the story, a Jewish doctor dresses in a Reaper costume in order to take revenge on a Nazi war criminal. The doctor's quest for vengeance ends up spiraling out of control, which leads him into a deadly confrontation with Batman.

The Phantasm's actions in *Batman: Mask of the Phantasm* were every bit as puzzling as the character's basic premise. Throughout the film, the Phantasm disappears and reappears at will in clouds of smoke, performs near-superhuman feats of strength and speed, and appears to be able to float. When the Phantasm is revealed to be Andrea, a woman of seemingly average size and strength, it leaves one to wonder just how she was able to do all of those incredible things. Oddly, the film never addresses this question in any way.

And just what did Andrea end up doing with the defeated Joker at the end of the film? They disappear into one of her unexplained clouds of smoke, and we are left without the slightest idea of what they might do to one another. Will she kill him? Will he kill her? Their confrontation is left even *more* unresolved when we see Andrea on a cruise ship at the very end of the film—obviously, whatever ended up happening between the two of them did not stop Andrea from being able to get a chance to take a relaxing sea voyage to "get away from it all!"

But *Batman: Mask of the Phantasm*'s few weaknesses do not even come close to compromising the overall high quality of the film. All of the elements that made *Batman: The Animated Series* such an incredible program are very much in evidence in *Batman: Mask of the Phantasm*. Timm, Radomski and company present a powerful interpretation of Batman and his world in the film, and that unquestionably makes its release a high watermark in the character's history.

There are a few elements of the sound of *Batman: Mask of the Phantasm* that should be singled out for praise as well. Shirley Walker's musical score for the film is excellent, matching the quality of the music she had composed for *Batman: The Animated Series*. And of course, the movie's voice talent is top-notch, especially Kevin Conroy as Bruce Wayne/Batman, Mark Hamill as the Joker, and Efrem Zimbalist, Jr. as Alfred.

It is worth noting that *Batman: Mask of the Phantasm* was influenced by Frank Miller and David Mazzucchelli's *Batman: Year One* almost as much as it was influenced by *Batman: Year Two*. In fact, two of the most memorable sequences in the film were obviously inspired by Miller and Mazzucchelli's series. Those sequences are the one in which a pre–Batman Bruce makes his very first attempt at fighting crime, and the one in which Batman is cornered by an aggressive Gotham Police SWAT team. These sequences do not follow their *Batman: Year One* counterparts panel-for-panel, but they are so similar that there is no doubt that they were directly based on Miller's work.

Batman: Mask of the Phantasm may not have found the audience it deserved during its theatrical run, but it did find that audience once it was released on home video. Warner Bros. first made the film available to the home video market on VHS tape in spring 1994. All of the Batman fans who missed the film's bow on the big screen got to experience it in the comfort of their own homes, and the word spread as to just how good it was very quickly. *Batman: Mask of the Phantasm* has been highly regarded by Batman fans ever since that initial home video release. Warner first released a DVD version of the film in late 1999, and the film has remained available in that format up to the present day.

The success of *Batman: The Animated Series* came at a very opportune time for the Batman character. It kept the character in the public eye as Warner Bros. decided just how to move forward with their Batman franchise after their dissatisfaction with *Batman Returns*. Next chapter, we'll examine what was happening on the Batman landscape as Warner was making plans for their next Batman feature film.

12

Between Burton and Schumacher, 1993–1995

Not surprisingly, the success of *Batman: The Animated Series* dominated the Batman character's world as Warner Bros. was making plans for their next live-action Batman feature film after director Tim Burton's 1992 film *Batman Returns*. First off, the series spawned several well-received Batman comic titles. Debuting in October 1992, *The Batman Adventures* featured stories created in the visual and narrative style of the TV series. *The Batman Adventures* eventually gave way to the new title *Batman and Robin Adventures*, which eventually gave way to another new title, *Gotham Adventures*, which eventually gave way to yet *another* new title that bore the comic's original 1992 title, *Batman Adventures*. But regardless of the title, all of these comics stayed true to the tone established in *Batman: The Animated Series*.

In 1994, a stand-alone comic inspired by the series, *Mad Love*, was released. Written by Paul Dini and illustrated by Bruce Timm, it provided their Harley Quinn character with a detailed origin. The story revealed that Harley was a psychiatrist named Harleen Quinzel who fell in love with the Joker in the process of trying to rehabilitate him. So she designed her Harley Quinn costume in order to become the Joker's partner, both in love and in crime.

Of course, *Mad Love* shows that being in love with the Joker is no easy task. The Joker becomes annoyed with Harley and throws her out of their hideout. Harley decides that her problems with the Joker are not due to the fact that he is an insane murderer — they are due to the fact that Batman continues to make the Joker's life so miserable. So Harley alone concocts a scheme to capture Batman and kill him. She almost succeeds, but Batman convinces her to call the Joker to come and witness her moment of triumph.

The Joker comes, and actually *saves* Batman from Harley's deathtrap; if *he* isn't going to kill Batman, then no one is, especially not his lowly assistant. In fact, the Joker is so enraged with Harley's ambition that he knocks her out of a window, almost killing her. *Mad Love* ends with Harley vowing to end her relationship with the Joker — but when she receives a rose from him, she is smitten all over again. *Mad Love*'s tale of Harley's self-destructive love was so wonderfully written and illustrated that it won the prestigious Eisner Award for the best single comic issue of 1994.

The success of *Batman: The Animated Series* also had a tremendous impact on the manufacturing and sale of Batman toys. Throughout the 1990s, Kenner Toys released dozens upon dozens of *Batman: The Animated Series* action figures and accessories, creating the most comprehensive collection of Batman toys ever offered by a single toy company. Batman,

Robin, Batgirl, Joker, Penguin, Riddler and Catwoman had been offered for sale in action figure form by a number of companies throughout the years, but the variety of Kenner's *Batman: The Animated Series* line was truly staggering. Along with the aforementioned characters, Batman fans could collect action figures of virtually every major character ever featured in the series. And since the series got around to featuring most every major character that had ever appeared in Batman's comic book world, this meant that Kenner's *Animated Series* line literally covered a huge portion of Batman's 50-plus year history.

Batman was faced with one of the biggest challenges of his crimefighting career in 1993. In an ongoing series entitled *Knightfall* which ran in the character's monthly comic book titles, Batman faced a villain known as Bane, who had been created by writers Chuck Dixon and Doug Moench, and artist Graham Nolan. Bane had become incredibly powerful after being injected with an experimental steroid known as "Venom." In an effort to wear Batman down and eventually destroy him, Bane set all of the hero's most deadly foes loose from Arkham Asylum, the mental hospital where they were being held. For a number of weeks, Batman labored to capture all of the escapees, which left him in a severely weakened physical and mental state. Bane, having deduced Batman's real identity, then attacked the fatigued crimefighter at Wayne Manor in *Batman* #497, July 1993. Batman tried to fight the criminal, but it was no use — Bane overpowered him and broke his back, leaving him totally paralyzed.

Obviously, Batman could no longer fight crime in his condition, so in a continuation of the *Knightfall* series entitled *Knightquest*, he asked a superhuman hero named Azrael to assume the guise of Batman for him. Azrael, whose real identity was Jean Paul Valley, agreed to take over as Batman — but his Batman was very different from Bruce's Batman. First off, Jean Paul adopted a heavily armored costume that looked nothing like Bruce's costume. Also, Jean Paul's Batman showed none of the regard for human life that Bruce had shown over the years; he eventually became so violent that Bruce demanded that he give up being Batman. Jean Paul refused to give up his new identity without a fight, so Bruce rehabilitated himself over time, and eventually donned his old costume to confront his successor. In the final part of the *Knightfall* series (*KnightsEnd*), the "Bruce Batman" battled the "Jean Paul Batman," and the "Bruce Batman" emerged victorious; in *Batman: Legends of the Dark Knight* #63, August 1994, Jean Paul relinquished the mantle of Batman once and for all.

The early 1990s also saw the Batman character enter into a whole new realm of entertainment — the amusement park. During this time, the Six Flags Corporation was acquired by Time Warner, the parent company of DC Comics and Warner Bros. (As we discussed earlier in the book, Warner Communications had been the parent company of DC and Warner for a number of years— Warner Communications merged with Time in 1990, forming Time Warner.) So Six Flags was able to start using the likenesses of all of the characters owned by Time Warner at their amusement parks. Of course, Batman was one of these characters, and Six Flags made him a *big* part of many of their rides and attractions.

One of the first and most ambitious Batman-themed projects undertaken by Six Flags was the roller coaster Batman: The Ride, which opened at Six Flags Great America near Chicago, Illinois in 1992. Batman: The Ride was the world's first inverted roller coaster, and it ended up being so popular that Six Flags built new versions of the ride at a number of their other parks throughout the United States. However, Batman: The Ride was only one of the many rides and attractions featuring the character that Six Flags developed. A Batman fan could take a trip to most any Six Flags park and ride a wide variety of Batman-themed rides, watch a live stage show featuring Batman and many of his supporting characters, and of course, buy a wealth of Batman merchandise at a park gift shop. In 1998, Time Warner sold Six Flags to another corporation — but Six Flags has continued to feature Batman and other Time Warner characters at their parks to this day.

Batman's continued popularity in many forms of entertainment certainly suggested that the public would welcome him back when he returned to the big screen — and that is just what happened when director Joel Schumacher's film *Batman Forever* was released in 1995. We'll discuss that film in detail in the next chapter.

13

Batman Forever (1995)

Cast: Val Kilmer (Batman/Bruce Wayne), Tommy Lee Jones (Harvey Dent/Two-Face), Jim Carrey (Edward Nygma/The Riddler), Nicole Kidman (Dr. Chase Meridian), Chris O'Donnell (Dick Grayson/Robin), Michael Gough (Alfred), Pat Hingle (Commissioner Gordon), Drew Barrymore (Sugar), Debi Mazar (Spice), Ed Begley, Jr. (Fred Stickley), Elizabeth Sanders (Gossip Gerty), Rene Auberjonois (Dr. Burton), Joe Grifasi (Bank Guard), Philip Moon (Newcaster), Jessica Tuck (Female Newscaster), Dennis Paladino (Crime Boss Moroni), Kimberly Scott (Margaret), Michael Paul Chan (Executive), Jon Favreau (Assistant), Greg Lauren (Aide), Ramsey Ellis (Young Bruce Wayne), Michael Scranton (Thomas Wayne), Eileen Seeley (Martha Wayne), David U. Hodges (Jack Napier), Jack Betts (Fisherman), Tim Jackson (Municipal Police Guard), Daniel Reichert (Ringmaster), Glory Fioramonti (Mom Grayson), Larry A. Lee (Dad Grayson), Bruce Roberts (Handsome Reporter), George Wallace (Mayor), Bob Zmuda (Electronic Store Owner), Rebecca Budig (Teenage Girl), Don "The Dragon" Wilson (Gang Leader), Sydney D. Minckler (Teen Gang Member), Maxine Jones (Girl on Corner #1), Terry Ellis (Girl on Corner #2), Cindy Herron (Girl on Corner #3), Dawn Robinson (Girl on Corner #4), Gary Kasper (pilot), Amanda Trees (Paparazzi Reporter), Andrea Fletcher (Reporter), Ria Coyne (Socialite), Jed Curtis (Chubby Businessman), William Mesnik (Bald Guy), Marga Gomez (Journalist), Kelly Vaughn (Showgirl), John Fink (Deputy), Noby Arden, Marlene Bologna, Danny Castle, Troy S. Wolfe (Trapeze Performers), Christopher Caso, Gary Clayton, Oscar Dillon, Keith Graham, Kevin Grevioux, Mark Hicks, Corey Jacoby, Randy Lamb, Maurice Lamont, Sidney S. Liufau, Brad Martin, Deron McBee, Mario Mugavero, Joey Nelson, Jim Palmer, Robert Pavell, Pee Wee Piemonte, Peter Radon, Francois Rodrigue, Joe Sabatino, Mike Sabatino, Ofer Samra, Matt Sigloch, Mike Smith (Harvey's Thugs). *Producers:* Tim Burton, Peter MacGregor-Scott. *Assistant Producer:* Mitchell Dauterive. *Executive Producers:* Benjamin Melniker, Michael Uslan. *Director:* Joel Schumacher. *Unit Production Manager:* Ralph Burris. *Screenplay:* Lee Batchler, Janet Scott Batchler, Akiva Goldsman (Story by Lee Batchler and Janet Scott Batchler, based on characters created by Bob Kane). *Cinematography:* Stephen Goldblatt. *Casting:* Mali Finn. *Production Designer:* Barbara Ling. *Art Directors:* Chris Burian-Mohr, James Hegedus, Joseph P. Lucky. *Set Designers:* James Bayliss, Richard Berger, Peter J. Kelly, Patricia Klawonn, Gene Nollmann, Brad Ricker. *Set Decorator:* Elise "Cricket" Rowland. *Costume Designers:* Bob Ringwood, Ingrid Ferrin. *Music:* Elliot Goldenthal. *Editor:* Dennis Virkler. *First Assistant Director:* William Elvin. *Second Assistant Director:* Alan Edmisten. *Sound:* Petur Hliddal. *Key Makeup Artist:* Ve Neill. *Special Makeup Designer:* Rick Baker. *Key Hair Stylist:* Yolanda Toussieng. *Visual Effects Supervisor:* John Dykstra. *Stunt Coordinator:* Conrad Palmisano. *Special Effects Supervisor:* Thomas L. Fisher. *Studio:* Warner Bros. *Length:* 122 minutes. *United States Release Date:* June 16, 1995.

As we discussed in Chapter 10, the bad press and disappointing box office numbers that Tim Burton's *Batman Returns* had inflicted on Warner Bros. led the studio to decide

Val Kilmer as Batman and Chris O'Donnell as Robin in *Batman Forever* (1995).

that its Batman film franchise needed to be taken in a different direction. So in June 1993, Warner hired Joel Schumacher to direct their third live-action Batman film instead of Burton. The studio believed that Schumacher would be able to steer the franchise back toward the generally lighter, more mainstream, audience-friendly tone of the 1989 *Batman*.

Warner's confidence in Schumacher was primarily based on the fact that the director had helmed a number of stylish and commercially successful films such as *St. Elmo's Fire* (1985), *The Lost Boys* (1987) and *Flatliners* (1990). Plus, these films had starred some of Hollywood's hottest young actors and actresses, which made them especially appealing to younger audiences. A director with a track record of making hit films that connected with

Tommy Lee Jones as Two-Face and Jim Carrey as the Riddler in *Batman Forever* (1995).

the sensibilities of a younger demographic seemed to be the perfect candidate to again make Batman "fun" for movie audiences of all ages.

This change in directors was a decision that made winners out of everyone involved. Of course, Warner Bros. benefited because the change gave them the chance to plot a new course for their Batman film franchise. And Schumacher benefited because the change instantly propelled his career to new heights—after all, he had just been handed the reins to a gargantuan film project that would surely command worldwide attention.

Ironically, Burton benefited from this change as well, even though he was the one who was in essence losing his job! While it was true that the Batman character had brought incredible success to the director, he had always been somewhat uncomfortable with this success, especially the success that stemmed from the 1989 *Batman*. Burton had made it clear on a number of occasions that he felt *Batman* wasn't *his* movie nearly as much as it was simply a Batman movie.[1]

The success of *Batman* allowed Burton to make *Batman Returns* into a film that truly was *his*—but that film's lack of interest in Batman himself made it fairly obvious that the character was simply no longer a part of what Burton really wanted to do as a filmmaker. Being freed from directing a third Batman film meant that the director would be given the chance to make films that were much more meaningful to him. And Burton would make the most of that chance—his post–Batman directorial success would prove that it was a positive artistic step for him to move on from the character.

Incidentally, Warner's decision to ease Burton out of their Batman film franchise did not mean that the director's ties to the franchise would be completely severed. The studio chose to credit Burton as producer of their third live-action Batman film, even though in reality Burton would hardly be involved in the film's creation. Burton's success had definitely led him to be recognized as a "name brand," so keeping that name connected to the franchise was a decision that benefited both Burton and the studio.

Warner Bros. and Schumacher chose the husband-and-wife team of Lee Batchler and Janet Scott Batchler to script their Batman film. The initial drafts of the screenplay were written by the Batchlers, and then Schumacher brought in Akiva Goldsman revise the Batchlers' work. The finished script was given an official title, *Batman Forever*, and it was startlingly different from Warner's previous Batman films.

One of the most obvious signs of how different *Batman Forever* would be from its predecessors was that the film would feature Robin/Dick Grayson. As we discussed earlier in the book, the character was supposed to be included in both *Batman* and *Batman Returns*, but was eventually cut from both films in order to simplify their storylines. This time around, Robin/Dick was going to be such a major focus of the film that there would no chance of him getting cut a third time. The character's presence would serve to "lighten" *Batman Forever* just as he had lightened countless Batman comic stories since his 1940 debut.

However, *Batman Forever*'s Robin was going to be considerably changed from his comic book counterpart. He would still be a circus trapeze artist named Dick Grayson who performed with his family in an act called "The Flying Graysons," and the murder of his family would lead him to become a masked crimefighter. But both his age and attitude would be quite different from that of the comic book Robin. In *Batman Forever*, Dick would be not a boy when his family was killed, but a young man in his late teens or early twenties. And unlike his comic book counterpart, his reaction to their deaths would fill him with a rage and thirst for revenge that practically eclipsed his sorrow. Obviously, *Batman Forever*'s Batman and Robin would have a very different partnership than the kind of "father-son" rapport they traditionally were shown to have in the comics.

Of course, this new version of Batman and Robin would need villains to face off against—and like *Batman Returns*, *Batman Forever* was going to feature two of Batman's classic comic book adversaries. One of these adversaries had already been brought to the big screen—the Riddler, one of the villains featured in the 1966 film *Batman*, was chosen to do battle with Batman and Robin in *Batman Forever*.

The other adversary was coming to the big screen for the very first time—Two-Face had remained one of Batman's most memorable comic book villains ever since his debut in the early 1940s, but he had never been depicted in a Batman motion picture. In fact, there had been only one screen version of the character of *any* kind in his 50 plus-year history—as noted in Chapter 11, he was memorably realized in animated form in *Batman: The Animated Series*.

Two-Face also had several near-misses in terms of screen depictions during his first half-century. The character had almost made it to the television screen in live-action form back in the 1960s—the creators of ABC's *Batman* briefly considered adding Two-Face to their roster of villains, but probably due to the fact that his appearance was so grotesque, he was deemed unacceptable for their lighthearted take on Batman and his world.[2] And of course, a pre–Two-Face Harvey Dent was featured in the 1989 *Batman*, the role being played by Billy Dee Williams. (We'll discuss Williams' version of Dent a bit more in just a moment.) At any rate, *Batman Forever* had guaranteed itself the distinction of presenting both the first live-action version *and* the first big screen version of Two-Face.

Another big difference between *Batman Forever* and its predecessors was going to be the manner in which Batman himself was depicted. In the *Batman Forever* script, the darkness of the Batman found in *Batman* and *Batman Returns* gave way to a Batman who was struggling to emerge from the shadows of mindless violence. *Batman Forever*'s take on Batman/Bruce Wayne was that the only way Bruce could cope with the murder of his parents when he was a boy was by adopting his fearsome Batman alter ego—but as the years passed, this alter ego began to completely consume him.

This element of Batman's character was played up to a far greater degree in *Batman Forever*'s original script than it would be in the finished movie. In the script, Batman was forced to confront the fact that his violent actions were responsible for a number of lives that were lost during his battles against the Joker in *Batman* and against the Penguin in *Batman Returns*.

For example, the script included a scene showing Bruce Wayne watching a TV talk show that featured a commentator who accused Batman of being no more heroic than these criminals because of all of the death and destruction that had been left in his wake. And during one of Batman's struggles with Two-Face, the villain implied that the crimefighter was every bit as much of a killer as *he* was. The Batchler team–Goldsman Batman realized that during his previous film adventures, he had sometimes stepped over the line separating a vigilante from an out-and-out murderer. And he also realized that if he kept stepping over this line, before long his whole life would be given over to violence.

In this author's opinion, this development of Batman's character in *Batman Forever* was a highly significant and welcome change from the manner in which he had been portrayed in Warner's first two Batman films, especially *Batman Returns*. As we discussed in Chapter 10, Batman was basically depicted as a remorseless killer in *Batman Returns*, which was very upsetting for many longtime fans of the character. *Batman Forever*'s script seemed to represent a conscious decision on the part of Warner Bros. to give their Batman the moral high ground he had always held in the comics. In fact, one could almost interpret the script as a direct apology to Batman fans for the scenes in *Batman* and *Batman Returns* that depicted the character as being willing, if not eager, to take human lives in his fight against crime.

At any rate, the Batman/Bruce Wayne of the *Batman Forever* script was trying to reconcile his two identities into one life that both identities could live with. The arrival of Dick Grayson, a young man facing a tragedy so much like Bruce's own, served to highlight the fact that if Bruce wanted to hold onto his sanity, he had to come to grips with the anger and grief inside him that had led him to become Batman.

Batman's/Bruce's characterization in *Batman Forever*'s script was made all the more intriguing by including scenes that depicted him directly blaming himself for his parents' deaths. In the script, Bruce was haunted by the fact that shortly after his parents' murders, he had read in the very last entry of his father's diary that the only reason they were going out at all that fateful night was because Bruce insisted on seeing a movie. Late in the script, Bruce gets the chance to re-read the diary, and he realizes that when he was a boy, he had misread what his father wrote—it was not Bruce, but his parents who wanted to go out to see a movie that night. This revelation helps him to move past blaming himself for the loss of his parents—and by letting go of this self-blame, he is able to come to terms with his dual identity. At the end of the script, Bruce is finally able to perceive his life as Batman as a means to seek justice instead of simply as a means to inflict violence.

Simply put, *Batman Forever*'s original script was undoubtedly a far deeper character study of Batman than any previous big screen adaptation of the character to date. Unfortunately, a substantial amount of this character material would not actually make it into the final cut of the film. Many of the scenes depicting Batman trying to come to grips with his long-held anger and grief were filmed, and they were even included in preliminary cuts of the movie. But these scenes were removed from the final version of *Batman Forever* in order to shorten the film and simplify its narrative. The script's diary scenes and most of its direct references to *Batman* and *Batman Returns* were particularly affected by these cuts. Ironically, these cuts would actually end up not simplifying, but *confusing Batman Forever*'s narrative—we'll discuss this in greater detail later in the chapter.

All of the changes that Warner's Batman film franchise was going through evidently convinced the face of the franchise that it was time for him to move on to new opportunities. In late June 1994, Michael Keaton announced that he had decided not to reprise his role as Batman/Bruce Wayne in *Batman Forever*. This split between Keaton and Warner Bros. was presented to the public as one that was completely amicable—both parties issued statements that spoke of Keaton's time with the franchise in very positive terms. However, in reality the split was not without some disagreement—reportedly Keaton did not see eye-to-eye with Schumacher over the new direction in which *Batman Forever* was taking his character.[3]

Schumacher chose 33-year-old Val Kilmer to replace Keaton. In many respects, Kilmer was an ideal choice. He bore a much closer physical resemblance to the Batman/Bruce Wayne of the comics than did Keaton; he was six feet tall, in possession of a good physique and, most importantly, he had the same kind of classic "leading man" good looks as the character in the comics. Also, he had proven himself to be an intense, charismatic actor in films such as *The Doors* (1991), in which he re-created the Doors' singer Jim Morrison's troubled life with startling realism and power.

If Kilmer had any real drawback in terms of playing Batman/Bruce Wayne, it was that he didn't really seem particularly interested in the role itself. In some of the interviews he did before *Batman Forever* was released, he indicated that he took the part simply to beef up his film resume. After all, *Batman Forever* would almost surely be a colossal hit once it was released, and the movie's success would obviously help to propel his film career to new heights. Simply put, it appeared that Kilmer considered the role to be a wise career move, but not one that held any personal significance for him.[4]

Kilmer's expressed ambivalence, if not downright glibness, about playing Batman/Bruce Wayne was somewhat troubling for some longtime fans of the character. After all, how good could Kilmer be as Batman if he cared nothing at all about the part? That said, however, while Kilmer might have been publicly flippant about portraying Batman/Bruce Wayne in *Batman Forever*, that attitude did not manifest itself in his actual performance.

Chris O'Donnell was hired for the role of Robin/Dick Grayson in *Batman Forever*. The handsome 24-year-old actor was best known for starring alongside Al Pacino in the acclaimed drama *Scent of a Woman* (1992). Like Kilmer, O'Donnell was seen as a fresh talent whose career was definitely on its way up—consequently, their pairing as Batman and Robin generated a good deal of buzz.

The casting of *Batman Forever*'s villains was also bringing the project a good deal of pre-production attention. Tommy Lee Jones was picked to play the role of Harvey Dent/Two-Face. Jones was a veteran performer who was known for his no-nonsense, almost deadpan acting style, so the role of Two-Face, with his dramatically split appearance and personality, was seen as something of a departure for the actor.

As mentioned earlier in this chapter, the pre–Two-Face Harvey Dent had been played by Billy Dee Williams in the 1989 *Batman*. Williams probably took the small part of Dent in *Batman* in the hopes that there would be a meatier part for him as Two-Face if a Batman sequel was ever produced. But when it came time to cast the role for *Batman Forever*, Schumacher chose to hire Jones over Williams. Consequently, Williams was denied the chance to expand his minor portrayal of Dent into one of Batman's most memorable villains.

Another actor by the name of Williams turned out to be one of *Batman Forever*'s nearmisses in terms of casting the film's villains. Ever since the release of the 1989 *Batman*, rumors had persisted that Robin Williams would play the part of the Riddler if the character was ever featured in a Batman sequel. But when it came time to cast *Batman Forever*, Williams passed on the role, so it was given to Jim Carrey. Carrey was a manic, rubberfaced comedian best known for starring in the comedies *Ace Ventura: Pet Detective* and *The Mask* (both 1994). Given that the general public's perception of the Riddler was still so closely associated with Frank Gorshin's delightfully hammy portrayal of the character in the 1960s *Batman* TV show and film, Carrey's nonstop comedic energy seemed like a great fit for the part.

Batman/Bruce Wayne would be given a new love interest in *Batman Forever*, one created specifically for the film. Nicole Kidman was cast as Dr. Chase Meridian, a beautiful psychologist who has moved to Gotham City to consult with the Gotham Police about Two-Face's crimes. Like all the rest of *Batman Forever*'s principal performers, Kidman was very much a "hot commodity" at the time. She had starred in a wide variety of high-profile films during the late 1980s and early 1990s, including the 1992 drama *Far and Away*, which also featured her superstar husband Tom Cruise.

Along with Batman, Robin, Two-Face, Riddler and Chase, most everything else about *Batman Forever* would be "new"— Schumacher cut loose basically all of the major creative forces behind *Batman* and *Batman Returns* in order to bring a new sensibility to his Batman film. *Batman Forever* was going to look and sound very different from its predecessors.

Well, there were a *few* holdovers from *Batman* and *Batman Returns*. Perhaps the most notable of these holdovers was costume designer Bob Ringwood. Ringwood really had his work cut out for him in *Batman Forever* just designing costumes for the film's four main characters—he designed two new Batman costumes, a Robin costume, and multiple Two-Face and Riddler costumes!

Schumacher had Ringwood make substantial changes to Batman's costume in *Batman Forever*. There were actually two distinctly different Batman costumes featured in the film. The first (the one Batman wore for the majority of the movie) was similar to the Batman costumes featured in *Batman* and *Batman Returns*. It was all black except for its bat emblem, which featured a yellow oval around a black bat silhouette. However, it differed from the earlier Warner bat costumes in that its utility belt was black, and its muscled body armor sported nipples that were molded onto its chest!

Longtime Batman fans were generally very perturbed by Schumacher's decision to have Ringwood put nipples on the Batman costume — Batman's costume was supposed to strike terror into the hearts of criminals, and nipples certainly did not help to accomplish this goal in any way. In fact, Batman's creator even weighed in on the "nipple" controversy. Bob Kane made a number of visits to the *Batman Forever* set, and during one of these visits he made it clear to Schumacher and company that he was very unhappy about this new addition to Batman's costume.[5]

Ringwood's second Batman costume featured during *Batman Forever*'s final scenes did not feature those troublesome nipples. In Batman's final confrontation with Two-Face and the Riddler, he wore an experimental costume he had been developing with sonar equipment built into its headgear. This costume was not flat black in color like Batman's earlier film costumes, but shiny gunmetal gray. It also did not feature the classic bat emblem of a black bat silhouette inside of a yellow oval like Batman's earlier film costumes had—its bat emblem was a much larger bat silhouette with no yellow oval, and it was actually molded into the costume's muscled chest armor.

Ringwood's Robin costume in *Batman Forever* was crafted out of the same kind of shiny material as Batman's second, "experimental" costume. It featured colors that were similar to the comic book Robin's 1990s look—its cape was black with yellow lining, its full bodysuit was red and green, and its mask, gloves and boots were black. The costume had the letter "R" molded into its chest armor just like the bat insignia was molded into the Batman costume's chest armor. And, like *Batman Forever*'s first Batman costume, the Robin costume sported nipples on its chest armor.

As evidenced by the nipples on Batman and Robin's costumes, Schumacher was intent on lightening the mood of Warner's Batman franchise, and bringing some humor back to the character that had been lacking in Warner's earlier Batman films, especially *Batman Returns*. This philosophy extended to the costuming of *Batman Forever*'s villains. Ringwood outfitted Two-Face and the Riddler in outrageously garish, brightly colored costumes that recalled the villains of the 1960s screen *Batman*.

Batman Forever's Two-Face was outfitted in his normal comic book–style clothes—namely, suits that were half well-tailored and conservative (to match the unscarred handsome side of his face) and half-gaudy and gangster-like (to match the scarred side of his face). However, these suits were far wilder than Two-Face's comic book garb—his "gangster side" was adorned at times with purple tiger stripes, and at other times with rhinestone and sequin patterns. And the prosthetic makeup designed for the scarred side of his face was not the deep green color of the comic book Two-Face's scarred side, but rather an almost fluorescent purple-magenta. Two-Face's makeup was designed by the noted film makeup artist Rick Baker.

The Riddler's appearance was every bit as crazy as Two-Face's. The character wore a number of different costumes in *Batman Forever*, each one gaudier than the last. His first one resembled the character's traditional comic book garb of a skintight green bodysuit emblazoned with black question marks, but as the film went on, his costumes grew more and more outlandish. One of them even featured a coat with lights woven into its fabric that flashed a pattern of green question marks.

Not only were all of *Batman Forever*'s costumes brand new, but all of the equipment in Batman and Robin's crimefighting arsenal was given a makeover as well. The Batmobile was completely redesigned by production designer Barbara Ling, illustrator Tim Flattery and special effects supervisor Tommy Fisher. The car was built by the custom vehicle construction company TFX under the supervision of Charley Zurian and Allen Pike.

Batman Forever's Batmobile featured a ribbed body highlighted with blue and white lights built into its sides, illuminated bat insignias on its hubcaps and three scalloped batwing-like tailfins. The left and right sides of the car had one tailfin each, and the third and largest tailfin jutted back from the center of the car's cockpit. The car was far more flamboyant and fanciful than any screen version of the Batmobile to date. While it might have lacked some of the real-world practicality found in the 1966 and 1989 screen Batmobiles, its dramatic design made it every bit as memorable.

Ling and Flattery also designed *Batman Forever*'s Batboat, which like their Batmobile featured a ribbed body and a batwing-like tailfin. And also like their Batmobile, it was a real, operating vehicle — it was constructed by VIP Marine, an Oregon-based boat construction company. Unfortunately, for all the time and expense that went into crafting the Batboat, it was only seen in *Batman Forever* for several moments near the end of the film. *Batman Forever* also featured a Batwing that was very similar in appearance to the Batwing used in the 1989 *Batman*. However, Ling and illustrator Matt Codd redesigned it with a ribbed body and tailfin to match the film's Batmobile and Batboat. Like *Batman*'s Batwing, this Batwing was not a full-size, operational craft but a miniature model that could only be made to fly through the magic of special effects.

In fact, special effects played a larger role in the making of *Batman Forever* than they had in Warner's previous Batman motion pictures, mainly because the art of superimposing computer-generated graphics onto film had taken a quantum leap since the late 1980s and early 1990s. In order to use this new technology to its fullest potential, Schumacher brought veteran special effects expert John Dykstra on board as *Batman Forever*'s visual effects supervisor. A substantial amount of *Batman Forever*'s action and sets ended up being realized through Dykstra's special effects team.

Dykstra's work was an important element of *Batman Forever*'s visual style, but it by no means overshadowed the film's incredible real-life sets. Ling designed dozens of sets for *Batman Forever*, and they were so ambitious that Warner's Burbank, California studios could not hold them all. Sets such as the Gotham Police Headquarters rooftop, the Gotham Hippodrome Circus, the Riddler's lair, and the Arkham Asylum exterior were built at Warner. When Warner ran out of available space for the film, several sets were built at Universal Studios in California, including the interior of Arkham. Incidentally, *Batman Forever* would end up holding the distinction of being the first live-action Batman screen work to feature a depiction of Arkham Asylum.

Batman Forever needed still *more* room, so the Dome in Long Beach, California originally built by Howard Hughes for his aviation and nautical projects housed several of the film's sets. *Batman Forever*'s Dome sets included the Batcave and Two-Face's lair.[6] The film's Batcave set was particularly impressive — with its huge amount of high tech equipment, including a sunken turntable for the Batmobile, it dwarfed the Batcave sets used in Warner's two previous live-action Batman films.

Ling's real-life sets and Dykstra's visual effects meshed so perfectly with one another that it was impossible to tell where one ended and the other began. Nowhere was this fact more apparent than in Dykstra's incredibly complex and detailed miniature Gotham City sets that were constructed for the film at one of Hughes' former aircraft hangars in Marina del Rey, California. Many of the buildings in these sets stood at over fifteen feet tall, and they were crafted with such precision that they seamlessly blended with all of Ling's life-size sets.[7]

Schumacher's decision to realize Batman's world on such a grand scale in *Batman Forever* was undoubtedly a very wise one, especially in terms of the film's depiction of Gotham City. One of *Batman Returns*' biggest problems was that its Gotham sets were far too cramped to capture the city as the gigantic, bustling metropolis that it had always been in Batman comic books. In *Batman Forever*, Schumacher and company created a massive, eye-popping version of Gotham that was unlike any other that had ever been realized on screen.

Since *Batman Forever* was going to look so different from its predecessors, Schumacher decided the film should sound different as well, so composer Elliot Goldenthal was hired to write a new musical score. Goldenthal was entrusted with the unenviable task of writing a score that would capture the dark, adventurous nature of the Batman character, but at the same time would not sound too similar to Danny Elfman's wonderful Batman music. Goldenthal actually managed this task quite well. His Batman music was perhaps not as memorable as Elfman's, but it still meshed nicely with *Batman Forever*'s larger-than-life images. Goldenthal's *Batman Forever* score even contained some blaring staccato brass notes that brought to mind the lighter spirit of the 1960s *Batman* theme music written by Neal Hefti.

Like the 1989 *Batman*, *Batman Forever* featured a pop soundtrack as well as an orchestral soundtrack. But while the 1989 *Batman* pop soundtrack consisted of songs all written and performed by Prince, the *Batman Forever* pop soundtrack would consist of songs performed by a number of different contemporary artists. Two of these songs, "Hold Me, Thrill Me, Kiss Me, Kill Me" by U2 and "A Kiss from a Rose" by Seal became substantial radio hits. These songs definitely helped to promote *Batman Forever*, even though they were not prominently featured in the film itself — they only played during the film's final credits.

Considering that *Batman Forever* was so different in so many ways from *Batman* and *Batman Returns*, it seemed like somewhat of a surprising choice on Schumacher's part to retain Michael Gough as Alfred and Pat Hingle as Commissioner Gordon. After all, the movie was going to have a new Batman, a new Harvey Dent, a new Gotham City, a new Batmobile and a new Batcave — what was the point of having *any* carryover from Warner's previous Batman films? That said, however, it was enjoyable seeing these two veteran actors return to their familiar roles. This was especially true in terms of Michael Gough — his role would be even more important in *Batman Forever* than it had been in *Batman* or *Batman Returns*, because he would be called upon to act as sympathetic council to not one, but *two* heroes.

Production of *Batman Forever* commenced in mid–1994 in grand fashion — the Batmobile was filmed driving at high speeds on the streets of lower Manhattan in New York City. After the New York scenes were wrapped up, filming moved to the California sets. The *Batman Forever* shoot generally went quite smoothly — Schumacher remained loose and calm during filming, and most of his actors responded well to his affable style. However, there was at least some degree of offstage drama — reportedly both Kilmer and Jones proved to be difficult to work with, which led Schumacher to publicly criticize the actors after the film was released.[8]

Still, both Schumacher and Warner Bros. seemed to have a tremendous amount of confidence in *Batman Forever* while the film was being made. A good deal of this confidence likely stemmed from the fact that the director and the studio were so much more in synch with one another than Tim Burton and Warner had been with each other during the making of *Batman Returns*. Schumacher perfectly understood that Warner wanted him to strike a balance between the darker and the lighter elements of the Batman character so that the film would be appropriate for audiences young and old. In fact, Schumacher not only understood this assignment, he actually welcomed it — in a number of interviews he gave while the film was being made, he discussed his desire to shape *Batman Forever* into a film that would appeal to a very wide audience, one made up of both children and adults.[9]

Obviously, striking a balance between the darker and the lighter elements of the Batman character in order to attract larger audiences was not something that Burton had been willing to do while he was making *Batman Returns*. So as Schumacher was meeting, and perhaps even surpassing, all of Warner's expectations during the making of *Batman Forever*, the studio must have felt that they had found exactly the right ingredient they needed to restore their Batman film franchise to the heights it had reached in 1989. The studio had to consider this to be *very* good news, considering how much money they were shelling out for *Batman Forever*—the cost to make the film ended up reaching about $100 million.[10]

Perhaps the most telling sign of the confidence Schumacher and Warner Bros. had in *Batman Forever* was the manner in which the film was being marketed. The public criticism that Warner had suffered over their efforts to develop merchandising tie-ins to *Batman Returns* aimed at younger audiences was not deterring the studio from aggressively marketing *Batman Forever*. On the contrary, Warner had secured just as many merchandising tie-ins for *Batman Forever* as they had for *Batman Returns*, and a substantial number of these tie-ins were products designed for children. Warner knew that marketing *Batman Forever* in such a manner would pose no risk of repeating the *Batman Returns* merchandising fiasco—Schumacher's work on *Batman Forever* had ensured the studio that the film could be marketed to younger audiences without any hint of impropriety.

The biggest problem that Schumacher and Warner Bros. had with *Batman Forever* was actually getting the film done. The large number of special effects shots the film contained made it a very complicated project, and it was made even trickier by the fact that only about three months had been allotted for its postproduction phase. But Dykstra's special effects team performed brilliantly for Schumacher and Warner during postproduction, completing every scene that the director and the studio had requested from them.[11]

Batman Forever's world premiere was held in Los Angeles on June 9, 1995. Most all of the film's principal onscreen and offscreen talent attended the event, including Kilmer, Kidman, O'Donnell, Jones, Carrey and Schumacher. Many celebrities not connected to the film also attended, making the premiere a huge media event. A week later, on June 16, *Batman Forever* opened in theatres throughout the United States.

Batman Forever opens with a series of quick shots of Batman in the Batcave, readying himself for battle. He speeds off in the Batmobile, headed for the Second National Bank in Gotham City where Two-Face is attempting a daring robbery. When Batman arrives, he meets the beautiful Dr. Chase Meridian, a psychologist consulting with Commissioner Gordon on the Two-Face case. Two-Face captures a bank guard and places him in a giant vault located on one of the bank's upper floors. Batman bursts in and Two-Face's thugs attack him. Batman overpowers the thugs and jumps in the vault to rescue the guard.

But it turns out the guard was merely bait to get Batman to enter the vault — the vault is closed, and then pulled high into the sky by a chain connected to Two-Face's helicopter. As the vault rises, acid that Two-Face has placed inside starts to spill everywhere, almost scalding Batman and the guard. But Two-Face's plan to kill Batman with the acid fails when Batman breaks out of the vault, saves the guard and starts climbing the chain to confront Two-Face in the helicopter. Batman and Two-Face fight aboard the helicopter, which is headed straight for the Lady Gotham statue in Gotham Harbor. (Obviously, the statue is Gotham's version of the Statue of Liberty in New York City!) The helicopter crashes into the statue, but not before both Two-Face and Batman leap to safety.

The next day, Bruce Wayne inspects Wayne Enterprises' electronics division and meets a brilliant but unstable Wayne employee named Edward Nygma. Nygma, who completely idolizes Wayne, tells Wayne he has invented a device that beams television signals directly into people's minds. Wayne tells Nygma that he does not want his company to pursue such a project because it is unethical to manipulate people's brains in such a manner. Nygma is crushed by Wayne's rejection, and plots revenge against him.

Bruce quickly leaves the inspection because he sees the Batsignal in the sky. He arrives at the Gotham Police headquarters as Batman, but is surprised to find that it is not Gordon that has summoned him, but Chase. She tells him that Two-Face's lucky coin, with one side scarred and one side clean, might somehow be able to be used to trap the criminal. Also, infatuated by Batman since their first meeting, she wastes no time in trying to seduce him. But her efforts are cut short when Commissioner Gordon shows up. Meanwhile, Nygma knocks out Fred Stickley, his supervisor at Wayne Enterprises, and then tries out his television signal device on him. Nygma is surprised to learn that not only is he able to transmit signals into Stickley's brain, but he is also able to absorb Stickley's knowledge into his *own* brain during the process.

Nygma murders Stickley, covers up the crime and quits his job at Wayne Enterprises. He then starts sending Bruce anonymous threatening messages in the form of riddles. Bruce takes them to Chase to ask her what she makes of them. Bruce is as taken with Chase as she is with his alter ego, so he asks her to attend a circus performance benefiting Gotham Hospital with him.

Two-Face hijacks the circus benefit while the trapeze artists the Flying Graysons are performing. Still intent on killing Batman, he assumes that one of Gotham's elite in attendance must know Batman's true identity. Rather than reveal his identity to Two-Face, Bruce simply starts single-handedly fighting the criminal's thugs. He gets help from the flying Graysons, who work to remove a bomb that Two-Face has planted in the center ring. Dick Grayson is able to throw the bomb off the roof, but while he is doing so Two-Face murders all of the other flying Graysons—Dick's father, mother and brother.

Bruce, remembering the horror of his own parents' murders, offers to let Dick stay at Wayne Manor for a few days. Troubled by Dick's loss, Bruce begins having recurring visions of events relating to his parents' deaths. These visions involve a large, unidentified red book. Dick tells Alfred that his father had nicknamed him "Robin" years ago after he had saved his brother from a serious trapeze fall. Alfred comforts Dick by assuring him that, even after the terrible loss he has suffered, "Robin" will fly again someday.

Dick is immediately curious about just where Bruce goes every night, and why one particular room in the house is always locked. Meanwhile, Nygma adopts the guise of the Riddler, and convinces Two-Face to team up with him to destroy Batman. They go on a crime spree to raise funds for Nygma to start a company that sells his invention, which he simply calls "The Box."

Bruce, still having visions about his parents' murders, goes to see Chase. Chase tells him that he has repressed memories that are trying to surface. While they are talking, Alfred calls Bruce to tell him that Dick has learned Bruce is really Batman; worse yet, he has broken into the Batcave and stolen the Batmobile. While driving around Gotham, Dick stops a bunch of street punks from abducting a woman. When the punks attack him, Batman comes to his rescue. Later, Dick tries to convince Bruce to let him be his partner so that they can find Two-Face and kill him, but Bruce refuses. Bruce tells Dick that killing Two-Face will not take away the pain he feels over the loss of his family—in fact, Bruce knows from experience that such vengeance will actually make the pain worse.

Nygma holds a party to unveil a new version of his "Box," and Bruce, Dick and Chase attend. Bruce inadvertently allows the "Box" to scan his brain, revealing to Nygma the fact that he is Batman. When Two-Face crashes the party, Bruce changes into Batman to try to capture him. Two-Face and his men escape through an under-construction subway tunnel. Batman follows them into the tunnel, and Two-Face shoots out a support beam that leaves Batman buried in gravel. Dick, dressed in his Flying Graysons costume and a mask, comes to his rescue. Even though Dick has saved his life, Bruce still refuses to let Dick become his partner.

Bruce, in his Batman costume, goes to see Chase, who says that her infatuation with him is over because she has fallen in love with Bruce. Bruce has the same feelings for Chase, so he decides to give up being Batman and to try to lead a "normal" life with her. He invites her to Wayne Manor to tell her about his secret life. He talks about the red book he has been recalling in his visions relating to his parents' murders—it was his father's diary. After his parents were killed, Bruce realized his father would never write in the diary again, and it was at that point Bruce saw how truly alone in the world he was. In his grief and rage, he ran out of his house and fell into a hole located on the Wayne acreage that led down to a huge cave under the house. As a giant bat flew at him in the cave, he vowed to use the bat's image to fight crime, to avenge his parent's deaths.

But while Bruce has been revealing his secret identity to Chase, Two-Face, Riddler and their goons have knocked out Alfred and forced their way into the house. Bruce and Chase put up a good fight against them, but Bruce is knocked unconscious after a bullet fired by Two-Face grazes his head. The Riddler finds the entrance to the Batcave and uses explosives to destroy most all of Batman's crimefighting equipment. Leaving Alfred and Bruce unconscious and the Batcave in ruins, the villains take Chase hostage and flee.

After Bruce and Alfred regain consciousness, they examine all of the riddles that have been sent to Bruce and determine that Nygma is the Riddler. Several new experimental Bat-costumes and Bat-vehicles were not destroyed by the villains, so Bruce prepares to confront the Riddler and Two-Face as Batman at Nygma's "Box" transmission headquarters on an island in Gotham Harbor. Dick appears in his Robin costume that Alfred has made for him, and Batman finally decides to take him on as a partner. Batman and Robin speed off, Batman in the Batwing and Robin in the Batboat, to face Two-Face and the Riddler.

The villains, waiting for the heroes, detonate bombs to destroy the Batwing and the Batboat, but Batman and Robin are still able to make their way to Nygma's island headquarters. Robin fights Two-Face and defeats him—though Dick originally wanted to kill Two-Face to avenge the deaths of his family, he decides that justice would be better served by seeing Two-Face sent to prison. But Two-Face unexpectedly pulls a gun on Robin and takes him hostage.

Batman finally catches up with the Riddler deep inside his lair, but he finds that the villain has set up an elaborate deathtrap for both Chase and Robin. At the touch of a button, both will fall through trapdoors and plummet to the rocky shore far below. The Riddler tells Batman he will have to choose between saving the love of his life or his junior partner. But Batman does neither—he flings a Batarang at the Riddler's huge "Box" antenna, smashing it and causing the Riddler's lair to be destroyed in a series of powerful explosions. The Riddler sets in motion his deathtrap for Chase and Robin, and Batman dives through the trapdoor after them. Using his grappling hook, he saves them both.

As the trio climb out of the trap, Two-Face confronts them with a gun. He flips his coin to determine whether he will shoot them or not. At the same moment, Batman flings a handful of coins into the air. Unable to tell which coin is actually his, Two-Face loses his balance and falls to his death. Batman stands in triumph over the Riddler, whose mind has become completely unhinged through absorbing the thoughts of so many different people. In fact, the Riddler has even forgotten that he learned Batman's secret identity—Chase discovers this fact when she checks in on the criminal after he has been imprisoned at Arkham Asylum. The film ends with Batman and Robin shown in silhouette, running in front of the lit Batsignal.

Batman Forever received decent but generally unspectacular reviews. The film did not fare quite as well critically as *Batman Returns*— but as discussed last chapter, *Batman Returns* turned out to be more popular with critics than it did with general audiences. The reverse turned out to be true for *Batman Forever*. While critics might not have thought too much of the film, moviegoers of all ages responded quite well to it. So from Warner Bros.' perspective, *Batman Forever* was very much a success because it brought them excellent box office returns. It earned over $52 million in its U.S. opening weekend alone, and ended up grossing over $184 million during its U.S. theatrical run. With a worldwide total gross of over $335 million, *Batman Forever* outperformed *Batman Returns* in its initial theatrical run by around $60 million.[12]

And just as importantly to Warner Bros., *Batman Forever*'s lighter overall tone made the film much more enjoyable for younger audiences than *Batman Returns* had been. Much to Warner's relief, *Batman Forever* made their Batman film franchise "family friendly" again.

Interestingly, serious Batman fans seemed to be split over whether or not *Batman Forever*'s lighter tone was a step in the right direction as far as the future of Warner's Batman film franchise was concerned. Some felt that the film's more heroic portrayal of Batman was a marked improvement over the manner in which the character was portrayed in the Burton-directed Batman films, especially *Batman Returns*. Others felt that with all of its bright colors and tongue-in-cheek humor, *Batman Forever* marked an unwelcome return to the kind of campiness found in the Batman screen works of the 1960s.

Batman fans might not have been so divided over *Batman Forever*'s merits if so much of its Batman/Bruce Wayne character material had not been removed from the final cut of the film. As previously mentioned, many of *Batman Forever*'s scenes depicting Batman trying to come to grips with his long-held anger and grief were removed from the final version of the film in order to shorten it and simplify its narrative. The scenes that were particularly affected by these cuts were the ones involving Bruce's father's diary and the ones that made direct references to *Batman* and *Batman Returns*. If these scenes had remained in the film, the majority of Batman fans might well have seen *Batman Forever* as a more serious character study of their hero. But without these scenes, many Batman fans perceived the film as being an often shallow and rather silly exercise in pyrotechnics.

Ironically, these cuts actually ended up not simplifying, but *confusing Batman Forever*'s narrative. The finished film still included scenes that centered on Bruce's father's diary, but these scenes made no reference to the fact that Bruce had read a passage in the diary that led him to blame himself for his parents' deaths. Consequently, the diary keeps re-appearing in Bruce's visions relating to the loss of his parents in the film, but its importance is never satisfactorily explained. At the end of the film Bruce finally says that seeing the diary sitting on his father's desk made him realize how truly alone in the world he was. But this offhand line does not seem like anywhere near a big enough payoff for as much as the diary has been built up in the film. Obviously, if the diary scenes were going to be kept in *Batman Forever* at all, they should have been given the proper weight accorded to them in the film's original script.

As we noted in our discussions of the 1989 *Batman* and *Batman Returns*, the success of Warner's 2005 film *Batman Begins* led the studio to release their four previous Batman live-action features on 2-disc DVD sets late that same year. The 2-disc DVD set of *Batman Forever* revealed the importance of these deleted scenes by including them in the set's collection of bonus material. We'll go over the full content of the *Batman Forever* DVD set later in the chapter, but these deleted scenes are so crucial to the film's overall vision that we need to examine them as a stand-alone entity.

The scene entitled "Two-Face's Hate" is an extended version of the Batman/Two-Face helicopter fight scene at the beginning of the film. In the scene, Two-Face taunts Batman, implying that the crimefighter is every bit as much of a killer as *he* is. The scene entitled "Dick's Pain" shows a discussion between Bruce and Dick at Wayne Manor that takes place just after Dick's family has been murdered. Bruce tells Dick that he should not let the love of his family twist into hatred for Two-Face.

In the scene "Bruce's Dilemma," Bruce sits in the Batcave watching a Gotham City TV news report. The report features a commentator who accuses Batman of being no more heroic than the criminals he fights because his self-declared war on criminals has caused a huge amount of destruction throughout Gotham and put all of the city's inhabitants at risk. Bruce then talks to Alfred about the night of his parents' wake. He remembers being frightened by something and running from it, but he can't remember what it was that frightened him.

"The Secret of the Batcave" is by far the most important and compelling of the deleted scenes. It begins with Bruce and Alfred entering the Batcave after it has been destroyed by the Riddler. They go to the area of the cave that has always frightened Bruce for no apparent reason. Bruce goes into a chamber by himself, and there he finds his father's diary. Bruce had left the diary in the chamber when he fell into the cave on the night of his parents' wake, but he was so traumatized by the incident that he completely forgot the diary was there. He reads the diary's last entry, and finds that it was not him who insisted on the family seeing a movie the night his parents were murdered — it was actually his father and mother who had their hearts set on seeing a film.

Bruce then realizes that the murder of his parents was in no way his fault. As he comes to this realization, a giant bat flies through the chamber at him and holds itself motionless right at his face. This bat is obviously not real, it is a figment of Bruce's imagination that symbolizes his anguish over losing his parents and his decision to adopt the guise of Batman. Now that Bruce has learned that he was not at all responsible for his parents' deaths, his imaginary bat no longer frightens him. In fact, it actually comforts him — he can finally move past blaming himself for the loss of his parents, and he can perceive his life as Batman as a means to seek justice instead of simply as a means to inflict violence. Bruce walks out of the chamber and confidently says to Alfred, "I'm Batman."

Given the fact that *Batman Forever* was basically a straight-ahead action movie that was so much lighter in tone than Warner's previous Batman films, perhaps the heavy symbolism of "The Secret of the Batcave" would have seemed out of place if the scene had been included in the film's final cut. That said, however, the scene is both emotionally powerful and visually striking — the serious Batman fans that dismissed Schumacher's take on the character in *Batman Forever* as shallow and silly might not have been so dismissive if the scene had remained in the film. At least the scene was eventually released in some form so that these fans could have the chance to see that Schumacher tried to give Batman more substance than the final cut of *Batman Forever* ended up showing.

But even though all of this deeper character material relating to the film's depiction of Batman was excised, *Batman Forever*'s portrayal of Batman was far closer to his comic book form than was the Batman of *Batman Returns*. The biggest difference between *Batman Returns*' Batman and *Batman Forever*'s Batman was that *Forever*'s Batman unequivocally did not kill. This difference was made crystal clear within the first major fight scene of the film. As Batman fights Two-Face's hoods in the Second National Bank, one of the hoods runs at Batman. When Batman steps out of the way, the hood almost falls down an open elevator shaft. The Batman of Burton's films would have just let the hood fall down the shaft to his doom, but Schumacher's Batman grabs the hood by the collar and saves him. Of course, he then knocks him out of action so that he can continue his pursuit of Two-Face, but he does not use lethal force.

Much of *Batman Forever*'s material that directly referenced the 1989 *Batman* and *Batman Returns* was cut from the final version of the film — but the film still contained scenes that made it clear Batman was remorseful over the fact that he had tried to kill Jack Napier/The Joker. He realized that his willingness to take a human life had led him down a path of endless vengeance — and he needed to turn away from that path in order to stop his whole life from being given over to darkness and violence.

Batman Forever drew on a substantial amount of classic Batman comic imagery to illuminate its depiction of its title character. For example, one of the film's flashback scenes depicting the murder of Bruce's parents showed the boy kneeling over his parents' bodies, starkly illuminated by a street light. This image was drawn from the cover of the first issue of the 1987 Frank Miller–David Mazzucchelli comic series *Batman: Year One*. The scene depicting young Bruce falling down a hole and into the cave on the Wayne acreage that would eventually become the Batcave, and then being confronted by a giant bat flying right at him, was drawn from Miller's 1986 graphic novel series *Batman: The Dark Knight Returns*. (However, the circumstances surrounding Bruce's fall into the cave in *Batman Forever* were very different from the circumstances surrounding Bruce's fall in *Batman: The Dark Knight Returns*— in *Forever*, the fall happened right after Bruce's parents had been murdered, while in *Returns*, the fall happened while his parents were still alive and well.)

Batman Forever's depiction of its title character was made all the better by Val Kilmer's excellent acting. He captured the essence of Batman/Bruce Wayne's character in the film, realizing the character as both a hero and a man wrestling with his inner demons in an attempt to hang onto his sanity. And as previously mentioned, he was physically far more suited for the part than was Michael Keaton in Burton's Batman films. The combination of the film's thoughtful treatment of Batman and Kilmer's strong performance made *Batman Forever*'s Batman a very good live-action version of the character.

However, *Batman Forever*'s Batman portrayal was not without its problems. The use of computer graphics technology perhaps gave the filmmakers *too* much freedom, because it allowed them to stray far beyond the boundaries of what a hero like Batman could do if he were actually a real person. In the film, Batman is able to jump off of 40-story buildings by using his cape to slow his fall, and to drive his Batmobile up the walls of buildings — in other words, he is able to do things that are not physically possible.

From Batman's very first story back in 1939, the thing that made him such a memorable character was that he was a regular human being that could theoretically exist in real life. Batman appealed to people because Bruce Wayne was an ordinary man doing extraordinary things. As Batman, he pushed himself to be as strong, as fast and as smart as humanly possible — but when all was said and done, his humanity kept his adventures rooted in reality. *Batman Forever*'s decision to throw all semblance of reality out the window for the sake of spectacular visual effects undercut the main premise of the character that had made him so popular for so long.

Chris O'Donnell's earnest portrayal of Robin/Dick Grayson was every bit as good as Kilmer's Batman/Bruce Wayne. O'Donnell was given the benefit of very strong material to work with. His origin scene depicting the death of his family was nicely adapted from the very first Robin comic story "Robin — the Boy Wonder" (*Detective Comics* #38, April 1940).

However, the film did make one major change to Robin's origin — in the comics, Two-Face had never been depicted as having anything to do with the Grayson murders.

Of course, O'Donnell was not a boy, but a young man in his mid-twenties when *Batman Forever* was filmed, so the film's relationship between Dick Grayson and Bruce Wayne was very different from the kind of "father-son" rapport the characters traditionally were shown to have had in the comics. In *Batman Forever*, fate throws Bruce and Dick together, and neither of them really know what to make of the other. But Dick's reaction to the murder of his family, the rage and thirst for revenge that he feels, touches a nerve in Bruce. Bruce wants to help Dick come to grips with the anger and grief inside him, and perhaps by helping Dick, he can find a way to help himself come to grips with his *own* anger and grief. The bond between the two men that forms in the film comes from the fact that they have both faced the same kind of tragedy in their lives — and now they both must find a way to move beyond these tragedies. Consequently, their relationship seems very plausible.

The only real problem with O'Donnell's performance is one that the actor had no control over — he is not featured in enough scenes as Robin in *Batman Forever*. He does not appear in full costume until the final scenes of the film, so audiences never really get much of a chance to see Batman and Robin working together as a team.

After *Batman Forever* was released, much discussion arose regarding Schumacher's infusing his cinematic version of the Batman and Robin characters with a considerable amount of sexual subtext. The characters' costumes, with their bulging crotches and exaggerated musculature complete with nipples, set many a tongue wagging, calling the characters' sexuality into question in much the same way the 1954 book *Seduction of the Innocent* by Fredric Wertham had. There is no doubt that in *Batman Forever*, Schumacher was trying to "sex up" the characters in a subtle, playful way that would raise the eyebrows of adult audiences. But at the same time, Schumacher made sure the film still contained plenty of action so that younger audiences could enjoy the film as a straight-ahead adventure piece. In this regard, *Batman Forever* was quite similar to the 1960s screen Batman — as we discussed earlier in the book, the 1960s *Batman* television show and film had been designed to entertain adults as a tongue-in-cheek comedy, and children as an action show.

Whether Schumacher pushed the envelope too far in terms of sexing up Batman and his world in *Batman Forever* is a matter of personal opinion. One might argue that having to put up with a few sexual references and costume nipples was a small price for Batman fans to pay in order to see a film that provided a generally intelligent portrayal of their hero. But one might also argue that Schumacher's sexual politics had no place in a Batman film in the first place, so the inclusion of *any* such material was unacceptable.

Batman Forever's villains the Riddler and Two-Face turned out to be a major highlight of the film. Jim Carrey's Riddler/Edward Nygma was far and away the more compelling of the two. Prancing around in his bizarre costumes and twirling his question mark cane like some kind of crazed drum major, he brought the Riddler to life in a way that was both funny and creepy. He was also very good in his Edward Nygma scenes, which featured him by turns both idolizing and despising Bruce Wayne. Incidentally, the film's Riddler origin story was in no way tied to the character's comic book origin — but the Riddler's first comic book appearances were fairly undistinguished, so the film's embellished Riddler backstory in no way detracted from the character's overall impact.

However, the Riddler/Edward Nygma character in general suffered from one major drawback in *Batman Forever*. His "Box" technology that was featured so prominently in the film obviously had no basis in reality, and it dumbed down the plot of the film to a level of silliness that rivaled the 1940s Batman serials and the 1966 *Batman*. And not only was the very concept of the "Box" technology completely ridiculous, but Nygma's ability to invent it, mass produce it and mass market it within a few short weeks further divorced it from any semblance of reality.

Tommy Lee Jones's performance as Two-Face was also quite good — though to be honest, his character was often overshadowed by Carrey's manic portrayal of the Riddler. Still, Jones made an admirable effort to leave behind his almost deadpan acting style and bring Two-Face to life in a manner in keeping with the overall flamboyance of the film. Jones's portrayal of Two-Face was definitely helped by the fact that *Batman Forever* chose to depict the character in a manner that recalled Two-Face's classic comic book stories. His half-scarred/half-unscarred appearance wonderfully captured the character's comic book look. In fact, the Two-Face makeup created by Rick Baker successfully performed quite a tricky balancing act — it made the character grotesque, but not to a point that younger audiences would have been completely terrified by it.

Batman Forever even gave a neat little nod to the character's comic book origin. Near the opening of the film, Bruce is seen watching a Gotham City TV news report that shows a video clip of Gotham City crime kingpin "Boss" Moroni throwing acid at Harvey Dent's face. The acid hits only one side of Dent's face, and this injury leads him to adopt his Two-Face persona. The TV images of Dent being hit with acid were directly drawn from Two-Face's first comic book story "The Crimes of Two-Face," originally published in *Detective Comics* #66, August 1942.

Nicole Kidman's performance as Dr. Chase Meridian was generally as strong as the performances of all the rest of *Batman Forever*'s major players. Perhaps her best scene is when she meets Bruce for the first time. Her irritation with his seemingly foppish behavior subtly gives way to a curiosity about exactly what it is he is hiding behind his "bored playboy" facade.

As strong as all of *Batman Forever*'s principal actors were, it was Joel Schumacher who perhaps acquitted himself most handsomely out of everyone involved with the film. In taking over Batman directorial duties from Tim Burton, Schumacher had delivered a film that had given Warner Bros. exactly what their Batman film franchise needed after the disappointing performance of *Batman Returns*. Still, Schumacher had proven to have his drawbacks in terms of directing a Batman film — as we just noted, his coy sexual subtext and his tendency to at times favor spectacular visual effects over reality did not sit well with many serious Batman fans.

Though Schumacher's *Batman Forever* was far from perfect, it was certainly a step in the right direction after the *Batman Returns* misstep. Warner Bros. seemed to have every reason to be optimistic that they had found the right director to oversee their Batman film franchise. As we will discuss later in the book, this judgment would prove to be very wrong.

But before we leave *Batman Forever*, let's examine the movie's home video release history. The film's box office success led to a very high demand for *Batman Forever* VHS tapes and laserdiscs when Warner first released it to the home video market in late October 1995. The first DVD version of *Batman Forever* was released by Warner in 1997. The DVD offered the film in its original widescreen format as well as in a format cropped to fit a standard television screen, but it offered no bonus features or printed material dealing with the making of the film.

As we noted earlier in this chapter, the success of Warner's 2005 film *Batman Begins* led the studio to release their four previous Batman live-action features on 2-disc DVD sets late that same year. Each of these sets were loaded with special features that detailed their particular film's creation. The *Batman Forever* DVD set included a 1995 television documentary hosted by Chris O'Donnell entitled *Riddle Me This: Why Is Batman Forever?* The short program was designed to introduce the public to Warner's new cinematic vision of Batman, and featured commentary from members of *Batman Forever*'s cast and crew, including Schumacher, Kilmer, Carrey, Jones and Kidman. *Riddle Me This: Why Is Batman Forever?* had an overall upbeat tone that was undoubtedly meant to assure viewers that *Batman Forever* would be a much more "family friendly" film than *Batman Returns* had been.

The DVD set also included newly-produced documentaries. The program *Shadows of the Bat: The Cinematic Saga of the Dark Knight Part 5* chronicled the making of *Batman Forever*. The program featured insights from many of the individuals who played a major role in the film's creation, including Joel Schumacher, Lee Batchler, Janet Scott Batchler, Akiva Goldsman, Val Kilmer, Chris O'Donnell, Jim Carrey, Tommy Lee Jones and Nicole Kidman. These insights were accompanied by a good deal of behind-the-scenes footage shot on the *Batman Forever* set showing the film's cast and crew at work.

The DVD set's program *Beyond Batman* consisted of featurettes about some of the specific elements of *Batman Forever*. The titles of the featurettes were "Out of the Shadows: The Production Design of *Batman Forever*," "The Many Faces of Gotham City," "Knight Moves: The Stunts of *Batman Forever*," "Imaging Forever: The Visual Effects of *Batman Forever*," and "Scoring Forever: The Music of *Batman Forever*." The set also included featurettes on the main heroes and villains of the film.

As we also noted earlier in the chapter, the DVD set also included a substantial number of scenes deleted from the final cut of *Batman Forever*. In addition to the four Batman/Bruce Wayne character scenes we already examined, there were three other scenes included in the set. The most notable of these was the film's original opening scene which showed one of Arkham Asylum's doctors discovering that Two-Face had escaped from the facility.

Incidentally, the doctor in this scene was given the last name of "Burton," and had a wild mop of black hair that looked just like Tim Burton's unruly coiffure. Obviously, the character was designed to be a slightly quirky tribute to Warner's first Batman director. This particular scene with Dr. Burton did not make it into the final cut of *Batman Forever*, but the character still ended up making a brief appearance in the film — he was featured in the Arkham Asylum scene at the very end of the movie.

This 2005 DVD set remained the definitive home video version of *Batman Forever* until Warner released the movie on Blu-ray disc in early 2009. The *Batman Forever* Blu-ray included all of the special features found on the DVD set, but it did not contain any new bonus material. Of course, the Blu-ray's main selling point was not its special features, but its presentation of the film itself. On Blu-ray, *Batman Forever* looked and sounded far better than it ever had on any other home video format.

I'll close my discussion of *Batman Forever* with these thoughts. Serious Batman fans have continued to be very divided over the film's merits since the film was released almost two decades ago. In fact, *Batman Forever*'s reputation among Batman fans has not really improved at all during this time — if anything, it has *worsened*. I suspect that this has less to do with the film itself than it does with Joel Schumacher's second Batman film, the disastrously bad *Batman and Robin* (1997). I believe that *Batman and Robin* ended up being so reviled by serious Batman fans that many of them reached a point where they could not give Schumacher even the slightest credit for any of the good things found in his first Batman film.

And make no mistake, I am of the opinion that there *are* many good things to be found in *Batman Forever*. I suppose this opinion will come as no surprise to those of you that have read this entire chapter, since I've spent a good deal of it favorably discussing the film. Still, please allow me a moment to recap what I consider to be *Batman Forever*'s main strengths. The film presents a thoughtful, heroic depiction of Batman/Bruce Wayne. It features Robin/Dick Grayson in a manner that is well-adapted from the classic comic version of the character. It features well-realized depictions of two of Batman's most recognizable comic villains. It features the first live-action version of Arkham Asylum. All in all, I feel that there is a lot in *Batman Forever* for a serious Batman fan to like, and that is in large part due to the work of Joel Schumacher. Unfortunately, the things I'll be saying about the second half of Schumacher's Batman directorial tenure won't be as nearly as positive. We'll get to that story a bit later in the book.

14

Between Schumacher's Batman Films, 1996–1997

Only two years passed between the release of Joel Schumacher's Batman films *Batman Forever* (1995) and *Batman and Robin* (1997), but that was still enough time to allow several important events in Batman history to occur. The most notable of these was the release of DC's four-part *Elseworlds* graphic novel entitled *Kingdom Come* in 1996. *Kingdom Come* would set the comics industry abuzz much like the first graphic novels such as *Batman: The Dark Knight Returns* had a decade earlier.

Written by Mark Waid and illustrated by Alex Ross, *Kingdom Come* set all of DC's major heroes in a world far more closely tied to reality than had ever been attempted in a comic work. In *Kingdom Come*, DC's aging heroes are struggling to come to terms with their place in society in a not-too-distant future. Their powers and talents obviously set them apart from "normal" people, but how do they best use these gifts to better humankind? If they interfere with the workings of "normal" society too much, they run the risk of becoming nothing more than super-powered dictators. If they interfere too little, they run the risk of being perceived as being unresponsive to the needs of that society.

The series opens on a pessimistic note: DC's legendary heroes have not been able to find this balance that allows them to both consistently help and harmoniously co-exist with "normal" people, so they have largely removed themselves from everyday society. A new breed of super beings, "metahumans," have taken over for titans such as Superman, Batman, Robin, Wonder Woman and Green Lantern, and these metahumans care nothing for the concerns of everyday society. They roam the earth fighting among themselves like super-powered street gangs, terrorizing anyone who gets in their way.

This situation finally reaches a breaking point when some of these metahumans incite a confrontation that unleashes a nuclear bomb–like blast in Kansas, killing millions of innocent people. The Kansas tragedy spurs Superman, Wonder, Woman, Green Lantern, Robin and a number of other heroes back into action. They return from their self-imposed exile to bring these metahumans under control and to finally find that elusive balance that will allow super beings and ordinary people to peacefully co-exist.

Of course, one hero is conspicuously absent from this reformed Justice League — Batman. Bruce Wayne does not believe that a bunch of old heroes simply swooping down from out of the sky is going to suddenly put an end to the tensions that have arisen between super beings and ordinary people, so he refuses Superman's offer to join the League. Besides, Bruce has his own loose crimefighting organization with a number of heroes such as Green Arrow and Black Canary.

The League has even bigger problems than Bruce's opposition: Sinister forces led by Lex Luthor plan on undermining their efforts, because they want to see an all-out war erupt between super beings and ordinary people. Luthor's organization believes that humans need to reclaim their planet by forcefully ridding it of super beings, no matter what the cost of waging such a war might be terms of human life. In fact, Luthor has brainwashed and gained control over one particularly powerful super being in order to help him bring about this conflict—Billy Batson, otherwise known as Captain Marvel.

Bruce joins forces with Luthor, seemingly to oppose Superman—but in reality, Bruce has thrown in with Luthor in order to keep tabs on him. When Bruce learns that Luthor is planning on using Captain Marvel to incite his human-metahuman war, Bruce turns on Luthor and his forces, incapacitating them. But Captain Marvel escapes Bruce's grasp and makes his way to a metahuman prison where a battle has erupted between the Justice League and the incarcerated metahumans. Bruce changes to Batman and makes his way to the prison with his forces. A tremendous battle ensues between the League, the metahumans and Batman's forces. The United Nations, terrified that this conflagration will eventually destroy the entire world, fires nuclear missiles at the prison to rid the world of super beings once and for all.

Superman is able to convince Captain Marvel that Luthor has been brainwashing him. The two heroes reach a moment of understanding and Captain Marvel intercepts the missiles at the last second, saving many of the super beings, but losing his own life. Superman, furious that the people of the world have turned on him, races to the U.N. Headquarters intent on punishing those responsible for firing the missiles.

All of the activity depicted in *Kingdom Come* up to this point has been monitored by the otherworldly hero the Spectre and a mild-mannered minister by the name of Norman McKay. All along, the Spectre has had the power to intervene in the crisis, but not being of the Earth, he is unsure of the best way to proceed. So he has brought McKay with him to bear witness to all of these events so that McKay can pass judgment on them and tell the Spectre what action should be taken.

McKay tells the Spectre what to do: McKay wants the Spectre to take him to Superman. McKay then tells the Man of Steel that being Superman is not just about being "Super," it is every bit as much about being a "Man." The conflict between super beings and ordinary people can yet be mended if Superman can remember this fact and work side by side with humans instead of above them to better the planet. Superman agrees, and with help from the likes of Wonder Woman and Batman, he begins the task of trying to achieve a better understanding between regular humans and super beings.

Kingdom Come's potent mix of mythological and religious themes coupled with time-honored DC comic book history made the series an instant classic. *Kingdom Come* obviously owed much to Frank Miller's *Batman: The Dark Knight Returns*—its setting of a not-too-distant future, its moral complexities and its apocalyptic final battle between former allies were drawn from Miller's work at least to some extent. But what set the series apart was that Miller's take on the DC Universe was far more pessimistic than that of Waid and Ross. *Kingdom Come* ended on a very optimistic note, depicting most all of the DC titans alive and well and ready to stand shoulder-to-shoulder in an effort to make the world a better place. *Batman: The Dark Knight Returns* ended with Batman giving up his cape and cowl, and still very much in conflict with Superman and the society he represented.

The uplifting spirit of *Kingdom Come*'s story was brought to life by Alex Ross' jaw-dropping, almost photographically realistic artwork. As opposed to being rendered in the traditional comic book style of pen and ink, Ross painted all of the art in *Kingdom Come* using a form of watercolor paint known as gouache. His painting style owed much to the realism found in works by Norman Rockwell and Andrew Loomis. Ross actually used live models to create most of the characters featured in *Kingdom Come*; Ross' inspiration for the Norman McKay character was his own father Clark, a minister in real life.

As previously mentioned, *Kingdom Come*'s depiction of Batman/Bruce Wayne was quite similar to the way the character was portrayed in *Batman: The Dark Knight Returns*. He was about the same age in both works, and Miller and Ross visually rendered his physical appearance in a similar manner. However, Waid and Ross came up with the inspired idea of making the character dependent on bionic enhancements. Since he was just an ordinary man, years of crimefighting had taken his toll on him physically, and now he needed these enhancements just to perform everyday tasks. Depicting the character in this manner allowed Waid and Ross to design a futuristic Batman costume complete with jet-propelled wings. The runaway success of *Kingdom Come* led Alex Ross to provide illustrations for a number of other Batman-related works, some of which we'll discuss later in the book.

Another comic work that debuted in 1996 ended up having a sizeable impact on the history of the Batman character. The 13-issue graphic novel series *Batman: The Long Halloween* was very well-received by comic fans when it was first published between late 1996 and late 1997. The series was written by Jeph Loeb and illustrated by Tim Sale, who had previously created three popular stand-alone graphic novel specials for the Batman comic title *Batman: Legends of the Dark Knight*. (These specials were collected together and released as a single-volume graphic novel entitled *Batman: Haunted Knight* in 1996.)

Batman: The Long Halloween told a story that basically picked up right where Frank Miller and David Mazzucchelli's 1987 series *Batman: Year One* left off. In *Batman: The Long Halloween*, Batman is still working to break the stranglehold that crime boss Carmine Falcone has on Gotham City. But Falcone ends up being only a part of the trouble that the crimefighter has to face — an unknown killer is murdering members of the Falcone family on major holidays. Because of the timing of these murders, the killer is dubbed "Holiday."

As Batman tires to deduce who Holiday is, he also has to deal with a number of costumed criminals that have recently appeared in Gotham, including the Joker, the Riddler and the Scarecrow. The crimefighter does have his allies to help him in his struggle to bring Gotham's crime problems under control, especially Commissioner James Gordon and District Attorney Harvey Dent. He also has one other mysterious ally — the Catwoman's actions often border on the criminal, but she has a knack for coming to his aid when he needs it the most.

Batman soon ends up with even *more* trouble — Dent is disfigured when Boss Maroni, a mobster with connections to Falcone, throws a vial of acid onto one side of Dent's face. Dent's injury unhinges his mind, leading him to a life of crime as Two-Face. One of Dent's first actions as Two-Face is to kill Falcone, the man he feels is the most responsible for Gotham's evils.

Eventually Holiday is seemingly brought to justice when Falcone's son Alberto confesses to the killings. But things are not at all what they seem — at the end of the series, it is revealed that Dent's wife Gilda began the Holiday murders in order to destroy the Falcone family so that she and her husband could have a normal life together. Gilda believes that Dent himself might have committed several of the later Holiday murders, and that Alberto's confession is a lie.

Loeb wrote *Batman: The Long Halloween* as an intricate, logical crime drama—in other words, it was very similar in style and spirit to the work that directly inspired it, *Batman: Year One*. Interestingly, though the plot of the series was generally very realistic in nature, its art was not—Sale's work was very expressive, to the point of being almost cartoonish. Still, there was a dark sensibility in Sale's renderings that perfectly meshed with Loeb's suspenseful narrative. *Batman: The Long Halloween* was released as a single-volume book not long after its initial premiere, and it has remained one of the most popular Batman graphic novels ever created. Its success inspired Loeb and Sale to create another Batman series that ended up being quite popular in its own right—*Batman: Dark Victory* (1999–2000) explored the introduction of Dick Grayson into Batman's world. *Batman: The Long Halloween* also ended up having a very large influence on director Christopher Nolan's Batman films—we'll discuss that influence in more detail later in the book.

The 1996 release of the excellent 4-issue comic series *Batman: Black and White* ended up being a noteworthy event in the history of the Batman character as well. The premise of *Batman: Black and White* was a simple one—the series presented a collection of short, black-and-white Batman comic stories created by many of the comic book industry's most admired writers and artists. The variety of stories found in *Batman: Black and White* was truly amazing—there were action-packed adventures, intimate character studies and otherworldly fantasies. Some stories were intensely moving, some were downright chilling, and some were just plain silly. As different as all of these stories were from one another, they all offered affectionate and thought-provoking takes on the Batman character. *Batman: Black and White* was first released as a single-volume book in 1997—it ended up being so well-received that more black-and-white Batman comic stories were created over the years in order to allow for the release of two more *Batman: Black and White* volumes. The quality of these two volumes matched the high standard set by the original *Batman: Black and White*.

The year 1996 also marked the first publication of a unique Batman book that was not a comic work. A marvelous coffee table book, *Batman Collected* by Chip Kidd examined the history of Batman merchandise such as toys, clothes and trading cards. The book consisted mainly of photographer Geoff Spears' beautifully shot pictures of Batman merchandise dating from the 1960s through the '90s. *Batman Collected* was the first major work to explore the importance of Batman non-comic items to the overall Batman fan experience.

We'll touch on one other aspect of Batman's comic history in this chapter. It is an aspect that is by no means specifically confined to the time period between Joel Schumacher's Batman films, but it fits here as well as it does anywhere else in this book. In the 1990s, Batman began to be featured in a growing number of intercompany crossover comic books—in other words, comic books that featured characters from more than one major comic book company.

For example, Batman shared adventures with many of Marvel Comics' most famous characters in a host of joint DC/Marvel comic projects. In 1995, he teamed up with Spider-Man in *Spider-Man and Batman: Disordered Minds*. In 1996, he teamed up with Captain America in *Batman and Captain America*. In 1997, he teamed up with Daredevil in *Daredevil and Batman: Eye for an Eye*, and he again teamed up with Spider-Man in *Batman and Spider-Man: New Age Dawning*. This is just a small sampling of all of the intercompany crossovers that Batman has been featured in since the 1990s—over the past two decades, the character has crossed paths with literally dozens of characters owned by major comic book companies other than DC.

At any rate, in early 1997 the Batman character was going so strong in so many different kinds of works that there seemed to be no chance his next big screen adventure would be anything less than a huge success. As we will discuss next chapter, Joel Schumacher's film *Batman and Robin* released in June of that year blew that assumption into a million pieces.

15

Batman and Robin (1997)

Cast: George Clooney (Batman/Bruce Wayne), Arnold Schwarzenegger (Mr. Freeze/Dr. Victor Fries), Chris O'Donnell (Robin/Dick Grayson), Uma Thurman (Poison Ivy/Dr. Pamela Isley), Alicia Silverstone (Batgirl/Barbara Wilson), Michael Gough (Alfred Pennyworth), Pat Hingle (Commissioner Gordon), Elle MacPherson (Julie Madison), Jeep Swenson (Bane), John Glover (Doctor Jason Woodrue), Vivica A. Fox (Ms. B. Haven), Vendela K. Thommessen (Nora Fries), Elizabeth Sanders (Gossip Gerty), John Fink (Aztec Museum Guard), Michael Reid McKay (Antonio Diego), Eric Lloyd (Young Bruce Wayne), Jon Simmons (Young Alfred), Christian Stogie Kenyatta, Andy Lacombe (Snowy Cones Thugs), Joe Sabatino (Frosty), Michael Paul Chan (Observatory Scientist), Anthony E. Cantrall (Observatory Press), Alex Daniels, Peter Navy Tuiasosopo (Observatory Guards), Harry van Gorkum (M.C.), Sandra Taylor, Elizabeth Guber (Debutantes), Patrick Leahy (Himself), Jesse Ventura, Ralph Moeller (Arkham Asylum Guards), Doug Hutchinson (Golum), Tobias Jelinek, Greg Lauren, Dean Cochran (Motorcycle Gangs), Coolio (Banker), Nicky Katt (Spike), Lucas Berman (Tough Boy Biker), Uzi Gal, Howard Velasco (Cops), Bruce Roberts (Handsome Cop), John Ingle (Doctor). *Producer:* Peter MacGregor-Scott. *Executive Producers:* Benjamin Melniker, Michael E. Uslan. *Director:* Joel Schumacher. *Screenplay:* Akiva Goldsman (Based on characters created by Bob Kane). *Cinematography:* Stephen Goldblatt. *Editors:* Dennis Virkler, Mark Stevens. *Music:* Elliot Goldenthal, Danny Bramson. *Music Editor:* Michael Connell. *Sound:* Petur Hliddal, Joe Iwataki. *Sound Editors:* Bruce Stambler, John Leveque. *Casting:* Mali Finn. *Production Designer:* Barbara Ling. *Art Directors:* Richard Holland, Geoff Hubbard. *Set Designers:* James Bayliss, Richard Berger, Dawn Brown, John P. Bruce, R. Gilbert Clayton, Mick Cukurs, Keith Cunningham, Eric C. Sundahl, Mindi Toback, Stella Furner, Peter J. Kelly, Nancy Mickelberry. *Set Decorator:* Dorree Cooper. *Special Effects:* Matt Sweeney. *Visual Effects:* John Dykstra. *Costumes:* Ingrid Ferrin, Robert Turturice. *Key Makeup:* Ve Neill. *Mr. Freeze Makeup:* Jeff Dawn. *Stunt Coordinators:* Pat E. Johnson, Alex Daniels. *Studio:* Warner Bros. *Length:* 125 minutes. *United States Release Date:* June 20, 1997.

Because Joel Schumacher's *Batman Forever* had turned out to be such a resounding commercial success, Warner Bros. was happy to bring the director back to helm their next live-action Batman film. Schumacher decided that the film would be titled *Batman and Robin*, and that it would feature three of Batman's well-known comic book villains, Mr. Freeze, Poison Ivy and Bane. Schumacher also decided that *Batman and Robin* would introduce the Batgirl character into the Warner Batman film series for the first time. The director called on Akiva Goldsman, co-writer of *Batman Forever*, to write *Batman and Robin*'s screenplay. Goldsman would have his work cut out for him trying to fit all of these new characters, not to mention the film's title characters, into his script.

We've discussed both Mr. Freeze and Bane earlier in the book, but this is the first time

George Clooney as Batman, Chris O'Donnell as Robin, and Alicia Silverstone as Batgirl in *Batman and Robin* (1997).

we've noted the character of Poison Ivy. Clad in a green costume designed to look like leaves from a tree, Poison Ivy first appeared in *Batman* #181, June, 1966, in a story entitled "Beware of — Poison Ivy!" The story did not provide Poison Ivy with any kind of origin — she was just presented as a villainess who was anxious to prove herself as the world's female public enemy number one.

As the years went on, Poison Ivy would be given several different origin stories. The

Arnold Schwarzenegger as Mr. Freeze and Uma Thurman as Poison Ivy in *Batman and Robin* (1997).

one that finally stuck was first published in *Secret Origins* #36, January 1989, in a story entitled "Pavane." The story revealed her real identity to be Pamela Isley, a timid botanical science student who had been injected with poisons during experiments conducted by her crazed professor, Dr. Jason Woodrue. The poisons did not kill her, but they left her body full of plant-like toxins, giving her the ability to kill someone just by kissing them.

Both Poison Ivy and Bane had been featured in episodes of the television program *Batman: The Animated Series*, but *Batman and Robin* would mark the first time that the characters would make it to the screen in a live-action work. This was not the case with Mr. Freeze — as we discussed in Chapter 6, the character had been featured in six episodes of the 1960s *Batman* television series. At any rate, it seemed like a safe bet to assume that Schumacher would do a good job bringing Poison Ivy and Bane to the screen in live-action form for the first time — after all, in *Batman Forever* the director and Tommy Lee Jones had handled the live-action screen debut of Two-Face quite well.

Even before *Batman Forever* finished its initial theatrical run, Goldsman began work on crafting a script for *Batman and Robin*. Goldsman's screenplay for the film turned out to be strictly a solo effort — he did not collaborate with any other writers, and no other writers were ever called upon to make revisions to his finished work. This was the first time that a Warner Batman film script had been created in such a manner — all of the studio's previous Batman movies had been written by more than one screenwriter.

Schumacher might have had no trouble finding his screenwriter for *Batman and Robin*, but he ended up having quite a bit of trouble finding his Batman for the film. Val Kilmer was under contract with Warner Bros. to reprise his role as Batman/Bruce Wayne in the studio's follow-up to *Batman Forever*, but it was obvious that the actor was not particularly interested in honoring that contract. He had signed with Paramount Pictures to play the title role in their film *The Saint*, and this commitment ended up leading to the possibility of Kilmer being required to work on *The Saint* and *Batman and Robin* at virtually the same time. Warner Bros. and Schumacher were understandably upset with Kilmer over his willingness to take on another film that could compromise his ability to work on *their* film. After a few initial attempts to resolve the situation with Kilmer and Paramount, Warner and Schumacher decided that it would be a better choice to simply find a different actor to play Batman in *Batman and Robin*.[1]

In fact, Schumacher already had someone in mind for the part — the director called on George Clooney to replace Kilmer. Clooney was a handsome, 35-year-old actor best known for starring in the hit NBC television drama *ER*. Clooney was actually a hotter property than was Kilmer at the time *Batman and Robin* was going into production, so it seemed as if Schumacher had actually been able to "trade up" in terms of selecting a new Batman.

As happy as Schumacher was to secure Clooney for *Batman and Robin*, he probably was every bit as happy about the fact that he would not have to work with Kilmer again. As we discussed in Chapter 13, Schumacher found Kilmer difficult to work with during the making of *Batman Forever*. And the actor's decision to take on *The Saint* seemed like a very clear indication that he would have continued to be a disruptive presence if he had been forced to honor his contract and star in *Batman and Robin*. Ironically, there would end up being no clear winner in the battle between Schumacher and Kilmer. *The Saint* was released in 1997, and the film did Kilmer no good at all when it turned out to be a commercial and critical failure. And Schumacher's *Batman and Robin* — well, I think we all know where *this* story is going to end up!

But let's not get too far ahead of ourselves here. Schumacher scored a number of casting triumphs to go along with his new Batman. Chris O'Donnell, whose Robin/Dick Grayson portrayal had been very effective in *Batman Forever*, signed on to reprise his role in *Batman and Robin*. And *Batman and Robin*'s other main characters were going to be portrayed by actors who were sure to generate every bit as much attention as Clooney and O'Donnell. Megawatt action star Arnold Schwarzenegger was cast as Mr. Freeze/Dr. Victor Fries, and Uma Thurman was chosen to play Poison Ivy/Dr. Pamela Isley. Thurman had become a major star in her own right after her memorable performance in the commercially and critically successful 1994 crime film *Pulp Fiction*. Alicia Silverstone, best known for starring in the 1995 hit comedy *Clueless*, was cast as Batgirl/Barbara Wilson. The part of Bane was given to professional wrestler/actor Robert "Jeep" Swenson.

Not surprisingly, Schumacher elected to retain the Warner Batman film series' two most dependable actors for *Batman and Robin*—Michael Gough was again cast as Alfred, and Pat Hingle was again cast as Commissioner Gordon. Gough's role had been expanded in *Batman Forever*, and it would be expanded even further in *Batman and Robin*—in fact, this time around, his character would end up driving much of the film's plot.

Like *Batman Forever*, *Batman and Robin* was primarily filmed at Warner's Burbank studios. Also like its predecessor, *Batman and Robin* used a blend of gargantuan real-life sets and computer-generated images to realize its spectacular vision of Gotham City and its equally spectacular action sequences. These sets and computer graphics were again tied together by incredibly complex and detailed miniature sets that were even more elaborate than the miniature sets used for *Batman Forever*. The miniature Gotham City set created for *Batman and Robin* featured twice as many structures as *Batman Forever*'s miniature Gotham set, and its tallest buildings were over thirty feet tall, twice as tall as *Batman Forever*'s tallest building model.[2]

Production of *Batman and Robin* took place from early 1996 through early 1997, with most of the principal photography taking place between September 1996 and February 1997. Schumacher and Warner Bros. seemed to feel every bit as optimistic about the film while it was in production as they had felt about *Batman Forever* while it was being made. This optimism appeared to be very well-founded — the film's cast and crew all got along wonderfully with one another, working so smoothly together that principal photography wrapped ten days earlier than scheduled.[3]

The calm, positive atmosphere surrounding the movie was undoubtedly helped along by the fact that Schumacher had been able to retain much of his behind-the-camera talent from *Batman Forever*, including producer Peter MacGregor-Scott, production designer Barbara Ling, visual effects supervisor John Dykstra, and composer Elliot Goldenthal. Simply put, everything about *Batman and Robin* seemed to indicate that Warner's Batman franchise was about to chalk up another tremendous success.

The film had ended up to be the studio's most expensive Batman film to date — the price tag of the production was about $125 million.[4] But Warner had to have considered that price tag to be money well spent, because Schumacher and company definitely seemed to be on a roll with their Batman franchise. How could *Batman and Robin* end up being anything but a huge blockbuster for them?

But after the first preview trailers for *Batman and Robin* ran in spring 1997, many serious Batman fans sensed that something had gone very wrong with the film. First off, many of the scenes in the preview were lit in outrageously garish shades of magenta, orange and lime green. These colors did not seem to match up with the images of the dark, shadow-lined streets of Gotham City found in Warners' previous Batman films.

Also, some of the film's costumes seemed all wrong. Chris O'Donnell wore a Robin costume that was all blue with an abstract red bird logo on its chest — in other words, a costume that did not even slightly resemble any costume the character had ever worn in his almost 60-year history. Alicia Silverstone's Batgirl costume consisted of nothing more than a rather undefined all-black bodysuit and a black cape — the costume did not even have the bat-eared cowl that the character had always worn in the comics. Finally, the preview featured Clooney as Batman rather jocularly saying "Hi Freeze, I'm Batman" upon meeting Mr. Freeze for the first time. Judging from this scene, there was not going to be near enough darkness in Clooney's Dark Knight for most longtime Batman fans' tastes.

Of course, previews can be misleading, so these fans had to wait for the film's nationwide premiere on June 20, 1997, just like the rest of the general movie going public to see how good or bad the film would actually be. When they actually got to see *Batman and Robin* in its entirety, most of them were mortified — the film was so day-glo bright, so goofy, so utterly "un–Dark Knightish" that it seemed to have far more in common with the campy 1960s *Batman* TV show and film than with Warner's previous Batman films. Granted, these earlier films did not by any means paint a consistent portrait of their title character — elements of the "dark" Batman found in Burton's *Batman Returns* were certainly at odds with elements of Schumacher's *Batman Forever*'s "light" Batman. But even still, *Batman and Robin* was *so* completely off the mark in terms of portraying the post-camp Batman that it made the majority of serious Batman fans raging mad. What in the world had Joel Schumacher done to their hero?

Batman and Robin opens with a series of quick shots of Batman and Robin in the Batcave, readying themselves for battle. Batman speeds off in the Batmobile and Robin speeds off on his Redbird motorcycle, both headed for the Gotham Museum of Art where Mr. Freeze is attempting to steal a rare diamond. Freeze has used his freeze gun to cover most everything in the museum with ice. Batman and Robin burst in and use ice skates that are built into the soles of their boots to fight Freeze's thugs. The fight becomes a wild game of hockey with the rare diamond as the puck. As the heroes overpower the thugs, Mr. Freeze tries to escape in his small rocket-powered capsule.

Batman and Robin also climb on board the capsule right before it launches. As the capsule rises, Freeze shoots his freeze gun at Batman's arms and traps him. Freeze jumps out of the capsule right before it leaves the Earth's atmosphere, gliding toward the Earth using wings built into the back of his costume. Robin frees Batman from his icy trap, and the pair uses the capsule's doors to "skyboard" back to earth, fighting Freeze on the way down. Back on solid ground, Freeze blasts Robin with his freeze gun and encases him in a block of ice. Rather than pursue Freeze any further, Batman thaws out his partner.

The scene shifts to a South American rain forest, where Dr. Pamela Isley is developing a chemical concoction called "Venom," so that plants will be able to protect themselves like animals. However, the Venom is being used without her knowledge by her supervisor Dr. Woodrue in an attempt to create an army of "super soldiers." Woodrue injects one of his human guinea pigs with Venom and creates his first super soldier, whom he calls "Bane." When Isley discovers Woodrue's plans for corrupting her research, he pushes her into her research table. She falls to the floor, covered with plant toxins and poisonous creatures. But incredibly, she does not die — instead, these toxins and poisons fuse with her own chemistry, turning her into Poison Ivy. In the ruins of her lab, she notices a Wayne Enterprises beaker. Since Wayne was the original backer of Woodrue's and Isley's work, Poison Ivy decides to travel to Gotham City and confront Bruce Wayne. She brings Bane along with her in case she might need some extra muscle.

Back in Gotham City, Bruce and Dick discuss the origin of Mr. Freeze. Freeze was originally Dr. Victor Fries, a molecular biologist working to find a cure for a disease known as MacGregor's Syndrome. Fries was particularly committed to ending the disease, because it was killing his wife Nora. To slow the progress of the disease in Nora, Victor placed her in a water-filled tank and suspended her in a cryogenic sleep. But one night while he was conducting his research, a lab accident left him unable to withstand any temperature above the most freezing cold. His mind unhinged by the impending loss of his wife and his accident, he adopted the guise of Mr. Freeze. He needs diamonds due to the fact that his extreme-cold suit is powered by diamond enhanced lasers. But Mr. Freeze is momentarily forgotten at Wayne Manor because of the unexpected arrival of Barbara Wilson, Alfred's young niece, who is on break from her studies at a school in England. Bruce tells Barbara she is welcome to stay and visit her uncle as long as she likes.

The next day, Bruce attends a press conference to announce Wayne Enterprises' donation of a powerful telescope to the Gotham Observatory. Pamela Isley crashes the dedication and tries to get Wayne Enterprises to adopt a series of extreme environmental policies designed to protect the world's plants. Bruce rejects her proposal, telling her that his company puts the needs of people first, not plants. Pamela angrily tells him that she will help plants to reclaim the world.

That night, Batman and Robin attend a charity event to raise money to go toward the protection of the Earth's rainforests. Part of the charity event is an auction in which the highest bidders win dates with beautiful women dressed in plant-themed attire. Poison Ivy crashes the party and, though she is not supposed to be on the auction block, she enters herself in the bidding. Through the use of a fairy dust–like mix of pheromones, she drives all the bidders wild with desire, including Batman and Robin. The bidding finally ends when Batman whips a Batman credit card out of his utility belt.

The auction is interrupted when Mr. Freeze crashes the party to steal a rare diamond that is on display there. He makes off with the diamond and drives away in his armored Freeze mobile. Batman and Robin pursue him, Batman in the Batmobile and Robin on his Redbird cycle. Freeze drives off of a bridge and onto one of Gotham's giant statues. As he drives down the arm of the statue, Batman and Robin follow closely behind him. Freeze jumps his vehicle from the statue's hand to a nearby rooftop, and Batman also makes the jump in the Batmobile. But Batman does not allow Robin to make the jump for fear that he might get hurt; via computer, he shuts the Redbird cycle's engine down. Batman slams into Freeze on the rooftop, capturing him.

Back at the Batcave, Batman and Robin argue — Robin says that if they are ever to truly work as a team, Batman needs to trust him. Later, Bruce talks to Alfred about his troubles with Dick. Alfred tells Bruce that he believes Bruce has never really learned to trust *anyone*— he has used his Batman guise to try to control fate, and to shield himself from tragedies like the one that took his parents from him. Alfred also tells him that trying to control fate, even death itself, is a struggle that no one can win — not even someone as formidable as Batman.

Meanwhile, Dick spots Barbara taking one of Bruce's motorcycles and sneaking it out of the Wayne Manor garage late at night. Curious to see what the girl is up to, Dick follows her and learns that she is entering illegal and highly dangerous street races in downtown Gotham. This night's race is so dangerous that Dick has to save Barbara from plummeting off of a bridge that is under construction. Back at Wayne Manor, Barbara tells Dick that she was expelled from school for motorcycle racing, but racing earned enough money to allow her to take Alfred away from his life of servitude and take care of him for the rest of his days. But there may not be too many of these days left — Bruce walks in to tell Dick that Alfred is gravely ill.

The captured Freeze has been taken to Arkham Asylum, but just as soon as he arrives, Ivy and Bane show up to break him out. Upon hearing the news of Freeze's escape, Batman and Robin race to meet with Commissioner Gordon at Freeze's old hideout. Freeze, Ivy and

Bane have also made their way to the hideout. Upon finding the police and Batman and Robin there, Freeze turns on the hideout's ultra freezing air vents in order to chase the cops out, and Ivy and Bane battle Batman and Robin. Ivy uses her pheromones to attract the heroes to her, and they end up quarreling over her rather than capturing her. They escape, but not before Ivy disconnects the power to the cryo-chamber holding Freeze's wife.

Ivy lies to Freeze, telling him that Batman has killed his wife. Enraged, Freeze plans on using the new Gotham Observatory telescope in conjunction with his newly developed freeze cannon to blanket the city in endless winter, making everyone in Gotham pay for the misery Batman has inflicted on him. Back at Wayne Manor, the heroes learn that, like Nora Fries, Alfred is dying of MacGregor's Syndrome. Bruce and Dick again quarrel over Bruce's refusal to consider Dick an equal partner — Dick says he is tired of living in Bruce's shadow, and he wants his own Robin light in the sky.

Through a computer disc created by Alfred, Barbara has learned that Bruce and Dick are actually Batman and Robin. Barbara now understands that the reason Alfred has remained in servitude for so long is that he was tending to heroes, not just a couple of spoiled bachelors. Barbara sneaks into the Batcave, where a computer simulation of Alfred tells the girl that he suspected she might learn Wayne's secret, so he took the liberty of designing her own crimefighting costume. She will be "Batgirl."

Ivy, realizing that Robin is unhappy about living in Batman's shadow, steals the Batsignal and changes it into a Robin signal. Robin answers the signal, but not alone — Batman has convinced him that Ivy is setting a trap for him, so the two heroes put aside their differences to try to capture Ivy. Ivy ends up capturing *them* with her specially bred, super strong vines. Batgirl rushes in to save the day, defeating Ivy in hand-to-hand combat. Batman and Robin are surprised by Barbara's transformation, but they figure they will need all the help they can get to stop Freeze and his freeze cannon. So the newly formed team of Batman, Robin and Batgirl, wearing brand-new matching black and silver costumes, race off to confront Freeze at the Gotham Observatory, located high atop a huge statue above the streets of the city.

From the Observatory, Freeze uses his cannon and the telescope to begin covering the city in ice. The trio of heroes arrive on the scene and begin work on reversing the freezing process, but Freeze attacks them, sending Robin and Batgirl plummeting off the observatory. Using their grappling hooks, the young heroes stop their fall and make their way back up to the observatory. They are now attacked by Bane, but they are able to defeat the villain by disconnecting the tube that supplies his brain with Venom.

Atop the telescope, Batman and Freeze fight. Batman is able to defeat the villain, but Freeze ignites a number of bombs he has placed in the observatory, completely destroying the telescope. Using the telescope's undamaged computer to realign a number of satellites orbiting the Earth, the heroes are able to reflect the rays of the sun throughout downtown Gotham to reverse the damage Freeze has caused. Batman tells the defeated Freeze that he did not kill Nora — in fact, he restored the power to her cryo-chamber, actually saving her life. In gratitude, Freeze resolves to give up his life of crime and re-dedicate himself to helping humanity. He starts by giving Batman vials of medication that can cure MacGregor's Syndrome in its early stages. Freeze is then returned to Arkham, where he is to share a cell with Poison Ivy. Ivy, whose mind has seemingly become completely unhinged, stares in unbelieving terror at her new cellmate.

Back at Wayne Manor, Bruce administers Freeze's medication to Alfred and cures him of MacGregor's Syndrome. Bruce agrees not only to treat Dick as more of an equal, but also to take Barbara on as a partner as well. The film ends with Batman, Robin and Batgirl shown in silhouette, running in front of the lit Batsignal.

There is so much wrong with *Batman and Robin* that it is hard to decide where to begin discussing the film's problematic elements. But one of the main things that jumped out at this Batman fan upon seeing it for the first time was that so much of the film was such a literal retread of *Batman Forever*. *Batman and Robin* was so close to *Batman Forever* in terms of plot, pacing and character development that one cannot help but come to the conclusion that the film was consciously pieced together to be as similar to its predecessor as possible.

What follows is a breakdown of major events that occur in *both* movies—notice how these events even occur at almost exactly the same *time* in each movie!

Batman Forever opening—WB shield morphs into a bat logo, the principal actor credits roll in a "letters whooshing across the screen" motif, and a bat symbol is shown with the words "FOREVER" superimposed over it.

Batman and Robin opening—WB shield morphs into a bat logo, the principal actor credits roll in a "letters whooshing across the screen" motif, and a bat symbol is shown with a "Robin" symbol superimposed over it.

Batman Forever 1 minute, 10 seconds—Batman is in the Batcave, putting on his costume and readying his weapons for battle.

Batman and Robin 1 minute, 10 seconds—Batman and Robin are in the Batcave, putting on their costumes and readying their weapons for battle.

Batman Forever 1 minute, 30 seconds—The Batmobile rises out of a sunken turntable.

Batman and Robin 2 minutes—The Batmobile rises out of a sunken turntable.

Batman Forever 1 minute, 45 seconds—Batman and Alfred exchange quips before Batman drives off in the Batmobile.

Batman and Robin 2 minutes, 20 seconds—Batman, Robin and Alfred exchange quips before Batman drives off in the Batmobile, and Robin drives off on his Redbird motorcycle.

Batman Forever 2 minutes—The Batmobile races into Gotham City.

Batman and Robin 3 minutes—The Batmobile and the Redbird motorcycle race into Gotham City.

Batman Forever 2 minutes, 30 seconds—Two-Face terrorizes a helpless bank security guard.

Batman and Robin 4 minutes—Mr. Freeze terrorizes a helpless museum security guard.

Batman Forever 6 minutes—Batman enters and battles Two-Face's thugs.

Batman and Robin 6 minutes—Batman and Robin enter and battle Mr. Freeze's thugs.

Batman Forever 7 minutes, 15 seconds—Batman is locked in a safe that is attached to Two-Face's helicopter and pulled into the sky high above Gotham City.

Batman and Robin 9 minutes, 45 seconds—Batman is trapped in Mr. Freeze's rocket-powered capsule which launches into the sky high above Gotham City.

Batman Forever 12 minutes—Batman and Two-Face jump out of the helicopter to safety right before it crashes.

Batman and Robin 11 minutes–12 minutes, 30 seconds—Batman, Robin and Mr. Freeze jump out of the capsule to safety right before it leaves the Earth's atmosphere.

Batman Forever 13 minutes—Edward Nygma, the disgruntled Wayne Enterprises employee who will murder his immediate supervisor and become the costumed villain the Riddler, is introduced.

Batman and Robin 15 minutes—Pamela Isley, the disgruntled Wayne Enterprises employee who will murder her immediate supervisor and become the costumed villain Poison Ivy, is introduced.

Batman Forever 24 minutes, 45 seconds—The origin of Two-Face is shown via a television news video clip.

Batman and Robin 21 minutes—The origin of Mr. Freeze is shown via a security camera video clip.

Batman Forever 33 minutes—Dick Grayson, the young trapeze artist who will become Batman's junior partner Robin, is introduced.

Batman and Robin 29 minutes—Barbara Wilson, Alfred's young niece who will become Batman's junior partner Batgirl, is introduced.

Batman Forever 33 minutes—A lavish circus to benefit a charitable cause is held for Gotham's elite, and the event is crashed by Two-Face.

Batman and Robin 40 minutes—A lavish ball to benefit a charitable cause is held for Gotham's elite, and the event is crashed by Poison Ivy and Mr. Freeze.

Batman Forever 1 hour, 5 minutes—Dick steals the Batmobile from the Batcave after learning that Bruce is Batman. He fights a bunch of street punks with neon paint on their faces who are trying to abduct a young woman. When they start to overwhelm him, Batman comes to his rescue.

Batman and Robin 1 hour, 1 minute—Barbara steals one of Bruce's motorcycles and enters herself in an illegal street gang race being run by street punks with neon paint on their faces. When the punks sabotage her during the race, Dick comes to her rescue.

Batman Forever 1 hour, 38 minutes—Batman suits up in his new glossy-black hi-tech suit for the first time. A quick camera shot playfully focuses on his rear end.

Batman and Robin 1 hour, 36 minutes—Batgirl suits up in her new glossy-black hi-tech suit for the first time. A quick camera shot playfully focuses on her rear end.

Batman Forever 1 hour, 40 minutes—The newly established team of Batman and Robin head off in separate Bat vehicles to confront the Riddler and Two-Face.

Batman and Robin 1 hour, 42 minutes—The newly established team of Batman, Robin and Batgirl head off in separate Bat vehicles to confront Mr. Freeze.

Batman Forever 1 hour, 54 minutes—After defeating the Riddler, Batman stands over his foe in triumph.

Batman and Robin 1 hour, 55 minutes—After defeating Mr. Freeze, Batman stands over his foe in triumph.

Batman Forever 1 hour, 55 minutes—Edward Nygma is shown incarcerated in Arkham Asylum, completely out of his mind, wearing dirty black and white-striped prison clothes.

Batman and Robin 1 hour, 56 minutes—Pamela Isley is shown incarcerated in Arkham Asylum, completely out of her mind, wearing dirty black and white-striped prison clothes.

Batman Forever 1 hour, 57 minutes—Batman and Robin are shown in silhouette running in front of the lit Batsignal.

Batman and Robin 1 hour, 59 minutes—Batman, Robin and Batgirl are shown in silhouette running in front of the lit Batsignal.

Obviously, it should be pointed out that sequels by their very nature often tend to be very similar to the films that inspired them—after all, they almost always involve the same characters, as well as the same styles of plot and pacing. It should also be pointed out that the motion picture industry as a whole is guilty of an appalling lack of creativity—year after year, Hollywood turns out plenty of big-budget, big-studio films that are short on originality and long on derivativeness. But as illustrated above, *Batman and Robin* is *so* similar to *Batman Forever* that it feels about as imaginatively constructed as a child's "paint by numbers" set.

But as bad as *Batman and Robin*'s formulaic nature is, the film has an even bigger problem — namely, it is completely divorced from any sense of reality. As discussed last chapter, *Batman Forever*'s use of computer graphics technology perhaps gave Schumacher and company *too* much freedom, because it allowed them to stray far beyond the boundaries of what a hero like Batman could do if he were actually a real person. This problem was magnified tenfold in *Batman and Robin*. Characters are flying through the air at impossible speeds and trajectories, cars are being driven over wildly uneven terrain, and roads suddenly dead end right in the middle of bridges that look to be 50 stories off of the ground. At different points in the film, Batman, Robin, Mr. Freeze, Poison Ivy and Bane are all shown leaping off of buildings or flying vehicles and plummeting thousands of feet back to earth without any means to slow their descent, and none of them suffers so much as a scratch.

Ironically, Schumacher himself concisely summed up this problem in an interview he gave to a film special effects magazine entitled *Cinefex*. In the article "Freeze Frames" (September 1997), Schumacher spoke excitedly of the liberties that computer-generated special effects had allowed the *Batman and Robin* team to take: "We were able to create the kind of excitement and fantasy you don't normally see in an action movie, simply because we didn't have to concern ourselves with reality."[5] The idea that Schumacher considered not having to concern himself with reality a plus when making a Batman film shows how poorly the director actually understood his subject. Because without reality, Batman was simply not Batman.

One of the most bizarre manifestations of *Batman and Robin*'s unreality was the film's Batmobile designed by production designer Barbara Ling. The car had always been depicted in a fanciful manner since the 1960s *Batman* film and TV show, but *Batman and Robin*'s Batmobile was not so much fanciful as it was absurd. It was about 30 feet long from its front bumper to its gigantic rear tailfins, and all it had in terms of cockpit space was a tiny little opening that was barely even big enough for one person! The whole point of Batman ever having a Batmobile was so that he could transport not only himself, but also other passengers and crimefighting equipment. A Batmobile that was about as long as a mobile home and could only carry one person made no sense whatsoever.

Batman and Robin's unreality was made all the more unbearable by Akiva Goldsman's self-consciously campy script. *Batman Forever*'s generally strong script had actually been co-written by Goldsman with Lee Batchler and Janet Scott Batchler — but *Batman and Robin* proved beyond the shadow of a doubt that Goldsman was not up to the task of creating a decent Batman film script all on his own. The film was full of appallingly "cute" touches such as Batman pulling a Batman credit card out of his utility belt, and Batman and Robin producing ice skates from the soles of their boots to fight Freeze's thugs. Also, *Batman and Robin*'s terrible disease that was supposedly threatening the life of Nora Fries and Alfred was nothing more than a silly in-joke — "MacGregor's Syndrome" was completely made-up disease named after the film's producer, Peter MacGregor-Scott. Goldsman left the "MacGregor's Syndrome" plotline so underdeveloped that the film never even bothered to explain what part of the body the disease attacked, or what its symptoms were!

Another of *Batman and Robin*'s major problems was the film's costuming. Schumacher decided to completely revamp the costumes of Batman, Robin and Batgirl, with predictably disastrous results. The film's title might have been *Batman and Robin*, but given Robin's basically all-blue costume, it sure did not *look* like Robin up there on the screen. And the first Batgirl costume Alicia Silverstone wore in the film consisted of nothing more than a rather plain all-black bodysuit and black cape. It had no color to it to give it any definition — it would have looked far better if it had remained truer to the character's time-honored costume and sported a yellow bat emblem, boots and gloves. Worst of all, the costume did not even have the bat-eared cowl that the character had always worn in the comics. Schumacher and company decided to let Silverstone's beautiful hair fly free when dressed as Batgirl. And her hair *was* lovely — she just didn't look anything like Batgirl.

The Batman costume George Clooney wore for the majority of the film was generally similar to the Batman costumes Val Kilmer wore in *Batman Forever*. Clooney's costume was completely blue-black in color, and featured a bat emblem molded into the costume's chest armor. It was the least jarring of the film's hero costumes because it basically stayed true to the character's "movie look" established in Warner's previous Batman films.

Amusingly, both of these Batman and Robin costumes featured sharply-defined nipples molded onto their chest armor just like the costumes in *Batman Forever*, but poor Batgirl didn't get any sharply-defined nipples on *her* costume! Obviously, giving Batgirl's costume a "topless" look was not even remotely an option for the filmmakers, considering they were looking to make *Batman and Robin* a family friendly Batman film like its predecessor *Batman Forever* had been. But the film's decision to have "some nipples here, but no nipples there" served to illustrate just how completely ridiculous a decision it was to ever outfit *any* of the costumes with nipples in the first place.

The hero costuming situation degraded even further during *Batman and Robin*'s climax. When the three heroes confront Mr. Freeze at Gotham Observatory, they have all changed into new, matching costumes. (Since Alfred was always depicted as being the "costume maker" in Schumacher's Batman films, one can assume that the early stages of MacGregor's Syndrome do not affect tailoring skills.) The costumes were dark gray in color with silver highlights molded into their armor. Once these costumes appeared on the screen, Batman, Robin and Batgirl lost almost all visual connection to their comic book counterparts. With no elements of design or color to separate them from one another, they might has well have been stormtroopers in a *Star Wars* film.

Batman and Robin's lighting did nothing to help this feeling that Batman, Robin and Batgirl were actually no longer Batman, Robin and Batgirl in the film. As previously mentioned, much of the film was lit in outrageously garish shades of magenta, orange and lime green, and these colors did not seem to match up with the images of the dark, shadow-lined streets of Gotham City found in Warner's previous Batman films. This combination of "non–Batman costumes" and "non–Batman colors" made *Batman and Robin* feel like a — well, like a "non–Batman film."

The criticisms of Schumacher infusing his cinematic version of the Batman character with inappropriate sexual subtext that arose with the release of *Batman Forever* continued with the release of *Batman and Robin*. As discussed last chapter, these criticisms of *Batman Forever* had some validity — and since *Batman and Robin* was so similar to its predecessor, the criticisms applied equally well to this new film. But the film had far bigger problems than simply the inclusion of a few sexual in-jokes.

With all of *Batman and Robin*'s problems, poor George Clooney really had no chance of establishing himself as a good Batman/Bruce Wayne. At 5'11" and of average build, he was by no means physically perfect for the part, but had he been given a better Batman film to appear in, he likely would have been far better in the role than he was in *Batman and*

Robin. At any rate, Clooney played the part in the film with the same detached charm he had displayed in many of his other movie and TV roles. His amiable performance was enjoyable enough, but given the overall absurdity of the film he was not given any chance to display the kind of intensity that Michael Keaton or Val Kilmer had in their best Batman screen moments.

Perhaps Clooney's strongest scenes in *Batman and Robin* were the ones he played opposite Michael Gough. As Alfred faces his own mortality with dignity and grace in the film, Bruce must face the prospect of losing the person who has been closest to him since his parents died. It is at this profound moment that both men truly realize what they have meant to each other throughout the years. Both Clooney and Gough acted these scenes with sincerity and warmth, making the scenes just about the only ones in the film with any emotional resonance.

In *Batman and Robin*, Chris O'Donnell's Robin/Dick Grayson character took a gigantic step backward from his debut in *Batman Forever*. His Robin costumes were nothing like any of the costumes the Robin comic character had ever worn. And in his scenes as Dick Grayson, his shrill bickering with Bruce over wanting his own Robin signal in the sky made him sound not like a determined crimefighter, but like a Las Vegas nightclub performer who is unhappy over not receiving star billing in his act. Like Clooney, O'Donnell never really had a chance of making his character work in *Batman and Robin* since he was saddled with such atrocious material.

As Batgirl/Barbara Wilson, Alicia Silverstone fared no better. Her scenes as both Batgirl and Barbara were about as badly written as most every other scene in the film. Plus, for many longtime Batman fans, Silverstone's Batgirl just did not seem like Batgirl because the character's origin was so different from the comic book Batgirl's. In the film, instead of being Barbara Gordon, the daughter of Commissioner Gordon, she was Barbara Wilson, Alfred's niece. This change made good narrative sense in the context of the film because Alfred was such a major part of the film's storyline and Gordon was not. But even still, it was a change that did not sit well with many Batman fans, so consequently they had little use for Silverstone's performance.

Arnold Schwarzenegger's Mr. Freeze/Dr. Victor Fries was arguably the most grating of *Batman and Robin*'s major characters. The development of Freeze had started out promisingly enough — his origin revolving around his attempts to save his wife Nora was nicely adapted from the Mr. Freeze origin story created for "Heart of Ice," a standout episode of the television program *Batman: The Animated Series*. (We discussed that episode in some detail in Chapter 11.) Also, Schwarzenegger's silvery-blue makeup that covered every inch of his exposed skin, and his imposing metallic costume with neon blue highlights, made the character visually very interesting.

But the character was completely spoiled by his obnoxious tendency to speak dialogue that consisted of little more than an unending barrage of bad puns and one-liners relating to ice and cold. It seemed as if Schumacher and Goldsman wanted to capitalize on Arnold's tradition of uttering pithy, instantly memorable phrases in his films, such as his deathless line "I'll be back" from *The Terminator* (1984). Consequently, almost every line that Schwarzenegger spoke in *Batman and Robin* sounded like it was designed to be printed on a souvenir Mr. Freeze T-shirt that kiddies would want to rush out and buy just as soon as they had seen the movie. Here is just a sampling of these lines — "The Iceman cometh," "Cool party" and "Chilled to perfection." And they say comic book dialogue is corny!

Uma Thurman's Poison Ivy/Dr. Pamela Isley was perhaps the strongest of *Batman and*

Robin's main characters. Her origin was well-adapted from the comic book Poison Ivy's origin story "Pavane" we discussed at the beginning of this chapter. Also, the mainly bright green plant-themed costumes Thurman wore were faithful to the character's appearance both in the comics and in episodes of *Batman: The Animated Series*. Thurman made the most of the decent material she was given to work with in the film, hamming up her part with a nice blend of sexuality and humor.

The Bane character's inclusion in *Batman and Robin* seemed like nothing more than an afterthought. Schumacher and company evidently decided that since Bane had become such a popular character in Batman comic books, they would find a way to tie him into Poison Ivy's origin so they could use him in the film. But they certainly did not use him to great effect — he was depicted as being little more than a dimwitted henchman for Ivy. Given the character's popularity in Batman comics, many fans were disappointed to see him reduced to such a simple background character. One final, and tragic, note regarding *Batman and Robin*'s Bane — Robert "Jeep" Swenson, the actor who played the role, died of heart failure caused by steroid abuse not long after the film was released.

Incredibly, there were other characters in *Batman and Robin* that were even *less* developed than Bane! Far and away the most puzzling of these characters was Bruce's girlfriend Julie Madison, played by Elle MacPherson. Schumacher and Goldsman went *way* back to find the Julie Madison character in Batman comic stories — she was featured in a number of Batman's adventures that were first published between late 1939 and early 1941! In those stories, she was a beautiful socialite who was engaged to Bruce Wayne, but she eventually broke off their engagement because she hated seeing him waste his life away as a self-centered, lazy playboy. (Obviously, Bruce never revealed his secret life as Batman to her.)

Julie only appeared in several scenes in *Batman and Robin*, and she was so peripheral that there was really no point in including her in the film at all. In fact, you'll notice that it wasn't necessary for me to even *mention* the character when providing a very detailed account of the film's plot! Bruce Wayne's other love interests that made the leap from the comics to the screen such as Linda Page and Vicki Vale might not have been the most memorable movie characters ever created, but even they managed to make an infinitely bigger impression than Julie Madison did in *Batman and Robin*. Perhaps Schumacher thought so highly of MacPherson that he wanted to find some way to include her in one of his movies — but he certainly didn't do her any favors by giving her this particular part.

Unfortunately, Commissioner Gordon ended up being another of *Batman and Robin*'s woefully underdeveloped characters. Pat Hingle as Gordon was only given a handful of lines in the film, reducing Batman's most trusted ally on the Gotham City Police Department to nothing more than one of *Batman and Robin*'s bit players.

Like *Batman Forever*, *Batman and Robin* was designed to be a family friendly Batman film that would attract audiences of all ages — in other words, a film that would make Warner Bros. lots and lots of money. But because of all the movie's shortcomings, it took a terrible critical and commercial beating. *Batman and Robin* received overwhelmingly negative reviews, and only ended up grossing only about $107 million during its U.S. theatrical run — about $75 million less than *Batman Forever* had grossed during its U.S. theatrical run two years earlier. After *Batman and Robin* finished its worldwide run it had grossed about $238 million, so it had finally made Warner Bros. enough money for the studio to call the film a "hit."[6] But of course, Warner did not really consider the film a hit at all. It was their lowest-grossing Batman film yet. With the release of *Batman and Robin*, Joel Schumacher had let the studio down even worse than Tim Burton had with the release of *Batman Returns*.

Warner Bros. aggressively marketed the home video release of *Batman and Robin* in October 1997, likely hoping that the film would be able to bring in some extra revenue in the wake of its disappointing box office numbers. While all of Warner's previous Batman movies had first premiered in the home video market on videotape or laserdisc formats, *Batman and Robin*'s initial home video release was on DVD format. The movie was also released on VHS tape and laserdisc for consumers who had not yet upgraded to DVD technology. The DVD offered the film in its original widescreen format as well as in a format cropped to fit a standard television screen, but it offered no bonus features or printed material dealing with the making of the film. Incidentally, Warner chose to release its previous three live-action Batman movies, *Batman* (1989), *Batman Returns* (1992), and *Batman Forever* (1995), to the home video market on DVD for the first time upon the home video premiere of *Batman and Robin*. (We discussed the home video release history for each of those films in detail in their individual chapters.)

As we also discussed in those chapters, the success of Warner's 2005 film *Batman Begins* led the studio to release their four previous Batman live-action features on 2-disc DVD sets late that same year. Each of these sets were loaded with special features that detailed their particular film's creation. The *Batman and Robin* DVD set included a number of newly-produced documentaries about the movie. The program *Shadows of the Bat: The Cinematic Saga of the Dark Knight Part 6* chronicled the making of *Batman and Robin*, featuring insights from many of the individuals who played a major role in the film's creation such Joel Schumacher, Akiva Goldsman, Peter MacGregor-Scott, George Clooney, Chris O'Donnell, Arnold Schwarzenegger, Uma Thurman, and Alicia Silverstone. These insights were accompanied by a good deal of behind-the-scenes footage shot on the *Batman and Robin* set showing the movies's cast and crew at work. Perhaps the most unusual moment of the documentary was when Schumacher literally offered an apology to anyone who had been disappointed by the film!

The DVD set's program *Beyond Batman* consisted of featurettes about some of the specific elements of *Batman and Robin*. The titles of the featurettes were "Bigger, Bolder, Brighter: The Production Design of *Batman and Robin*," "Maximum Overdrive: The Vehicles of *Batman and Robin*," "Dressed to Thrill: The Costumes of *Batman and Robin*," "Frozen Freaks and Femme Fatales: The Makeup of *Batman and Robin*," and "Freeze Frame: The Visual Effects of *Batman and Robin*." The set also included featurettes on the main heroes and villains of the film.

The DVD set featured one scene that was deleted from the final cut of *Batman and Robin*. The scene was entitled "Alfred's Lost Love," and it revealed that Barbara was not truly Alfred's niece, she was the daughter of a woman named Margaret Clark, a woman that Alfred had fallen in love with many years ago. In the scene, Alfred, Barbara, Bruce and Dick are strolling the grounds of Wayne Manor, and Alfred tells everyone that he broke off his relationship with Margaret because he was so much older than her. Schumacher must have decided that he didn't care for this "Alfred's lost love" backstory—for the final cut of the film, this scene was re-shot with dialogue that completely changed the relationship between Alfred, Margaret and Barbara. The re-shot scene revealed Margaret to be Alfred's sister, making her daughter Barbara his actual niece.

This 2005 DVD set remained the definitive home video version of *Batman and Robin* until Warner released the movie on Blu-ray disc in early 2009. The *Batman and Robin* Blu-ray included all of the special features found on the DVD set, but it did not contain any new bonus material. Of course, the Blu-ray's main selling point was not its special features, but its presentation of the film itself. On Blu-ray, *Batman and Robin* looked and sounded far better than it ever had on any other home video format.

Here are my final thoughts on *Batman and Robin*. As I mentioned earlier in this chapter, the film made many serious Batman fans raging mad when it was released. Over the years, this particular Batman fan's anger over the movie has given way to an equal amount of bewilderment. This is the question I always ponder when I think of *Batman and Robin*—just how did a film project that looked to have all of the right ingredients for success turn out to be so catastrophically bad?

Of course, there is no simple answer to this question. But one thing is certain—Schumacher and company were not *trying* to make a film that would end up to be regarded as one of the worst superhero movies of all time. They genuinely thought they were making a Batman film that would appeal to audiences young and old, one made up of Batman fans and non–Batman fans alike. But for some reason, they just couldn't resist the temptation to camp up the character and his world in a manner that recalled the 1960s *Batman* TV show and movie. They just didn't seem to grasp the fact that the camp version of Batman wasn't the way modern movie audiences appreciated the character anymore. Beginning with the release of the 1989 *Batman* film, these audiences had begun to see Batman as a serious character, and there was no going back. So in an ironic twist, Schumacher's failure turned out to be the serious Batman fan's victory—the world was seeing Batman *our* way now, and it would not settle for the camp Batman found in *Batman and Robin*.

But this victory certainly came at a very high price—the *Batman and Robin* debacle so unnerved Warner Bros. that the studio would not undertake the production of a new big-screen Batman movie for the better part of six years. Those six years were a *long* wait for us serious Batman fans. But as we will discuss later in the book, our patience would be rewarded by the 2005 release of *Batman Begins*, an incredible new Batman film that would put the character on the road to truly unimaginable big screen success.

16

Iconic Character, Dormant Film Franchise, 1998–2004

After the very disappointing critical and commercial performance of *Batman and Robin*, Warner Bros.' once-mighty Batman film franchise fell into disarray. Surprisingly, as flawed and uninspired as *Batman and Robin* was, Warner was still planning on bringing Joel Schumacher back to helm another Batman film shortly *after* the release of *Batman and Robin*. In the weeks surrounding the film's premiere, there was much discussion of the director's next Batman opus, *Batman Triumphant*, which was to have featured the Scarecrow and Harley Quinn as its villains. But once the studio realized just how poorly received *Batman and Robin* was going to be, Schumacher was relieved of his Batman directorial duties and plans for *Batman Triumphant* were scrapped.[1]

In the years that have passed since *Batman and Robin*'s failure, the viewpoint that Tim Burton was a far better fit for Warner's Batman film franchise than was Joel Schumacher has become increasingly popular among Batman fans and film buffs. But as we have seen over the course of this book, this viewpoint is far from accurate. Burton's 1989 *Batman* did indeed begin the dynasty, but his second Batman film, *Batman Returns*, was so dark and unsettling that it put many moviegoers off—consequently, *Returns* turned out to be a box office disappointment for Warner. Schumacher was brought in to direct Warner's third Batman film, *Batman Forever*, in order to make Batman "fun" again, and bring moviegoers back to the franchise. And Schumacher was successful in this regard; while *Batman Forever* was not as big of a blockbuster as the 1989 *Batman*, the film outgrossed *Batman Returns* by over $50 million.

Unfortunately for Schumacher, the good that the director did for Warner's Batman film franchise was all but forgotten upon the release of his disastrous *Batman and Robin*. But in all fairness, it should be pointed out that the franchise might have fallen apart even faster if it had been left solely in the hands of Tim Burton.

In fact, it can be argued that even though Burton and Schumacher brought Batman to the screen in radically different manners, their basic approach to directing Batman films was quite similar. Both directors stayed relatively close to the time-honored traditions of the Batman character for their Batman directorial debuts. But emboldened by the success of these films, both directors unwisely chose to stray much too far from those traditions when making their sophomore Batman efforts. Of course, both directors ended up in the same predicament when they tried to put their "personal" stamp on the Batman mythos—they both had to face the dramatically lower box office returns their second Batman films earned.

At any rate, after four movies that featured a substantial number of the major characters in the Batman universe, Warner's Batman film franchise appeared to be completely dead. The movies had run through the heroes Batman, Robin and Batgirl, and the villains the Joker, the Penguin, the Catwoman, the Riddler, Two-Face, Mr. Freeze, Poison Ivy and Bane. Many in the general public knew the long line of characters that had been used in the films and assumed that everything that could be squeezed out of the Batman universe for the big screen had been squeezed out — they figured that Batman simply had no more to offer in terms of further movie projects.

Of course, we serious Batman fans vehemently disagreed with this line of thinking. The Batman character had an incredibly rich history that spanned generations — with all of the great Batman comic stories that had been published over the decades, we knew that there were *hundreds* of films to be made that featured the character, not *four*. And certainly not *these* four movies — let's be honest, none of them were likely to be remembered as cinematic masterpieces. In fact, at least one of them had a legitimate shot of being remembered as a cinematic misstep of historic proportions! Serious Batman fans knew that with these four films, Warner's Batman film franchise had barely scratched the surface of the character's big screen potential. Batman had *so* much more to offer in terms of further movie projects — Warner was really missing out creatively and financially by letting their franchise lie dormant.

And Warner Bros. was in complete agreement with us on this subject. Given the Batman character's ongoing success in multiple forms of media, the studio knew that the character's absence from the big screen represented a giant missed opportunity for them. Warner would continue to try to find a way to bring Batman back to the movies in the wake of *Batman and Robin*, but it would be awhile before they found the right project and the right director to accomplish this goal. (Next chapter, we'll discuss a few of Warner's post–*Batman and Robin* Batman film projects that never made it past the early planning stages.)

Luckily, we serious Batman fans had other new Batman projects to enjoy while we waited for Warner Bros. to rethink their Batman film franchise. One of them was a new *Batman: The Animated Series* film entitled *Batman & Mr. Freeze: SubZero*, which was scheduled to premiere on home video in spring 1997 as a tie-in to *Batman and Robin*. *SubZero* featured most of *Batman and Robin*'s main characters and its plot found Batman, Robin and Barbara Gordon engaged in an epic struggle against Mr. Freeze. But only weeks before *SubZero*'s release, Warner suddenly and quietly postponed it. The film was not released on home video until a full year later, in spring 1998.

Warners' reason for shelving *SubZero* for a year and then releasing it with very little fanfare was likely the simple fact that *SubZero* was a far superior work to the abysmal *Batman and Robin*. Had *SubZero* and *Batman and Robin* been released in conjunction with one another, film critics would have had a field day pointing out the fact that the grandiose, ridiculously expensive *Batman and Robin* paled in comparison to its relatively modestly priced animated companion. As it turned out, *Batman and Robin* took a terrible critical beating anyway. But one can imagine how much worse that beating would have been if major film critics had been able to screen *Batman and Robin* and *SubZero* side by side, and then write headlines to their reviews like "MEMO TO WARNER BROS. — NEXT TIME AROUND, SAVE YOUR MONEY AND JUST RELEASE THE CARTOON." Of course, Warner would never publicly acknowledge the fact that this line of reasoning led them to sit on *SubZero* for a year, but it seems to be the most likely explanation for the studio's decision to (pardon the pun) give the film the cold shoulder.

So not only did *Batman and Robin* prove to be a terrible disappointment for longtime

Batman fans, but it also probably forced these fans to wait an additional year for the release of a *good* Batman screen work. In fact, *SubZero* was more than good — it was great. Produced, written and directed by Boyd Kirkland and co-produced and co-written by Randy Rogel, the film continued the tradition of wonderful visuals and storytelling established in previous *Batman: The Animated Series* works.

In *SubZero*, Victor Fries' wife Nora, who has been suspended in a cryogenic sleep for a number of years in order to keep her from dying from an incurable disease, requires an immediate organ transplant just to maintain her tenuous existence. But since she has a rare blood type, there are no organs available. In desperation, Fries suits up as Mr. Freeze and kidnaps Barbara Gordon, who has Nora's blood type. Freeze plans on killing Barbara and using her organs to save Nora, but Batman and Robin discover Freeze's plan and race to Barbara's rescue. *SubZero* ends with a dramatic confrontation between the heroes and Freeze on an abandoned offshore oil rig, as Batman and Robin save Barbara from Freeze's clutches.

SubZero turned out to be the swan song for the original version of *Batman: The Animated Series*. In late 1997, a new version of *Batman: The Animated Series* premiered on the Kid's WB Network. Entitled *The New Batman/Superman Adventures*, the Batman portion of the series consisted of 25 episodes that originally aired between fall 1997 and fall 1998.

Despite the series title, Batman and Superman were generally featured working separately from one another in *The New Batman/Superman Adventures*. In 1996, Alan Burnett, Paul Dini and Bruce Timm had created a Superman animated series done in a similar style to their animated Batman works, so *The New Batman/Superman Adventures* was really a pairing of their separate Batman and Superman series. However, *The New Batman/Superman Adventures* did include a special three-part episode entitled "World's Finest" which depicted Batman and Superman working together to defeat the Joker and Lex Luthor. ("World's Finest" was eventually released on home video under the title *The Batman Superman Movie* in 1998.)

The Batman episodes in *The New Batman/Superman Adventures* picked up several years after the continuity established in the original *Batman: The Animated Series*. These years had brought major changes to Batman's world. First off, Dick Grayson had ended his partnership with Batman after the two had a falling-out; he then adopted the identity of Nightwing and continued to fight crime on his own. In Dick's absence, Batman decided to take on two new partners. First, he finally took Batgirl into his confidence, revealing his secret identity to her and regularly working with her on cases. (Barbara Gordon's transformation from Batgirl to Oracle as depicted in the comics was a plot development that was never incorporated into this animated version of Batman's world.)

He also took on a new Robin, Tim Drake, a tough street kid whose father Steven was working for Two-Face. After Two-Face murdered Steven, Batman took in Tim and made him his ward just as he had done with Dick. Interestingly, the animated Tim's origin was much more similar to the second origin of the much-hated Jason Todd Robin comic character than it was to the comic book Tim's origin! But as we discussed earlier in the book, a hallmark of the original *Batman: The Animated Series* was to synthesize different elements of Batman history into a powerful, singular vision of the character's world — so this decision to tinker with Tim's origin a bit was not particularly jarring for Batman fans.

The Batman episodes in *The New Batman/Superman Adventures* were visually quite different from the original *Batman: The Animated Series*. The new series had a much simpler, decidedly cartoonish look to it; the realism found in many episodes of *Batman: The Animated Series* gave way to an expressive style that at times bordered on slightly absurd caricature. For example, Batman's shoulders were so broad and the Joker's chin was so pointed in *The*

New Batman/Superman Adventures that the characters seemed about as far removed from real life as characters in a Looney Tunes cartoon.

Not only were the Batman characters in *The New Batman/Superman Adventures* rendered in a different style from the way they were rendered in *Batman: The Animated Series*, but their costumes were also markedly different as well. For example, the deep blue shades found in the Batman costume of *Batman: The Animated Series* gave way to a basically all-black and gray Batman costume in *The New Batman/Superman Adventures*. And Robin's costume was radically changed as well: No longer red, green and yellow like the character's traditional comic book costume, it was a red, black and yellow design unlike any Robin costume that had ever appeared in the comics over the years.

The Batman episodes featured in *The New Batman/Superman Adventures* might have looked substantially different from the original *Batman: The Animated Series*, but these new episodes were just like the original series in many other respects. For example, their scripts were every bit as well-written as the scripts for the original series. Dini and Timm even adapted their Eisner Award–winning comic tale *Mad Love* into a standout episode of the program. Also, most of the *Batman: The Animated Series* voice talent reprised their roles in *The New Batman/Superman Adventures*. And these new episodes also treated the Batman character and his comic book history with the same respect and affection that the original series did.

Nowhere was this fact more apparent than in the episode "Legends of the Dark Knight," written by Timm and Robert Goodman, and directed by Dan Riba. In "Legends of the Dark Knight," a group of Gotham kids discuss what they think Batman is really like, and realize that they all hold wildly varying views of the crimefighter. One young man sees Batman as a cheerful public servant with an enthusiastic Robin by his side. This view is illustrated by an animated sequence inspired by the 1940s Batman comic art of Dick Sprang which shows Batman and Robin fighting the Joker. A young girl sees Batman as a fearsome, savage combatant who is aided by a street-wise female Robin. This view is illustrated by an animated sequence inspired by Frank Miller's 1986 graphic novel series *Batman: The Dark Knight Returns* which shows Batman and Robin (the Carrie Kelley version of the character) fighting a dangerous gang leader. The kids eventually find themselves in the middle of a crime in progress, and they find out what Batman is *really* like when he comes to their rescue. (Incidentally, this episode was based on the classic comic story "The Batman Nobody Knows" by writer Frank Robbins and artist Dick Giordano which was first published in *Batman* #250, July 1973. In that story, three kids share their varying visions of Batman with Bruce Wayne.)

"Legends of the Dark Knight" also contains one priceless Batman in-joke. As the kids discuss Batman, they happen upon a kid named Joel who offers his opinion that the crimefighter wears a costume made of tight rubber armor and has a car that can drive up walls. The kids instantly dismiss Joel's thoughts with complete derision. Obviously, Joel is meant to represent a young version of director Joel Schumacher, and the character's thoughts on Batman are pulled directly from Schumacher's Batman films! Poor Joel Schumacher — not only did he have to deal with *real* Batman fans that were angry at him over his cinematic version of Batman, he even had to deal with angry *fictional* Batman fans!

On November 3, 1998, Batman's creator Bob Kane died at the age of 83. As we noted earlier in the book, Kane had the good fortune to spend the last decade of his life enjoying the spoils of his creation's continued success, the majority of that success stemming from Warner's Batman film franchise. Kane was survived by his daughter Debbie from his first marriage, and his second wife Elizabeth Sanders Kane. Though Kane had no substantial involvement in the making of any of Warner's Batman films, he always offered his public support for the franchise — he spoke of all of the franchise's films in glowing terms whenever he was interviewed by the media, and he also made occasional visits to the film's sets.

Kane's enthusiasm for Warner's Batman film franchise probably continued to remain so high because the franchise elected to cast his second wife, an aspiring actress, in most of its films. Elizabeth Sanders Kane was given a one-line part in *Batman Returns* (she was billed as "Gothamite 4") and she was given the role of Gossip Gerty in both *Batman Forever* and *Batman and Robin*. The Gossip Gerty part only consisted of a few lines in each film, and was modeled after an old-fashioned entertainment gossip columnist.

In addition to supporting Warner's Batman film franchise, Kane also spent his final years preparing his autobiography *Batman and Me* for publication. The book was co-written by Tom Andrae, and it was first released in 1989. A revised and expanded edition of the book entitled *Batman and Me: The Saga Continues* was released in 1996. As we also noted earlier in the book, Kane was often guilty of shameless self-interest, leading him to falsely claim that he was basically the sole architect of Batman's success. Unfortunately, both editions of *Batman and Me* reveal this deficit in Kane's personal character — they are filled with fanciful, unsubstantiated anecdotes that appear to be nothing more than rather transparent attempts to make Kane's achievements seem even more grand than they actually were.[2]

The loss of Bob Kane was definitely a reminder of how far the Batman character had come and how much the world had changed since the time of his creation — but Kane's death was by no means the *only* big change that the world was bringing to Batman in the late 1990s. During this time, the exploding popularity of the Internet revolutionized the way that people shared information with one another. And of course, Batman had continued to be such a popular commodity over the decades that it was no surprise that the character instantly became a hot Internet topic.

Through the Internet, Batman fans were able to become Batman *producers*—countless fan-made websites dedicated to the character seemed to pop up on the World Wide Web almost overnight. This new form of communication linked Batman fans together in a manner that they had ever been linked before. There was a now an online "Batman community" that stretched all around the world, a community that was infinitely larger and more unified than the isolated clusters of Batman fans that had gathered at individual comic stores and comic conventions over the years.

A number of these fan-made Batman websites became so popular with the online Batman community that DC Comics and Warner Bros. were compelled to seriously pay attention to them. The wealth of reviews and opinions found on these sites offered the companies an excellent way to gauge how well Batman fans were responding to their various Batman products.

One of these fan-made Batman websites that turned out to be particularly popular and influential was Batman-on-Film, and its focus made it a special favorite of this author over the years. Batman-on-Film was created in 1998 by a 33-year-old Batman fan from Texas named Bill Ramey. Ramey was so disappointed with the direction that Warner's Batman film franchise had taken with the release of *Batman and Robin* that he created his website as a means to lobby for "the long-term continuation of the Batman film franchise and the production of *quality* Bat-movies," as he succinctly phrased it.

Batman-on-Film had decidedly humble beginnings — it was originally launched as a very small site under the name of "JettD60's BATMAN 5 Page." Ramey gave the site its much catchier name in 2000, and its presentation of news and opinion relating to Warner's efforts to relaunch their Batman film franchise in the wake of *Batman and Robin* really clicked with the Batman community. Batman-on-Film expanded its scope as it grew in size and popularity, offering coverage of non-film Batman works such as TV programs and comic books.

By 2005, when Warner was releasing *Batman Begins*, the site had become *so* popular with the Batman community that it was being visited hundreds of thousands of time a day! Warner definitely appreciated all of the attention that Batman-on-Film was bringing to their Batman cinematic efforts. The studio even made a point of giving Ramey special behind-the-scenes media access while he was covering their later Batman films *The Dark Knight* (2008) and *The Dark Knight Rises* (2012).

In the interest of full disclosure, I should point out that over the years I have contributed a number of articles to Batman-on-Film. But even if I had never been associated with the site, I would still be noting it in this book because of the very positive impact it has had on the history of Batman big screen works.

Obviously, not all Batman-related Internet websites were fan-made. DC Comics and Warner Bros. developed many different websites in order to advertise and sell their various Batman products. Warner created particularly elaborate sites for Christopher Nolan's Batman films *Batman Begins*, *The Dark Knight* and *The Dark Knight Rises* that were packed with material designed to enhance the viewing experience of each film. We'll discuss those sites in detail later in the book.

The concept of extremely long Batman story arcs first realized in the 1993 series *Knightfall*, *Knightquest* and *KnightsEnd* continued to gain in popularity during the late 1990s. DC found that Batman fans tended to stick with tales that ran in Batman's regular monthly comic titles, so they devised several more epic plots to keep those fans coming back for more. Among these were a 1998 series entitled *Cataclysm* that depicted Gotham City being destroyed by a major earthquake, and a 1999 follow-up series entitled *No Man's Land* that depicted post-quake Gotham as a lawless territory that has been abandoned by the federal government. In *No Man's Land*, Batman struggled to bring the city back under control, as portions of it had been claimed by criminals like the Joker and Two-Face. Gotham City was eventually rebuilt with the aid of Superman's old foe, Metropolis mogul Lex Luthor. (Luthor's rebuilding of Gotham was not by any means an act of charity—his efforts were motivated by a desire to improve his pubic image so that he could run for president!)

During the *No Man's Land* saga, a new Batgirl character was introduced. Cassandra Cain had been trained from a very young age to be an assassin by her adopted father, who was himself a professional killer. Cassandra hated the terrible life that was being forced on her, so she fled, making her way to Gotham City. In the midst of the *No Man's Land* crisis, she aided the former Batgirl Barbara Gordon, now known as the computer expert Oracle, and eventually convinced Batman to take her on as one of his partners. As the new Batgirl, she adopted a faceless, almost completely black costume with a cape and bat-eared cowl. This new Batgirl proved to be such a popular character that in April 2000 she was given her own monthly comic title, simply titled *Batgirl*.

As previously mentioned, artist Alex Ross' vision of the DC Universe in *Kingdom Come* created such a sensation that the artist was asked to provide paintings for a number of other DC publications during the late 1990s. Some of these images were of Batman—for example, Ross provided a series of stunning paintings for the cover of part one of *No Man's Land* that were enhanced with lenticular animation. These images revealed Ross' visual concept of the "classic Batman" for the first time. (*Kingdom Come* was an *Elseworlds* title set in the future, so Ross' *Kingdom Come* Batman was far removed from the character's regular continuity.)

16—Iconic Character, Dorman Film Franchise, 1998–2004

Stripped of *Kingdom Come*'s science fiction–fantasy elements, Ross' regular continuity Batman was far and away the most realistic visual interpretation of the character ever created for a comic book work. His costume was entirely black and gray with the exception of his dark yellow-gold utility belt, and it seemed to have real-life texture and weight. When one looked closely enough at Ross' Batman paintings, one could make out the furrows pressed into his latex-style cowl and the heavy stitching on his cape.

In 1998, Ross teamed with *Batman: The Animated Series* writer Paul Dini to create an oversize graphic novel work entitled *Superman: Peace on Earth*. The book explored a theme similar to the main theme of *Kingdom Come*—namely, what course of action should an individual with incredible powers take in order to best help the world? However, unlike *Kingdom Come*, *Superman: Peace on Earth* depicted Superman in a regular continuity setting as opposed to an *Elseworlds* setting.

In the 1999 oversize graphic novel work *Batman: War on Crime*, Dini and Ross gave Batman the same kind of treatment they had given Superman in *Superman: Peace on Earth*. Set in Batman's regular continuity, the book examined the character's motivation for fighting crime, as well as the tremendous physical and mental toll that the fight had taken on him over the years. In *Batman: War on Crime*, Batman encounters Marcus, a young inner city boy whose parents are murdered in front of him, a tragedy mirroring Bruce Wayne's loss of his parents. In grief, the boy turns to a life on the streets, joining a gang and participating in criminal activities. Batman is able to convince the boy that to rebuild his shattered life and cope with the loss of his parents, he must not become part of the cycle of violence that took their lives—because turning to crime can never be a remedy for crime.

Batman: War on Crime's story eloquently showed that the reason Batman continued his relentless quest for justice was for people like Marcus; the hero considered his struggle worthwhile if he could help to rescue even one person from the evil of crime. Dini and Ross accomplished something else in the book that was just as profound as telling a story about one of Batman's small victories in his ongoing crusade. In the book's real world setting, they were almost miraculously able to sum up Batman's six-decade history by using many of the elements and supporting characters that had helped to make him such an icon for generations.

For example, almost *every* one of Batman's major villains appears in the pages of *Batman: War on Crime*—if you look closely enough when you read the book, you will spot the Joker, the Penguin, the Riddler, the Catwoman, Two-Face, and Harley Quinn! (I won't tell you where all of these villains are in the book, but I will give you this hint if you want to look for them—many of them are not in their usual outlandish costumes, but in more "civilian" garb.) Other time-honored Batman characters and traditions show up in *Batman: War on Crime* as well—Alfred is seen tending to Bruce in the Batcave, and Commissioner Gordon is seen making an arrest relating to one of the cases Batman is working on. In this author's opinion, no other Batman work ever created, either print or non-print, has captured Batman in a real world setting as brilliantly as Dini and Ross did *Batman: War on Crime*.

The year 1999 also saw the release of an excellent book by Les Daniels that commemorated the Batman character's sixtieth anniversary. *Batman: The Complete History* provided a concise summation of the Dark Knight's 60-year history, both in the comics and on the screen. The book's visuals were every bit as strong as its text—it was designed and art directed by Chip Kidd, author of the 1996 book *Batman Collected*.

Having left behind the classic version of Batman with the last episodes of *The New Batman/Superman Adventures*, Bruce Timm, Paul Dini and Alan Burnett developed a new

Batman in *Batman: War on Crime* (1999). Art by Alex Ross.

animated series entitled *Batman Beyond*, which premiered on the Kid's WB Network in early 1999. Set in Gotham City well into the twenty-first century, *Batman Beyond* followed the adventures of a new Batman. In the series, Bruce Wayne (again voiced by Kevin Conroy), now 80 years old and long retired from crimefighting, has taken on a young man named Terry McGinnis as his protégé. Terry (voiced by Will Friedle) fights crime in a futuristic jet-propelled Batman costume, and Bruce monitors Terry's exploits from the Batcave.

Batman Beyond was a substantial success for Warner Bros.—over 50 episodes were produced over the course of its three-season run. However, some longtime Batman fans did not wholeheartedly embrace the series because they felt it strayed a bit too far from the mythos that had made Batman such an enduring character in the first place. But even the most ardent old school Batman fans could find enjoyment in *Batman Beyond*'s constant references to characters and events relating to the continuity established by *Batman: The Animated Series* and *The New Batman/Superman Adventures*.

The *Batman Beyond* movie released directly to home video in 2000 entitled *Batman Beyond: Return of the Joker* contained more than just passing references to Bruce Wayne's Batman years. In the film, the Joker has seemingly returned from the dead to plague both Bruce and Terry. Barbara Gordon, now Gotham's Police Commissioner, tells Terry about the Joker's last and perhaps most hideous crime, which took place while Bruce was still Batman. The Joker captured Robin (the Tim Drake version), tortured him, and brainwashed him into becoming his protégé instead of Batman's. The madman went so far as to surgically alter Tim's face so that the boy would look like him.

Batman was able to rescue Tim from the Joker's clutches, but their lives were irrevocably changed by the villain's actions. Tim was left severely emotionally scarred, and Bruce was so shaken by what had happened to the boy that he would never again let Tim don the guise of Robin. The Joker paid the ultimate price for his horrendous crime—he was killed during this final struggle with Batman.

Of course, Bruce and Terry eventually discover the secret forces behind the Joker's "return," and put a stop to them. But even still, the lingering memory of Tim's anguish keeps *Batman Beyond: Return of the Joker* from having what could be considered a truly "happy" ending. Consequently, the film stands as one of the darkest screen depictions of Batman and his world ever created.

In fact, Warner Bros. felt that the original version of *Batman Beyond: Return of the Joker* was going to be *too* dark and disturbing for younger audiences, so the film was edited for its initial release. The flashback sequence showing the manner in which the Joker was killed was the part of the film that was most drastically changed. The original flashback sequence revealed that Tim fatally shot the Joker in the chest with a hand-held spear gun while Batman was trying to rescue the boy. Not surprisingly, the image of Batman's junior partner murdering the Joker made Warner uncomfortable, so the sequence was reworked to show the Joker accidentally being electrocuted by some loose cables during his struggle with Batman. (*Batman Beyond: Return of the Joker* was first released on home video in its edited form, but the unedited version of the film was subsequently released as well.)

Batman fans got another chance to see the classic animated Batman in action the in Dini and Timm series *Justice League*, which premiered on the Cartoon Network in late 2001. As we noted earlier in the book, the Justice League of America got its comic book start back in 1960, and Batman was one of its founding members. Since that debut, DC published a number of *Justice League* comic titles, and Batman was often depicted as being on the League's roll call. So when Dini and Timm put together their version of the League, it was no surprise that Batman was included. Though the character was usually not the main focus of *Justice League* episodes, it was still enjoyable for Batman fans to watch him working alongside DC heroes such as Superman, Wonder Woman, Flash and Green Lantern. After two seasons, the series was retitled *Justice League Unlimited*—it ran for another three seasons under this new title. (Of course, Kevin Conroy was called on to voice the part of Batman in the series.)

Batman fans got a chance to *be* the classic animated Batman by playing as the character in the video game *Batman: Vengeance*, which was released on major gaming platforms such as PlayStation 2 and Xbox in late 2001. Many Batman video games had been released since the late 1980s, most of them arcade-style games designed as tie-ins to particular Batman screen works—for example, all of Warner's Batman films had accompanying video games released with them. But *Batman: Vengeance* was far more ambitious than these early games—it presented its players with a long, complex plot that was filled with many characters from the classic animated Batman's world, making it an immersive experience from start to finish.

Much of the major voice talent from *Batman: The Animated Series* and *The New Batman/Superman Adventures* reprised their roles for *Batman: Vengeance*, including Kevin Conroy (Batman/Bruce Wayne), Mark Hamill (The Joker) and Arleen Sorkin (Harley Quinn). *Batman: Vengeance* enjoyed a considerable amount of success when it was released, and it helped to pave the way for several later Batman video games that would go on to achieve spectacular success. We'll discuss those games later in the book.

In addition to all of the new Batman comics, screen works, and video games being released, the Batman merchandising machine that started with the first wave of Batmania back in 1966 continued to roll on. In the late 1990s, DC itself moved beyond the print medium in terms of creating merchandise based on their characters. The company formed a collectibles division known as DC Direct that manufactured and sold high-quality DC character statues and action figures. These items were targeted toward the serious comic fan, so they almost always had an extremely narrow focus—for example, one would not buy a generic Batman action figure through DC Direct, one would buy a "*Batman: The Dark Knight Returns* Batman," or a "*Kingdom Come* Batman." The range of Batman collectibles offered through DC Direct was truly impressive — a serious Batman fan could basically create their own miniature museum of Batman history by collecting DC Direct's products.

That museum did not have to be limited to just DC Direct products, however. In 2002, Mattel obtained the rights to manufacture toys and action figures based on DC Comics characters. Mattel's first line of Batman figures came out in 2003, and since then the company has produced scores of Batman products based on various comic and screen versions of the character.

Batman: The Dark Knight Strikes Again, Frank Miller's long-awaited sequel to his classic work *Batman: The Dark Knight Returns*, made its debut as a three-part graphic novel series in 2002. Bruce Wayne once again suits up as Batman to confront Superman's foes Lex Luthor and Brainiac, who are scheming to imprison all super beings and ultimately take over the world. And Batman has to square off against one more surprise enemy as well — his old partner Dick Grayson! Full of jagged art, crazy kaleidoscopic colors and wicked wit, the series was in many respects every bit as daring and thought-provoking as its predecessor.

Even though the series sold extremely well, *Batman: The Dark Knight Strikes Again* was perceived by many Batman fans as somewhat of a letdown, probably because it was up against unbeatable competition — namely, *Batman: The Dark Knight Returns*. Miller's first

Batman graphic novel series was unquestionably a landmark event in comics history. But by 2002, all of the elements that had made *Batman: The Dark Knight Returns* seem like such a revelation when it was first published (fine quality printing, intricately colored artwork, complex storytelling, etc.) were commonplace in the comic book industry. So there was really no possible way for *Batman: The Dark Knight Strikes Again* to make anywhere near the kind of impact on readers that *Batman: The Dark Knight Returns* had.

That said, however, there were aspects of *Batman: The Dark Knight Strikes Again* that some Batman fans found to be unpalatable. Much of the series' apocalyptic action and tirades against the powers that be in America seemed like a tired rehash of Miller's first Batman graphic novel series. Plus, the "Luthor vs. super beings" plot came across as being far too similar to the plot of Mark Waid and Alex Ross' 1996 graphic novel series *Kingdom Come*. (Of course, *Kingdom Come* offered an optimistic spin on this plot, while *Batman: The Dark Knight Strikes Again* offered a pessimistic spin.) Finally, the series' climax which revealed Dick Grayson to be one of the storyline's main villains seemed to be nothing more than a chance for Miller to once again express his intense dislike for the traditional version of the Robin character. (As we discussed earlier in the book, Miller started the "let's have the Joker kill the Jason Todd Robin!" movement in *Batman: The Dark Knight Returns*.) At any rate, Miller's long-awaited Batman sequel was by no means a total failure, but it was ultimately met with ambivalence as much as anything else.

In late 2002, the Batman character returned to television in live-action form, albeit in a very peripheral manner, in a WB Television Network series entitled *Birds of Prey*. The series was based on the same-name DC comic title that featured Oracle in its group of heroes. *Birds of Prey* had an intriguing, yet ultimately very frustrating premise. In the series, Batman has retired and left Gotham City, leaving Oracle (Dina Meyer) to continue his fight. She is aided by Helena Kyle (Ashley Scott), the illegitimate child of Batman and Catwoman who fights crime as the Huntress. Though Batman is out of the picture, his faithful butler Alfred (Ian Abercrombie) has remained in Gotham to attend to the needs of Oracle and the Huntress.

The Huntress was a DC Comics character that had made semi-regular appearances in various comic titles since 1977. Her real name was Helena Wayne, and she came from an alternate DC universe known as Earth-Two where Bruce Wayne and Selina Kyle were her father and mother. Over the years, DC revised Helena's backstory a number of times—but all of the different versions of the character maintained some sort of connection to Batman and his world.

In *Birds of Prey*'s pilot episode, a number of brief flashbacks showed Batman (Bruce Thomas) and Batgirl in action; it also showed the Joker shooting Barbara Gordon and leaving her paralyzed as depicted in the 1988 graphic novel *Batman: The Killing Joke*. (We discussed that graphic novel in detail in Chapter 7.) These scenes were stylishly realized in the manner of Warner's Batman films, and left Batman fans hungry for more. But unfortunately, there basically *wasn't* any more. After the pilot episode, *Birds of Prey* settled into a mind-numbing hodgepodge of trite action, teen angst and unbearably slow-paced, soap opera–style romance. With Batman gone and Barbara paralyzed, there was not a cape or cowl in sight to help liven things up.

However, one episode of *Birds of Prey*, "Lady Shiva," featured Batgirl back in action. In the episode, Barbara employs an untested and potentially dangerous bionic enhancing device to allow her to walk again so that she can confront one of her old foes, Lady Shiva. The episode devoted a generous amount of screen time to Batgirl's exploits, which allowed

Dina Meyer to demonstrate what a tremendous screen Batgirl she could have been if she had been able to play the part in a better-realized production.

"Lady Shiva" also allowed viewers to appreciate the fabulous Batgirl costume that had been designed for the show. Its black bodysuit, cape and cowl were crafted in the style of the Batman and Batgirl costumes found in the Warner films. The costume also sported a yellow bat insignia, yellow boots, yellow gloves and a yellow utility belt. The *Birds of Prey* Batgirl costume is the most faithful live-action screen depiction of the Barbara Gordon Batgirl's comic book look to date.

Unfortunately, the excellent bat-moments found in the *Birds of Prey* pilot and in "Lady Shiva" were among the series' only bright spots. Not even the first ever live-action portrayal of the popular character Dr. Harleen Quinzel, better known as the Joker's assistant Harley Quinn (Mia Sara), could bring any sort of spark to the program. The WB Network canceled *Birds of Prey* in early 2003, after only 13 episodes.

A long story arc entitled *Hush* that first ran in monthly issues of *Batman* comics from late 2002 to late 2003 ended up having a large impact on the history of the Batman character. *Hush* was written by Jeph Loeb, author of the 1996–97 graphic novel series *Batman: The Long Halloween*, and illustrated by Jim Lee, Scott Williams and Alex Sinclair. The story arc presented the tale of Batman confronting a mysterious criminal known as "Hush." The criminal's face is hidden under bandages, and he is determined to bring an end to Batman's crimefighting exploits. Hush has even formed an alliance with one of Batman's most dangerous foes, the Riddler, in order to take down the crimefighter.

Hush is eventually revealed to be a close friend of Bruce Wayne's named Thomas Elliot who has deduced that Bruce is actually Batman. Elliot has long held a grudge against the Wayne family, because Thomas Wayne unknowingly foiled Elliot's plot to murder his parents in order to gain their inheritance. Elliot is murdered by Two-Face before Batman can bring him to justice. But Batman is left with a far more disturbing problem than his confrontation with Hush — the crimefighter learns that the body of Jason Todd, his second Robin who was murdered by the Joker, is missing from his grave.

Hush's run in *Batman* was so well-received by Batman fans that the story arc was eventually collected into a two-volume graphic novel set, as well as a single-volume graphic novel. And *Hush*'s resurrection of the Jason Todd character turned out to be a plot element that would be expanded upon in a number of later Batman works. We'll discuss a few of those works later in the book.

Earlier in this chapter, we discussed the impact that the growing popularity of the Internet had on the Batman character starting in the late 1990s. The Internet continued to revolutionize the way serious Batman fans shared information with one another — for example, it played an integral part in the improbable success of a 2003 independent short film entitled *Batman: Dead End*. Director Sandy Collora made the film starring Clark Bartram in the title role, and its depiction of Batman was inspired by artist Alex Ross' visual interpretation of the character. In *Batman: Dead End*, the crimefighter first squares off against the Joker (played by Andrew Koenig), but he then has to face even deadlier competition — namely, creatures from the *Alien* and *Predator* film series!

Batman: Dead End, with its striking visuals and exciting action scenes, was originally intended to basically serve as a resume piece for Collora — in fact, Collora did not even have permission from Warner Bros. or DC Comics to use the Batman character, so the film was never supposed to reach a wide audience. But after *Batman: Dead End* was made available to the general public via the Internet, many Batman fans applauded it as one of the best live-action portrayals of the character ever created! Collora's film inspired the creation of scores of fan-made Batman films that could be viewed on the Internet. Most of these unofficial films were forgettable, amateurish efforts, but a precious few of them were so elaborate and well-made that they ended up winning critical praise and drawing huge online audiences. We'll discuss several of these standout fan-made Batman films later in the book.

In 2003, an animated Batman movie entitled *Batman: Mystery of the Batwoman* was released directly to home video. Set in the continuity established in the Batman episodes of *The New Batman/Superman Adventures*, *Mystery of the Batwoman* told of a mysterious new crimefighter known as Batwoman appearing in Gotham City. Clad in a gray costume with a cape and cowl like Batman's, this Batwoman is targeting a weapons smuggling operation run by Rupert Thorne and the Penguin. Of course, her exploits bring her face-to-face with Batman (again voiced by Kevin Conroy), who tries to deduce her true identity.

He has no shortage of suspects—the hero crosses paths with three young women who have both the skills and motive to go up against Thorne and the Penguin. One of them is a gangster's daughter named Cathy Duquesne (pronounced "DuCane"—a clever reference to the Kathy Kane Batwoman character who appeared in Batman comic stories from the mid–1950s to the early 1960s), with whom Bruce becomes romantically involved. At the end of *Mystery of the Batwoman*, all of the bat-heroes go up against Thorne, the Penguin and also Bane, who has been brought into town by the other villains to provide some extra muscle.

Though rendered in the visual style of *The New Batman/Superman Adventures*, *Mystery of the Batwoman* was considerably lighter in tone than was its predecessor. The film's producer-director Curt Geda and writers Alan Burnett and Michael Reaves set out to create an animated work that focused on the more "fun" aspects of the Batman character. So *Mystery of the Batwoman* contained no small amount of amusing banter between its main characters, as well as a light romance for Bruce that even had a happy ending. (After all of Bruce's romantic troubles with the likes of Catwoman, Talia and Andrea Beaumont over the years, Geda and company evidently decided to give the poor guy a break for once!)

As successful as *Batman: The Animated Series*, *The New Batman/Superman Adventures* and *Batman Beyond* had been, it seemed like somewhat of a surprising decision on the part of Warner Bros. to create a new Batman animated TV show that had no connection whatsoever to their earlier shows. But that is just what the studio did—in late September 2004, Warner premiered *The Batman* on the Kid's WB Network. The creative forces behind the series were supervising producers Michael Goguen and Duane Capizzi. In *The Batman*, the part of Batman/Bruce Wayne was voiced by Rino Romano. The series kicked off with the basic premise that Bruce Wayne was 26 years old, and he had only been fighting crime as Batman for several years.

In *The Batman*, the crimefighter's exploits become increasingly dangerous and dramatic because more and more costumed criminals keep showing up in Gotham City. And Batman has even more problems to deal with other than villains such as the Joker, the Penguin, the Catwoman, Mr. Freeze, Bane, and the Riddler. Gotham City Police Commissioner Angel Rojas believes that Batman is a menace to his city, so he orders his force to apprehend the crimefighter at all costs. Batman eventually ends up forming an alliance with the Gotham Police through their newly-appointed Commissioner James Gordon. Gordon's daughter Barbara turns out to be an even closer ally of Batman—she dons the disguise of Batgirl and proves to be a valuable partner to the crimefighter.

Obviously, even this brief synopsis of *The Batman*'s basic premise makes it obvious

Batman in the animated television series *The Batman* (2004–08).

that the series was radically different from Warner's earlier Batman animated TV shows. In fact, it is really no exaggeration to state that the series went out of its way to change many of the cherished traditions that had helped to make Batman such a popular character for decades. We just noted a major change that *The Batman* made to one of these traditions—in the series, Batgirl was introduced into Batman's world relatively quickly, but Robin was not.

Many of *The Batman*'s characters underwent changes that were far more sweeping than merely having their timelines altered. Several of them were given new origin stories that were significantly different from their comic book origins. For example, the series created an odd backstory for the Penguin that involved both the Wayne family and Alfred—the Penguin harbored a deep hatred for the Waynes because many years ago, Alfred's family chose to be servants for the Waynes instead of for *his* family!

In fact, many of the characters in *The Batman* even *looked* almost nothing like their comic book counterparts. The most notable exception to this trend was Batman himself—he was outfitted in a dark blue and gray costume with a flowing cape that resembled the character's costume in *Batman: The Animated Series*. But the rest of the characters in *The Batman*—well, let's just say that their visual designs gave longtime Batman fans a *lot* to get used to. The Joker was by far the most jarring of *The Batman*'s characters—he ran around in his bare feet, he had huge red eyes, and he sported a hairstyle of long green dreadlocks. His triangular face was shaped every bit as sharply as the blade of a shovel, and he had gigantic yellow teeth. The character didn't look like a real-life person at all—he looked more like some sort of abstract statue that had been constructed out of Lego building blocks.

Simply put, *The Batman* tried so hard to distance itself from previous Batman works, especially Warner's earlier Batman animated TV shows, that it essentially wound up not seeming like a Batman show at all. During the course of the series' 65 episodes which aired from late 2004 to early 2008, it moved toward a slightly more traditional interpretation of Batman and his world. For example, *The Batman* introduced the Dick Grayson version of Robin about three-quarters of the way through its run. And the climactic episodes of the series featured Batman working with members of the Justice League such as Superman, Flash and Green Lantern. But even with these changes, *The Batman* still remained too far removed from traditional Batman mythos to win over many longtime fans of the character.

The Batman spawned one movie that was released directly to home video by Warner Bros. in late 2005. *The Batman Vs. Dracula* featured the crimefighter in a fight to the death with the vampire lord Count Dracula. In the film, Dracula is reborn in Gotham City, and he quickly makes good use of several of Batman's regular villains. He recruits the Penguin to be his servant, and he attacks the Joker, turning the madman into a vampire.

Batman quickly realizes that Dracula poses a terrible threat to everyone living in Gotham, so he feverishly works on developing an antidote for vampirism. The crimefighter's antidote cures all of the Gothamites that have been turned into vampires, including the Joker, and Batman is eventually able to destroy Dracula by striking him with beams emanating from a machine designed to store solar energy. *The Batman Vs. Dracula* was a modest success upon its release, but it certainly did not capture the attention of Batman fans like Warner's earlier animated Batman movies had.

At any rate, neither *The Batman* nor *The Batman Vs. Dracula* ever had much of a chance to create a significant amount of buzz among serious Batman fans anyway—those fans were much more interested in another new Batman screen work that was premiering in 2005. As we will discuss in the next chapter, Warner's dormant Batman film franchise came roaring back to life with the theatrical release of *Batman Begins*.

17

Batman Begins (2005)

Cast: Christian Bale (Batman/Bruce Wayne), Michael Caine (Alfred), Liam Neeson (Ducard), Katie Holmes (Rachel Dawes), Gary Oldman (Jim Gordon), Cillian Murphy (Dr. Jonathan Crane), Tom Wilkinson (Carmine Falcone), Rutger Hauer (Earle), Ken Watanabe (Ra's Al Ghul), Mark Boone Junior (Flass), Linus Roache (Thomas Wayne), Morgan Freeman (Lucius Fox), Larry Holden (Finch), Gerard Murphy (Judge Faden), Colin McFarlane (Loeb), Sara Stewart (Martha Wayne), Gus Lewis (Bruce Wayne — age 8), Richard Brake (Joe Chill), Rade Sherbedgia (Homeless Man), Emma Lockhart (Rachel Dawes — age 8), Christine Adams (Jessica), Catherine Porter (Blonde Female Reporter/Assassin), John Nolan (Fredericks), Karen David (Courthouse Reporter #1), Jonathan D. Ellis (Courthouse Reporter #2), Tamer Hassan (Faden's Limo Driver), Ronan Leahy (Uniformed Policeman #1), Vincent Wong (Old Asian Prisoner), Tom Wu (Bhutanese Prison Guard #1), Mark Chiu (Bhutanese Prison Guard #2), Turbo Kong (Enormous Prisoner), Stuart Ong (Chinese Police Officer), Chike Chan (Chinese Police Officer), Tenzin Clive Ball (Himalayan Child), Tenzin Gyurme (Old Himalayan Man), Jamie Cho (Stocky Chinese Man), David Murray (Jumpy Thug), John Kazek (Dock Thug #2), Darragh Kelly (Dock Thug #3), Patrick Nolan (Dock Cop #1), Joseph Rye (Dock Cop #2), Kwaku Ankomah (Dock Cop #3), Jo Martin (Police Prison Official), Charles Edwards (Wayne Enterprises Executive), Lucy Russell (Female Restaurant Guest), Tim Deenihan (Male Restaurant Guest), David Bedella (Maitre D), Flavia Masetto (Restaurant Blonde #1), Emily Steven-Daly (Restaurant Blonde #2), Martin McDougall (Gotham Dock Employee), Noah Lee Margetts (Arkham Thug #1), Joe Hanley (Arkham Thug #2), Karl Shiels (Arkham Thug #3), Roger Griffiths (Arkham Uniformed Policeman), Stephen Walters (Arkham Lunatic), Richard Laing (Akham Chase Cop), Matt Miller (Gotham Car Cop #3), Risteard Cooper (Captain Simonson), Shane Rimmer (Older Gotham Water Board Technician), Jeremy Theobald (Younger Gotham Water Board Technician), Alexandra Bastedo (Gotham City Dame), Soo Hee Ding (Farmer), Con Horgan (Monorail Driver), Phill Curr (Transit Cop), Jack Gleeson (Little Boy), John Judd (Narrows Bridge cop), Sarah Wateridge (Mrs. Dawes), Charlie Kranz (Basement Club Manager), Terry McMahon (Bad Swat Cop #1), Cedric Young (Liquor Store Owner), Tim Booth (Victor Zsaz), Tom Nolan (Valet), Leon Delroy Williams (Pedestrian), Roger Yuan (Hazmat Technician), Joe Sargent (Narrows Teenager #1), Mel Taylor (Narrows Resident), Ilyssa Fradin (Barbara Gordon), Andrew Pleavin (Uniformed Policeman #2), Jeff Christian (Driving Cop), John Burke (Arkham Lunatic Cell Mate), Earlene Bentley (Arkham Asylum Nurse), Alex Moggridge (Arkham Asylum Orderly), Jay Buozzi (Asian Man/Ra's Al Ghul), Jordan Shaw (African Boy in Rags), Omar Mostafa (Falafel Stand Vendor), Patrick Pond (Opera Performer #1 Faust — Bass), Poppy Tierney (Opera Performer #2 Margaret — Soprano), Rory Campbell (Opera Performer #3 Mefistofle — Tenor), Fabio Cardascia (Caterer), Spencer Wilding, Mark Smith, Khan Bonfils, Dave Legeno, Ruben Halse, Rodney Ryan (League of Shadows Warriors), Dominic Burgess (Narrows Cop), Nadia Cameron-Blakey (Additional Restaurant Guest #1), Mark Straker (Male Restaurant Guest #2), TJ Ramini (Crane Thug #1), Kieran Hurley (Crane Thug #2), Emmanuel Idowu (Narrows Teenager #2), Jeff Tanner (Bridge Cop). *Producers:* Charles Roven, Emma Thomas, Larry Franco. *Executive Producers:* Benjamin Melniker, Michael E. Uslan. *Director:* Christopher Nolan. *Screenplay:* Christopher Nolan, David S. Goyer (Story by David S. Goyer, based upon characters appearing

17—Batman Begins (2005)

in comic books published by DC Comics, Batman created by Bob Kane). *Director of Photography:* Wally Pfister. *Production Designer:* Nathan Crowley. *Editor:* Lee Smith. *Music:* Hans Zimmer, James Newton Howard. *Visual Effects Supervisors:* Janek Sirrs, Dan Glass. *Special Effects Supervisor:* Chris Corbould. *Costume Designer:* Lindy Hemming. *Casting:* John Papsidera, Lucinda Syson. *Studio:* Warner Bros. *Length:* 140 minutes. *United States Release Date:* June 15, 2005.

As we've noted in the past two chapters, the 1997 release of Joel Schumacher's *Batman and Robin* left Warner Bros.' Batman film franchise in a creative and commercial sinkhole. After the film's disappointing performance, the studio scuttled plans for a third Schumacher-directed Batman film that was to be titled *Batman Triumphant*, and they began trying to reimagine their franchise.[1] That proved to be no easy task—the studio attempted to launch a number of Batman film projects that never made it past the early planning stages. All of these projects were designed to completely reboot the franchise—in other words, they would have had little or no connection to Warner's previous Batman films.

Several of these projects were notable enough to mention here. In 2000, Warner began developing a big screen, live-action version of the animated TV series *Batman Beyond*. (We discussed that series last chapter.) The series' co-creators Paul Dini and Alan Burnett were tapped to co-write the film's script. Also in 2000, the studio worked on developing *Batman: Year One*, a film based on Frank Miller and David Mazzucchelli's 1987 comic series of the same name. (We discussed that series in Chapter 7.) The film was to be scripted by Miller himself and directed by Darren Aronofsky. In 2001, Warner began developing a film that would have rebooted both Batman and Superman—unlike *Batman Beyond* and *Batman: Year One*, this project was not derived from any previous comic or screen work. The film was to be titled *Batman vs. Superman*, and directed by Wolfgang Petersen.[2]

As intriguing as these projects might have sounded, they did not end up impressing Warner Bros. enough to move forward on committing them to film. In early 2003, the studio finally found a filmmaker with a cinematic approach to Batman that they were willing to back

Christian Bale as Batman in *Batman Begins* (2005).

wholeheartedly. Christopher Nolan was a 33-year-old director who was a dual citizen of both the United Kingdom and the United States. Nolan had first gained wide attention through his 2000 film *Memento*, a gripping, complex psychological thriller that became a surprise critical and commercial hit. The director followed up this success with the 2002 Warner Bros. film *Insomnia*, a thriller starring Al Pacino, Robin Williams and Hilary Swank that also turned out to be critically and commercially well-received.

Nolan presented Warner with his idea for a Batman film that was both true to the character's comic book roots, and markedly different from their four previous Batman films. He would tell the story of Batman's origin in a manner that was far more connected to the real world than Tim Burton's and Joel Schumacher's cinematic takes on the character had been. Through the studio, Nolan found the perfect screenwriter to help him script his Batman film — David S. Goyer had written the screenplays for the films *Blade* (1998) and *Blade II* (2002) that were based on the Marvel Comics character of the same name, and had been a staff writer for DC Comics.

Interestingly, Nolan and Goyer basically started their Batman film at the same jumping-off point as *Batman Triumphant*, Schumacher's canceled Batman film. Both films had planned on using the Scarecrow as one of their main villains. The Scarecrow character exemplified the tricky balancing act that Nolan and Goyer had to perform in putting together their Batman film — the movie would have to totally reinvent Batman from the ground up, but it could not feature any of the character's most recognizable villains because they had all been used in Warner's previous Batman films. So Nolan and Goyer were basically left with the unenviable task of starting Batman completely over without being able to start over any of his most well-known villains. Since the Joker, the Penguin, the Catwoman, the Riddler and Two-Face were out, Nolan and Goyer were just going to have to make do with a secondary villain like the Scarecrow in their film.

The Scarecrow was by no means a poor character, mind you — he had just never been as regularly-used or well-known as any of the villains listed above. Back in Chapter 7, we discussed the Scarecrow's appearance in "The Fear," a 1985 episode of the television program *Super Powers Team: The Galactic Guardians*, but we didn't really examine the character's history. We'll go ahead and do that now. The Scarecrow was first introduced in Batman comic stories in the early 1940s — he was actually a professor of psychology named Jonathan Crane who became obsessed with inflicting fear on people. He donned a Scarecrow costume that looked quite a bit like Ray Bolger's Scarecrow costume in the classic 1939 film *The Wizard of Oz* and found all sorts of ways to paralyze his victims with fear. His most common method was to spray these victims with a hallucinogen usually referred to as "fear gas."

The Scarecrow's comic appearances were well-received enough, but the character's stock began to rise quite a bit higher in the 1990s when he was featured in several standout episodes of the television programs *Batman: The Animated Series* and *The New Batman/ Superman Adventures*. In fact, Nolan and Goyer would borrow from these episodes quite liberally when they created their version of the Scarecrow for their Batman film. (We'll discuss this in more detail later in the chapter.)

Nolan and Goyer decided to use another lesser-known Batman villain for their film, one that was a relatively new creation — still, the villain's comic appearances had been so revered by serious Batman fans that he rated a much loftier place in Batman history than a character like the Scarecrow. That villain was the eco-terrorist Ra's Al Ghul. As we also discussed in Chapter 7, Ra's was created by writer Denny O'Neil and artist Neal Adams, and he first appeared in Batman comic stories published in the early 1970s.

As they began scripting their Batman film, Nolan and Goyer drastically changed the Scarecrow and Ra's from their classic comic incarnations. The characters lost their fanciful costumes and sci-fi elements in order to better mesh with Nolan and Goyer's realistic interpretation of Batman and his world. (We'll discuss these changes in more detail later in the chapter.) Batman himself did not undergo anywhere near as large of a transformation for the film as the Scarecrow and Ra's did — Nolan and Goyer drew extensively on a number of noteworthy Batman comic stories to construct their version of the crime-fighter.

Two comic works had a particularly large effect on their interpretation of Batman. The first of these was a story entitled "The Man Who Falls," which was written by Denny O'Neil and illustrated by Dick Giordano. "The Man Who Falls" was originally published in the 1989 DC trade paperback *Secret Origins of the World's Greatest Super-Heroes*, and it provided a chronicle of the events that led Bruce Wayne to adopt his Batman persona.[3]

Interestingly, the story was not really an original work, but more of a retelling of a number of earlier Batman comic stories. For example, in the story young Bruce takes a fall into a large cave under Wayne Manor — this was pulled from Frank Miller's 1986 graphic novel series *Batman: The Dark Knight Returns*. And in the story, Bruce serves as an apprentice to a ruthless bounty hunter named Henri Ducard — this was pulled from a 1989 comic series entitled *Blind Justice* written by the screenwriter of the 1989 *Batman* film, Sam Hamm. Also in the story, a pre–Batman Bruce makes his very first attempt at fighting crime, and that attempt does not go particularly well — this was pulled from Frank Miller and David Mazzucchelli's 1987 comic series *Batman: Year One*.

We discussed both *Batman: The Dark Knight Returns* and *Batman: Year One* in detail in Chapter 7, but this is the first time we've noted *Blind Justice*. In 1988, DC called on Hamm to write a three-part Batman adventure for *Detective Comics* in order to commemorate the character's upcoming 50th anniversary. *Blind Justice* was the result of this collaboration between Hamm and DC, and it was originally published in *Detective Comics* #598, March 1989 through *Detective Comics* #600, May 1989. The series was by no means as successful or influential as works such as *Batman: The Dark Knight Returns* and *Batman: Year One* — that is why we had not discussed it earlier in the book. Still, its introduction of the Henri Ducard character makes it worthy of note in this particular chapter.

Batman: Year One's influence on Nolan and Goyer went far beyond the series simply being referenced in "The Man Who Falls." The series as a whole ended up being the second comic work that had a profound effect on Nolan and Goyer's interpretation of Batman.[4] In fact, their script would feature a number of sequences that were pulled almost directly from the pages of *Batman: Year One*. It is hardly surprising that Nolan and Goyer regularly turned to the series for inspiration, given the fact that Warner had come close to actually making a *Batman: Year One* film. (We'll examine the similarities between the comic works we've just mentioned and Nolan's finished film later in this chapter.)

As Nolan and Goyer wrote the first draft of their Batman script, they decided on a catchy name for the film that perfectly captured its focus — *Batman Begins*. Both Warner Bros. and DC Comics were very pleased with the direction that Nolan and Goyer were taking with their character in the screenplay. After years of frustrating cinematic false starts, the Warner Batman film franchise was finally back in business with *Batman Begins*.

After Nolan and Goyer finished the first draft of the *Batman Begins* script, Goyer had to leave the project in order to return to his work on the Blade film franchise. Goyer had written the screenplay for the third installment of the franchise, *Blade: Trinity*, and he had been assigned to direct the film as well. After Goyer's departure, all of the changes that were made to the script were done solely by Nolan.[5]

Nolan had started to form his production team for *Batman Begins* while he and Goyer were working on the first draft of the film's screenplay. His wife Emma Thomas, who was an associate producer on *Memento*, would serve as a producer on *Batman Begins*. And Nathan Crowley, who was the production designer for *Insomnia*, would serve in that same capacity for *Batman Begins*.

From the very first moments that *Batman Begins* was becoming a reality, Nolan had a vision of what his version of the Batmobile would look like in the film. Nolan's Batmobile was a very clear indication of just how different *Batman Begins* was going to be from Warner's previous Batman movies. He imagined Batman's auto not as the flamboyant sports car that it had been in those earlier films, but as a tank-like urban assault vehicle that still managed to possess incredible power and speed. Nolan and Crowley worked on making a three-dimensional model of Nolan's imagined Batmobile, using pieces pulled from various model car and airplane kits to build it from scratch.[6]

The Batmobile model that Nolan and Crowley ended up creating was startlingly original — they described their car as "a cross between a Lamborghini and a Hummer," and that description was a perfectly accurate one.[7] It sat low to the ground atop huge all-terrain tires, and its armor gave it a streamlined look that suggested both the sleek design of a sports car and the no-nonsense durability of a military vehicle. The practicality and realism of Nolan's Batmobile perfectly summed up where the director was going with *Batman Begins* as a whole, and Warner Bros. loved Nolan's vision of the car — right after seeing Nolan and Crowley's Batmobile model, they approved the construction of a full-sized, fully functioning prototype.[8]

Nolan's version of the Batmobile was a radical departure from previous screen versions of the auto, but it did have a precedent in Batman comics. Frank Miller's 1986 graphic novel series *Batman: The Dark Knight Returns* depicted Batman using a massive tank-like Batmobile in his adventures. The Batmobile of *Batman: The Dark Knight Returns* was much more of a tank than a car, but it still undoubtedly served as an inspiration to Nolan and Crowley as they designed the *Batman Begins* Batmobile.

Nolan's Batmobile served as a hugely promising start for *Batman Begins*, but the director was just getting warmed up. His choice for the actor to portray Batman in the film was every bit as inspired as his vision of Batman's car. In September of 2003, Warner Bros. announced that *Batman Begins* would star Christian Bale as Batman/Bruce Wayne. Bale was a 29-year-old Welsh actor who had a long and very diverse film resume. As a teenager, he had starred in Steven Spielberg's acclaimed World War II drama *Empire of the Sun* (1987), and he went on to appear in movies such as *Henry V* (1989), *Newsies* (1992), *Swing Kids* (1993), and *Little Women* (1994).

Bale's reputation as an actor was further solidified by his performance as a crazed serial killer named Patrick Bateman in the 2000 film *American Psycho*. Bale's riveting, intense turn as Bateman showcased a darker side of his talent that would serve him well when playing Nolan's version of Batman/Bruce Wayne. Bale's physical attributes made him perfectly suited for the role as well — he was very handsome, stood at six feet tall, and possessed an athletic build.

Warner's confidence in *Batman Begins* was evidenced by the huge budget they gave to the film — $180 million.[9] This budget meant that Nolan would not have to spare any expense while he was making the movie. The casting of *Batman Begins* certainly reflected the film's high-profile nature—Nolan loaded the movie with a truly stellar ensemble of well-known actors. The director's casting choices included Michael Caine as Alfred, Katie Holmes as Bruce's longtime friend Rachel Dawes, Morgan Freeman as Bruce's Wayne Enterprises confidant Lucius Fox, Gary Oldman as Jim Gordon, Cillian Murphy as Dr. Jonathan Crane/The Scarecrow, and Liam Neeson as Ducard. (Obviously, there ended up being a lot more to Neeson's role than him simply being "Ducard"—we'll discuss that fact in detail later in the chapter.)

As *Batman Begins* continued to take shape, Crowley worked on bringing Nolan's vision of Gotham City to life. The film's Gotham would end up reflecting Nolan's desire to present Batman and his world in a much more realistic manner than Warner's previous Batman films had. Crowley's Gotham City designs were inspired not by the fanciful images of Gotham found in Tim Burton's and Joel Schumacher's Batman films, but by real-life American cities such as New York City and Chicago.

Crowley was also busy helping to shape the *Batman Begins* Batmobile model into a real-life, working auto. He closely worked with the film's Special Effects Supervisor Chris Corbould and Corbould's mechanical engineer Andy Smith to accomplish this formidable task. The most unusual aspect of the car was that it did not have a single front axle like a normal auto—it had two sub-axles, one for each front wheel, which allowed the car to turn. The Batmobile was designed to be almost as functional in real life as it would appear on screen—it could perform jumps of up to 60 feet, and race at speeds of nearly 100 miles per hour. Eventually, a number of Batmobiles ended up being built so that at least one would always be on hand for filming.[10]

Batman Begins would outfit Batman with a new costume and crimefighting equipment to go along with his new Batmobile. The film's costume designer Lindy Hemming created a Batsuit that was different from the Batsuits featured in Warner's previous Batman films. However, this Batsuit was not as radically different from its predecessors as the *Batman Begins* Batmobile was from its predecessors. The *Batman Begins* Batsuit was completely black in color from its cowl to its boots, and featured a bat emblem molded into the costume's chest armor—in other words, its style was somewhat similar to the Batsuits used in Tim Burton's and Joel Schumacher's Batman films. This likely came as a surprise to many longtime Batman fans, because obviously Nolan was going to great lengths to distance his Batman film from Warner's previous Batman efforts. (Of course, there was one major and *very* welcome difference between the *Batman Begins* Batsuit and the Schumacher film Batsuits—the *Begins* Batsuit was not outfitted with nipples!)

The *Batman Begins* Batsuit did feature a new cape design that set it apart from previous Warner film Batsuits. Hemming created a cape for the costume that was cut from nylon parachute silk. The silk was then put through a process referred to as "electrostatic flocking," which meant that the silk was covered with glue, electrically charged, and sprinkled with fine material. The material was held to the silk through the glue and the electric charge, giving the cape a flat black, velvety appearance.[11]

The plot of *Batman Begins* would end up giving the cape an added dimension. The film called for the cape to be able to become rigid so that Batman could use it like a hang-glider. Consequently, Hemming's cape underwent a second design that transformed it into a bat-winged glider that was well over fifteen feet wide.

The *Batman Begins* Batsuit also featured a utility belt that was a completely original design. The belt was dark gold in color, and outfitted with magnetic strips that allowed Batman to easily carry his grapple gun and Batarangs. Its appearance and functionality meshed very well with Nolan's desire to place Batman in a real-world setting in the film.

In March 2004, the *Batman Begins* cast and crew began shooting its first scenes in Iceland, which featured Bruce and Ducard swordfighting on a frozen lake. The shoot turned out to be every bit as adventurous as the action depicted in the film — the lake they were filming on sat at the foot of Iceland's Vatnajokull Glacier, which was in the process of melting. Luckily, they captured the footage they needed before the lake's icy surface completely melted away. The Iceland shoot continued to be very challenging — Bruce's journey to Ra's Al Ghuls's headquarters was filmed there, and during the filming the crew had to brave winds of over 70 miles an hour.[12]

Huge sets for the film were built at Shepperton Studios in England, including a Batcave set that was 250 feet long, 120 feet wide and 40 feet tall. The set was outfitted with scores of water pumps to create a huge waterfall that ran through the set. The Batcave sets used for Warner's previous Batman films had been impressive, but still, they paled in comparison to the *Batman Begins* Batcave set.[13]

As vast as the film's Batcave set was, even it was dwarfed by the gigantic Gotham City set built for the film inside of Cardington Sheds, a former airship hangar located near London, England. At Cardington, Nolan and company had an indoor space to work with that allowed them to create the largest indoor film set that had ever been constructed. Cardington's Gotham set was a staggering 900 feet long, 240 feet wide, and 160 feet tall! The Gotham locations that were built at Cardington included a run-down neighborhood known as the Narrows, a section of the base of the Gotham Monorail System, and the exterior of Arkham Asylum.[14]

The size of the Cardingon set allowed Nolan and company to film some of the movie's most ambitious and spectacular action scenes in a controlled indoor setting. These scenes included Batman falling five stories from an apartment building while engulfed in flames, and Batman using his grapple gun to board a speeding Gotham Monorail train. Both of these dangerous stunts were performed by Christian Bale's stunt double Buster Reeves.[15]

Batman Begins utilized miniature sets to realize its vision of Batman's world as well. Incredibly detailed miniatures were constructed in order to capture several of the film's most impressive action sequences — these sequences included the Batmobile's journey across the rooftops of Gotham, and the destruction of a Gotham Monorail train.[16]

A real-life glacier, a massive Batcave set with a giant man-made waterfall, the largest indoor set in the history of moviemaking — what more could Nolan bring to the table for *Batman Begins*? But the director had plans for the film that were even *more* ambitious. In late July 2004, after finishing most of the movie's England shoot, the *Batman Begins* cast and crew traveled to the United States for about two weeks of location shooting in Chicago, Illinois. The majority of the movie's Batmobile chase scenes were filmed on Chicago's Lower Wacker Drive and Amstutz Highway. These scenes involved very little special effects — the Batmobile was filmed while actually driving at speeds of around 100 miles an hour. Several scenes featuring Gordon and Batman were also filmed on the rooftops of the city. These scenes used some of the buildings found in Chicago's impressive skyline as their backdrop.

While Nolan was directing *Batman Begins*, he did something that was quite unusual for a filmmaker to do on such a big-budget movie. Nolan directed every one of the film's scenes himself, never using a second film unit with a second director to help him speed up the movie's shooting schedule. Consequently, every last scene in *Batman Begins* would reflect the director's personal artistic vision.[17]

As principal photography for *Batman Begins* wrapped up, there was still a considerable amount of work to be done in terms of completing computer-generated images for the film. The movie's computer-generated images included a number of scenes showing Batman gliding through the air using his cape, and a scene showing thousands of bats flying around the huge cave located under Wayne Manor.[18]

Not surprisingly, Nolan made decisions regarding the musical scoring of *Batman Begins* that took the film's soundtrack in a very different direction from the music found in Warner's previous Batman films. The soundtracks for those films had featured lush, sweeping orchestral compositions, as well as contemporary pop music from artists such as Prince and U2. Nolan called on Hans Zimmer and James Newton Howard to create the *Batman Begins* soundtrack, and the music they wrote for the film was nothing at all like those previous soundtracks. Zimmer and Howard's *Batman Begins* compositions were very ambient in nature, often consisting of hypnotic percussion patterns and long-held musical tones that suggested the constant jumble of city sounds — sounds such as automotive traffic, commuter trains, and large electric generators. Their score might not have had a memorable main title theme like Danny Elfman's "Batman Theme" written for the 1989 *Batman* — but even still, the power and intensity of the score as a whole perfectly meshed with *Batman Begins'* real world interpretation of Batman.

Batman Begins was the first Batman big screen work to be released after the Internet had truly reached massive global popularity. Consequently, it ended up being the first Batman film that was promoted through an elaborate official website that could be easily accessed by millions of people all over the world. The *Batman Begins* website was launched by Warner Bros. in mid–2004, about a year before the movie's actual premiere date. In the months leading up to the film's release, the site featured a wealth of *Batman Begins* information — visitors could look at production photos, watch videos of the film's theatrical previews, and read biographies of the film's cast and crew. Incidentally, Warner has continued to maintain and update the site right up to the present day, so it still functions as a marvelous resource designed to enhance one's appreciation of the film.

The world premiere of *Batman Begins* was held at Grauman's Chinese Theatre in Los Angeles on June 6, 2005. Most all of the film's principal onscreen and offscreen talent attended the event, including Bale, Caine, Holmes, Freeman, Oldman, Neeson and Nolan. The film's Batmobile was also in attendance — it was parked out front of the theatre for everyone to see as they made their way inside. A week later, on June 15, *Batman Begins* opened in theatres throughout the United States.

Batman Begins opens with a shot of bats swarming in a sepia-toned twilight sky — for an instant, the bats form a huge bat silhouette. We are then transported back to Bruce Wayne's childhood, when he is 8 years old. Bruce and his friend Rachel Dawes are playing in a greenhouse at Wayne Manor. Bruce hides from Rachel, standing on an abandoned well. The boards covering the well give way, and Bruce tumbles in. As Bruce lies injured at the bottom of the well, a terrifyingly large swarm of bats fly at him.

Cut to the present day — Bruce is in his late twenties, dirty and unshaven, and he is incarcerated in a Bhutanese prison. He has just awoken from a nightmare about his encounter with the bats in the well, and his reality is no better than his nightmare. Some other prisoners attack Bruce, and he beats them savagely. After the fight, prison guards put him in solitary confinement — in solitary, Bruce is visited by a man named Ducard, who speaks on behalf of Ra's Al Ghul. Ducard tells Bruce that Ra's can offer him a path in his life — this path will lead to true justice through Ra's' organization The League of Shadows.

Ducard tells Bruce that he will have him released from prison, and then Bruce will need to pick a rare blue flower and take it to the top of a mountain near the prison. Bruce does this, and at the top of the mountain he finds a huge structure that houses the League. Inside, Ra's and Ducard are waiting—Bruce gives Ducard the flower, and Bruce's League training quickly begins when Ducard unexpectedly attacks him. Ducard sees that Bruce is a skilled fighter, but he wonders what fears are driving Bruce.

A series of flashback scenes reveal those fears. Bruce's father Thomas rescues Bruce after his fall into the well, but the boy is left terrified of bats. Days later, Thomas takes Bruce and Bruce's mother Martha to a performance of the opera *Mefistofle*. The opera features a scene with batlike creatures on the stage, which frighten Bruce so much that he asks to leave. The Wayne family exits the opera through the rear of the theatre, which leads out to a seedy alley. In the alley, a mugger confronts them. Thomas tries to give the mugger his wallet, but the mugger panics and fatally shoots Thomas and Martha.

After the murders, Bruce sits alone in a Gotham City Police Station. A cop comes in to try to comfort the boy—the young officer is named Jim Gordon. Another officer named Loeb comes in to tell Bruce that the mugger has been apprehended. Sometime later, a funeral is held for the Waynes at Wayne Manor. After the funeral, Bruce is in the manor with only the Wayne butler, Alfred. Bruce tells Alfred that he thinks the murder of his parents was *his* fault because the opera scared him so badly. Alfred assures the boy that his actions were in no way responsible for the murders, and comforts the boy the best he can.

Back to the present day—a montage shows how daunting the League's training of Bruce is. Ducard and Bruce are swordfighting on a frozen lake—during their combat, Ducard tells Bruce that his parents' deaths were the fault of *Thomas*, because he did not take action against the mugger.

Another flashback sequence reveals that Bruce himself tried to take revenge against the mugger. Bruce returns from his studies at Princeton to attend a parole hearing for the mugger, whose name is Joe Chill. Chill is being considered for parole because he will testify against Carmine Falcone, a powerful mobster he once shared a jail cell with. Bruce goes to the hearing with a gun hidden in his coat so that he can murder Chill—but as Chill is being led out of the courtroom, a Falcone-hired assassin posing as a reporter shoots and kills him first.

Rachel, who now works as an intern for Gotham City's district attorney, drives Bruce from the scene of Chill's murder. Bruce shows her his gun and tells her that he was going to kill Chill. Rachel slaps Bruce, and says that Thomas would be ashamed of him. Bruce jumps out of the car, throws his gun away, and goes into a restaurant where Falcone is dining in order to confront the mobster.

Inside the restaurant, Falcone tells Bruce that he commands such incredible power because everyone fears him so much. Falcone says that his power is so great that he wouldn't even think twice about shooting and killing Bruce right then and there. Bruce now realizes that the problem of crime is much bigger than the actions of petty criminals like Chill—it is the monstrous actions of criminals like Falcone that truly need to be stopped. Bruce resolves to disappear from Gotham and learn about the criminal mind so that he can learn how to take on the evil that is destroying his city.

Back to the present day—Bruce's training with the League is almost complete, and their last test for him proves to be his most daunting. Ducard crushes the blue flower that Bruce brought to him and heats it so that it can be inhaled—Ducard instructs Bruce to breathe in the flower's scent, which Bruce does. Bruce quickly realizes that the flower is a powerful fear-inducing hallucinogen. While Bruce is under the effects of the hallucinogen, he battles Ducard—even as he faces his deepest fears, he maintains his mental control and defeats his mentor.

Ra's applauds Bruce's efforts, and then Ra's and Ducard direct Bruce to execute a man accused of murder that the League has imprisoned. Bruce refuses, and they tell him he needs to do this to prove that he is ready for the challenge they are about to give him. They want Bruce to lead the League into Gotham in order to attack and destroy the city—they feel that Gotham has become so corrupt and unjust that the city is beyond saving. Bruce is horrified by this plan, so he starts a fire in the compound in order to escape from the League. The entire League then attacks Bruce, including Ra's—Bruce is able to fight them off, and Ra's is killed during the struggle. Bruce is able to save the unconscious Ducard before the compound burns to the ground.

Bruce decides that it is now time to return to Gotham, so he has Alfred pick him up via a private jet. During their flight home, Bruce talks to Alfred about wanting to become some sort of symbol in his fight against crime in Gotham. Bruce has not decided what this symbol should be, but he knows that he wants it to be something terrifying. Back in Gotham, Dr. Jonathan Crane testifies in court on behalf of a crazed killer named Victor Zsaz. Rachel, who is now Gotham's Assistant District Attorney, is furious with Crane for doing this, because Zsaz has connections to Falcone. Rachel suspects that Crane is connected to Falcone as well.

Back at Wayne Manor, Bruce starts researching Gotham's cops and criminals. As he works, a bat flies into the room. This leads Bruce to go back down into the well where he fell as a boy, and he finds that the well leads to a huge, bat-filled cave under the Manor. As he stands in the cave, bats flying all around him, it is obvious that he has found the symbol he is looking for. He can strike fear into the hearts of criminals by disguising himself as the creature that frightened him so badly when he was young.

Meanwhile, Crane meets with Falcone, and tells the mobster that Rachel is a problem that needs to be handled. The next day, the Wayne Enterprises Board meets to discuss the future of the company, and Bruce walks in—since Bruce has been gone from Gotham without a trace for six years, everyone is shocked to see him. Bruce tells the Wayne C.E.O. William Earle that he wants to work in the company's Applied Sciences division, which is run by Lucius Fox.

Bruce goes to see Fox, who shows him some of the division's projects, including high-powered grapple guns and armored suits. Bruce asks Fox if he could "borrow" some of this equipment, but he doesn't tell Fox about his plans to become a crimefighter. Later, Bruce and Alfred work down in the cave under Wayne Manor, transforming it into a base of operations. Alfred mentions that Bruce is likely not the first Wayne to be in the cave—the Wayne home was a stop on the Underground Railroad, so Bruce's ancestors probably shielded runaway slaves by hiding them in the cave. Bruce also begins work on modifying one of the armored suits into a costume for himself.

Wearing this costume, along with a ski mask to hide his face, Bruce sneaks into the office of Gotham City Police Sergeant Jim Gordon. Gordon thinks he is being accosted by some lunatic when Bruce asks him how they can bring down Falcone. Bruce then tells Gordon to watch for his signal. The sergeant tries to apprehend Bruce as he flees the station, but Bruce gets away.

Bruce goes to see Fox again, who sets him up with some more high tech equipment. This equipment includes a fabric known as "memory cloth" which can be used to design a glider-like cape, and a tank-like armored automobile known as "the Tumbler." Later, in the cave Bruce and Alfred put the finishing touches on Bruce's first Batman costume, which includes a cape, a bat-eared cowl, and bat-shaped weapons.

Falcone meets with a crooked Gotham cop named Flass at the Gotham docks, where Falcone is having a large amount of illegal drugs shipped in. Flass checks in on the shipment, and tells Falcone that everything seems in order. Flass' assessment turns out to be very wrong when Batman attacks the thugs Falcone has hired to carry out the shipment. Batman takes all of the thugs down, and then attacks Falcone in his car. Right before Batman bears down on Falcone, the mobster says "What the hell are you?" under his breath. Batman answers him by pulling him out of the car, saying "I'm Batman," and knocking him out.

Meanwhile, Rachel is riding a Gotham Monorail train to her home, and several of Falcone's hitmen make an attempt to kill her. Batman stops them, and gives Rachel information that will help her to prosecute Falcone. Gordon arrives at the docks to find Falcone tied to a searchlight that is powered up — the light casts a batlike silhouette on the clouds in the sky.

The next day, Gotham Police Commissioner Loeb instructs his force to bring this vigilante to justice. Also, Earle learns that a microwave emitter weapon has been stolen from a Wayne Enterprises shipment — the weapon is designed to vaporize large amounts of water. That night, Bruce goes out on the town to build his "eccentric playboy" image. He runs into Rachel for the first time since returning to Gotham — she is very disappointed in his lifestyle.

Later that night, Crane goes to see Falcone in jail. Crane shows Falcone a scarecrow mask that he uses to torment his patients, and then he sprays the mobster with a form of the hallucinogen used by the League of Shadows. Batman attacks Flass in order to get information about Falcone's drug shipment — Flass tells the crimefighter that some of the drugs had something hidden in them, and those drugs were taken to a run-down Gotham neighborhood known as the Narrows.

Batman goes to the Narrows to find out about the drugs. There, a young boy sees him, and Batman gives the boy a small flexible periscope from his utility belt as a kind of "souvenir." Batman finds the apartment where the drugs are being hidden, and Crane is there to destroy them. Crane, in his scarecrow mask, sprays Batman with the hallucinogen and sets his costume on fire. The crimefighter jumps out of the apartment window to escape, and he calls Alfred for help.

The hallucinogen is so damaging to Bruce's mental state that Alfred has to call Fox for help. Fox is able to synthesize an antidote for the hallucinogen in order to save Bruce. Bruce tells Fox that he had better prepare a lot more of the antidote, because it is obvious that the hallucinogen is being used by Gotham's underworld and is somehow connected to Falcone's drug shipment. (Obviously, by this point Fox has figured out that Bruce is spending his nights fighting crime as Batman.)

Rachel stops by Wayne Manor to wish Bruce a happy 30th birthday. A big party is planned for Bruce at the Manor later in the day, but Rachel will not be able to attend. She needs to go to Arkham Asylum, located in the Narrows, because Crane has moved Falcone there. Worried that Rachel is heading into a very dangerous situation, Bruce races to Arkham as Batman. At Arkham, Crane realizes that Rachel is suspicious of his actions, so he sprays her with the hallucinogen. Batman bursts in on Crane and sprays him with the hallucinogen. The drugged Crane now sees Batman as a fearsome monster, and he tells the crimefighter that he has been working for Ra's Al Ghul. Batman is shocked by this confession, since he himself had watched Ra's die.

As Batman struggles to digest this information, he hears sirens — scores of Gotham Police officers have arrived at Arkham to arrest him. Gordon goes in to the asylum before the rest of the police, and Batman tells him that the hallucinogen is the work of Crane and someone even *worse* than Falcone. Before the rest of the Gotham Police enter the asylum, Batman activates a transmitter that emits a frequency that will attract bats. Thousands of bats swarm the asylum, allowing Batman and Gordon to exit the building with the gravely injured Rachel.

Batman puts Rachel in his car — it is the Tumbler, painted all black. In the car, Batman leads the Gotham Police on a high-speed chase through the streets of Gotham. The crimefighter is able to elude the police and make it back to his headquarters in the cave. There he is able to give Rachel the antidote for the hallucinogen. Batman tells Rachel that for the safety of Gotham, she needs to get what is left of the antidote to Gordon.

At Arkham, Gordon learns that a huge amount of the hallucinogen has been put into Gotham's water supply by Crane's thugs. At the same time, Bruce arrives at his birthday party at Wayne Manor, which is already in progress. Fox is at the party, and as Bruce and Fox talk they realize that the hallucinogen could be dispersed throughout Gotham by using the stolen microwave emitter to turn the poisoned water into vapor.

Bruce is shocked to see that Ducard is also at the party, and that Ducard is not who he seems to be at all — in reality, *he* is Ra's Al Ghul. Ra's has come to Gotham to make good on his promise to destroy the city — he is the one who has stolen the microwave emitter, and he will use it to unleash his hallucinogen on all of Gotham's citizens. Bruce pretends to be drunk, and he throws everyone out of his party so that Ra's cannot hurt them. Ra's and his men attack Bruce and set the Manor ablaze — luckily, Alfred is able to save Bruce before he is burned in the fire, and the two men escape into the cave. Ra's has other members of the League positioned throughout Gotham — some of them free all of the inmates in Arkham, including Crane.

Rachel finds Gordon, who is still at Arkham, and she gives him the antidote. She then rescues a little boy who has lost his parents — it is the boy whom Batman gave his periscope to. Ra's has arrived on the scene, and he loads the microwave emitter onto a Gotham Monorail train. He turns on the emitter, which vaporizes the water in all of the nearby water pipes — the dispersion of the hallucinogen has begun.

Batman arrives in the Narrows to confront Ra's. The crimefighter gives Gordon the keys to the Tumbler, saying he will need the Sergeant's help to stop Ra's. Before Batman engages Ra's, he rescues Rachel and the boy from a number of escaped Arkham inmates, including a horseback-riding Crane dressed in his scarecrow mask. As Rachel talks to Batman, she realizes that he is actually Bruce. Batman is able to intercept Ra's' train by latching onto it with his grapple gun. He climbs up his grapple line to board the train as it speeds down the track, and once he is on board he fights Ra's. While they are fighting, Gordon uses missiles in the Tumbler to destroy one of the bridges that the train will be passing over. Batman jumps out of the train just before it crashes — Ra's is killed, and the microwave emitter is destroyed.

Batman has brought Gotham through a tremendous ordeal, but his story is really just beginning. Bruce has gained control of his family's company, and he plans on rebuilding his burned-out home. Rachel comes to visit him as he works on the Manor — they are in love with one another, but Rachel feels there is no way for them to be together because of Bruce's double life.

Batman then meets with Gordon on the roof of the Gotham Police building. There, Gordon has installed a spotlight with a bat silhouette on it that can be used to signal the crimefighter. They still have much to do to fix all of the damage that Ra's, Falcone and

Crane have caused. And to make matters worse, they have new criminals to worry about. A bank robbery/double murder has just been committed by someone who leaves a Joker playing card at the scene of his crimes. Batman tells Gordon that he'll look into this crime. As the crimefighter turns to leave, Gordon says to him, "I never said thank you." Batman says that Gordon will never have to as he jumps off of the roof and into the night sky.

Christopher Nolan's plan to make a Batman film that would tell the story of the character's origin in a real world setting had succeeded spectacularly. *Batman Begins* took the Batman character and his world much more seriously than any previous Batman feature film had — and as a result, the movie turned out to be a complex, richly detailed crime drama that was truly light years ahead of any previous big screen adaptation of the Batman character. Another thing that really set the film apart from its predecessors was that it was about what a Batman film should be about — namely, Batman himself. The previous Warner Batman movies had all seemed to be more interested in the gaudily costumed villains they featured than they were in their title character. *Batman Begins* put an end to this line of thinking, placing Bruce Wayne's quest for justice and his transformation into Batman squarely at the center of the film's plot.

Nolan's reinvention of Warner's Batman film franchise received a resoundingly positive response from both the critics and the general moviegoing public. *Batman Begins* garnered better reviews than had any previous Batman big screen work, and it performed very well at the box office. The film made over $48 million during its opening weekend in the U.S., and it went on to take in well over $200 million in the United States alone. It also made almost $170 million in foreign box office returns, bringing its worldwide total gross to over $370 million.[19]

The success of *Batman Begins* was made all the more impressive by the fact that the movie had to convince critics and the general public to give Warner's Batman film franchise another chance after they had been so disappointed by Joel Schumacher's *Batman and Robin*. As we discussed earlier in the book, many people knew the long line of characters that had been used in Warner's previous Batman films and assumed that everything that could be squeezed out of the Batman universe for the big screen had been squeezed out — they figured that Batman simply had no more to offer in terms of further movie projects. *Batman Begins* proved what all of us serious Batman fans had known all along — that Warner's Batman film franchise had barely scratched the surface of the character's big screen potential, and that Batman had *so* much more to offer in terms of further movie projects.

In spite of all of Warner's efforts to make it clear that *Batman Begins* was a complete restart of their Batman film franchise, there were those critics and moviegoers that had somewhat of a difficult time understanding this fact. They thought that the film was a *prequel* to all of Warner's previous Batman films, not a brand new cinematic interpretation of the character. This confusion would definitely be cleared up by Nolan's two later Batman films *The Dark Knight* (2008) and *The Dark Knight Rises* (2012), since so many of the characters featured in those films were completely different interpretations of characters that had been featured in Warner's previous Batman films.

Batman Begins has so many strengths that it is hard to decide where to begin an analysis of the film. We'll start with an in-depth examination of the Batman comics, graphic novels and screen works that inspired Christopher Nolan and David S. Goyer's screenplay. As mentioned earlier in this chapter, Nolan and Goyer drew on a number of classic Batman works when crafting the script. What follows is a list of scenes from the film and the Batman works they can be directly traced to. (Incidentally, we have discussed all of these works at one point or another earlier in the book.)

Young Bruce takes a fall into a cave under Wayne Manor, and a terrifyingly large swarm of bats fly at him — this was pulled from the 1986 graphic novel series *Batman: The Dark Knight Returns*, and the 1989 comic story "The Man Who Falls."

While training himself to be a crimefighter, Bruce is mentored by a skilled combatant named Ducard — this was pulled from the 1989 comic series *Blind Justice*, and the 1989 comic story "The Man Who Falls."

Thomas and Martha Wayne are murdered by a mugger as Bruce looks on — this was pulled from numerous Batman works such as the 1939 comic story "Legend — The Batman and How He Came to Be," the 1948 comic story "The Origin of Batman," the 1986 graphic novel series *Batman: The Dark Knight Returns*, the 1987 comic series *Batman: Year One*, and the 1989 comic story "The Man Who Falls."

A bat flies into Wayne Manor while Bruce formulates his crimefighting strategy — this was pulled from the 1939 comic story "Legend — The Batman and How He Came to Be."

Batman interrogates Flass in order to find out what he knows about Falcone's illegal drug shipment. The crimefighter does this by suspending Flass high above the city streets in an upside-down position — this was pulled from the 1996 graphic novel *Batman: Haunted Knight*.

Batman interrogates Jonathan Crane after Crane has been sprayed by his own fear-inducing hallucinogen. The drugged Crane then sees Batman as a fearsome bat-like monster — this was pulled from "Nothing to Fear," a 1992 episode of the television series *Batman: The Animated Series*.

At the end this interrogation, the drugged Crane says to Batman that "Dr. Crane isn't here right now" as if he is out of his body, and his body has somehow become his personal answering machine — this was pulled from the 1996 graphic novel *Batman: Haunted Knight*.

Batman escapes from the Gotham Police by activating a transmitter that attracts a swarm of bats — this was pulled from the 1987 comic series *Batman: Year One*.

Crane attempts to poison Gotham's water supply by dispersing fear toxin into water pipes located under Arkham Asylum — this was pulled from "Dreams in Darkness," a 1992 episode of the television series *Batman: The Animated Series*.

Crane, in his scarecrow mask, sits astride a horse that is performing a leaping maneuver known as a levade — this was pulled from the 1996–97 graphic novel *Batman: The Long Halloween*.

Gordon and Batman meet on the rooftop of the Gotham City Police Department to discuss a new criminal who calls himself the Joker — this was pulled from the 1987 comic series *Batman: Year One*.

It is interesting to note that while Nolan and Goyer publicly acknowledged the Batman print works that *Batman Begins* was inspired by (particularly "The Man Who Falls" and *Batman: Year One*), they apparently chose not to publicly acknowledge any inspiration they might have drawn from *Batman: The Animated Series*. This is somewhat surprising, because it seems almost a certainty that the television series had a substantial influence their work — after all, the similarities I've just noted between episodes of the series and scenes from the film are striking.

At any rate, no previous Batman big screen work had ever drawn on such a wide array of classic Batman material. By crafting their *Batman Begins* screenplay in this manner, Nolan and Goyer showed more respect for the time-honored traditions of Batman character than any filmmaker had ever shown. Of course, it should be pointed out that they still chose to take quite a few liberties with this material. For example, in the film the Waynes were leaving a performance of the opera *Mefistofle* because Bruce was scared of the batlike creatures on the stage when Thomas and Martha were shot and killed. In the comics, neither the opera nor bats ever had anything to do with the Wayne murders — the family was always shown leaving a movie theatre right before the tragedy.

Most all of the liberties that Nolan and Goyer took with Batman mythos were decidedly small ones, so the film's depiction of Batman generally stayed very close to the character's time-honored traditions. However, there was one noticeable exception to this rule — Nolan and Goyer chose to portray Bruce Wayne as not being particularly skilled in the disciplines of science and technology. Since Batman's very first origin story "Legend — The Batman and How He Came to Be" was published in 1939, Bruce was depicted as having developed his mind every bit as much as his body in order to become Batman. In fact, that story even stated that he had trained himself to become a "master scientist."

In *Batman Begins*, Bruce is shown to be unapologetically ignorant of scientific and technological matters. For example, when Lucius Fox tells Bruce what steps he had to take in order to synthesize an antidote for Crane's hallucinogen, Bruce implies that he does not understand a word that Fox is saying. Also, all of the high tech equipment that Bruce uses to fight crime as Batman is not developed by Bruce — rather, he obtains it from the Wayne Enterprises archives through Fox. In this author's opinion, Nolan and Goyer's decision to slightly "dumb down" the Bruce Wayne character in the film is an unnecessary and unwelcome one.

Incidentally, this decision leads to Fox being a much more integral character in *Batman Begins* than he had ever been in any previous Batman work. Ever since Fox was first introduced into Batman comic stories in the late 1970s, he had played a decidedly peripheral role in Batman mythos — he was a Wayne Enterprises executive who was a close confidant of Bruce's, but he had no knowledge of Bruce's exploits as Batman. Obviously, the *Batman Begins* Fox not only knows that Bruce is Batman, but he also sets Bruce up with all of his crimefighting gear. This new version of Fox is basically a shameless copy of the character known as Q from the James Bond film series — over the years, Q provisioned Bond with an endless array of high tech spy gadgetry. Here is perhaps the most concise way to sum up the manner in which Fox is depicted in *Batman Begins* — Fox seems to have been given all of the intelligence that Nolan and Goyer decided to take away from Bruce!

But this "dumbing down" of Bruce is basically the only objection I have with Nolan and Goyer's take on Batman/Bruce Wayne in the film. In my opinion, the Batman/Bruce Wayne of *Batman Begins* is the most definitive big screen version of the character ever created. He is grim and determined, but he is still very much in control of his actions and emotions. There is darkness in his soul because he is born from great tragedy, but he can still take some satisfaction in the fact that his mission is truly helping Gotham City and its citizens. As we've just discussed, Nolan and Goyer formed their version of Batman/Bruce Wayne by piecing together elements drawn from classic incarnations of the character — but their version of Batman/Bruce Wayne ended up being so well-constructed that he *himself* ended up being a classic incarnation of the character.

Nolan and Goyer's powerful vision of Batman/Bruce Wayne is acted to perfection by Christian Bale. As we've made our way through the history of Batman feature films, we've examined all of the actors who have played the role on the big screen — Lewis Wilson, Robert Lowery, Adam West, Michael Keaton, Val Kilmer and George Clooney. Bale's incredible performance in *Batman Begins* is head and shoulders above all of the Batman performances given by these actors.

What really sets Bale apart from these actors is that he is equally marvelous at playing both Batman and Bruce Wayne. His striking good looks, muscular physique, and psychological intensity capture both of the character's identities to a degree that is almost startling. It is difficult for me to find words to convey just how good I think Bale is in *Batman Begins*, but I'll give it a try. To me, Bale *is* Batman/Bruce Wayne during every moment he is on the screen in the film — I can't think of a higher compliment to give his performance.

There is one more element of the *Batman Begins* Batman that is worthy of high praise. The Batsuit that costume designer Lindy Hemming created for the film is every bit as impressive as Nolan and Goyer's writing and Bale's acting. As we noted earlier in this chapter, the costume is perhaps more similar to the Batman costumes used in Warner's previous Batman films than one might have expected in a franchise restart. But the costume still has enough differences in style and design to set it apart from these earlier costumes. At any rate, here are the most important observations that need to be made regarding Hemming's Batsuit — it looks flat-out spectacular on film, and it captures the character's iconic appearance as well as any movie Batman costume ever created.

The high quality of Bale's performance as Batman/Bruce Wayne in *Batman Begins* is matched by the film's supporting cast. Michael Caine's interpretation of Alfred is particularly stellar — Caine bears no physical resemblance to the Alfred of the comics, but his acting brings a warmth and humanity to Bruce's closest confidant that is both believable and touching. The interplay between Bale and Caine in their scenes together gives the film some of its best quiet, character-driven moments.

Liam Neeson is excellent as Ducard, though obviously he really is not so much "Ducard" as he is Ra's Al Ghul. In this author's opinion, Nolan and Goyer's decision to fold Ducard and Ra's into one single character does not work particularly well. Elements of both characters are incorporated into Neeson's portrayal of Ducard/Ra's, but combining them together does not allow for *either* of them to be explored with any great depth.

This is not especially disappointing in terms of the Ducard character — as we noted earlier in this chapter, the character never had made much of an impact on Batman mythos since he was first introduced in 1989. It is more disappointing that Ra's is shortchanged — he had become one of Batman's truly classic villains since his creation in the early 1970s, so he could have been more richly developed if he had not been shoehorned into a "surprise ending" kind of a plot device.

That said, however, Nolan and Goyer's decision to lose the sci-fi/fantasy elements of Ra's like his ability to achieve immortality through the use of his Lazarus Pit made the character fit in very well with the film's real world interpretation of Batman. (We discussed the origin of Ra's and his Lazarus Pit back in Chapter 7.) And Nolan and Goyer did stay very true to the overall spirit of the character in the film — Ra's' determination to wipe out millions of lives in order to restore the planet to what he considered to be its "natural balance" perfectly captured the essence of the comic book Ra's.

I should probably say at least a few words about the film's "decoy Ra's" played by Ken Watanabe. Watanabe's acting, looks and wardrobe nicely convey that Ra's is a man of far eastern descent who is in possession of great wisdom and strength — in other words, he is perhaps more similar to the comic book Ra's than the film's *real* Ra's! Of course, this misdirection was a very intentional one on the part of Nolan so that he could outfit *Batman Begins* with a whopper of a plot twist.

Katie Holmes turns in a solid performance as Rachel Dawes in *Batman Begins*. Rachel is the only major character in the film that has no origin in Batman's comic book roots. Her ties to Bruce that go all the way back to their childhood together and her strong moral convictions make her a more interesting character than the heroines in Warner's previous Batman films — in other words, she is definitely an upgrade over Vicki Vale and Chase Meridian! Holmes does a very nice job with the strong material that Nolan and Goyer have given her to work with.

As excellent as all of *Batman Begins*' supporting cast is, one would be hard pressed to pick out just one cast member as being the best of the bunch. But if I were forced to do just that, I think I would choose Gary Oldman's performance as Jim Gordon. Like Bale, Oldman completely disappears into his part — this allows him to bring Gordon to life in a richly detailed manner that makes all previous big screen versions of the character look laughingly simplistic by comparison. Of course, Oldman's performance benefits greatly from Nolan and Goyer's thoughtful interpretation of Gordon — it is drawn almost exclusively from Frank Miller and David Mazzucchelli's version of the character found in their 1987 comic series *Batman: Year One*. Oldman's appearance in the film is meant to reflect this version of the character as well — he is made up to look *exactly* like the *Batman: Year One* Gordon.

By contrast, Cillian Murphy's depiction of Dr. Jonathan Crane/The Scarecrow in *Batman Begins* has little to do with *any* comic version of the character. Nolan and Goyer made the decision to lose the character's Ray Bolger–like scarecrow costume and outfit him with nothing more than a business suit and a burlap mask. In keeping with the film's real world sensibilities, the burlap mask has a practical function — it houses a gas mask that Crane wears while spraying his victims with fear toxin. Murphy's creepy performance both in and out of the burlap mask makes Crane a very memorable character even though he is so far removed from the Scarecrow of the comics.

As we discussed just a bit ago, Lucius Fox is made to be a very integral character in *Batman Begins*. Nolan wisely chose to entrust this important role to the acclaimed veteran actor Morgan Freeman. Freeman gives a likable, low-key performance as Fox in the film — by investing Fox with a sense of quiet wisdom and a wonderfully wry sense of humor, Freeman effectively conveys what a valuable ally Fox is to Bruce.

There are several characters in *Batman Begins* that were first introduced into Batman's world through Frank Miller and David Mazzucchelli's 1987 comic series *Batman: Year One*. Tom Wilkinson plays Gotham crime boss Carmine Falcone, Mark Boone Junior plays Gotham City Police Detective Flass, and Colin McFarlane plays Gotham City Police Commissioner Loeb. None of these characters are carbon copies of their *Batman: Year One* counterparts in terms of their actions or appearance — still, they greatly enhance the film because they are so well-written and acted.

There is one more character in the film that I just have to examine in some detail. Jack Gleeson plays the young boy who receives a small flexible periscope from Batman as a kind of "souvenir." At the end of the film, Batman rescues both Rachel and the boy from the clutches of a number of escaped Arkham inmates. The boy is by Rachel's side when she realizes Batman's true identity and calls the crimefighter "Bruce."

All right, I realize that I might be reading too much into this character, but doesn't he appear to be a *lot* like a very young Robin? He has equipment given to him by Batman in his possession — he might even have Batman's *real identity* in his possession as well, for goodness' sake! It appears than he might have been orphaned due to Ra's' attack on Gotham City. (Of course, most all classic versions of the Robin character featured origins in which they were orphaned.) I mean, come on — just look at all of these signs! You want more? Well, here's one more for you — the boy is even wearing a red t-shirt that looks a bit like a Robin tunic in his scenes!

Did Nolan find a very subtle way to incorporate the Robin character into his vision of Batman and his world in *Batman Begins*? Well, the director went out of his way not to give us any hints as to just who this boy might be — Gleeson is billed simply as "Little Boy" in the film's credits. And Nolan chose not to feature the character in either of his Batman sequels, so we'll probably never know any more about the character than we do right now. And not only did Nolan never revisit this character, but he also found a way to incorporate a new character with the name of "Robin" into one of his Batman sequels — we'll discuss that "Robin" in detail later in the book. Still, I wonder — that "Little Boy" sure seems a lot like a Robin to me!

It is interesting to note that even though Batman is such a quintessential American character, much of the *Batman Begins* cast and crew hail from countries in and around the United Kingdom. For example, Christopher Nolan, Michael Caine, Tom Wilkinson and Gary Oldman are English, Christian Bale is Welsh, and Liam Neeson and Cillian Murphy are Irish. But even though so much of *Batman Begins*' creative talent is U.K.-based, the film still has a decidedly "American" feel to it. Bale, Oldman, Wilkinson and Murphy in particular adopt flawless American accents when they assume their roles — so all of their characters convincingly come across as having been born and raised in the United States.

One of *Batman Begins*' most potent strengths is the film's incredible production design. The collaboration between Nolan and his production designer Nathan Crowley ended up bringing Batman's world to life in a way that was both wonderfully atmospheric and strikingly realistic. All of the film's massive sets are a wonder to behold — Gotham City, Arkham Asylum, Wayne Manor and the Batcave are realized in such spectacular fashion that audiences are totally drawn into the production. The scale and detail of these sets makes one feel as if they are standing right next to Batman during his adventures. The *Batman Begins* sets are so ambitious that most all of the sets used in Warner's previous Batman films are left looking claustrophobic by comparison — and given how elaborate many of the sets were for Burton's and Schumacher's Batman films, that *really* is saying something!

The gigantic scope of the film's sets is matched by the scope of the film's location shooting. The scenes filmed in Iceland and in Chicago help to bring Batman's world to life in an immersive manner that would not be possible by filming on cramped soundstages. These scenes definitely showcase the incredible work of the film's director of photography Wally Pfister. Pfister's Chicago shots that depict Batman standing on top of skyscrapers are the ones are particularly unforgettable — as a lifelong Batman fan, I can truly say that I had been waiting for iconic scenes like these to show up in a Batman movie all of my life!

Interestingly, so much of the production design and cinematography of *Batman Begins* seemed to be tied to one particular color. Many of the film's Gotham scenes are bathed in light that appears to come from the common overhead street lights that emit an orange/brown color — as a result, these scenes have a decidedly sepia tone to them. This color doesn't just show up in the film itself — it was also the dominant color in most of the theatrical posters used to advertise the film's release.

Of course, far and away the most striking element of the film's production design is its Batmobile. (Incidentally, the Batmobile was always referred to by the name of "the Tumbler" in the film, but we'll stick with tradition and call it by its time-honored name here!) When Nolan and Crowley decided to realize the Batmobile in such a utilitarian, no-nonsense manner during the early planning stages of the film, they really were on to something—the incredible car really is every bit as much of a star in the film as its lead actors, and its design is a perfect summation of the film's real world approach to Batman. The true genius of the auto lies in the fact that its appearance is so memorably unrefined—if one would outfit it with a long handle coming off the back, it would look a lot like a giant push lawn mower!

Hans Zimmer and James Newton Howard's excellent musical score is another essential component in establishing *Batman Begins*' overall atmosphere. Their ambient compositions have a power and intensity that perfectly complements the film's real world interpretation of Batman. Incidentally, Zimmer and Howard titled these compositions in an unusual way—all of the pieces were named with Latin words that describe various species of bats.

In the end, most all of the things that are so wonderful about *Batman Begins* can be traced directly to Christopher Nolan. The film is definitely based on a wide variety of classic Batman material, but it is Nolan's vision that pulls all of that material together to form an unforgettable cinematic portrait of Batman and his world. *Batman Begins* is by turns savage, sensitive, tragic, and funny, and it rarely loses sight of the fact that Batman's real strength as a character lies in his close ties to reality.

That said, however, I do still have a few quibbles with the film. First, I feel that some of its scenes suffer from very hyperactive editing—there are moments in the movie when one has to process so many ridiculously quick cuts that it is hard to keep up with what is happening onscreen. This is especially true of the film's action sequences—after all of my repeated viewings of the movie, I still find some of its action difficult to follow. For example, one of the film's signature scenes is when Batman leaps from the top floor of Arkham Asylum and uses his cape to glide to the bottom of the Asylum's ornate circular stairwell. There are a total of *seven* different camera angles cut into Batman's seven-second glide! In my opinion, a few less angles would have allowed viewers to better take in this iconic scene.

Another problem that I have with *Batman Begins* involves one of the film's major plot points. The climax of the movie revolves around Ra's Al Ghul's fear hallucinogen being dispersed into Gotham's water system — the poisoned water is then turned into vapor by some sort of powerful microwave emitter. This scenario is physically impossible for a variety of reasons. First, because water pipes are highly pressurized, they cannot be opened they way they are opened under Arkham Asylum where the hallucinogen is being poured into the water system. If a real water pipe was opened in that manner, the water inside of it would not keep flowing through the pipe like a fast-moving stream — instead, it would quickly flood the entire area.

Furthermore, if the city's water pipes started rupturing because the water inside of them was vaporized, the overall water pressure in the system would *lower*, not raise. So the idea of the microwave emitter somehow being able to generate enough water pressure to cause a chain-reaction explosion of the city's entire water system is at odds with real physical science.

Nolan had repeatedly stated that he wanted to keep *Batman Begins* as closely tied to reality as possible — so it seems like a very odd decision on his part to have set up the entire climax of the film around a scenario that could not possibly happen in real life. In my opinion, *Batman Begins* could have been an even better movie than it turned out to be if it had given a plausible climax that was more in keeping with its real world sensibilities.

All right, that's enough of my quibbling—let's go back to saying good things about *Batman Begins*. During the film's initial theatrical run, it was treated to a cinematic upgrade that no previous Batman screen work had ever received—it was remastered so that the film could be shown in IMAX theatres. Just in case anyone is unfamiliar with the IMAX film format, I'll take a moment here to give a quick rundown of what it is and what it does.

In the late 1960s, a Canadian film company called the IMAX Corporation began creating its own motion picture film format and corresponding set of cinema projection standards. Movies that were filmed in the IMAX format were able to capture images of far greater size and clarity than movies using conventional film formats. At first, the format was used almost exclusively for the creation and screening of documentary films. Giant-sized IMAX theatres constructed at museums and science centers around the world showed IMAX films about animals, nature, science, travel, and a host of other topics.

But the format started to be used to produce and screen non-documentary films as well—for example, Walt Disney Pictures released their animated film *Fantasia 2000* on IMAX format in early 2000. Not long after the release of *Fantasia 2000*, IMAX developed technology to remaster non–IMAX films so that they could be shown in IMAX theatres. Since the IMAX format was crossing over from the world of documentary works to the world of entertainment works more and more frequently, multiplex cinemas around the world started outfitting their facilities with IMAX theatres.

In the early 2000s, Warner Bros. started releasing a number of their high-profile movies in IMAX format—*Batman Begins* was one of those movies. Simply put, the film looked absolutely dazzling when it was screened in the IMAX format. As I mentioned earlier in this chapter, *Batman Begins* realized Batman's world in such spectacular fashion that audiences were totally drawn into the production—the movie became even *more* immersive once it was transferred onto high-resolution IMAX film and projected onto giant IMAX screens.

Incidentally, this assessment of the film having even more of an impact when screened in IMAX is based on personal experience. During the summer of 2005, I attended IMAX showings of the movie in Cincinnati, Ohio, Indianapolis, Indiana and my hometown of Columbus, Ohio—these showings definitely took my *Batman Begins* viewing experience to a whole new level. The showing that was particularly memorable was the one in Indianapolis—I saw the film at the massive IMAX theatre at the Indiana State Museum, and I left the theatre feeling like I had been standing shoulder-to-shoulder with Batman during most every second of the time he was on the screen.

Obviously, I was not the only one who was so impressed with how incredible *Batman Begins* looked in IMAX. When Christopher Nolan began work on his sequel to the movie, he decided to actually *film* a sizeable portion of the sequel with IMAX cameras. That sequel was the stunningly successful *The Dark Knight* (2008), and it was the first non-documentary feature film ever made to include scenes that were shot using IMAX technology. (We'll discuss the film and its IMAX scenes in detail later in the book.)

Let's take *Batman Begins* from the big screen to the small screen and examine the movie's home video release history. The film's box office success led to a high demand for *Batman Begins* DVDs and VHS tapes when Warner Bros. first released it to the home video market in October 2005. Incidentally, *Batman Begins* was the last Batman big screen work to be made commercially available on VHS before the format was put on the road to obsolescence by the DVD format. There were several different DVD versions of the film released by Warner. It was offered as two separate single-disc releases, one in its original widescreen format and one in a format cropped to fit a standard television screen. *Batman Begins* was also released as a 2-disc set—the set contained the widescreen version of the film, as well as a wealth of bonus material.

This bonus material was very similar to the bonus material found on the 2-disc DVD sets of Warner's previous Batman films. (As we've discussed a number of times earlier in the book, these DVD sets were also released in 2005 in the wake of *Batman Begins*' success.) Highlights of this material included eight featurettes about the making of the film — the featurettes were entitled "Batman: The Journey Begins," "Shaping Mind and Body," "Gotham City Rises," "Cape and Cowl," "Batman: The Tumbler," "Path to Discovery," "Saving Gotham City," and "Genesis of the Bat." These featurettes included commentary from many of the individuals who played a major role in the movie's creation, including Christopher Nolan, David S. Goyer, Nathan Crowley, Emma Thomas, Chris Corbould, Wally Pfister, Lindy Hemming, Christian Bale, Gary Oldman, and Katie Holmes. Their commentary was accompanied by a good deal of behind-the-scenes footage shot on the *Batman Begins* set showing the film's cast and crew at work.

This 2005 DVD set remained the highest-quality home video version of *Batman Begins* until Warner released the movie on HD DVD in October 2006. However, the HD DVD format turned out to be a short-lived one. The majority of consumers ended up choosing Blu-ray over HD DVD as their preferred high definition video format, so HD DVD production was completely suspended less than two years after the release of the *Batman Begins* HD DVD.

Warner released *Batman Begins* on Blu-ray in July 2008 to coincide with the theatrical release of *The Dark Knight*, Nolan's sequel to *Batman Begins*. The *Batman Begins* Blu-ray included all of the special features found on the DVD set, as well as several new special features. Far and away the most notable of these was "*The Dark Knight* IMAX Prologue," the bank robbery sequence featuring the Joker that opened *The Dark Knight*. Since that sequence had actually been filmed in IMAX, those who purchased the *Batman Begins* Blu-ray got the opportunity to see the extraordinary level of visual quality that high-resolution IMAX film was going to bring to *The Dark Knight*. And needless to say, the *Batman Begins* Blu-ray flawlessly reproduced all of the incredible sights and sounds found in both *Batman Begins* and "*The Dark Knight* IMAX Prologue." (Of course, the Blu-ray really couldn't deliver the kind of overwhelming viewing experience that IMAX showings of these films could — but hey, let's not get *too* greedy here!)

There is one more screen version of *Batman Begins* that we should take note of here. The video game *Batman Begins* was released on major gaming platforms such as PlayStation 2 and Xbox in June 2005 to coincide with the theatrical release of the actual film. *Batman Begins* presented its players with a long, complex plot that closely adhered to the plot of the film, and its graphics were designed to capture the look of the film's characters, props and sets. The game's connection to the film was made even stronger due to the fact that all of the film's principal actors provided the voices for their characters in the game's audio. Interestingly, even though the *Batman Begins* video game enjoyed a reasonable amount of commercial and critical success when it was released, it did not end up inspiring Warner Bros. to release video game tie-ins to Nolan's two later Batman films — so to date, *Batman Begins* is the only modern, immersive video game based on a live-action Batman film ever to be produced.

It is also interesting to note how Warner Bros. chose to handle general merchandising tie-ins to promote the release of *Batman Begins*. Obviously, the film was intended for adult audiences — indeed, it was the most complex, mature Batman film that Warner had produced to date. But even still, the film's release was supported by the usual amount of merchandise intended for children — there was a wide variety of *Batman Begins* action figures, toys, books, comics, trading cards, clothing, etc., in stores as the film first hit theatres. Thankfully, this merchandising blitz did not create the kind of controversy that the merchandising blitz for the adult-oriented *Batman Returns* had. The reason for this was simple—even though *Batman Begins* was also an adult-oriented film, it was nowhere near as dark and disturbing as *Batman Returns* had been. Consequently, it did not seem at all inappropriate to help promote the film through some products designed for children. (Plus, how could you ever stop a kid from wanting a toy version of a cool car like the Tumbler?)

I'll close my discussion of *Batman Begins* with these thoughts. This reboot of Warner's Batman film franchise certainly did not reach the incredible, history-making level of success that the studio's first Batman film did back in 1989—but it still undoubtedly stands as one of the greatest achievements in the history of the Batman character. To date, *Batman Begins* is the only Batman big screen work that draws on a wide array of classic Batman material—and as a result, it is widely considered to be one of the best cinematic portraits of the character ever created.

I think that I can best sum up what an important milestone *Batman Begins* is in the history of the character with these following sentences. Most all previous Batman big screen works had their moments for us serious Batman fans, moments that gave us a glimpse of the iconic character that we loved. But sitting through an entire Batman film just to enjoy a moment or two was by no means a truly satisfying experience for us—wasn't there a filmmaker out there who could give us a Batman movie that contained more than just "moments?" We longed for a well-constructed, intelligently-written Batman film that would really take the character seriously—one that would capture the spirit of Batman's greatest comic adventures by staying true to the time-honored traditions of the character from fade in to fade out. Christopher Nolan delivered that film to us—it was *Batman Begins*.

In other words, I consider *Batman Begins* to be the best Batman big screen work ever created. I realize that Nolan's next two Batman films *The Dark Knight* (2008) and *The Dark Knight Rises* (2012) ended up being so staggeringly successful that most people see them as being far greater triumphs than *Batman Begins*. I personally do not agree with this line of thinking—in fact, even though I very much enjoyed *The Dark Knight* and *The Dark Knight Rises*, I feel that neither film lived up to the promise established by *Batman Begins*. I'll lay out my case for this argument in the next few chapters of the book.

18

The Dark Knight (2008)

Cast: Christian Bale (Batman/Bruce Wayne), Michael Caine (Alfred), Heath Ledger (The Joker), Gary Oldman (Jim Gordon), Aaron Eckhart (Harvey Dent), Maggie Gyllenhaal (Rachel Dawes), Morgan Freeman (Lucius Fox), Monique Gabriela Curnen (Ramirez), Ron Dean (Wuertz), Nestor Carbonell (Mayor), Chin Han (Lau), Eric Roberts (Maroni), Ritchie Coster (Chechen), Anthony Michael Hall (Engel), Keith Szarabajka (Stephens), Joshua Harto (Reese), Melinda McGraw (Barbara Gordon), Nathan Gamble (James Gordon, Jr.), Michael Jai White (Gambol), Beatrice Rosen (Natascha), Cillian Murphy (Scarecrow), Colin McFarlane (Loeb), Michael Vieau (Rossi), Michael Stoyanov (Dopey), William Smillie (Happy), Danny Goldring (Grumpy), Matthew O'Neill (Chuckles), William Fichtner (Bank Manager), Olumiji Olawumi (Drug Dealer), Greg Beam (Drug Buyer), Erik Hellman (Junkie), Vincenzo Nicoli (Crime Boss), Edison Chen (LSI VP), Nydia Rodriguez Terracina (Judge Surrillo), Andy Luther (Brian), James Farruggio (Man No. 1), Tom McElroy (Man No. 2), Will Zahrn (Assistant DA), James Fierro (Thug at Party), Patrick Leahy (Gentleman at Party), Sam Derence (Male Guest), Jennifer Knox (Female Guest), Patrick Clear (Judge Freel), Sarah Jayne Dunn (Maroni's Mistress), Chucky Venn, Winston Ellis (Bodyguards), David Dastmalchian (Joker's Thug), Sophia Hinshelwood (Reporter), Keith Kupferer (Heckler), Joseph Luis Caballero (Cop Heckler), Richard Dillane (Acting Commissioner), Daryl Satcher (Officer at Intersection), Chris Petschler (Convoy Leader), Aidan Feore (Fat Thug), Philip Bulcock (Murphy), Paul Birchard (Cop with Fat Thug), Walter Lewis (Medic), Vincent Riotta (Cop at 250 52nd Street), Nancy Crane (Nurse), K. Todd Freeman (Polk), Matt Shallenberger (Berg), Michael Andrew Gorman (Cop at Hospital), Lanny Lutz (Bartender), Peter DeFaria (Civilian), Matt Rippy (First Mate), Andrew Bicknell (Prison Ferry Pilot), Ariyon Bakare (Guard Commander), Doug Ballard (Businessman), Helene Wilson (Mother), Tommy Campbell, Craig Heaney, Lorna Gayle, Lisa McAllister, Peter Brooke (Passengers), Joshua Rollins (SWAT Sniper), Dale Rivera (SWAT Leader), Matthew Leitch (Prisoner on Ferry), Tiny Lister (Tattooed Prisoner), Thomas Gaitsch (Reporter #3), William Armstrong (Evans), Adam Kalesperis (Honor Guard Man), Tristan Tait (Uniform Cop), Bronson Webb, David Ajala (Bounty Hunters), Gertrude Kyles (Fox's Secretary), Jonathan Ryland (Passenger Ferry Pilot), James Scales (Guardsman), Nigel Carrington (Warden), Ian Pirie (Corrections Officer), Lateef Lovejoy, Grahame Edwardes, Roger Monk, Ronan Summers (Prisoners), Wai Wong (Hong Kong Detective), Michael Corey Foster (Honor Guard Leader), Hannah Gunn (Gordon's Daughter), Brandon Lambdin (Armored Car SWAT). *Producers:* Emma Thomas, Charles Roven, Christopher Nolan. *Executive Producers:* Benjamin Melniker, Michael E. Uslan, Kevin De La Noy, Thomas Tull. *Director:* Christopher Nolan. *Screenplay:* Jonathan Nolan, Christopher Nolan (Story by Christopher Nolan and David S. Goyer, based upon characters appearing in comic books published by DC Comics, Batman created by Bob Kane). *Director of Photography:* Wally Pfister. *Production Designer:* Nathan Crowley. *Editor:* Lee Smith. *Music:* Hans Zimmer, James Newton Howard. *Visual Effects Supervisor:* Nick Davis. *Special Effects Supervisor:* Chris Corbould. *Costume Designer:* Lindy Hemming. *Casting:* John Papsidera. *Studio:* Warner Bros. *Length:* 152 minutes. *United States Release Date:* July 18, 2008.

Obviously, the strong commercial and critical success of *Batman Begins* led Warner Bros. to hope that Christopher Nolan would want to write and direct a sequel to the film. Nolan obliged the studio in this regard, although not right away—his first project after *Batman Begins* was the 2006 mystery thriller *The Prestige* starring Hugh Jackman and two of his *Batman Begins* actors, Christian Bale and Michael Caine. But after *The Prestige* was finished, Nolan went to work figuring out just how he was going to follow up his first Batman film. His first order of business was to recruit David S. Goyer for the movie, and he and Goyer laid out a story for the movie's screenplay.

Since Warner's Batman film franchise was now officially rebooted, Nolan and Goyer were now given much more latitude in terms of just what characters they could use in their new Batman movie. They wouldn't have to pass on any of Batman's classic comic villains just because they had been used in either Tim Burton's or Joel Schumacher's Batman films. *Batman Begins* had established that Warner's cinematic Batman was unquestionably in Nolan and Goyer's world now, and the two men had the power to shape that world in most any way that they saw fit.

Not surprisingly, these new rules led them to choose two of Batman's all-time greatest villains for their film. Nolan and Goyer decided that they would create brand-new interpretations of the Joker and Two-Face for the movie—interpretations that were light years removed from the manner in which the Joker was depicted in Burton's *Batman* and Two-Face was depicted in Schumacher's *Batman Forever*. (Of course, having the Joker in the film

Christian Bale as Batman in *The Dark Knight* (2008).

was really a foregone conclusion—after all, his first appearance in Gotham had been discussed by Batman and Gordon during the final scene of *Batman Begins*.)

As Nolan and Goyer put together their film's story, they did not draw on nearly as much classic Batman material as they had when they were writing *Batman Begins*. However, they were greatly influenced by one particular Batman comic work—that work was the 1996–97 13-part graphic novel series *Batman: The Long Halloween*, which was written by Jeph Loeb and illustrated by Tim Sale.[1] (We'll examine the similarities between *Batman: The Long Halloween* and Nolan's finished film later in this chapter.)

Nolan brought another writer onto the project as well—the finished script would end up being penned by the director and his brother Jonathan. The Nolan brothers and Goyer decided on a title for their new Batman film—it would be called *The Dark Knight*. Of course, "The Dark Knight" was a nickname for Batman that dated all the way back to *Batman* #1, Spring 1940. The phrase essentially became DC Comics' official second name for Batman after the 1986 publication of Frank Miller's groundbreaking graphic novel series *Batman: The Dark Knight Returns*.

Interestingly, longtime Batman fans knew just what the phrase "The Dark Knight" meant when the film was given this title, but the title ended up causing some confusion among moviegoers with a much more casual interest in the character. A Batman movie called *The Dark Knight*? Just who was this "Dark Knight," anyway? (Of course, the film would end up being so incredibly successful that most everyone in the world would come to understand just who "The Dark Knight" was—but let's not get ahead of ourselves here!)

Nolan was able to retain most all of the creative team that had worked with him on *Batman Begins*. That team included producer (and wife!) Emma Thomas, production designer Nathan Crowley, special effects supervisor Chris Corbould, costume designer Lindy Hemming, and cinematographer Wally Pfister. All of these talented individuals had come together to shape *Batman Begins* into a truly great film, so they were confident that they could do the exact same thing for *The Dark Knight*.

Nolan was also able to retain many of *Batman Begins*' principal actors for *The Dark Knight*. In the film, Christian Bale would play Batman/Bruce Wayne, Michael Caine would play Alfred, Gary Oldman would play Jim Gordon, Morgan Freeman would play Lucius Fox, and Cillian Murphy would make a cameo appearance as the Scarecrow. However, one major cast member decided not to make a return appearance in *The Dark Knight*—Katie Holmes bowed out of the project, so the part of Rachel Dawes was given to Maggie Gyllenhaal.

Nolan's choices to play the film's main villains were every bit as inspired as his casting of *Batman Begins* had been. In August 2006, Warner Bros. announced that Heath Ledger had been picked to play the role of the Joker. Ledger was a 26-year-old Aus-

Heath Ledger as the Joker in *The Dark Knight* (2008).

tralian actor who was an extremely hot property mainly due his memorable performance as Ennis Del Mar in the 2005 drama *Brokeback Mountain*. Ledger's turn as Del Mar, a Wyoming ranch hand who enters into a deep yet troubled homosexual relationship with another ranch hand, was a major component of the film's resounding critical and commercial success. In fact, Ledger's performance in *Brokeback Mountain* was so well-received that it earned him an Academy Award nomination for best actor. *Brokeback Mountain* certainly proved that Ledger was an actor of great depth and emotional power — so Nolan's decision to cast him as the Joker in *The Dark Knight* seemed like one that crackled with dramatic possibility.

Nolan chose Aaron Eckhart to play the role of Harvey Dent/Two-Face. Like Ledger, Eckhart was a very charismatic and talented actor whose career had been on a steep upward trajectory. Eckhart had won critical praise for his roles in high-profile films such as *Erin Brockovich* (2000) and *Thank You for Smoking* (2005).

As Nolan and Goyer had drastically changed the Scarecrow and Ra's Al Ghul from their classic comic incarnations for *Batman Begins*, the Nolan brothers and Goyer drastically changed the Joker and Two-Face from *their* classic comic incarnations for *The Dark Knight*. In terms of the characters' appearance, they looked generally similar their classic comic book counterparts — but their origins and actions definitely deviated from the comic book Joker and Two-Face quite a bit. (We'll discuss these changes in more detail later in the chapter.)

Nolan made the decision to outfit Batman with a new costume in *The Dark Knight*. The *Batman Begins* Batsuit had looked great on film, but it ended up being so cumbersome that it had greatly compromised Bale's mobility. So Nolan had costume designer Lindy Hemming create a new Batsuit for *The Dark Knight*, one that would allow Bale much more freedom of movement. This new Batsuit was comprised of far more separate pieces of body armor than the *Batman Begins* Batsuit — there were over 100 pieces that fitted together to make up the costume.[2]

One of the main differences between the *Batman Begins* Batsuit and the *Dark Knight* Batsuit was that the *Dark Knight* Batsuit had a cowl allowed Bale to actually turn his head — none of the previous Warner film Batsuits had allowed its wearers to perform that simple movement. One part of the *Dark Knight* Batsuit that was unchanged from the *Batman Begins* Batsuit was the costume's cape — Nolan and Hemming felt that they had gotten the cape just right the first time around, so it was not changed in any way.[3] Incidentally, the changes that were made to the Batsuit for *The Dark Knight* turned out to be more than just a design element of the film — they were actually written into the film's plot.

In *The Dark Knight*, Hemming had another character to costume whose visual appearance was every bit as iconic as Batman himself — of course, that character was the Joker. For the Joker's main costume, Hemming stuck very close to the character's time-honored comic look — he was outfitted in a suit with a long purple coat, purple pants and a green vest.

The most surprising aspect of the Joker's appearance in *The Dark Knight* was not his clothes, but his makeup. The traditional version of the character usually had an evenly chalky white face, a broad red-lipped smile, and neatly slicked-back green hair. The *Dark Knight* Joker sported unevenly applied white facial makeup that was referred to as "war paint" in the film, heavy smears of blood red lipstick on his lips, and hideous scars at the corners of his mouth that gave the impression of a smile cut into his face. His hair was a dirty, disheveled mane streaked with green dye. The *Dark Knight* Joker's face gave the impression that the character was decomposing before your very eyes, and seemed to be a direct window into a corrosive soul.

The scars at the corners of Ledger's mouth were accomplished through the use of subtle silicone prosthetics. Ledger's prosthetics were *far* less elaborate than the ones Jack Nicholson had to wear when he played the Joker in the 1989 film *Batman*—consequently, Ledger's Joker ended up being a much more visually realistic version of character than Nicholson's Joker had been.

The first photos of Ledger as the Joker that were released to the public made it very clear that his version of the character in *The Dark Knight* was going to be completely different from any previous version of the Joker. This definitely came as a surprise to most everyone, both serious Batman fans and casual Batman fans alike—after all, the character had remained almost totally unchanged for almost seven decades. From his debut in *Batman* #1, Spring 1940, to Cesar Romero's Joker in the 1960s *Batman* film and TV show, to Nicholson's Joker, the character's appearance and demeanor had basically remained a constant. Of course, the Joker had stopped killing his victims during the 1950s and 1960s thanks to Comics Code Authority regulations—but hey, *all* of Batman's villains had to do that! At any rate, everyone's long-held perceptions of the Joker were about to change thanks to Nolan and Ledger's interpretation of the character.

Aaron Eckhart's Two-Face was less of a departure from the traditional comic book version of the character than was Ledger's Joker—his grotesque appearance reflected the character's comic book look that dated back to the early 1940s. Of course, given the fact that *The Dark Knight* was going to be much more adult and realistic in nature than many other Batman works, the film's Two-Face looked even *more* grisly than many previous versions of the character, especially Tommy Lee Jones' Two-Face in *Batman Forever* (1995). The appearance of the *Dark Knight* Two-Face was accomplished not so much with makeup and prosthetics as it was through digital effects—Eckhart performed his Two-Face scenes wearing a skull cap and partial prosthetics, and the scarred side of his face was digitally added in after filming.[4]

Incidentally, while Ledger's Joker would end up being a large part of the film advertising strategy, Eckhart's Two-Face would not be revealed to the public until the actual release of the film. All of the movie's publicity material would only show Eckhart as the unscarred Dent, allowing Dent's eventual transformation into Two-Face to have even more impact on its audiences.

In addition to the Tumbler version of the Batmobile, Nolan would dream up another unusual vehicle for Batman to use in *The Dark Knight*. The film's script called for the Batmobile to have a kind of "escape pod" that could detach from the car if it ended up being catastrophically damaged—that "escape pod" was a two-wheeled, motorcycle-like vehicle that was formed out of the detachable front tires and suspension of the car. This vehicle became known as the "Bat-Pod."

Much like he did with the Batmobile, Nolan had come up with something startlingly original when he conceived of the Bat-Pod. Though it looked much like a motorcycle, its design was completely unlike any motorcycle ever built. The Bat-Pod was well over ten feet long, it sat atop two huge tires, and it had no handlebars—it was driven by stunt rider Jean-Pierre Goy, who had to operate it from an almost horizontal, face-down position.[5] Some of *The Dark Knight*'s most exciting action scenes would prominently feature this innovative new vehicle.

The biggest innovation found in *The Dark Knight* was one that wasn't just a first in the history of Batman films, it was one that was a first in the history of *all* film. As we noted last chapter, Nolan decided to actually film a sizeable portion of the movie with IMAX cameras. *The Dark Knight* was the first non-documentary feature film ever made to include scenes that were shot using IMAX technology. Filming in IMAX certainly posed a number of technical problems for Nolan and his cinematographer Wally Pfister, because the huge IMAX cameras were so much heavier and more unwieldy than standard 35mm film cameras. Also, their depth of focus was much different from a standard 35mm film camera's depth of focus, so setting up shots with them required extra care and calculation.

All of this extra work was definitely worth it. Nolan's decision to shoot some of *The Dark Knight* in IMAX would make the movie a viewing experience that was unlike any other in the history of filmed entertainment. The movie's IMAX sequences ended up being more expansive and detailed than any images ever created for a non-documentary feature film.

The first scenes to be filmed for *The Dark Knight* were ones that were shot in IMAX — in December 2006, the bank robbery sequence featuring the Joker was filmed at the Old Post Office on Congress Parkway in Chicago, Illinois. This sequence would end up opening the film, and it would also end up being one of the film's major promotional tools — dubbed "*The Dark Knight* IMAX Prologue," Warner Bros. released the sequence with selected IMAX screenings of the film *I Am Legend* in December 2007. And as noted in the previous chapter, "*The Dark Knight* IMAX Prologue" was also included as a special feature on the *Batman Begins* Blu-ray which was released in July 2008, the same month as the theatrical premiere of *The Dark Knight*. These advance releases of "*The Dark Knight* IMAX Prologue" allowed the public to see firsthand the extraordinary level of visual quality that high-resolution IMAX film was going to bring to *The Dark Knight*.

After the filming of the bank robbery sequence was completed, the film's cast and crew returned to Cardington Sheds, the former airship hangar located near London, England, where much of *Batman Begins* had been filmed. The Cardington shoot for *The Dark Knight* commenced in January 2007, using a number of new sets that had been constructed for the film there. Among these sets were the "Bat-Bunker," Batman's temporary headquarters that he had to use while Wayne Manor was being rebuilt. (Remember, in *Batman Begins* Ra's Al Ghul had burned the Manor to the ground when he tried to destroy Gotham.) Also, an interior set of a skyscraper under construction was built — the film's climax featuring the final showdown between Batman and the Joker would be filmed on this set.[6]

Nolan had been so pleased with the Chicago location shooting he had done for *Batman Begins* that he decided to use the city to even greater effect in *The Dark Knight*. So once the Cardington shoot was finished, the film's cast and crew returned to United States for an extended shoot in Chicago — over three months. From early June to early September 2007, "The Windy City" became "Gotham City" — Nolan and company filmed in a myriad of locations throughout Chicago, capturing many incredible scenes for their film.

The work that went into filming these scenes was often every bit as adventurous as the action *in* the scenes themselves. Christian Bale stood atop the 110-story Sears Tower in full costume to capture an unforgettable image of Batman watching over Gotham. On LaSalle Street right in the heart of the city, one of the film's most breathtaking stunts was performed — special effects supervisor Chris Corbould devised a way to flip the Joker's large circus truck end-over-end and have it land upside-down! This was accomplished by rigging a large pole to fire out from the bottom of the truck's cab, forcing the entire truck high into the air.[7]

As incredible as the film's truck stunt was, Nolan had another stunt lined up for the film that was even more epic. An abandoned building that had once been used by Brach's candy company was outfitted with signage to turn it into Gotham General Hospital — and then the building was completely blown up with powerful explosives. Like the bank robbery sequence featuring the Joker, all of these eye-popping action sequences were filmed with IMAX cameras. (We'll do a rundown of just which of the movie's scenes were filmed in IMAX later in the chapter.)

One of *The Dark Knight*'s most memorable action sequences was enhanced with scenes filmed on a miniature set. The Batmobile's pursuit of an armored police truck being attacked by the Joker was partially realized through the use of incredibly detailed miniature vehicles, including an over five-foot-long Batmobile model.[8]

The Dark Knight could certainly qualify as one of the largest film projects ever undertaken — it had a budget of over $180 million, and it was using complex IMAX technology in a way that it had never been used before.[9] But in spite of the film's almost overwhelming size and scope, its cast and crew still enjoyed a confident, relaxed working relationship with one another. Unfortunately, the production's remarkably positive atmosphere would end up being darkened by several shocking tragedies.

The first of these occurred at a racetrack near Chertsey, England, on September 24, 2007. Corbould and his special effects crew were at the racetrack to do test runs for one of the film's stunts involving a police car. Cinematographer Conway Wickliffe was operating a camera from the back seat of a vehicle following the police car. That vehicle crashed into a tree during one of the test runs, and Wickliffe was killed in the collision.[10]

The film's cast and crew were very shaken by Wickliffe's death, but they quickly had to get back to work in order to wrap up the production. In early November 2007, Nolan and company traveled to Hong Kong for a week of location shooting. Nolan had decided that he wanted to take Batman outside the realm of Gotham City in *The Dark Knight*, and this decision turned out to be a wise one — the movie's scenes showing Batman high atop the skyscrapers in Hong Kong ended up providing the production with some of its most iconic Batman images.

By December 2007, principal photography for *The Dark Knight* had been completed and Nolan was overseeing the film's post-production in Los Angeles. Like *Batman Begins*, *The Dark Knight* would end up featuring many scenes that were created using computer-generated images. These images included Batman using his cape to glide between Hong Kong skyscrapers, and the Bat-Pod detaching from the catastrophically damaged Batmobile.[11] And as we noted earlier in the chapter, Two-Face's grotesque appearance was also accomplished through digital effects.

Another shocking tragedy connected to *The Dark Knight* occurred on January 22, 2008, and this one was so sensational and unexpected that it ended up affecting the entire world's perception of the film. Heath Ledger was found dead of a drug overdose in his New York City apartment — it was eventually discovered that the 28-year-old actor had accidentally ingested a lethal combination of prescription medications.[12] Not surprisingly, Ledger's tragic death instantly became a huge news story — after all, he had come to be recognized as one of the movie industry's most charismatic and promising acting talents. Plus, the fact that he had just completed filming his intense, disturbing portrayal of the Joker in *The Dark Knight* made his untimely passing all the more morbidly fascinating to the public.

Obviously, Warner Bros. was put in a very difficult position in terms of aggressively promoting *The Dark Knight* after Ledger's death. The theatrical previews of the film had been so spectacularly-received by the public that there was never really any doubt the film was going to be hugely popular once it was released — and the unavoidable truth was that Ledger's passing would definitely make the film even *more* buzzworthy. But the studio certainly did not want to appear as if they were callously trying to use Ledger's death to build up even more anticipation for *The Dark Knight*. So Warner wisely elected to fashion a promotional campaign for the movie that was a little less Joker-centric, and continue planning for the movie's release in July.

And the studio had already created quite a bit of very innovative promotion for the film. For example, in 2007 Warner and DC Comics had launched a direct-to-video animated film series known as DC Universe Animated Original Movies, and their first Batman film in that series was designed to be a tie-in to the release of *The Dark Knight*. *Batman: Gotham Knight* was released to the home video market on Blu-ray and DVD on July 8, 2008, less than two weeks before *The Dark Knight*'s U.S. premiere.

The premise of *Batman: Gotham Knight* was very intriguing. Warner and DC described it as a collection of "six spellbinding chapters chronicling Batman's transition from novice crimefighter to The Dark Knight." Each chapter was a stand-alone story created by different screenwriters and animators, so they each basically presented their own unique vision of Batman. But these chapters did have several unifying factors. First, all of the chapters were based on stories originally written by Jordan Goldberg. And all of the chapters featured the same actor voicing the part of Batman/Bruce Wayne — the role was well-played by Kevin Conroy, who of course had previously voiced the character in *Batman: The Animated Series* and several other animated works. Finally, since *Batman: Gotham Knight* was designed to be a tie-in to *The Dark Knight*, all of the chapters were obviously inspired by Nolan's cinematic vision of Batman.

This is not to say that *Batman: Gotham Knight* was totally in synch with Nolan's Batman universe. In fact, the subject matter of most of the film's chapters had only passing connections to Nolan's Batman movies. And since the visual style of the film varied wildly from chapter to chapter, the film often did not look much like Nolan's Batman movies either. Truth be told, the most memorable elements of *Batman: Gotham Knight* really had almost nothing to do with Nolan's work — the film's powerful storytelling and incredible visuals made it a very satisfying Batman screen production in its own right.

Several of *Batman: Gotham Knight*'s individual chapters were noteworthy enough to warrant specific mention here. *In Darkness Dwells* was written by David S. Goyer, who of course co-wrote both *Batman Begins* and *The Dark Knight* with Nolan. In the chapter, Batman ventures down into the Gotham City sewers to rescue a priest kidnapped by Killer Croc and the Scarecrow — while in the sewers, the crimefighter engages the villains in fierce combat and saves the priest. *Deadshot* was written by Alan Burnett, who wrote some of the most memorable episodes of *Batman: The Animated Series*. In the chapter, Batman is targeted by an incredibly skilled assassin known as Deadshot — the crimefighter brings the assassin to justice by besting him in combat atop a fast-moving train. *In Darkness Dwells* and *Deadshot* were so brilliantly written and animated that they will probably always be remembered as two of the finest Batman animated works ever created.

The Blu-ray and 2-disc DVD set of *Batman: Gotham Knight* included some interesting bonus material along with the film — strangely, perhaps the most memorable item found in this material had nothing to do with either the film itself or *The Dark Knight*! The 2008 documentary *Batman and Me: A Devotion to Destiny* examined the life of Batman's creator Bob Kane. The production was based on Kane's autobiography *Batman and Me* that was first published in 1989. What really made the documentary so fascinating was that it did not shy away from addressing the fact that Kane was a highly unusual, self-centered man who likely stretched the truth on many occasions in order to make his achievements seem even more grand than they actually were.

Of course, Warner Bros. had planned on using the Internet to promote *The Dark Knight* in a number of different ways. *The Dark Knight*'s official website was launched by Warner Bros. about a year before the movie's actual premiere date. In the months leading up to the film's release, the site featured a wealth of *The Dark Knight* information—visitors could look at production photos, watch videos of the film's theatrical previews, and read biographies of the film's cast and crew. Incidentally, Warner has continued to maintain and update the site right up to the present day, so it still functions as a marvelous resource designed to enhance one's appreciation of the film.

The Dark Knight's official website was only one part of Warner's strategy to market the film via the Internet. Warner also developed a number of ingenious fictional websites based on *The Dark Knight*—these websites were designed to introduce their visitors to the movie's vision of Gotham City. For example, the "I Believe in Harvey Dent" website supported Dent's political campaign, and the "Gotham Cable News" website offered a wide variety of news stories about the city.

The highlight of the "Gotham Cable News" material was *Gotham Tonight*, a series of six short video programs first broadcast on the Internet in June and July of 2008. The series was hosted by Gotham Cable News anchors Mike Engel and Lydia Filangeri—of course, Engel and Filangeri were not *real* news anchors, they were characters played by Anthony Michael Hall and Lauren Sanchez, respectively. (Incidentally, Hall's character would be featured in a number of scenes in *The Dark Knight* itself.) *Gotham Tonight* caught viewers up on what had been happening in Gotham during the roughly year-long period between *Batman Begins* and *The Dark Knight*.

Viewing *Gotham Tonight* was not an absolute requirement to fully appreciate the intricacies of *The Dark Knight*. That said, however, the series greatly enhanced one's appreciation for the film because they presented so much information relating to the film's complex plot. And this information was not simply created from footage pulled from *Batman Begins* and *The Dark Knight*—rather, *Gotham Tonight* contained newly-filmed scenes featuring some of *The Dark Knight*'s integral characters. The actors who appeared in the series included Gary Oldman (as Jim Gordon), Aaron Eckhart (as Harvey Dent), Eric Roberts (as Sal Maroni) and Colin McFarlane (as Gotham City Police Commissioner Loeb). So in effect, *Gotham Tonight* played like a stand-alone Batman mini-movie that could well have been entitled *The Dark Knight Begins*!

And *Gotham Tonight* perfectly dovetailed into the film itself. The sixth and final episode of the program featured Engel interviewing Harvey Dent, but that interview had to be cut off so that Engel could allow Filangeri to report on a breaking news story. Filangeri then reported that a daring bank robbery had just taken place in Gotham — of course, the robbery Filangeri was speaking of was the Joker's bank heist that opened *The Dark Knight*!

Warner Bros. was also able to promote the film through two documentary programs produced for the cable television network The History Channel. *Batman Tech* and *Batman Unmasked: The Psychology of The Dark Knight* both were originally broadcast on the network in July 2008, right around the time of *The Dark Knight*'s U.S. premiere date. *Batman Tech* explored forms of modern technology that might allow some of Batman's crimefighting equipment to exist in real life. *Batman Unmasked: The Psychology of The Dark Knight* examined how the real-life discipline of psychology might be used to interpret the thoughts, actions, and motivations of Batman character. Both programs featured a wealth of footage drawn from *Batman Begins* and *The Dark Knight*, as well as commentary from some of the individuals who played a major role in the creation of the films, including Nolan and Bale.

Let's get back to discussing *The Dark Knight* itself. Hans Zimmer and James Newton Howard's musical score for *Batman Begins* had turned out to be so effective that Nolan brought the composers back to create the soundtrack for *The Dark Knight*. Like their *Batman Begins* music, the music they wrote for *The Dark Knight* was very ambient in nature, often consisting of hypnotic percussion patterns and long-held musical tones. But unlike their *Batman Begins* music, the composers chose to give their compositions for *The Dark Knight* titles that were related to scenes in the film, titles such as "I Am the Batman" and "Harvey Two-Face." (As we discussed last chapter, all of Zimmer and Howard's *Batman Begins* compositions were named with Latin words describing various species of bats.)

The world premiere of *The Dark Knight* was held in the IMAX theatre at AMC Loews Lincoln Square in New York City on July 14, 2008. Much of the film's principal onscreen and offscreen talent attended the event, including Bale, Caine, Eckhart, Oldman, Gyllenhaal and Nolan. The film's Bat-Pod was also in attendance — it was parked out front of the theatre for everyone to see as they made their way inside. Several days later, on July 18, *The Dark Knight* opened in theatres throughout the United States.

The Dark Knight opens with an image of a bat silhouette coming through a wall of blue flame and smoke. We are then taken to the streets of Gotham in the daylight hours, where a bank robbery is being staged by a gang of criminals in rubber clown masks. Several of the criminals talk about their unknown leader who has orchestrated the heist — he calls himself "the Joker." The Joker's target is a bank that the Gotham mob has been funneling their money through. The robbery goes off like clockwork — the Joker has ruthlessly set up the heist so that his henchmen will be killing each other off one by one just as they each perform their appointed tasks.

In the end, it turns out that the Joker himself was one of the clown-masked criminals, and he is the last one left alive. He reveals his face to one of the mob bank employees just before he escapes. His stringy hair is colored green, his face is covered with white makeup, his eyes are ringed with black makeup, and his lips are painted with bright red lipstick— he looks like some sort of ghoulish clown. His appearance is made even more frightening by the hideous long scars at the corners of his mouth that seem to force his face into a grotesque parody of a smile. The Joker escapes the bank in a school bus he has loaded with the mob's money.

That night, Gotham Police Sergeant Jim Gordon shines his spotlight with a bat silhouette on it into the sky above the city. Gordon is now the head of his own unit known as the Major Crimes Unit. But Batman doesn't come to meet with Gordon — Gordon hopes this is because Batman is "busy." It has been a year since Batman has appeared in Gotham, and he has already helped to dramatically lower the city's crime rate.

It turns out that the crimefighter is indeed busy — in a nearby parking garage, a mob boss known as the Chechen is meeting with Dr. Jonathan Crane, who is wearing his scarecrow mask. The Chechen is angry because Crane sold him illegal drugs laced with Crane's fear-inducing hallucinogen. The conversation is interrupted when Batman confronts them. Or rather, *Batmen* confront them — it is not actually Batman, but a group of gun-wielding Batman copycats dressed in capes and cowls.

The real Batman arrives on the scene, driving his tank-like armored automobile known as the Tumbler through one of the garage's walls. As the Tumbler fires missiles meant to intimidate everyone, Batman jumps into the battle between the criminals and the copycats, subduing all of the combatants. Crane tries to escape the scene in a van, and Batman leaps off of one of the garage's ramps and lands on the van's roof, crushing it.

Later, Gordon arrives at the mob bank that the Joker robbed. Batman is there as well, and the two men discuss the fact that much of the cash that was in the bank was currency that they had been tracking — it had been used in illegal drug buys. So they know for certain that they have found one of the banks where the mob's dirty cash is being held. They have tracked these bills to four other Gotham banks as well, so they actually know where most *all* of this cash is being held. They agree that it is time to move on the mob and seize all of this money.

Gordon wonders if they need to step up their efforts to find the Joker — the criminal has hit a few other mob banks before this current heist. Batman tells him going after the mob is top priority, and the Joker can wait. Gordon tells Batman that Gotham's new District Attorney Harvey Dent is going to want to join this fight against the mob — Batman wonders whether or not Dent can be trusted.

The next morning, Bruce is at his underground bunker that serves as a makeshift Batman headquarters while Wayne Manor is being rebuilt. (Remember, Ra's Al Ghul burned the Manor to the ground when he tried to destroy Gotham.) He talks to Alfred about taking Dent into his confidence — Alfred wonders if Bruce's interest in Dent stems from the fact that the D.A. is dating Gotham's Assistant District Attorney Rachel Dawes, the woman that Bruce would have ended up with if not for his double life as Batman. Alfred also worries that Bruce is pushing himself too hard as Batman, and that he should know his limits.

Later that day, Dent and Rachel are in court to try to secure a conviction for Sal Maroni, the mob boss who took over Carmine Falcone's operations. (Remember, Falcone was driven insane when Crane gave him an overdose of his fear-inducing hallucinogen.) Their case against Maroni falls apart when their star witness changes his testimony — in fact, the witness even tries to shoot Dent with a smuggled-in gun while on the stand. That same day, Dent meets with Gordon — Dent doesn't like the fact that Gordon has been put in charge of his own unit, and that this unit contains some cops that Dent had investigated for corruption. Still, Dent tells Gordon that he will give him the warrants he needs to raid the mob bank. Dent also says that he wants to meet Gordon's shadowy ally the Batman.

That same day, a businessman named Lau tries to sell Wayne Enterprises on going into a joint venture with his company Lau Security Investments. After meeting with Lau, Bruce reveals to his right-hand man at Wayne Enterprises Lucius Fox that he did not really want to go into business with Lau. Bruce just wanted a closer look at Lau's books because he had figured out that Lau was the mob's main money launderer. Bruce also tells Fox that he needs to make some modifications to his Batsuit, and Fox says he will oblige. (Remember, Fox was the one who first outfitted Bruce with crimefighting gear from technology stockpiled at Wayne Enterprises.)

That night, Dent and Rachel are dining at a fancy restaurant, and Bruce is there as well. They talk, and Bruce is so impressed with Dent that he tells the D.A. that he will throw him a fundraiser. A different kind of gathering is happening in Gotham at about the same time — the leaders of the mob, including the Chechen, Maroni, and another boss named Gambol, are meeting to discuss their cash storage problem. Lau meets with them via a video hookup, and tells them that he has moved their money and fled for Hong Kong before Gordon could carry out his raid.

The Joker crashes the mob's meeting. He kills a mob henchman by performing a "magic trick"— that is, smashing a pencil through the henchman's skull. The Joker says he will take care of the mob's *real* problem, the Batman, by killing him. The Joker goes on to say that will perform this service for a steep price — half the mob's take. Enraged by this brazen offer, Gambol puts a bounty on the Joker's life.

Later, Dent, Gordon and Batman meet on the roof next to Gordon's spotlight with a bat silhouette on it. In order to bring down the mob, Batman says that he will go to Hong Kong to apprehend Lau. The crimefighter will have a new costume and new equipment for this challenge — Fox has made all of the Batsuit modifications that Bruce asked of him. This new Batsuit sports lighter armor, and a cowl that allows Bruce to turn his head much easier.

Meanwhile, a group of thugs report to Gambol, saying they have killed the Joker. These thugs have the Joker's body in a bag to prove this to the crime boss. But the thugs actually *work* for the Joker, who is very much alive — he jumps up, grabs Gambol, and holds him at knifepoint. The Joker tells Gambol that the scars on his face were inflicted on him by his father, who assaulted him on a drunken rampage while saying "why so serious?" After telling this chilling tale, the Joker kills Gambol.

Bruce and Fox travel to Hong Kong — Fox meets with Lau, and tells him that his deal with Wayne Enterprises is dead. But Lau's problems are just beginning — Batman swoops from out of the sky into Lau's office building, apprehends the crooked businessman, and uses a ground-to-plane cable system known as "skyhook" to pull them both into a huge cargo aircraft. Back in Gotham, Rachel interrogates the imprisoned Lau, who agrees to testify against the mob if he is granted immunity and a plane back to Hong Kong. Maroni and the Chechen now know that the Joker was right, Batman is their real problem — the Chechen says that the only way to fix this problem is to "hire the clown." After the Chechen makes this assessment, Gordon arrests him, Maroni, and all of their underlings.

Gordon, Dent and Gotham Police Commissioner Loeb meet with Gotham City Mayor Anthony Garcia to discuss all of these arrests. Their discussion is interrupted by a corpse dressed as Batman, its face smeared with Joker makeup, hitting the outside of the Mayor's window. It is not the real Batman, but one of the Batman copycats, that the Joker has killed. The Joker has killed this copycat to send a message to Batman — the madman says that until Batman reveals his true identity, he will keep killing people.

Bruce makes good on his promise to throw a fundraiser for Dent — at the event, he says that he believes in Dent, and that the D.A. has the power to bring Gotham's crime problem under control. Meanwhile a Major Crimes Unit officer named Ramirez tells Gordon that there is DNA from three people on the Joker card that had been pinned to the dead copycat's body. The DNA is from Dent, Loeb, and Judge Surrillo, the judge who is hearing the cases against the mob. Gordon thinks the DNA is meant to be a tip-off as to who the Joker will target next, so he orders protection for all three people. Gordon is too late to save two of them — Loeb dies from drinking poisoned whiskey, and Surrillo is killed by a car bomb.

And the third is in grave danger — the Joker crashes Bruce's fundraiser, hoping to kill Dent there. Bruce gets to Dent before the Joker can — he puts the D.A. in a sleeper hold, knocks him out, and hides him. The Joker then grabs Rachel, telling her a story about how he got his scars that is completely different from the story he told Gambol. Bruce quickly spirits away to change into his Batman costume, and then bursts back on the scene to confront the Joker. Batman saves Rachel by engaging the Joker and his men in hand-to-hand combat, but the confrontation ends when the Joker throws Rachel out of a window, which is many stories above the ground. Batman dives after her, and using his glider-like cape, he is able to stop her from falling to her death.

The next day, Dent goes to the Major Crimes Unit to bring Lau to trial. But Lau now refuses to cooperate given the fact that Gotham can't even seem to protect its own police officers and judges. Meanwhile, Bruce and Alfred discuss the Joker's motives in their makeshift Batman headquarters. Alfred tells Bruce that the Joker is a man that can't be reasoned with — some men "just want to watch the world burn." Later, Gordon gets a phone message from the Joker about where to find Harvey Dent. Batman and Gordon rush to the site of the Joker's tip, but it is not really Dent they find there — it is two other men that the Joker has murdered, one with the last name of Harvey and one with the last name of Dent. They also find a paper that announces the Joker's next target — Mayor Garcia.

The next day, Fox meets with a Wayne Enterprises employee named Coleman Reese. In examining the company's records, Reese has figured out that Bruce is Batman. Reese tells Fox that he wants Wayne to pay him a huge amount of money to keep quiet about his double life. Reese gives up on his bribery scheme when Fox gently reminds him that Bruce is not someone to be trifled with — after all he *is* bringing down the city's most dangerous men with his bare hands.

Bruce and Fox are able to use advanced computer technology to get a fingerprint off of a bullet fired at the scene of Joker's recent double murder. Bruce traces the fingerprint to someone who owns an apartment overlooking the route that Commissioner Loeb's funeral procession will take that day. In that apartment, Bruce finds members of the Gotham Police's Honor Guard, bound and blindfolded — the Joker and his men have taken the Guard's place in the funeral procession. Dressed as a Guard member, the Joker tries to shoot Mayor Garcia. Gordon jumps in to shield the Mayor, and he is struck and killed by the Joker's bullets.

Dent tries to interrogate one of the Joker's men that has been captured, with no success. Dent then spirits the man away to an undisclosed location to interrogate him quite a bit more roughly. At the same time, Batman performs some rough interrogation of his own — he tries to get Maroni to tell him where the Joker is by throwing him off of a fire escape and breaking his legs. Maroni says that the only way Batman is going to find the Joker is by taking off his mask and letting the madman come to *him*.

A gun-wielding Dent threatens to kill the Joker's henchman if he will not reveal where the Joker is. Dent flips a coin, saying that if it comes up heads he will not shoot, but if it comes up tails, he *will* shoot. As the coin comes up heads, Batman arrives on the scene and stops this interrogation. Batman tells Dent that the D.A. is Gotham's hope now — the Joker's reign of terror has convinced him that it is time to hang up his cape and cowl and leave the city in Dent's care.

Bruce tells Rachel of his plans to quit being Batman — since Rachel had told Bruce she would be there for him when he gave up his double life, she now will have to choose between her old love (Bruce) and her new love (Dent.) Bruce and Alfred shut down their makeshift Batman headquarters and prepare to reveal their secret to the world. The next day, Dent holds a press conference to reveal Batman's decision to turn himself in to the authorities. Dent defends Batman, while everyone else at the conference thinks that Batman should turn himself in to appease the Joker. Dent then turns the tables on everyone, including Bruce — Dent says that *he* is Batman, and the police take him into custody. Rachel, angry that Bruce did not turn himself in like he said he would, gives Alfred a letter for Bruce before going to see Dent in jail.

18—The Dark Knight (2008)

Dent is going to be transferred to jail via an armored police truck. When Rachel asks Dent why he falsely confessed to being Batman, he says that now Batman will be able to bring the Joker down as the Joker tries to bring *him* down. Rachel tries to talk Dent out of this plan—he pulls a coin out of his pocket and says, "Heads I go through with it." He then flips the coin to Rachel, and she sees that it is a two-headed coin—obviously this is the coin he used while interrogating the Joker's henchman.

On the streets of Gotham, the police convoy that is escorting Dent's armored truck encounters a fire truck engulfed in flames, forcing them to turn onto an underground road. On that road, the convoy is ambushed by the Joker and his men. The Joker is in the semi-trailer of a large circus truck that has the words "Laughter is the best medicine" painted on it—an "S" has been sloppily painted in front of the word "Laughter" so that the truck actually reads "*Slaughter* is the best medicine." Just as the Joker is about to shoot Dent's armored truck with a bazooka, Batman races up next to the truck in the Tumbler and blocks the Joker's shot. The Tumbler absorbs the full blast of the bazooka, destroying the car. Batman is able to escape from the vehicle when its two front wheels disengage to form a motorcycle-like vehicle.

The Joker keeps chasing Dent's armored truck in his circus truck—Batman uses cables fired from his motorcycle to bring the circus truck to a halt, flipping it completely over. The Joker gets out of the truck unharmed, and Batman charges him on his motorcycle—the crimefighter does not hit him, but goes into a skid and wrecks. The Joker goes to Batman lying on the pavement, and just at that moment, Gordon comes out of the armored truck and holds a gun on the madman.

The Joker is taken to a cell at the Major Crimes Unit, where Gordon tells Mayor Garcia that he faked his death because he didn't want to risk his family's safety. The Mayor appoints Gordon the new Gotham Police Commissioner in front of everyone, including the Joker. Gordon goes home, but goes right back to the M.C.U. when Dent turns up missing. Gordon unsuccessfully tries to interrogate the Joker—Batman has been hiding in the interrogation room, so he tries to find out what happened to Dent. The Joker tells Batman that he kidnapped Dent *and* Rachel and hid them in separate locations. The madman tells Batman where they are located—Batman goes to rescue Rachel, and Gordon goes to rescue Dent.

Dent is bound in a warehouse wired with explosives, and Rachel is bound in a different warehouse wired with explosives. Batman makes it to *his* warehouse, but it turns out the Joker lied about which person was held at which warehouse—so Batman saves Dent, not Rachel. Gordon does not make it to his warehouse in time—it explodes, killing Rachel. Batman's warehouse explodes as he is rescuing Dent, and the flames horribly burn the D.A. on one side of his face.

At the same time, the Joker escapes from the M.C.U. by detonating explosives rigged in the stomach of one of his henchmen. The madman is able to take Lau with him as he escapes. As Batman surveys the damage caused by the explosion that killed Rachel, he finds Dent's lucky two-headed coin. He leaves the coin for Dent as he lays unconscious in the hospital. Later, Bruce and Alfred discuss Rachel's death, and Alfred hides the letter that Rachel had left for Bruce—in it, she had told Bruce that she was going to marry Dent, not him.

Gordon goes to see Dent in the hospital, who is now awake. Dent makes Gordon say the nickname that M.C.U. officers had for Dent while he was investigating them—Harvey Two-Face. Dent turns to reveal the half of his face that is burned—he truly *is* Two-Face now. Gordon wants to know which of his officers took Rachel to the Joker, but Dent won't tell him. At the hospital, Maroni is there to talk to Gordon. The mobster has decided that the Joker is so dangerous that it is time to turn him over to the police in the hope that they can stop him. He tells Gordon that he knows where the Joker will be that afternoon, because he is supposed to meet with him. He gives Gordon this location, and Gordon starts to organize a police detail to apprehend the Joker there.

It turns out that the Joker is in a warehouse loaded with the mob's money. The criminal has Lau sitting atop the huge pile of cash. The Chechen comes in—the Joker kills him, takes over his men, and sets the pile of money ablaze. The Joker then calls a TV talk show that Coleman Reese has decided to appear on in order to reveal Batman's real identity. The Joker puts a bounty on Reese's life—he says that if Reese is not dead within one hour, he will blow up one of Gotham's hospitals. The madman does not specify just which hospital he will target.

Gordon calls off his search for the Joker that was based on Maroni's tip, and sends all of his officers to the city's hospitals. Gordon himself goes to find Reese, who is already faced with scores of Gotham citizens trying to kill him. Bruce also races to Reese to ensure that he is not harmed—he even crashes his Lamborghini into a pickup truck that is trying to ram the police van Reese is riding in.

Dressed as a nurse, the Joker visits Dent at Gotham General Hospital—the madman convinces the D.A. to give up his war on crime, and to give into chaos. Dent flips his now-scarred two-headed coin to decide whether or not to kill the Joker—it lands good side up, so Dent lets the Joker live. As the Joker leaves the hospital, he detonates the explosives he has hidden there, reducing it to rubble. The Joker then delivers a new threat to Gotham via hijacked TV cameras. He says that he is taking over the whole city, and anyone that doesn't want to play by his rules should flee.

Batman meets with Fox at Wayne Enterprises—the crimefighter has set up a spy system that taps into all of the cell phones in Gotham that he will use to find the Joker. Fox is troubled by the ethical ramifications of the system, but he will still use it to help Batman save Gotham. At the same time, Dent goes on a rampage, attacking everyone that set up Rachel and himself—he violently beats Ramirez (the M.C.U. cop who took Rachel to the Joker), and kills Maroni and Wuertz (the M.C.U. cop who took him to the Joker). Dent also sets a trap for Gordon since Wuertz and Ramirez were his officers—the two-faced killer kidnaps Gordon's wife and children.

Large ferryboats are being used to transport Gotham's citizens out of the city. The Joker rigs two of these ferryboats with explosives. One of these boats is carrying average people, and the other is carrying inmates from Gotham's prisons. The Joker has given a detonator to each boat, giving each boat the chance to destroy the *other* boat. The Joker tells the boat passengers that the first boat to destroy the other boat will be allowed to live. The "average people" boat starts a paper vote to decide whether or not to blow the "inmate" boat up—the final tally is in favor of blowing the "inmate" boat up, but no one will actually use the detonator. In the "inmate" boat, a prisoner convinces the prison warden to give him the detonator—but instead of using it, the prisoner surprisingly throws it off the boat and into the water.

Meanwhile, Batman races to an under-construction high rise building where the Joker is overseeing his ferryboat takeover. Batman fights his way up to the Joker's position, subduing henchmen and saving hostages along the way. The crimefighter makes it to the Joker, but the madman overpowers him and prepares to blow up the boats himself. Batman hits the Joker in the face with spikes from his gauntlets and throws him off of the building. The

Joker is saved from certain death when Batman uses his grapple gun to catch the madman on his way down. The Joker is captured, but he still takes delight in telling Batman what he did to Dent.

Gordon has raced to the site of the explosion that killed Rachel because Dent is holding his family there. Dent decides that the best way to take his revenge on Gordon is to kill the cop's young son. Before Dent can do this, Batman arrives on the scene and knocks Harvey off of the charred building. Dent is dead, and Gordon and Batman worry that their dreams of reforming Gotham have died with the city's once-heroic D.A. Batman convinces Gordon to accuse *him* of killing all of Dent's victims so that they can maintain Dent's spotless reputation. Gordon does this, and Gotham's true hero, its "dark knight," is made out to be the city's biggest villain in an attempt to give its citizens hope in the wake of Dent's demise.

The critical and commercial success of *The Dark Knight* was so overwhelming that the film created a wave of Batmania that surpassed even the incredible phenomena surrounding the 1960s screen Batman and Tim Burton's 1989 *Batman*. It won almost universally rave reviews from major film critics all over the world — and its box office numbers weren't just tremendous, they were downright historic. *The Dark Knight* earned over $150 million in its U.S. opening weekend alone, and ended up grossing over $530 million during its U.S. theatrical run. When the film finally finished its worldwide theatrical run, it had reached a pinnacle that only a handful of films had ever been able to reach — its worldwide total gross ended up topping just over a *billion* dollars![13] Before the release of *The Dark Knight*, there might have been a fair number of people in the world who did not know that "The Dark Knight" was a commonly-used name for Batman — but the film most definitely made sure that practically every last person on the planet knew *exactly* who "The Dark Knight" was!

I personally found it fascinating that the initial success of *The Dark Knight* led to the general public occasionally perceiving "Batman" and "The Dark Knight" as somewhat separate entities. The most striking example of this phenomenon I ever encountered occurred in October 2008, when my family and I were attending a Halloween event at the Columbus Zoo in our hometown of Columbus, Ohio. I was intrigued to learn from Zoo publicity material that on the day of our visit "Batman (From DC Comics)" would be appearing in live shows, and "Batman, The Dark Knight" would be appearing in the Zoo's character parade!

These character appearances were officially licensed by Warner Bros. and DC Comics — so I was a bit surprised that the companies were willing to market their iconic character in a manner that basically split him into two separate personas. But sure enough, that is just what they did — that day at the Columbus Zoo, "Batman" and "The Dark Knight" were markedly different from one another. The same actor played both characters, but "Batman" was dressed in a comic-style costume that looked a lot like Alex Ross's interpretation of Batman in the 1999 oversize graphic novel *Batman: War on Crime*, and "The Dark Knight" was dressed in a costume that looked just like Christian Bale's movie costume.

All of the people that I saw interacting with either "Batman" or "The Dark Knight" on that day didn't seem to care just which version of the character they were getting — to them "Batman" was just, well, *Batman*, whether he looked to be from a comic book page or a movie screen. And the general public has seemed to hold onto that perspective in the years following the release of *The Dark Knight* — some people might have been making a distinction between "Batman" and "The Dark Knight" right after the movie came out, but that distinction did not ever become a common way to view the character. Like the words "autumn" and "fall," "Batman" and "The Dark Knight" have remained words that are just two different ways of saying the same thing.

Whether he was referred to as "Batman" or "The Dark Knight," the character brought in a *lot* of money from the sale of merchandise inspired by the film. The wide variety of *The Dark Knight* action figures, statues, toys, books, clothing, etc., available for purchase made the summer of 2008 a very enjoyable (and expensive!) time for *all* Batman collectors.

Obviously, the breathtaking success of *The Dark Knight* was thrilling to most all of us serious Batman fans. That said, however, I must say that I personally have always had very conflicted feelings about the film. I was thrilled by its success, and there was a *lot* about the film that I loved—but there were just as many things about the film that left me deeply disappointed. Here's the best analogy I can come up with to explain how I feel about *The Dark Knight*. Many of us have a close relative who is in possession of a number of really annoying traits—we love that relative dearly, but often they just drive us out of our minds. *The Dark Knight* is my own personal film version of that relative!

I realize that I will probably have a very hard time convincing many of you to see *The Dark Knight* as a noticeably flawed work, which is obviously the way that I see it. But before I start laying out my case against *The Dark Knight*, let me assure you that I have not come to this conclusion about the film lightly. This is a film about a character I have loved most all of my life, and it was so staggeringly successful that it was seen by millions upon millions of people around the world. It made over a billion dollars—a billion! It stands as such a stunning achievement in the history of the Batman character that I wish I could love it without any reservations at all. However, I personally cannot overlook the film's many flaws just because it was such an incredible success.

But before we get into examining these flaws, I'd like to go over the many things that I love about *The Dark Knight*. The cinematic vision of Batman that Christopher Nolan kicked off in *Batman Begins* is continued in grand fashion in *The Dark Knight*. In the film, Nolan takes the character and his world every bit as seriously as he did in his first Batman film. Because of this, so much of *The Dark Knight* ends up being exactly what a great Batman story should be—it is thrilling, thought-provoking, tragic, and ultimately uplifting.

Probably my very favorite part of the film is Christian Bale's portrayal of Batman/Bruce Wayne. As I said last chapter, I felt that Bale's performance in *Batman Begins* captured both of the character's identities to a degree that was almost startling—and I believe that he is every bit as wonderful in *The Dark Knight* as he was in *Batman Begins*. (However, I feel that *The Dark Knight*'s overall interpretation of Batman/Bruce Wayne is nowhere near as good as *Batman Begins*' interpretation of the character—but we'll get to that later in the chapter.) Bale's legacy as a truly great screen Batman is further cemented by his incredible work in *The Dark Knight*.

There is one aspect of Bale's Batman performance in *The Dark Knight* that is markedly different from his Batman performance in *Batman Begins*. When Bale is wearing the cape and cowl in *The Dark Knight*, he speaks in a deep, throaty whisper that sounds nothing like his regular voice. Bale did not change up his voice nearly as much in his *Batman Begins* Batman scenes. This change in the character's voice in *The Dark Knight* received a fair amount of criticism from moviegoers who felt that it was too absurdly dramatic. I personally find the change to be quite appropriate—to me, it captures the physical and emotional strain that being Batman is starting to have on Bruce.

Bale's performance in *The Dark Knight* is definitely helped by the new Batsuit that Lindy Hemming created for the film. This new costume obviously allows Bale much more freedom of movement in his Batman scenes—and every bit as importantly, it looks just as great on film as the *Batman Begins* costume did.

As tremendous as Bale was in *The Dark Knight*, the performance in the film that really transfixed audiences was Heath Ledger's turn as the Joker. Sadly, it must be pointed out that at least some of the public's fascination with Ledger's Joker stemmed from the actor's untimely death not long before the movie was released. But even if this tragedy had not occurred, Ledger's electrifying interpretation of Batman's greatest foe would almost certainly still have been the most talked-about aspect of the film. Both Ledger's appearance and his acting ended up painting a portrait of the Joker that was *very* unexpected.

In *The Dark Knight*, Ledger's Joker is light years removed from the traditional comic book version of the character. Gone is the villain's nerve toxin that causes his victims to die with a grotesque smile on their faces, and in its place is nothing more than a knife. In the film, that knife turns out to be a horrifyingly realistic way for the Joker's victims to "go out with a smile," because the villain often cuts "smiles" into the faces of his victims. But just because the Joker often chooses to murder his victims with a knife, that doesn't mean that there aren't other weapons he relishes using as well. He every bit as lethal when using guns and explosives— and in *The Dark Knight*, he uses a *lot* of guns and explosives.

And as we noted earlier in the chapter, gone is the comic books Joker's evenly chalky white face, broad smile, and neatly slicked-back green hair in *The Dark Knight*. Instead, the character sports unevenly applied "war paint," hideous self-inflicted scars at the corners of his mouth that give him his own "cut smile," and a dirty, disheveled mane streaked with green dye.

Obviously, Nolan chose not to use one of the most time-honored elements of the Joker character for *The Dark Knight*—namely, the explanation of how the villain had ended up with his bizarre appearance. In the classic comic story "The Man Behind the Red Hood!" which was first published in *Detective Comics* #168, 1952, it was revealed that the Joker had ended up with white skin and green hair after he had fallen into a vat of acid. That origin was incorporated into some of the most famous versions of the character, such as the Joker found in the 1988 graphic novel *Batman: The Killing Joke*, and the Joker found in the 1989 film *Batman*. (Obviously, we discussed these different Jokers earlier in the book.) But even if Nolan's Joker is markedly different from the conventional depiction of the Joker in terms of origin, appearance and choice of weapons, the essence of character is unchanged — he is an insane, murderous and diabolically clever criminal. And it should be pointed out that Nolan did choose to hang onto one crucial element of the comic book Joker's origin. Like the comic book Joker, *The Dark Knight* Joker has no known pre–Joker identity, so no one knows where he came from or who he originally was. His villainy just seems to materialize from out of nowhere.

Ledger's acting is every bit as unsettling as his appearance in the film. He brings the Joker's insanity to life in a manner that is almost casual, as if the Joker sees hurting and killing people as nothing more than an instinctive act, like breathing. I must admit that it makes me uncomfortable that Ledger is so effortlessly creepy in the role — his frightening performance, coupled with his tragic death right after the film was released, makes his performance hard to watch and even harder *not* to watch. Ledger's amazing work in *The Dark Knight* won the actor a number of posthumous awards. The most notable of these was an Academy Award for Best Supporting Actor, which members of his family accepted on his behalf on February 22, 2009.

I'm sure there are those serious Batman fans who feel that Ledger's performance as the Joker in *The Dark Knight* is less than satisfying because it is so far removed from the traditional comic version of the character. I do not count myself among those fans. To tell you the truth, I *do* find the traditional comic version of the Joker to be a generally more compelling character than Ledger's version of the character. In fact, you asked me to pick my own personal favorite interpretation of the Joker, I would probably point to the version of the character found in one of the works we just mentioned, *Batman: The Killing Joke*. That said, however, I feel that Ledger's performance as the Joker in *The Dark Knight* has a gritty realism that meshes perfectly with Nolan's real world take on Batman.

Aaron Eckhart gives a very strong performance as Harvey Dent/Two-Face in *The Dark Knight*. His acting wonderfully captures the earnest determination of Dent, as well as the unimaginable physical and emotional pain that the character is put through when he is transformed into Two-Face.

However, in this author's opinion, Nolan kind of misses the mark with his interpretation of Dent/Two-Face in *The Dark Knight*. In the comics, it has often been suggested that Dent has had to struggle with a dark side to his personality even before his transformation into Two-Face. This makes his slide into villainy much more logical. But in *The Dark Knight*, Dent is so good and incorruptible throughout most of the film that it seems completely improbable for him to become so evil just because of Rachel's death and his own disfigurement.

I personally feel that the version of Dent/Two-Face found in the outstanding animated TV series *Batman: The Animated Series* captured the essence of the character much better than *The Dark Knight*. As we noted in Chapter 11, that series depicted Dent as a person plagued by dual personality disorder long before the accident that disfigured half of his face and turned him to a life of crime. So the dark side of Dent was very much there even before his disfigurement — his transformation into Two-Face basically just revealed the troubled person that he had *always* been. *The Dark Knight* would have done well to borrow this page from *Batman: The Animated Series* when constructing their real world interpretation of the character.

Michael Caine, Gary Oldman and Morgan Freeman are every bit as wonderful in their respective roles of Alfred, Gordon, and Fox in *The Dark Knight* as they were in *Batman Begins*. The actors settle right back into their characters without missing a beat, and their performances are definitely enhanced by the powerful material that the Nolans have given them to work with. And of course, there is another *Batman Begins* actor who ends up making quite an impression in *The Dark Knight* as well — Cillian Murphy's repeat performance as the Scarecrow might be very brief, but it is still a real pleasure to see the actor's memorable interpretation of the villain on the big screen again.

Maggie Gyllenhaal does a nice job of taking over the role of Rachel Dawes in *The Dark Knight*— of course, the part was originally played by Katie Holmes in *Batman Begins*. Gyllenhaal conveys Rachel's conflicted feelings about both Bruce and Dent in a manner that is very believable. That said, however, the character as a whole still comes off as rather forced — this is because her main function in the film is to lead Bruce to the conclusion that he should give up being Batman. (I personally am very uncomfortable with Bruce being led to this conclusion in *The Dark Knight*— I'll explain just why I feel this way when we discuss *The Dark Knight*'s interpretation of Batman/Bruce Wayne a bit later in the chapter.)

There is one more cast member of *The Dark Knight* who I feel warrants special mention. Patrick Leahy, the longtime U.S. senator from Vermont, plays the small part of "Gentleman at Party" quite nicely in the film — he is the one who says "We're not intimidated by thugs" to the Joker when the villain crashes Wayne's fundraiser for Dent. The Senator had been an avid Batman fan ever since he was a child — the film not only gave him the chance to share the screen with his boyhood hero, but also to be threatened by that hero's greatest villain.

One of *The Dark Knight*'s most potent strengths is the film's incredible production design. The collaboration between Nolan and his production designer Nathan Crowley yields the same spectacular results that it did when the two were realizing *Batman Begins* together—in *The Dark Knight*, they bring Batman's world to life in a way that is both wonderfully atmospheric and strikingly realistic. Interestingly, *The Dark Knight* chooses to step away from two of the Batman character's most iconic locales—the film features no Wayne Manor set or Batcave set. But even without these familiar places, *The Dark Knight* still constructs a meticulously-detailed world for the character that totally draws audiences into the production. Perhaps the most memorable aspect of the film's production design is the Bat-Pod—the vehicle's odd yet imposing presence definitely heightens the excitement of all the action scenes it is featured in.

The high quality of the film's production design is matched by the incredible scope of its location shooting. The scenes filmed in Chicago and Hong Kong help to bring Batman's world to life in a grand manner that would not be possible by filming on cramped soundstages. Of course, *Batman Begins* featured a number of scenes that were filmed in Chicago as well—but the Chicago location shooting that Nolan chose to do for *The Dark Knight* went well beyond the scope of the *Batman Begins* Chicago location shooting. In fact, *The Dark Knight* Chicago location shooting ended up producing some of the most spectacular scenes ever to appear in a motion picture. The flipping of the Joker's large circus truck and the Gotham General Hospital explosion were just two of the unforgettable Chicago-shot scenes in the film.

And of course, these incredible scenes in *The Dark Knight* were made even *more* incredible due to the fact that they were filmed in IMAX format. As we noted earlier in the chapter, the movie was the first non-documentary feature film ever made to include scenes that were shot using IMAX technology. *The Dark Knight*'s IMAX sequences ended up being more expansive and detailed than any images ever created for a non-documentary feature film. The sequences not only gave you a much clearer image, they also gave you a much wider frame—so it is really no exaggeration to say that they made the movie into a viewing experience that was unlike any other in the history of filmed entertainment.

But the only way to get that experience was to actually see *The Dark Knight* in an IMAX theatre. Those theatres were the only ones with the projection equipment to screen IMAX prints of the film with the enhanced picture quality. In this author's opinion, there was a *huge* difference between seeing the film in a regular movie theatre and seeing the film in an IMAX theatre—I saw *The Dark Knight* once or twice in a regular movie theatre just for comparison, but my IMAX screenings of the film went well into double digits!

Many establishing shots filmed in IMAX were used throughout *The Dark Knight*, but less than ten of the movie's sequences were actually filmed entirely in the format. Those sequences included the Joker's bank heist, Batman's capture of Lau in Hong Kong, Batman's pursuit of the Joker using the Batmobile and the Bat-Pod, the aftermath of the explosion that killed Rachel, Bruce's Lamborghini crash, the Gotham General Hospital explosion, the battle between Batman and the Joker on the under-construction high rise building, and the film's closing montage.

Both *The Dark Knight*'s IMAX and non–IMAX scenes were brilliantly captured by the film's director of photography Wally Pfister. Pfister's work on *Batman Begins* had been unforgettable, but this time around his work could only be described as "history-making" since he was using IMAX technology in a way that it had never been used before.

Last chapter, we noted that so much of the production design and cinematography of

Batman Begins seemed to be tied to a sepia-toned color. The production design and cinematography of *The Dark Knight* changes up that color design — this time around, much of Batman's world is bathed in shades of deep blue. In this author's opinion, this is the perfect color for the Batman character, because it gives his black costume an overall blue/black color — much like the costume appears in the comics. And this color also works well visually for the Joker's purple-toned costume. *The Dark Knight*'s shades of blue don't just show up in the film itself — blue was also the dominant color in most of the theatrical posters used to advertise the film's release.

Hans Zimmer and James Newton Howard's excellent musical score is another essential component in establishing *The Dark Knight*'s overall atmosphere. Like the music they composed for *Batman Begins*, their music for *The Dark Knight* has a power and intensity that perfectly complements the Nolan's real world interpretation of Batman. And one other aspect of *The Dark Knight*'s audio landscape needs to be noted here as well — sound editor Richard King won an Academy Award for Best Sound Editing for his fine work on the film.

In the end, I feel that *The Dark Knight* is an amazing movie — and I give Christopher Nolan all the credit in the world for creating such a powerful cinematic interpretation of Batman. And with those words of praise, I will end my long list of things that I like about the film.

But as I warned you just a bit earlier, there are just about as many things about *The Dark Knight* that I *don't* like that I feel we need to discuss. Most all of these things are connected to what I consider to be *The Dark Knight*'s two most troubling flaws. The first of these flaws is the film's woefully inconsistent story construction. The second is the film's poorly-thought-out portrayal of Batman.

I want to start off my analysis of *The Dark Knight*'s shortcomings by looking at the film's story construction issues, because I feel these issues are what *really* bog the film down. I am not talking about elements of its plot that simply go against my own personal interpretation of the Batman character — I am talking about elements of its plot that simply make no sense whatsoever. To put it bluntly, there are many times in *The Dark Knight* when its characters end up saying and doing things that completely defy real world logic. And the longer *The Dark Knight* goes on, the more convoluted its plot seems to get — in fact, by the time the film has reached its final scenes, even the film itself can't seem to keep up with everything that is going on! I will now take some time to lay out the elements of *The Dark Knight*'s story construction that I find to be the most ridiculous and unrealistic.

I can point to a very specific moment in *The Dark Knight* when I feel the film really starts to lose command of its ambitious narrative. That moment is the very end of the first face-to-face confrontation between Batman and the Joker at Bruce's fundraising event for Dent. For some reason, Nolan chooses to leave this critical sequence in the film completely unresolved.

Please allow me to lay this moment out for you in detail. The Joker throws Rachel out the window, and Batman saves her from falling to her death. After this scene, the film never returns to the fundraising event to see just what happened after the Joker was left alone at the event with many of Gotham's most wealthy and powerful citizens. Are we to assume that the Joker chose not to menace them at all? Did he just gather up his men and walk out? It certainly seems highly implausible that the Joker would have not further threatened these citizens in some way or another in an attempt to get to Dent. And after saving Rachel, wouldn't Batman have raced back up to the event to try to keep the Joker from harming

Dent or anyone else? No matter *what* Batman and the Joker chose to do after their initial confrontation, the film should have found some way to inform us of their actions.

Interestingly, the film was originally supposed to do just that. The final shooting script of *The Dark Knight* included a scene that showed the Joker leaving the event in a car driven by one of his henchmen. In the scene, the henchman asked the Joker, "What do we do about Dent?" and the Joker replied to him, "I'm a man of my word."[14] This concise scene would have been more than enough to let us know that the Joker left the event before he could find Dent, and that the villain was still intent on trying to murder the D.A. The scene would also have let us know that Batman was not able to race back up to the event in time to fight the Joker again. Presumably, this brief scene was cut from the film in the interest of time—but in this author's opinion, this scene was so essential in helping to clarify a pivotal moment in the film that it *never* should have been cut.

And while we are on the subject of this sequence, why are we never informed of just what Dent's reaction was to everything that happened at the fundraising event? Wasn't Dent the least bit curious about finding out just who put him in a sleeper hold and hid him away right before the Joker arrived? Also, wasn't he curious about Rachel's encounter with the Joker, or how traumatized she was by the madman's assault on her? After all, he did throw her out of a window that was hundreds of feet off the ground! *The Dark Knight* should have slowed down and filled in all of the blanks regarding this sequence, not just breathlessly rushed on to continue its narrative.

Unfortunately, this sequence only marks the beginning of the film's unfortunate lack of narrative clarity. Here is another sequence that ended up leaving me completely baffled. Dent holds a press conference to reveal Batman's decision to turn himself in to the authorities. Dent defends Batman, while everyone else at the conference thinks that Batman should turn himself in to appease the Joker. So, *the Joker* is the one killing public officials and ordinary citizens, and there are Gothamites who think that *Batman* is the problem that needs to be dealt with immediately? Worse yet, they think that following the Joker's instructions regarding how the city should deal with Batman is a sound idea? You've got to be kidding me! All of the evidence points to the fact that *the Joker* is the problem, not Batman—so why in the world would these people at the press conference be demanding action against Batman instead of the Joker? This simply makes no logical sense at all.

The Dark Knight's story continues to get even *more* confusing. Right before the movie's climax starts, Maroni goes to Gordon and tells him exactly where he can find the Joker that afternoon. Maroni knows where the Joker will be because he is supposed to meet with him—but the mobster decides that this madman is so dangerous that it is time to turn him over to the police in the hope that they can stop him. Based on this information, Gordon starts to organize a police detail to apprehend the Joker.

We then see the Joker in a warehouse, which is the location where Maroni said the madman would be. The Joker lights a huge pile of mob money with Lau atop it on fire, and then calls a talk show in order to threaten to blow up a Gotham hospital. Gordon then switches gears to deal with the Joker's new threat—but incredibly, he completely gives up on his plan to send a police detail to check out the location where he *knows* the Joker is! Now, Gordon has solid information that will lead him directly to the man who is the source of all of the city's trouble, and he doesn't bother to send at least a *few* officers to go after the man? Again, you've got to be kidding me!

Unbelievably, *The Dark Knight* ends up making no attempt whatsoever to explain just what happens at this warehouse. It appears that Lau will be killed by the Joker's fire—but instead of letting the viewer know just what happens to this character, the film's narrative breathlessly rushes on to its climax. Did Lau die? Did Gordon *ever* get some officers to this location to find out just what went down there? In this author's opinion, this entire sequence suffers from poor storytelling.

We are now getting to what I consider to be one of The Dark Knight's most baffling sequences. The whole scenario of the Joker pitting one ferryboat packed full of average people against one ferryboat packed full of prison inmates is so poorly-conceived that there is simply no way to make much sense out of it. In the sequence, we see a relatively small number of people on each boat talking over whether or not they should blow the other boat up. Now, the boats that are used in the sequence actually hold over *four thousand* people. So there would be no way in the world to have effective communication between all of the passengers on either boat — that being the case, how could these passengers possibly reach a consensus about how to handle their predicament?

And let's take just a moment to consider the numbers that the film comes up with when the "average people" boat takes a paper vote on whether or not to blow the "inmate" boat up. Three hundred forty people vote to blow the boat up, and 196 people vote *not* to blow the boat up. So the votes are cast by a total of a little over five hundred people — and as I just mentioned, that boat would have had over four thousand people on it! This discrepancy in numbers certainly does not help to clarify just how many people are on the boat, and how they are able to communicate with one another.

Furthermore, why would so many passengers on the "average people" boat ever come to the conclusion that it was morally defensible to blow up the "inmate" boat just because it was packed with inmates? Obviously, the "inmate" boat would have been carrying a lot of people *other* than inmates—so blowing up the "inmate" boat would have also meant blowing up scores of noble individuals such crew members, police officers, and National Guardsmen. One would think that anyone with a basic capacity for rational thought would have grasped this fact — but evidently, the Nolans chose to stock the "average people" boat with a large number of passengers that did *not* have this capacity!

And on the flip side of this coin, just why does one of the most fearsome prisoners on the "inmate" boat throw their boat's detonator into the water, effectively saving everyone on the "average people" boat? It seems that the Nolans wanted to use the whole ferryboat sequence to make some sort of social commentary about how "good" people and "bad" people are really not that far removed from one another. But whatever commentary they were trying to make was certainly obscured by the overall silliness of the sequence. In fact, I find the sequence to be such a head-scratcher that I can't believe that audiences generally accepted it without question.

The Joker's actions in this ferryboat sequence bring me to another problem I have with The Dark Knight's narrative, one that is more general in nature. I find it ridiculous that the film endows the Joker with a seemingly all-powerful capability to commit evil. In fact, I feel that The Dark Knight Joker eventually stops being a believable character because he is constantly doing things that no one could *ever* do in real life. In order to best illustrate my point, take a moment to consider the following questions regarding the Joker's actions that the film raises.

How can the Joker find a way to get himself and his henchmen, all of them disguised as Gotham Police, into a very prominent spot into the funeral procession for Commissioner Loeb? And then once they are in the procession, how is it that *none* of the real policemen standing right next to them ever take notice of them?

How can the Joker steal a Gotham fire engine and set it ablaze in the middle of a major Gotham street, and do this completely undetected? And how can the Joker set enough explosive charges in Gotham General Hospital to bring the entire structure to the ground without *any* of these charges being detected by the police and hospital workers who are swarming through the building? And finally, how can the villain fill those large ferryboats with massive amounts of explosives without *any* of these explosives being detected by the boats' crew members?

Let's move on to the last few problems I have with *The Dark Knight*'s story construction. I feel that by the time the film is reaching its final climax, its ambitious narrative has really fallen into disarray. Batman has stopped Dent from killing Gordon and his family, Dent has fallen to his death, and so much of what has transpired between those characters makes very little sense.

First off, Gordon talks to Batman about the consequences of Dent's murderous actions being "five dead, two of them cops." How could Gordon possibly know about any of the people Dent had killed? Gordon had been occupied trying to save all of the hostages taken by the Joker during the villain's assaults on the hospital and the ferryboats—and then things got even *more* frantic for the poor man as he tried to save his family from Dent. And just who are these "five dead" in the first place? The film showed Dent killing Officer Wuertz and the driver at the wheel of Maroni's car—that's *two* victims. And we assume that Maroni was also killed while riding in that car—that's *three* victims. But who in the world are the other two?

But wait, let's go back to the three victims we *do* know about for a second. All of those murders took place with no witnesses present—so how could Gordon find out about the murders so quickly? And even if he *could* have found out about them, how could he have known that it was Dent that committed them? Simply put, this exchange between Gordon and Batman about the people that Dent murdered is a narrative mess.

The solution that Gordon and Batman come up with to hide Dent's transformation into a villain makes even less sense than the "five dead, two of them cops" scenario. The men think that Dent's murderous actions will cause the citizens of Gotham City to totally lose hope, so they decide to blame Batman for Dent's villainy. Excuse me? Why in the world would Gothamites be moved to not lose hope because Batman, their onetime hero, is now a villain? And make no mistake, most Gothamites *would* have been perceiving Batman as a hero after the events of both *Batman Begins* and *The Dark Knight*. After all, by now *thousands* of Gothamites have seen him in action firsthand, gallantly fighting dangerous criminals.

In fact, it probably would have been easier for Gothamites to accept the fact that *Dent* had snapped and committed several murders rather than Batman. After all, the emotional and physical trauma he had endured from the Joker's attack had left him in a horrifying state—wouldn't most people understand that he was not in his right mind when he did the terrible things he did? At any rate, one would think that if the actions of any one person were going to make Gothamites lose hope, it would not be the actions of either Batman or Dent—it would be the actions of the Joker. Wasn't it the Joker who left countless people dead and dozens of buildings burned to the ground?

Simply put, Nolan's fixation on the Dent character is a major impediment to *The Dark Knight*'s narrative. The character's transformation into Two-Face is shoehorned into the film way too late, and then way too much importance is placed on the character's actions. It just doesn't make any sense that Gordon and Batman would sacrifice Batman's reputation, not to mention his crimefighting mission, in order to hide the truth about Dent from all of Gotham City. Incidentally, Nolan's odd fascination with the Dent character would carry over into *The Dark Knight Rises*— obviously, the character was not even alive during the events of that film, and he *still* ended up playing much larger of a role in its plot than seemed logical. (We'll discuss this in detail a bit later in the book.)

All right, *The Dark Knight*'s story construction problems have probably taken up enough of our time by this point. Let's move on to my other major problem with the film — its poorly-thought-out portrayal of Batman/Bruce Wayne really troubles me. Nolan obviously decided to rely on his own artistic sensibilities rather than classic Batman material when creating the film's interpretation of Batman and his world — and in this author's opinion, Nolan did the character no favors when he made this decision. As we discussed last chapter, Nolan drew on a wide array of classic Batman material when he created *Batman Begins*, showing more respect for the time-honored traditions of the character than any filmmaker had ever shown. *The Dark Knight* does not draw on *nearly* as much classic Batman material as *Batman Begins* did — in fact, there is really only one classic Batman work that really inspires the film in any direct way. That work is the 1996–97 13-part graphic novel series *Batman: The Long Halloween* written by Jeph Loeb and illustrated by Tim Sale.

And even then, *The Dark Knight* only borrows bits and pieces from the series. The first scene in the film that is directly pulled from *Batman: The Long Halloween* is the one that shows Batman, Gordon and Dent standing by the Batsignal, discussing their plan to attack organized crime in Gotham City. And the scene showing the Joker burning a huge pile of mob money stored in a warehouse is also inspired by the series— though in the series, it is not the Joker but Batman and Dent who set fire to the money. And the phrase "I Believe in Harvey Dent" that is repeated a number of times in the film as both a campaign slogan and a personal vote of confidence for Gotham's new D.A. is pulled directly from dialogue found in *Batman: The Long Halloween*.

Obviously, *The Dark Knight* has many scenes that recall classic Batman comic stories, especially its scenes showing Batman and the Joker fighting one another. Still, there is no way to escape the fact that the Batman of *The Dark Knight* is almost solely a Nolan creation, with very little connection to any previous versions of the character. This in itself is not a problem — the problem is that there are elements of *The Dark Knight* Batman that run counter to time-honored traditions of the character.

Far and away the most troubling aspect of *The Dark Knight* Batman is the notion that he would *ever* consider ending his war on crime in order to appease the demands of the Joker. I don't think I can overstate just how wildly off base this notion is to the character's basic principles. For generations, Batman has seen the Joker for just what he is— he is a cold-blooded killer, a maniac who is a danger to every last soul in Gotham if he is not locked up. If the Joker is on the loose, Batman has to track him down, subdue him and lock him up again — the situation is as simple as that, there are no other options.

In *The Dark Knight*, the Joker may be new to Gotham, but Batman has already seen enough of him to know the evil he is capable of. So Batman is going to try to stop that evil by simply giving in to it? He is going to leave the Joker, this maniac that has already killed a large number of Gothamites, out on the streets where he can have the potential to kill again and again? The Batman character as I understand and appreciate him would *never* do this. I see this aspect of *The Dark Knight*'s depiction of Batman as a total affront to everything that the character stands for.

And it should be mentioned that the person who seems to be truly at the heart of Batman's decision to cease fighting crime in *The Dark Knight* is Rachel — apparently he loves her so much that he can't stand the thought of her being harmed in any way. This also runs counter to the time-honored traditions of the Batman character — for generations, Batman has not allowed his personal feelings to completely compromise his mission as a crimefighter. At any rate, Batman should know that *no one* is really safe if the Joker is on the loose — and that includes Rachel. So if Batman wants Rachel and every last person in Gotham to be as safe as possible, he needs to get going and stop the Joker!

In discussing this problem I have with *The Dark Knight*'s depiction of Batman, I am reminded of a scene from the 1989 film *Batman*. Near the end of the movie, Vicki Vale presses Bruce about the status of their relationship. Bruce can't really give her a definitive answer because he has much bigger worries — the Joker is at large. All he can say to her is "He's out there right now — and I've got to go to work." We sure could have used *that* kind of determination in the *The Dark Knight* version of Batman, Mr. Nolan!

All right, I think I'm done airing all of my grievances against *The Dark Knight*! Let's take the film from the big screen to the small screen and examine its home video release history. Needless to say, *The Dark Knight* was such a gigantic box office hit that it was also tremendously successful when it was first made available to the home video market by Warner Home Video in early December 2008. At that time, Warner released the film on both Blu-ray and DVD format.

There were several different DVD versions of the film. It was offered as two separate single-disc releases, one in its original widescreen format and one in a format cropped to fit a standard television screen. *The Dark Knight* was also released as a 2-disc set which contained the widescreen version of the film, as well as several bonus features. One of these bonus features was a collection of mini-documentaries called *Gotham Uncovered: The Creation of a Scene*, which contained over 80 minutes of material detailing the making of the film — this material included commentary from members of the film's cast and crew, and behind-the-scenes footage showing that cast and crew at work. None of the DVD versions of *The Dark Knight* presented the film with its IMAX sequences in their original large-frame format — however, one of the 2-disc set's other bonus features was a stand-alone presentation of those IMAX sequences in large-frame.

The Blu-ray version of *The Dark Knight* was the one that really delivered the goods. The high-definition Blu-ray format allowed viewers to truly appreciate the extraordinary level of visual quality that high-resolution IMAX film had brought to the movie. And needless to say, the movie was presented with its IMAX scenes in their original large-frame format. The Blu-ray also contained the bonus features found on the 2-disc DVD set, as well as a number of exclusive bonus features. This wealth of material included the just-mentioned *Gotham Uncovered: The Creation of a Scene*, the History Channel programs *Batman Tech* and *Batman Unmasked: The Psychology of The Dark Knight*, and all six episodes of the Internet video series *Gotham Tonight*. (We discussed *Batman Tech*, *Batman Unmasked: The Psychology of The Dark Knight*, and *Gotham Tonight* earlier in the chapter.)

I think I'll close my discussion of *The Dark Knight* with these thoughts. The film left a legacy that was every bit as far-reaching as Tim Burton's groundbreaking 1989 film *Batman*. The staggering success of *The Dark Knight* catapulted the Batman character to a level of artistic and commercial prominence in the entertainment industry that few could have ever imagined. The character that not too long ago could be dismissed as nothing more than a silly diversion for kids was now the subject of dramatic film with an Oscar-winning acting performance and a billion dollar gross. How could this be anything less than thrilling to a serious Batman fan? As for me, I will love *The Dark Knight* for the rest of my days—though its annoying traits will continue to drive me crazy! I'm afraid that I can't be quite as positive about Nolan's third and final Batman film, *The Dark Knight Rises* (2012). We'll get to that story a bit later in the book.

19

"Non-Nolan" Batman Works During the Nolan Cinematic Batman Era

Christopher Nolan's three Batman films form such a cohesive narrative that I really would prefer to examine them in direct order in this book. That said, however, quite a few notable "non–Nolan" Batman works were released during the period of Nolan's Batman films. So in this chapter, we are going to take a bit of a break from Nolan in order to examine those works.

From early 2005 to early 2006, the *Batman* comic title featured a story arc called "Batman: Under the Hood" written by Judd Winick. The story arc introduced a mysterious character known as the Red Hood—the Red Hood fought crime like Batman, but unlike Batman he was more than willing to kill the criminals he fought. Batman eventually learned the Red Hood's true identity, and it was a real shocker—he was really Batman's second Robin Jason Todd, who was thought to have been killed by the Joker years ago.

Jason *was* killed by the Joker, but he was brought back to life through a fairly convoluted plot trick that allowed DC Comics to change the fates of a number of their characters. It is hardly worth trying to sum up that plot trick because it is so confusing, but here goes—in the 2005–06 comic series *Infinite Crisis*, a character known as Superboy-Prime assaulted the barrier of reality, causing a number of past events in the DC Universe to be altered. Truth be told, it is probably just easier to say that DC elected to revise the histories of some of their characters!

At any rate, in "Batman: Under the Hood," Jason adopted the Red Hood persona, brutally fought crime, and was eventually confronted by Batman after he had kidnapped the Joker. Jason held the madman at gunpoint and tried to convince Batman that they needed to kill him, but Batman was able to disarm Jason before he could pull the trigger. Both Jason and the Joker escaped from Batman after their altercation, leaving both characters free to plague the crimefighter in the future.

Jason's resurrection spawned an enjoyable 2010 direct-to-video DC Universe Animated Original Movie called *Batman: Under the Red Hood*. (We'll examine that project in detail later in the chapter.) Incidentally, it should be pointed out that the work that laid the foundation for Jason's return was the 2002–03 *Batman* comic story arc entitled *Hush*—as we discussed in Chapter 16, *Hush* ended with Batman discovering that Jason's body was missing from his grave. And it should also be pointed out that the inspiration for Jason's Red Hood persona came from a classic Batman comic story from *many* years back—as we discussed in Chapter 5, a 1951 *Detective Comics* story called "The Man Behind the Red Hood!" revealed the Joker to have originally been an unnamed criminal who called himself the Red Hood.

The *Infinite Crisis* series helped to bring about another change to Batman's comic world. DC's 2006–07 series called *52* chronicled the 52-week period of time directly after the events of *Infinite Crisis*—during that time, Superman, Batman and Wonder Woman stopped fighting crime, and other DC heroes stepped in to fill the void that the three legendary heroes had left. Some new heroes were even created for *52*—the series introduced a new version of Batwoman into the DC Universe. The character initially created quite a stir—her real identity was Kate Kane, and she was a lesbian. Many major news media outlets ran stories about the Kate Kane Batwoman's comic debut, because she was one of the first openly gay comic book characters ever created.

Obviously, the character was a reworking of the Kathy Kane Batwoman character that had appeared in Batman comic stories of the 1950s and early 1960s. (We discussed her back in Chapter 5.) In fact, this new Batwoman's black and red bat-themed costume even looked a bit like the original Batwoman's costume. Ironically, the original Batwoman was introduced into Batman's world in order to refute the assertions made by Fredric Wertham in his book *Seduction of the Innocent* that Batman and Robin were homosexual—and a half century later, this new Batwoman was a champion of gay rights! Take *that*, Wertham! At any rate, the Kate Kane Batwoman's debut was well-received by comic fans, so she became a fairly regular fixture of Batman's comic book world.

In late 2005, DC launched a highly unusual and controversial Batman comic series called *All Star Batman and Robin the Boy Wonder*. The premise of the series was that it would retell the history of Batman and his world in continuity that was in no way bound to the character's regular comic book continuity. The reason that DC was willing to give this particular series such latitude on what it could do with Batman was simple—it was going to be created by a "dream pairing" of one of the greatest comic book writers of all time and one of the comic industry's hottest artists. *All Star Batman and Robin the Boy Wonder* was written by Frank Miller and illustrated by Jim Lee, and comic fans were extremely anxious to see how these huge talents would end up interpreting Batman when they joined forces. The series' first issue released in September 2005 was a smash hit, selling hundreds of thousands of copies.

Ironically, the series quickly became one of the most widely hated Batman comic works ever created even though it sold remarkably well right out of the gate. To put it bluntly, DC entrusted the wrong creative team with such an open-ended project—Lee's art was spectacular as usual, but Miller's writing was completely off the mark. *All Star Batman and Robin the Boy Wonder* was shockingly mean-spirited and violent, even more brutal than any of Miller's previous Batman comic works—and those works contained their fair share of violent and disturbing images.

Miller's earlier interpretations of Batman showed the character to be in possession of a very troubled psyche, and obviously those interpretations resonated resoundingly well with serious Batman fans. But Miller's take on Batman's mental state in *All Star Batman and Robin the Boy Wonder* pushed the envelope *way* too far for many of those fans. The series' Batman was in the very early stages of his crimefighting career, and he was well beyond "troubled"—he was actually downright psychotic. For example, he took delight in seriously injuring the criminals he fought, and he basically held a grieving Dick Grayson prisoner in the Batcave after Dick's parents had been murdered. He even told Dick to eat freshly-caught rats in the Batcave instead of letting Alfred give the boy a proper meal!

When we discussed several of Miller's previous Batman comic book works earlier in this book, we noted his intense dislike for the traditional version of the Robin character. Apparently, Miller's hatred of Robin had gotten so out of control by the time he was writing *All Star Batman and Robin the Boy Wonder* that he was intent on piling as much abuse on the poor kid as he possibly could!

At any rate, most comic book readers were incensed by Miller's antics in the pages of *All Star Batman and Robin the Boy Wonder*, which brought the series both bad press and declining sales. It ended up running for only ten issues, the last of which was published in late 2008. In 2010, DC announced that Miller and Lee would return to the series for a number of issues in order to wrap up its storyline, but this return never ended up happening. Lee has continued to provide illustrations for Batman-related works in the years since *All Star Batman and Robin the Boy Wonder* folded, but to date Miller has not undertaken any new Batman-related projects.

As always, new Batman works kept right on being released — so those fans disappointed by *All Star Batman and Robin the Boy Wonder* had plenty of new Batman comic stories that they could turn their attention to. In fact, the early years of Batman's crimefighting career were re-interpreted in a separate series of comics released between late 2005 and early 2006, right around the time that *All Star Batman and Robin the Boy Wonder* debuted. The six-issue tale *Batman and the Monster Men* written and illustrated by Matt Wagner was an expanded retelling of a story that was first published in *Batman* #1, Spring 1940 — in that story, Batman faced off against the evil scientific genius Hugo Strange for the first time. Wagner followed up *Batman and the Monster Men* with another six-issue series called *Batman and the Mad Monk*, which was released between late 2006 and early 2007. The series retold a two-part story that was first published in *Detective Comics* #31 and #32 in late 1939 — in that story, Batman battled a vampire known as the Monk. Wagner's take on Batman's early years in these two series was very well-received, and both were eventually released as stand-alone graphic novels.

In 2006, the Batman character entered a new realm of merchandising that ended up winning over both the young and the young at heart. Lego Toys began manufacturing Batman-related building block sets that offered a whimsical interpretation of the character and his world. Lego fans could create their own Batman adventures one block at a time by assembling Batcave, Batmobile, Batwing, and Batboat kits. Each kit included several different Batman-related figures, so these fans could collect a wide variety of figures to use with their Lego Batman structures and vehicles.

Lego Batman toys ended up becoming so popular that they entered the world of video gaming — *Lego Batman: The Videogame* was released on major gaming platforms such as PlayStation 3, Xbox 360 and Wii in late 2008. The game's lighthearted take on Batman and his world could be enjoyed both by younger players and longtime fans of the character. *Lego Batman: The Videogame* enjoyed enough success to spawn a sequel — *Lego Batman 2: DC Super Heroes* was released in mid–2012, and it featured DC heroes such as Superman and Wonder Woman fighting crime alongside of Batman. That game was adapted into an animated film entitled *Lego Batman: The Movie — DC Super Heroes Unite* that was released directly to home video in mid–2013.

Grant Morrison became the writer of the *Batman* comic title in 2006, and he quickly began to shake up Batman's comic world. In a story arc called "Batman & Son" that ran in *Batman* #655 through #658, Morrison brought Bruce Wayne's pre-teen son Damian into Batman's life. Damian sprang from a comic work that was almost two decades old — he was the child of Bruce and Talia Al Ghul that Talia gave up for adoption in the 1987 graphic novel *Batman: Son of the Demon*. (We discussed that graphic novel in detail in Chapter 7.) In "Batman & Son," Damian was a spoiled, violent child who made things very difficult for Bruce and his allies when he first came to live at Wayne Manor—but he eventually became an important part of their crimefighting team.

Bringing Damian into Batman's world was a big change, but Morrison was just getting warmed up. In his 2008 DC crossover storyline called *Final Crisis*, he had the villain Darkseid kill Batman! Of course, it was quickly revealed that Batman was not really *killed*—Darkseid was actually sent him into past worlds. So Batman had to make his way through time and return to the present in order to truly resume his stature as Batman. As Bruce made his way back, Dick Grayson and Tim Drake disagreed over who should take his place as Batman—eventually Dick assumed the role, Damian became his Robin, and Tim assumed the guise of Red Robin. Bruce was eventually able to return to the present and again become Batman, but it took him a couple of years to do that—not comic years, *our* years. We'll get to the return of the Bruce Wayne Batman later in the chapter.

Incidentally, the idea of Red Robin character actually originated in the 1997 graphic novel series *Kingdom Come*—in that series, Robin donned a new costume that featured a full Batman-like cowl, and was then known as "Red Robin." In the years after *Kingdom Come* was released, there were a number of characters that donned the Red Robin mantle, but none of them stuck. With Tim Drake, Morrison finally found an established character to fill the Red Robin costume.

Let's step away from Morrison's complicated storylines now. *The Essential Batman Encyclopedia* by Robert Greenberger was released in 2008; it was the most comprehensive reference work on Batman comic history ever created. The book provided a wealth of information on the thousands of characters appearing in Batman comic stories between 1939 and 2007. *The Essential Batman Encyclopedia* was a welcome reference tool for serious Batman fans. There had been only one other attempt at creating a Batman encyclopedia before, the 1976 book *The Encyclopedia of Comic Book Heroes Volume 1: Batman* by Michael J. Fleisher—and obviously, it was woefully out of date. (We discussed that book in Chapter 7.)

Another fascinating Batman book released in 2008 was *Bat-Manga!: The Secret History of Batman in Japan*, which was designed by Chip Kidd. The book was a collection of Japanese comic works (known as "manga" in Japan) that featured Batman—these works were created by the famed manga artist Jiro Kuwata in the 1966 and 1967, during the height of the camp Batman craze. *Bat-Manga!: The Secret History of Batman in Japan* gave Batman fans a rare opportunity to see the character interpreted in a manner that had almost no connection to his creators in the United States.

Interestingly, even though Batman's return to the big screen through Christopher Nolan's films had been so tremendously successful, Warner Bros. elected to keep their Batman animated TV series completely separate from Nolan's Batman universe. As we discussed in Chapter 16, the 2004–08 series *The Batman* offered a take on the character that was markedly different from the one offered by the classic 1990s series *Batman: The Animated Series*—and that take never connected to Nolan's Batman films in any way.

When *The Batman*'s run ended, Warner developed a new Batman animated series called *Batman: The Brave and the Bold*. The series premiered on the Cartoon Network in November 2008, and it ran for 65 episodes before it ended its run in November 2011. The creative forces behind the series were producers James Tucker and Michael Jelenic. In *Batman: The Brave and the Bold*, the part of Batman/Bruce Wayne was voiced by Diedrich Bader.

19—"Non-Nolan" Batman Works During the Nolan Era 261

Batman in the animated television series *Batman: The Brave and the Bold* (2008–11).

Batman: The Brave and the Bold's take on Batman was light years removed from Nolan's Batman universe, and the series' title was a perfect indication of what its interpretation of Batman was all about. As we discussed way back in Chapter 6, *The Brave and the Bold* was a DC comic title that featured Batman in "team-up" stories from late 1966 all the way up until 1983—these stories gave the character the chance to interact with DC heroes he would not normally have worked with in his other comic titles. In fact, Batman ended up sharing adventures with most every major hero in the DC universe in the pages of *The Brave and the Bold*.

Basically, *Batman: The Brave and the Bold* was a screen version of that classic comic title. Throughout the series, Batman shared adventures with dozens of DC characters—and not just well-known characters such as Robin, Superman, Wonder Woman, the Flash, and Green Lantern. Batman also teamed up with lesser-known characters such as the Atom, Hawkman, Black Lightning, Plastic Man, and the Elongated Man—good grief, even the goofy 1950s characters Bat-Mite and Ace the Bat-Hound showed up in a number of episodes!

Obviously, *Batman: The Brave and the Bold* was designed to be a lighthearted action show that harkened back to the more kid-friendly comics of the 1960s and 1970s—in fact, many of its episodes were so absurdly wholesome and fantasy-oriented that they ended up being every bit as comedic in nature as the 1960s *Batman* TV show and film. But that did not stop the series from being a hugely enjoyable viewing experience for longtime Batman fans—it was loaded with subtle Batman references and in-jokes that only a serious Batman fan would be able to understand and appreciate.

Plus, the series' flamboyant visual design could be enjoyed by both younger viewers and longtime Batman fans. Batman himself was rendered in a style that recalled both the 1940s comic art of Dick Sprang and Adam West's 1960s screen Batman—he wore a blue and gray costume with a flowing cape and short ears on its cowl that was a perfect summation of the character's basic appearance from the 1940s through the 1960s. Most of the series' heroes and villains were designed to reflect the way they looked during that time period in Batman history as well—for example, the Joker, the Penguin, the Riddler, Two-Face and the Catwoman all looked as if they had been pulled from the colorful pages of a 1940s comic story.

And even though the tone of *Batman: The Brave and the Bold* was normally very light-hearted, it was also capable of delivering some astonishingly powerful episodes from time to time. One of the series' most unforgettable episodes was "Chill of the Night!" which was written by Paul Dini, one of *Batman: The Animated Series*' most noted writers, and directed by Michael Chang. The episode told the story of Batman hunting down Joe Chill, the villain who murdered Thomas and Martha Wayne.

In "Chill of the Night!" Batman's pursuit of Chill is being followed by two of DC's ghostly crimefighters, the Spectre and the Phantom Stranger. The Spectre believes that Batman should go down the path of vengeance and kill Chill, while the Phantom Stranger believes that Batman should continue on the path of justice and simply apprehend Chill. They even make a very high-stakes wager on just which path Batman will follow. They agree that if Batman kills Chill, the crimefighter will become an agent of the Spectre and continue to wreak murderous vengeance on criminals—and if Batman does not kill Chill, he will be free to continue making his own moral choices.

The Phantom Stranger takes Batman back into the past to reveal just why Chill killed the Waynes—the crimefighters travel to the night the Waynes were holding a charity masquerade ball at their home. Batman is shocked to see that his father is dressed in a bat-like costume that looks so much like his own. During that event, a gangster named Lew Moxon tries to rob the Waynes—Batman and Thomas fight and capture Moxon, and the gangster is sent to prison. The Spectre then takes Batman to another moment in the past to reveal more details relating to the Wayne murders. Seeking revenge against the man who sent him to prison, Moxon had ordered his henchman Joe Chill to murder Thomas Wayne. The night of the hit, Chill ended up panicking and killing both Thomas and Martha.

Once Batman knows that it was Chill who killed his parents, he tracks the criminal down—he finds Chill in a Gotham warehouse, where the criminal is trying to sell a high tech weapon called a "sonic disrupter" to a number of Batman's most dangerous foes, including the Joker, the Penguin and Two-Face. Batman corners Chill in a secluded room, takes off his mask, and tells Chill that he is the son of the man Chill murdered so many years ago. At this moment, Batman makes his moral choice—he does not kill Chill. In panic, Chill runs away from Batman, but he is killed when a stray blast from the sonic disrupter brings part of the warehouse down on top of him. At the end of the episode, it is implied that the Spectre had made sure that Chill would pay for his crimes with his life, even if Batman himself did not actually do the killing.

"Chill of the Night!" is every bit as good as the very best episodes of *Batman: The Animated Series*—in other words, it is unquestionably one of the finest Batman animated works ever produced. Dini seamlessly blends several classic Batman comic stories into the episode—for example, the episode's opening scenes depicting the Wayne murders and Bruce's transformation into Batman are drawn from 1939 comic story "Legend—The Batman and How He Came to Be." And the scenes depicting Batman's quest to bring Joe Chill to justice are drawn from the 1948 comic story "The Origin of Batman." (We discussed both of these stories earlier in the book.)

Finally, the scenes involving a bat-costumed Thomas Wayne fighting Lew Moxon, and Moxon ordering Chill to kill Wayne, are drawn from the 1956 comic story "The First Batman." This is the first time we've mentioned "The First Batman" in the book—the story was originally published in *Detective Comics* #235, September 1956. The reason we had not discussed it earlier is because its embellishment of the Wayne murder story did not really take root in Batman mythos. Most of the Batman comic stories dealing with Batman's origin that were created after the publication of "The First Batman" did not feature Thomas Wayne's bat-like costume or the Lew Moxon character in any way. That said, however, the story did fit very nicely into the plot of "Chill of the Night!"

And Dini's decision to work the Spectre and the Phantom Stranger into the episode gives Batman an opportunity to face the moral conflict that has so often been a major element of his character—does Batman stand for justice or vengeance? To this particular Batman fan, the character's decision to choose justice over vengeance in "Chill of the Night!" perfectly sums up what Batman is really all about.

"Chill of the Night!" is made even more special by its stellar voice cast, which spans several generations of Batman history. Adam West, the legendary 1960s screen Batman, voices the part of Thomas Wayne. Julie Newmar, the actress who played the Catwoman during the *Batman* TV show's first two seasons, voices the part of Martha Wayne. Kevin Conroy, the voice of Batman/Bruce Wayne in *Batman: The Animated Series*, voices the part of the Phantom Stranger. Mark Hamill, the voice of the Joker in *Batman: The Animated Series*, voices the part of the Spectre. And Richard Moll, the voice of Harvey Dent/Two-Face in *Batman: The Animated Series*, voices the part of Lew Moxon. Of course, all of these actors are excellent in their respective roles.

I've discussed the voice cast of "Chill of the Night!" at length and I haven't even gotten around to mentioning the actor voicing Batman/Bruce Wayne yet! Diedrich Bader does a wonderful job voicing the part both in this episode and in the entire *Batman: The Brave and the Bold* series.

And I need to point out that even though I've gone over "Chill of the Night!" in great detail, that does not mean I believe that it is the only *Batman: The Brave and the Bold* episode that is worthy of praise. In fact, there is one more episode that was also written by Dini that I just *have* to take note of before we move on. In "Bat-Mite Presents: Batman's Strangest Cases!," the interdimensional imp Bat-Mite introduces several priceless Batman-mini-adventures—one is based on the Batman manga works found in the book *Bat-Manga!: The Secret History of Batman in Japan* that we just discussed. Another is a team-up of Batman, Robin and the Scooby-Doo gang that is a parody of the Batman/Scooby team-ups found in the 1970s animated TV series *The New Scooby-Doo Movies*.

We did not discuss *The New Scooby-Doo Movies* earlier in the book, so here's just a bit of background information on the series—it featured Scooby and the gang sharing adventures with a host of guest stars, including Batman and Robin. The series' silly plots and poor animation made it forgettable at best, so having Batman mixed up in it certainly did not thrill most longtime fans of the character. But Batman fans could certainly get a kick out of seeing *Batman: The Brave and the Bold* do such a wickedly funny spoof of the series.

Examining "Chill of the Night!" and "Bat-Mite Presents: Batman's Strangest Cases!" back-to-back is probably the perfect way to sum up just how wide-ranging of a series *Batman: The Brave and the Bold* really was. The series' generally sunny depiction of Batman might have run counter to the tastes of many serious Batman fans—still, its engaging and affectionate take on the character and his world ended up making it a high point in the history of Batman screen works.

Earlier in the book we discussed a number of Batman video game titles that helped to further the character's overall popularity. As well-received as these games had been, their success paled in comparison to the spectacular success of video game *Batman: Arkham Asylum*, which was released on major gaming platforms such as PlayStation 3 and Xbox 360 in late 2009. *Batman: Arkham Asylum* had a number of notable connections to *Batman: The Animated Series*—the game was written by Paul Dini, and it featured some of the series' major voice talent. In the game, Kevin Conroy voiced Batman, Mark Hamill voiced the Joker, and Arleen Sorkin voiced Harley Quinn.

In *Batman: Arkham Asylum*, the Joker hatches a diabolical plot to create an army of chemically-enhanced henchmen to terrorize Gotham City. These henchmen are created through the use of a drug known as Titan, which is a variation of the Venom drug used to create the villain Bane. Batman must fight his way through Arkham Asylum and defeat some of his most dangerous foes in order to thwart the Joker's plan.

Simply put, most everything about *Batman: Arkham Asylum* was flat-out stunning. Its incredibly lifelike graphics, intricate plot, excellent voice acting, and wonderful attention to detail took the Batman video game genre to a level of sophistication that it had never come close to reaching before. The game's spectacularly-rendered version of Batman was one of its primary strengths—the character looked like an Alex Ross Batman painting set in motion. And of course, since the character was voiced by Kevin Conroy, he sounded every bit as good as he looked. *Batman: Arkham Asylum* was richly rewarded for its extremely high quality—the game enjoyed almost universally positive critical reviews, and it sold over 4 million copies.

In fact, *Batman: Arkham Asylum* was so successful that it spawned a sequel—the game *Batman: Arkham City* was released on major gaming platforms such as PlayStation 3 and Xbox 360 in late 2011. It was co-written by Dini, Paul Crocker and Sefton Hill, and featured the voices of Kevin Conroy as Batman and Mark Hamill as the Joker. (Arleen Sorkin did not return to voice Harley Quinn, so the part was played by Tara Strong.)

In *Batman: Arkham City*, Batman is locked up in Arkham City, a newly-formed prison that encloses some of Gotham's worst slums. The reason that Batman is being held in the prison is because it is being run by Hugo Strange, a warden who is as unbalanced and dangerous as any of the prison's inmates. (As we noted earlier in the book, Strange was a villain that had been featured in Batman comic stories since the early 1940s—but in the game's storyline, Batman had no prior history with the character.)

While Batman is in the prison, he learns of Strange's initiative known as "Protocol 10," which is a plan to murder all of the prison's inmates. As Batman works to keep Protocol 10 from being carried out, he ends up clashing with some of his longtime foes who are being held in Arkham City, including the Joker, Harley Quinn, Two-Face, Mr. Freeze, and the Penguin. Luckily, Batman has some allies to help him with his mission—Robin comes to his aid, and so does his occasional adversary the Catwoman.

Batman: Arkham City lived up to the very high standards set by *Batman: Arkham Asylum* in every way—it was just as brilliantly written, animated and acted as its predecessor. And like *Batman: Arkham Asylum*, *Batman: Arkham City* enjoyed almost universally positive critical reviews. Commercially, *Batman: Arkham City* performed even *better* than *Batman: Arkham Asylum*—it sold over 6 million copies. Playing the two games back-to-back created a completely immersive experience for serious Batman fans that was unprecedented in the history of the character.

Batman in the video game *Batman: Arkham Asylum* (2009).

All right, it's finally time to get the comic book version of Bruce Wayne back into his Batman costume. In Grant Morrison's 2010 comic series *Batman: The Return of Bruce Wayne*, Bruce adopted all sorts of crimefighting personas as he traveled forward in time. He eventually returned to the present, where he learned that Darkseid's attack on him was never meant to kill him — it was designed to load him up with a form of negative energy as he made his way through time. That energy would then completely destroy reality when Bruce returned to the present. (Oh, and it should be pointed out that Bruce was not able to travel through time by himself — a servant of Darkseid's had been sent to follow Bruce and initiate his time jumps.) But Bruce did not destroy reality when he returned to the present because he devised a plan to have his Justice League allies briefly stop his heart just as he returned — this allowed the energy to leave his body.

So Bruce was back in the present day again, and ready to resume the mantle of Batman. Of course, the present already had a Batman now — remember, Dick Grayson had taken over the role upon Bruce's "death." Well, Morrison had an answer for this problem as well. In his ongoing comic series *Batman Incorporated* launched in late 2010, Morrison had Bruce take his Batman crimefighting operation worldwide — the series followed the exploits of the Bruce Batman, the Dick Batman who fought crime with the Damian Robin, the Tim Drake Red Robin, as well as a host of Batman-led costumed operatives around the globe.

A few of these operatives were noteworthy enough to warrant specific mention here. In 2009, Cassandra Cain passed her Batgirl mantle on to a character named Stephanie Brown. This is the first time in the book we've mentioned the Stephanie Brown character — she was first introduced into Batman's world back in 1992, and over the years she went through a *lot* of changes. At first she assumed the guise of a costumed adventurer known as the Spoiler, then she became Robin for a very short time when Tim Drake vacated the position, and then she was killed in the 2004–05 Batman comic story arc *Batman: War Games*. But we're not done yet — then it was revealed that Stephanie's death was faked, and *then* she became Batgirl. Talk about a nomadic character! At any rate, Cassandra eventually returned to fighting crime after giving her Batgirl role to Stephanie — she adopted a new bat-themed persona known as Black Bat.

For those of you who have been determined enough to keep up with all of these developments, here's a snapshot of Batman's comic world in late 2010. Dick Grayson was now the main Batman character in the long-running comic titles *Detective Comics* and *Batman*, as well as in a newer comic title, *Batman and Robin*. And Bruce was now the main Batman character in two newer comic titles, *Batman Incorporated* and *Batman: The Dark Knight*. These Batmen shared their adventures with allies such as Robin, Red Robin, Batgirl, Black Bat, and Batwoman. (Things have gotten so hectic that I'll bet many of you have already forgotten about the new Batwoman we discussed earlier in the chapter!) And a number of these characters not only appeared in Batman comic titles, but also had comic titles of their own. So needless to say, it had gotten pretty crowded and confusing in Batman's comic book world by this point. In late 2011, DC would undertake a revamp and relaunch of *all* of their comic titles in an attempt to sort out the continuities of their characters. We'll discuss how this revamp and relaunch (known as *The New 52*) affected Batman and his world a bit later in the chapter.

Last chapter, we discussed Warner and DC's direct-to-video animated film series known as DC Universe Animated Original Movies and the first Batman film in that series, *Batman: Gotham Knight* (2008). Over the past several years, DC Universe Animated Original Movies has continued to produce new films based on DC comic works. A number of these productions were ensemble stories that featured Batman working with a host of other DC heroes—these productions included *Superman/Batman: Public Enemies* (2009) and *Superman/Batman: Apocalypse* (2010).

In *Superman/Batman: Public Enemies*, Superman and Batman teamed up to stop a gigantic meteorite from destroying the earth, and in *Superman/Batman: Apocalypse*, Superman and Batman witnessed the arrival of Superman's cousin Kara to the earth. (Of course, by the end of *Superman/Batman: Apocalypse*, Kara would adopt the character's traditional guise of Supergirl.) Kevin Conroy, who had voiced the part of Batman/Bruce Wayne in *Batman: Gotham Knight*, returned to voice the role in these two films. Both productions were based on story arcs that had appeared in *Superman/Batman*, a comic title that featured Superman and Batman appearing in adventures together much like the old *World's Finest* comic title. (*Superman/Batman* ran from 2003 to 2011.)

The series released its second Batman film, *Batman: Under the Red Hood*, on Blu-ray and DVD in July 2010. The film's screenplay was written by Judd Winick, author of the 2005–06 *Batman* comic story arc "Batman: Under the Hood" that the film was based on. (Remember, we discussed that story arc at the beginning of this chapter.) The production was directed by Brandon Vietti. In *Batman: Under the Red Hood*, the part of Batman/Bruce Wayne was voiced by Bruce Greenwood, the part of the Red Hood was voiced by Jensen Ackles, and the part of the Joker was voiced by John DiMaggio.

Batman: Under the Red Hood opens with Batman's second Robin Jason Todd being killed by the Joker—the madman severely beats the young man with a crowbar, and then leaves him in a building he has wired with explosives. Batman arrives on the scene after the explosion goes off, but he is too late to save his partner. Five years later, Batman faces a dangerous new adversary in Gotham City known as the Red Hood. The Red Hood has taken over Gotham's illegal drug trade, and is intent on wielding even more power in the city—he wants to take over the operations of the Gotham crime lord Black Mask. When Batman confronts the Red Hood, he is surprised to learn that the Red Hood considers himself not a criminal, but a crimefighter. He feels he is taking the drastic measures needed to bring Gotham's rampant crime under control—measures that Batman himself should have taken years ago.

But Batman's problems with the Red Hood turn out to be much bigger than just a struggle with an out-of-control vigilante—the crimefighter is shocked to learn that the Red Hood is really Jason Todd. Batman's quest to find out how Jason came back from the dead leads him to his longtime adversary Ra's Al Ghul. Ra's tells Batman the truth about Jason—five years ago, Ra's had hired to Joker to fight Batman in order to distract the crimefighter from one of Ra's' terrorist plots. The Joker ended up killing Jason, and Ra's was so remorseful over Jason's death that he tried to bring the young man back to life with his Lazarus Pit. Ra's' attempt to resurrect Jason went horribly wrong—the young man came out of the pit severely mentally damaged.

Armed with this knowledge, Batman again confronts the Red Hood—but that confrontation has become much more complicated, because Black Mask has freed the Joker from Arkham Asylum. Black Mask has done this so that he can hire the Joker to take down the Red Hood. Instead of the Joker taking down the Red Hood, the Red Hood abducts the Joker, and Batman sets off in pursuit of both of them. Batman and the Red Hood engage in a fierce fight in an abandoned apartment which ends with an unmasked Jason holding the Joker at gunpoint, trying to convince Batman to kill the madman. Batman refuses, and disarms Jason—this leads Jason to set off a bomb he has planted in the building. After the explosion, Batman is able to find the still-alive Joker in the rubble, but there is no sign of Jason.

Winick changed quite a few of the plot details found in "Batman: Under the Hood" for *Batman: Under the Red Hood*. The most notable of these changes was that Jason's resurrection in the film had nothing to do with Superboy-Prime assaulting the barrier of reality—instead, Ra's Al Ghul was responsible for Jason being brought back to life. And "Batman: Under the Hood" featured a complex storyline that was filled with a wide variety of DC characters, both heroes and villains. The storyline of *Batman: Under the Red Hood* featured far fewer DC characters, and was greatly simplified to fit the film's 75-minute running time.

Also, the film's depiction of the Joker was obviously greatly influenced by Heath Ledger's interpretation of the character in the film *The Dark Knight*. Like *The Dark Knight* Joker, *Batman: Under the Red Hood*'s Joker was much more quietly sinister than his usually over-the-top comic book counterpart, and he sported a dark, disheveled mane of hair. The way that the character was used in the film's plot was obviously inspired by *The Dark Knight* Joker as well. In *Batman: Under the Red Hood*, the Joker was called on by other criminals to work with them, but these other criminals had no idea what they were really getting themselves into when they forged ties with such a dangerous madman.

Batman: Under the Red Hood was very well-received by critics and longtime fans of the character when it was released—in fact, it ended up being considerably more popular than the comic work that inspired it. It is easy to see why the film was so successful—it was beautifully animated, and its voice cast was excellent. It also contained a wealth of interesting bonus material, including a short documentary about the evolution of the Dick Grayson Robin character entitled *Robin: The Story of Dick Grayson*. The Blu-ray release of the film included all of this bonus material as well as a short documentary about the evolution of the Jason Todd character called *Robin's Requiem: The Story of Jason Todd*. (Given the fact that *Batman: Under the Red Hood* was basically about the Jason Todd character more than any other character, it seems that *all* releases of the film should have contained this documentary, not just the Blu-ray!)

The third Batman title produced by DC Universe Animated Original Movies was far more faithful to its source material than *Batman: Under the Red Hood* had been. *Batman: Year One* was released on Blu-ray and DVD in October 2011, and it was almost a panel-for-panel adaptation of Frank Miller and David Mazzucchelli's 1987 groundbreaking comic series of the same name. It was written by Tab Murphy, and directed by Sam Liu and Lauren Montgomery. The film featured Benjamin McKenzie as the voice of Batman/Bruce Wayne and Bryan Cranston as the voice of Jim Gordon. Obviously, since *Batman: Year One* was such a literal reworking of a classic Batman comic series, it was heartily embraced by most serious fans of the character. And the fact that it was as well-animated and acted as all of the other films in the DC Universe Animated Original Movies series made those fans appreciate it all the more.

Also like the other films in the DC Universe Animated Original Movies series, *Batman: Year One* contained a wealth of interesting bonus material. A short documentary called *Heart of Vengeance: Returning Batman to His Roots* chronicled the character's Denny O'Neil–Neal Adams led revamp of the 1970s, and Frank Miller's 1980s reinvention of the character through his works *Batman: The Dark Knight Returns* and *Batman: Year One*. Ironically, even though so much of the documentary was about Miller's work, Miller himself declined to take part in the production in any way. He obviously chose to continue his separation from the Batman character that began with the 2008 cancellation of his controversial comic title *All Star Batman and Robin the Boy Wonder*.

In November 2010, the Cartoon Network premiered a new Warner Bros. animated TV series called *Young Justice* created by Greg Weisman and Brandon Vietti. It featured a new animated version of Batman, though the character was not really the focal point of the series. The premise of *Young Justice* was that the Dick Grayson Robin was leading a team of young DC superheroes that was basically an offshoot of the Justice League. Batman often stepped in to counsel Robin and the team during their adventures. In the series, the part of Batman/Bruce Wayne was voiced by Bruce Greenwood, and the part of Robin/Dick Grayson was voiced by Jesse McCartney.

The series underwent a number of major changes for its second season, which premiered in April 2012. It was retitled *Young Justice: Invasion*, and it was set five years in the future from the events of the first season. By this point in time, Dick Grayson had become Nightwing, Tim Drake had become Robin, and the Barbara Gordon version of Batgirl had begun to work with the crimefighters. In *Young Justice: Invasion*, Greenwood and McCartney reprised their roles from the first season, Cameron Bowen voiced the part of Robin/Tim Drake, and Alyson Stoner voiced the part of Batgirl/Barbara Gordon. Obviously, the continuity of *Young Justice* was in no way connected to Batman's official comic book continuity, and Batman himself did not play a very large role in the series—but the series still contained moments that provided a very enjoyable depiction of the character and his world.

As we noted in Chapter 16, director Sandy Collora's 2002 independent short film *Batman: Dead End* inspired the creation of scores of fan-made Batman films that could be viewed on the Internet. And the exploding popularity of video-sharing websites such as YouTube made these films readily available to anyone with Internet access—so Batman fans were essentially given a new format that allowed them to sample a wide variety of unofficial screen interpretations of the character. As we also noted in Chapter 16, most of these Batman fan films were forgettable, amateurish efforts, but a precious few of them were so elaborate and well-made that they ended up winning critical praise and drawing huge online audiences.

For example, in 2003 a filmmaker named Aaron Schoenke formed his own production company called Bat in the Sun Productions and started making his own Batman films. Schoenke's first few Batman films such as *Dark Justice* (2003) were very well-received by the online Batman community, which led his subsequent Batman productions to become more and more ambitious. In fact, Schoenke's *City of Scars* (2010) was a *tremendously* ambitious work—it was 30 minutes in length, it was shot on high definition video cameras, and it had a budget of over $25,000. The film starred Kevin Porter as Batman and Paul Molnar as the Joker, and it chronicled Batman's efforts to stop one of the Joker's murderous crime sprees in Gotham City. *City of Scars* was certainly not a production that rivaled the overall scope and quality of Warner's best Batman films. But even still, it could be argued that its powerful interpretation of Batman and his world was far closer in look and spirit to the character's best comic adventures than *any* of Warner's Batman efforts.

I feel that in the interest of full disclosure, I should state that the Batman fan film movement took hold of me several years ago. I became fascinated with the idea of being able to create my own screen interpretation of Batman, so in 2007 I decided to make my own Batman fan film with my sons Taylor and Keaton. The result of our efforts was a three-and-a-half minute video called *Batman: Watching Over Gotham* that was inspired by my all-time favorite Batman work, the 1999 oversize graphic novel *Batman: War on Crime* by

Paul Dini and Alex Ross. I just used the word "amateurish" to describe the majority of the Batman fan films that have been produced, and I suppose that word could be used to accurately describe our little film. Still, it was great fun for me to prowl the rooftops of Columbus, Ohio late at night dressed as Batman while we made our movie. (Of course, given my lifelong Batman obsession, you know that I just *had* to play the part in my own Batman film!)

In September 2011, DC Comics premiered *The New 52*, which was a revamp and relaunch of all of the company's comic titles. *The New 52* was designed to follow the events of DC's 2011 system-wide crossover *Flashpoint*, in which the Flash reset the timeline of the entire DC Universe. *The New 52* was an ambitious project, to say the least — DC canceled all of their monthly comic titles and replaced them with 52 new comic titles, all of them starting with a ceremonial "issue number 1." Of course, this project was not really as radical of a restart as DC made it out to be. For example, the comic titles *Batman* and *Detective Comics* continued to feature Batman stories just like they had been doing for over 70 years — they just had their issue numbers reset back to 1.

That said, however, *The New 52* did bring some major changes to Batman's comic book continuity. Some of the complicated plotlines that Grant Morrison had set in motion over the last few years were negated — Bruce Wayne was again the only Batman, and Dick Grayson was again Nightwing, having adopted that persona after stepping down from being the original Robin. But some of Morrison's other plotlines stayed intact — Damian Wayne remained Robin and Tim Drake remained Red Robin, even though both of their backstories were greatly revised.

The New 52 also retained Jason Todd as the character who had been killed by the Joker when he was Robin, and then brought back from the dead to assume the persona of the Red Hood. But the details of Jason's story as laid out in Judd Winick's story arc "Batman: Under the Hood" were significantly altered, much like the backstories of Damian Wayne and Tim Drake had been.

No member of Batman's crimefighting team was changed as much for *The New 52* as the character of Batgirl was. The injuries that Barbara Gordon suffered when she was shot by the Joker in the classic 1988 graphic novel *Batman: The Killing Joke* no longer left her permanently paralyzed — instead, she was able to regain the use of her legs and return to her crimefighting activities as Batgirl. This retooled Barbara Gordon Batgirl was given a costume that looked much like the costume the character wore when she debuted all the way back in 1967 — and then she was given her own *The New 52* comic title, simply titled *Batgirl*. Incidentally, the Cassandra Cain and Stephanie Brown versions of Batgirl basically just disappeared from the DC Universe after the Barbara Gordon Batgirl was reintroduced. The new Kate Kane version of Batwoman fared much better than Cain and Brown — *The New 52* gave the character her own comic title (simply titled *Batwoman*), and did not change her backstory in any way.

All of the changes that the Batman character had been put through over the years were very difficult to keep up with — even for serious Batman fans. The excellent 2012 reference book *Batman: The World of the Dark Knight* by Daniel Wallace helped to accomplish this task. The lavishly-illustrated book followed the history of Batman and his world from his 1939 origin all the way through *The New 52*, and provided a concise overview of the many incarnations of the character created over the decades.

Batman was prominently featured in the DC Universe Animated Original Movies production *Justice League: Doom*, which was released on Blu-ray and DVD in February 2012.

The film was based on Mark Waid's story arc "JLA: Tower of Babel" that had appeared in the DC comic title *JLA* in 2000. In *Justice League: Doom*, Batman has developed a plan to incapacitate League should they ever go rogue and threaten the human race. These plans are stolen by the villain Vandal Savage, who attempts to destroy the League with them. Batman is able to stop Savage, but the League's faith in having Batman as a teammate is seriously shaken. Kevin Conroy provided the voice of Batman/Bruce Wayne in *Justice League: Doom*, just as he had for several previous DC Universe Animated Original Movie projects.

I'm going to close out this chapter with a bit of an "author's choice"—that is, a few sentences about one of my own personal all-time favorite Batman works that debuted during the Nolan cinematic Batman era. The graphic novel *Batman: Noel* written and illustrated by Lee Bermejo was released in November 2011, and it told a tale of Batman hunting down the Joker that was blended with Charles Dickens' 1843 novella *A Christmas Carol*.

Batman: Noel was a remarkable work on a number of levels—first and foremost, Bermejo's incorporation of *A Christmas Carol* into the book's plot was beautifully done. The other aspect of the book that was so amazing was that Bermejo's story and artwork managed to take in huge amount of Batman history in just over 100 pages. The book was not tied to any particular Batman continuity, so Bermejo was free to draw on a wide variety of notable interpretations of the character.

For example, some scenes in *Batman: Noel* invoked the look and spirit of the 1960s screen Batman, while others invoked the look and spirit of Christopher Nolan's Batman films. The book contained scenes that recalled Batman's team-ups with Superman in their long running comic title *World's Finest*, as well as scenes that recalled Batman's classic comic battles with villains such as the Catwoman and the Joker. Bermejo used his incredible talent to create his own unique vision of Batman and his world in *Batman: Noel*, one that struck just the right balance between being innovative and being respectful of the character's rich history.

Speaking of Nolan, I think it is probably about time for us to return to his cinematic vision of Batman. In the next chapter, we'll discuss the final film in his Batman trilogy, *The Dark Knight Rises* (2012).

20

The Dark Knight Rises (2012)

Cast: Christian Bale (Batman/Bruce Wayne), Michael Caine (Alfred), Gary Oldman (Jim Gordon), Anne Hathaway (Selina Kyle), Tom Hardy (Bane), Marion Cotillard (Miranda), Joseph Gordon-Levitt (Blake), Morgan Freeman (Lucius Fox), Matthew Modine (Foley), Ben Mendelsohn (Daggett), Burn Gorman (Stryver), Alon Moni Aboutboul (Dr. Pavel), Juno Temple (Jen), Daniel Sunjata (Captain Jones), Chris Ellis (Fr. Reilly), Tom Conti (Prisoner), Nestor Carbonell (Mayor), Brett Cullen (Congressman), Aidan Gillen (CIA Op), Sam Kennard (Special Ops Sergeant), Aliash Tepina (Hooded Man #2), Nick Julian (Caterer), Miranda Nolan (Maid #2), Claire Julien (Maid #3), Reggie Lee (Ross), Joseph Lyle Taylor (DWP Man), Tyler Dean Flores (Mark), Duane Henry (SWAT in Dive Bar), James Harvey Ward (SWAT in Alley), Gonzalo Menendez (Cop in Manhole), Cameron Jack (Sewer Thug #1), Lex Daniel (Sewer Thug #2), Thomas Lennon (Doctor), Trevor White (Yuppie), Rob Brown (Allen), Fredric Lehne (Exchange Security Chief), Courtney Munch (Female Security Guard), Chris Hill (Paparazzi #1), Travis Guba (Paparazzi #2), Jay Benedict (Rich Twit), Will Estes (Officer Simon Jansen), David Dayan Fisher (Shoe Shine Man at GSE), P. J. Griffith (Sniper at Exchange) Glen Powell (Trader #1), Ben Cornish (Trader #2), Russ Fega (Trader #3), Andres Perez-Molina (Valet at Museum), Brent Briscoe (Veteran Cop), John Nolan (Fredericks), Oliver Cotton (2 Star Air Force General), Mark Killeen (Airport Cop), Sarah Goldberg (Analyst #1), John Macmillan (Analyst #2), Robert Wisdom (Army Captain at Bridge), Ronnie Gene Blevins (Cement Truck Driver), John Hollingworth (CIA Analyst), Ian Bohen (Cop with Gordon), Uri Gavriel (Blind Prisoner), Noel G. (Ex-Prisoner at River), Max Schuler (Foley's Kid), Daina Griffith (Foley's Wife), Hector Atreyu Ruiz (Gangbanger), Patrick Cox (Huge Inmate), Aramis Knight (Kid with Apple), Josh Stewart (Barsad), William Devane (President), Harry Coles (Younger Prison Child), Joey King (Older Prison Child), Liam Neeson (Ra's Al Ghul), Julie Mun (Reporter at Stadium), Cillian Murphy (Dr. Jonathan Crane), David Gyasi (Skinny Prisoner), Patrick Jordan (Special Forces #2), Joshua Elijah Reese (Mercenary at City Hall), Desmond Harrington (Uniform), Mychael Bates (Bomb Truck Driver), Rory Nolan (Little Boy at Bridge), Tomas Arana (Wayne's Lawyer), Peter Holden (Applied Sciences Tech #1), David Monahan (Applied Sciences Tech #2), Jillian Armenante (Lawyer's Clerk), Aja Evans (Greeter at Museum), Aldous Davidson (Valet at Wayne Enterprises), Michael James Faradie (Guard at Blackgate), Wade Williams (Warden at Blackgate), Antwan Lewis (Reporter at Wayne Enterprises), Jake Canuso (Waiter in Florence Café), Josh Pence (Young Ra's Al Ghul), India Wadsworth (Warlord's Daughter), Kevin Kiely (Thug #1 in Basement), Daniel Newman (Thug #2 in Basement), Massi Furlan (Janitor at GSE), Warren Brown (Mercenary Security #1), Luke Rutherford (Mercenary Security #2), Phillip Browne (Mercenary Security #3), Christopher Judge (Mercenary Security #4), Aldo Bigante (2nd Cop with Gordon), Charles Jackson Coyne (Anthem Singer), Patrick Leahy (Board Member #2), Todd Gearhart (Uniform #2). *Producers:* Emma Thomas, Christopher Nolan, Charles Roven. *Executive Producers:* Benjamin Melniker, Michael E. Uslan, Kevin De La Noy, Thomas Tull. *Co-Producer:* Jordan Goldberg. *Director:* Christopher Nolan. *Screenplay:* Jonathan Nolan, Christopher Nolan (Story by Christopher Nolan and David S. Goyer, based upon characters appearing in comic books published by DC Comics, Batman created by Bob Kane). *Director of Photography:* Wally Pfister. *Production Designers:* Nathan Crowley, Kevin Kavanaugh. *Editor:* Lee Smith. *Music:* Hans Zimmer. *Visual Effects Supervisor:* Paul Franklin. *Special Effects Supervisor:* Chris Corbould. *Costume Designer:* Lindy Hemming. *Casting:* John Papsidera. *Studio:* Warner Bros. *Length:* 165 minutes. *United States Release Date:* July 20, 2012.

Obviously, the history-making success of *The Dark Knight* led Warner Bros. to give Christopher Nolan free rein in terms of exactly where he would decide to take the studio's Batman film franchise next. After the release of *The Dark Knight*, the director did exactly what he did after the release of *Batman Begins*— he chose to tackle a non–Batman film project before returning to his cinematic vision of Batman. This particular project brought Nolan almost as much mind-boggling success as *The Dark Knight* had brought him — the 2010 science fiction film *Inception* starring Leonardo DiCaprio, Ken Watanabe, Joseph Gordon-Levitt, Marion Cotillard, Ellen Page and Tom Hardy was a gigantic commercial and critical hit, grossing over $820 million worldwide.[1]

Inception's triumph had to be a deeply personal one for Nolan, because the film was truly *his* in almost every way. It was written by him from the ground up — in other words, he did not have to work with a bunch of characters created by someone else like he had to do when he was scripting his Batman films. And of course, it was directed and co-produced by him as well. (His wife Emma Thomas was the film's other producer.) *The Dark Knight* and *Inception* had catapulted Nolan to the very top of the motion picture industry, and the director was now considered to be one of the most influential and respected filmmakers in the world.

Nolan decided that he only had one more Batman film in him, and he wanted to bring his cinematic vision of the character to a definite close with that film. As he had done with his two previous Batman movies, he laid out a story for the film with David S. Goyer. That story was turned into a finished script by Nolan and his brother Jonathan. Of course, this was the second Batman screenplay the two brothers had written together — they had previously collaborated on the script for *The Dark Knight*. The classic Batman villains that the Nolan brothers and Goyer decided to feature in this new screenplay were Selina Kyle/the Catwoman and Bane. Of course, both of these characters had been used in Warner's Batman film franchise before — Catwoman had appeared in Tim Burton's *Batman Returns*, and Bane had appeared in Joel Schumacher's *Batman and Robin*.

While the script was still taking shape, the Nolan brothers decided that the title of

Christian Bale as Batman in *The Dark Knight Rises* (2012).

the finished film would be *The Dark Knight Rises*. This title hinted at the film's overall concept — its plot would center around Batman coming out of a long, self-imposed retirement, and rising to prominence in Gotham City once more.

Most all of the creative team that had been with Nolan throughout his directorial career was back on board for *The Dark Knight Rises*. That team included producer (and wife!) Emma Thomas, production designer Nathan Crowley, special effects supervisor Chris Corbould, costume designer Lindy Hemming, and cinematographer Wally Pfister. Nolan also retained many of the principal actors who appeared in *Batman Begins* and *The Dark Knight* for *The Dark Knight Rises*. In the film, Christian Bale would play Batman/Bruce Wayne, Michael Caine would play Alfred, Gary Oldman would play Jim Gordon, Morgan Freeman would play Lucius Fox, and Cillian Murphy would make a cameo appearance as Dr. Jonathan Crane, a.k.a. the Scarecrow. The cast and crew of Nolan's Batman films already had two incredibly successful productions under their belt, and they were very confident that this third production would also be a smash hit.

Nolan's choices to play the new main characters appearing *The Dark Knight Rises* were definitely influenced by the casting choices he had made for *Inception*. Indeed, three of those roles went to actors who had received top billing in that film. Tom Hardy was picked to play Bane, Marion Cotillard was picked to play Miranda Tate, and Joseph Gordon-Levitt was picked to play John Blake. (Obviously, there ended up being a lot more to both Cotillard's and Gordon-Levitt's roles than them just being "Tate" and "Blake," respectively — we'll discuss the full nature of their roles in detail later in the chapter.)

However, the role of Selina Kyle/the Catwoman went to someone who would be working with the director for the first time — the director chose Anne Hathaway for the part. Hathaway had first achieved wide recognition through her starring roles in light comedies such as *The Princess Diaries* (2001), but she showcased her range as a dramatic actress when she appeared in the critically acclaimed film *Brokeback Mountain* (2005).

In casting *The Dark Knight Rises*, Nolan had definitely followed the pattern he had established for *Batman Begins* and *The Dark Knight* — he had loaded the film with a truly stellar ensemble of well-known actors. And once again, cost was certainly no issue in terms of Nolan picking the actors he wanted for the film. Given the director's recent track record at the box office, Warner Bros. gave him an even bigger budget for *The Dark Knight Rises* than they had for *The Dark Knight* — about $250 million.[2]

The Dark Knight Rises' gigantic budget also allowed Nolan to shape the film into an even more grandiose production than *The Dark Knight* had been. This time around, Nolan's cinematic vision of Batman would take on the feel of an epic war movie rather than an urban crime drama. In this author's opinion, Nolan's decision to realize Batman and his world in this fashion in *The Dark Knight Rises* did not end up meshing very well with the time-honored traditions of the character — but we'll get to that later in the chapter.

As he had done with his previous two Batman films, Nolan dreamt up a brand-new unusual mode of transportation for Batman to use in *The Dark Knight Rises*. In the movie, Batman would take to the skies in a futuristic wingless aircraft that was kind of a hybrid between a jet and a helicopter. The aircraft was dubbed "the Bat," and it looked very much like a flying version of the Tumbler. A full-size model of the Bat was constructed for use in the film — but like the Batwings featured in Burton's and Schumacher's Batman films, the Bat could not actually fly in real life. So all of *The Dark Knight Rises*' scenes showing the aircraft in action were realized through the use of special effects. (We'll discuss the different special effects that were used to create the film's Bat scenes a bit later in the chapter.)

20—The Dark Knight Rises *(2012)*

Anne Hathaway as Selina Kyle/The Catwoman in *The Dark Knight Rises* (2012).

Like *The Dark Knight*, *The Dark Knight Rises* would be partially shot in IMAX format. But the film's IMAX footage would not be limited just to establishing shots and a relatively few number of sequences like *The Dark Knight*'s IMAX footage had been — Nolan would end up using roughly *twice* as much IMAX footage in the film as he did in *The Dark Knight*. So IMAX would bring even more grandeur and detail to *The Dark Knight Rises* than it had brought to *The Dark Knight*.

Shooting for *The Dark Knight Rises* commenced in May 2011, when Nolan and company traveled to Jaipur, Rajasthan, a rural area of India. In Jaipur, scenes showing Bruce escaping from an underground prison run by Bane were filmed. The production then returned to film in the United Kingdom at the massive Cardington Sheds hangar. That hangar had served Nolan very well during the making of *Batman Begins* and *The Dark Knight*, and it was again used to great effect for *The Dark Knight Rises*. Two massive sets were constructed there — those sets were Bane's lair located deep in the sewers of Gotham City, and parts of Bane's underground prison located in an unspecified foreign country.[3]

The interior shots of a CIA plane hijacked by Bane were filmed just outside of Cardington Sheds. The fuselage of the plane was mounted on a hydraulic lift which allowed it to be tilted into a near-vertical position — this was done in order to show Bane's men wrecking the plane by attaching cables to it from a much larger plane flying above. The exterior shots of the plane hijacking were filmed in the skies over Inverness in the Scottish Highlands.[4]

Christian Bale as Batman and Tom Hardy as Bane in *The Dark Knight Rises* (2012).

This spectacular sequence was filmed entirely in IMAX, and it would end up opening the film. It was completely finished up well before the release of *The Dark Knight Rises* so that it could be used as one of the film's major promotional tools—dubbed "*The Dark Knight Rises* IMAX Prologue," Warner Bros. released the sequence with selected IMAX screenings of the film *Mission: Impossible — Ghost Protocol* in December 2011. (As we noted earlier in the book, this marketing strategy was first employed to promote the release of *The Dark Knight*—"*The Dark Knight* IMAX Prologue" was released with selected IMAX screenings of the film *I Am Legend* in December 2007.)

After nine weeks of shooting in the United Kingdom, the film's cast and crew traveled to the United States for about a month of location shooting in Pittsburgh, Pennsylvania. Nolan had used the city of Chicago to realize his vision of Gotham City in his first two Batman films, but he decided that it was time for a change of scenery in *The Dark Knight Rises*—so for several weeks during the summer of 2011, "the Steel City" became "Gotham City."[5]

Some of the film's most memorable sequences were filmed in Pittsburgh. Bane's attack on the Gotham Rogues' football stadium was filmed at Heinz Field, the home of the Pittsburgh Steelers football team. In the sequence, Bane detonates massive explosives in the stadium as the Rogues face off against the Rapid City Monuments in front of a huge hometown crowd. This sequence was filmed with over ten thousand extras in the stadium, most all of them wearing the Rogues' team colors of black and yellow. Some of the Rogues football players were portrayed by real-life Steelers—in fact, the Rogues player that returns the Monument's kickoff for a touchdown in the film is the team's longtime wide receiver Hines Ward.

Of course, the explosives that destroy the stadium in the sequence were all created through the use of special effects—the only explosives that were actually detonated while the scene was being filmed were relatively small charges set in piles of turf located on the stadium field. Incidentally, I can't resist pointing out that my wife and I traveled from our hometown of Columbus, Ohio to Pittsburgh in order to be extras in this sequence—it was fascinating to watch Nolan and company work on such an incredibly large and complex scene. Oh, and if you want to pick us out in one of the sequence's crowd scenes, we are two of the yellow dots!

Several important sequences found in the climax of *The Dark Knight Rises* were filmed in Pittsburgh as well. The fight between Batman and Bane that takes place in the middle of the battle between the Gotham City Police and Bane's men was filmed at Carnegie Mellon University, and the Bat's pursuit of a truck carrying a nuclear bomb was filmed on several of the city's downtown streets. These shots of the Bat in action were accomplished by mounting the aircraft atop a crane truck. Cameras filmed the Bat being driven around by the truck—and then the truck was digitally removed from the shots, making it appear as if the Bat was really flying.[6]

Most all of the film's scenes that were shot in Pittsburgh were supposed to be taking place in the cold of late fall and winter—since these scenes were being shot in the stifling summer heat, drastic measures had to be taken to get them into the "right" season. Those measures included a lot of heavy clothes being worn by cast members and extras in near-100 degree temperatures, and a lot of fake snow on the ground!

After the Pittsburgh shoot was complete, Nolan and company headed to Los Angeles, California for about nine weeks of filming. There was one particularly important set for the film constructed in Los Angeles—the rebuilt Batcave was a gigantic set that rivaled the scope and size of the Batcave set built for *Batman Begins* at Shepperton Studios in England. Like the *Batman Begins* Batcave, *The Dark Knight Rises* Batcave was outfitted with scores of water pumps to create a huge waterfall and underground river that ran through the set.[7] The main thing about the set that was so different from the *Batman Begins* set was that it housed Batman's costume and crimefighting equipment *under* the river—Batman's costume and equipment were encased in waterproof cubes that could be hydraulically lifted out of the water when needed.

The Dark Knight Rises wrapped up filming in New York City in November 2011. The movie's climactic battle between the Gotham City Police and Bane's men was shot on Wall Street using over a thousand extras. The New York City shoot also included scenes showing the Bat in flight—these scenes were accomplished by suspending the aircraft from cables.[8]

After the principal photography for *The Dark Knight Rises* had been completed, Nolan began work on overseeing the film's post-production in Los Angeles. Like his previous two Batman movies, *The Dark Knight Rises* would end up featuring many scenes that were created using computer-generated images. These images included scenes showing the Bat in flight, and scenes featuring Catwoman performing incredible maneuvers on the Bat-Pod.[9]

And also like Nolan's previous two Batman movies, *The Dark Knight Rises* utilized miniature sets to realize several of its spectacular scenes. The previously-mentioned sequence in which Bane wrecks a CIA plane used a miniature of the plane in the filming of the actual crash scene. Also, a scene showing Bane using explosions to gain access to Wayne Enterprises from his underground lair was shot using a one-third scale model of that lair.[10]

Hans Zimmer and James Newton Howard had worked together to compose musical scores for both *Batman Begins* and *The Dark Knight*—but this time around Howard bowed out of the project, so Zimmer composed the score for *The Dark Knight Rises* on his own. Like the soundtracks for Nolan's first two Batman films, the soundtrack for *The Dark Knight Rises* was very ambient in nature, featuring compositions that consisted of hypnotic percussion patterns and long-held musical tones.

However, this new score was different from its predecessors in one noticeable way— Zimmer chose to feature human voices performing a rhythmic Moroccan chant as part of the score. The chant's loose English translation was "he rises," which fit in very nicely with the film's concept of Batman rising to prominence in Gotham once more.

The manner in which Zimmer decided to record the chant was a very novel one — he invited fans of Nolan's Batman films to record themselves performing the chant, and then send those recordings to him via the Internet. Zimmer received an overwhelming response to this invitation — around 180,000 people ended up chanting for him! All of these chant recordings were then mixed together to realize the final chant heard in the film.[11]

As we discussed earlier in the book, Warner Bros. created quite a bit of very innovative promotion for *The Dark Knight* such as the direct-to-video animated movie *Batman: Gotham Knight*, several History Channel documentaries, and a number of fictional websites based on the film. The studio's promotion for *The Dark Knight Rises* was nowhere near as diverse as this promotion for *The Dark Knight*—still, Warner did end up producing one Batman television documentary that tied into the film. *The Batmobile* premiered on the CW Network (a network partially owned by Warner) in mid–July, 2012, and it examined the history of Batman's famous ride in the comics and on the screen. The highlight of the program was footage showing the first-ever gathering of the five big screen Batmobiles that took place in Burbank, California in April 2012. The Batmobiles in attendance were the 1966 *Batman* Batmobile, the 1989 *Batman* Batmobile, the *Batman Forever* Batmobile, the 1997 *Batman and Robin* Batmobile, and the Tumbler.

And of course, Warner Bros. promoted *The Dark Knight Rises* by creating an elaborate official website for the film — the site was launched by the studio about a year before the movie's premiere date. In the months leading up to the film's release, the site featured a wealth of *The Dark Knight Rises* information —visitors could look at production photos, watch videos of the film's theatrical previews, and read biographies of the film's cast and crew. Incidentally, Warner has continued to maintain and update the site right up to the present day, so it still functions as a marvelous resource designed to enhance one's appreciation of the film.

The world premiere of *The Dark Knight Rises* was held in the IMAX theatre at AMC Loews Lincoln Square in New York City on July 16, 2012. Much of the film's principal onscreen and offscreen talent attended the event, including Bale, Oldman, Hathaway, Hardy, Cotillard, Gordon-Levitt, Freeman, and Nolan. Several days later, on July 20, *The Dark Knight* opened in theatres throughout the United States.

Tragically, the U.S. opening of *The Dark Knight Rises* cannot be recounted without taking note of the horrifying events that took place in Aurora, Colorado, on the night of the film's premiere. During a midnight showing of the film at a movie theatre in that city, a crazed gunman opened fire on the audience inside the theatre, killing 12 people and injuring 58 others. The terrible attack shocked the entire world, and cast a pall over the movie's highly-anticipated release. Needless to say, the tragedy deeply affected the cast and crew of *The Dark Knight Rises*. Bale chose to reach out to the victims of the shooting personally— he visited with a number of them at an Aurora hospital several days after the incident.[12]

It is hard to move on after having to discuss this awful event—but let's try to do just that and go through the film itself. *The Dark Knight Rises* opens with an image of a bat silhouette coming through layers of ice. We are then taken to a memorial service for Harvey Dent for just a moment, where Gotham City Police Commissioner Jim Gordon is speaking. The meaning of Gordon's words might not be clear to those in attendance, but they are certainly clear to us—he says "I *believed* in Harvey Dent." Obviously, Dent's murderous actions as Two-Face right before his death shattered Gordon's belief in Gotham's heroic D.A. into a million pieces.

The scene shifts to an airstrip somewhere in Eastern Europe, where a CIA plane is taking a nuclear physicist named Dr. Leonid Pavel into their custody. The CIA agent in charge of the operation is persuaded to take several other men wearing shackles and hoods into custody as well, because he is told that the men worked for a dangerous mercenary known only as "Bane." Once aboard the plane, the CIA agent interrogates the men, trying to gain information about Bane. He is shocked to learn that Bane himself is actually one of the men—Bane's demeanor is oddly serene, and he wears a strange-looking mask over his nose and mouth.

For a moment, the CIA agent thinks he has bagged himself a major prize, but Bane has orchestrated a daring plan to grab Pavel for himself and crash the CIA plane. Bane's own plane, a much larger aircraft, swoops in and drops cables that connect to the CIA plane. The cables force the CIA plane to tip forward, ripping its wings off. Right before the CIA plane is completely destroyed, Bane grabs Pavel and spirits him onto his plane using one of the cables. Just what Bane intends to do with Pavel is not made clear at this point.

Back in Gotham City, a new holiday known as "Harvey Dent Day" is being celebrated. It has been eight years since Dent's death, and a bill called the "Dent Act" passed after Dent was killed has virtually ended organized crime in Gotham. At Wayne Manor, a charity event honoring Dent's memory is being held, but Bruce Wayne is nowhere to be found—he has become a total recluse over the past few years, hiding in his rebuilt mansion. (Remember, Ra's Al Ghul burned the Manor to the ground when he tried to destroy Gotham, and it was still being rebuilt at the time of Dent's death.) Batman has also vanished from Gotham as well—the crimefighter completely disappeared after he supposedly murdered Harvey Dent.

Gordon prepares to speak at the Wayne Manor event. He has written a speech telling the truth about Dent—the speech will reveal that *Dent* was the insane murderer the night he was killed, not Batman. But as Gordon steps to the podium, he changes his mind about delivering the speech, instead slipping it back into his pocket. Gordon then says that Dent's death was not in vain because there are over a thousand inmates being held without bail in Blackgate Prison as a result of the Dent Act. As Gordon speaks, a shadowy figure watches him from the roof of Wayne Manor—it is Bruce.

Inside the Manor, a waitress named Selina Kyle delivers a plate of food to Bruce's room on Alfred's order. Bruce confronts Selina there, because she has stolen his mother's pearls from a high-tech safe that was supposedly uncrackable. Bruce's years as a recluse have not been kind to him—he is bearded, disheveled, and using a cane to help him walk. Selina kicks Bruce's cane out from under him and jumps out of the window, making off with the pearls. She hitches a ride with a congressman who is leaving the party.

Bruce examines the safe that Selina robbed, and he realizes that for some unknown reason she had dusted it for prints. Meanwhile, Gordon is back at the Gotham City Police Station, where a rookie cop named John Blake talks to him. Blake tells the Commissioner that the congressman never made it home after leaving the Wayne event. Blake also asks

Gordon about Batman — it is obvious that Blake doesn't buy the story that Batman killed Dent eight years ago.

Back at Wayne Manor, Alfred finds Bruce in the Batcave, where he is investigating Selina Kyle. He learns that she was only posing as a waitress — in reality she is a master cat burglar, and she had dusted the safe for *his* prints while she was robbing it. Alfred interrupts Bruce's investigation to tell him that Bruce needs to get back out into the world, but Bruce says that there is nothing out there for him since Rachel Dawes died. Alfred responds to this by telling Bruce a story. During the seven years that Bruce had left Gotham, Alfred would take a summer holiday to Florence, Italy. Alfred hoped to see Bruce there, maybe with a wife and children — then he would know that Bruce had made it out of his tragic life. Alfred ends this story by saying that he never wanted to see Bruce return to Gotham because there was nothing there for him but pain.

The next day, Officer Blake goes to the scene of a mysterious death — the body of a young man from a Gotham orphanage has washed out of one of the city's sewers. Blake goes to the orphanage to inform them of the boy's death — coincidentally, it is the same one where he grew up after his parents were killed. Blake learns that boys have been going down into the sewers because they have heard that there is some sort of "work" for them down there.

That night, Selina goes to a seedy bar to take copies of Bruce's fingerprints to a man named Stryver, who works for a powerful but corrupt Gotham businessman named John Daggett. Daggett runs his own very successful construction company, and he also sits on the board of Wayne Enterprises. Stryver is supposed to have something for Selina in return for the fingerprints, but instead of giving her anything he is simply going to have some of Daggett's henchmen kill her. But Selina has planned ahead — she brought the missing congressman with her and used his cell phone so that the Gotham Police will track the number and immediately storm the bar. They do just that, and some of the cops pursue Daggett's henchmen as they try to escape into the sewers under Gotham. Selina is then able to escape the scene unnoticed.

Gordon is one of the cops that go into the sewers, and down there he is overpowered by a number of men. The men are working for Bane, who has established a headquarters in the sewers. They take Gordon to Bane — the mercenary searches the Commissioner, and takes his speech that tells the truth about Dent from him. Gordon is able to escape from Bane by rolling into the sewer waters, which carry him out to the sewer tunnel where the young man's body had recently washed up. Blake, playing a hunch that Gordon might end up at that tunnel as well, goes to the tunnel and finds the Commissioner there, gravely wounded. Deputy Commissioner Foley, one of Gordon's friends on the Gotham Police force, takes command of the force after Gordon is hurt.

The next day, Blake goes to see Bruce at Wayne Manor to tell him that Gordon has been injured, and that Gordon spoke of a masked man with an underground army. Blake tells Bruce that Gordon needs Batman. Bruce wonders why Blake is telling him all of this, and Blake responds by saying that he knows Bruce is Batman. Blake met Bruce at his orphanage years ago, and somehow during this meeting Blake just instinctively knew that Bruce was the crimefighter.

Blake's visit spurs Bruce into action — he learns that Bane is financially connected to Daggett. Bruce surmises that Daggett must have brought the mercenary to Gotham so that the two men could join forces. Bruce also goes to the hospital to have his leg examined, but his doctor's appointment is only part of the reason why he has gone there. He puts on a mask and sneaks into Gordon's hospital room in order to visit his wounded ally. Bruce tries to convince Gordon that "Batman wasn't needed anymore" after the passage of the Dent Act, but Gordon says that Batman must return to fight this new evil that has come to Gotham.

Bruce follows Selina to a charity ball held by Miranda Tate, who had been working with Bruce on a Wayne Enterprises nuclear fusion energy project some years ago. Miranda chides Bruce for giving up on the project and going into seclusion, but Bruce has more pressing concerns than Miranda's disapproval. He finds Selina, dances with her, and takes back his mother's pearls. But Selina still ends up getting the better of Bruce—she leaves the party before him and steals his Lamborghini!

The next day, Bruce goes to see Lucius Fox at Wayne Enterprises because he wants to know why the company has been in such dire financial straits as of late. Fox tells Bruce that all of the company's fiscal woes stem the fact that Bruce spent so much money on the energy project and then completely mothballed it. Fox also sees Bruce's visit as a chance to show him some of the new Wayne Enterprises equipment that Fox has been safekeeping over the years. Bruce tells Fox that he has retired from crimefighting, and that he has no interest in such equipment—even still, Bruce cannot help but be impressed by a futuristic aircraft that Fox shows to him. Fox says that the aircraft has a long, uninteresting name, so he has just taken to calling it "the Bat." The Bat has a problem with its autopilot system, so Fox suggests that Bruce look into fixing it.

Back at the Batcave, Bruce straps on a futuristic knee brace that gives his leg full mobility again. Alfred then tells Bruce what he has learned about Bane—the mercenary was born and raised in a horrible prison on the other side of the world. Bane managed to escape the prison, and he was taken in by Ra's Al Ghul—Ra's trained him to be a part of his band of mercenaries known as the League of Shadows, but Bane was so extreme that Ra's excommunicated him from the League. Alfred is afraid that Bruce will not be able to defeat Bane as Batman—in fact, Alfred believes that Bruce has become so troubled that he will *want* Bane to defeat him. In other words, Alfred sees Bruce's potential return to the cape and cowl as nothing more than an elaborate suicide attempt.

At the Gotham Stock Exchange, traders are frantically doing their business as usual when they are attacked by Bane and his men. They shoot their way in with automatic weapons, killing at least one person in the process, and then Bane hacks into the Exchange's computer system. The Gotham City Police Department rushes to the scene, but Bane and some of his men escape on motorcycles while carrying hostages. The police give chase, and so does Batman on his Bat-Pod. Batman is armed with an electromagnetic pulse gun that enables him to shut down all types of machinery, so he brings several of the motorcycles that Bane's men are riding to a dead stop.

Deputy Commissioner Foley gets word that Batman is back, and he immediately suspends the force's pursuit of Bane and his men in order to apprehend the crimefighter. Blake is skeptical of this decision, but Foley says to him, "Who do you want to catch? Some robber, or the son-of-a-bitch that killed Harvey Dent?" Just as scores of police are bearing down on him, Batman overpowers one of Bane's men—he is carrying the laptop computer that was used to hack into the Exchange's computer system. The crimefighter is able to drive off on his Bat-Pod with the laptop just before the police reach him. Batman rides into a dead-end alley, and Foley thinks he has the crimefighter trapped. The assumption turns out to be spectacularly wrong when Batman files out of the alley in the Bat.

While Batman has been in action, Selina has been at Daggett's home dressed in her black cat burglar outfit. She is trying to steal a computer program known as the "clean slate," which can erase a person from every computer database in the world — the program is the item that Daggett had promised her if she could come up with Bruce's fingerprints. Daggett interrupts her burglary and tells her that the clean slate is nothing more than a myth — it does not exist. Selina does not believe Daggett, and she whisks him out of his home to interrogate him further. But she is not able to do this when Daggett's heavily-armed men arrive on the scene and begin firing on her. Batman bursts into the fray — he and Selina fight off the men, jump into the Bat, and make their escape. Bane arrives on the scene just in time to see them fly away.

Batman learns from Selina that she sold Bruce's fingerprints to Daggett, and the crimefighter quickly realizes the connection between the stolen prints and the stock market raid. Back at the Batcave, Alfred scolds Bruce for assuming the guise of Batman again — Alfred still believes that Bruce simply cannot defeat Bane as Batman. Alfred is so convinced that Bruce is wrong to again don the cape and cowl that he leaves Bruce for good. Before he leaves, Alfred reveals to Bruce that he burned the letter that Rachel had written to Bruce before she was killed by the Joker — in that letter, Rachel had told Bruce that she was leaving him for Harvey Dent. Bruce, crushed by Alfred's deception, bids a tearful goodbye to his closest confidant.

The next day, Fox comes to Wayne Manor to see Bruce. Scores of fake trades were made using Bruce's stolen fingerprints, and these trades have completely bankrupted Wayne Enterprises. Bruce, fearing that the company will fall under the control of Daggett, arranges a meeting with Miranda Tate to show her their nuclear fusion reactor. It turns out that the reactor is completely operable — Bruce chose to shut the project down several years earlier because Leonid Pavel had published a report that detailed how the reactor could be converted into a nuclear bomb. After showing Miranda the reactor, Bruce convinces her to run his company while he sorts out the fake trade problem.

Later, Daggett meets with Bane — Daggett is angry that Miranda was chosen to run Wayne Enterprises over him, but he has no idea of the trouble he has put himself in by aligning with Bane. Bane no longer needs Daggett's help to take over Gotham City, so he casually breaks the corrupt businessman's neck, killing him instantly. Meanwhile, Bruce goes to Selina's apartment, and he asks her to help Batman find Bane's sewer headquarters. At the same time, Officer Blake meets with Gordon in his hospital room — Gordon promotes Blake to the rank of detective in order to help him track down Bane.

That night, Bruce arrives back at Wayne Manor to find Miranda waiting for him. They give into their attraction for one another and sleep together. But Bruce does not stay at the Manor with Miranda for long — he dons his Batman costume and meets Selina down in the Gotham sewers. Selina takes him to Bane's headquarters, but it turns out that she has set a trap for the crimefighter — Bane knows she is bringing Batman to him. In fact, Bane even knows that Batman's true identity is Bruce Wayne. Batman and Bane engage in a ferocious fight, but the crimefighter is defeated by the mercenary — Bane lifts Batman into the air and brings Batman down hard on his knee, breaking the crimefighter's back. Bane then sets off a series of explosions that allow him to gain access to Wayne Enterprises — he then commandeers all of the equipment Bruce had used to fight crime as Batman, including several Tumblers.

The next day, Blake tries to locate Bruce, but he instead finds Selina, who is trying to flee the city. Selina is taken into custody and held at Blackgate Prison. Bruce, who has survived his backbreaking encounter with Bane, is also taken into custody — Bane takes him to the horrible underground prison where the mercenary was born and raised. Bane tells Bruce that he is going to torture all of Gotham and eventually destroy the city entirely, and Bruce will be forced to watch his actions from prison.

Back in Gotham, Bane breaks into a Wayne Enterprises board meeting, kidnaps Fox and Miranda, and takes them into the sewers. Gordon learns of the kidnappings and sends every Gotham cop into the sewers to find Bane. Bane makes Fox and Miranda power up the nuclear fusion reactor, and then he makes his other hostage Dr. Pavel turn the reactor into a nuclear bomb. But Bane's insane scheme to destroy Gotham has only just begun. For months, he had been directing Daggett's construction crews to pour cement mixed with explosives all over the city. This allows him to detonate explosives throughout Gotham that destroy every bridge and tunnel that connects the city with the rest of the world. These explosions also trap most all of Gotham's police officers in the sewers. In an instant, Bane is able to separate Gotham from the world and hold the entire city hostage.

In order to make everyone in Gotham aware of what he has done to the city, Bane has also had his explosive cement poured underneath the field of the Gotham Rogues' football stadium. So as he detonates all of his explosives, the Rogues' football field is blown to bits along with all of the city's bridges and tunnels. Bane's timing is horrifyingly perfect — the field is blown up just as the Rogues are facing off against the Rapid City Monuments in front of a huge hometown crowd. Bane walks out to address the stunned crowd after the field has been blown up — he has Dr. Pavel explain how powerful the nuclear bomb really is, and then he kills Pavel. Bane then tells the crowd that the bomb can be detonated by an anonymous citizen who is in possession of a remote trigger to the bomb, and that person *will* trigger the bomb if anyone should try to enter or to leave the city.

Luckily, there are still some people in Gotham who are trying to oppose Bane's takeover of the city. Blake is able to rescue Gordon from his hospital room, and the two do their best to stay hidden from Bane's men and to work on piecing together a resistance movement.

Some time later, Bane goes to Blackgate Prison to hold a makeshift press conference. He reads Gordon's speech that tells the truth about Harvey Dent and Batman. Bane then declares that since the Dent Act is based on a lie, all of the prisoners in Blackgate should be set free. So Bane frees all of these prisoners, including Selina. People all over Gotham start rioting and taking over the posh homes that belong to wealthy Gothamites.

In Bane's prison, an inmate tells Bruce the story of how Ra's Al Ghul and his wife were once held there. Ra's married the daughter of a wealthy warlord, but the warlord did not approve of Ra's, so he sentenced Ra's to the prison. The daughter took Ra's' place in the prison, and she was pregnant with Ra's' child. But before Bruce can find out just who Ra's' child was, the inmate works on fixing Bruce's broken back by punching his displaced vertebrae back into place. Bruce can walk again, and he begins to work on rebuilding his body so that he can escape from the prison and save Gotham. During this time, Bruce also learns that Bane wears his mask because he was injured in a prison fight, and his injuries never healed properly — so the mask helps to keep his constant pain under control.

To escape the underground prison, Bruce has to climb up a well-like pit that leads to the outside world, and then leap from one ledge to another ledge that appears to be impossibly far from the first ledge. Bruce makes the climb with a rope tied around his waist, but he cannot make the jump between the ledges, so he takes a very hard fall. Bruce learns that the child of Ra's made this jump and escaped the prison many years ago — Bruce assumes that this child must have been Bane himself.

Back in Gotham, U.S. Special Forces officers manage to infiltrate the city, and they meet with Gordon and Blake. All of these lawmen are briefed by Fox and Miranda, who have been working to keep themselves hidden from Bane. They explain that the bomb's fuel cells are decaying — this means that the bomb will go off in a matter of weeks if it is not reconnected to its reactor. And the bomb has been almost impossible to locate, because it is constantly being transported in a lead-lined truck. The Special Forces officers have no time to digest all of this bad news, because they are attacked and killed by Bane and his men.

Bruce makes another attempt to escape the prison, but he again fails to make the jump between the ledges. However, the third time he is successful — he is able to rise from the prison, and make his way back to Gotham so that he can try to save his city. Once he is back in Gotham, he finds Selina, and he asks her to find a way to get him to Fox. Bruce even has a present for Selina — it turns out that the clean slate program is real, and he gives her a copy of it so that she will be able to start her troubled life over. Meanwhile, Gordon is out on the streets of Gotham, trying to figure out where the bomb is, and he is captured by Bane's men. Selina gets Bruce to Fox, but the men are also captured by Bane's men. Selina is able to free them so that they can formulate a plan to disable the bomb's remote trigger.

Gordon is forced to stand trial in front of Bane's perverse version of a court that is presided over by none other than Dr. Jonathan Crane, a.k.a. the Scarecrow. Crane sentences Gordon to "death by exile," which means Gordon will have to walk across the dangerously thin ice covering the river that separates Gotham from the rest of the world. Batman shows up just in the nick of time to save Gordon — he attacks Bane's men that are sending the Commissioner out onto the ice. Batman then gives Gordon a device that will block the remote trigger to the bomb — the crimefighter instructs Gordon to find the bomb and place the device on it.

Batman is also able to save Blake from Bane's men, and the two clear a path out of the sewers that allows all of the Gotham police to finally get above ground again. Batman then sets Selina up on his Bat-Pod so that she can clear a path out of one of Gotham's tunnels so that Gothamites can get free of the city before the bomb goes off.

The entire Gotham Police force plans an attack on Bane's men, who are stationed at Gotham City Hall. As Batman flies over the building in the Bat, the officers race down the street on foot, attacking Bane's men and engaging them in hand-to-hand combat. Batman suddenly emerges in the middle of the fray to battle Bane, and the mercenary does not get the best of the crimefighter this time. Batman punches Bane repeatedly, and the mercenary is rendered helpless when his mask is damaged by Batman's blows. Batman then tries to get Bane to tell him where the trigger to the bomb is, when all of a sudden he is attacked by a *very* unexpected assailant — Miranda stabs Batman in the side with a long knife. Batman is shocked to learn that *she* is the child of Ra's Al Ghul who made the climb out of the prison many years ago, not Bane. And her name is not really Miranda — it is Talia. Bane was her protector in the prison, and she returned to the prison with her father to free Bane after she had escaped.

Talia tells the wounded Batman that both she and Bane have come to Gotham to carry out Ra's' plan to destroy the city — the crimefighter might have been able to stop Ra's, but he won't stop them. Talia is the person that Bane had entrusted with the bomb's remote trigger, and she shows Batman the trigger right before she pushes its button. But the bomb does not go off, because Gordon has been able to find the bomb and disable its remote trigger mechanism with the device given to him by Batman. In fact, Gordon has climbed into the truck carrying the bomb, so he is right in the middle of all of the action.

Talia leaves City Hall in one of the Tumblers in order to find the truck with the bomb and keep Gordon from returning the bomb to its power source at the reactor. Bane is just about to kill Batman when Selina comes charging in on the Bat-Pod—she shoots Bane with the vehicle's guns, killing him. Batman and Selina go to find the truck carrying Gordon and the bomb, Selina on the Bat-Pod, Batman in the Bat. A furious chase takes place, and Talia is able to climb on board the truck—Batman and Selina are able to crash the truck and bring it to a stop, and Talia is killed in the crash. But the bomb cannot be returned to the reactor—just as she was about to die, Talia was able to send a remote command to the reactor that destroyed it. So now there is no way to keep the bomb from exploding.

Batman has no choice but to tether the bomb to the Bat, and fly the bomb out into the middle of the ocean so it does not destroy Gotham City. Right before he does this, he lets Gordon know who he really is. He then flies off, and the bomb explodes far away from Gotham. It is assumed that Batman was killed in the blast.

Some time later, Gordon, Blake, Fox and Alfred hold a memorial service for Bruce at Wayne Manor. Bruce's will leaves most everything to Alfred, but the Manor itself is left to Gotham City to be used for the care of orphans. An intriguing item is left for Blake, who turns out to have a legal first name that is different from John, the name he normally uses—his real first name is Robin. The item is a bag that contains directions leading to the Bat-cave—Bruce has left Blake the tools to carry on his work as Batman. At Wayne Enterprises, Fox looks into what he could have done to fix the Bat's autopilot, because it would have saved Bruce's life. Fox is surprised to learn that Bruce himself fixed the autopilot months ago. Could it be that Bruce is not really dead?

Yes, it turns out that Bruce is actually alive and *very* well. Alfred visits Florence, Italy, just like he used to do during the years that Bruce was away from Gotham. At a Florence café he spots Bruce sitting with Selina, looking happy and contented. The two men smile at each other, neither of them saying a word. Batman may endure in Gotham, but it seems very unlikely that Bruce Wayne will ever again be the one donning the cape and cowl.

The critical and commercial success of *The Dark Knight Rises* was so gargantuan that it was even able to top the overwhelming success of *The Dark Knight* in some respects. The film won resoundingly positive reviews from major film critics all over the world, and its box office returns kept pace with the historic box office returns of *The Dark Knight*. *The Dark Knight Rises* earned over $160 million in its U.S. opening weekend alone, and ended up grossing almost $450 million during its U.S. theatrical run. Actually, that U.S. box office total actually ended up being over $80 million *less* than the U.S. box office total of *The Dark Knight*, but the film more than made up for this deficit in foreign box office returns. Those returns totaled well over $630 million—so when *The Dark Knight Rises* finally finished its worldwide theatrical run, its worldwide total gross reached over one billion, 80 million dollars, even *higher* than the worldwide total gross of *The Dark Knight*.[12]

In our discussion of *The Dark Knight* earlier in the book, I spent a good deal of time explaining my love/hate relationship with the film. Its iconic Batman scenes and its staggering success thrilled me, but its woefully inconsistent story construction and its poorly-thought-out portrayal of Batman seriously disappointed me. I'm sorry to have to say that my feelings about *The Dark Knight Rises* are far less ambiguous. I feel that the film also suffers from these two flaws that so compromised *The Dark Knight*—but *this* time around these flaws are so prevalent that they end up preventing me from being able to truly enjoy the film.

Don't get me wrong, I'm glad that *The Dark Knight Rises* was such an incredible commercial and critical success—after all, it *was* a Batman film, and I'm always going to be happy when a film about my all-time favorite character does so well. But my enthusiasm for the film pretty much ends there. In my opinion, the movie's story construction is so haphazard, and its portrayal of Batman is so completely off the mark, that I frankly am baffled as to why so many people liked the film so much in the first place.

I want to start off my analysis of *The Dark Knight Rises* by looking at the film's story construction issues, because I feel these issues are what really make the film such a mess. I am not talking about elements of its plot that simply go against my own personal interpretation of the Batman character—I am talking about elements of its plot that simply make no sense whatsoever. To put it bluntly, characters in the film are constantly saying and doing things that completely defy real-world logic. I will now take some time to lay out the elements of *The Dark Knight Rises* that I find to be the most ridiculous and unrealistic.

First off, Bruce Wayne's physical condition is a variable that is laughably inconsistent throughout the entire film. At the opening of *The Dark Knight Rises*, we are led to believe that Bruce's exploits as Batman have left him nearly crippled—when he is examined by a doctor, the doctor tells him he has no cartilage in his knee, very little cartilage in his elbows and shoulders, scar tissue on his kidneys, and residual concussive damage to his brain tissue. Bruce supposedly sustained all of this damage during the time he was fighting crime as Batman, which was a period of about *one* year! Many real-life professional athletes take about as much physical abuse in a year as Bruce ended up taking as Batman, and they are left in far less deplorable condition.

Furthermore, in the film Bruce has had a full *eight* years of rest to recover from his Batman-related injuries, but those years appear to have done him no good at all. And then when Bruce all of a sudden decides to return to action as Batman, he appears to be able to regain full strength and mobility just by strapping on a futuristic knee brace—the film never makes any sort of attempt to explain just how this miraculous brace works so many wonders for Bruce.

Things get far more confusing in terms of Bruce's physical condition as the film goes on. Looking much like his old self, he ferociously fights crime as Batman until Bane breaks his back. Barely able to move or even turn his head, he is taken to Bane's prison—but his broken back is totally fixed when a prison inmate punches his displaced vertebrae back into place! So for eight years, Bruce could not get over some relatively minor injuries he suffered while fighting crime as Batman, but he could get over a broken back in a matter of a few months without receiving any skilled medical attention? You've got to be kidding me!

And things get even stranger from there. To escape the underground prison, Bruce has to climb up a well-like pit that leads to the outside world, and then leap from one ledge to another ledge that appears to be impossibly far from the first ledge. Bruce makes the climb with a rope tied around his waist, but he cannot make the jump between the ledges, so he takes a very hard fall. This fall is so hard that it looks like it would seriously injure *anyone*—so it would almost certainly kill a man who just had his back broken a few weeks before! But Bruce not only survives this fall, he survives it *twice*—when he makes a second attempt to escape the prison, he falls when he fails to make the jump between the ledges. Again, you've got to be kidding me!

Finally, Bruce escapes the prison and makes his way back to Gotham for his final confrontation with Bane. He is again looking much like his old self, decisively defeating Bane in hand-to-hand combat, until Talia stabs him in the side with a long knife. But this serious knife wound doesn't slow Batman down one bit — he is able to board the Bat, pilot it on a wild chase through Gotham, and fly the bomb out into the middle of the ocean so it does not destroy the city! In fact, Batman appears to be almost completely unaffected by his wound — we never even see *one* drop of blood from it!

This observation about Batman's knife wound leads me to another huge problem I have with *The Dark Knight Rises* — this is a movie that is filled with hundreds, if not thousands, of casualties, and the entire movie only shows very few people actually bleeding during its running time. The only people who are shown with blood on them are Bruce, Bane and Talia — and even *they* have barely more than a few drops they have to deal with.

I am not bothered by the lack of blood in *The Dark Knight Rises* because I am bloodthirsty and I like to see a lot of gore in movies. I am bothered by this because I feel that violence in movies should not be presented in a manner that is so sanitized that it appears to have no consequences. One of the most important elements of the Batman character is that violence *does* have terrible consequences — the character would not even exist if his parents had not been murdered. *The Dark Knight Rises* is a film that is loaded top to bottom with a shocking amount of violence, but that violence is presented in such glossed-over fashion that it ends up having very little meaning or emotional impact — it plays out like some sort of elaborately-choreographed dance that exists only for the sake of grand spectacle.

For example, the climactic battle between Bane's men and the Gotham Police at Gotham City Hall is so glossed-over in terms of its violence that it ends up having no connection whatsoever to the horrifying results of real-world violence. Policemen charge up a relatively narrow city street to face an army of men who are directly firing on them with scores of automatic weapons — a few of these policemen fall, but the vast majority of them keep on running, sustaining no injuries. In real life, a charge such as this would be akin to suicide — in just a few minutes of unimaginable carnage, all of the policemen would be killed or wounded. Again, a scene such as this seems to exist only for the sake of grand spectacle, and its unwillingness to acknowledge the terrible consequences of gun violence strikes this author as not only illogical, but also somewhat irresponsible.

So far, we've only scratched the surface of *The Dark Knight Rises*' story construction problems. I will now lay out a large number of these problems in rapid-fire fashion by asking you to consider all of the following questions that the film raises upon viewing it.

Why would a CIA agent ever take men into his custody without making even the most rudimentary checks to see just who these men were, or what they might have been hiding on their person? One quick peek under the hoods covering the heads of Bane and his men sure would have saved that CIA agent and everyone on board his plane a whole lot of trouble!

How in the world could John Blake have deduced that Batman was actually Bruce Wayne? After all, Blake only met Bruce one time in his entire life, and that meeting took place when he was a young man — plus, the meeting only lasted for a minute or two!

How could the "clean slate" computer program possibly erase a person from every computer database in the world? And even if such a program could be created, wouldn't paper records still exist that could provide information about the people who were trying to "erase" themselves?

Why would Deputy Commissioner Foley pull *every* cop off of the pursuit of the criminals who perpetrated the takeover of the Gotham Stock Exchange, and order all of those cops to pursue Batman? Those criminals terrorized hundreds of people with deadly weapons during their attack—worse yet, their attack left a number of people dead or seriously injured. Wouldn't Foley think that it would be wise to at least have a *few* cops continue their pursuit of a group of criminals who had proven themselves to be so dangerous?

Wouldn't the fake trades that were made using Bruce's stolen fingerprints be instantly nullified since they were executed during the takeover of the Gotham Stock Exchange?

Why in the world would Commissioner Gordon ever order every one of his available cops to go into the city sewers at the exact same time? Wouldn't he want to keep a reasonable number of cops above ground in case of emergency?

How could both Gordon and the nuclear bomb not be smashed to bits as they were bouncing around the inside of a truck trailer that was in such a violent wreck? And wouldn't all of that impact somehow have affected the bomb's functionality?

How could Batman possibly have survived the nuclear bomb blast? He was still piloting the aircraft connected to the bomb just before it was set to explode, and the bomb was said to have a *six-mile* blast radius!

Wouldn't *everyone* in the world make the connection that Bruce was Batman when the two ended up "dying" at the exact same time? And wouldn't someone other than Alfred recognize the world-famous, supposedly recently-deceased ex-billionaire casually sitting in a café in Florence, Italy?

Christopher and Jonathan Nolan wrote the script for *The Dark Knight Rises* with the intention that they were going to make a deadly serious Batman film that was deeply rooted in reality, one that was filled with thought-provoking social and political commentary. If the Nolan brothers wanted *The Dark Knight Rises* to be a truly realistic, serious and thought-provoking movie, then they should not have loaded it to the brim with so many outrageously illogical scenes. In this particular Batman fan's opinion, *The Dark Knight Rises* is such a silly exercise in screenwriting that the film cannot be taken much more seriously than Tim Burton's *Batman Returns* or Joel Schumacher's *Batman and Robin*.

And I haven't even gotten into my objections over how the Nolan brothers chose to interpret Batman and his supporting characters yet! I believe that the Nolan's Batman in *The Dark Knight Rises* runs counter to several important, long-cherished elements of the Batman character. My main disagreement with the Nolans about the film's Batman is over these following questions. Why does Bruce Wayne don the disguise of Batman? What satisfaction does Bruce get from being Batman? In *The Dark Knight Rises*, the Nolans answered these questions very differently from the way that I would answer them, and very differently from the manner in which Batman has been portrayed in comics for generations.

As to this first question, in the comics Bruce becomes Batman to fight crime in order to avenge his parents' deaths—*all* crime. His relentless quest for justice can never end, because there will always be *someone* in the world who is being adversely affected by crime. Simply put, as long as there's a breath left in Bruce's body, he will don his costume in order to fight crime and seek justice.

In order to best illustrate my point here, I'm going to cite a classic Batman comic story that we did not get around to discussing earlier in the book. "There Is No Hope in Crime Alley" was written by Denny O'Neil and illustrated by Dick Giordano, and was first published in *Detective Comics* #457, March 1976. The story chronicles a pilgrimage that Batman makes every year on the anniversary of his parents' murders—he visits the street where they were gunned down, which has come to be known as "Crime Alley" in the years since their deaths.

On these visits, he always makes a point of meeting with an elderly woman named

Leslie Thompkins, who runs a shelter there. Leslie does not know why Batman always seeks her out, but readers of the story are let in on that secret. Leslie has lived on that street ever since she was young, and she was there the night Bruce's parents were murdered—in fact, she was the first person who reached out to comfort Bruce after his parents were so brutally taken from him. Even in the face of his terrible loss, Batman believes that there is still hope left in Crime Alley—that hope is embodied in Leslie's kindness.

I cannot think of a better way to sum up why Bruce dons the disguise of Batman than to quote the following dialogue from "There Is No Hope in Crime Alley." Early in the story, Batman stops a mugger from robbing a poor old man in Crime Alley, and the man asks Batman why he would bother with such a small crime. Batman tells the man that "crime is crime ... and to you the loss of a dollar is more important than the loss of thousands to a banker."

The Batman of *The Dark Knight Rises* is nowhere near as focused or determined as this classic comic Batman. In the film, Bruce actually tells Gordon that he quit being Batman for eight years because "Batman wasn't needed anymore." Batman wasn't needed? You've got to be kidding me! In the movie, crime in Gotham City has become less rampant because of the passage of the Dent Act. But obviously, there is still crime in the city—for example, the bodies of young men who died under mysterious circumstances are regularly being discovered in Gotham's sewer system.

Batman as I understand and appreciate him would be down in those sewers in a heartbeat investigating those deaths, but that is not what the Batman of *The Dark Knight Rises* does. In the film, Bruce is in the prime of his life and has a lot of fight left in him—yet in the face of adversity, he chooses to give up being Batman, hide out in his mansion, and ignore mysterious deaths such as the bodies being found in the sewers. This is just not what my vision of what the character's basic motivation is.

I'll bet a lot of you would counter this viewpoint by bringing up Frank Miller's classic 1986 Batman graphic novel *Batman: The Dark Knight Returns* to me—in that work, Batman has retired for a decade, much like he did in *The Dark Knight Rises*. I would answer you by saying that Miller's graphic novel takes place much later in Batman's career, after he has fought crime for *decades*—in fact, Bruce is all the way up in his mid–50s when he decides to again don the cape and cowl. *The Dark Knight Rises*' interpretation of a younger Batman who fights crime for about a year and then quits for *eight* years is a far cry from the determined, relentless Batman of the comics—and that includes the version of the character found in *Batman: The Dark Knight Returns*.

This leads me to second question I posed—what satisfaction does Bruce get from being Batman? In the comics, Bruce is most always able to take some satisfaction in knowing that his mission is truly helping Gotham City and its citizens. This mission has helped him to make sense of his life in the wake of terrible tragedy. In other words, Bruce sees being Batman as doing something positive with the hand that fate has dealt him.

In *The Dark Knight Rises*, both Bruce and Alfred look upon Bruce's costumed adventures as some kind of curse. Alfred even suggests that Bruce is nowhere near up to the task of being Batman, so he is in effect trying to commit suicide by donning the cape and cowl. This line of thinking is about 180 degrees removed from how Bruce and Alfred view Bruce's Batman persona in the comics. In the comics, Bruce and Alfred are very much partners in Batman's amazing, ongoing adventures. Bruce is a hero as Batman, and Alfred's ability to aid and care for Bruce makes him very much a hero as well. There are times when Alfred is bemused or even alarmed by Bruce's obsession—but on the whole, both men see Batman as a very noble, worthwhile endeavor. I feel that the film's premise that Bruce and Alfred view Batman as an overwhelming negative is a giant and unwelcome departure from the character's time-honored mythos.

The film's interpretation of Batman is certainly further degraded by the fact that the character is barely in the film. The movie has a running time of 2 hours and 45 minutes, and its scenes that actually feature Batman clock in at not much over a half hour! Call me crazy, but I expect to be able to see Batman on the screen when I go to see a movie that is supposed to be about Batman! I find this to be perhaps the most telling sign of how disinterested Christopher Nolan had become in the character by the time he was making *The Dark Knight Rises*—the director certainly had an ax to grind in terms of the social and political commentary that he wanted to make in the film, but all of his heavy-handed musings left him with little time to deal with the character that the film was actually supposed to be about.

In fact, repeated viewings of *The Dark Knight Rises* have led me to believe that Nolan wasn't interested in making a Batman movie nearly as much as he was in making an epic war movie. And in my opinion, this is a problem—the character just does not mesh all that well with the trappings of an epic war movie. Now don't get me wrong, it is not the *worst* kind of movie for Batman to be in—it's not like Nolan put the character into a light romantic comedy, a western, or a musical! But in my opinion, the overall feel of *The Dark Knight Rises* is just too big and bombastic to fit with the classic interpretation of Batman as a lone crimefighter, a creature of the night.

As we noted in our discussion of *The Dark Knight*, Nolan chose to draw on a very small amount of classic Batman material for that particular film. The director followed that same course of action for *The Dark Knight Rises*—very few of the film's scenes were inspired by great Batman works of the past. Obviously, the Batman work that had the most profound influence on the movie was the 1993 comic book series *Knightfall*—in that series, Bane broke Batman's back, forcing the crimefighter to give up the mantle of Batman for a time. Obviously, the film's scenes showing Bane breaking Batman's back were directly inspired by *Knightfall*. (We discussed that series in detail in Chapter 12.)

And in the scene when Batman is sighted in Gotham for the first time in eight years, a veteran cop says to a rookie cop, "You're in for a show tonight, son." That line of dialogue is pulled from Miller's *Batman: The Dark Knight Returns*. Finally, in the scene when Catwoman abruptly disappears from Batman's sight, Batman says to himself, "So that's what that feels like." That line of dialogue is pulled from the 1996 graphic novel series *Kingdom Come* written by Mark Waid and illustrated by Alex Ross. (But in *Kingdom Come*, Bruce says it to himself when *Superman* abruptly disappears from his sight.) These three Batman scenes in *The Dark Knight Rises* are basically the only ones that have any ties to classic Batman material.

It should be pointed out that in *The Dark Knight Rises*, the Nolans seemed to be trying to capture the spirit of the *Batman: The Dark Knight Returns* Batman, even if they were not using many of the particular aspects of that character. After all, the idea of Batman returning to action after a long retirement was basically the very essence of what *Batman: The Dark Knight Returns* was all about. I would argue that the Nolan's plan to draw on the *Batman: The Dark Knight Returns* Batman for their *The Dark Knight Rises* Batman was ill-fated from the very start. To have Batman properly return to action after a long retirement, you really need to let the character have a decent career as Batman in the first place—and I would hardly call the year that Bruce spends wearing the cape and cowl in Nolan's Batman film series a "decent career!"

Christian Bale gives his usual stellar performance as Batman/Bruce Wayne in *The Dark Knight Rises*, though the impact of that performance is definitely compromised by the substandard quality of the material he is given to work with. Who knows, Bale might well have enjoyed making the film far more than he enjoyed making *Batman Begins* or *The Dark Knight*— after all, he didn't have to put up with wearing that cumbersome Batman costume nearly as much as he had to when he made those earlier films!

Michael Caine, Gary Oldman and Morgan Freeman also turn in their usual excellent performances in *The Dark Knight Rises*, though they too are adversely affected by the lackluster material handed to them. Caine's performance as Alfred is particularly moving at the end of the film, when he cries over Bruce's "death" as if he had lost his own son. (Of course, when I give into my cynical side, I think that it serves Alfred right to be so heartbroken — after all, he didn't support Bruce's decision to return to action as Batman at all!) And Oldman's performance as Gordon is every bit as earnest as his earlier turns in the role — I just wish that Gordon wouldn't have had to make stupid decisions like sending most all of Gotham's police force into the sewers! Freeman fares a bit better than Caine and Oldman — his scenes as Fox are infused with the same kind of wry humor that made his scenes in *Batman Begins* and *The Dark Knight* so effective.

Anne Hathaway's self-assured, sultry performance as Selina Kyle in *The Dark Knight Rises* is definitely one of the film's high points. The actress is definitely helped by the film's wonderful characterization of Selina — she is sharply realized as the complex antihero that the character has been in the comics for decades. The Nolan brothers definitely based their version of the character on the Selina found in Frank Miller and David Mazzucchelli's 1987 comic series *Batman: Year One*. Like the *Batman: Year One* Selina, the film's Selina is a not so much an out-and-out criminal as she is a wily, Robin Hood–like thief — and she is so unpredictable that she is every bit as likely to come to Batman's aid as she is to fight him.

Interestingly, Selina is never referred to as "Catwoman" by name in the film, but she does not need to be. Without question, she simply *is* the Catwoman — she is a master cat burglar, and she wears a skintight black outfit with black night vision goggles that look like cat ears when she flips them on top of her head. In this author's opinion, the Nolans were decidedly unsuccessful in their attempts to bring Batman and his world to life in *The Dark Knight Rises*— but they sure found a perfect way to work the Catwoman into their cinematic vision of Batman. In fact, *The Dark Knight Rises* paints a portrait of the Catwoman that is far closer in spirit to the modern comic book version of the character than any of the previous big screen Catwomen had been. Thank goodness the character finally got a chance at big screen redemption after the disastrous 2004 feature film *Catwoman* starring Halle Berry! (We briefly discussed that movie in Chapter 10.)

Tom Hardy's performance as Bane isn't bad, though it is nowhere near as memorable as Hathaway's performance as Selina. Truthfully, it seems unlikely that Hardy really could have found a way to do much more with his role than he did — Bane's mask obscures the actor's facial expressions and his dialogue to the point that his character comes across as rather bland. To make matters worse, much of Hardy's dialogue is delivered in a pleasant, almost cheerful voice that is presumably supposed to serve as a chilling counterpoint to his character's murderous actions. But in this author's opinion, this cheerfulness makes the character seem far less menacing than he ought to be.

The serum that Bane ingests in *The Dark Knight Rises* is very different from the serum that the character ingests in the comics. In the comics, an experimental drug known as "Venom" is dispensed into Bane's body, and this is what gives him his incredible strength.

In the film, Bane's industrial-looking, tubed mask dispenses some sort of anesthetic that gives him relief from the constant pain he is in—that pain stems from unhealed injuries he suffered while he was in prison. In this author's opinion, changing the purpose of Bane's serum also negatively impacts the character's sense of menace.

The most problematic aspect of the Bane character in *The Dark Knight Rises* has nothing to do with Hardy's performance. The main thing that is wrong with Bane in *The Dark Knight Rises* is that the film's screenplay ends up leaving the character so poorly developed. Exactly what injuries did he suffer that led him to need his mask? Just how did he find out that Batman was actually Bruce Wayne? And why did he spend so much time and effort trying to torment Bruce instead of just carrying out his former mentor Ra's Al Ghul's plan to destroy Gotham? After all, Ra's' original goal was simply to bring down Gotham, and that goal had nothing to do with wreaking vengeance on Bruce—Ra's just believed that the city had become so corrupt and unjust that it needed to be destroyed. The film's screenplay could have answered all of these questions about Bane's actions and motivations very easily, but it didn't.

Incidentally, the close connection between Ra's and Bane in *The Dark Knight Rises* was an invention of the Nolans—in the comics, Bane's origin was in no way tied to Ra's. And before we leave the Bane character behind, I can't resist making this last observation. We have just noted that *The Dark Knight Rises* version of Bane has been drastically changed from the comic version of Bane in terms of the character's origin and appearance. So it really is not too much of an exaggeration to say that the Bane in Joel Schumacher's *Batman and Robin* might actually be a *bit* more faithful to the comic version of the character than *The Dark Knight Rises* Bane! (This is probably one of the most positive things I've said about *Batman and Robin* in the entire book, by the way.)

The Dark Knight Rises leaves the Miranda Tate/Talia Al Ghul character even *more* underdeveloped than Bane. As Miranda, the character is heroically working to save the world through the Wayne Enterprises clean energy project. Miranda's actions throughout the film clearly reflect the fact that she passionately cares about finding a way to better the lives of everyone around the world. And then right at the end of the film the character suddenly is revealed to actually be Talia, and she only cares about exacting revenge on Bruce and killing millions of people in a giant nuclear blast! If Talia's main goal all along was to carry out her father's plan of destroying Gotham and all of its citizens, then she certainly could have worked toward that goal a lot faster by curtailing all of her admirable activities!

And speaking of her activities, just why did she sleep with Bruce? Was that just a bit of a recreational break from her plan to destroy both Bruce and Gotham? Again, the film could have better explained the character's actions and motivations very easily, but it didn't. Presumably the Nolan brothers tried to keep Miranda/Talia a mysterious figure so that she could provide them with a whopper of a plot twist just like the Ra's character did in *Batman Begins*. But in this author's opinion, *both* of the Al Ghuls would have been much stronger characters if they had been allowed to be known by the name of Al Ghul from the beginning of their respective films—enough with the labored Al Ghul plot twists already, Mr. Nolan!

At any rate, Marion Cotillard as Miranda/Talia looks lovely on the screen in *The Dark Knight Rises*, but her performance cannot possibly rise above the half-baked material she is given to work with. Simply put, both Cotillard and the Talia character deserved much better than what the Nolan brothers had prepared for them.

Joseph Gordon-Levitt gives a very solid, likeable performance as John Blake in the film. That said, however, the Blake character falls so far outside the realm of Batman mythos that the idea of him taking over the mantle of Batman from Bruce Wayne does not sit well at all with this particular Batman fan. And giving the character the legal name of Robin certainly does not instantly give him some sort of "Batman legitimacy"—in fact, it could be argued that throwing the Robin name into *The Dark Knight Rises* is nothing more than a rather cheap plot trick on the part of the Nolan brothers. Plus, as we discussed earlier in the chapter, the manner in which Blake deduces that Batman is actually Bruce Wayne makes practically no sense at all—this poorly-thought out aspect of the character certainly makes him even more difficult to warm up to.

Interestingly, in *Batman Begins* Nolan put a lot more time and care into setting up a separate character that could have ended up being Robin. As we noted in our discussion of that film earlier in the book, the character of the "Little Boy" played by Jack Gleeson certainly seemed to be on a fast track to becoming Batman's junior sidekick. The boy received a small flexible periscope from Batman as a kind of "souvenir." And then at the end of the film, the boy was by Rachel Dawes' side when she realized Batman's true identity and called the crimefighter "Bruce." This character undoubtedly had a much more concrete connection to Batman/Bruce Wayne in *Batman Begins* than Blake has to Batman/Bruce Wayne in *The Dark Knight Rises*. But we have to play by Nolan's rules in his Batman films, so Blake is the character who gets to be Batman's official Robin, not the "Little Boy!"

Nolan does find a way to incorporate a number of other characters from his previous Batman films into *The Dark Knight Rises*. Perhaps the most memorable of these Dr. Jonathan Crane, a.k.a. the Scarecrow, played by Cillian Murphy—the scenes showing Crane serving as a judge for Bane's perverse version of a court are both chilling and funny. Crane turns out to be the only Batman villain that appears in all three of Nolan's Batman films, by the way. And Ra's Al Ghul, played by Liam Neeson, shows up in the film as well. However, he is not really a physical part of the film's action—he appears as a hallucination that Bruce is having while he is being held in Bane's prison. Harvey Dent, played by Aaron Eckhart, is also very briefly in the film—he appears in several quick flashback scenes in his Two-Face form.

It is worth pointing out here that Dent's importance in the film seems very forced. As we discussed earlier in the book, Nolan started this trend of focusing an inordinate amount attention on the character in *The Dark Knight*, and this trend continues into *The Dark Knight Rises*. Why are so many of Gotham's major policy decisions based around this long-dead man who really spent so little time as a city official there? It is this author's opinion that Nolan's fixation on the actions and legacy of the Dent character in *The Dark Knight* greatly compromises the logic of the film, especially when there is *another* character that Nolan should be focusing on.

And just who is that character? Well, I'm sure all of you know just who I am referring to! It is simply inexcusable that Nolan did not find some way to account for the whereabouts of the Joker in *The Dark Knight Rises*. The character's effect on the psyche of Gotham as depicted in *The Dark Knight* was so devastating that it certainly would have carried over to the time period of *The Dark Knight Rises*. So how in the world could Nolan have ever thought it was appropriate not to refer to the character in some way, shape or form in the film?

Obviously, Nolan felt uncomfortable dealing with the Joker in the film due to the death of Heath Ledger, the actor who played the character in *The Dark Knight*. But pointing out what happened to Ledger in no way answers the question of what ended up happening to the Joker in Nolan's cinematic Batman world. What was the Joker doing during the years that Bruce Wayne stopped fighting crime as Batman? Was he simply locked up in Arkham Asylum? Did he ever try to escape? Was he ever tried in court for all of his hideous crimes?

Here is a Joker-related question that is even *more* pertinent to *The Dark Knight Rises*. What were the Joker and all of the inmates being held at Arkham doing during Bane's takeover of Gotham City? We know that all of the inmates being held at Blackgate Prison were set free by Bane — so wouldn't Bane have had at least *some* sort of interest in all of the Arkham inmates? And wouldn't Bane have had even *more* interest in the Joker, undoubtedly Gotham's most notorious criminal? As I just mentioned, we have to play by Nolan's rules in his Batman films — but even still, it must be pointed out that his stubborn refusal to find at least *some* way to acknowledge the Joker in *The Dark Knight Rises* is a huge impediment to the film.

Well, I've spent quite a bit of time knocking *The Dark Knight Rises* around — I think it is time to focus on some of the positive things to be found in the film. Lindy Hemming's costume designs for the movie are every bit as wonderful as the work she did for Nolan's first two Batman films. *The Dark Knight Rises* sticks with the exact same Batman costume found in *The Dark Knight*, so there are no wardrobe surprises to be found in terms of the film's cape and cowl scenes. Hemming's best work in the film is probably her sleek, no-nonsense design for Anne Hathaway's cat burglar outfit.

The movie's production design also matches the same high standards set by Nolan's first two Batman films. Batman's new ride the Bat helps to bring a heightened level of excitement to the film's action scenes, and his redesigned Batcave is wonderfully atmospheric. Plus, *The Dark Knight Rises'* many scenes shot on location around the world make the film just about as visually spectacular as any movie ever made.

And of course, the film's scenes shot in IMAX are every bit as breathtaking as the IMAX scenes featured in *The Dark Knight*. As mentioned earlier in the chapter, there is far more IMAX footage in *The Dark Knight Rises* than there was *The Dark Knight* — so it is not really possible to specifically list all of the film's IMAX sequences like we did in our discussion of *The Dark Knight*. At any rate, seeing *The Dark Knight Rises* in IMAX format made the film into an immersive experience that most any serious Batman fan would find unforgettable. I'm including myself in that category, by the way — obviously, I was not too crazy about the film from the very first time I saw it, but I still saw it in IMAX format multiple times and always hugely enjoyed its spectacle.

Hans Zimmer's musical score for *The Dark Knight Rises* also is every bit as memorable and effective as the music he had written for *Batman Begins* and *The Dark Knight*. One of the most powerful moments in the score occurs when Alfred spots Bruce at the café in Florence right at the end of film. Zimmer's music delivers a marvelously powerful, percussive burst of sound just as Alfred realizes that Bruce has been able to cheat death and leave his tragic life in Gotham behind.

I should point out that even though I was not that thrilled with *The Dark Knight Rises* itself, I still greatly enjoyed all of the enthusiasm there was for the character during the summer of 2012. And being the serious Batman fan that I am, I also very much enjoyed looking over all of the merchandise inspired by the film that was for sale that summer. The wide variety of *The Dark Knight Rises* action figures, statues, toys, books, clothing, etc., available for purchase certainly kept the Batman merchandising machine chugging along at full steam.

There is one more thing about *The Dark Knight Rises* that I just have to point out here. It is by no means something that I picked up on before anyone else, but it is so oddly funny that I can't resist making mention of it. At the end of the film, Batman has to tether Bane's nuclear bomb to the Bat, and fly the bomb out into the middle of the ocean so it does not destroy Gotham City. This scene is strikingly similar to one of the most memorable scenes in the 1966 film *Batman*!

As we noted way back in Chapter 6, in that particular scene Batman has to find a way to dispose of a large lit bomb. Batman grabs the bomb and dashes outside to try to find a place to throw it where it will not hurt anyone when it explodes. As he runs around a waterfront area, he dodges crowds of people, mothers pushing babies in strollers, and even a Salvation Army band! He is finally able to throw the bomb into a deserted area and take cover just before it explodes. Just before he does this he says to himself in exasperation, "Some days you just can't get rid of a bomb!" This line would have worked every bit as well if it had been spoken by Batman during the climax of *The Dark Knight Rises*!

We have one more bit of business to attend to relating to *The Dark Knight Rises* before we finish up our discussion of the film. Because the movie was so incredibly successful, it sold extremely well when it was first made available to the home video market by Warner Home Video in early December 2012. At that time, Warner released the film on both Blu-ray and DVD format.

There were two different DVD versions of the film — it was offered both as a single-disc release and as a 2-disc set. Both versions presented the entire movie in basic widescreen format — in other words, they did not include the movie's IMAX sequences in their original large-frame format in any way. The 2-disc set included a number of interesting bonus features along with the film. The most notable of these features was *Ending the Knight*, a collection of 17 mini-documentaries about the making of the film. These mini-documentaries included commentary from members of the film's cast and crew, and behind-the-scenes footage showing that cast and crew at work. Another of the set's bonus features was the 2012 television documentary *The Batmobile* that we discussed earlier in the chapter. The set's version of *The Batmobile* was greatly expanded from its original broadcast version — it was able to include more information on Batman's iconic car due to the fact that it had a much longer running time.

As was the case with *The Dark Knight* Blu-ray, the Blu-ray version of *The Dark Knight Rises* was the one that really delivered the goods. The high-definition Blu-ray format allowed viewers to truly appreciate the extraordinary level of visual quality that high-resolution IMAX film had brought to the movie. And needless to say, the movie was presented with its IMAX scenes in their original large-frame format. The Blu-ray also included all of the bonus features found on the 2-disc DVD set.

Throughout this book, I've had a difficult time deciding just what my final thoughts would be for each of the Batman feature films we've examined. Strangely enough, I've known exactly how I wanted to close out my discussion of *The Dark Knight Rises* from my very first screening of the film. So without further ado, here is that closer. I will always be grateful that Christopher Nolan shared his cinematic vision of the Batman character with the world — but after the release of *The Dark Knight Rises*, I would be every bit as grateful if Nolan stood by his decision to never again make another Batman movie.

As we noted at the beginning of this chapter, Nolan has reached truly incredible heights as a filmmaker with his last several productions. So when it comes right down to it, he doesn't really need Batman to help him make powerful artistic statements anymore. I personally think that road runs both ways. *The Dark Knight Rises* is all the proof I need to lead me to the opinion that Warner's Batman film franchise will be better off without Nolan in the future. So let me just say this to you, DC Comics and Warner Bros.—if Nolan really does elect to walk away from the Batman character for good, I wish you luck in finding a new filmmaker to carry on your cinematic version of Batman. I may not love everything that Nolan has done with your great character on the big screen, but I will say this—he has left you with one incredible act to follow.

21

The Adventure Goes On and On

And so we have reached the end of our journey through the history of Batman feature films. Of course, we *have* to stop because we're all out of that history now — we have followed it right up to the present day. But because all of the character's recent big screen adventures have been so successful, it is a certainty that more Batman feature films will be made in the years to come. Personally, I just can't wait to see what the future holds for the big screen Batman.

I feel that the best way for me to close out this book is to offer an observation about just how important of a role Batman feature films have played in the overall history of the character. Here is that observation. For many years, the Batman character really only appealed to a small percentage of the population, and that percentage was made up almost solely of children and hardcore comic book fans. But during the past quarter of a century, Batman's popularity has taken a quantum leap — the character has now reached a level of appeal that is almost universal. And the main reason the character has grown so staggeringly popular with people from all walks of life over those years? That's a very simple question to answer — the reason is Batman feature films. Warner Bros.' Batman film series reached millions upon millions of people that would otherwise have never been exposed to the character.

And even better, these people were exposed to a version of the character that was based on the dark hero we serious Batman fans had always loved. For the most part, the Warner films brought Batman to the big screen in a manner that was in keeping with Bob Kane and Bill Finger's original vision of the character. And because of that, Batman has moved beyond being just kid stuff or a campy joke — millions of people see him as an iconic, multi-layered character with both a rich history and a limitless future. So thank you, Warner Bros. — you brought Batman to a level of success that is absolutely thrilling to us serious Batman fans.

Let's take a second to consider just how limitless Batman's future truly is. Think about the huge variety of Batman merchandise that is readily available to the public at this point in time. For example, right now Mattel Toys has a line of popular Batman toys out through their Fisher-Price subsidiary that is designed for children aged 1 and up. That's right — a person can start becoming a Batman fan by owning cool Batman toys before they have to worry about doing things like walking or eating solid foods!

On the other end of the spectrum, DC Universe Animated Original Movies recently released their productions *Batman: The Dark Knight Returns Part 1* and *Batman: The Dark Knight Returns Part 2* to the home video market on Blu-ray and DVD. (*Part 1* was released in late 2012 and *Part 2* was released in early 2013.) These videos are wonderfully produced, very faithful adaptations of Frank Miller's groundbreaking 1986 graphic novel series *Batman: The Dark Knight Returns*. Of course, given their source material, these productions are undoubtedly intended for an adult audience — they are incredibly sophisticated, and they contain their fair share of violent and disturbing images.

So, there is no arguing the fact that Batman has become an entertainment icon with remarkably broad appeal — after all, he can hold the attention of 1 year olds every bit as well as he can hold the attention of sophisticated adults. And of course, the character's growth into such a universal artistic force has made him an increasingly potent commercial force as well. In other words, he can *really* bring in the money — the character's Warner feature films alone have made billions of dollars. (In fact, as we discussed earlier in the book, both *The Dark Knight* and *The Dark Knight Rises* made over a billion dollars *each*!) And the sale of Batman comics, books, toys, clothing, television productions, and home videos has raked in many more millions of dollars over the decades. Simply put, Batman is not just big — he is also big business.

In fact, the world of Batman has grown to be so vast and far-reaching that I must reluctantly admit that now I have a difficult time keeping up with it. The character's comic titles alone often bewilder me — there are so many of them, and their complicated ongoing story arcs almost require an owner's manual to keep up with. Case in point — toward the end of the book we discussed the Damian Wayne character assuming the mantle of Robin in Batman's comic book world. The character made his debut as Robin in mid–2009, and before he got the chance to make much of an impression on readers, his place in Batman mythos was being tinkered with as DC Comics premiered their 2011 system-wide revamp/relaunch *The New 52*.

And the world of *The New 52* ended up giving the Damian Robin even *less* of a chance to make an impression on readers— he was killed off by a genetically-altered clone of himself in early 2013. All in all, Damian's turn as Robin lasted about as long as the unpopular Jason Todd Robin. In fact, when you really think about it, Damian had been given even more of an uphill battle to get noticed than Jason ever had — after all, Damian had to share the stage with multiple Batmen, a separate version of Robin (Tim Drake's Red Robin), and numerous other bat-costumed heroes. In other words, I feel like the hustle and bustle of Batman's comic world never really allowed me to get used to the Damian Robin — and now he's gone already!

Incidentally, this thought leads me to think what a truly impossible task it has been to try to briefly sum up Batman's comic book history in this book. Even though we discussed a great number of incredible Batman comic works in this book, there are many, many more equally fabulous Batman comic tales out there that we couldn't get around to discussing in order to hold the book to a reasonable length. So if I neglected to note your favorite Batman comic work in the book, please don't be angry with me — I probably think as highly of that work as you do!

In closing, I'm sad to say that the difficulty I'm having in terms of keeping tabs on the character probably has a lot to do with where I am in my life. My Batman obsession started when I was in preschool, and the character had only been around for less than three decades. Now Batman is nearing his 75th year, and I am nearing my 50th year — Batman is going stronger than ever at 75, but the half-century mark has weighed me down a bit more than I thought it would!

But even if keeping up with Batman's ongoing exploits both on and off of the screen has gotten to be more of a challenging task for me, I'm far from done with the character.

21—The Adventure Goes On and On

As I write these words, a life-size mannequin outfitted in an Alex Ross–style Batman costume looks across the room at me—the grim, determined look in his eyes seems to say, "You're still with me, aren't you?" And of course, my answer to that question is "Yes." I feel that being an avid Batman fan is simply way too much fun of a pastime to ever give up on. An avid Batman fan is a person who always has something to look forward to, because there is great new Batman stuff being released all the time. (Of course, our home is *already* filled with Batman stuff, including a life-size Batman mannequin, but there is always room for more!)

Here's one of the main reasons why I could never even consider giving up on Batman just yet. Just recently, Warner Bros. obtained the rights to use the likenesses of the characters from the 1960s *Batman* film and TV show—so for the very first time in history, Batman fans will soon be able to purchase an official *Batman* action figure that actually looks like Adam West in costume! I have been waiting ever since I was three years old to have my very own Adam West Batman action figure. How could I possibly walk away from Batman right now when I have the chance to bring this over four-decade-long wait to a happy end in just a matter of weeks?

So keep those adventures coming, Dark Knight—keep them coming on the printed page, on the screen, on the toy shelves, on amusement park rides, even on the first T-shirt I put on when I wake up in the morning. There is no doubt that you'll long outlast me, but I'll keep prowling the shadowy rooftops of Gotham with you in my imagination for just as long as I can.

Chapter Notes

Chapter 1

1. Les Daniels, *Batman: The Complete History* (San Francisco: Chronicle Books, 1999), pp. 17–18.
2. Bob Kane with Tom Andrae, *Batman & Me: The Saga Continues* (Van Nuys: Zanart Entertainment, 1996), p. 38.
3. Daniels, p. 23.
4. Anthony Tollin, *The Shadow Volume 9* (San Antonio: Sanctum Books, 2007), "Foreshadowing the Batman."
5. Daniels, p. 37.
6. Kane, p. 46.
7. Daniels, pp. 39–41.
8. Ibid., p. 40.
9. Kane, pp. 45–46.
10. Daniels, p. 47.

Chapter 2

1. Bob Kane, *Batman: The Dailies Volume 1 1943–1944* (New York: DC Comics and Princeton: Kitchen Sink Press, 1990), p. 4 (introduction by Joe Desris).
2. Les Daniels, *Batman: The Complete History* (San Francisco: Chronicle Books, 1999), p. 57.
3. "The Return of Batman," *Time,* November 26, 1965, pp. 60–61.
4. Bob Kane with Tom Andrae, *Batman & Me: The Saga Continues* (Van Nuys: Zanart Entertainment, 1996), pp. 125–27.

Chapter 3

1. Bob Kane, *Batman: The Dailies Volume 1 1943–1944* (New York: DC Comics and Princeton: Kitchen Sink Press, 1990), pp. 7–8 (introduction by Joe Desris).
2. Bruce Scivally, *Billion Dollar Batman: A History of the Caped Crusader on Film, Radio and Television from 10 Cent Comic Book to Global Icon* (Wilmette, IL: Henry Gray, 2011), pp. 36–43.

Chapter 4

1. Bruce Scivally, *Billion Dollar Batman: A History of the Caped Crusader on Film, Radio and Television from 10 Cent Comic Book to Global Icon* (Wilmette, IL: Henry Gray, 2011), pp. 50–52.
2. Bob Kane with Tom Andrae, *Batman & Me: The Saga Continues* (Van Nuys: Zanart Entertainment, 1996), pp. 130–131.
3. Ibid., pp. 127–31.

Chapter 5

1. Fredric Wertham, *Seduction of the Innocent* (London: Museum Press), p. 190.
2. Les Daniels, *Batman: The Complete History* (San Francisco: Chronicle Books, 1999), p. 88.
3. Ibid., pp. 95–97.

Chapter 6

1. Joel Eisner, *The Official Batman Batbook* (Chicago: Contemporary Books, 1986), pp. 5–6.
2. Ibid., p. 52.
3. Ibid., p. 8.
4. James Van Hise, *Batmania II* (Las Vegas: Pioneer Books, 1992), "Burt Ward: Ever at Batman's Side."
5. "The Return of Batman," *Time,* November 26, 1965, pp. 60–61.
6. Eisner, p. 52.
7. Van Hise, "George Barris: Building the Batvehicles."
8. Bruce Scivally, *Billion Dollar Batman: A History of the Caped Crusader on Film, Radio and Television from 10 Cent Comic Book to Global Icon* (Wilmette, IL: Henry Gray, 2011), p. 102.
9. Eisner, pp. 58–59.
10. Scivally, p. 118.
11. Van Hise, "The Year of the Bat."

Chapter 7

1. Michael Evry and Michael Kronenberg, *The Batcave Companion* (Raleigh: TwoMorrows Publishing, 2009), pp. 53–55.
2. Les Daniels, *Batman: The Complete History* (San Francisco: Chronicle Books, 1999), p. 117.
3. Michael E. Uslan, *The Boy Who Loved Batman* (San Francisco: Chronicle Books, 2011), pp. 183–184.

Chapter 8

1. Michael E. Uslan, *The Boy Who Loved Batman* (San Francisco: Chronicle Books, 2011), p.183.
2. Ibid., pp. 183–185.
3. Ibid., pp. 191–193.
4. Ibid., p. 193.
5. Gary Collinson, *Holy Franchise, Batman! Bringing the Caped Crusader to the Screen* (London: Robert Hale, 2012), pp. 66–67.
6. Uslan, p. 186.
7. Jon B. Cooke, ed., *Comic Book Artist Collection Volume 2* (Raleigh: TwoMorrows Publishing, 2002), pp. 11–12.
8. Ken Hanke, *Tim Burton: An Unauthorized Biography of the Filmmaker* (Los Angeles: Renaissance Books, 1999), pp. 75–76.
9. Bruce Scivally, *Billion Dollar Batman: A History of the Caped Crusader on Film, Radio and Television from 10 Cent Comic Book to Global Icon* (Wilmette, IL: Henry Gray, 2011), pp. 157–160.
10. Ibid., p. 167.
11. Nancy Griffin and Kim Masters, *Hit and Run: How Jon Peters and Peter Guber Took Sony for a Ride in Hollywood* (New York: Touchstone, 1997), p. 166.
12. Scivally, pp. 225–226.
13. Ibid., p. 161.
14. Ibid., pp. 161–163.
15. Collinson, p. 71.
16. Ibid., p. 71.
17. James Van Hise, *Batmania II* (Las Vegas: Pioneer Books, 1992), "The Year of the Bat."
18. Scivally, pp. 182–183.
19. "*Batman* (1989)," *Internet Movie Database* (www.imdb.com), retrieved 1-25-13.
20. Griffin and Masters, pp. 168–69.
21. Ibid., pp. 171–172.
22. Scivally, p. 189.
23. "*Batman* (1989)," *Box Office Mojo* (www.boxofficemojo.com), retrieved 1-25-13.
24. Van Hise, "The Making of the Batmobile 1990."

Chapter 10

1. Ken Hanke, *Tim Burton: An Unauthorized Biography of the Filmmaker* (Los Angeles: Renaissance Books, 1999), pp. 117–119.
2. Though Hamm's *Batman 2* script has never been published in any official form, it can be found on a number of websites such as *The Internet Movie Script Database* (www.imsdb.com).
3. Bruce Scivally, *Billion Dollar Batman: A History of the Caped Crusader on Film, Radio and Television from 10 Cent Comic Book to Global Icon* (Wilmette, IL: Henry Gray, 2011), p. 205.
4. Ibid., p. 207.
5. Mark Cotta Vaz, "A Knight at the Zoo," *Cinefex*, August 1992, p. 25.
6. Jeffrey Ressner, "Three Go Mad in Gotham," *Empire*, August 1992.
7. Hanke, pp. 120–21.
8. Ibid., pp. 118–19.
9. "Batman Returns," *Internet Movie Database* (www.imdb.com), retrieved 1-25-13.
10. "Batman Returns," *Box Office Mojo* (www.boxofficemojo.com), retrieved 1-25-13.
11. Steve Daly and Anne Thompson, "Batlash," *Entertainment Weekly*, July 31, 1992, pp. 32–35.
12. Ibid., pp. 32–35.

Chapter 11

1. Paul Dini and Chip Kidd, *Batman Animated* (New York: HarperEntertainment, 1998), "Mask of the Phantasm."

Chapter 13

1. Ken Hanke, *Tim Burton: An Unauthorized Biography of the Filmmaker* (Los Angeles: Renaissance Books, 1999), p. 95.
2. Bruce Scivally, *Billion Dollar Batman: A History of the Caped Crusader on Film, Radio and Television from 10 Cent Comic Book to Global Icon* (Wilmette, IL: Henry Gray, 2011), p. 90.
3. Mitchell Fink, "*Batman*'s Star Wars," *People*, July 18, 1994, p. 27.
4. Bruce Bibby, "Riddle Me This, Batman," *Premiere*, May 1995.
5. Ibid.
6. Scivally, p. 248.
7. Mark Cotta Vaz, "Forever and a Knight," *Cinefex*, September 1995, pp. 94–97.
8. Benjamin Svetkey, "Holy Happy Set!" *Entertainment Weekly*, July 12, 1996.
9. Scivally, p. 253.
10. "Batman Forever," *Internet Movie Database* (www.imdb.com), retrieved 1-25-13.
11. Vaz, p. 113.
12. "Batman Forever," *Box Office Mojo* (www.boxofficemojo.com), retrieved 1-25-13.

Chapter 15

1. Bruce Scivally, *Billion Dollar Batman: A History of the Caped Crusader on Film, Radio and Television from 10 Cent Comic Book to Global Icon* (Wilmette, IL: Henry Gray, 2011), pp. 273–274.

2. Mark Cotta Vaz, "Freeze Frames," *Cinefex,* September 1997, p. 18.
3. Scivally, p. 291.
4. *"Batman and Robin,"* Internet Movie Database (www.imdb.com), retrieved 1-25-13.
5. Vaz, p. 176.
6. *"Batman and Robin,"* Box Office Mojo (www.boxofficemojo.com), retrieved 1-25-13.

Chapter 16

1. Gary Collinson, *Holy Franchise, Batman! Bringing the Caped Crusader to the Screen* (London: Robert Hale, 2012), pp. 120–121.
2. Bob Kane with Tom Andrae, *Batman & Me: The Saga Continues* (Van Nuys: Zanart Entertainment, 1996).

Chapter 17

1. Gary Collinson, *Holy Franchise, Batman! Bringing the Caped Crusader to the Screen* (London: Robert Hale, 2012), pp. 120–121.
2. Simon Reynolds, "Escape from the Batcave," *Cinefantastique,* July 2005, pp. 32–33.
3. Jody Duncan Jesser and Janine Pourroy, *The Art and Making of The Dark Knight Trilogy* (New York: Abrams, 2012), pp. 38–40.
4. Ibid., p. 40.
5. Bruce Scivally, *Billion Dollar Batman: A History of the Caped Crusader on Film, Radio and Television from 10 Cent Comic Book to Global Icon* (Wilmette, IL: Henry Gray, 2011), p. 334.
6. Jesser and Pourroy, p. 60.
7. Claudia Kalindjian, *Batman Begins: The Official Movie Guide* (New York: Time, 2005), p. 94.
8. Jesser and Pourroy, p. 60.
9. *"Batman Begins,"* Internet Movie Database (www.imdb.com), retrieved 1-25-13.
10. Joe Fordham, Starting Over," *Cinefex,* October 2005, p. 101.
11. Kalindjian, p. 82.
12. Ibid., p. 144.
13. Ibid., p. 145.
14. Ibid., p. 144.
15. Ibid., p. 147.
16. Fordham, pp. 108–112, 118.
17. Jesser and Pourroy, pp. 131–132.
18. Fordham, pp. 95–96, 108.
19. *"Batman Begins,"* Box Office Mojo (www.boxofficemojo.com), retrieved 1-25-13.

Chapter 18

1. Jody Duncan Jesser and Janine Pourroy, *The Art and Making of The Dark Knight Trilogy* (New York: Abrams, 2012), p. 49.
2. Ibid., pp. 113–115.
3. Bruce Scivally, *Billion Dollar Batman: A History of the Caped Crusader on Film, Radio and Television from 10 Cent Comic Book to Global Icon* (Wilmette, IL: Henry Gray, 2011), pp. 374–375.
4. Jody Duncan, "Batman Grounded," *Cinefex,* October 2008, pp. 84–86.
5. Jesser and Pourroy, p. 177.
6. Scivally, p. 381.
7. Duncan, pp. 82–83.
8. Ibid., pp. 73–75.
9. *"The Dark Knight,"* Internet Movie Database (www.imdb.com), retrieved 1-25-13.
10. Scivally, pp. 386–387.
11. Duncan, pp. 71, 80–81.
12. James Barron, "Medical Examiner Rules Ledger's Death Accidental," *The New York Times,* February 7, 2008 (www.nytimes.com), retrieved 1-25-13.
13. *"The Dark Knight,"* Box Office Mojo website (www.boxofficemojo.com), retrieved 1-25-13.
14. Christopher Nolan, Jonathan Nolan and David S. Goyer, *The Dark Knight Trilogy* (New York: Opus, 2012), p. 227.

Chapter 20

1. *"Inception,"* Box Office Mojo (www.boxofficemojo.com), retrieved 1-25-13.
2. *"The Dark Knight Rises,"* Internet Movie Database (www.imdb.com), retrieved 1-25-13.
3. Jody Duncan Jesser and Janine Pourroy, *The Art and Making of The Dark Knight Trilogy* (New York: Abrams, 2012), pp. 194–197.
4. Ibid., pp. 198–202.
5. Ibid., pp. 202–203.
6. Ibid., pp. 208–210.
7. Ibid., pp. 213.
8. Ibid., pp. 213–217.
9. Jody Duncan, "A Farewell to Arms," *Cinefex,* October 2012, pp. 53–55, 64.
10. Ibid., pp. 46–48, 57–58.
11. Jesser and Pourroy, pp. 257–260
12. *"The Dark Knight Rises,"* Box Office Mojo (www.boxofficemojo.com), retrieved 1-25-13.

Bibliography

Collinson, Gary. *Holy Franchise, Batman! Bringing the Caped Crusader to the Screen.* London: Robert Hale, 2012.

Cowsill, Alan, Alexander Irvine, Matthew K. Manning, Michael McAvennie, and Daniel Wallace. *DC Comics Year by Year: A Visual Chronicle.* New York: DK Publishing, 2010.

Daniels, Les. *Batman: The Complete History.* San Francisco: Chronicle Books, 1999.

_____. *DC Comics: A Celebration of the World's Favorite Comic Book Heroes.* New York: Billboard Books, 2003.

Darius, Julian. *Batman Begins and the Comics.* Honolulu: Sequart.com, 2005.

Dini, Paul, and Chip Kidd. *Batman Animated.* New York: HarperEntertainment, 1998.

_____ (writer), and Alex Ross (artist). *Batman: War on Crime.* New York: DC Comics, 1999.

_____ (writer), Bruce Timm (artist) and various other artists. *The Batman Adventures: Dangerous Dames and Demons.* New York: DC Comics, 2003.

Eisner, Joel. *The Official Batman Batbook.* Chicago: Contemporary Books, 1986.

Englehart, Steve, and Len Wein (writers), Terry Austin, Dick Giordano, Al Milgrom, Marshall Rogers and Walt Simonson (artists). *Strange Apparitions.* New York: DC Comics, 1999.

Evry, Michael, and Michael Kronenberg. *The Batcave Companion.* Raleigh: TwoMorrows Publishing, 2009.

The Greatest Batman Stories Ever Told. New York: DC Comics, 1988.

Greenberger, Robert. *The Essential Batman Encyclopedia.* New York: Ballantine, 2008.

Jesser, Jody Duncan, and Janine Pourroy. *The Art and Making of The Dark Knight Trilogy.* New York: Abrams, 2012.

The Joker: Stacked Deck. Stanford: Longmeadow Press, 1990.

Kalindjian, Claudia. *Batman Begins: The Official Movie Guide.* New York: Time, 2005.

Kane, Bob, with Tom Andrae. *Batman & Me: The Saga Continues.* Van Nuys: Zanart Entertainment, 1996.

_____, various writers and artists. *The Batman Archives, Volume 1.* New York: DC Comics, 1990.

_____. *The Batman Archives, Volume 2.* New York: DC Comics, 1991.

_____. *Batman: The Dailies.* Introduction by Joe Desris. New York: DC Comics and Princeton: Kitchen Sink Press, 1990.

_____. *Batman: The Dark Knight Archives, Volume 1.* New York: DC Comics, 1992.

_____. *Batman: The Dark Knight Archives, Volume 2.* New York: DC Comics, 1995.

_____. *Batman: The Dynamic Duo Archives, Volume 1.* New York: DC Comics, 2003.

_____. *Batman: The Dynamic Duo Archives, Volume 2.* New York: DC Comics, 2006.

_____. *Batman: The Sunday Classics.* Introduction by Joe Desris. New York: DC Comics and Princeton: Kitchen Sink Press, 1991.

_____. *Batman: The World's Finest Comics Archives, Volume 1.* New York: DC Comics, 2002.

_____. *Batman: The World's Finest Comics Archives, Volume 2.* New York: DC Comics, 2004.

Kidd, Chip. *Batman Collected.* Boston: Bullfinch Press, 1996.

_____, and Geoff Spear. *Mythology: The DC Comics Art of Alex Ross.* New York: Pantheon Books, 2003.

Loeb, Jeph (writer) and Jim Lee (artist). *Batman: Hush.* New York: DC Comics, 2002–2003.

_____ (writer) and Tim Sale (artist). *Batman: The Long Halloween.* New York: DC Comics, 1996–1997.

Marriott, John. *Batman: The Official Book of the Movie.* New York: Bantam Books, 1989.

Miller, Frank. *Batman: The Dark Knight Returns.* New York: DC Comics, 1986.

_____. *Batman: The Dark Knight Strikes Again.* New York: DC Comics, 2002.

_____ (writer), and David Mazzucchelli (artist). *Batman: Year One.* New York: DC Comics, 1988.

Moore, Alan (writer), and Brian Bolland (artist). *Batman: The Killing Joke.* New York: DC Comics, 1988.

Nolan, Christopher, Jonathan Nolan and David S. Goyer. *The Dark Knight Trilogy.* New York: Opus, 2012.

O'Neil, Dennis (writer), various artists including Neal Adams and Dick Giordano. *Batman: Tales of the Demon.* New York: DC Comics, 1991.

Pearson, Roberta E., and William Uricchio, eds. *The Many Lives of the Batman.* London: Routledge, 1991.

Schoell, William. *Batman and Robin: The Making of the Movie.* Nashville: Rutledge Hill Press, 1997.

_____. *Batman Forever: The Official Movie Book.* New York: Modern Publishing, 1995.

_____. *Comic Book Heroes of the Screen.* New York: Citadel Press, 1991.

Scivally, Bruce. *Billion Dollar Batman: A History of the Caped Crusader on Film, Radio and Television from 10 Cent Comic Book to Global Icon.* Wilmette, IL: Henry Gray, 2011.

Singer, Michael. *Batman Returns: The Official Movie Book.* New York: Bantam Books, 1992.

Uslan, Michael E. *The Boy Who Loved Batman.* San Francisco: Chronicle Books, 2011.

Van Hise, James. *Batmania II.* Las Vegas: Pioneer Books, 1992.

Vaz, Mark Cotta. *Tales of the Dark Knight: Batman's First Fifty Years 1939–1989.* New York: Ballantine Books, 1989.

Waid, Mark (writer), and Ross, Alex (artist). *Kingdom Come.* New York: DC Comics, 1996.

Wallace, Daniel. *Batman: The World of the Dark Knight.* New York: DK Publishing, 2012.

_____. *The Joker.* New York: Universe, 2011.

West, Adam, with Jeff Rovin. *Back to the Batcave.* New York: Berkley Books, 1994.

Index

Numbers in **_bold italics_** indicate pages with photographs.

ABC Television Network 59, 60, 61, 62, 65, 67, 75
Abercrombie, Ian 203
Abraham Lincoln on Screen (2009 book) 3, 4
"Accidentally on Purpose" (*Detective Comics* #83, January 1944 story) 21
Ace the Bat-Hound **_55_**, 56, 261
Ace Ventura: Pet Detective (1994 film) 158
Ackles, Jensen 267
Action Comics (comic book title) 5
Acton Lane Power Station, West London, England 107
"Adam West: Behind the Cowl" (television documentary on *Batman: Holy Batmania!* DVD set) 77
Adams, Jane 42
Adams, Neal 3, 82, 84, 85, 87, 102, 115, 140, 210, 268
The Adventures of Batman (home movie version of 1943 movie serial *Batman*) 30
The Adventures of Batman and Robin (1994–1995 television series) 139
Adventures of Captain Marvel (1941 movie serial) 18
The Adventures of Superman (radio program) 32–33
Alfred *see* Pennyworth, Alfred
Al Ghul, Ra's 84, 85, 93, 141, 210, 211, 223, 224, 226, 233, 267, 268, 292, 293
Al Ghul, Talia 85, 93, 205, 260, 286, 292
Alien (film series) 204
"All My Enemies Against Me" (*Detective Comics* #526, May 1983 story) 90
The All-New SuperFriends Hour (1977 television series) 86
All Star Batman and Robin the Boy Wonder (2005–2008 comic series) 258–259, 269
Alteri, Kevin 141
Alyn, Kirk 36
AMC Loews Lincoln Square, New York City, New York 239, 278
American Psycho (2000 film) 212
Andrae, Tom 197
Aparo, Jim 85, 87, 90
Aquaman 56, 86
Arkaham, Amadeus 121
Arkham Asylum 121, 150, 160, 170, 214, 225, 226, 264, 267, 294
Arkham Asylum: A Serious House on Serious Earth (1989 graphic novel) 121–122
Arnold, Captain 21
Aronofsky, Darren 209
"Assembling the Arctic Army" (featurette on *Beyond Batman* video documentary) 138
Atom 261
Aurora, Colorado 278
Austin, Terry 87, 88, 92, 103
Austin, William 20, 21
Austin, Texas 70
Azrael 150

Back to the Batcave (1994 book) 78
Bader, Diedrich 260, 263
Baker, Rick 169
Bale, Christian **_209_**, 212, 214, 215, 222, 223, 224, 225, 228, **_231_**, 232, 235, 239, 245, 246, **_273_**, 274, **_276_**, 278, 291
Bane 150, 177, 179, 180, 181, 190, 194, 205, 264, 273, 274, 275, **_276_**, 277, 286, 287, 290, 291, 292, 293, 294
Barbeau, Adrienne 142
Barr, Mike W. 93, 146
Barris, George 66
Bartram, Clark 204
Basinger, Kim 106, 109, 114, 116, 119
The Bat 274, 277, 287, 294, 295
The Bat (1920 stage play) 6
Bat-Girl 54, **_55_**, 56, 75
"Bat-Girl" (*Batman* #139, April 1961 story) 54
Bat in the Sun Productions 269
Bat-Manga!: The Secret History of Batman in Japan (2008 book) 260, 263
Bat-Mite 54, **_55_**, 56, 86, 261, 263
"Bat-Mite Presents: Batman's Strangest Cases" (*Batman: The Brave and the Bold* television series episode) 265
Bat-Pod 234, 239, 277
The Bat, the Cat and the Penguin (1992 television documentary) 137
The Bat Whispers (1930 film) 6
Batarang 5, 116
Batboat 61, 62, 65, 70, 136, 159, 160, 259
Batcave 20, 32, 33, 41, 61, 66, 79, 142, 160, 214, 225, 249, 258, 259, 277, 294
Batchler, Janet Scott 155, 156, 170, 187
Batchler, Lee 155, 156, 170, 187
Batcopter 61, 62, 65, 69, 70, 79
Batcycle 61, 62, 65, 70
"Batdance" (Prince song) 117
Bateman, Patrick 212
BatFilm Productions 88, 89, 102
Batgirl (Barbara Gordon alter ego) 75, 76, 98, 150, 195, 203, 204, 205, 206, 270

307

Index

Batgirl (Barbara Wilson alter ego) 177, *178*, 181, 189, 194
Batgirl (Cassandra Cain alter ego) 198, 266, 270
Batgirl (comic book title) 198
Batgirl (Stephanie Brown alter ego) 266, 270
Batman: comic illustrations *6*, *9*, *55*, *57*, *83*, *88*, *91*, *93*, *96*, *200*; costume 5, 58; creation 5, 6; debut 7; fiftieth anniversary of character 108, 109; as home video game character *265*; mental state of character 98; merchandising 67–68, 109, 202, 297–298; as motion picture character *17*, *37*, *60*, *100*, *125*, *140*, *153*, *178*, *209*, *231*, *273*, *276*; origin of character 7, 33, 34; popularity as an Internet subject 197; relationship with Dick Grayson Robin 53, 82, 168; relationship with Gotham City Police Department 12; relationship with Superman 93; as television character *206*, *261*; use of lethal force 11, 12, 115, 133–134; visual appearance 5, 108
Batman (comic book title) 9, 10, 11, 12, 13, 84, 90, 93, 122, 150, 232, 234, 257, 259, 266, 270
Batman (1943 movie serial) 1, 14, *17*, 32, 35, 36, 37, 38, 39, 40, 41, 42, 47, 48, 50, 51, 65; box office performance 29; as camp piece 17, 29; costuming 18; fight scenes 18–19; filming 16; home video release history 30–31; impact on history of Batman character 31; music 20, 117; opening credits 20; performance of principal actors 19; popularity of film among Batman fans 36; production credits 15; scripting 16; serial's invention of Alfred 20–21; serial's invention of Batcave 20; synopsis 22–29; as World War II propaganda piece 16, 22
Batman (1966 film) 1, 58, *60*, *69*, 81, 87, 155, 158, 192, 234, 261, 278, 295, 299; box office performance 74; filming 68; home video release history 76–77; as means to facilitate production of *Batman* television program 61–62; music 70; performance of principal actors 73–74; popularity of film among Batman fans 79; premiere 70; production credits 59; reviews 74; synopsis 70–73
Batman (1966–1968 television series) 2, 29, 60, 73, 74, 77, 80, 81, 82, 87, 88, 89, 99, 101, 108, 114, 155, 158, 179, 182, 187, 192, 234, 261, 263, 299; casting 62, 64–65; costuming 62–63; development 59–62; music 68; as national craze 67; premiere 67; production 65; second season 74; sets 66; third season 75–76
Batman (1989 album) 117, 161
Batman (1989 film) 1, 3, 30, 42, 51, 52, 77, 78, 81, 89, 98, *100*, *101*, 121, 123, 124, 126, 128, 132, 133, 134, 143, 156, 157, 161, 165, 167, 191, 192, 193, 211, 215, 231, 234, 245, 247, 255, 278; Academy Award won by film 116; box office performance 112; budget 107; casting 105, 106; controversy surrounding casting of Michael Keaton as Batman 105–106; costuming 108, 117; filming 106–107; home video release history 119–120; impact on history of Batman character 100–101, 120; music 20, 109, 117; performance of principal actors 113–115; premiere 109; production credits 99; production design 106, 107, 116; props 116–117; regard for established Batman comic book mythos 113, 115; reviews 112; scripting 104, 105; sets 106–107, 116; special effects 118; suitability for children 133; synopsis 109–112; Tim Burton's direction 117–119
The Batman (2004–2008 television series) 2, 205–207, *206*, 260
The Batman (unfilmed script by Tom Mankiewicz) 103
Batman Adventures (comic book title) 149
The Batman Adventures (comic book title) 149
Batman and Captain America (1996 graphic novel) 175
Batman and Me (1989 book) 29, 42, 197, 238
Batman and Me: A Devotion to Destiny (2008 documentary) 237–238
Batman and Me: The Saga Continues (1996 book) 197
Batman & Mr. Freeze: SubZero (1997 video) 194–195

Batman and Robin (comic book title) 266
Batman and Robin (1943–1946 newspaper comic strip) 32
Batman and Robin (1949 movie serial) 1, 30, 34, *37*, 59; choice of shooting locations 39; costuming 40; dialogue 40; fight scenes 41; filming 36; home video release history 50–51; music 39; performance of principal actors 41; popularity of film among Batman fans 36; production credits 35; regard for established Batman comic book mythos 36, 41–42; scripting 38–39; synopsis 42–50
Batman and Robin (1997 film) 1, 170, 172, 176, *178*, *179*, 193, 194, 195, 197, 209, 220, 273, 278, 288, 292; box office performance 190; budget 181; casting 180; costuming 187–188; deleted scene 191; filming 181; home video release history 191–192; lack of realism in film 187; lighting 181, 188; performance of principal actors 188–190; popularity of film among Batman fans 192; premiere 182; production credits 177; scripting 180, 187; sets 181; sexual subtext 188; similarity to *Batman Forever* 185–187; special effects 181, 187; suitability for children 190; synopsis 182–185
The Batman and Robin Adventures (comic book title) 149
"Batman & Son" (2006 comic story arc) 259–260
Batman and Spider-Man: New Age Dawning (1997 graphic novel) 175
Batman and the Mad Monk (2006–2007 comic series) 259
Batman and the Monster Men (2005–2006 comic series) 259
Batman: Animated (1999 book) 2
Batman: Arkham Asylum (2009 video game) 3, 264, *265*
Batman: Arkham City (2011 video game) 3, 264
Batman Begins (2005 film) 1, 3, 31, 119, 137, 165, 169, 191, 192, 198, 207, *209*, 231, 232, 235, 237, 238, 246, 248, 249, 250, 253, 273, 274, 275, 277, 278, 291, 293, 294; box office performance 220; budget 212–213; casting 212–213;

Christopher Nolan's direction 214, 226; cinematography 225; costuming 213, 220; design and construction of film's Batmobile 213; editing 226; filming 214, 225; home video release history 227–228; IMAX screenings 227; impact on history of Batman character 229; lack of realism in film 226; merchandising tie-ins 228–229; music 215, 226, 239; official website 215; performance of principal actors 222–224; premiere 215; production credits 208–209; production design 225; regard for established Batman comic book mythos 220–222, 254; reviews 220; scripting 211–212; sets 214; special effects 214–215; suitability for children 228; synopsis 215–220
Batman Begins (2005 home video game) 228
Batman Beyond (1999–2001 television series) 201, 209
Batman Beyond: Return of the Joker (2000 video) 201
Batman: Black and White (1996 comic series) 175
Batman Collected (1996 book) 2, 175, 199
Batman: Dark Victory (1999–2000 graphic novel series) 175
Batman: Dead End (2003 film) 204–205, 269
"Batman: Double for Superman!" (*World's Finest Comics* #71, July–August 1954 story) 54
Batman Forever (1995 film) 1, 151, **153**, **154**, 172, 177, 180, 185, 186, 187, 191, 193, 197, 231, 234, 278; box office performance 165, 190; budget 162; casting 157–158; costuming 158–159; deleted scenes 165–166, 170; filming 161; home video release history 165, 169–170; Joel Schumacher's direction 169; makeup 159; merchandising tie-ins 162; music 160–161; performance of principal actors 167–169; popularity of film among Batman fans 165, 166, 170; premiere 162; production credits 152; production design 159; regard for established Batman comic book mythos 156, 166–167, 171; reviews 164–165; scripting 155–157; sets 160; sexual subtext 168; special effects 160, 162, 167; suitability for children 165; synopsis 162–164
Batman from the 30s to the 70s (1971 book) 85
Batman: Gotham by Gaslight (1989 graphic novel) 121
Batman: Gotham Knight (2008 video) 237, 266, 267, 278
Batman: Haunted Knight (1996 book) 174, 221
Batman: Holy Batmania! (DVD set) 77
"Batman: Holy Batmania!" (television documentary on *Batman: Holy Batmania!* DVD set) 77
Batman Incorporated (comic book title) 266
Batman: Legends of the Dark Knight (comic book title) 121, 150, 174
Batman: Mask of the Phantasm (1993 film) 117, 138, **140**; box office performance 146; home video release history 148; music 147; premiere 139, 143; production credits 139; synopsis 143–146; voice acting 148; Warner Bros.' decision to release film as theatrical work 143
"Batman Meets Bat-Mite" (*Detective Comics* #267, May 1958 story) 54
Batman: Mystery of the Batwoman (2003 video) 205
"The Batman Nobody Knows" (*Batman* #250, July 1973 story) 196
Batman: Noel (2011 graphic novel) 271
Batman-on-Film (Internet website) 197–198
Batman Original Motion Picture Score (1989 album) 117
Batman: Red Rain (1991 graphic novel) 121
Batman Returns (1992 film) 1, 120, 121, 122, **125**, 141, 142, 146, 148, 149, 152, 154, 156, 162, 167, 169, 182, 191, 193, 197, 273, 288; box office performance 132–133, 165; budget 129; casting 127–128; costuming 134; fight scenes 134; filming 128; home video release history 137–138; merchandising tie-ins 126–127, 129, 229; moviegoers' negative reaction to film 132–133; music 128, 137; performance of principal actors 134–136; premiere 129; production credits 123; regard for established Batman comic book mythos 133–134; reviews 132, 165; scripting 124, 126, 127; sets 128; suitability for children 126–133; synopsis 129–132; Tim Burton's direction 137
Batman: Son of the Demon (1987 graphic novel) 93, 260
The Batman–Superman Hour (1968 television series) 86
The Batman Superman Movie (1998 video) 195
"Batman Takes Over" (1949 movie serial *Batman and Robin* chapter) 42–43
Batman Tech (2008 documentary) 238, 255
Batman: The Animated Series (1992–1995 television series) 2, 87, 117, 138, 149, 155, 179, 189, 190, 194, 195, 196, 199, 201, 202, 210, 221, 237, 248, 262, 263, 264; animation 142; design 142; development 139; initial television run 139; music 143; regard for established Batman comic book mythos 140–141; toys based on series 149–150; voice acting 142–143
Batman: The Blue, the Grey and the Bat (1992 graphic novel) 121
Batman: The Brave and the Bold (2008–2011 television series) 2, 260–264, **261**
Batman: The Complete History (1999 book) 199
Batman: The Complete Robin Storyboard Sequence (program on 1989 *Batman* DVD set) 119
Batman: The Dark Knight (comic book title) 266
Batman: The Dark Knight Returns (1986 graphic novel series) 3, 91–92, 93, 95, 98, 102, 103, 104, 118, 167, 173, 174, 196, 202, 203, 211, 212, 221, 232, 289, 290, 298
Batman: The Dark Knight Returns Part 1 (2012 video) 297–298
Batman: The Dark Knight Returns Part 2 (2013 video) 297–298
Batman: The Dark Knight Strikes Again (2002 graphic novel series) 202–203
"Batman: The Journey Begins" (2005 video documentary) 228

Batman: The Killing Joke (1988 graphic novel) 52, 96–97, 98, 203, 247, 248, 270
Batman: The Long Halloween (1996 graphic novel series) 174–175, 221, 232, 254
Batman: The Return of Bruce Wayne (2010 comic book series) 266
Batman: The Ride (roller coaster) 150
"Batman: The Tumbler" (2005 video documentary) 228
Batman: The World of the Dark Knight (2012 book) 270
"Batman Theme" (1966 *Batman* musical piece) 67, 70
"Batman Theme" (1989 *Batman* musical piece) 20, 109, 117, 128, 143, 215
"Batman Trapped" (1949 movie serial *Batman and Robin* chapter) 44–45
Batman Triumphant (unproduced Batman film) 193, 209, 210
Batman 2 (unfilmed script by Sam Hamm) 124, 127
"Batman: Under the Hood" (2005–2006 comic book story arc) 257, 267, 268, 270
Batman: Under the Red Hood (2010 video) 257, 267, 268
Batman Unmasked: The Psychology of the Dark Knight (2008 documentary) 238–239, 255
Batman: Vengeance (2001 home video game) 202
The Batman Vs. Dracula (2005 video) 207
Batman Vs. Superman (unproduced Batman film) 209
"The Batman Vs. the Cat-Woman" (*Batman* #3 story) 11
"Batman Vs. Wizard" (1949 movie serial *Batman and Robin* chapter) 49
"Batman Victorious" (1949 movie serial *Batman and Robin* chapter) 49–50
Batman: War Games (2004–2005 comic book story arc) 266
Batman: War on Crime (1999 graphic novel) 3, 199, **200**, 245, 269
"Batman Wars Against the Dirigible of Doom" (*Detective Comics* #33, November 1939 story) 7
Batman: Watching Over Gotham (2007 film) 269
Batman with Robin the Boy Wonder (1969 television series) 86

Batman: Year One (1987 comic book/graphic novel series) 93, **94**, 95, 142, 148, 167, 174, 175, 209, 211, 221, 224, 268, 291
Batman: Year One (2011 video) 268
Batman: Year Two (1987 comic book/graphic novel series) 146, 148
Batmania (Batman fanzine) 80
"Batman's Last Chance" (1949 movie serial *Batman and Robin* chapter) 47
Batmobile 12, 18, 30, 36, 37, 38, 58, 61, 65, 66, 70, 76, 78, 79, 95, 107, 114, 116, 117, 136, 137, 142, 159, 160, 187, 212, 213, 215, 225, 226, 234, 235, 249, 259
The Batmobile (2012 documentary) 278, 295
Batrope 5
"The Bat's Cave" (1943 movie serial *Batman* chapter) 23–24
"Bats, Mattes, and Dark Knights: The Visual Effects of *Batman Returns*" (featurette on *Beyond Batman* video documentary) 138
Batsignal 13, 41, 118, 136
Batson, Billy 173
Batwing 116, 134, 160, 259
Batwoman (*Batman: Mystery of the Batwoman* character) 205
Batwoman (comic book title) 270
"The Batwoman" (*Detective Comics* #233, July 1956 story) 54
Batwoman (Kate Kane alter ego) 258, 266, 270
Batwoman (Kathy Kane alter ego) 54, **55**, 56, 75, 81, 205, 258
Beaumont, Andrea 143, 147, 205
Beetlejuice (1988 film) 104, 105, 106
Begley, Ed, Jr. 143
Bell Helicopter Company 69
Bening, Annette 127
Bennet, Spencer 36, 41
Bermejo, Lee 271
Berry, Halle 135, 291
"Beware of—Poison Ivy!" (*Batman* #181, June 1966 story) 178
"Beware the Gray Ghost" (*Batman: The Animated Series* television series episode) 143
Beyond Batman (multi-part video documentary on Warner Bros.' Batman film DVD sets) 119, 138, 170, 191

"Bigger, Bolder, Brighter: The Production Design of *Batman and Robin*" (featurette on *Beyond Batman* video documentary) 191
Bingham, Jerry 93
Biography Channel 77
Birds of Prey (comic book title) 203
Birds of Prey (2002 television series) 203
Black Bat 266
Black Canary 172
Black Lightning 261
Black Mask 267
Blackgate Prison 294
Blade (1998 film) 210
Blade Trinity (2004 film) 211
Blade II (2002 film) 210
Blake, John 274, 287, 292, 293
Blick, Hugo E. 113
Blind Justice (1989 comic book series) 211, 221
Bolger, Ray 210, 224
Bolland, Brian 96, 97
Bond, James 59, 6, 222
Bookworm 64
Boone, Jean 70
Boone, Mark Junior 224
Bowen, Cameron 269
Boy Wonder: My Life in Tights (1995 book) 78
Brainiac 202
The Brave and the Bold (comic book title) 56, 68, 85, 261
Brokeback Mountain (2005 film) 233, 274
Bronson Cave, California 66
Brown, Stephanie 266, 270
"Building the Batmobile" (featurette on *Beyond Batman* video documentary) 119
Burbank, California 128, 160
Burnett, Alan 87, 139, 141, 143, 195, 199, 205, 209, 237
Burnette, Smiley 20
Burton, Tim 103, 104, 106, 107, 109, 117, 118, 119, 120, 121, 124, 126, 127, 128, 133, 134, 135, 136, 137, 138, 149, 152, 153, 154, 155, 161, 169, 170, 182, 193, 210, 213, 225, 231, 245, 255, 273, 274, 288
Byrne, John 90

Cain, Cassandra 198, 266, 270
Caine, Michael 213, 215, 223, 225, 231, 232, 239, 248, 274, 291
"Cape and Cowl" (2005 video documentary) 228
Capizzi, Duane 205
Captain America 175

Captain Marvel 173
Cardington Sheds, London, England 214, 235, 275
Carnegie Mellon University 277
Carrey, Jim **154**, 158, 162, 168, 169, 170
Cartoon Network 56, 201, 260, 269
Casablanca FilmWorks 102, 103, 104
"The Case of the Chemical Syndicate" (*Detective Comics* # 27, May 1939 story) **6**, 7
"Case of the Costume-Clad Killers" (*Detective Comics* #60, February 1942 story) 13
Caspian, Judson 146
Caspian, Rachel 146
Cataclysm (1998 comic book series) 198
Catwoman 9, 11, 38, 61, 64, 68, **69**, 86, 124, **125**, 127, 135, 141, 150, 174, 194, 199, 205, 210, 262, 263, 264, 271, 273, 274, **275**, 277, 291
Catwoman (2004 film) 135, 291
Cavendish, Dr. Charles 121
CBS Television Network 78
"Cesar Romero: In a Class by Himself" (television documentary on *Batman: Holy Batmania!* DVD set) 77
"The Challenge" (*Legends of the Super Heroes* episode) 89
Challenge of the SuperFriends (1978 television series) 86
Chang, Michael 262
Chertsey, England 236
Chicago, Illinois 213, 214, 225, 235, 249, 276
Chill, Joe 33, 34, 105, 113, 146, 262, 263
"Chill of the Night!" (*Batman: The Brave and the Bold* television series episode) 262–263
Chinatown (1974 film) 105
A Christmas Carol (1843 novella) 271
Cincinnati, Ohio 227
Cinefex (magazine) 187
City of Scars (2010 film) 269
Claridge, Henry 9, 10
Clooney, George **178**, 180, 181, 182, 188, 189, 191, 222
Clueless (1995 film) 181
Cobblepot, Oswald Chesterfield 13, 127, 135
Codd, Matt 160
Cole, Royal K. 36
Collora, Sandy 204, 205, 269
Columbia Pictures 16, 29, 30, 34, 35, 36, 39, 42, 50, 61, 65, 124

Columbia Pictures: The Condensed Features Collection (home movie series) 30
Columbus, Ohio 70, 227, 245, 270, 277
Columbus Zoo, Columbus, Ohio 245
Comics Code Authority 52, 53, 234
Conan Doyle, Sir Arthur 6
Condors, Jim 82
Conroy, Kevin 142, 148, 201, 202, 205, 237, 263, 267, 271
Conway, Gerry 90
Corbould, Chris 213, 228, 232, 235, 274
Corvette (Chevrolet) 107
Cotillard, Marion 273, 274, 278, 292
Craig, Yvonne 76
Crane, Jonathan 210, 221, 224, 274, 293
Cranston, Bryan 268
"The Crimes of Two-Face" (*Detective Comics* #66, August 1942 story) 169
Crocker, Paul 264
Croft, Douglas 16, **17**, 19, 29, 41
Crowley, Matt 32
Crowley, Nathan 212, 213, 225, 228, 232, 249, 274
Cruise, Tom 158
Cushenbery, Bill 66
CW Network 278

Daka, Doctor 16, 17, 39, 65
Daniels, Les 199
Daredevil 175
Daredevil and Batman: Eye for an Eye (1997 graphic novel) 175
Dark Justice (2003 film) 269
"The Dark Knight" (nickname for Batman) 10, 8, 232, 245–246
The Dark Knight (2008 film) 1, 198, 220, 227, 228, 229, **231**, **232**, 268, 273, 274, 275, 276, 278, 285, 290, 291, 293, 294, 298; Academy Awards won by film 247, 250; box office performance 245; budget 236; casting 232–233; Christopher Nolan's direction 250; cinematography 249; costuming 233, 246; filming 235–236, 249; home video release history 255; IMAX screenings 249; IMAX-shot scenes 249; impact on history of Batman character 255–256; makeup 233–234; merchandising tie-ins 246; music 239, 250; official website 238; performance of principal actors 246–248; premiere 239; production credits 230; production design 249–250; promotion 237–239; regard for established Batman comic book mythos 247, 254–255; reviews 245; scripting 232, 233; sets 235; sound editing 250; special effects 234, 236; story construction problems 250–254; synopsis 239–245; worldwide popularity 245
The Dark Knight IMAX Prologue (2007 film) 228, 235, 276
The Dark Knight Rises (2012 film) 1, 198, 220, 229, 254, 256, 271, **273**, **275**, **276**, 298; Aurora, Colorado shooting on night of film's premiere 278; box office performance 285; budget 274; casting 274; Christopher Nolan's direction 290; costuming 294; filming 275–277; home video release history 295; IMAX screenings 294; IMAX-shot scenes 275–276, 294; merchandising tie-ins 294; music 277–278, 294; official website 278; performance of principal actors 291–293; premiere 278; production credits 272–273; production design 274, 294; regard for established Batman comic book mythos 288–290; reviews 285; scripting 273; sets 275, 277; special effects 274, 277; story construction problems 286–288; synopsis 279–285
The Dark Knight Rises IMAX Prologue (2011 film) 276
Darkseid 260, 266
"Daughter of the Demon" (*Batman* #232, June 1971 story) 84–85
Dawes, Rachel 213, 224, 232, 248, 249, 250 251, 255, 293
DC Comics 5, 20, 21, 29 52, 53, 61, 68, 80, 82, 86, 88, 90, 92, 95, 101, 102, 150, 175, 197, 202, 203, 204, 210, 237, 245, 257, 266, 270, 296, 298
DC Universe Animated Original Movies (animated film series) 237, 266, 268, 270, 271, 297
Deadshot (*Batman: Gotham Knight* video episode) 237
A Death in the Family (1988–1989 comic book/graphic novel series) 95, 96
Del Mar, Ennis 233

Dempski, Dan 70
Dent, Gilda 174
Dent, Harvey 13, 106, 116, 141, 155, 157, 158, 169, 174, 248, 250, 251, 253, 254, 263, 293
"Designing the Batsuit" (featurette on *Beyond Batman* video documentary) 119
Detective Comics (comic book title) 5, 9, 12, 13, 94, 85, 87, 88, 90, 98, 101, 103, 211, 258, 259, 266, 270
DeVito, Danny *125*, 127, 135, 137, 138, 141
Deyell, Peter 63, 77
DiCaprio, Leonardo 273
Dick Tracy (newspaper comic strip) 8
Dickens, Charles 271
"Did Robin Die Tonight?" (*Batman* #408, June 1987 story) 95
DiMaggio, John 267
Dini, Paul 2, 3, 139, 141, 143, 149, 195, 196, 198, 199, 201, 209, 262, 263, 264, 269
Dixon, Chuck 150
Dr. No (1962 film) 59
Dome, Long Beach, California 160
"The Doom of the Rising Sun" (1943 movie serial *Batman* chapter) 28–29
The Doors (1991 film) 157
Dozier, William 60, 61, 62, 64, 65, 66, 67, 68, 75
Dracula 121, 207
Drake, Steven 195
Drake, Tim 122, 126, 141, 195, 260, 266, 269, 270, 298
"Dreams in Darkness" *Batman: The Animated Series* television series episode) 221
"Dressed to Thrill: The Costumes of *Batman and Robin*" (featurette on *Beyond Batman* video documentary) 191
Ducard, Henri 211, 213, 221, 223
Duncan, Johnny 35, *37*, 41, 51
Duquesne, Cathy 205
Dykstra, John 160, 162, 181

Eckhart, Aaron 233, 234, 238, 239, 248, 293
Egghead 64
"Eight Steps Down" (1943 movie serial *Batman* chapter) 27–28
Eisner, Joel 2
Eisner Award 149
"The Electrical Brain" (1943 movie serial *Batman* chapter) 22–23, 47
Elfman, Danny 20, 109, 117, 128, 137, 143, 161, 215

Elliot, Thomas 204
Ellsworth, Whitney 11
Elongated Man 261
Elseworlds (DC Comics irregular graphic novel series) 121, 172, 198, 199
"Embers of Evil" (1943 movie serial *Batman* chapter) 27
Empire (magazine) 126
Empire of the Sun (1987 film) 212
The Encyclopedia of Comic Book Heroes Volume 1: Batman (1976 book) 85, 260
Ending the Knight (2012 documentary collection) 295
Engel, Mike 238
Englehart, Steve 87, 88, 92, 102, 103, 115, 141
Entertainment Weekly (magazine) 133
ER (television program) 180
Erin Brockovich (2000 film) 233
The Essential Batman Encyclopedia (2008 book) 260
Evans, John 116, 117
An Evening with Batman and Robin (1965 re-release of 1943 movie serial *Batman*) 29, 30, 50, 65
"Executioner Strikes" (1943 movie serial *Batman* chapter) 28

Fairbanks, Douglas 6
Falcone, Alberto 174
Falcone, Carmine 94, 174, 224
Fantasia 2000 (1999 film) 233
Far and Away (1992 film) 158
"The Fatal Blast" (1949 movie serial *Batman and Robin* chapter) 46
"The Fear" (*Super Powers Team: The Galactic Guardians* television series episode) 87, 210
52 (2006–2007 comic series) 258
Filangeri, Lydia 238
Filmation 86
Final Crisis (2008 comic book series) 260
Finger, Bill 5, 6, 7, 8, 11, 81, 84, 102, 115, 120, 297
"The First Batman" (*Detective Comics* #235, September 1956 story) 263
Fisher, Tommy 159
Fisher-Price Toys 297
Flash 56, 207, 261, 270
Flashpoint (2011 comic book series) 270
Flass, Arnold 221, 224
Flatliners (1990 film) 153

Flattery, Tim 159
Fleisher, Michael 85, 260
Florence, Italy 288, 294
"Flying Spies" (1943 movie serial *Batman* chapter) 27
Foley 287, 288
Ford, Glenn 66
Fox, Gardner 8, 82
Fox, Lucius 213, 222, 224, 232, 248, 274, 291
Fox Kids Network 139
Fox Television Network 143
Fraser, Harry 16
Freeman, Morgan 213, 215, 224, 232, 248, 274, 278, 291
Freeze, Mr. 56, 64, 141, 177, **179**, 189, 194, 205, 264
"Freeze Frame: The Visual Effects of *Batman and Robin*" (featurette on *Beyond Batman* video documentary) 191
"Freeze Frames" (*Cinefex* September 1997 story) 187
Friedle, Will 201
Fries, Nora 141, 189, 195
Fries, Dr. Victor 141, 189, 195
"From Jack to the Joker" (featurette on *Beyond Batman* video documentary) 119
"Frozen Freaks and Femme Fatales: The Makeup of *Batman and Robin*" (featurette on *Beyond Batman* video documentary) 191
Furst, Anton 106, 107, 116, 117, 128
Futura (1955 experimental Lincoln automobile) 66

Geda, Curt 205
"Genesis of the Bat" (2005 video documentary) 228
Gervis, Bert, Jr. *see* Ward, Burt
Gibson, Walter 6
Giordano, Dick 82, 85, 87, 196, 211
Glastron Boat Company 70
Gleeson, Jack 224, 225, 293
Glover, John 142
Goguen, Michael 205
Goldberg, Jordan 237
Goldenthal, Elliot 160, 161, 181
Goldsman, Avika 155, 156, 170, 177, 187, 189, 190, 191
Goodman, Robert 196
Gordon, Barbara 75, 76, 96, 97, 195, 198, 201, 203, 205, 269, 270
Gordon, Commissioner James 7, 12, 13, 21, 41, **55**, 64, 75, 87, 94, 95, 96, 97, 98, 106, 116, 127, 141, 161, 174, 181, 190, 199, 205, 213, 221, 224, 232, 238, 248,

251, 252, 253, 254, 268, 274, 288, 289, 291
Gordon-Levitt, Joseph 273, 274, 278, 292
Gorshin, Frank 59, 64, *69*, 78, 89, 158
Gossip Gerty 197
Gotham Adventures (comic book title) 149
Gotham City 12, 25, 33, 39, 41, 53, 67, 82, 87, 106, 107, 116, 121, 128, 136, 142, 160, 198, 201, 205, 213, 214, 225, 235, 237, 253, 254, 264, 274, 299
Gotham City Police Department 12, 13, 21, 277, 287
"Gotham City Revisited: The Production Design of *Batman Returns*" (featurette on *Beyond Batman* video documentary) 138
"Gotham City Rises" (2005 video documentary) 228
Gotham Rogues 276
Gotham Tonight (2008 internet video series) 238, 255
Gotham Uncovered: The Creation of a Scene (2008 documentary collection) 255
Gough, Michael 106, 115, 127, 161, 181, 189
Gould, Chester 8
Goy, Jean-Pierre 234
Goyer, David S. 210, 211, 212, 220, 221, 222, 223, 224, 228, 231, 232, 233, 237, 273
Grauman's Chinese Theatre, Los Angeles, California 215
Gray Ghost 143
Grayson, Dick 90, 96, 122, 141, 156, 175, 195, 202, 203, 207, 258, 260, 266, 268, 269, 270
Green Arrow 172
Green Lantern 56, 172, 207, 261
Greenberger, Robert 260
Greene, Sid 82
Greenway Productions 60
Greenwood, Bruce 267, 269
Griffith, D.W. 64
Grissom, Carl 106, 116
Guber, Peter 102, 103, 104, 119, 124
Gyllenhaal, Maggie 232, 239, 248

Hall, Anthony Michael 238
Hamill, Mark 142, 148, 202, 263, 264
Hamilton, Neil 64
Hamm, Sam 104, 105, 107, 119, 124, 126, 127, 138, 211
Hanna-Barbera 86, 89

Hardy, Tom 273, 274, *276*, 278, 291, 292
Harris, Stacy 32
"Harvey Two-Face" (2008 *The Dark Knight* musical piece) 239
Hastings, Bob 142
Hathaway, Anne 274, *275*, 278, 291, 294
Hayes, Gabby 20
"Heart of Ice" (*Batman: The Animated Series* television series episode) 141, 189
Heart of Vengeance: Returning Batman to his Roots (2011 documentary) 268–269
Hefti, Neil 67, 70, 161
Heinz Field, Pittsburgh, Pennsylvania 276
Hemming, Lindy 213, 223, 228, 232, 233, 247, 274, 294
Henry V (1989 film) 212
"Here Comes Alfred" (*Batman #16*, April–May 1943 story) 20–21
"Hi Diddle Riddle" (*Batman* television series episode) 61, 63, 67
Hill, Sefton 264
Hillyer, Lambert 19
Hingle, Pat 106, 116, 127, 161, 181, 190
Hirohito 23
The History Channel 238, 255, 278
"Hold Me, Thrill Me, Kiss Me, Kill Me" (U2 song) 161
Holiday 174
Hollywood, California 42
Holmes, Katie 213, 215, 224, 228, 232, 248
Holmes, Sherlock 6
Hopwood, Avery 6
Howard, James Newton 215, 226, 239, 250, 277, 278
Hudson University 82
Hughes, Howard 160
Hugo, Victor 11
Hummer (General Motors truck) 212
"Hunt for a Robin-Killer" (*Detective Comics* #374, April 1968 story) 82
"Hunt the Dark Knight" (*Batman: The Dark Knight Returns* story, 1986) *91*
Huntress 203
Hush 204
Hush (2002–2003 comic book story arc) 204, 257

I Am Legend (2007 film) 235, 276

"I Am the Batman" (2008 *The Dark Knight* musical piece) 239
"The Ice Crimes of Mr. Zero" (*Batman* #121, February 1959 story) 56
Image Entertainment 77
"Imaging Forever: The Visual Effects of *Batman Forever*" (featurette on *Beyond Batman* video documentary) 170
IMAX Corporation 227
"In Darkness Dwells" (*Batman: Gotham Knight* video episode) 237
Inception (2010 film) 273, 274
Indiana State Museum, Indianapolis, Indiana 227
Indiana University 101, 102
Indianapolis, Indiana 227
Infantino, Carmine 56, 58, 75, 80, 81
Infinite Crisis (2005–2006 comic book series) 257–258
"Inside the Elfman Studios: The Music of *Batman Returns*" (featurette on *Beyond Batman* video documentary) 138
Insomnia (2002 film) 210, 212
Inverness, Scotland 275
Isley, Pamela 179
It Started with a Kiss (1959 film) 66

Jack the Ripper 121
Jackman, Hugh 231
Jaipur, Rajasthan, India 275
Jeffries, Dean 65
Jelenic, Michael 260
JLA (comic book title) 271
"JLA: Tower of Babel" (2000 comic book story arc) 271
The Joan Rivers Show (television series) 127
Johnson, Lyndon B. 73
Joker 38, 50, 53, 58, 61, 64, 84, 86, 87, 88, 104, 105, 121, 122, 134, 135, 141, 142, 149, 150, 174, 194, 195, 196, 198, 199, 201, 204, 205, 206, 207, 210, 231, 233, 234, 235, 236, 247, 248, 249, 250, 251, 252, 253, 254, 255, 258, 262, 263, 264, 267, 268, 269, 270, 271, 293, 294; comic illustrations *10*, *91*, *96*; debut 9; as motion picture character *69*, *101*, *140*, *232*; origin 52, 96–97, 247; romance with Harley Quinn 142, 149; visual appearance 9, 11
"The Joker" (*Batman* #1, Spring 1940 story) *9*, *10*, 11, 113

"The Joker Returns" (*Batman* #1, Spring 1940 story) 10, 11
"The Joker's Five-Way Revenge" (*Batman* #251, September 1973 story) 84
Jones, Tommy Lee **154**, 157, 158, 161, 162, 169, 170, 234
"Julie Newmar: The Cat's Meow" (television documentary on *Batman: Holy Batmania!* DVD set) 77
Justice League (2001–2002 television series) 201–202
Justice League: Doom (2012 video) 270
Justice League of America 56, 68, 201, 269
Justice League of America (comic book title) 56, 86
Justice League Unlimited (2003–2005 television series) 202

Kane, Betty 54
Kane, Bob 5, 6, 7, 8, 11, 13, 16, 29, 30, 32, 42, 56, 80, 81, 84, 102, 106, 109, 115, 119, 120, 134, 140, 196, 237, 238, 297
Kane, Debbie 196, 197
Kane, Elizabeth Sanders 196
Kane, Gil 82
Kane, Kate 258, 270
Kane, Kathy 54, 205, 258
Kasem, Casey 77, 86
Katzman, Sam 36
Keaton, Michael 98, **100**, 104, 105, 106, 107, 108, 109, 113, 114, 118, 119, **125**, 127, 128, 134, 137, 138, 157, 167, 189, 222
Kelley, Carrie 91, 92, 196
Kemp, Jan 62, 63
Kenner Toys 126, 149
Kent, Harvey 13
Kerns, Hubie 70
Kidd, Chip 2, 175, 199, 260
Kidman, Nicole 158, 169, 170
Kid's WB Network 195, 201, 205
Killer Croc 90, 141, 237
Killer Moth 75
Kilmer, Val **153**, 157, 161, 162, 167, 170, 180, 188, 189, 222
King Lear (play) 100
King Tut 64
Kingdom Come (1996 graphic novel series) 172–174, 198, 202, 203, 260, 290
Kirkland, Boyd 195
"A Kiss from a Rose" (Seal song) 161
Kitt, Eartha 68
Knebworth House, London, England 107
"Knight Moves: The Stunts of *Batman Forever*" (featurette on *Beyond Batman* video documentary) 170
Knightfall (1993 comic book series) 150, 198, 290
Knightquest (1993 comic book series) 150, 198
KnightsEnd (1994 comic book series) 150, 198
Knox, Alexander 106, 116, 119
Koenig, Andrew 204
Krypto the Superdog 56
Krypto the Superdog (2005–2006 television series) 56
Kuwata, Jiro 260
Kyle, Helena 203
Kyle, Selina 11, 95, 127, 135, 273, 274, 291

Lady Shiva 203
"Lady Shiva" (*Birds of Prey* television series episode) 203–204
Lamborghini Automobile Company 212
Lane, Lois 42
Larry Darmour Productions 16
Lau 249, 251, 252
Laurel and Hardy 29
Leahy, Patrick 248
Ledger, Heath 11, **232**, 233, 234, 236, 237, 247, 248, 268, 293
Lee, Jim 204, 258, 259
"Legend — The Batman and How He Came to Be" (preface to "Batman Wars Against the Dirigible of Doom") 7, 221, 222, 262
"Legends of the Dark Knight" (*New Batman/Superman Adventures* television series episode) 196
Legends of the Dark Knight: The History of Batman (video documentary on 1989 *Batman* DVD set) 119
Legends of the Super Heroes (1979 television program) 77, 89
Lego Batman: The Movie— DC Super Heroes Unite (2013 video) 259
Lego Batman: The Videogame (2008 home video game) 259
Lego Batman 2: DC Super Heroes (2012 home video game) 259
Lego Toys 259
Leonardo da Vinci 6
Lester, Loren 142
Lichtenstein, Roy 59
Life (news magazine) 67
Lincoln, Abraham 4
Lincoln Automobile Company 66
Ling, Barbara 159, 160, 181, 187

Liss, Ronald 32
Little Barford Power Station, Bedfordshire, England 107
Little Women (1994 film) 212
Liu, Sam 268
"The Living Corpse" (1943 movie serial *Batman* chapter) 24–25
Locklear, Heather 143
Loeb, Gillian 94, 224, 238, 252
Loeb, Jeph 174, 175, 204, 232, 254
London, England 106, 214, 235
Lone Ranger 18
A Lonely Place of Dying (1989 comic book/graphic novel series) 122
Loomis, Andrew 174
Looney Tunes cartoons 196
Los Angeles, California 16, 25, 36, 39, 277
The Lost Boys (1987 film) 153
Lowery, Robert 35, **37**, 41, 51, 222
"Lured by Radium" (1943 movie serial *Batman* chapter) 26
Luthor, Lex 173, 195, 198, 202, 203

MacCurdy, Jean 139
MacGregor-Scott, Peter 181, 187, 191
MacPherson, Elle 190
Mad Love (1994 comic book) 149, 196
"Mad Love" (*The New Batman/Superman Adventures* television series episode) 196
Madison, Julie 190
"Making-Up the Penguin" (featurette on *Beyond Batman* video documentary) 138
"The Malay Penguin" (*Detective Comics* #473, November 1977 story) **88**
"The Man Behind the Red Hood" (*Detective Comics* #168, February 1951 story) 52, 97, 113, 247, 258
"The Man Who Falls" (*Secret Origins of the World's Greatest Super-Heroes*, 1989 story) 211, 220
The Man Who Laughs (1928 film) 11
Mankiewicz, Tom 103
"The Many Faces of Gotham City" (featurette on *Beyond Batman* video documentary) 170
Marina Del Ray, California 160
Marineland, Palos Verdes, California 69

"Mark of the Zombies" (1943 movie serial *Batman* chapter) 24
The Mark of Zorro (1920 film) 6
Maroni, Sal 238, 251, 253
Martian Manhunter 56
Martinson, Leslie 68, 74
Marvel Comics 101, 175, 210
The Mask (1994 film) 158
"Master of Fear" (*Batman* #457, December 1990 story) 122
Mattel Corporation 202, 297
Mazzucchelli, David 93, 95, 148, 167, 174, 209, 211, 224, 268, 291
McCartney, Jesse 269
McClure Syndicate 32
McCuistion, Michael 143
McCulley, Johnston 6
McDonald's Restaurants 129
McDowell, Malcolm 143
McFarlane, Colin 224, 238
McFarlane, Todd 146
McGinnis, Terry 201
McMahon, Ed 89
McKay, Norman 173, 174
McKean, Dave 121, 122
McKenzie, Benjamin 268
McLeod, Victor 16
Mefistofle (1868 opera) 222
Mego Toys 87
Melniker, Benjamin 88, 89, 92, 102, 103, 104, 119
Memento (2000 film) 210, 212
Meredith, Burgess 59, 64, **69**, 70
Meridian, Dr. Chase 158, 169, 224
Meriwether, Lee 59, 68, **69**, 70
Merrill, Gary 32
Meyer, Dina 203, 204
MGM Studios 102
Miller, Frank 91, 92, 93, 95, 98, 102, 103, 115, 118, 119, 140, 146, 148, 167, 173, 174, 196, 202, 203, 209, 211, 212, 224, 232, 258, 259, 268, 289, 291, 298
"The Million Dollar Debut of Batgirl" (*Detective Comics* #359, January 1967 story) 75, 76
Mission: Impossible — Ghost Protocol (2011 film) 276
Mr. Mom (1983 film) 106
Mister Rogers' Neighborhood (television program) 100
Moench, Doug 150
Moldoff, Sheldon 56, 81
Moll, Richard 142, 263
Molnar, Paul 269
Monk 259
Monroe, Marilyn 42
Montgomery, Lauren 268
Moore, Alan 96, 97, 98

Moroni, Boss 169, 174
Morrison, Grant 93, 121, 122, 259, 260, 266, 270
Morrison, Jim 157
Moxon, Lew 262, 263
Murphy, Cillian 224, 225, 232, 248, 274, 293
Murphy, Tab 268
Mutual Broadcasting System 32
Mxyzptlk, Mr. 54
"The Mystery of the Menacing Mask" (*Detective Comics* #327, May 1964 story) 58
"The Mystery of the Waxmen" (1945 radio serial) 32

Naish, J. Carrol 16
Napier, Alan 64
Napier, Jack 104, 105
National Helicopter Service 69
NBC Television Network 77, 180
Neeson, Liam 213, 215, 223, 225, 293
Nestle Quik 62
The New Adventures of Batman (1977 television series) 77, 86
The New Batman/Superman Adventures (1997–1998 television series) 195–196, 199, 201, 202, 205, 210
The New 52 (2011 revamp and relaunch of all DC Comics titles) 266, 270, 298
The New Scooby-Doo Movies (1972–1974 television series) 263
The New Titans (comic book title) 122
New York City, New York 5, 39, 128, 161, 213, 236, 239, 277, 278
New York ComicCon, 1980 102
The New York Times (newspaper) 133
Newmar, Julie 59, 68, 78, 263
Newsies (1992 film) 212
Nicholson, Jack 11, 98, **101**, 103, 105, 107, 108, 109, 113, 115, 119, 135, 234
"Night of the Reaper" (*Batman* #237, December 1971 story) 147
Nightwing 90, 95, 195, 270
Nigma, Edward *see* Nygma, Edward
"A Nipponese Trap" (1943 movie serial *Batman* chapter) 27
No Man's Land (1999 comic book series) 198
Nock, Eugene 69
"Nocturnal Overtures: The Music of *Batman*"(featurette

on *Beyond Batman* video documentary) 119
Nolan, Christopher 3, 175, 198, 210, 211, 212, 213, 214, 215, 220, 221, 222, 223, 224, 225, 226, 227, 228, 229, 231, 232, 233, 234, 235, 236, 237, 238, 239, 246, 247, 248, 249, 250, 253, 254, 255, 256, 257, 260, 261, 271, 273, 274, 275, 276, 277, 278, 288, 290, 292, 293, 295, 296, 297
Nolan, Graham 150
Nolan, Jonathan 232, 273, 288
Norvick, Irv 82
"Not Yet He Ain't" (*Batman* television series episode) 68
"Nothing to Fear" (*Batman: The Animated Series* television series episode) 221
Nygma, Edward 58

O'Donnell, Chris **153**, 157, 162, 167, 170, **178**, 180, 181, 189, 191
The Official Batman Batbook (1986 book) 2
O'Hara, Chief 64
Ohio State Fair 70
Oldman, Gary 213, 215, 224, 225, 228, 232, 238, 239, 248, 274, 278, 291
"One Bullet Too Many" (*Batman* #217, December 1969 story) 82, 85
One Flew Over the Cuckoo's Nest (1975 film) 105
O'Neil, Denny 3, 82, 84, 85, 87, 95, 102, 115, 119, 141, 210, 211, 268
Oracle 98, 195, 198, 203
"The Origin of Batman" (*Batman* #47, June–July 1948 story) 33, 105, 221, 262
Ornithopter (da Vinci invention) 6
"Out of the Shadows: The Production Design of *Batman Forever*" (featurette on *Beyond Batman* video documentary) 170

Pacino, Al 157, 210
Page, Ellen 273
Page, Linda 21, 22, 190
Palance, Jack 106, 116
Palos Verdes, California 69
Paramount Pictures 180
Paramount Theatre, Austin, Texas 70
Paris, Charles 32
"Partners of Peril" (1936 story) 7
Pasko, Martin 143

"Path to Discovery" (2005 video documentary) 228
Patterson, Shirley 22
Paul, Victor 70
"Pavane" *Secret Origins* #36, January 1989 story) 179, 190
PBS Network 100
Pearl Harbor, Hawaii 22
Pee Wee's Big Adventure (1985 film) 103, 109
Penguin 13, 38, 53, 58, 61, 64, **69**, 86, 87, 124, **125**, 127, 135, 141, 150, 194, 199, 205, 206, 207, 210, 262, 264
"The Penguin Goes Straight" (*Batman* television series episode) 68
Pennyworth, Alfred 20, 21, 42, **55**, 64, 87, 106, 115, 127, 141, 161, 181, 199, 203, 206, 213, 223, 232, 248, 274, 289, 290, 291, 294
"The People vs. the Batman" (*Batman* #7, October/November 1941 story) 12
Peters, Jon 102, 103, 104, 107, 124, 128
Petersen, Wolfgang 209
Pfeiffer, Michelle **125**, 127, 135, 137, 138
Pfister, Wally 225, 228, 232, 235, 249, 274
Phantasm **140**, 143, 146
Phantom Stranger 262, 263
"The Phoney Doctor" (1943 movie serial *Batman* chapter) 25–26
Pike, Allen 159
Pinewood Studios, London, England 106, 128
Pittsburgh, Pennsylvania 276, 277
Pittsburgh Steelers 276
Plastic Man 261
PlayStation 2 202, 228
PlayStation 3 259, 264
Plympton, George H. 36
Poison Ivy 177, 178, **179**, 180, 194
"Poison Peril" (1943 movie serial *Batman* chapter) 25
Poland, Joseph F. 36
PolyGram Pictures 103
Porter, Kevin 269
Predator (film series) 204
The Prestige (2006 film) 231
Preminger, Otto 64
Prince 109, 117, 215
The Princess Diaries (2001 film) 274
Pulp Fiction (1994 film) 180

Q 222
Qayin 93

Quinn, Harley 142, 149, 193, 199, 204, 264
Quinzel, Harleen 142, 149, 204

Radomski, Eric 139, 140, 141, 143
Ramey, Bill 197–198
Rapid City Monuments 276
Reaper 146, 147
Reaves, Michael 143, 205
Red Hood (Jason Todd alter ego) 257, 267, 270
Red Hood (Joker alter ego) 52, 97, 258
Red Robin (Dick Grayson alter ego) 260
Red Robin (Tim Drake alter ego) 260, 266, 270, 298
Reeve, Christopher 88
Reeves, Buster 214
Reinhart, Keaton 269
Reinhart, Taylor 269
Relentless (1948 film) 39
Repp, Stafford 64
"The Return of the Batman" (unfilmed script by Michael Uslan) 102
Return to the Batcave: The Misadventures of Adam and Burt (2003 television program) 78
Reynolds, Debbie 66
Riba, Dan 196
Riddle, Nelson 67, 70
Riddle Me This: Why Is Batman Forever? (1995 television documentary) 170
"The Riddle of the Missing Card" (*Batman* #5, Spring 1941 story) 12
Riddler 38, 58, 61, 63, 64, **69**, 86, 89, 141, 150, **154**, 155, 174, 194, 199, 204, 205, 210, 262
Rienzi (1840 opera) 20
Rinehart, Mary Roberts 6
Ringwood, Bob 108, 134, 158, 159
Ritmanis, Lolita 143
"The Roast" (*Legends of the Super Heroes* episode) 89
Robbins, Frank 82, 196
Roberts, Eric 238
Robin (Carrie Kelley alter ego) 91, 196
Robin (Damian Wayne alter ego) 260, 266, 270, 298
Robin (Dick Grayson alter ego): adopting Batman persona in wake of Bruce Wayne's death 260, 266; appearances in *Star Spangled Comics* 33; comic illustrations **9**, **55**, **57**, **88**; costume of character 8; inclusion of character in *Batman 2* and

Batman Returns scripts 124, 126; inclusion of character in 1989 *Batman* script 104, 105, 119; as motion picture character **17**, **37**, **60**, **153**, **178**; origin of character 8, 141, 15, 167; popularity of character among Batman fans 9; relationship with Batman 53, 82, 168
Robin (Jason Todd alter ego): death of character 96, 97, 203, 267; origin of character 90; popularity of character among Batman fans 90–91, 95; resurrection as the Red Hood 257, 267, 270; second origin of character 95
Robin (1991 comic book series) 122
Robin (Stephanie Brown alter ego) 266
Robin (Tim Drake alter ego): costume 122; Joker's capture of character in *Batman Beyond: Return of the Joker* 201; origin of character 122; origin of character as depicted in TV series *The New Batman/Superman Adventures* 195; popularity of character among Batman fans 122
Robin Hood 8, 18, 40
"Robin Meets the Wizard" (1949 movie serial *Batman and Robin* chapter) 46–47
"Robin Rescues Batman" (1949 movie serial *Batman and Robin* chapter) 45
"Robin Rides the Wind" (1949 movie serial *Batman and Robin* chapter) 48
"Robin — The Boy Wonder" (*Detective Comics* #38, April 1940 story) 8, 141, 167
Robin: The Story of Dick Grayson (2010 documentary) 268
"Robin's Reckoning" (*Batman: The Animated Series* television series episode) 141
Robin's Requiem: The Story of Jason Todd (2010 documentary) 268
"Robin's Ruse" (1949 movie serial *Batman and Robin* chapter) 47–48
"Robin's Wild Ride" (1949 movie serial *Batman and Robin* chapter) 44
Robinson, Jerry 8, 11, 81
Rockwell, Norman 174
Rogel, Randy 141, 195
Rogers, Marshall 87, 88, 92, 102, 103, 115, 140

Rojas, Angel 205
Romano, Andrea 142
Romano, Rino 205
Romero, Caesar 11, 69, 64, **69**, 70, 234
Ross, Alex 3, 172, 173, 174, 198, 199, 203, 204, 245, 264, 269, 290, 299
Ross, Clark 174

The Saint (1997 film) 180
St. Cloud, Silver 87, 88, 103
St. Elmo's Fire (1985 film) 153
Sale, Tim 174, 175, 232, 254
Sanchez, Lauren 238
Sanders, George 64
Santa Claus 4, 18
Sara, Mia 204
Savage, Vandal 271
"Saving Gotham City" (2005 video documentary) 228
Scarecrow 38, 87, 174, 193, 210, 211, 224, 232, 233, 237, 248, 274, 293
Scent of a Woman (1992 film) 157
Schoenke, Aaron 269
Schumacher, Joel 151, 153, 154, 157, 158, 159, 160, 161, 162, 167, 168, 169, 170, 172, 175, 176, 177, 180, 181, 182, 187, 188, 190, 191, 192, 193, 196, 209, 210, 213, 220, 225, 231, 273, 274, 288, 292
Schwartz, Julius 56, 58, 75
Schwarzenegger, Arnold **179**, 180, 189, 191
Scooby-Doo 263
"Scoring Forever: The Music of *Batman Forever*" (featurette on *Beyond Batman* video documentary) 170
Scott, Ashley 203
Seal 161
Sears Tower, Chicago, Illinois 235
"The Secret Cavern" (*Detective Comics* #48, February 1941 story) 12
"The Secret of the Waiting Graves" (*Detective Comics* #395, January 1970 story) 84, 85
Secret Origins of the World's Greatest Super-Heroes (1989 book) 211
Seduction of the Innocent (1953 book) 28, 52, 53, 54, 168, 258
Semple, Lorenzo, Jr. 61, 67, 68, 72
Shadow 6, 7
Shadows of the Bat: The Cinematic Saga of the Dark Knight (multi-part video documentary on Warner Bros.' Batman film DVD sets) 119, 138, 170, 191
"Shaping Mind and Body" (2005 video documentary) 228
Shepperton Studios, Shepperton, Surrey, England 214, 277
The Shining (1980 film) 105
Shreck, Max 127, 135
"The Sign of the Sphinx" (1943 movie serial *Batman* chapter) 26–27
Silver 18
Silverstone, Alicia **178**, 180, 181, 189, 191
Sinclair, Alex 204
Six Flags Corporation 150, 151
Six Flags Great America, Chicago, Illinois 150
Skaaren, Warren 104, 105, 107, 113, 126, 127
"Slaves of the Rising Sun" (1943 movie serial *Batman* chapter) 24, 48
"Sleek, Sexy and Sinister: The Costumes of *Batman Returns*" (featurette on *Beyond Batman* video documentary) 138
"Smack in the Middle" (*Batman* television series episode) 67
Smith, Andy 213
Sony Corporation 124
Sony Pictures Home Entertainment 30–31, 51
Sorkin, Arleen 142, 202, 264
Soule, Olan 86
Spears, Geoff 175
Spectre 173, 262, 263
Spider-Man 175
Spider-Man (2002 film) 115
Spider-Man and Batman: Disordered Minds (1995 graphic novel) 175
Spielberg, Steven 212
Spoiler 266
Sprang, Dick 13, 81, 196, 261
Star Spangled Comics (comic book title) 13
Star Wars (film series) 116, 188
Stoner, Alyson 269
Strange, Dr. Hugo 87, 259, 264
Strange Apparitions (1999 book) 88
Strick, Wesley 124, 126, 127
Strong, Tara 264
Stryker, Alfred 7
Subcommittee to Investigate Juvenile Delinquency in the United States 52
Sullivan, Vin 5
Super Powers Team: The Galactic Guardians (1985 television series) 77, 86, 87, 210
Superboy Prime 257, 268
SuperFriends (1973 television series) 86, 89
SuperFriends: The Legendary Super Powers Show (1984 television series) 77, 86
Supergirl 267
Superman 5, 7, 9, 12, 32, 33, 42, 54, 56, 60, 81, 86, 93, 108, 172, 173, 195, 199, 207, 209, 258, 259, 261, 267, 271, 290
Superman (1948 movie serial) 18, 36
Superman (1978 film) 88, 102, 103, 115
Superman/Batman (comic book title) 267
Superman/Batman: Apocalypse (2010 video) 267
Superman/Batman: Public Enemies (2009 video) 267
Superman: Peace on Earth (1998 graphic novel) 199
Superman II (1980 film) 103
Swabacker, Leslie 16
Swank, Hilary 210
Swenson, Jeep 181, 189
Swing Kids (1993 film) 212

Talbot, Lyle 41
"Target: Robin" (1949 movie serial *Batman and Robin* chapter) 45–46
Tate, Miranda 274, 292
The Terminator (1984 film) 189
TFX Company 159
Thank You for Smoking (2005 film) 233
"There Is No Hope in Crime Alley" (*Detective Comics* #457, March 1976 story) 288–289
Thomas, Bruce 203
Thomas, Emma 212, 228, 232, 273, 274
Thompkins, Leslie 289
Thorne, Rupert 87, 103, 141, 205
"Those Wonderful Toys: The Props and Gadgets of *Batman*" (featurette on *Beyond Batman* video documentary) 119
"Three Go Mad in Gotham" (*Empire* magazine article) 126
Thurman, Uma **179**, 180, 189, 191
Time (news magazine) 29, 65
Time Corporation 150
Time Warner Corporation 150, 151
Timm, Bruce 139, 140, 141, 143, 146, 149, 195, 196, 199, 201

Tinsley, Theodore 7
Todd, Jason 90, 95, 122, 203, 204, 257, 267, 268, 270, 298
Todd, Joseph 90
Todd, Trina 90
Tracy, Dick 60
Trent, Simon 143
Tucker, James 260
Tumbler (nickname of Batmobile in Nolan Batman film series) 225, 234, 274, 278
"Tunnel of Terror" (1949 movie serial *Batman and Robin* chapter) 43–44
20th Century–Fox 61, 68
Two-Face 13, 38, 116, 151, *154*, 155, 174, 180, 194, 198, 199, 210, 231, 233, 234, 248, 253, 262, 263, 264, 293
"Two-Face" (*Batman: The Animated Series* television series episode) 141

U2 161, 215
United Artists Studios 102
United Nations 173
United States Senate 52
The Untold Legends of the Batman (1980 comic book series) 90
Urich, Robert 137
Uslan, Michael 88, 89, 92, 101, 102, 103, 104, 109, 119

Vale, Vicki 42, 106, 116, 124, 127, 190, 224, 255
Valley, Jean Paul 150
Van Nuys, California 69
Vatnajokull Glacier, Iceland 214
Veight, Conrad 11
Vietti, Brandon 267
Village Roadshow Pictures 135
VIP Marine 160
"Visualizing Gotham: The Production Design of *Batman*" (featurette on *Beyond Batman* video documentary) 119

Waggoner, Lyle 63, 77
Wagner, Matt 259
Wagner, Richard 20
Waid, Mark 172, 173, 174, 203, 271, 290
Walken, Christopher 127, 135
Walker, Shirley 117, 143, 147
Wallace, Daniel 270
Wallach, Eli 64
Walt Disney Pictures 227
"War Is Declared" (*Batman: Year One* story, 1987) **94**

Ward, Burt 58, 59, *60*, 62, 63, 70, 76, 77, 78, 86, 89
Ward, Heinz 276
Warhol, Andy 59
Warner Books 92, 103
Warner Brothers Animation 139
Warner Brothers Pictures 78, 88, 89, 92, 98, 102, 103, 104, 105, 106, 107, 108, 109, 118, 123, 124, 126, 127, 128, 132, 135, 137, 143, 148, 150, 152, 153, 154, 155, 156, 157, 161, 162, 165, 169, 177, 180, 181, 182, 190, 191, 192, 193, 194, 196, 197, 198, 201, 202, 203, 204, 205, 206, 207, 209, 210, 212, 215, 220, 227, 228, 231, 232, 235, 237, 238, 245, 260, 266, 269, 274, 275, 278, 296, 299
Warner Brothers Studios, Burbank, California 128, 181
Warner Communications 92, 102, 103, 150, 160
Warner Home Video 119, 255, 295
Watanabe, Ken 223, 273
Waters, Daniel 124, 127, 138
Wayans, Marlon 126
Wayne, Bruce: decision to adopt Batman identity 8, 48, 288–289; decision to take Dick Grayson as junior partner 8; decision to take Jason Todd as junior partner 90; decision to take Tim Drake as a junior partner 122; murder of parents 7, 33, 34, 156, 167, 221, 222, 262–263; romance with Andrea Beaumont 143; romance with Julie Madison 190; romance with Linda Page 21–22; romance with Silver St. Cloud 87
Wayne, Damian 93, 259, 260, 270, 298
Wayne, Helena 203
Wayne, Martha 7, 34, 105, 118, 221, 222, 262, 263
Wayne, Thomas 7, 33, 34, 105, 204, 221, 222, 262, 263
WB Television Network 203, 204
Wein, Len 90
Welch, Bo 128
Wertham, Fredric 28, 52, 53, 54, 56, 168, 258
West, Adam 3, 58, 59, *60*, 62, 63, 65, 70, 73, 74, 76, 77, 78, 86, 87, 89, 100, 102, 106, 222, 261, 263, 299
West, Roland 6

Westwood, California 109
Wickliffe, Conway 236
Wii 259
Wilkinson, Tom 224, 225
Williams, Billy Dee 106, 116, 155, 157, 158
Williams, Paul 142
Williams, Robin 158, 210
Williams, Scott 204
Wilson, Barbara 189
Wilson, Charles 21, 222
Wilson, Lewis 16, *17*, 19, 29, 30, 41
Winick, Judd 257, 267, 268, 270
Wizard 38, 39
The Wizard of Oz (1939 film) 210
"The Wizard Strikes Back" (1949 movie serial *Batman and Robin* chapter) 47
"The Wizard's Challenge" (1949 movie serial *Batman and Robin* chapter) 48–49
Wonder Woman 56, 86, 172, 173, 258, 259, 261
Woodrue, Dr. Jason 179
World War II 16, 22
World's Best Comics (comic book title) 12
"World's Finest" (*The New Batman/Superman Adventures* television series episode) 195
World's Finest Comics (comic book title) 12, 13, 33, 54, 93, 271
The World's Greatest Super-Friends (1979 television series) 86
Writer's Guild of America 104
Wuertz 253
Wuhl, Robert 106, 116

Xbox 202, 228
Xbox 360 259, 264

Yamaha Motorcycle Company 70
Young, Peter 116
Young, Sean 106, 127
Young Justice (2010–2011 television series) 269
Young Justice: Invasion (2012–2013 television series) 269

Zahler, Lee 20, 117
Zero, Mr. 56, 64
Zimbalist, Efrem, Jr. 142, 148
Zimmer, Hans 215, 226, 239, 250, 277, 278, 294
Zorro 6
Zurian, Charley 159

www.ingramcontent.com/pod-product-compliance
Lightning Source LLC
Chambersburg PA
CBHW081538300426
44116CB00015B/2680